THE NEW TESTAMENT

THE NEW TESTAMENT

AN INTRODUCTION TO BIBLICAL SCHOLARSHIP

Arthur J. Bellinzoni

WIPF & STOCK · Eugene, Oregon

THE NEW TESTAMENT
An Introduction to Biblical Scholarship

Copyright © 2016 Arthur J. Bellinzoni. All rights reserved. Except for brief quotations in critical publications or reviews, no part of this book may be reproduced in any manner without prior written permission from the publisher. Write: Permissions. Wipf and Stock Publishers, 199 W. 8th Ave., Suite 3, Eugene, OR 97401.

Wipf & Stock
An Imprint of Wipf and Stock Publishers
199 W. 8th Ave., Suite 3
Eugene, OR 97401

www.wipfandstock.com

ISBN 13: 978-1-4982-3511-2

Manufactured in the U.S.A.   01/05/2016

CONTENTS

PREFACE | xiii
ABBREVIATIONS | xvii

INTRODUCTION | 1
    The Origins of Modern Biblical Scholarship | 1
    The Historical Method | 13
    The Rules of Evidence | 16
    Conclusions | 20

CHAPTER 1: TEXTUAL CRITICISM | 23
    What is Textual Criticism? | 24
    Applying the Method to the Text of the New Testament: Some Examples | 32
        Mark 1:1 | 32
        Mark 6:3 | 33
        John 1:34 | 35
        Matthew 24:36 | 36
        Romans 8:28 | 36
        1 John 4:19 | 37
    Conclusions | 38
    Appendix to Chapter 1 | 41

CHAPTER 2: LITERARY CRITICISM AND PHILOLOGY | 46
    Literary Criticism | 47
        The Literary Forms of the Books of the New Testament | 47
        Applying the Method to the Text of the New Testament: Some Examples | 51
    Philology | 56
        The Meaning of Words in their Original Contexts | 58
        The Authenticity of Ephesians and Colossians | 60
    Conclusions | 65

CONTENTS

CHAPTER 3: SOURCE CRITICISM | 67
    The Priority of Mark | 69
        The Triple Tradition | 70
        Luke's Great Omission of Markan Material | 76
        The Double Tradition | 78
    The Sayings Source Q | 82
        Do Not Worry | 84
        Jesus' Exhortation to Fearless Confession | 87
    Special M and Special L | 88
    Conclusions | 92

CHAPTER 4: THE APOSTOLIC PREACHING AND ITS DEVELOPMENTS | 95
    The Apostolic Preaching | 96
    And Its Developments | 107
    Conclusions | 113

CHAPTER 5: THE CRUCIFIXION OF JESUS AND THE PASSION NARRATIVE | 117
    The Emergence and Development of a Passion Narrative | 117
    The Crucifixion of Jesus in Mark | 121
    Conclusions | 128

CHAPTER 6: FORM CRITICISM | 132
    What is Form Criticism | 132
    The Forms | 133
        Pronouncement Stories | 134
        Miracle Stories | 138
        Parables | 144
        Sayings | 145
        Legends | 147
    Conclusions | 156

CHAPTER 7: REDACTION CRITICISM | 159
    What is Redaction Criticism? | 159
    Examples of Redaction Criticism | 160
        Peter's Confession | 160
        The Rejection of Jesus at Nazareth | 167
    Conclusions | 173

CHAPTER 8: JESUS OF NAZARETH: THE ESCHATOLOGICAL PROPHET | 177
    The Quest for the Historical Jesus: The Sources | 178

CONTENTS

Jesus Outside the Canonical Gospels | 180
Jesus, the Eschatological Prophet of God's Imminent Rule | 183
    The Quest for the Historical Jesus: The Criteria | 183
    The Quest for the Historical Jesus: A New Look at Old Texts | 185
Conclusions | 197

CHAPTER 9: JESUS OF NAZARETH: THE TEACHER OF WISDOM | 203
The "Sayings Gospel" Q | 203
    References to the Son of Man in Kloppenberg's Q1 | 211
    References to God's Rule in Kloppenberg's Q1 | 213
    Looking at Q as an Integral Whole | 215
The Gospel of Thomas | 222
    An Early Date for the *Gospel of Thomas* | 225
    A Late Date for the *Gospel of Thomas* | 227
    The *Gospel of Thomas*, Eschatology, and Gnostic Thought | 230
Conclusions | 233

CHAPTER 10: THE EARLY CHRISTIAN CHURCH | 238
The Earliest Jesus Movement: Our Sources | 239
Pentecost | 241
Early Practices | 244
The Hellenists | 246
The Jesus Movement in Judea and Samaria and Beyond | 246
The Earliest Preached Message: The Primitive *Kerygma* | 247
The Spread of Christianity | 251
Disagreements between Paul and Acts | 257
Messengers of the Gospel | 258
The Message of the Earliest Apostles | 262
House Churches | 264
Authorship, Audience, and the Place and Date of Composition
    of the Acts of the Apostles | 265
Conclusions | 267

CHAPTER 11: PAUL: THE MAN, THE MISSION, AND THE MESSAGE | 271
Paul the Man | 272
    The Early Years | 272
    The Conversion of Paul and the Acts of the Apostles | 273
    The Psychology of Paul | 278
Paul's Mission | 279
    Paul's Early Travels | 279

A Proposed Chronology | 281
The Ethnic Composition of the Early Christian Community | 283
The Jerusalem Council | 284
The Incident at Antioch | 287
The Collection | 289
Paul's Message | 290
1 Thessalonians | 290
1 Corinthians | 291
2 Corinthians | 292
Galatians | 293
Philippians | 294
Philemon | 295
Romans | 295
Summary of Paul's Gospel | 296
Problems and Conclusions | 300
Chronology | 300
Paul and Acts | 301
The Pauline Letters and Their Transmission | 301
The Period Before 49 | 302
The Antioch Question | 303
Paul's Message | 303
Paul's Death as a Martyr | 304

CHAPTER 12: EARLY CHRISTIAN GOSPELS, PART 1 | 305
The Canonical Gospels | 306
Early Witnesses to the Four Gospels | 306
Papias of Hierapolis | 306
Marcion, Justin Martyr, and Others | 307
Irenaeus | 308
The Muratori Canon | 309
The Synoptic Gospels | 310
The Gospel of Mark | 311
The Gospel of Matthew | 317
The Gospel of Luke | 323
The Gospel of John | 329
Conclusions | 335

CHAPTER 13: EARLY CHRISTIAN GOSPELS, PART 2 | 340
The *Gospel of Thomas* | 340
The *Gospel of Peter* | 344

Jewish Christian Gospels: The Testimony | 346
    Irenaeus | 346
    Clement of Alexandria | 346
    Origen | 347
    Eusebius of Caesarea | 347
    Epiphanius | 348
    Jerome | 348
Jewish Christian Gospels: The Fragments | 349
    The *Gospel of the Hebrews* | 349
    The *Gospel of the Nazoreans* | 350
    The *Gospel of the Ebionites* | 351
Jewish Christian Communities: Their Social Location | 352
The *Infancy Gospel of James* | 352
The *Infancy Gospel of Thomas* | 353
The *Gospel of Mary* | 356
The *Gospel of Truth* | 357
Tatian's *Diatessaron* | 359
Conclusions | 361

CHAPTER 14: POST APOSTOLIC CHRISTIANTIES | 366

Jewish Christianities | 367
    The Letter of James | 368
    The Gospel of Matthew | 369
    The Letter to the Hebrews | 370
    The *Didache* | 371
    Jewish Christianities in the East | 372
Deutero-Pauline or Post-Pauline Christianity | 375
    Pseudepigraphy in the Ancient World | 376
    Ephesians | 377
    Colossians | 377
    2 Thessalonians | 378
    1 and 2 Timothy and Titus | 380
    Marcion | 381
Johannine Christianity | 382
    The Gospel of John | 383
    The Johannine Letters | 384
Petrine Christianity | 386
    The Primacy of Peter | 387
    1 Peter | 387
    2 Peter and Jude | 388
    Other Petrine Writings | 389

CONTENTS

    Gnostic Christianities | 389
        The Origins of Gnosticism | 389
        References to Gnosticism in the New Testament | 390
        Christian Gnostics | 392
    Conclusions | 393

CHAPTER 15: THE REVELATION OF JOHN | 397
    Authorship, Date and Place of Composition,
        and Literary Genre of Revelation | 398
        Authorship | 398
        Date | 400
        Place of Composition | 401
        Genre: Apocalypse, Letter, and Prophecy | 402
    Structure of the Revelation of John | 402
    Understanding the Message of Revelation | 404
    The Letters to the Seven Churches | 406
    John's Revelation and Ancient Literature | 407
    Conclusions | 408

CHAPTER 16: THE CANON OF THE NEW TESTAMENT | 410
    The Beginnings of Christian Writings | 411
    Other Christian Writings of the Period | 413
    The Formation of the Canon | 414
    Early Collections of Christian Books | 414
        Paul's Letters | 414
        The Gospels | 416
        The Catholic Letters | 418
        Acts and Revelation | 418
    Canonical Lists | 418
        Marcion | 419
        The Canon of Origen | 419
        The Muratori Canon | 421
        Eusebius of Caesarea | 421
        Constantine | 422
        The Catalogue of Uncertain Date and Provenance Inserted in Codex
            Claromontanus | 423
        The Cheltenham Canon | 423
        Athanasius's List | 424
        The Canon of Cyril of Jerusalem | 424
        The Canon of the Synod of Laodicea | 425

CONTENTS

    The Canon Approved by the Apostolic Canons | 425
    The Canon of Gregory of Nazianus | 426
    The Council of Amphilochius of Iconium | 426
    The Canon of the Third Synod of Carthage | 428
    The Decretum Gelasianum | 429
    The Catologue of Sixty Canonical Books | 430
    The Stichometry of Nicephorus | 430
    Jerome and Augustine | 430
Factors Significant in the Formation of the Canon | 431
Conclusions | 432

BIBLIOGRAPHY | 437
SCRIPTURE INDEX | 443
AUTHOR INDEX | 469

PREFACE

THERE ARE MYRIAD INTRODUCTIONS to both the Old and the New Testaments that are committed to the historical critical method of investigation, but introductory textbooks rarely address directly the foundational principles of contemporary biblical scholarship.

Both as an undergraduate and as a graduate student, I was introduced to the historical-critical study of the Bible without actually understanding the basis of and the justification for the historical approach. A friend called to my attention a few years ago the value of having an introductory textbook that addresses issues of methodology in order to enable students of the Bible to understand better the reasons for and the implications of the best results of biblical scholarship.

Accordingly, this book has a twofold purpose: (1) to introduce readers to the origins of and the reasons for the basic methodology of biblical scholarship; and (2) to provide an overview of the beginnings and early evolution of Christianity by employing those methods in an examination of relevant literature. An unusual feature of this book is that I do not simply describe methodology in a way that is pedantic and difficult for the reader to understand, but, where possible, I lead the reader through a series of exercises to illustrate how biblical scholarship actually "works."

In writing this book, I have been mindful of college undergraduates, seminary students, graduate students, and scholars in the field of New Testament studies. I am also mindful of laypersons who have some knowledge of the Bible but who may be unaware of the methodological basis of biblical scholarship and its results. It is essential that people at every level of understanding have an awareness of the kinds of conclusions that come with the rigorous application of the historical method of biblical scholarship.

This volume is not an introduction to the Bible, or even to the New Testament. There are already many excellent introductions to the Bible as a whole, and separate introductions to the Old and the New Testaments. Typically such introductions afford basic information about all of the books of the Bible. I am, however, not aware of any introductory study that tries to accomplish what I am attempting with this volume.

In the opening chapter, the introduction, I provide the reader with insight into the origins and the foundational principles of the historical method of biblical scholarship, including a discussion of the rules of evidence for the writing of history,

PREFACE

whether biblical history or any other history. The rules and methods for the writing of history are always the same whatever the subject matter. Nonetheless, the systematic application of the historical method to the Bible has come only with a struggle that has spanned several centuries and that is still not deeply implanted in the minds of millions of people.

The opening chapter of this volume is among the most important and the most challenging, although it is this material that is generally lacking in introductions to the New Testament. An understanding of the origin, the emergence, and the method of biblical scholarship is, in my opinion, essential to an appreciation of what unfolds in subsequent chapters.

To present the reader with a book that is both faithful to the rigors of biblical scholarship and, at the same time, readable and engaging, I have focused on two issues:

First of all, I have developed somewhat detailed arguments for portions of the book in order to allow the reader to understand how an historical reconstruction is built upon the interpretation of relevant data. The work of biblical scholars is generally based on the study of original texts that require knowledge of ancient languages, minimally Hebrew and Greek, of which few laypersons have any comprehension. In the course of this volume, I will introduce some issues involving texts in their original languages in order to expose the reader to an understanding and an appreciation of the ways in which biblical scholars build detailed cases.

Secondly, I have in other instances avoided detailed arguments and discussion and have provided the reader instead with what are scholarly conclusions based on a careful reading of the evidence, at least as I understand the evidence and the consensus of sound scholarship. Without taking such shortcuts, it is simply not feasible to cover in detail one hundred and fifty years of history in a modest volume of the sort that I propose to offer here.

Nevertheless, my intention is to provide the reader with meaningful insight into both the methods of biblical scholarship and the results of the application of these methods to biblical texts in order to provide a reasoned and reasonable reconstruction of what likely happened in the earliest decades of the history of Christianity, which is after all our ultimate goal. Although not everyone will agree with my conclusions, hopefully all will agree with the value and the rigor of the method used to reach these conclusions. I hope that this blend of rigorous application of the historical method and introductory overviews of the history of early Christianity will stimulate the reader who wants more information about the subject to pursue individual issues in greater detail.

Writing an introduction means making compromises regarding what to include and what not to include, and I have made such compromises. I do not cover in detail every book of the New Testament, as most introductions attempt to do. I am more interested in addressing more deeply certain themes rather than in providing a summary of every book of the New Testament. In making the decisions I have made, I

PREFACE

hope to remain faithful to the text, to scholars who have written before me, and, most importantly, I hope to be faithful to the history that unfolded in the ancient past. It is essential in this regard to remind the reader that biblical scholarship is not an exact science in the way in which physics and astronomy are more-or-less exact sciences with strong foundations in mathematics.

The study of the origins of Judaism and Christianity is especially problematic, because the earliest periods of both religions are far removed from our earliest written sources, especially in the case of the Old Testament. We shall, in the course or what follows in this volume, have ample opportunity to understand the limitations of reconstructing the past.

The writing of history uses what we call the historical method, or the scientific method, and aims at objectivity to the extent that objectivity is possible in trying to reconstruct events that occurred thousands of years ago. Equally competent scholars often draw very different conclusions from the same evidence. The important word here is *evidence*. Ideally, scholars look at the same *evidence*, all of the available data, and at what other scholars have had to say in the past about that data. Then, and only then, do historians try to connect all of the dots in a way that is faithful both to the data and to the methodology of historical investigation. Scholars can do no more than draw conclusions within the limits of historical reason, but they can never be certain that their conclusions conform to what actually happened in the distant past. Rather scholars build models of the past or revisit and renovate models built by earlier scholars. The historical method is nothing more and nothing less; hence it is essential to understand at the outset the limits of the discipline.

Although the Bible represents both Israel's history and the history of early Christianity as "the acts of God," the doing of history is at all times a secular exercise. Accordingly, an historical study of the Bible poses serious concerns for many readers, because it is that impartial, detached, neutral, unbiased, dispassionate, and objective perspective that troubles some students of the text but that necessarily lies at the heart of all rigorous and serious biblical scholarship.

Although I am ultimately responsible for everything that I have gathered into this book, the final version is better because of the generous suggestions and criticisms of two good friends and colleagues: Marvin A. Breslow, professor emeritus of history at the University of Maryland and my roommate for four years at the Harvard University Graduate School of Arts and Sciences; and David M. Reis, formerly visiting assistant professor of religion at Wells College, where we first met, and currently visiting assistant professor of religion at the University of Oregon, Eugene. Both of these men labored tirelessly and unselfishly over every word of every chapter and made invaluable contributions to this volume. Only I can appreciate the ways in which they have influenced both my thinking and my writing. I want also to acknowledge the tireless technical assistance I received at every stage of this project from Dimitrios Dimopoulos; I could not have prepared this manuscript without him.

PREFACE

This book is respectfully dedicated to the two professors who most influenced me in my graduate study of the New Testament at Harvard University many years ago: Helmut Koester and Krister Stendahl, brilliant scholars and great men both.

Arthur J. Bellinzoni

Professor Emeritus of Religion
Wells College
Aurora, New York

"The lot of historical writers is hard; for if they tell the truth they provoke men, and if they write what is false they offend God."

—Matthew Paris, 13th century English Benedictine monk

ABBREVIATIONS

SCRIPTURE ABBREVIATIONS

Old Testament

Gen	Genesis	Eccl	Ecclesiastes
Exod	Exodus	Song	Song of Solomon
Lev	Leviticus	Isa	Isaiah
Num	Numbers	Jer	Jeremiah
Deut	Deuteronomy	Lam	Lamentations
Josh	Joshua	Ezek	Ezekiel
Judg	Judges	Dan	Daniel
Ruth	Ruth	Hos	Hosea
1-2 Sam	1-2 Samuel	Joel	Joel
1-2 Kgs	1-2 Kings	Amos	Amos
1-2 Chr	1-2 Chronicles	Obad	Obadiah
Ezra	Ezra	Jonah	Jonah
Neh	Nehemiah	Mic	Micah
Esth	Esther	Nah	Nahum
Job	Job	Hab	Habakkuk
Ps (*pl* Pss)	Psalms	Zech	Zechariah
Prov	Proverbs	Mal	Malachi

New Testament

Matt	Mathew	Eph	Ephesians
Mark	Mark	Phil	Philippians
Luke	Luke	Col	Colossians
John	John	1-2 Thess	1-2 Thessalonians
Acts	Acts	1-2 Tim	1-2 Timothy
Rom	Romans	Titus	Titus
1-2 Cor	1-2 Corinthians	Phlm	Philemon
Gal	Galatians	Heb	Hebrews

ABBREVIATIONS

Jas	James	Jude	Jude
1-2 Pet	1-2 Peter	Rev	Revelation
1-2-3 John	1-2-3 John		

Apocryphal Books

Tob	Tobit	Ep Jer	Epistle of Jeremiah
Jdt	Judith	Sg Three	Song of the Three Jews
Add Esth	Additions to Esther	Sus	Susanna
Wis	Widsom of Solomon	Bel	Bel and the Dragon
Sir	Sirach	1-2 Macc	1-2 Maccabees
Bar	Baruch	3-4 Macc	3-4 Maccabees
1-3 Esd	1-3 Esdras	Pr Man	Prayer of Manasseh

New Testament Aprocrypha and Church Fathers

Did	*Didache*	*Gos Pet*	*Gospel of Peter*
Gos Ebion	*Gospel of the Ebionites*	*Gos Truth*	*Gospel of Truth*
Gos Heb	*Gospel of the Hebews*	*Inf Jas*	*Infancy Gospel of James*
Gos Mary	*Gospel of Mary*	*Inf Thos*	*Infancy Gospel of Thomas*
Gos Thos	*Gospel of Thomas*		

Other Abbreviations

BCE	Before the Common Era
CE	Of the Common Era
Oxyr Pap	Oxyrhynchus Papyrus

INTRODUCTION[1]

THE TERM GENERALLY USED for biblical scholarship in professional circles is "biblical criticism." The English word "criticism"—which has its roots in the Greek verb κρίνειν (*krinein*), meaning "to separate," "to think," "to discern," "to decide," "to distinguish," "to judge"—unfortunately conjures up the English word "criticize" with its connotations of attacking, subverting, or undermining. The intention of biblical scholarship is, however, not to criticize, to attack, to subvert, or to undermine the Bible. Rather, biblical scholarship endeavors to better understand the Bible, by using the same methodology that historians use when they investigate documents from ancient Greece, medieval Europe, or modern America. In other words, the goal of the historian is always the same: to analyze available evidence in order to make informed and discriminating judgments about the past.

THE ORIGINS OF MODERN BIBLICAL SCHOLARSHIP

Already in antiquity, Jews and Christians applied critical methods to establish the canons of the Hebrew Bible (what Christians call the Old Testament) and of the New Testament. Ancient Jewish scribes were not only copyists, jurists, and lawyers; they were also teachers and scholars who established rules for copying manuscripts in a conscious effort to standardize biblical texts. Nevertheless, different versions of the books of the Hebrew Bible continued to exist as late as 70 CE[2] in manuscripts known as the Dead Sea Scrolls, and also in the so-called Septuagint, a translation into Greek of ancient Hebrew manuscripts undertaken in Alexandria, Egypt, ca. 250–150 BCE. It was likely sometime around 500 CE that the text of the Hebrew Bible was standardized by the scholars known as Masoretes, whose responsibility it was to maintain the

---

1. This chapter is revised from Arthur J. Bellinzoni, *The Old Testament: An Introduction to Biblical Scholarship* (Amherst NY: Prometheus Books, 2009). Copyright © 2009 by Arthur J. Bellinzoni. All rights reserved.

2. In using the designations BCE (Before the Common Era) and CE (of the Common Era), I am using terminology that is more current and more inclusive than the designations BC (Before Christ) and AD (*Anno Domini*, in the year of the Lord), which are specifically Christian. There is, otherwise, no difference between BCE and BC, or between CE and AD.

tradition and rules that governed the production of all copies of the Hebrew Bible (the so-called Masoretic text, the basis of all modern Hebrew Bibles, or Old Testaments).

In the second and third centuries CE and even later, Fathers of the Christian Church exercised judgments when deciding which Christian writings to include in the canonical New Testament and whether to defend the authority of the Jewish Bible and include it in the Christian canon of sacred scripture. Accordingly, in one form or another, critical study of the Bible reaches back about two thousand years. Nonetheless, although Jewish scribes and early Christian Fathers were encouraged by intellectual curiosity, they were clearly motivated more by doctrinal presuppositions than by what we would consider today to be impartial inquiry and objective research.

Ancient Jewish rabbis and early Christian Fathers essentially assumed that individual books of the Old and New Testaments ultimately had God as their author, although they acknowledged several stages in the development of these books. First there was the divine utterance itself, the words that God actually spoke in the past; second, there was the hearing of that divine utterance by an inspired prophet or mediator chosen or otherwise designated by God to deliver his divine utterance to the people; and third, there was the faithful transcription of the prophet's or the mediator's words into writings by competent and trustworthy scribes, presumably under the inspiration of the Spirit of God or the Holy Spirit, whose role it was to guarantee the authenticity and the accuracy of the written word and its faithfulness to the divine utterance. This process, it was believed, guaranteed the authenticity, the accuracy, and the authority of these writings as "holy books," set apart by God himself as the record of his message for the Jews, and later for Christians, and ultimately for the whole of humankind.

It is not sufficient to rely on the fanciful conjectures of ancient authors or even on long-standing traditions regarding such serious matters as the authorship and date of composition of ancient books. The criterion for such determination rests rather on a critical examination of internal evidence furnished by the individual books themselves and on relevant and available external evidence that can assist in the process of making informed judgments.

Many early Fathers of the Church were aware of problems that have become focuses of modern biblical scholarship. These men were, however, generally concerned with the content and the authority of the church's sacred scripture and, for the most part, simply accepted traditions of Judaism and of the early Christian church regarding matters of authorship, date, and place of composition of the books of the Bible.

In his monumental *Introduction to the Old Testament*, Robert Pfeiffer maintained that

> The crude beginnings of a critical and historical investigation of the Old Testament reach back at least to the second century of our era, when Celsus maintained that the Pentateuch could not have been written by a single author, and Ptolemy (a disciple of the Gnostic teacher Valentinus), in his epistle to Flora,

distinguished in the Pentateuchal law parts inspired by God, parts written by Moses, and parts written by the elders.³

Pfeiffer notes that several ancient writers, some of them early Christian Fathers, made significant contributions to historical criticism of the Bible, but he confers especially strong praise on Porphyry:

> Porphyry, a Syrian Neoplatonist philosopher who lived in Alexandria (ca. 233–304), attacked the historicity of the Book of Daniel, proving conclusively that it was written in the Maccabean period, and that chapter 11 was not a prophecy, but a veiled history of Syria from Alexander to Antiochus Epiphanes.⁴

Likewise,

> Jerome (died 420) refused to commit himself to the view either that Moses wrote the Pentateuch or that Ezra published it, but by identifying Deuteronomy as the lawbook discovered in the Temple during the reign of Josiah (*Commentary on Ezekiel, ad* 1:1) he unwittingly found the key to Pentateuchal criticism.⁵

So too,

> Theodore of Mopsuestia, a theologian belonging to the school of Antioch (died ca. 428), not only perceived that the titles and superscriptions of the Psalms were added to the original compositions, but also that a number of psalms (seventeen, in his opinion) were Maccabean in date.⁶

In addition to these examples cited by Pfeiffer, Origen (185–254), one of the greatest of all Christian theologians, concluded on the basis of internal evidence, specifically stylistic criteria, that Paul was likely not the author of Hebrews (cf. Eusebius, *Church History* 6.25.11ff.), and Origen's disciple Dionysius of Alexandria (ca. 190–265) found linguistic and stylistic reasons to dismiss the traditional view that the apostle John was the author of the book of Revelation (Jerome, *De Viris Illustribus* 1).

These learned and critical Fathers of the Church were exceptions in their times, and there is no uninterrupted line of succession to connect them and their findings to modern biblical scholarship. Their observations had to be rediscovered many centuries later.

Modern biblical scholarship had its earliest foundations in the sixteenth century. The invention of printing about 1440, the advent of the Protestant Reformation in 1517, and the revival of scholarship during the Renaissance in the fourteenth, fifteenth, and sixteenth centuries all contributed to the rediscovery of a method that had long since been set aside, perhaps even forgotten. Print disseminated texts as never before, accelerating the spread of information.

---

3. Pfeiffer, *Introduction*, 43.
4. Ibid., 43.
5. Ibid., 43.
6. Ibid., 43.

The humanistic revival of critical scholarship meant that Europeans rediscovered and relearned biblical Hebrew, classical and biblical Greek, and other languages of the ancient Near East. The convergence of these movements resulted in the emergence and spread of modern biblical scholarship, although the road to the future proved to be extremely treacherous, because the Church surrendered authority in critical areas only after a series of fierce fights.

With a new focus on impartial inquiry, scholars for the first time asked with authority whether the beliefs and the practices of the medieval Roman Catholic Church reflected faithfully the beliefs and practices of their ancient forebears. With that question in his mind, Martin Luther and other Protestant reformers maintained that there should be a return to the authority of the scriptures and an abandonment of the authority heretofore vested in the church, most especially in the bishop of Rome, the Pope. The renewal of interest in the Old and New Testaments in their original Hebrew and Greek was imperative.

The German Protestant reformer Andreas Rudolph Bodenstein (1477–1541), known also as Andreas Carlstadt, or simply as Karlstadt after the city of his birth, presented theses denying free will as early as 1516. He asserted the doctrine of salvation by grace alone and was, by 1518, an ardent supporter of Martin Luther. Karlstadt was apparently the first person since Celsus and Jerome, more than a thousand years earlier, to break with the ancient tradition that Moses was the author of the Pentateuch, because, he argued, the account of Moses' death in Deuteronomy 34 is in the same style as the rest of the Pentateuch and could not have been written by Moses.

Louis Cappel (1585–1658), a French Protestant theologian and Hebrew scholar, was the first trained specialist who had the requisite skills and the courage to carry out, with meticulousness, insight, and reason, a systematic and linguistic investigation of the text of the Hebrew Bible. In his *Arcanum Punctationis Revelatum* (*The Secret of the Pointing Revealed*; 1624), Cappel proved that vowels had been added to the text of the Hebrew Bible during the Christian period and that until that time the text of the Hebrew Bible consisted only of consonants. In his *Critica Sacra* (*Sacred Literary Criticism*; 1650), Cappel proved that even the earlier consonantal text without vowel pointings had not been transmitted without errors and required correction with help from ancient translations as well as some measure of speculation on the part of biblical scholars.[7]

---

7. The Hebrew language is written from right to left and was originally written only with consonants. Vowel sounds between the consonants were understood but not written. Only later, when Hebrew was no longer a spoken language and when Jews spoke Aramaic, or Greek, or Latin, or some other vernacular language did rabbinic scholars add the requisite vowel signs to the Hebrew text in the form of dots and dashes above and below the consonants. These vowel pointings were standardized about 500 CE. Imagine the confusion in trying to understand an English text without vowels. For example, try to pronounce the English word NTRL. That could, of course, be NeuTRaL, or NaTuRaL, or even NoT ReaL, words with very different meanings, yet all written with the same consonants. The opportunity for confusion in reading a text without vowels is enormous. The adding of vowel pointings to the Hebrew Bible much later than when the books were originally written means that those

INTRODUCTION

Jean Morin (1591–1659), a French Roman Catholic priest, has been called the most learned Roman Catholic author of the seventeenth century. Born a Calvinist, Morin converted to Roman Catholicism and in 1618 joined the Oratory at Paris. Several of Morin's writings address questions of the text of the Old Testament: *Exercitationes ecclesiastiae in utrumque Samaritorium Pentateuchum* (*Ecclesiastic Exercises in the Samaritan Pentateuch*; 1631), in which he argued that the Samaritan text and the Greek Septuagint are often superior to the extant Hebrew text of the Old Testament, a position he took up once again in his *Exercitationes biblicae de Hebraei Graecique textus sinceritate* (*Exercises Regarding the Reliability of the Text of the Hebrew and Greek Bibles*; 1663, 1669, 1686). Morin also published the text of the Greek Septuagint in *Biblia graecae sive Vetus testamentum secundum Septuaginta* (*The Greek Bible of the Old Testament According to the Septuagint*; 1628) and the text of the Hebrew-Samaritan Pentateuch in *Pentateuchus hebraeo-samaritanus* (*The Hebrew-Samaritan Pentateuch*; 1645) and *Pentateuchus samaritanus* (*The Samaritan Pentateuch*; 1645).

In 1637, French philosopher René Descartes (1596–1650) published *Discours de la Méthode* (*Discourse Concerning Method*), in which he elevated the principle of doubt to a valid historical, philosophical, and scientific principle. Descartes's approach involved three principles:

1. Man, as a thinking being, stands at the center of all investigation. Descartes's famous phrase *cogito, ergo sum* (I think, therefore I am) summarizes that standpoint.
2. Tradition alone is not a legitimate or convincing reason for acknowledging something as true. It is necessary to question everything except what is so patently obvious that there can be no reasonable basis for doubt.
3. Human reason is the one and only criterion of all truth.

A consequence of Descartes's philosophy was that human reason became a legitimate principle, indeed *the* legitimate principle, for examining religion and the Bible.

Frenchman Isaac La Peyrère (1596–1676) published in Amsterdam in 1655 *Prae-Adamitae* (*Humans before Adam*), in which he concluded that the biblical time span of six thousand years since creation was insufficient to derive Turkish, Chinese, Arabic, and the European languages from a single original language. La Peyrère also argued that Adam was not the first man but merely the earliest ancestor of the Israelites. He also attacked, although only in passing, the Mosaic authorship of the Pentateuch.

La Peyrère's work was considered heretical by the French clergy, by the faculty at the Sorbonne, and by the violent crowd that burned his book and that tried also to burn him—presumably just treatment for the first scientist to extend the age of the earth beyond the restrictive mathematics of the Bible. Religious orthodoxy responded predictably and dogmatically by requiring a *sacrificium intellectus*, a submission of the intellect or of reason to the authority of the Bible and the church. The argument was

---

later rabbinical scholars added the vowels that suited their understanding of the texts. There is, of course, no guarantee that their vowels reflected the intentions of the original authors.

made that fallen reason could serve as no guide to knowledge, and certainly not as a guide to sacred scripture.

In chapter 33 of *The Leviathan* (1660), English philosopher of natural law Thomas Hobbes (1588–1679) summarized the purposes and the methods of the critical study of the Bible by asking such questions as: Who were the actual authors and what were the dates of composition of the several books of the Bible? How did the books of the New Testament gain authority as scripture, if not through the decisions of bishops assembled in 354 at the Council of Laodicea? How can we judge the source of the authority by which we interpret scripture? Hobbes concluded that Moses wrote only a few chapters of the book of Deuteronomy and that most of the books of the Old Testament were written following the Babylonian Exile in the late-sixth century BCE.

One of the most influential figures in the development of historical criticism of the Bible was the Jewish philosopher Baruch Spinoza (1632–1677), whose invaluable contribution to the subject appears in chapters 7–10 of his *Tractatus theologico-politicus* [*Theological-Political Treatise*]. By the time of the publication of this work in 1670, there was nothing particularly new about the claim that Moses was not the author of the whole of the Pentateuch. What was new, however, was Spinoza's claim that the issue of authorship has major importance with regard to determining how scripture is to be understood and interpreted. Specifically, Spinoza was troubled by the fact that the scripture itself had become an object of veneration and that more attention was sometimes paid to the words on the printed page than to the message conveyed by those words.

Spinoza maintained that if the Bible is a historical (i.e. natural) document, then it should be examined like any other phenomenon. The study of the Bible should, therefore, be conducted as one would conduct the study of any other object in nature: by collecting and evaluating empirical data within the book itself and by then setting that data within the context of its time and place of composition.

Spinoza states his position clearly in chapter 7 of the *Tractatus*:

> I hold that the method of interpreting Scripture is no different from the method of interpreting Nature, and is in fact in complete accord with it. For the method of interpreting Nature consists essentially in composing a detailed study of Nature from which, as being the source of our assured data, we can deduce the definitions of the things of Nature. Now in exactly the same way the task of Scriptural interpretation requires us to make a straightforward study of Scripture, and from this, as the source of our fixed data and principles, to deduce by logical inference the meaning of the authors of Scripture. In this way—that is, by allowing no other principles or data for the interpretation of Scripture and study of its contents except those that can be gathered only from Scripture itself and from a historical study of Scripture—steady progress can be made without any danger of error, and one can deal with matters that surpass our understanding with no less confidence than those matters that are known to us by the natural light of reason.[8]

---

8. Spinoza, *Tractatus*, 177.

INTRODUCTION

In precisely the same way in which knowledge about nature is derived from nature alone, so too knowledge about scripture, for Spinoza, must be derived from scripture alone, and in both instances that is accomplished only through the clear and un-theological exercise of rational inquiry. Spinoza maintained that the universal message conveyed in the scripture was a simple moral message, namely, "to know and love God, and to love one's neighbor as oneself." This and this alone is the *true* word of God, and it lies unadulterated in a defective, flawed, distorted, and corrupted text (the Bible), articulated imperfectly and imprecisely in the words of men (the authors of the various books of the Bible). This simple message preserved within the Bible requires no philosophical or metaphysical speculation about the universe or about God; it requires no formal training in philosophy or history. "Scriptural doctrine," Spinzoa maintained, "contains not abstruse speculation or philosophic reasoning, but very simple matters able to be understood by the most sluggish mind."[9]

Another major figure in the emergence of biblical scholarship is Richard Simon (1638–1712), a French Roman Catholic priest and biblical scholar. Simon studied theology at Paris, where he developed an interest in Hebrew and other ancient Near Eastern languages. Simon's *Histoire critique du Vieux Testament* (*Critical History of the Old Testament*; 1678, 1685) raised once again the question of whether Moses could have written material in the books traditionally attributed to him. Simon's views raised strong opposition within France leading to the issuance of a council of state that ordered the seizure and destruction of the total impression of thirteen hundred copies of Simon's book, and Simon himself was expelled by his colleagues from his religious order. The book was republished in the Netherlands in 1685. In his study, Simon called attention to the fact that there is sometimes more than one version of the same story and that these doublets show variations in their literary styles. Consequently, apart from the legal portions of the Pentateuch, which Simon attributed to Moses, the remainder of the Pentateuch was the work of several different authors.

Simon's study was in three volumes. The first dealt with issues of biblical scholarship, such as the transmission of the text of the Hebrew Bible from ancient until modern times and the question of the authorship of the Pentateuch and of other books of the Hebrew Bible. Volume 2 provided an account of the principal translations of the Old Testament, both ancient and modern. Volume 3 consisted of an examination of the Old Testament's principal commentators.

Although many critical positions had been advanced earlier by scholars such as Cappel and Morin, the special value of Simon's work was that it brought together in one place the established results of Old Testament scholarship up to his time. Simon's work provoked considerable hostility not only from the Roman Catholic Church but also from Protestants, who saw in Simon's work a frontal attack on their single most important stronghold, an infallible Bible. Simon responded to attacks leveled against his work in his *Réponse aux Sentiments de quelques théologiens de Hollande* (*Response*

---

9. Ibid.

to the Opinions of Some Theologians from Holland*) (1685). Simon's later work consisted of his *Histoire critique du texte du Nouveau Testament* (*Critical History of the Text of the New Testament*; 1689), in which he discussed the origin and character of the various books of the New Testament, and by his *Histoire critique des versions du Nouveau Testament* (*Critical History of the Versions of the New Testament*; 1690), in which he provided an account of the various translations of the New Testament, both ancient and modern.

In 1693, Simon published what was perhaps his most valuable contribution to biblical scholarship, *Histoire critique des principaux commentateurs du Nouveau Testament depuis le commencement du Christianisme jusques à notre temps* (*Critical History of the Principal Commentators of the New Testament from the Beginning of Christianity until the Present Time*), and in 1695 he published *Nouvelles Observations sur le texte et les versions du Nouveau Testament* (*New Observations on the Text and the Versions of the New Testament*). Simon's contribution to the emerging discipline of biblical scholarship cannot be overestimated. Simon's use of internal evidence has led to his being regarded as the father of modern biblical criticism.

In addition to challenges from philosophy and from the emerging field of biblical scholarship, science began to deal a series of blows to the inerrancy of scripture. Although it was not intentional, a major assault on the Bible came in the sixteenth and seventeenth centuries from the field of astronomy. Polish astronomer Nicolaus Copernicus (1473–1543) began his work on *De revolutionibus orbium coelestium* (*On the Revolutions of the Heavenly Spheres*) in 1515, but it was not until 1543, the year of his death, that he published his findings and in a crushing blow displaced the earth, and therefore humankind, from the center of the universe, and even from the center of our solar system, and advanced the model of a heliocentric universe.

Italian philosopher, poet, and Roman Catholic priest Giordano (Filippo) Bruno (1548–1600) spread Copernicus's system as well as his own view that there were infinite worlds in the physical universe and that the stars are other suns. Bruno was rewarded for his work by being burned at the stake for heresy.

Galileo Galilei (1564–1642) was an Italian mathematician, astronomer, and physicist, who published in 1632 *Dialogo sopra i due massimi sistemi del mondo* (*Dialogue Concerning the Two Chief Systems of the World* [Ptolemaic and Copernican]). For his support of Copernicus's theory, Galileo was tortured at Rome both physically and mentally and remained under house arrest for the remainder of his life, ironically to be absolved by the Roman Catholic Church more than three hundred fifty years later in 1989.

Copernicus's model of the universe was substantially strengthened by German mathematician Johannes Kepler (1571–1630), who was the first to recognize that the planets go around the sun in elliptical rather than in circular orbits. Kepler formulated the laws of planetary motion that describe mathematically the elliptical orbits of all celestial objects. By working independently of the Bible and the church, Copernicus,

INTRODUCTION

Bruno, Galileo, and Kepler diminished significantly the influence of the Bible as a source for scientific knowledge.

As a result of the growing influence of reason during the seventeenth century, science, philosophy, and history began to emerge as separate and distinct branches of learning, increasingly independent of biblical and ecclesiastical authority. These new approaches to knowledge were certain to spill over increasingly into the field of biblical studies. Although the Bible was acknowledged as the final word in virtually all fields of knowledge at the beginning of the seventeenth century, by the end of that century the Bible's universal authority was being eroded, and it was being treated increasingly like any other historical document.

The eighteenth century brought additional support for the progressive views of these earlier scientists and scholars. In 1753, prominent French Roman Catholic physician Jean Astruc (1684–1766) published *Conjectures sur les mémoires originaux dont il paraît que Moïse s'est servi pour composer le livre de Genèse* (*Conjectures on the Original Memoirs that Moses Appears to Have Used in Composing the Book of Genesis*), in which he postulated the existence of two distinct sources in the book of Genesis, based on the alternating use of two names for God, one of which sources used Elohim, and the other Yahweh or Jehovah.

This thesis of two sources in the book of Genesis received little attention until Johann Gottfried Eichhorn (1752–1827) published the first great modern introduction to the Old Testament, his *Einleitung in das Alte Testament* (*Introduction to the Old Testament*, 3 volumes; 1780–83). Eichhorn built on Astruc's hypothesis of two documents in Genesis and expanded the theory by noting that the separate documents have other characteristics, both literary and substantive, and applied his analysis of the sources to the whole of the Pentateuch (Genesis, Exodus, Leviticus, Numbers, and Deuteronomy). Eichhorn's analysis was more radical than Astruc's because Eichhorn was also writing under the influence of eighteenth century German rationalism, English deism, and skepticism and was, therefore, asking questions and raising doubts much more penetrating than the relatively innocuous issue of multiple sources of the book of Genesis.

In doing so, Eichhorn may have been aware of the writings of Englishman Charles Blount (1654–1693), most especially his short pamphlet on the nature of miracles, *Miracles, No Violation of the Laws of Nature* (1683), the publication of which attracted a great deal of hostile criticism; and of Anthony Collins (1676–1729), an English theologian who defined the position of the English deists and defended the cause of rational theology in his *A Discourse Concerning Free-Thinking* (1713). In their writings, Blount and Collins dismissed out of hand specifically both miracles and predictive prophecy and, in addition, the authority of the Old Testament. The writings of Blount and Collins likely afforded Eichhorn the philosophical underpinning for his more radical positions on these issues.

THE NEW TESTAMENT

It was, however, Hermann Samuel Reimarus (1694–1768), German philosopher, man of letters, and professor of Oriental languages, who first expressed an unequivocal and uncompromising opposition to the supernatural in the Bible. Reimarus studied theology, ancient languages, and philosophy and in 1720–21 visited Holland and England, where he likely encountered the English deist movement. Reimarus is best known for his *Apologie oder Schutzschrift für die vernünftigen Verehrer Gottes* (*Apology or Defense for the Rational Worshippers of God*), carefully withheld from publication during his lifetime, but from which, following his death, his friend Gotthold Ephraim Lessing published several chapters under the title of *Fragmente eines Ungennannten* (*Anonymous Fragments*), generally referred to as the *Wolfenbüttel Fragments* (1778). The position of the *Apologie* is pure naturalistic deism, allowing for no miracles and no intrusion of the supernatural into the natural order. Natural religion advances everything that is the opposite of revealed religion and uses doubt with its rationalist presuppositions as the basic principle of all historical investigation. The basic Truths of this natural religion are the existence of a good and wise Creator and the immortality of the human soul, truths that are discoverable only on the basis of human reason and that can and should constitute the foundation of universal religion.

Reimarus's work is the starting point of Albert Schweitzer's masterpiece *The Quest of the Historical Jesus* (1968) (*Von Reimarus zu Wrede*, 1906 [*From Reimarus to Wrede* is the title in the original German]). Schweitzer opens his chapter on Reimarus with these words: "Before Reimarus, no one had attempted to form a historical conception of the life of Jesus."[10] Reimarus's bold work was the first effort to apply systematically and consistently the tools of historical criticism to the life of Jesus, and its results were devastating to Christian orthodoxy of the time. According to Schweitzer, Reimarus stated "we are justified in drawing an absolute distinction between the teaching of the Apostles in their writings and what Jesus Himself in His own lifetime proclaimed and taught."[11] Schweitzer goes on to state: "What belongs to the teaching of Jesus is clearly to be recognized. It is contained in two phrases of identical meaning, 'Repent, and believe in the Gospel,' or, as it is put elsewhere, 'Repent, for the Kingdom of Heaven is at hand.'"[12] According to Reimarus, Jesus took his personal stand within first-century Judaism and accepted its Messianic expectations without modifying or correcting them in any way. What is new in Jesus' teaching is the timetable, namely, that the arrival of the Kingdom (or Rule) of God was imminent.

According to Reimarus, Jesus had no intention of setting aside Judaism and putting a new religion, Christianity, in its place. Drawing a clue from the difficulty that the Easter event was first proclaimed at Pentecost, fifty days after Jesus' death, Reimarus came to the conclusion that following Jesus' unexpected and inexplicable death, his disciples stole his body, hid it, and proclaimed a spiritual resurrection as well as

---

10. Schweitzer, *Quest of the Historical Jesus*, 13.
11. Ibid., 16.
12. Ibid., 16.

INTRODUCTION

Jesus' second coming in glory in the very near future. It is no wonder that Reimarus chose not to publish his work during his lifetime; his conclusions struck at the very heart of Christianity.

In spite of Reimarus's sometimes far-fetched conclusions, his work is extraordinarily significant because of his remarkable eye for detail and his systematic application of the principle of historical reason to the texts of the canonical gospels. Many of Reimarus's insights still remain at the center of biblical scholarship two hundred fifty years after his death: the understanding of Jesus as an eschatological prophet; the problem of the Messianic Secret; the difficulties associated with Jesus' prediction of his own passion, death, and resurrection, the *miracle stories* of the gospels as opposed to the *miracles* of Jesus, the striking difference between the Jesus of the gospel of John and the Jesus of the synoptic gospels (Matthew, Mark, and Luke), and much more.

Reimarus's work was followed by a series of rationalist lives of Jesus to which Schweitzer devotes several chapters in his *Quest*. It was, however, David Friedrich Strauss (1808–74) who provided for New Testament scholars a critical key that is essentially still a working principle of contemporary biblical scholarship. "Religion," Strauss maintained, "is not concerned with supra-mundane beings and a divinely glorious future, but with present spiritual realities which appear as 'moments' in the eternal being and becoming of Absolute Spirit."[13] Strauss maintained "immortality is not something which stretches out into the future, but simply and solely the present quality of the spirit, its inner universality, its power of rising above everything finite to the Idea."[14]

Strauss's masterpiece, *Das Leben-Jesu* (*The Life of Jesus*), published in two volumes of 1,480 pages in 1835 and 1836, when Strauss was still in his twenties, is one of the most brilliant works in the entire corpus of biblical scholarship. Although the concept of myth had frequently been applied by scholars to the Old Testament, prior to the work of David Friedrich Strauss it had never been fully appreciated or consistently applied to the life of Jesus. The word myth was, and to many Christians still is, an offense to religious belief. However, as used by Strauss, religious myth is "nothing else than the clothing in historic form of religious ideas, shaped by the unconscious power of legend, and embodied in a historic personality."[15]

For Strauss, Christianity introduced into history the Idea of God-manhood as that idea was realized and expressed in the historical personality of Jesus of Nazareth. For early Christians, it was frankly impossible to advance a purely historical representation of Jesus, because the early church was confident that Jesus was the incarnation of God-manhood, an ideal that, they believed, is now open to everyone and that remains the ultimate goal of all humanity. As a thoroughgoing Hegelian, Strauss sought, through his mythological interpretation of the New Testament, to bring together and synthesize the *thesis*, as represented by the supernaturalistic explanation of the Bible,

13. Ibid., 73.
14. Ibid., 73.
15. Ibid., 79.

with its opposite or *antithesis*, as represented by the rationalistic interpretation of the Bible, both of which were in Strauss's opinion unacceptable ways of reading and understanding the text.

For Strauss, all of the stories relating to Jesus before his baptism are myths, woven on Old Testament prototypes. As for the accounts of the baptism of Jesus in the four gospels, the historical residue of these stories is only that Jesus was baptized by John the Baptist and was, for a period of time, probably a disciple of John. In their present forms, however, the stories of Jesus' baptism serve to state that either for Jesus or more likely for the early church, the baptism was the moment in Jesus' life in which his messiahship either dawned on him, or served, more probably, as the moment from which Jesus' messiahship was traced by his followers. So too the story of the temptation of Jesus is primitive Christian legend, woven out of stories from the Old Testament, designed to show Jesus' inner struggle concerning his own self-identity.

As for the healing miracles, some of them may have their roots in actual exorcisms that Jesus performed, but in their present form, in which evil spirits or demons recognize Jesus as Messiah, these stories reflect the church's effort to show that the supernatural powers of evil recognized and submitted themselves to Jesus' supernatural power during his lifetime. Reports of healings of the blind, of the deaf, of paralytics, of the dumb, and raisings of the dead belong to the expectations of contemporary Judaism regarding what will transpire in the Messianic age and have their roots not in history, but in passages in the Old Testament (e.g. Isa 35:5–6a, "Then the eyes of the blind shall be opened, and the ears of the deaf unstopped; then shall the lame man leap like a deer, and the tongue of the speechless sing for joy").

Strauss maintained, moreover, that the stories of the resurrection appearances of Jesus to his disciples and to others are all mythical. Matthew knew of such appearances only in Galilee, Luke of appearances only in Jerusalem, and Mark of no appearances at all. For Strauss, if there were appearances of the risen Lord, then he had, indeed, not died; and if Jesus had actually died, then there were, pure and simple, no such appearances. The mythical character of the ascension into heaven is, for Strauss, self-evident.

What Strauss did, story by story, gospel by gospel, was to demonstrate down to the most minute detail that what we have in the gospels of the New Testament are not reliably historical accounts of virgin births, theophanies at baptisms, healings of the sick, and raisings of the dead, culminating in Jesus' own resurrection from the dead and ascension into heaven. Rather what we have are "stories" that *clothe in historical form* the Church's claim or idea that Jesus was a divinely ordained messenger of God. The *stories about Jesus* in the gospels are the "historicizing" of that Idea.

Going a step farther, Strauss was the first to take the position that the Gospel of John has little historical value. The Jesus of the Gospel of John is dominated by the theological conviction of the early church. Unlike the gospels of Matthew, Mark, and Luke, in which history is carefully interwoven with myth, in John there is little more than dogma pretending to be history:

John represents a more advanced stage in the mythopoeic process, inasmuch as he has substituted for the Jewish Messianic conception, the Greek metaphysical conception of the Divine Sonship, and, on the basis of his acquaintance with the Alexandrian Logos doctrine, even makes Jesus apply to Himself the Greek speculative conception of pre-existence.[16]

It has not been my purpose in this section to trace the long and detailed history of the emergence of modern biblical scholarship.[17] I have, however, tried to point to some of the major players who made particularly significant contributions to the emergence of the modern method of biblical scholarship with its deference to rationalism as the primary criterion of historical reason.

THE HISTORICAL METHOD

As we have already seen, the historical method (or what I prefer to call the tools of biblical scholarship) emerged and evolved over a period of several centuries and in the larger context of learning nourished by the Renaissance, the Reformation, and the Age of Reason.[18] However, the basic tenets of that method, the canons of biblical scholarship, have been firmly in place for more than a century, although some scholars and many Christians refuse to acknowledge that fact. Although the war is over, the battle against biblical scholarship rages on in some quarters because of the perceived threat of biblical scholarship to Christian orthodoxy.

Before the rules of biblical scholarship were entirely clear, a number of smaller streams had to flow into a single great river. The first and the simplest of these small streams was an examination of internal evidence within the books of the Bible themselves. That methodology was already evident almost two thousand years ago in the early work of Celsus, Ptolemy, Porphyry, Jerome, Theodore of Mopsuestia, Origen, and Dionysius of Alexandria. The findings of these men had to be rediscovered, relearned, and further developed in the last few centuries. That work began with Karlstadt in Germany in the early sixteenth century, and continued with Cappel, Morin, and La Peyrère in France in the seventeenth century. Even Hobbes writing in England in the seventeenth century built his arguments essentially on an examination of evidence internal to the Bible.

---

16. Ibid., 86.

17. A good summary of that history can be found in succinct form in Krentz, *Historical-Critical Method*.

18. The reader can find a brilliant and comprehensive treatment of the history of Western thought in Tarnas's *Passion of the Western Mind*. Of special interest for our purposes here is chapter 5: "The Modern World View," in which Tarnas discusses the Renaissance, the Reformation, the Scientific Revolution, the Philosophical Revolution, Foundations of the Modern World View, and the Triumph of Secularism. What Tarnas accomplishes in five hundred pages is monumental and far more than I can hope to communicate in a short chapter.

THE NEW TESTAMENT

It was likely Spinoza, a Portuguese Jew, born and raised in Amsterdam, who first understood the importance of examining the Bible as one would study any other object in nature. Spinoza appealed to much more than the issue of internal evidence. He claimed that the Bible was a collection of books written by men and that it was, therefore, subject to the same vicissitudes as any other human endeavor. The Bible is simply one more object within the natural order.

In the late-eighteenth century in his introduction to the Old Testament, Eichhorn embraced for the first time the systematic philosophical perspective of German rationalism and English deism. At about the same time, Lessing published Reimarus's application of an unequivocal opposition to supernaturalism to the books of the New Testament and, more specifically, to the life of Jesus. The final nails were being hammered into the coffin of the old order of biblical interpretation. The rules of biblical scholarship were changing dramatically; they now had an uncompromising philosophical foundation: rationalism.

To understand the significance of this final blow to the old order, it is important to look briefly at the foundational contribution of movements variously called German rationalism, the German Enlightenment, English deism, and skepticism to see how they collectively provided the philosophical underpinning for modern biblical scholarship. German scholarship began to question and eventually to reject the divine authority of the traditional canon of the Bible and, more specifically, the inspiration and presumed correctness of the texts of the Old and New Testaments. It questioned whether it was appropriate to equate scripture with revelation.

The term Rationalism was used to designate the view that human reason, or human understanding, is the sole source, the final test, and the competent judge of all truth. As these insights invaded the study of the Bible, this seemly destructive criticism was leveled especially against the miracles recorded in the Bible and against the inerrancy and authenticity of the scriptures. Most specifically, David Hume (1711–76) directed his celebrated critique of miracles against the justification of religion by any means other than the rational. Hume weighed the possibility of error on the part of the observer of miracles or the historian against the possibility of miraculous occurrences themselves.[19] Human experience, affected by ignorance, fancy, and the imaginings of fear and hope, explains sufficiently the growth of religion and the presence of the element of the miraculous and the supernatural in virtually all religious traditions.

Once the special authority of the Bible had been questioned and its place in the natural order firmly established, it was essential to understand more clearly the original meanings of the ancient texts in their ancient contexts. Scholars understood that

---

19. Trying to find historical evidence to support the miracles of the Bible is like trying to find evidence to refute Darwin. The methodology of much evangelical Christian biblical scholarship is the historical equivalent of intelligent design in the realm of natural science. There is no distinction between bad biblical scholarship and bad science, because the presuppositions of biblical historians and of all historians and of all scientists are and must remain essentially the same. All employ a "scientific" (i.e., a secular, naturalist, non-supernatural) methodology in their work.

INTRODUCTION

a detached and objective reading of the Bible, free from dogmatic preconceptions and with special attention to the ancient languages and the original historical circumstances, would alone produce a more informed and less biased reconstruction and appreciation of the origins of ancient Judaism and early Christianity. Once scholars had established the principle that ancient documents should be examined in their own historical contexts, in a spirit of impartial inquiry and total freedom without predisposition or prejudice, it was only a matter of time until the methodology and tools of modern biblical scholarship emerged.

By the nineteenth century, archeological discoveries in Palestine, Egypt, and Mesopotamia and the decipherment of Egyptian hieroglyphs and ancient cuneiform[20] scripts aroused even greater interest in setting the Bible and biblical religion within the historical, social, and religious contexts of the ancient Near East. Scholars soon understood that ancient Israelite religion could and should be understood within the larger context of ancient Semitic religions and that early Christianity could and should be understood within the historical, social, and religious contexts of the Greco-Roman Hellenistic world. The issue of *contextuality* was paramount to the new method. It was evident that it was essential to look at the Bible itself and the historical figures in the biblical narratives within the historical, social, and religious contexts of the world in which these individuals lived and out of which these written documents arose.

It was suddenly obvious that each of the sixty-six books of the Christian Bible (thirty-nine from the Old Testament and twenty-seven from the New Testament) had its own unique history. Each of the sixty-six books was written in a particular time, in a particular place, by a particular author, and for a particular purpose, and it fell to historians to develop the particular tools and skills needed to discover the origin and history of each book.

Ulrich Wilckens has provided an excellent formal definition of the historical method of biblical scholarship:

> The only scientifically responsible interpretation of the Bible is that investigation of the biblical texts that, with a methodologically consistent use of historical understanding in the present state of its art, seeks via reconstruction to recognize and describe the meaning these texts have had in the context of the tradition history of early [Judaism and] Christianity.[21]

In other words, biblical scholarship is committed to providing a systematic statement of what probably happened in the past after assessing carefully and objectively the authenticity, the reliability, and the veridicality of the ancient sources, free from centuries of interpretative theological overlay. The biblical scholar must be a person

---

20. Cuneiform refers to the wedge-shaped characters in the inscriptions of ancient Akkadians, Assyrians, Babylonians, and Persians. It is the method of writing, not a particular language, just as many people in the world use the convention of the Roman alphabet to write their own individual languages.

21. Wilckens, *The Historical Method*, 33.

of integrity with a passionate and unqualified commitment to the truth, wherever that may lead.

Before proceeding to discuss the rules of evidence for what I consider sound biblical scholarship, it might be helpful to clarify what does and what does not constitute the purview of biblical scholarship by focusing on just two examples: one from the Old Testament and one from the New Testament.

However much evidence conservative Jewish or Christian scholars may muster to argue that God led the people of Israel out of Egypt in the Exodus, the exercise is doomed to failure. No body of evidence can possibly authenticate an act of God, or even the purported "events" described in the book of Exodus. Historians can establish the likelihood that there was an escape from Egypt by a relatively small band of Hebrew slaves, but the magnitude of the event as described in Exodus falls beyond the purview of the historian, who cannot deal with miraculous crossings of seas or with voices from burning bushes, as if they were actual events subject to verification or falsification. They are the language of ancient myth. At best historians can discuss the ways in which a simple event might have been interpreted by Moses and others as an act of Israel's God Yahweh and how such a simple event was exaggerated in the oral retelling and subsequently by authors in their writings. Scholars can discuss the biblical accounts of the exodus, but they can never know from those accounts that they reflect a reliable retelling of what actually happened.

Likewise no body of evidence can ever establish the historicity of Jesus' birth from a virgin. Science dictates that all children are born of a mother and a father, and there is a great deal of evidence in the New Testament that suggests, in fact, that Mary and Joseph were Jesus' biological parents. Historians can also speculate about how and why the early Church initially created oral traditions and then somewhat later written accounts in two different gospels, Matthew and Luke (which, by the way, disagree in significant details as to what is purported to have "happened"). What we have in the early chapters of the gospels of Matthew and Luke are *birth narratives* that demand our attention, but we obviously do not have *reliable accounts* of Jesus' birth. There is a fundamental difference between *miracle stories* and *miracles*. The latter falls totally outside the purview of the historian, who would properly characterize such *stories* as legends that served a particular purpose for early Christian communities.

THE RULES OF EVIDENCE

It should be eminently clear that biblical scholars make no assumptions about the Bible except that they are committed to studying its books in the same manner in which they would study any literature from antiquity, or from any other period. Indeed, because the Bible focuses on *history* and purports to tells the *story* of God's active involvement in *history*, then *history* must be a primary concern, a sine qua

INTRODUCTION

non, for anyone who wants to understand the Bible in as full and objective a way as is humanly possible.

Biblical scholars apply to the books of the Bible the same critical tools that they would apply to any writing that is a human production. In doing so, scholars apply greater value to evidence found within the books themselves than they do to external traditions *about* the Bible, which are generally considerably later than the writing of the books themselves and which often reflect the biases of subsequent generations.

Scholars assume that the books of the Bible were composed by men in specific historical environments of both time and place and that those documents will, therefore, almost always betray some evidence about the time and place of their composition. It is essential to acknowledge that these ancient documents will reflect methods of composition and worldviews contemporary with the world in which they arose and that those methods of composition and those worldviews will be substantially alien to our own. This simple fact means that the reader will have to try to place himself or herself into the time and place in which these books were written in order to be able to understand them properly.

Biblical scholars have determined that there are vast differences in the historical value of the books of the Old and New Testaments, and even differences within specific books insofar as history is the paramount concern. Having said that, it is important to lay out the rules and criteria whereby we can reasonably determine what likely did and did not happen in the ancient past. That is, however, not an easy task, and equally competent unbiased scholars will sometimes examine the same evidence and come to very different conclusions. The problem sometimes lies in the inadequacy or the insufficiency of the evidence, when drawing conclusions leaves a great deal of room for reasonable doubt. We shall, therefore, often speak about what is probable and even possible *within the limits of historical reason*.

Whatever else there may be in the sixty-six books that Christians call their canon of sacred Scripture, there is a human component, and that human component suffers from the same limitations, deficiencies, shortcomings, errors, and biases that we find in any body of literature from which we attempt to reconstruct what likely happened at some time in the past, in our case at various times in the very distant past. That endeavor poses enormous but not insurmountable challenges. It is, however, essential to approach our task with a measure of humility, because there is so much that we do not know and will probably never know with any degree of certainty.

Biblical scholars with a strong personal religious predisposition sometimes fall into the trap of exercising the principles of biblical criticism until they reach the point where the application of rationalist principles appears to conflict with what they consider revealed truth. For the historian as historian, nothing, not even so-called "revealed truth," can stand in the way of the consistent application of the canons of historical reason. There are no exceptions, no exemptions, no bending of the rules, and no retreating from the consistent application of the principles of historical reason.

At this juncture, it is important to state clearly and unequivocally that history and theology are by no means the same. The historian attempts to reconstruct the past; the theologian tries to identify and unfold the meaning and relevance of the texts. Although the two are closely interrelated, they are distinct. Our purpose in this volume will be to focus exclusively on the question of history, what we can and cannot know, and with what measure of certainty.

Whatever the historian's particular subject matter, history is much more than a simple retelling of what is written in the sources. History is a narrative account of the past, based on the sources, but only after their reliability, their competence, their authenticity, their truthfulness, and their clarity have been carefully examined and critically questioned. Biblical scholars must hone their analytical acumen in examining and evaluating the relevant biblical and non-biblical texts in order to provide the best possible explanation of what happened in the past.

In order to appreciate better the methodology used by biblical scholars, let me by analogy consider the example of the courtroom, because historical sources are like witnesses in a courtroom and must be questioned and have their testimony evaluated. John Smith is on trial for murdering Mary Jones, and you, the reader, are a member of the jury. It is, on the one hand, the burden of the state, through the office of the district attorney, to set forth persuasively the evidence needed to convince you and the other jurors that John is guilty. It is, on the other hand, the responsibility of John's defense attorney to cast doubt in the minds of the jurors that John is, in fact, guilty. Typically, witnesses are introduced, examined, and cross-examined to build the case and to influence the jury. Wherever appropriate, physical evidence is admitted for consideration. In the end, the jurors retreat to the privacy of a room, where they are expected to discuss and evaluate the evidence and ultimately to pass judgment on John's guilt, which the state must establish in their minds *beyond reasonable doubt*.

The standard by which the historian makes judgments is understandably less than the courtroom threshold of *beyond reasonable doubt*. Nevertheless, the principle for making judgments is basically the same: to collect and evaluate the evidence (the witnesses) impartially and without bias in order to make an informed and reasoned decision or determination about what actually happened at some time in the past.

Just as there are basic rules of evidence in the courtroom, so too there are basic rules of evidence for the historian as well. Typically, historians, in dealing with a primary source, ask of that source the *who*, the *where*, the *when*, and the *why* questions. To use the book of the Gospel of Matthew as an example, is there either internal or external evidence that enables the historian to determine *where, when, why*, and *by whom* the Gospel of Matthew was written?

The time and place criterion generally affirms that the closer in time and place a source or the author of a source is to an event, the more reliable that source is likely to be. Conversely, the farther in time and place a source or the author of a source is from an event, the less reliable that source is likely to be. The historian looks for

INTRODUCTION

direct testimony of an event. Most reliable are accounts from multiple independent eyewitnesses. Next in reliability would be accounts of an event, created after the event itself, by multiple individuals who themselves had direct access to independent eyewitnesses to the actual event. Obviously, the farther removed a source is from the purported event, the less reliable the testimony is likely to be.

A second criterion to which historians generally appeal is the bias rule. Every source is biased in some way. Documents invariably tell us what the author of the document thought happened, or perhaps in all too many instances what the author of the document wanted his audience to believe happened. Accordingly, every source and every piece of evidence must be examined critically and skeptically. No evidence and no testimony can be taken entirely at its face value, especially evidence or testimony whose primary purpose is to advance the agenda of the witness (or the author) or the agenda of the in-group to which the source is addressed. The Bible is especially problematic in this regard, because it is a collection of in-group writings for in-group readers and does not purport to be objective.

Wherever possible, evidence from external written sources and circumstantial evidence, such as linguistic studies and archaeological data, can and should be called upon to confirm or to question what we find in our biblical sources. Fortunately, we have many written sources from ancient Mesopotamia, ancient Egypt, ancient Canaan, and the Greco-Roman world, which enable us to read the Old and New Testaments against the background and within the context of ancient Near Eastern history, religion, and culture. In addition, we now know much more about the languages of the ancient world and we have substantial raw data from archaeological excavations that we can use as objective, perhaps even scientific and unbiased, evidence in reconstructing the past.

We are in a better position today than we have ever been before to understand the Bible. It would appear, therefore, that we have an obligation to use all of the available methodologies and tools to the fullest extent possible in order to place our feet firmly on as solid a foundation of history as is humanly reasonable. What distinguishes the Bible from most other great religious literature is that throughout the sixty-six books, from Genesis to Revelation, the Bible claims that God has revealed himself in *history*. History is, therefore, paramount for both Jews and Christians, and a clear understanding of the ancient history can and will only enrich our understanding of the origins of both Judaism and Christianity. Faith is, of course, very different from history and science. Nevertheless, history can and should afford an important corrective to unexamined and uncritical religious faith.

Throughout this volume, I will be applying the basic principles of the historical method of biblical scholarship and the rules of evidence as outlined above. I hope to show how these principles work by applying them to particular stories and traditions. At times, I will also introduce or allude to additional principles or criteria that have guided biblical scholars in their efforts to reconstruct the past. At every step, our single-minded objective must always be a quest for the truth—an honest reconstruction of the past within the limits of historical reason. That quest will sometimes lead us to likely conclusions, sometimes to possible conclusions, and sometimes to no conclusion at all. We must be prepared to know when there is not sufficient evidence to know what happened in the past, just as there is in the courtroom sometimes insufficient evidence to convict a suspect. My goal in this volume is to lead the reader, wherever possible, through the method of biblical scholarship to what I consider the best conclusions based on a rigorous application of that method.

CONCLUSIONS

In this chapter, I examined the ways in which the Renaissance, the Reformation, and the Enlightenment increasingly gave rise to reason as the single most important criterion in the search for truth. It was inevitable that the fundamental principles that surfaced as a result of the human effort to understand the universe, our own earth, and human history should and would eventually be applied to a study of the world's religions, an more specifically to a study of the Bible, the life and ministry of Jesus of Nazareth, and the history of Christianity.

We have seen that the historical-critical method, as it has evolved and matured in the course of the human endeavor to understand the beginnings of Christianity, employs unreservedly and unconditionally the same secular methodology that is appropriate to the historical study of any period of history. Why would historians use a different methodology to study the life and ministry of Jesus and the origins of Christianity than they use to study the history of the ancient Mediterranean world of which Christianity was, at least initially, a relatively small part? Why would historians of religion use a different methodology to study the Tao Te Ching, the Bhagavad Gita, the Qu'ran, and the New Testament or to understand the lives and teachings of Confucius, Moses, Lao Tzu, Mohammed, and Jesus? The rules of historical investigation are obviously the same whatever the subject matter.

As we have observed, it was in the eighteenth century that the historical method first forged a serious and consistent path into the study of the New Testament with the appearance of Herman Samuel Reimarus's *Fragmente eines Ungenannten* (*Fragments of an Unknown Writer*), published posthumously by Reimarus's friend Gotthold Ephraim Lessing between 1774 and 1778.

Reimarus made it eminently clear that many of the fundamental claims of Christianity lie outside the realm of historical reason and require an alternative, a rational explanation. Most specifically, Reimarus made it clear that there is no way for historians, as historians, to deal with *miracles* or *resurrections*. Such presumed "events" are, in fact, faith claims that cannot be regarded as representations of what actually happened in the past. What we have here are *stories*, not *events*; what we have are early

INTRODUCTION

Christian *written accounts* of what the early church wanted its followers to believe about Jesus of Nazareth.

In the shadow of the Enlightenment, the intellectual revolution of the nineteenth century changed forever all thought and all study on just about every subject. Geology provided indisputable proof for the antiquity of the earth and of most animal species, including our own species, *homo sapiens*. By the end of the nineteenth century Charles Darwin's theory of evolution based on the mechanism of natural selection was commonplace not only in scientific circles but in educated circles in Europe and America. The fierce debate that had sometimes raged between religion and science throughout much of the nineteenth century died down toward the end of the century with science the clear and unmistakable, if not undisputed, victor. Although the war is over, the battle still rages on, especially in the United States, in evangelical Christian circles.

It is difficult to overestimate the importance of nineteenth century biblical scholarship for the contribution it made to the emerging methodology. Historical criticism became the only approved method of investigation and brought about a revolutionary change in the way in which the Bible is studied. The Bible, Jesus of Nazareth, and the two-thousand-year history of the Christian church had, effectively, been secularized and humanized, and there was no turning back. The books of the Bible were no longer simply sacred scriptures; they were very old documents that required secular study and analysis like every other ancient written source. The Bible was no longer the undisputed solitary criterion for the writing of history. Rather the historical method was now the single undisputed criterion for understanding the Bible. By the end of the nineteen century, Jesus of Nazareth was clearly and unequivocally a man to be studied, analyzed, and examined by using the critical tools of historical reason. Scholars had clearly embarked on a rigorous quest for the historical Jesus as someone distinct from the Christ of Christian faith.

Biblical scholars, educated clergy, and enlightened laypersons had come to an understanding that historical analysis of the Bible is not the same as the retelling of Bible stories. An historical analysis of the New Testament attempts to provide an objective narrative based on what the sources say, but only after their competence, their reliability, and their intelligibility have been scrupulously and meticulously examined, scrutinized, analyzed, and probed. Like a prosecuting attorney in a courtroom, the historian of the New Testament rigorously cross-examines and questions each and every witness or piece of evidence to determine within the limits of historical reason what may have actually happened in the course of the life and ministry of Jesus. Biblical scholarship is analytical and objective, systematic and methodical, because it uses all of the resources of the human mind to investigate all of the available evidence.

The historical-critical method effectively excludes the biblical view of a personal God who intervenes in human history. Such a preconception is an unacceptable and unscientific explanation for something that happened at some time in the distant past, just as it would be unsuitable to explain such an event in our contemporary world. That is the one simple and inviolable canon for the writing of any history—even the history of Christianity. The objective of all history is to promote a body of acknowledged and reputable information that addresses the question "What *actually* happened, when did it happen, and why did it happen?" What, when, and why are the focus of all historical investigation.

An historian cannot, of course, know all that there is to know about any subject or about any single event, however limited the focus might be. The historian is always limited by the reliability of the available evidence, the literary sources, and other data to which we have access. The goal of the biblical historian is to advance a body of information arranged in a narrative that provides an account, an explanation, and an interpretation of the past.

Simply stated, historical criticism is a process for (1) assembling all possible witnesses to an event, both oral and written sources; (2) assessing the value of these witnesses with the help of every available critical tool; (3) linking the data into a single coherent and consistent arrangement; and (4) advancing a conclusion, together with all its supporting evidence, in the form of a narrative. The art of collecting, evaluating, connecting, and presenting evidence is what we call historical criticism. This process constitutes the writing of most, if not all, history.

A good historian looks for every possible explanation for and interpretation of the significant data, looks at the facts in the light of various explanations and interpretations, and then eliminates the explanations and interpretations that fail to account adequately for the data. The explanation and interpretation of the data that best answers all of the questions and that deals most faithfully, most truthfully, and most objectively with all of the data is generally the best possible explanation. In drawing conclusions, the responsible historian presents the narrative explanation and interpretation with supporting information.

Clearly the good historian is a person of honesty and integrity, with no personal agenda, and with an uncompromising passion for the truth for its own sake. The goal of history is quite simply to advance the truth about the past. In addition, because the writing of history does not have the objectivity and precision of the physical and mathematical sciences, historians must have balance and humility and not overdraw their conclusions.

Fortunately, historians of the New Testament have developed several distinctive and specialized tools to assist them in their effort to reconstruct the past. It is essential in the next few chapters to introduce the reader to some of these basic tools and methods that are available to both amateur and professional students of the New Testament alike, as they attempt to understand better the life and ministry of Jesus and the history of early Christianity. We shall begin our study with an examination of textual criticism, philological study, literary criticism, source criticism, form criticism, and redaction criticism.

CHAPTER 1

TEXTUAL CRITICISM

Many years ago I attended a school board meeting with a group of citizens who were there to support the continued teaching of foreign languages in our local high school curriculum. In the course of the meeting, a gentleman stood up and said, "If English was good enough for Jesus, it's good enough for my kids." My friends and I looked at one another and knew that we had lost the day.

The truth of the matter is that Jesus did not speak English; neither was the New Testament written originally in English. Jesus spoke an ancient Semitic language called Aramaic, and the twenty-seven books of the New Testament were all written originally in Greek.

Readers who pick up the New Testament and open to the first book, the Gospel of Matthew, generally take for granted that they are reading a reliable English translation of an original Greek text written almost two thousand years ago by one of Jesus' twelve chosen apostles, Matthew, an eye-witness to events in the life and ministry of Jesus. The same might be said about the Gospel of John. The gospels of Mark and Luke, on the other hand, presumably reflect the teachings of disciples of Jesus' original twelve apostles—the author of the Gospel of Mark being a disciple of the apostle Peter, and the author of the Gospel of Luke being a disciple of Paul, who became an apostle of Jesus a few years after Jesus' death, when the risen Christ appeared to him on the road to Damascus.

The issue is, however, far more complicated than what most ingenuously assume. The four canonical gospels are actually all anonymous writings. Their ascription to Matthew, Mark, Luke, and John probably came much later than at the time of their original composition, likely as the result of a conscious effort on the part of some within the Christian community to assign to these books apostolic authority at a time when their actual authorship was unknown or had been forgotten.

The fact that we do not have the original text of the gospels, the so-called autographs, is even more disconcerting. What we do have are much later copies, usually several generations or even several centuries removed from the writing of the autographs. In fact, we have many thousands of ancient manuscripts of the books of the New Testament.

Still more troubling, it appears that each scribe, each copyist along the way, took lesser or greater liberties in editing and rewriting what he was copying. Just how much editing was done by the earliest scribes in the first century or two of the transmission of the books of the New Testament is not clear, but it is evident that most of the textual changes with which we are familiar were made during the second and third centuries, a time in which Christianity was still diverse and wide-ranging and in which some within the church were taking initial steps toward the establishment of a Christian orthodoxy. In fact, the freedom with which the books of the New Testament were reproduced after their original composition may have been considerable in the earliest decades of their transmission during the time before these books were considered "authoritative," long before they constituted the books of the canonical New Testament.

WHAT IS TEXTUAL CRITICISM?

To remind the reader of the opening paragraph of the Introduction, biblical criticism is the commonly used term for professional biblical scholarship. The term is neutral and does not suggest attack. It does, however, mean the employment of the same scholarly methods and tools that are used to examine historical documents everywhere. Textual Criticism is the particular scholarly discipline that has developed both the principles and the tools required to establish the best and most accurate Greek text of the twenty-seven books of the canonical New Testament.

That process is far more challenging than most readers of the New Testament realize. The discipline involves scrutinizing the ancient New Testament manuscript evidence in order to reconstruct, as accurately as possible, the texts of the books of the New Testament in the forms they had when they left the hands of their original authors.

Modern textual criticism originated and evolved to assist scholars in recreating from the myriad of different manuscripts a working Greek text of the New Testament as close as possible to the autograph, the earliest or original text of each book. Regrettably, we do not have access to the autographs themselves. They were presumably lost in the first decades after they were composed. What we do have in their stead are copies of copies of copies, etc., of which, in the case of the Greek manuscripts of the New Testament, no two are identical. Scholars must, therefore, attempt to reconstruct the autograph from later imperfect and sometimes widely divergent manuscripts.

Textual criticism is, of course, a challenge not only for the books of the New Testament but for virtually all ancient literature. The major difference is that there are many more manuscripts of the books of the New Testament than there are of any other writings from classical antiquity, making the task of reconstructing autographs of the books of the New Testament more challenging. Textual criticism also reveals the mutability with which ancient Christian copyists approached their texts, especially prior to the time they were regarded as canonical. It is important to acknowledge the simple fact that Christians did not begin to think of their texts as "static" or canonical until about 200 CE.

It is relatively easy to speculate about how differences in the manuscript tradition may have developed. We know, for example, that during early Christian worship services someone occasionally read from a letter of Paul or from one of the gospels. A Christian visiting from another church might decide to make or otherwise secure a copy of the relevant text to take to his home church. Alternatively, one church might take the initiative of sending a copy of a text of a gospel or a letter from Paul to another church. The quality of the copy would obviously depend on what an individual scribe hoped to accomplish in making that copy, but verbal exactness does not appear to have been the single most important criterion in copying a manuscript.

We find some hints of the process of disseminating early Christian books in the writings of some early church fathers. For example, 1 Clement, writing in Rome about 95, was obviously referring to a copy of Paul's first letter to the church at Corinth (1 Cor 1:12; 3:4–6, 22; 4:6) that had been circulated in Rome sometime before 95, when he wrote:

> Take up the epistle of the blessed Paul the Apostle. What did he first write to you at the beginning of his preaching? With true inspiration he charged you concerning himself and Cephas and Apollo, because even then you had made yourselves partisans (*1 Clement* 47:1–3).

Likewise, Polycarp, bishop of Smyrna, alludes to the way in which letters were circulated among Christian churches, when he wrote (ca. 120–140):

> Both you and Ignatius wrote to me that if anyone was going to Syria he should take your letters. I will do this if I have a convenient opportunity, either myself or the man I am sending as a representative for you and me. We send you, as you asked, the letters of Ignatius, which were sent to us by him, and others which we had by us. These are subjoined to this letter, and you will be able to benefit greatly from them. For they contain faith, patience, and all the edification which pertains to our Lord. Let us know anything further which you have heard about Ignatius himself and those who are with him (*The Letter of Polycarp to the Philippians* 13:1–2).

The church at Philippi had apparently written to Polycarp asking him to send them copies of letters of Ignatius that he may have had in Smyrna. This letter served as Polycarp's response to the Philippians' request.

Writing in Rome about 150, Justin Martyr refers several times to "the memoirs of the apostles, which are called Gospels" (*Apology* 66:3; *Dialogue with Trypho* 10:2; 100:1; 101:3; 103:8; 104:1; 105:5; 106:2; 107:1). Justin apparently had access to the gospels of Matthew and Luke, and perhaps also to Mark, and composed a harmony of those two (or three) gospels, indicating once again the instability of the text of the gospels in the second century.[1]

Early Christian scribes almost always made both inadvertent and intentional changes when they copied letters or gospels or any other written material. Conscious changes range from rather innocuous efforts to improve the grammar and the style of the text being copied to significant theological alterations, which were apparently intended to enhance or augment the understanding of Jesus or to advance a particular theological doctrine. It was presumably in this manner that manuscripts of the individual books of the New Testament spread from church to church throughout the ancient Roman world, especially in the earliest decades of the history of Christianity.

It was likely only when Christianity became the official religion of the Roman Empire in the early fourth century under the Roman Emperor Constantine that "authorized" copies of the New Testament were generated by professional scribes at the order of the emperor. That conscious decision came, however, more than 250 years after the writing of the autographs of many of the books. In any event, some 5,400 ancient manuscripts of the New Testament survive in their original Greek language, none of them exactly in the form of the autograph drafted by their original authors.

There are, in addition to our almost 5,400 Greek manuscripts, many additional thousands of manuscripts of early translations from the original Greek into other ancient languages—Syriac, Latin, Coptic, Armenian, Georgian, Ethiopic, Arabic, Nubian, Persian, Sogdian (a Middle Iranian language), Gothic, Old Church Slavonic, etc. The value of these translations or versions, as they are usually called, for textual criticism is somewhat limited because idiosyncrasies in each of these languages make it difficult for scholars to reconstruct the original Greek text that lay beneath these thousands of ancient versions.

There are also numerous quotations or allusions to New Testament books in the writings of early church fathers. However, alleged citations of the books of the New Testament in the writings of early church fathers raise additional concerns and challenges. Competent scholars disagree as to whether the earliest fathers (i.e. some of the Apostolic Fathers) were familiar with and quoted directly from specific books of the New Testament, quoted books of the New Testament from memory, or had independent access to oral tradition rather than to written books. With respect to citations from the New Testament in some of the later church fathers, we probably learn more about the kind of New Testament manuscript each was using than about the autographs of individual New Testament writings. Furthermore, we have multiple manuscripts of many of the patristic writings, so the process of trying to ascertain the original text of each church father further complicates the question of whether they had independent access to original readings of the text of the New Testament.[2]

---

1. Bellinzoni, *The Sayings of Jesus*. See also Koester, "Text," 19–37.

2. The names of many of these church fathers are listed in their approximate chronological order with their approximate dates in the Appendix at the end of this chapter.

TEXTUAL CRITICISM

In addition to Greek manuscripts, ancient translations or versions, and allusions in the writings of church fathers, there are about two thousand two hundred lectionaries or books containing readings for liturgical use during the course of the church's calendar year. Most of these lectionaries are Byzantine in origin, in other words historically relatively late, so unfortunately they afford little to no value in the effort to reconstruct the original text of the New Testament.

However interesting the ancient versions, the allusions in church fathers, and the lectionaries may be for appreciating the ways in which ancient copyists engaged their textual traditions, it is primarily the ancient Greek manuscripts that continue to serve as our primary resource for trying to recreate the original Greek text. Although our almost five thousand four hundred Greek manuscripts are all a bit different, they, nevertheless, provide the raw data from which textual critics have developed both the principles and the methodology required to reconstruct something close to the original Greek text of the canonical New Testament.

It is the assumption of most textual critics that the original reading of the text of the New Testament is, in virtually every instance, present somewhere in this vast storehouse of material with some three hundred thousand variant readings, most of which, fortunately, are very minor. In fact, only a few hundred variants are of important historical or theological significance.

Yet the task can be daunting, and some scholars have raised serious concerns about the possibility of success in this endeavor, especially with regard to the so-called synoptic gospels: Matthew, Mark, and Luke. In a study of the text of the synoptic gospels in the second century, Helmut Koester observed that:

> All of that evidence ... points to the fact that the text of the Synoptic Gospels was very unstable during the first and second centuries. ... With respect to Matthew and Luke, there is no guarantee that the archetypes of the manuscript tradition are identical with the original text of each Gospel. The harmonization of these two Gospels demonstrates that their text was not sacrosanct and that alterations could be expected, even if they were not always as radical as in the case of Marcion's revision of Luke, the *Secret Gospel*'s revision of Mark, and Justin's construction of a harmony.
>
> New Testament textual critics have been deluded by the hypothesis that the archetypes of the textual tradition which were fixed ca. 200 CE—how many archetypes for each gospel?—are (almost) identical with the autographs. This cannot be confirmed by any external evidence. On the contrary, whatever evidence there is indicates that not only minor, but also substantial revisions of the original texts [of the synoptic gospels] have occurred during the first hundred years of their transmission.[3]

To add to Koester's list of radical revisions to the gospels during the earliest decades of their transmission, I have called attention to the fact that scholars who

---

3. Koester, "Text," 19. See also Koester, *Ancient Gospels*.

subscribe to the priority of the Gospel of Mark could obviously consider the Gospels of Matthew and Luke as radical editorial (i.e., scribal) revisions of the Gospel of Mark.[4]

So too François Bovon:

> Copyists in the second century worked on the text [of Luke] with the best of intents, but thus concealed the original shape of the text. Theologians either tried to purify the work by abridgement (like Marcion) or to harmonize it with other Gospels (like Tatian). . . . The variant readings within the manuscript tradition have various causes: copyists' mistakes, the influence of oral tradition or of the other Gospels (esp. Matthew), recensions, and tendencies in theological development or ecclesiastic sensibilities."[5]

Moreover, William Petersen finds "profoundly flawed" the view that the text of the New Testament was fixed, for the greater part, at an early date in the form known to us today. Petersen asks poignantly: are we

> to presume that in the period when the text was *least* established, the *least* protected by canonical status, and the *most* subject to varying constituencies . . . vying for dominance within Christianity, the text was preserved in virginal purity, magically insulated from all those tawdry motives? To assent to this thesis not only defies common sense, but mocks logic and our experience with the texts of other religious traditions. . . . The text of the documents which would later be included in the New Testament was neither stable nor established.[6]

These comments about the instability of the text in the earliest period of its transmission aim at the very heart of an essential principle or assumption of most New Testament textual critics—namely, that the original reading of the text of the New Testament is present, in virtually every case, somewhere among the almost five thousand four hundred Greek manuscripts. Although this may be the case with many of the books of the New Testament, I contend that we simply cannot make that assumption with respect to the reconstruction of the autograph of the synoptic gospels.

With the exception of a very few papyrus fragments, the earliest manuscripts of the New Testament date to about 200, or more than a century after the autographs of most of the New Testament books were first written, and most of our extant manuscripts come from a time much later than that. In fact, our two earliest most complete manuscripts of the New Testament date from about 350. It may be that we have access not to the autographs of the books of the New Testament, but that, at least in the case of the synoptic gospels, we may have access to texts that were current about 200. Can

---

4. Bellinzoni, "Gospel of Luke," 47–48, especially n. 8. See also the informative preface to the Gospel of Luke 1:1–4: "Since many have undertaken to set down an orderly account of the events that have been fulfilled among us, just as they were handed down to us by those who from the very beginning were eyewitnesses and servants of the word, I too decided, after investigating everything carefully from the very first, to write an orderly account for you, most excellent Theophilus, so that you may know the truth concerning the things about which you have been instructed."

5. Bovon, *Luke 1*, 1.

6. Peterson, "What the Apostolic Fathers Tell Us," 45–46.

we honestly and realistically expect to close the glaring gap of those critical earlier decades about which we frankly know very little with regard to the transmission of the text of the twenty-seven books of the New Testament?

With that significant reservation in mind, it is important to note that textual criticism of the Bible made significant advances during the nineteenth century. Building upon the pioneering work of Erasmus in the sixteenth century, Karl Lachmann published in Germany in 1831 the first truly critical text of the New Testament, thereby setting aside the so-called *Textus Receptus*, or the Received Text. The *Textus Receptus* was an uncritical, essentially traditional Byzantine text that had served as the "normative" Greek New Testament for several centuries and that served as the basis for the New Testament portion of the King James Bible, published in English in 1611. A second edition of Lachmann's work appeared in 1842–50, together with an extensive critical apparatus and with suggestions on methodology.

With the emergence of textual criticism in the first half of the nineteenth century, with its effort to reconstruct the autograph of the books of the New Testament, German and English scholars began to write commentaries in the second half of the nineteenth century on virtually every book of the Bible, employing a methodology that was critical, linguistic, and historical, rather than a methodology designed to promote religious faith. These commentaries were virtually all written by Christians for Christians to advance Christianity. Most of those scholars assumed rather naïvely that historical study of the Bible would serve to advance rather than to diminish the uniqueness of Christianity.

One of the advances made by text critics was the recognition that manuscripts could be classified by the particular script used by ancient copyists. Scholars observed that the manuscripts of the Greek New Testament generally fall into three principal types: papyri, uncials, and minuscules. The term "papyri" is generally used to refer to papyrus pages that once belonged to codices or bound books but came loose from those books and, therefore, contain only portions of their original texts; papyri date from the second to the eighth centuries. The term "uncials" is generally used to refer to manuscripts written on parchment in uncial (or upper-case) continuous script—i.e. writing with no spacing between words and with no punctuation to mark the ends of sentences; uncials date from the fourth to the tenth century. The term "minuscule" is used of manuscripts written in lower case or cursive script on parchment, and later on paper, of which 80% are of the Majority or Byzantine text type; minuscules date primarily from the eighth to the fifteenth century.

This discovery led to the realization that manuscripts could be also classified into clusters or groups of manuscripts with sufficient similarities to suggest that they belong to a single family. Families of manuscripts apparently originated in the earliest centuries of the spread of Christianity in and around cities such as Alexandria, Antioch, Caesarea, Carthage, Constantinople, Rome, etc. that had especially large and important Christian communities. As additional new churches developed around these important urban centers, more manuscripts of Christian books were created for those new churches. These new manuscripts would obviously both preserve and amend local readings, thereby creating the families of manuscripts typical of a particular city, locality, or region.

Although textual critics have not always agreed on details of these clusters of manuscripts, these families of manuscripts usually include the following:[7]

1. The Alexandrian Text probably preserves some of the oldest readings of the New Testament. The text of Alexandrian manuscripts is generally shorter than that of other families of manuscripts and shows no significant evidence of the grammatical and stylistic improvements characteristic of most later readings.[8]

2. The Western Text is characterized by a tendency to paraphrase, to omit, to amend, and to add entire sentences, as well as a tendency for harmonization. It circulated particularly in Italy, Gaul, North Africa, and Egypt.[9]

3. A text type previously called the Caesarean Text probably originated in Egypt and may have been spread by Origen to Caesarea, and subsequently to Jerusalem. It is characterized by a conscious tendency to achieve literary excellence.[10]

4. The Byzantine Text is the latest of the families of manuscripts and is set apart by its precision and its completeness.[11] Because of its numerous manuscripts, the Byzantine Text was generally considered the most authoritative text and served as the basis for the printing of the *Textus Receptus*.

In an article on textual criticism, Eldon Jay Epp lays out a series of important criteria for reconstructing the earliest text of the New Testament based on both external and internal evidence.[12] In the following outline, Epp identifies these criteria as particularly significant for recognizing those variants that most likely reflect the autograph or the oldest text of the books of the New Testament:

---

7. Epp, "Textual Criticism," 431; Metzger, *Textual Commentary*, xvii–xxi. New Testament manuscripts are listed according to the following convention: papyri are all listed with a capital P or P and a numerical superscript (e.g. P66 and P45); uncials usually with a capital letter (e.g. ℵ and D), and minuscules generally with numbers (e.g. 1739 and 383).

8. The Alexandrian Text is represented by a line of manuscripts that includes P66, P75, B (Codex Vaticanus), ℵ (Codex Sinaiticus), C (Codex Ephraemi), A (Codex Alexandrinus), L (Codex Regius), 33, 1739; the Sahidic and Boharic Coptic versions from Upper and Lower Egypt respectively; and Alexandrian church fathers from Clement and Origen to Cyril. [The identification of these and other Greek manuscripts as well as manuscripts of the Latin, Syriac, Coptic, Armenian, Ethiopic, Georgian, and Old Church Slavonic versions that are mentioned in this chapter are identified with their approximate dates in the Appendix at the end of this chapter.]

9. The Western Text is represented by P29, P38, P48, 0171, D (Codex Cantabrigiensis), 1739 in the book of Acts, 383, 614; Marcion, Tatian, Irenaeus, Tertullian, Cyprian; and Old Latin versions.

10. The Caesarean Text is represented by P45, W (Codex Washingtonianus), Q (Codex Koridethi); Eusebius of Caesarea and Cyril of Jerusalem.

11. The Byzantine Text is represented by Codex A (Codex Alexandrinus) in the gospels, and the greatest number of miniscule manuscripts, including P42, P68, P84, and perhaps P74.

12. Epp, "Textual Criticism," 412-35; see 431 for the chart cited here.

TEXTUAL CRITICISM

A. *Criteria related to external evidence*

1. A variant's support by the earliest manuscripts, or by manuscripts assuredly preserving the earliest texts

2. A variant's support by the "best quality" manuscripts

3. A variant's support by manuscripts with the widest geographical distribution

4. A variant's support by one or more established groups of manuscripts of recognized antiquity, character, and perhaps location, i.e. of recognized "best quality"

B. *Criteria related to internal evidence*

1. A variant's status as the shorter or shortest reading in the variation unit

2. A variant's status as the harder or hardest reading in the variation unit

3. A variant's fitness to account for the origin, development, or presence of all other readings in the variation unit

4. A variant's conformity to the author's style and vocabulary

5. A variant's conformity to the author's theology or ideology

6. A variant's conformity to Koine (rather than Attic) Greek

7. A variant's conformity to Semitic forms of expression

8. A variant's lack of conformity to parallel passages or to extraneous items in the context generally

9. A variant's lack of conformity to Old Testament passages

10. A variant's lack of conformity to liturgical forms and usages

11. A variant's lack of conformity to extrinsic doctrinal views

A succinct summary of these criteria suggests that there are both external and internal criteria for establishing the oldest readings, or possibly even the autograph, of a New Testament book. The external evidence indicates that a textual reading or variant that is found in manuscripts that are the earliest, that are of the best quality, and that reflect the widest geographical distribution have the greatest claim to authenticity, especially if the reading is found in more than one "family" of manuscripts. The internal evidence indicates that a textual reading or variant that is shorter; that is harder (i.e. less orthodox); that can more easily account for other variant readings; that conforms to the author's style, vocabulary, and theology; that is written in Koine Greek; that contains Semitisms; that shows no harmonization to other texts; that lacks conformity to Old Testament parallels; that lacks conformity to liturgical texts; and that shows less predisposition to evolving doctrinal views has a greater claim to authenticity. These external and internal criteria have been developed and tested by scholars for almost two centuries since Lachmann began the work of Textual Criticism in 1831.

APPLYING THE METHOD TO THE TEXT OF THE NEW TESTAMENT: SOME EXAMPLES

With these criteria in mind and to illustrate the method and the importance of textual criticism, let us proceed to examine six passages in the New Testament with an eye to seeing more clearly how textual critics reconstruct the earliest form of the text and to understanding the specific results in these six instances. In each case, I will compare the best reconstructions with what actually appears in some of our most commonly used Bibles. The following sections might be considered "test cases," as they investigate both specific textual variants and the value of Epp's criteria.

MARK 1:1

"The beginning of the good news of Jesus Christ, the Son of God."[13]

This first example appears in the openng words of the Gospel of Mark, actually in the title or so-called superscription. In recent translations there is sometimes a footnote to this verse saying something to this effect: Some ancient authorities lack the words "the Son of God." A more accurate footnote would say that most textual critics agree that the words "the Son of God" probably did not appear in the autograph of Mark 1:1 but that they were added by later scribes to enhance the image of Jesus at the very outset of the gospel by advancing or making specific the doctrine of Jesus' divine sonship.

The fact that Jesus is referred to as the Son of God elsewhere in Mark (1:11; 3:11; 5:7; 9:7; 12:6; 14:61; 15:39) does not necessarily support its presence in Mark 1:1. Likewise, although several early manuscripts have the phrase "the Son of God"[14], "Son of God" is not found in many of the most important manuscript witnesses.[15]

The shorter reading ("The beginning of the good news of Jesus Christ") meets several of Epp's criteria as described above: A 1, 2, 3, 4; B 1, 2, 3. The longer reading fails on Epp's criteria. Simply stated, it is much easier to explain why an early scribe might have added the phrase "the Son of God" than it is to explain why an early scribe would have deleted those words. It is also difficult to explain why a scribe would unintentionally miss such an important phrase so early in his transcription of a manuscript, within the first six words of the very beginning of the gospel.

---

13. Unless otherwise noted, the Scripture quotations contained herein are from the New Revised Standard Version Bible, copyright © 1989 by the Division of Christian Education of the National Council of the Churches of Christ in the U.S.A. Used by permission. All rights reserved.

14. ℵ1, B, D, L, W; 2427; a few latt, sy, co versions; Irenaeuslat, Origenlat, and Augustine.

15. ℵ*, Θ, *l*, 28c, 2211; a few sams, syrp, arm, geo; Origen.

TEXTUAL CRITICISM

So why not simply print in our English translations of Mark 1:1 what most textual critics conclude was the original text: "The beginning of the good news of Jesus Christ"? Period! It is puzzling that contemporary translations of the New Testament still tend to avoid tampering with what has been the traditional reading since the appearance of the authoritative but (critically speaking) inferior King James Version, even when it is clear that the text they are printing in modern translation was almost certainly not in the text of the autograph. Quite frankly, this practice is misleading and unprofessional; yet it persists in many otherwise excellent modern editions.[16]

Proposed reading: "The Beginning of the good new of Jesus Christ."

MARK 6:3

"Is not this the carpenter, the son of Mary and brother of James and Joses and Judas and Simon, and are not his sisters here with us?"

The second example appears in Mark 6:3, a passage that reports that some people, upon hearing Jesus preach in the synagogue in Nazareth, expressed amazement at his teaching before asking who this Jesus was. A footnote to this passage often states something like: Other ancient authorities read: "Is not this *the son of* the carpenter and of Mary, etc.?" Once again, textual critics agree that what is in the footnote in some Bibles was probably in the autograph or the earliest version of Mark 6:3. The concern with this verse was that the more probable original text implies that both Joseph *and* Mary were Jesus' biological parents. Unthinkable! Most likely, later copyists deliberately changed the text because it contradicted the teaching of Matthew and Luke that Joseph was not Jesus' biological father and that Jesus was, in fact, born of a virgin.

The more difficult reading ("Is this not the son of the carpenter and of Mary?") is found in the earliest surviving fragment of Mark (P45), in a number of minuscules,[17] and in some early versions.[18] Once again, Epp's criteria are helpful, as the text of Mark 6:3 is informed by his criteria A 1, 2, 4; B 2, 3, 5, 11. The most compelling argument in support of this reading is that it is difficult to imagine why a scribe would change the text in a way that would imply that Jesus was the son of Joseph, but it is very easy to understand why a scribe would change the text in a way that would suggest that Jesus was not Joseph's son.

In Jewish tradition, the customary way of identifying anyone is through his patrilineal descent, e.g. Jesus, son of Joseph. Some have suggested that identifying Jesus as the son of Mary in this passage is actually a slur against Jesus' legitimacy, that Joseph was not Jesus' biological father, that Jesus was actually an illegitimate child. According

---

16. Bart Ehrman addresses this issue in his important study *The Orthodox Corruption of Scripture*, 72–75.
17. Specifically family *f*13, 33, 565, 579, 700, 2542.
18. Including a few it, vgmss, bomss, and eth; and in Origen.

to this view, the stories of the virgin birth in Matt 1:18–20 and Luke 1:34–35 were the church's subsequent response to the charge of Jesus' illegitimacy. Mark, of course, knows nothing of the tradition of the virgin birth, and there is nothing else in the Mark's gospel to suggest that Jesus was illegitimate.

Interestingly, this passage in Mark 6:3 raises another theological problem for Christians who believe in the perpetual virginity of Mary. The text refers specifically to Jesus' siblings, at least six in number: four named brothers and at least two and possibly more unnamed sisters:

> Is not this [Jesus] . . . the brother of James and Joses and Judas and Simon, and are not his sisters here with us?

The church's belief in the *perpetual* virginity of Mary appears to have originated in the middle of the second century, possibly with the writing of the *Protevangelium of James*, but apparently this doctrine did not result immediately and consistently in changes to the reference to Jesus' brothers and sisters in Mark 6:3.

Instead of tampering with this portion of the text, the church explained this problematic passage in one of two ways: either the six or more additional children were actually Jesus' more distant relatives (perhaps cousins) rather than his biological brothers and sisters, or they were Joseph's children from a previous marriage. Of course, there is no credible contemporary evidence to support either explanation. Rather, both are later, unconvincing, apologetic efforts to explain the data (the report of Jesus' brothers and sisters) in light of a prior theological commitment to belief in Mary's perpetual virginity.

The meaning of the original text of Mark 6:3 is eminently clear: Jesus had several brothers and sisters, all of whom were the children of Mary and Joseph. This view is also supported by the text of Luke 2:7, which reports that Mary "gave birth to her *firstborn* son [Jesus] and wrapped him in bands of cloth, etc." *Firstborn* clearly implies that Mary bore other children by Joseph. It would be curious to refer to an *only* child as a *firstborn* child. Jesus was apparently the eldest of Mary's and Joseph's seven (or more) children. Joseph's paternity of Jesus is also assumed in John 6:42a: They (the Jews) were saying, "Is not this Jesus, the son of Joseph, whose father and mother we know?" Interestingly, the Gospel of John does not contain a birth narrative such as what we find in Matt 1–2 and Luke 1–2 and shows no familiarity with the tradition of the virgin birth. Paul too knew that Jesus had brothers (1 Cor 9:5), although in his letters he identified by name only James (1 Cor 15:7; Gal 1:19).

With respect to this verse, once again theological orthodoxy in the form of intentionally modified manuscripts has relegated the probable text of the autograph to a footnote in many modern translations. More conservative or traditional translations, such as the King James Version and the New International Version, do not even include the footnote. It is interesting that the parallel to Mark 6:3 in Matt 13:55 reads "Is this not the carpenter's son? Is not his mother called Mary?" And the parallel to

Mark 6:3 in Luke 4:22 reads "Is not this Joseph's son?" It is difficult to explain why the gospels of Matthew and Luke, both of which report the virgin birth in their infancy narratives, would have identified Joseph as Jesus' father in these passages if they had not found this detail in the manuscripts of Mark to which they presumably had independent access.[19]

Proposed reading: "Is not this the son of the carpenter and of Mary and brother of James and Joses and Judas and Simon, and are not his sisters here with us?"

JOHN 1:34

> "And I myself [John the Baptist] have seen and have testified that this is the Son of God."

The Revised Standard Version includes the following footnote: Other ancient authorities read: "is God's chosen one" in lieu of the words "the Son of God."[20] Yet, the reading "Son of God" is found in far more manuscripts.[21] Even so, the manuscripts with the reading "God's chosen one," although a minority, reflect a more primitive theology, one bordering on theological adoptionism, the view that Jesus was "the chosen" or "the elect" of God, that he was "adopted" by God, some would say at the time of his baptism.

Changing the words "God's chosen one" to "the Son of God" clearly reflects a shift to the more exalted theology of Jesus' divine sonship. It is easy to imagine how Christian scribes might change "God's chosen one" to "the Son of God," a phrase that is actually more typical of Johannine theology. It is almost impossible to understand how a Christian scribe would change "the Son of God" to "God's chosen one," a phrase with a significantly more diminished (almost adoptionist) theology, especially in light of the Logos hymn in John 1. It is quite possible that this change in the reading was part of the larger polemic against the adoptionist theology that was rejected by several early Christian fathers and more formally at the Council of Nicaea in 325. Epp's criteria A 1, 2, 3, 4; B 2, 3 are helpful in determining what was likely the earliest form of this verse.[22]

Proposed reading:

> "And I myself have seen and have testified that this is God's chosen one."

---

19. In the following chapter I will present evidence to show that the authors of the gospels of Matthew and Luke almost certainly used the Gospel of Mark as their primary source.

20. These other ancient authorities include ℵ, P5, P106, 77, 218, b, e, *ff*2, sys.c, Ambrose—some of the earliest and best manuscripts of the Western tradition, as well as one of the earliest Byzantine papyri, and witnesses in Egypt, Syria, and the Latin-speaking West.

21. Including P55 and P66, as well as A, B, D, Θ, syh, bo.

22. See also Ehrman, *The Orthodox Corruption of Scripture*, 69–70.

MATTHEW 24:36

> "But about that day and hour no one knows, neither the angels of heaven, nor the Son, but only the Father."

This reading carries the footnote: other ancient authorities lack "nor the Son." The phrase "nor the Son" appears in the great majority of manuscripts of the Alexandrian, Caesarean, and Western manuscripts and in Origen, but it is omitted in several important manuscripts.[23] Although the phrase probably did not appear in the earliest form of the Markan parallel (Mark 13:32), it was apparently added by the author of the Gospel of Matthew; or it may have already appeared in the particular manuscript of Mark known to the author of the Gospel of Matthew. How otherwise can it be explained in some manuscripts of Matthew, but not in others? Why would later scribes add it to Matthew and, thereby, create theological difficulty by suggesting that God's divine son did not know when his second coming would occur? It appears more likely that the author of the Gospel of Matthew added it to his Markan source and that some scribes subsequently realized the theological embarrassment of the phrase and deleted it from their manuscripts of Matthew by harmonizing it with Mark. The problem for the scribes was that the phrase suggested that the Son of God was *not* all-knowing.

What is evident from this discussion is that the Christological controversies of the second and third centuries obviously influenced the ways in which scribes transmitted and intentionally modified the text of the New Testament. Ehrman is correct in referring to this tendency as "the orthodox *corruption* of scripture" in a conscious effort on the part of some scribes to replace the early church's "lower" Christology with the "higher" Christology that was beginning to point toward what would become Christian "orthodoxy" in the fourth century. This process of an orthodox corruption of scripture was fortunately not consistent, so some elements of this "lower" and more primitive Christology still survive in a number of manuscripts and in a number of passages in the New Testament. Epp's criteria A 1, 2, 3, 4; B 2, 3 are helpful in determining the earliest reading; this is, however, one instance in which the longer reading, not the shorter, is likely more original (therefore contrary to Epp's criterion B 1, which generally favors the shorter or the shortest reading).

Proposed reading: "But about that day and hour no one knows, neither the angels of heaven, nor the Son, but only the Father."

ROMANS 8:28

> "We know that all things work together for good for those who love God, and who are called according to his purpose."

---

23. Including ℵ, L, W, *f*1, 33, M, g1, vg, sy, co, and Jeromemss.

This is a particularly challenging verse, whose meaning is very different depending on which of two possible readings is regarded as original to Paul. The presence or absence of *ho theos* (God) as the subject of the main verb in various manuscript traditions affords very different interpretations of this verse.

If *ho theos* (God) is included as the subject,[24] the verse reads: "But we know that in all things God works for good with those who love God."

If *ho theos* (God) is omitted as the subject,[25] the verse would then read: "But we know that all things work together for good for those who love God."

The manuscript tradition weighs more heavily to omitting *ho theos* as the subject. So too, the appearance of the word "God" both toward the beginning of the sentence as the subject of one verb and at the end of the sentence as the object of a second verb is awkward. A simple masculine pronoun in the second instance would be both uncomplicated and more appropriate. Based on Epp's criteria A 1, 2, 3, 4, the preferred reading is:

"But we know that all things work together for good for those who love God."

1 JOHN 4:19

"We love because he first loved us."

There is a footnote that reads: other ancient authorities add "him" [after the word "love"]; others add "God" [after the word "love"]. This is a particularly challenging verse, depending on which reading is original to the author of 1 John.

The first question is whether the verb "we love" had as an object in the original text either "him" or "God" (the meaning would be the same in either case). Or was the object of the verb "one another" or "the brethren" (the meaning would once again be the same in either case)? Or did the verb "we love" have no object at all? The difference in meaning is significant.

Is our love of God the result of the fact that God loved us first? Such a tit-for-tat reciprocity sounds theologically offensive. Or does the sentence imply that we should love one another because God loved us first? That is certainly implied just a few verses earlier in 1 John 4:11 ("Beloved, since God loved us so much, we also ought to love one another"). The textual evidence is interesting:

"God" is found as the object of the verb "we love" in several manuscripts;[26]

24. As in P46, A, B, 81, sa, eth.

25. As in ℵ, C, D, F, G, K, L, P, Ψ, 6, 33, 69, 88, 104, 256, 263, 323, 326, 330, 424, 436, 451, 459, 614, 629, 945, 1175, 1241, 1243, 1319, 1505, 1506, 1573, 1735, 1739, 1836, 1852, 1874, 1877, 1881, 1912, 1962, 2127, 2200, 2464, 2492, 2495, M, latt, syp.h, bo, arm, geo, slav; Clement of Alexandria, Origengr.lat, Eusebius, Cyril of Jerusalem, Diodore, Didymus of Alexandria, Macarius/Symeon, John Chrysostom, Cyril of Alexandria, Hesychius, Theodoret of Cyrrhus, Lucifer, Ambrosiaster, Ambrose, Jerome, Pelagius, Augustine.

26. In ℵ, 048, 33, 81, 614, 630, 1505, vgcl, sy, bo.

"him" is found as the object of the verb in two traditions;[27]

a few very minor witnesses have "each other";

there is no object of the verb "we love" in several manuscripts;[28]

Codex Alexandrinus and the Vulgate, obviously by way of clarification, read "God" as the subject of the second verb, but this addition is clearly a later addition to the original text.

These emendations to such a brief sentence testify to the fact that the meaning of 1 John 4:19 was not always clear, even in antiquity.

As for the first verb, should it be read as a simple indicative "we love," or as a hortatory subjunctive "let us love" (as we find it translated in the Latin and in the Syriac Peshitta)? The hortatory subjunctive may be supported by what the author said just a few verses earlier in 1 John 4:7a: (Beloved, let us love one another, because love is from God).

The fact that the sentence begins with the pronoun *hēmeis* (we) places special emphasis on that word, suggesting a translation into English such as "as for us, we."[29]

Accordingly, on the basis of Epp's criteria A1, 2, 3, 4; B1, 3, 4, 5, I would suggest as the original reading:

"As for us, let us love, because he loved us first."

These illustrations indicate the profound importance of textual criticism in providing scholars with the tools needed to reconstruct the autographs or the earliest readings of the twenty-seven books of the New Testament. These six examples should give readers food for thought in their quest for the historical Jesus and for a clearer understanding of the theological and Christological perspectives of the earliest church. It is obviously essential to have available to scholars and to laypersons alike translations of the New Testament that are free from theological bias and that are consistently as close as possible to the autographs.

CONCLUSIONS

Any study of the New Testament must obviously focus on an examination of the text. It is not always clear, however, what constitutes the "authentic" text of the New Testament or what is the most appropriate way in which to examine and understand the

---

27. In Ψ and M.

28. In A, B, 323, 945, 1241, 1739; some vgst.ww, sa.

29. See also 1 John 2:20 2:24; 2:27, where we find the same emphatic use of the pronoun at the beginning of a sentence, but in these instances with the pronoun "you," suggesting that this is a common literary feature of the author.

text. In this chapter we have looked closely at a scholarly discipline whose purpose it is to scrutinize and understand more clearly the text of the New Testament: textual criticism. This discipline has a very specific purpose and a tested methodology designed to yield valuable and constructive results.

As we have seen, the purpose of textual criticism has been to develop both the principles and the tools required to establish the most accurate Greek text of the New Testament, the earliest version of each book or the autograph. Particularly important in textual criticism is identifying as accurately as possible the date and the place of origin of each ancient manuscript or manuscript fragment. The place of origin of a manuscript is often relatively easy to determine, as it is generally the same as the place where the manuscript was first discovered in modern times. Although manuscripts were obviously carried from one place to another, most manuscripts probably did not travel too far from the place in which they were first written, or at least we have little choice but to begin with that assumption in the absence of evidence to the contrary.

The science that provides scholars with the tools needed to determine the date of individual New Testament manuscripts is paleography, the science of "old writing," or the study of ancient writing. Paleographers examine the calligraphy of each manuscript and scrutinize the ways in which scribes formed individual letters. Scholars are then able to establish how the shape and form of individual lettering evolved over time. Such a change in calligraphy is evident in English, as cursive letters that we write today look quite different from many of the same letters found in documents a hundred or more years old.

Although few writings from antiquity come to us with a date inscribed on the manuscript, trained paleographers can date manuscripts fairly accurately based on the form of the various letters. Beyond that method of dating, science has provided another tool to confirm the work of paleography: carbon-14 dating, which determines the age of ancient artifacts of biological origin up to about 60,000 years old by measuring the proportion of radioactive carbon remaining in the artifact.

Although it was paleographers who initially dated the Dead Sea Scrolls, their results were subsequently confirmed by carbon-14 dating. Moreover the age of the legendary Shroud of Turin, the mantle that supposedly covered Jesus' body after his death, was tested in 1988 through carbon-14 dating and determined to come from the period 1260–1390, establishing beyond reasonable doubt that this relic is a medieval forgery. The downside of carbon-14 dating is that scientists must destroy a small amount the original material in order to determine its date, as was done in the case of the shroud. For that reason, scholars prefer to rely, whenever possible, on paleography.

An important assumption of textual criticism is that the original reading of the text of the New Testament is present somewhere, in virtually every case, among the almost 5,400 Greek manuscripts that have survived. As I indicated above, Helmut Koester, François Bovon, William Petersen, and I are less confident than most about this assumption. It is not self-evident that through the application of the principles of textual criticism we have undeniable and incontrovertible access to the autographs rather than to texts or to archetypes that were current in about 200, especially in the case of the synoptic gospels. Yet, it matters considerably whether we have access to something close to the autographs or access to archetypes that were current around 200, especially if texts were modified significantly by scribes during the earliest decades of their transmission. This is especially troublesome when we realize the degree to which conservative Christians put disproportionate emphasis on the Bible as the Word of God.

The truth of the matter is that we will never know definitively the answer to this troubling question. Accordingly, we have no choice but to work with the best text that scholars have made available to us without knowing exactly what it is that we are working with. It is to be hoped that we can continue to evaluate this dilemma as we look more closely at such issues as the literary relationship among the synoptic gospels, to which we will turn in a subsequent chapter.

Modern textual criticism began in 1831 with the publication of Karl Lachmann's critical text of the New Testament. Lachmann's study set aside the *Textus Receptus* from its heretofore unquestioned position as the most reliable Greek text of the New Testament, and thereby rendered obsolete all earlier translations of the New Testament from Greek into modern languages because they had all used inferior Greek manuscripts. Among those early translations rendered obsolete was the King James Bible of 1611, although its status as an "authorized" translation has not been seriously compromised in the eyes of many, if not most English-reading Christians. The second edition of Lachmann's Greek text appeared 1842–50 and contained an extensive critical apparatus and specific suggestions concerning methodology. Lachmann's work marks the beginning of modern textual criticism.

The subsequent identification of the several "families" of New Testament manuscripts—specifically Alexandrian, Western, Caesarean, and Byzantine types —was an important step in advancing an understanding of the ways in which scribes modified manuscripts which they were reproducing. The work of Lachmann and a century and a half of scholarly successors is reflected in Epp's criteria for ascertaining the oldest readings.

A succinct summary of Epp's criteria suggests that there is both external and internal evidence for determining what are probably the oldest readings. The external evidence can be summarized by saying that those manuscripts that are the earliest and that have broad geographical representation have the greater claim to authenticity. The internal evidence can be summarized by saying that those manuscripts that have the shorter and the harder (i.e. the less orthodox) readings are generally more reliable and are more likely closest to the autograph.

In the course of this chapter, we applied Epp's criteria to six verses in five different books of the New Testament and found the results of that exercise rewarding. In each instance, we were able to draw reasonable conclusions about what was likely the oldest form of the text, the task that is the ultimate objective of New Testament textual criticism.

APPENDIX TO CHAPTER 1

In order to understand more clearly the significance of the textual evidence discussed in this chapter, the following table of manuscripts is offered, based on material drawn primarily from Nestle-Aland, *Novum Testamentum Graece*, 27th edition (Stuttgart: Deutsche Bibel Gesellschaft, 2006).

Greek Manuscripts	
Manuscript (Papyri)	Century
P^5	3rd
P^{29}	3rd
P^{38}	circa 300
P^{42}	7th/8th
P^{45}	3rd
P^{46}	circa 200
P^{48}	3rd
P^{55}	6th/7th
P^{66}	circa 200
P^{68}	7th (?)
P^{74}	7th
P^{75}	3rd
P^{84}	6th
P^{106}	3rd
P^{108}	3rd

Uncial Codices	
ℵ	4th
A	5th
B	4th
C	5th
D	5th
F	9th
G	9th
K	9th
L	8th
P	6th
Q	5th
W	4th/5th
Θ	9th
Ψ	9th/10th
048	5th
0171	circa 300

Miniscule Codices	
6	13th
28	11th
28c = later correction of 28	
33	9th
69	15th
77	5th
81	6th
88	5th/6th

THE NEW TESTAMENT

104	7th	1874	?
218	5th	1877	14th
256	8th	1881	14th
263	6th	1912	10th
323	12th	1962	11th/12th
326	10th	2127	12th
330	1185	2200	14th
383	13th	2211	?
424	11th	2427	14th (?)
436	11th/12th	2464	9th
451	11th	2492	14th
459	?	2495	15th
565	9th	2542	13th
579	13th	l	12th
614	13th		
629	14th		
630	12th/13th		
700	11th		
945	11th		
1175	10th		
1241	12th		
1243	11th		
1319	?		
1505	12th		
1506	1320		
1555	13th		
1573	12th/13th		
1735	10th		
1739	10th		
1836	10th		
1852	13th		

M several hundred mss (Majority text)

f^1 = 1, 118, 131, 209, 1582 *et al*
f^{13} = 13, 69, 124, 174, 230, 346, 543, 788, 826, 828, 983, 1689, 1709 *et al*

$f\!f^2$	5th

Latin Manuscripts

Manuscript	Century
b	5th
e	5th
g^1	8th/9th
it = Old Latin witnesses as a group	2nd
latt = the entire Latin tradition	
vg = most editions of the Vulgate	4th–5th

vg^{cl} = Vulgate Clementina	1592	
vg^{mss} = individual Vulgate mss		
vgst = Vulgate Stuttgartiensis	1590	
vg^{ww} = Vulgate Wadsworth / White	1889–1954	

Other Versions

arm = Armenian

eth = Ethiopic

geo = Georgian

slav = Old Church Slavonic

Syriac Manuscripts

Manuscript	Century
sy and syr = Syriac (all the Syriac versions)	
sy^s = Syrus Sinaiticus	3rd/4th
sy^c = Syrus Curetonianus	4th/5th
sy^p = Syriac Peshitta	4th/5th
sy^{ph} = Syriac Philoxeniana	507/508
sy^h = Syriac Harklensis	615/616

Coptic Manuscripts

Manuscript	Century
bo = Bohairic Coptic	3rd
bo^{mss} = 2 to 4 Bohairic witnesses	
co = all the Coptic versions	
sa = Sahidic Coptic	3rd

THE NEW TESTAMENT
Church Fathers

Names of Church Fathers	Dates
The Apostolic Fathers	
1 Clement	95
Didache	100–120
Ignatius of Antioch	died 117
Papias of Hierapolis	70–150
Polycarp of Smyrna	69–155
2 Clement	140–160
Shepherd of Hermas	mid-second century
Epistle to Diognetus	late-second century
Justin Martyr	110–165
Marcion	second century
Tatian	second century
Irenaeus of Lyons	before 137–202
Clement of Alexandria	died about 215
Tertullian	circa 155–230
Hippolytus of Rome	died 236
Origen	185–254
Cyprian	circa 200–258
Eusebius of Caesarea	260–339
Lucifer of Cagliari	died 371
Athanasius of Alexandria	293–373
Titus of Bostra	died by 378
Basil the Great of Caesarea	329–379
Apostolic Constitutions	380
Cyril of Jerusalem	315–386
Gregory of Nazianzuz	329–390
Gregory of Nyssa	330–394
Ambrose	circa 338–397
Ambrosiaster	fourth century
Diodore	fourth century

Didymus the Blind	313–398
Epiphanius of Salamis	315–403
John Chrysostom	349–407
Jerome	circa 347–420
Augustine	354–430
Pelagius	circa 354–circa 420/440
Theodore of Mopsuestia	350–428
Cyril of Alexandria	375–444
Hesychius of Jerusalem	first half of the fifth century
Theodoret of Cyrrhus	circa 393–circa 460
Nonnus of Panopolis	fifth century
Macarius-Symeon	949–1022

CHAPTER 2

LITERARY CRITICISM AND PHILOLOGY

As we learned in the previous chapter, scholarly study of the text of the New Testament is called textual criticism, a discipline that serves as the foundation of all subsequent study of the twenty-seven books of the New Testament. Once scholars have established what they believe to be the earliest text of each book, it is still incumbent upon them to study that text carefully and impartially to determine the authenticity and the meaning of each book. In this chapter we will examine two more methods of studying the text: literary criticism and philology.

Literary Criticism is the scholarly discipline that examines the methods and the compositional devices (i.e. the literary genres) that early Christians drew upon to organize their thoughts and their beliefs, first in spoken words and eventually in written forms. The authors of the books of the New Testament were presumably familiar with and employed literary forms common in the ancient Jewish and Hellenistic world. Existing literary genres obviously affected the ways in which Christians organized both oral and written material as they composed the twenty-seven books that eventually became the church's canon of sacred scriptures.

In addition to such genre analysis, literary criticism also involves study of the text in ways that seek to illuminate the meaning of a passage. In this regard, we will examine two passages from letters of Paul: (1) a passage in Romans whose long-standing interpretation generally reflected the patriarchal bias of early and medieval Christians; and (2) a passage in 1 Corinthians whose meaning has been made clearer by applying to the text some of the methods of social science.

Philology is the scholarly study of the books of the New Testament in order to understand their authenticity and their original meaning. Once scholars have established the earliest text of the New Testament, it is still incumbent on them to study that text carefully and critically in order to determine the authenticity and the meaning of the several books. The grammatical syntax and vocabulary of a particular book might well afford clues regarding the book's authorship. Moreover, philology is helpful in establishing an understanding of the original meaning of many of the words that found their way into the New Testament. For example, in trying to understand who Jesus was and what he taught, students of the New Testament need to understand in their original historical, religious, and cultural contexts the meaning of such basic words and phrases as "kingdom of God," "Son of Man," Son of God," "Messiah," etc.

In order to understand Paul and the early Christian church, we need to understand the meaning of such words as "resurrection," "repentance," "salvation," "sin," "righteousness," "justification," etc. We may think that we already understand the meanings of these words and these concepts, but we need to understand them in the way in which Jesus and his earliest followers understood them if we are to be faithful to the principle that we want to examine the New Testament historically, i.e. in its own original context(s).

Let us now look more closely at each of these methods and their application to some specific texts.

LITERARY CRITICISM

Literary criticism is the discipline that examines the literary and compositional devices and methods used by authors to organize and compose their thoughts in order to present them in spoken and/or written forms. The books of the New Testament did not emerge from a vacuum. They had literary models or prototypes in the ancient world, and established literary forms or genres influenced early Christians who wrote not only our canonical books, but also the sources that lie behind many of the canonical books and ancient Christian writings that are not part of our canonical New Testament.

Very few of the books of the New Testament are the written product of a single author. Most underwent several stages in the course of their composition and subsequent editing; literary criticism attempts to uncover, where appropriate and where possible, the layers of the compositional process that resulted in our canonical books.

THE LITERARY FORMS OF THE BOOKS OF THE NEW TESTAMENT

In the earliest church, oral tradition met many if not most of the needs of the church, in some measure at least because the earliest Christians believed that they were living in the final generation of human history, that the world as we know it would come to an end within their lifetimes. But as time passed and the end did not come, the church began to generate written documents to serve the requirements of early Christian communities. The authors of these written documents adapted existing literary forms to express the needs of the nascent church. There are four basic literary genres among the books of the New Testament: gospels, history, letters, and an apocalypse.

1. Gospels. Our word *gospel* comes from the Old English word *godspel*, a combination of the word *god* (meaning *good*) and the word *spel* or *spiel* (meaning *news* or *tidings*).

The English word is, in fact, a translation of the Latin *evangelium*, which is a Roman transliteration of the New Testament Greek word εὐαγγέλιον (*euangelion*), meaning *good news* or *good tidings*.

In Greco-Roman sources, the word *euangelion* was used to describe a herald's announcement that an army had been victorious in battle, an interesting insight in light of its early Christian usage as the proclamation of the good news of God's victorious act of salvation through the death and resurrection of Jesus the Christ. Throughout the New Testament, that is consistently the meaning, namely: the preaching of the *good news* of God's salvific gift of Jesus the Christ and the consequences of that gift for humankind.

The earliest uses of the word *euangelion* (or of one of its cognates) appear in the New Testament in Paul's letters:

Gal 1:11 (possibly written as early as about 48–49, or in the opinion of most scholars in the mid-50s):

> For I want you to know, brothers and sisters, that the gospel (*euangelion*) that was proclaimed (*euangelisthen*) by me is not of human origin.

1 Thess 1:5 (written from Corinth about 52):

> . . . because our message of the gospel (*euangelion*) came to you not in word only, but also in power and in the Holy Spirit and with full conviction; just as you know what kind of persons we proved to be among you for your sake.

1 Cor 1:17 (written from Ephesus about 54):

> Christ did not send me to baptize but to proclaim the gospel (*euangelizesthai*), and not with eloquent wisdom, so that the cross of Christ might not be emptied of its power.

The word appears in the opening sentence of Mark (written in the late 60s)

> Mark 1:1 The beginning of the good news (*euangelion*) of Jesus Christ.

The author uses the word *euangelion* in the superscription or title to refer to the proclamation of the *good news* of God's saving act in Jesus the Messiah. In other words, the author does not refer to his own text as *a* gospel. Rather everything that follows this opening phrase in Mark is part of the *good news*, including not only Jesus' death and resurrection (as was the case in Paul's letters), but in the case of Mark, Jesus' life and ministry as well as his death and resurrection.

It is important to note that Papias (ca. 60–130), bishop of Hierapolis in Asia Minor and the earliest author to mention writings by Mark and Matthew does not use the word "gospel" (*euangelion*) to refer to the two writings (see Eusebius, *Church History* 3.39.15–16).

The earliest titles for our four canonical gospels were probably "According to Matthew," "According to Mark," etc. The earliest reference to the word *gospel* (*euangelion*) as the literary genre for the gospels of what would subsequently become the New

Testament appears in the mid-second century in the writings of Marcion (of which we have only fragments), Justin Martyr (*1 Apology* 66:3),[1] and *2 Clement* (8:5).[2] It is likely that at about this same time manuscripts of the gospels began to carry the longer notation "The Gospel according to Matthew," "The Gospel according to Mark," etc.

Although many scholars have traditionally argued that the author of the Gospel of Mark created the literary genre called *gospel*, New Testament scholars have more recently identified important similarities between the canonical gospels and Greco-Roman biographies, such as Plutarch's *Lives* and Suetonius' *Lives of the Caesars* (which date from the late first and early second centuries respectively). Both of these works are almost exactly contemporaneous with our four gospels. Scholars now recognize that the gospels of Matthew, Mark, Luke, and John are a particular kind of Greco-Roman biography with distinctive qualities that stem from their Christian character.

Like early Christian gospels, these Greco-Roman biographies were primarily concerned with portraying a person's qualities and character traits rather than with reporting what had actually happened during that person's lifetime. Ancient biography emphasized the positive aspects of a person's nature, primarily to inform readers or listeners about what kind of person he or she was and to encourage others to behave similarly. Typically, Greco-Roman biographies attempted to show how great an individual was.

2. History. The Acts of the Apostles, the second volume of the work Luke-Acts, is similar to other histories written in classical antiquity, although it has no parallel in the New Testament. Like most ancient historians, the author of Acts created for his book a number of speeches that he attributed to Peter and Paul, the two principal characters in the book. And like other ancient historians, the author of Acts was not so much concerned with historical accuracy as he was with similarity and plausibility as he reported the story of early Christianity, which is to say that he "historicizes" theology, or he "theologizes" history. The author of Acts composed a general history in which he traced developments in Christianity following Jesus' death down to the time of the book's composition by focusing on the spread of Christianity from its birthplace in Jerusalem until the time of its arrival in Rome, the seat of the Empire.

3. Letters. More than half of the books of the New Testament are epistles or letters. An epistle is a piece of public or private correspondence sent through the ancient equivalent of modern-day mail. In the ancient world, this generally meant sending

---

1. "For the apostles, in the memoirs composed by them, which are called *Gospels*, have thus delivered unto us what was enjoined upon them; that Jesus took bread, and when He had given thanks, said, 'This do ye in remembrance of Me, this is My body;' and that, after the same manner, having taken the cup and given thanks, He said, 'This is My blood;' and gave it to them alone."

2. "For the Lord says in the *Gospel*, 'If you did not guard that which is small, who shall give you that which is great? For I tell you that he who is faithful in that which is least, is faithful also in that which is much."

someone to hand-deliver a letter, or entrusting someone traveling in the right direction to deliver the correspondence.

In antiquity, letters generally began by identifying the sender of the correspondence, followed by the name of the person or persons being addressed, and a greeting at the outset. These opening remarks were then followed by the body of the letter.

Christian letter writing followed the basic form and conventions of non-Christian Greco-Roman tradition. The earliest extant Christian letters, which were written by the apostle Paul to Christian churches that he had either visited or intended to visit, followed the common Greco-Roman epistolary types of persuasion, admonition, rebuke, advice, exhortation, etc.

4. Apocalypse. An apocalypse or a revelation was a book that described the coming of the end time as that was disclosed or unveiled to a prophet in a vision. Apocalypses were often characterized by pseudonymity, symbolic imagery, numerology, and the expectation of an imminent cosmic cataclysm through which God would destroy the existing ruling powers of evil and raise the righteous to life in a future messianic kingdom.

Some scholars read the opening words of Revelation as the earliest surviving usage of the word *apocalypse* to refer to a work of a particular literary genre: "The revelation (Greek *apocalypsis*) of Jesus Christ" (Rev 1:1). I am not entirely convinced that this is the right way to read this verse. The use of the word *apocalypse* in this instance may be no different from its usage by Paul in Gal 1:11–12:

> For a want you to know, brothers and sisters, that the gospel that was proclaimed by me is not of human origin; for I did not receive it [the gospel] from a human source, nor was a taught it, but I received it through a revelation (*dia apocalypseos*) of Jesus Christ.

In this passage, Paul is, of course, not referring to *apocalypse* as a literary genre. He is referring to the manner in which God disclosed his Son *to* Paul (or *in* Paul, or *within* Paul) through a direct revelatory call:

> But when God, who had set me apart before I was born and called me through his grace, was pleased to reveal (ἀποκαλύψαι, apocalypsai) his Son to me (Greek *in me,* or *within me*), so that I might proclaim him among the Gentiles, I did not confer with any human being . . . (Gal 1:15–16)

This revelation to Paul should be understood as an appearance or manifestation of Christ "in Paul" or "within Paul." The text emphasizes the personal or inward quality of this revelation (*apocalypsis*).

Whatever the meaning of *apocalypsis* in Rev 1:1, it is clear that the book of Revelation became the prototype of Christian apocalypses.

It is important to recognize that the books of our canonical New Testament, when examined in the context of their own time, imitate literary forms or genres known to us from the ancient Greco-Roman and/or Jewish world. Nothing is more important to literary criticism of the Bible than looking at the biblical material in its own historical and literary context.

APPLYING THE METHOD TO THE TEXT OF THE NEW TESTAMENT: SOME EXAMPLES

To illustrate the methodology of Literary Criticism, it is worthwhile to look now at specific passages:

Romans 16:7 and Patriarchal Bias

Toward the end of his letter to the Romans, Paul extends greetings to friends and former associates now living in Rome as members of the Roman church. Rom 16:7 reads:

> Greet Andronichus and Junia, my relatives who were in prison with me; they are prominent among the apostles, and they were in Christ before I was.

Because of the way in which Paul speaks of the fifteen people in Rom 16:1–13 to whom he sends personal greetings, it is clear that he already knew all of them and had actually worked with some of them.

Among those whom Paul identified by name as being actively committed to the service of the gospel, seven were women: Prisca, Mary, Junia, Tryphaena, Tryphosa, Persis, and the mother of Rufus; and five were men: Aquila, Andronichus, Urbanus, Apelles, and Rufus. With regard to Andronichus and Junia (Rom 16:7), Paul mentions that they were his compatriots or fellow citizens (probably meaning fellow Jewish-Christians) in prison, that they were prominent among the apostles, and that they had become Christians before Paul's conversion (about 35), suggesting thereby that Andronichus and Junia may have been living in or near Jerusalem at the time of their conversions (1 Cor 15:5–7).

Andronichus is a Greek male name; Junia is a Latin or Roman female name. Both were names commonly given to freed slaves.[3] It seems possible (probable?) that Andronichos and Junia were a married couple and that they had served as evangelists (or as evangelizing apostles) somewhere in the eastern mission, where at some point they shared imprisonment with Paul.

There have been numerous efforts both in medieval and modern times to identify Junia as a man rather than as a woman. Although patristic evidence through the twelfth century consistently refers to Junia as a women, some ninth century manuscripts amended the Greek text to render the name as masculine (*Iouniân*), presumably a contracted form of the common masculine name Junianus. It was Martin Luther who popularized the reading of the masculine name.

---

3. Jewett, *Romans*, 961.

THE NEW TESTAMENT

Even the 2nd to the 27th (4th printing) editions of the prestigious Nestle(-Aland) critical edition of the New Testament read until very recently the accusative form of the male name *Iouniân*. The Nestle-Aland 27th (5th printing) edition of 1998 finally changed that to read *Iounían*, the accusative form of the female name Junia.[4] The masculine Junias is the preferred form in the Revised Standard Version, the New English Bible, the New International Version, and the New Jerusalem Bible. Some new translations read the feminine *Junia*: the New American Bible (Revised New Testament), the New Revised Standard Version, and the Revised English Bible.

The effort to render Junia as a man rather than as a woman appears to have been the result of patriarchal bias designed to suppress the idea that there could possibly have been a female apostle in the early church. It should be noted in this regard that the title "apostle" in the early church was applied not only to the twelve called by Jesus, but to others who had seen the risen Lord and had been commissioned as itinerant evangelists either by the risen Christ himself or by a church (Acts 13:1–3), specifically James (Gal 1:19; 1 Cor 15:7), Barnabas and Paul (Acts 14:1–4, 14; perhaps 1 Cor 9:6), unnamed persons (1 Cor 9:5; 12:28; 2 Cor 8:23; 11:13; Eph 4:11), perhaps Silvanus and Timothy (1 Thess 1:1; 2:7), and Andronicus and Junia (Rom 16:7).[5] Alternatively Paul apparently used the word *apostle* to refer to those who were early witnesses to the resurrection (1 Cor 15:5–9); in this regard, Paul apparently saw himself as the last to be so designated as an apostle (1 Cor 15:8–9).

Rom 16:7 is an excellent example of the way in which feminist criticism has led scholars to recognize once again the important role that women played in the early church.

---

4. It was Eldon J. Epp (*Junia: The First Woman Apostle*, 40–48), who pointed out that there has never been a shred of textual evidence to support the masculine form of the name in the text of Rom 16:7, and there is absolutely no evidence for a masculine name *Junias*.

5. See also *Did* 11:3–6 "And concerning the Apostles and Prophets, act thus according to the ordinance of the Gospel. Let every Apostle who comes to you be received as the Lord, but let him not stay more than one day, or if need be a second as well; but if he stay three days, he is a false prophet."; *Hermas, Vision* 3.5.1 "Listen then concerning the stones which go into the building. The stones which are square and white and which fit into their joins are the Apostles and bishops and teachers and deacons who walked according to the majesty of God, and served the elect of God in holiness and reverence as bishops and teachers and deacons; some of them are fallen asleep and some are still alive. And they always agreed among themselves, and had peace among themselves, and listened to one another; for which cause their joins fit in the building of the tower."; and *Hermas, Similitude* 9.15.4 "'But, Sir,' said I, 'what are the stones which were fitted into the building from the deep?' 'The first,' said he, 'the ten which were placed in the foundation, are the first generation; and the twenty-five are the second generation of righteous men; and the thirty-five are the prophets of God and his servants, and the forty are prophets and teachers of the preaching of the Son of God."; 9.16.5 "'Why, Sir' said I, 'did the forty stones also come up with them from the deep, although they had received the seal already?' 'Because,' said he, 'these apostles and teachers, who preached the name of the Son of God, having fallen asleep in the power and faith of the Son of God, preached also to those who had fallen asleep before them, and themselves gave to them the seal of the preaching."; 9.25.2 "Apostles and teachers who preached to all the world, and taught reverently and purely the word of the Lord, and kept nothing back for evil desire, but always walked in righteousness and truth, even as they had received the Holy Spirit. The passing of such is with the angels."

LITERARY CRITICISM AND PHILOLOGY
1 Corinthians 11:18–34 and the Significance of the Last Supper

Although Paul had written previously to the Corinthian Christians (1 Cor 5:9), that earlier letter is lost, although some scholars think that 2 Cor 6:14–7:1 may be a part of it. In the context of this second letter, known to us as 1 Corinthians, Paul addressed several issues of particular importance to the Corinthian Christians, who had written to Paul seeking his advice (1 Cor 7:1). In addition to whatever Paul learned from their letter to him, he admits to having heard rumors about problems and divisions within the church from "Chloe's people" (1 Cor 1:11; 5:1; 11:18).

In a subsequent chapter we shall consider details in the life and ministry of Paul. Suffice it to say here that Paul was in Ephesus (1 Cor 16:8) when in about 54 he wrote 1 Corinthians to the Corinthian church, which he himself had founded several years earlier.

Among the issues concerning which Paul afforded directions in this letter are marriage and virginity (1 Cor 7:1–40), meal-eating and the problem of food offered to idols (1 Cor 8:1–13; 10:14–32), spiritual gifts (1 Cor 12:1–31; 14:1–40), and the resurrection of Christ and the resurrection of the body (1 Cor 15:12–57). The matter of meals and, in particular, the issue of the celebration of the Lord's Supper was among the most problematic of the disputes between Paul and the Corinthian Christians. The text of 1 Cor 11:18–34 is sufficiently important to produce here in its entirety:

> [18]For, to begin with, when you come together as a church, I hear that there are divisions among you; and to some extent I believe it. [19]Indeed, there have to be factions among you, for only so will it become clear who among you are genuine. [20]When you come together, it is not really to eat the Lord's supper. [21]For when the time comes to eat, each of you goes ahead with your own supper, and one goes hungry and another becomes drunk. [22]What! Do you not have homes to eat and drink in? Or do you show contempt for the church of God and humiliate those who have nothing? What should I say to you? Should I commend you? In this matter I do not commend you!
>
> [23]For I received from the Lord what I also handed on to you, that the Lord Jesus on the night when he was betrayed took a loaf of bread, [24]and when he had given thanks, he broke it and said, "This is my body that is for you. Do this in remembrance of me." [25]In the same way he took the cup also, after supper, saying, "This cup is the new covenant in my blood. Do this, as often as you drink it, in remembrance of me." [26]For as often as you eat this bread and drink this cup, you proclaim the Lord's death until he comes.
>
> [27]Whoever, therefore, eats the bread or drinks the cup of the Lord in an unworthy manner will be answerable for the body and blood of the Lord. [28]Examine yourselves, and only then eat of the bread and drink of the cup. [29]For all who eat and drink without discerning the body, eat and drink judgment against themselves. [30]For this reason many of you are weak and ill, and some have died. [31]But if we judged ourselves, we would not be judged. [32]But when we are judged by the Lord, we are disciplined so that we may not be condemned along with the world.

> ³³So then, my brothers and sisters, when you come together to eat, wait for one another. ³⁴If you are hungry, eat at home, so that when you come together, it will not be for your condemnation. About the other things, I will give instructions when I come.

There are few issues that are as divisive in contemporary Christianity as the meaning and significance of the Last Supper, the church's Eucharist. Although there are accounts of the Last Supper in each of the synoptic gospels (Matt 26:26–30; Mark 14:22–26; Luke 22:14–23), there is none in the Gospel of John, which substitutes instead Jesus' washing of the feet of his disciples (John 13:1–5; cf. also John 6:48–58), a story that is found in no other gospel.

It appears from 1 Corinthians that the error of the Corinthians was essentially the result of a gentile (i.e. Corinthian) misunderstanding of what was originally a Jewish practice, namely a commemorative meal. If that is the case, then we must understand the original social and religious experience of the Jewish meal in order to appreciate Paul's admonition to the Corinthians.

Only when 1 Cor 11 is read against the background of the Jewish practice of a commemorative common meal is Paul's intention clear. Social science helps to clarify the importance of meals in Judaism and, hence, their intended importance to the Corinthians. In the first four chapters of his first letter to the Corinthians, Paul outlined how disruptive he found the divisions or schisms within the Corinthian church. He was particularly outraged by the divisions that had developed from the church's celebration of the Lord's Supper.

Paul maintained that the members of the Corinthian church were apparently coming together not to eat the Lord's Supper but to eat their own suppers (1 Cor 11:20). It is evident from Paul's account that the practice in the church at Corinth was for the people to bring their own food to the common meal, but then only to eat individually. Not only were the people not eating together, neither were they sharing their food. People were beginning to eat as soon as they arrived. Because some members of the church were very poor, they had little or nothing to eat and were still hungry after supper. Some, on the other hand, were fully satisfied and even drunk (1 Cor 11:21).

What concerned Paul most was the insensitivity and indifference of some Corinthian Christians to the circumstances of those among them who were the most poor. There was apparently no communal significance to the common meal, a situation that Paul found deplorable. Paul suggests that those who gorge themselves with food and drink should do so at home before they come to the communal meal. Apparently some of the Corinthian Christians were wealthy, whereas others were poor or perhaps even slaves, who could come to the supper only very late, missing thereby the communal significance of the meal.

By referring to the fact that he had "received from the Lord what [he] also handed on to [them]," Paul makes known that the abuses he perceives are the result of the church's failure to follow practices instituted by the Lord. In accordance with Jewish practice, Jesus began the meal by giving thanks and breaking bread and saying, "This is my body." Paul was convinced that everyone in the congregation should be present for this breaking of the bread and giving of thanks, for the bread was broken for them all. The giving of thanks was intended for the entire meal, not simply for the breaking of the bread, which begins the meal. The fact that the cup came "after supper" (1 Cor 11:25) suggests that the Eucharistic celebration originally framed the meal itself but that the Corinthians had deviated from this traditional practice. Paul believed that this supper should be a communal meal, a meaningful part of the Eucharistic celebration.

According to Jewish practice, the entire meal served as a recollection of Jesus' death, not just the broken bread. In Judaism the eating of meals often served as commemorations of past events, as in the cases of Passover, which commemorated the escape from Egypt (Exod 12:14), and Purim, which commemorated the deliverance of the Jews from a pogrom under the Persian official Haman (*1 Macc* 7:49; *2 Macc* 15:36; Josephus, *Antiquities* 11.6.13).

For Paul and in accordance with Jewish practice, the commemorative meal should be shared by the entire Corinthian church as they assembled in memory of Jesus. In the critical verse "This is my body," the demonstrative pronoun *this* is neuter, whereas the word *bread* is masculine in Greek, so the phrase presumably does *not* mean "This bread is my body." Rather, the body in which the risen Christ is present is the body of believers, the church, a theme that is common to Paul (Rom 12:5; 1 Cor 12:13, 27) and to the deutero-Pauline letters (Eph 1:22–23, 4:4, 12, 16; Col 1:18; 2:19; 3:15).

When Jesus was no longer with his followers in the flesh, he was still with them in the body of Christ, the body of believers, the church. For Paul, the chief act of common worship was the celebration of the Lord's Supper in which the body of believers, as Jesus' followers, share a common meal and receive the cup as a sign of their participation in the benefits of the new covenant. Each meal is a recollection and a proclamation of the gospel until Christ comes again.

In 1 Corinthians, the sacramental elements are not the bread and the wine, but rather the bread and the cup. Paul's words are not only older than what we find in the synoptic gospels, but they are likely more original as they lack the later parallelism of bread and wine. The cup is for Paul the celebration of the new covenant in Jesus' blood, and the bread and the cup together serve as a remembrance of Jesus in anticipation of his return (1 Cor 11:26).

Paul's condemnation of the community reflects Paul's judgment that the way in which the Corinthian Christians celebrated the meal commemorated not the unity of the body of believers, as it should, but rather reflected the brokenness of the community (1 Cor 10:16–17), most specifically the separation of the rich from the poor (1 Cor 11:21–22). The Corinthians failed to recognize the divine union of the fellowship of the body of Christ, which they were guilty of dividing and fragmenting.

For Paul the celebration of the Eucharist should mean that the Corinthian Christians were celebrating their fellowship together. Violation of the supper fractured the body of Christ, whose very purpose was to guarantee that the poor were fed, the sick were cared for, sinners were forgiven, and the church lived consistently in the love of Christ. It was for Paul the very fellowship of the church that was at stake. The body of Christ should be redemptive, not corrosive and broken.

Paul's final admonition is simple but profound, "So then, my brothers and sisters, when you come together to eat, wait for one another" (1 Cor 11:33). They mirror the final words of Paul's letter: "My love be with all of you in Christ Jesus" (1 Cor 16:24).

The meaning of 1 Cor 11:18–34 is clear only in the context of Jewish commemorative meals, something that was clearly unfamiliar to the Gentile Corinthian Christians.

PHILOLOGY

When applied to the Bible, philology refers to the study of the written documents in order to determine their authenticity and their meaning. More specifically, philological study is the discipline that attempts to ascertain the intended meaning of a text at the time it was first written.

In his *Essay on Criticism* (1711), Alexander Pope wrote:

> All seems infected that the infected spy,
> as all looks yellow to the jaundiced eye.

Pope was referring to the bias that people carry with them to an issue so that they then see exactly what they want to see rather than what is really there. In other words, we must be very careful not simply to see the world as we would like to see it through the eye of our biases; we must rather see the world as it really is. Pope's warning applies particularly to the study of the Bible: we must be very careful not simply to find in the Bible what we expect to or would like to find there; we need, rather, to read the Bible carefully to understand what it really said in its own time and in its own context.

Scholars often distinguish between two words that are Greek in origin: exegesis and eisegesis. The word "exegesis" refers to critical interpretation, explanation, or analysis of a text, specifically drawing *out* (Greek *ex*) of the text its original intended meaning. The word "eisegesis" has a negative connotation among biblical scholars. It implies reading *into* (Greek *eis*) the text a meaning that was not intended by the original author. Whether intentionally so or not, conservative Christians are often guilty of "eisegesis," reading *into* the text of the Bible meaning that is not there.

Philological study includes lexicography, grammar, the study of related foreign languages and of related texts. These are all essential elements in promoting a clearer and more accurate understanding of the books of the New Testament, all of which were originally written some two thousand years ago in Koine (or common) Greek, now a dead language, although an antecedent of modern Greek.

LITERARY CRITICISM AND PHILOLOGY

Once students of the Bible have established the most probable earliest text or the autograph of the books of the New Testament through the efforts of textual criticism, it is then essential to study that text carefully and critically. Only then can the reader hope to determine the authenticity and the meaning of the various books. Important to such study is developing an understanding of the original meaning of words and phrases that found their way into the New Testament. As mentioned in the introduction to this chapter, in order to understand who Jesus was and what he taught, students of the New Testament must understand in their original historical, cultural, and religious contexts the meaning of such basic words and phrases as "kingdom of God," "Son of Man," Son of God," "Messiah," etc. Likewise, in order to understand Paul, students must understand what Paul meant by such words and phrases as "salvation," "faith," "justification," "resurrection of the body," etc.

Unfortunately, many readers carry to the text of the New Testament their own preconceptions of what the New Testament is supposed to say and so find exactly what they are looking for without regard to what the New Testament may have meant to its original authors and their audiences two thousand years ago. It is not sufficient to think that we already understand what those words and phrases mean because we learned about them in Sunday school.

There are a number of excellent tools available to the reader interested in developing an understanding of the role of philology in the study of the New Testament. Specifically there are several invaluable dictionaries of the Bible, which contain scholarly articles on virtually every important word and every significant concept in the New Testament.

First and foremost is the invaluable one-volume Greek-English dictionary of New Testament Greek: Walter Bauer, *A Greek-English Lexicon of the New Testament and Other Early Christian Literature*, third edition, revised and edited by Frederick William Dankler (Chicago: University of Chicago Press, 2001).

There is also the single most important extended dictionary that deals with issues of philology in the New Testament and that contains scholarly articles on most Greek words found in the New Testament: Gerhard Kittel, *Theological Dictionary of the New Testament*, 10 volumes (Grand Rapids: William B. Eerdmans Publishing Co., 1964).

For those who are unfamiliar with the New Testament in its original Greek, there are excellent philological tools that require no knowledge of Biblical Greek:

The Interpreter's Dictionary of the Bible, 4 volumes and supplementary volume

The Anchor Bible Dictionary, 6 volumes

The New Interpreter's Dictionary of the Bible, 5 volumes

THE NEW TESTAMENT
THE MEANING OF WORDS IN THEIR ORIGINAL CONTEXTS

To illustrate the importance of philology to a study of the New Testament, I propose to introduce here a single example of a verse from the prophet Isaiah that may have inadvertently served as the basis for early Christian belief in the virgin birth of Jesus. Although Matt 1:23 is the crucial New Testament text for this belief, the matter extends back into the Old Testament to a passage in Isa 7:14, which the author of the Gospel of Matthew apparently misunderstood.

The text of Isa 7:14 in the New Revised Standard Version of the Bible reads:

> Therefore, the Lord himself will give you a sign. Look, a young woman is with child and shall bear a son, and shall name him Immanuel.

A footnote in the Revised Standard Version indicates that a third century BCE Greek translation of the original eighth century BCE Hebrew text of Isaiah identifies the future mother not as a "young woman," but as a "virgin."[6] In fact, that footnote is likely there because the King James Bible and many subsequent versions have mistakenly translated the passage in Isa 7:14 from Hebrew into English thus:

> Therefore the Lord himself shall give you a sign; Behold, a virgin shall conceive, and bear a son, and shall call his name Immanuel.

The passage in Isaiah has traditionally been understood by Christians as an Old Testament proof-text in which Isaiah prophesied or predicted Jesus' birth by the virgin Mary more than seven hundred years before the event. The author of the Gospel of Matthew quoted Isaiah as evidence that Jesus' birth by the virgin Mary was the fulfillment of Isaiah's prophecy. Matthew, however, did not use the Hebrew original of Isaiah but rather the Greek (mis)translation of this passage, when he wrote:

> Look, the virgin shall conceive and bear a son, and they shall name him Emmanuel (Matt 1:23).

So what exactly did Isaiah say and mean when he spoke these words in the eighth century BCE? It is here that philological study comes into play. The setting of the passage in Isa 7 is the political events in the southern kingdom of Judah in 734 BCE. Isaiah was apparently trying to persuade Judah's King Ahaz not to capitulate to Assyria in his effort to prevent an attack on his kingdom from the northern coalition of Syria and Samaria (Northern Israel). To encourage King Ahaz to accept his advice, the prophet Isaiah invited the king to ask him for a sign. When Ahaz refused Isaiah's request, the prophet offered the sign that "the young woman (Hebrew *'almâ*) is pregnant and about to give birth to a son; she will give him the name Immanuel." By the time the child is

---

6. Jewish scholars living in Alexandria, Egypt between 250 and 150 BCE translated the Hebrew Bible into Greek for the benefit of Jews whose families had been living in Egypt for several centuries. These Jews no longer understood the Jewish scriptures in the original Hebrew, hence the need for the Greek translation, commonly referred to as the Septuagint.

five or six years old, Isaiah said, the land of the threatening Syrian-Samarian alliance will be laid waste; the threat to Ahaz and the Kingdom of Judah will be removed.

Although it is not clear who the young woman or her about-to-be son were, it is clear that the passage does not and cannot refer to the virgin Mary and Jesus. For the sign to have had any meaning to King Ahaz, Isaiah must have been referring to a young woman already known to both the prophet and the king and to an impending birth that would take place within a few months time. The young woman was, after all, already pregnant. The meaning of the passage in Isa 7:14 is eminently clear to scholars who have studied the text in the original Hebrew. Jesus' birth to Mary more than seven hundred years in the future would obviously have had no significance whatsoever to King Ahaz and could not have served as a meaningful sign to him in 734 BCE.

With their jaundiced eyes, the translators of the King James Bible obviously assumed the validity of the connection between Isa 7:14 and Matt 1:23, because the translation of the passage in Isaiah in the King James Version (and in most subsequent conservative Christian translations) was influenced by the use of the Greek work *parthenos* (virgin), the third century BCE Septuagint's (mis)translation of Isaiah's Hebrew word *'almâ* (young woman). It is one thing to note that the author of the Gospel of Matthew apparently knew Isaiah not in the original Hebrew, but rather in the Greek (mis)translation. It is quite another thing to use Matthew's version of that Greek (mis)translation to render into English the text of the Hebrew of Isa 7:14. Yet that is exactly what happened in the King James Version and in many contemporary translations.

Philological study has made it clear that Isaiah was speaking about a pregnant young woman (Hebrew *'almâ*), not about a virgin (Hebrew *bĕthûlah*). It is evident that the pregnant woman about whom Isaiah was speaking was obviously not a virgin, as she was already pregnant. Yet, the translators of the King James Bible were determined to connect the text of Isaiah to the text of Matthew in order to reinforce Matthew's claim that Isaiah was referring to Mary and Jesus.

What is important in modern translations, however, is to translate into English as accurately as possible the meaning of the original text *in its own context*. Adding the footnote in the Revised Stand Version that the Greek (mistranslation) says "virgin" is misleading and only adds to the confusion. Stated simply, the author of the Gospel of Matthew made a mistake in quoting the Greek mistranslation of Isaiah as a proof-text for the virgin birth. The mistake resulted from the fact that the author of the Gospel of Matthew used not the original Hebrew text of Isaiah, which was clear on the matter, but that he used instead a Greek (mis)translation of Isaiah, the Septuagint. The author of the Gospel of Matthew may not have been able to read the text of Isaiah in the original Hebrew, so we cannot assign blame entirely to him. But we can assign blame to modern translators who can read Hebrew and who intentionally continue to perpetuate the error. Modern translators are sometimes still reluctant to acknowledge the simple truth that Isaiah was not referring to Mary and Jesus.

The following table illustrates the ways in which various translations of the Bible have rendered into English the Hebrew word *'almâ*:[7]

Bible Translation	Date	Character	Translation of *'almâ*
Douay-Rheims Bible	1609	translated from Vulgate	virgin
King James Version	1611	authorized Protestant	virgin
Revised Standard Version	1946	revision of KJV	young woman
Jerusalem Bible	1966	Roman Catholic	maiden
New International Version	1978	evangelical Christian	virgin
Anchor Bible Commentary	2000	non-denominational	young woman

Clearly, the study of lexicography, grammar, and the meaning of the words in related foreign languages has made it clear what this passage in Isaiah does and does not say. Although scholars have not been able to identify either the young woman or her son in Isa 7:14, it is clear that the author of the Gospel of Matthew unwittingly misused this passage as a proof-text for Jesus' birth from a virgin because he was relying on the Greek (mis)translation. In fact, it is very likely that the passage in Isa 7:14 in the Greek (mis)translation is the sole basis for the church's belief that Jesus was born of a virgin. As we have already seen, even in the New Testament itself there are passages that assume that Mary and Joseph were both Jesus' biological parents (see above, 34).

In subsequent chapters, we will have other opportunities to see how important it is to understand words in their contexts in order to develop a reliable understanding of the authentic teachings of Jesus and the beliefs of the early Christian church.

THE AUTHENTICITY OF EPHESIANS AND COLOSSIANS

There are in the New Testament seven unquestionably authentic letters of Paul: Romans, 1 and 2 Corinthians, Galatians, Philippians, 1 Thessalonians, and Philemon.

---

7. In addition to the translations listed in the chart, the website www.biblegateway.com lists numerous additional, presumably evangelical-approved, translations, which yield the following results: *New American Standard Bible* (NASB): "a virgin"; *The Message* (MSG): "a girl who is presently a virgin"; *Amplified Bible* (AMP): "the young woman who is unmarried and a virgin"; *New Living Translation* (NLT): "the virgin"; *English Standard Version* (ESV): "the virgin"; *Contemporary English Version* (CEV): "a virgin"; *New King James Version* (NKJV): "the virgin"; *21st Century King James Version* (KJ21): "a virgin"; *American Standard Version* (ASV): "a virgin"; *Young's Literal Translation* (YLT): "the Virgin"; *Darby Translation* (DARBY): "the virgin"; *New International Version – UK* (NIV-UK): "the virgin." A footnote to the CEV, in an attempt to be scholarly, clearly betrays its jaundiced eye of bias: "In this context the difficult Hebrew word did not imply a virgin birth. However, in the Greek translation made about 200 (BC) and used by many early Christians, the word parthenos had a double meaning. While the translator [of the Septuagint] took it to mean 'young woman,' Matthew understood it to mean 'virgin' and quoted the passage (Matt 1:23) because it was the appropriate description of Mary, the mother of Jesus." It is evident that in each and every one of these instances, the translation is colored by evangelical orthodox bias, not by scholarly philological study.

LITERARY CRITICISM AND PHILOLOGY

The authenticity of Ephesians, Colossians, 2 Thessalonians, 1 and 2 Timothy, and Titus has been questioned, and they are often referred to as deutero-Pauline letters, i.e., pseudonymous letters written by followers of Paul in Paul's name.

The word *philology* has, as one of its meanings, "the love of words" or "the study of words." Hence, philology can and should play a role in examining the question of the authenticity of Ephesians and Colossians. Although a study of vocabulary cannot be determinative in deciding the issue of Pauline authorship of these two letters, it is an important factor in this matter.

Although there are many similarities of vocabulary, literary style, and theological terminology between the unquestionably genuine letters of Paul and the disputed letters, the similarities need to be weighed along with the differences. This section is concerned only with differences of vocabulary as a means of illustrating the importance of philological studies in determining the matter of authorship. With regard to Colossians, Eduard Lohse has collected important data in this regard:[8]

1. There are in Colossians thirty-four words which appear nowhere else in the New Testament, so-called *hapaxlegomena* (Greek for "once spoken"):

Greek	transliteration	translation	reference
προακούειν	prŏakouein	to hear before	1:5
ἀρέσκεια	arĕskeia	good pleasure	1:10
ὁρατός	hŏratŏs	visible	1:16
πρωτεύειν	prōteuein	to be the first	1:18
εἰρηνοποιεῖν	eirēnŏpoiein	to make peace	1:20
μετακινεῖν	mĕtakinein	to be dissuaded, moved	1:23
ἀνταναπληροῦν	antanaplēroun	to complete	1:24
πιθανολογία	pithanŏlŏgia	beguiling speech	2:4
στερέωμα	stĕrĕōma	firm stability	2:5
συλαγωγεῖν	sulagōgein	to snare	2:8
φιλοσοφία	philŏsŏphia	philosophy	2:8
θεότης	thĕŏtēs	deity	2:9
σωματικῶς	sōmatikōs	bodily	2:9
ἀπέκδυσις	apĕkdusis	putting off	2:11
χειρόγραφον	cheirŏgraphŏn	certificate	2:14
προσηλοῦν	prŏsēloun	to nail	2:14
ἀπεκδύεσθαι	apĕkduĕsthai	to strip	2:15; 3:9
νεομηνία	nĕŏmēnia	new moon	2:16
καταβραβεύειν	katabrabeuein	to condemn	2:18
ἐμβατεύειν	ĕmbateuein	to enter into mystery rites	2:18

---

8. Lohse, *Colossians and Philemon*, 85–87.

THE NEW TESTAMENT

Greek	transliteration	translation	reference
δογματίζειν	dŏgmatizein	to have regulations imposed	2:20
ἀπόχρησις	apŏchrēsis	use	2:22
ἐθελοθρησκία	ĕthĕlŏthrēskia	self-chosen worship	2:23
ἀφειδία	apheidia	severity	2:23
πλησμονή	plēsmŏnē	indulgence	2:23
αἰσχρολογία	aischrŏlŏgia	abusive language	3:8
Σκύθης	Skuthēs	Scythian	3:11
μομφή	mŏmphē	complaint	3:13
βραβεύειν	brabeuein	to hold sway	3:15
εὐχάριστος	eucharistŏs	thankful	3:15
ἀθυμεῖν	athumein	to become timid	3:21
ἀνταπόδοσις	antapŏdŏsis	reward	3:24
ἀνεψιός	anĕpsiŏs	cousin	4:10
παρηγορία	parēgŏria	comfort	4:11

2. There are in Colossians twenty-eight words which appear elsewhere in the New Testament, but not in the unquestionably authentic Pauline letters:

Greek	transliteration	translation	reference
ἀποκεῖσθαι	apŏkeisthai	to lie prepared	1:5
σύνδουλος	sundoulŏs	fellow servant	1:7; 4:7
δυναμοῦν	dunamoun	to strengthen	1:11
κλῆρος	klērŏs	lot	1:12
θρόνος	thrŏnŏs	throne	1:16
συνεστηκέναι	sunĕstēkĕnai	to be established	1:17
ἀπόκρυφος	apŏkruphŏs	hidden	2:3
παραλογίζεσθαι	paralŏgizĕsthai	to delude	2:4
ἐξαλείφειν	ĕxaleiphein	to destroy utterly	2:14
ὑπεναντίος	hupĕnantiŏs	standing against	2:14
δειγματίζειν	deigmatizein	to put on display	2:15
ἑορτή	hĕŏrtē	festival	2:16
σκία	skia	shadow	2:17
θρησκεία	thrēskeia	worship	2:18
κρατεῖν	kratein	to adhere steadfastly	2:19
γεύεσθαι	geuĕsthai	to taste	2:21
θιγγάνειν	thinganein	to touch	2:21
ἔνταλμα	entalma	regulation	2:22

LITERARY CRITICISM AND PHILOLOGY

Greek	transliteration	translation	reference
τὰ ἄνω	ta anō	that which is above	3:1
κρύπτειν	kruptein	to hide	3:3
τελειότης	tĕleiŏtēs	perfection	3:14
πλουσίως	plousiōs	abundantly	3:16
πικραίνειν	pikrainein	to make bitter	3:19
ἅλας	halas	salt	4:6
ἀρτύειν	artuein	to season	4:6
ἀποκρίνεσθαι	apŏkrinĕsthai	to answer	4:6
πόνος	pŏnŏs	work	4:13
ἰατρός	iatrŏs	physician	4:14

3. There are fifteen words used in both Colossians and Ephesians and in other books of the New Testament, but which are not found in the genuine Pauline letters:

Greek	transliteration	translation	reference
αἰτεῖσθαι	aitesthai	to ask	1:9
κράτος	kratŏs	might	1:11
ἄφεσις	aphĕsis	forgiveness	1:14
κυριότης	kuriŏtēs	dominion	1:16
κατοικεῖν	katoikein	to dwell	1:19; 2:9
διάνοια	dianoia	mind	1:21
κατενώπιον	katĕnōpiŏn	before	1:22
θεμελιοῦν	thĕmĕlioun	to be firmly established	1:23
ἀπάτη	apatē	deceit	2:8
δόγμα	dŏwgma	regulation	2:14
σύνδεσμος	sundĕsmŏs	ligament	2:19; 3:14
αὔξειν	auxein	to grow	2:19
βλασφημία	blasphēmia	slander	3:8
ᾠδή	ōdē	song	3:16
ᾄδειν	adein	to sing	3:16

THE NEW TESTAMENT

4. There are numerous specifically Pauline terms, which are otherwise quite common, but which are missing from Colossians. Among them are:

Greek	Transliteration	translation
ἁμαρτία	hamartia (in the singular)	sin
ἀποκάλυψις	Apŏkalupsis	revelation
δικαιοσύνη, δικαιοῦν, δικαίωμα, δικαίωσις	dikaiŏsunē, dikaioun, dikaiōma, dikaiōsis	righteousness and related words
δοκιμάζειν, δοκιμή, δόκιμος	dŏkimazein, dŏkimē, dŏkimŏs	to examine and related words
ἐλευθερία, ἐλευθεροῦν	ĕleuthĕria, ĕleuthĕroun	freedom, to free
ἐπαγγελία, ἐπαγγέλλεσθαι	ĕpangĕlia, ĕpangĕllĕsthai	promise, to promise
κατεργάζεσθαι	Katĕrgazĕsthai	to achieve
καυχᾶσθαι, καύχημα	kauchasthai, kauchēma	to boast, boast
κοινός, κοινωνία	koinŏs, koinōnia	communal, community
λοιπός	loipŏs	other and related words
νόμος	nŏmŏs	law
πιστεύειν	pisteuein	to believe
πείθειν, πεποίθησις	peithein, pĕpoithēsis	to convince, confidence
σῷζειν, σωτηρία	sōzein, sōtēria	to save, salvation
ὑπακοή	hupakŏē	obedience

5. There are ten words which Colossians has in common only with Ephesians:

Greek	Transliteration	Translation	reference
ἀποκαταλλάσειν	apŏkatallasein	to reconcile	1:20, 22
ἀπαλλοτριοῦσθαι	apallŏtriousthai	to be alienated	1:21
ῥιζοῦσθαι	rhizousthai	to be rooted	2:7
συνεγείρειν	sunĕgeirein	to raise together	2:12
συζωποιεῖν	suzōpoiein	to make alive together	2:13
ἁφή	haphē	sinew	2:19
αὔξησις	auxēsis	growth	2:19
ὕμνος	humnŏs	hymn	3:16
ὀφθαλμοδουλία	ŏphthalmŏdoulia	eye-service	3:22
ἀνθρωπάρεσκος	anthrōparĕskŏs	pleaser of men	3:22

The collective evidence indicates important differences of vocabulary between Colossians and the unquestionably genuine letters of Paul. It has long been recognized that Colossians and Ephesians are very similar letters and that what applies to one likely applies to both. That is supported especially by the evidence in table 5 above.

Although the philological evidence concerning the vocabulary of Colossians (and Ephesians) is by itself not sufficient to establish that Colossians and Ephesians were not written by Paul, this evidence, together with an examination of important theological differences between Colossians and Ephesians and the indisputably Pauline letters, has led most scholars to identify these two writings as deutero-Pauline letters, written not by Paul himself but by a follower of Paul, who wrote pseudonymously in the name of Paul.

CONCLUSIONS

A glance at literary criticism of the New Testament enabled us to identify the literary genre of every book of the New Testament as an example of Greco-Roman literary forms that were current at the time: ancient biography, history, letters, and apocalypse. As we examine individual books of the New Testament in subsequent chapters, we will be able to understand these books better because we now understand more fully some of the common literary genres of the period. We understand also what these genres hoped to accomplish, and historical accuracy was *not* a primary consideration of ancient historians

We also found how feminist theology and social science have contributed to an understanding of the books of the New Testament. A strong patriarchal bias excluded for centuries a proper reading of Rom 16:7 and the identification of a woman, Junia, as an apostle, at least in the eyes of Paul. Were it not for the emergence of feminist theology, it is doubtful that anyone would have cared to make the case that has been made to identify more clearly the important role that women played in the early church

Study of the significance of the meal as a commemorative celebration in Judaism has afforded important insights into an understanding of the celebration of the Lord's Supper or the Eucharist in the Corinthian church to which Paul addressed several letters, some of which are unfortunately lost. Our study has shown that Gentile Christianity must be understood within the context of first century Judaism, or at least first century Hellenistic Judaism, especially in the case of those churches that Paul founded personally. As in the patriarchal bias that influenced the identification for centuries of the female apostle Junia as a male apostle Junias or Junianus, so too has theological controversy within Christianity over the meaning of the Eucharist clouded the way in which we have understood the place of the Eucharist in the Corinthian church.

Once we have agreed upon what is probably the oldest text, we can then rigorously apply the tools of literary criticism and philological criticism to the text to learn something about the authenticity of individual documents and their intended meaning within the context of the time in which each was written. The study of Isa 7:14 and Matt 1:23 illustrated the potential value of philology, as we have seen that the origin of the tradition of the virgin birth of Jesus may be attributable to nothing more than a mistaken reading of Isa 7:14 within the early Christian community, which was looking into the Jewish Bible for proof-texts to enable the church the build tradition around Jesus the messiah. We shall have ample opportunity to revisit this question in subsequent chapters.

We have also seen how the study of the vocabulary of a particular author might enable scholars to distinguish between authentic and inauthentic writings of that author. Specifically the study of the vocabulary of the corpus of Paul's unquestionably authentic letters (Romans, 1 and 2 Corinthians, Galatians, Philippians, 1 Thessalonians, and Philemon) afford a valuable tool in trying to address the questions of the authorship of letters, whose authenticity is less clear (Ephesians, Colossians, 2 Thessalonians, 1 and 2 Timothy, and Titus).

In the course of this chapter we have added to the collection of disciplines that scholars have mustered and refined in their attempt to understand better the text of the New Testament. Although not by any means an exact science, we are beginning to see that biblical scholars are very serious about their work and have honed a number of useful methodologies in the course of their study of the ancient text.

CHAPTER 3

SOURCE CRITICISM

As we saw in chapter 1, there are major challenges involved in attempting to establish or reconstruct the autograph or the earliest texts of the twenty-seven books of the New Testament, especially, so it appears, the texts of the gospels of Matthew, Mark, and Luke. To the extent that scholars can agree on the earliest texts of these three gospels, readers of the Bible might reasonably assume that a study of the gospels should begin with a look at the life and ministry of Jesus of Nazareth, the historical person who lies at the foundation of early Christianity. However desirable that task might seem, there are very serious methodological challenges involved in trying to reconstruct the life and ministry of Jesus.

Our only sources for such a reconstruction are the gospels of Matthew, Mark, Luke, and John; however, the process of moving through the gospels to Jesus is replete with problems that might make one think of trying to cross a mine field. The challenges are enormous, if not insurmountable. We need to begin our study of the gospels by analyzing them carefully in order to ascertain both what the gospels are and what they are not.

It was Herman Samuel Reimarus (1694–1768) who first realized that there is a striking difference between the Gospel of John and the three so-called synoptic gospels, Matthew, Mark, and Luke. The Gospel of John introduces the reader to a Jesus, who from the outset is the incarnation of the divine Word of God and whose message is primarily one of self-proclamation. Scholars refer to such statements in which gods and goddesses list their great deeds or virtues in the first person as aretalogies (meaning "lists of virtues"). Egyptian deities, especially the goddess Isis, commonly spoke in such aretalogies or hymns of self-praise. Many of Jesus' sayings, especially those found in the Gospel of John, share this aretalogical tendency.

For example, in marked contrast to the Jesus of the synoptic gospels, the Jesus of the Gospel of John is the subject of his own preaching. It is the Jesus of John only who says:

"I am he [Messiah], the one who is speaking to you." (John 4:26)

"I am the bread of life." (John 6:35, 48)

"I am the (living) bread that came down from heaven." (John 6:41, 51)

"You know where I am from." (John 7:28)

"I know him [the one who sent me, God] because I am from him, and he sent me." (John 7:29)

"I am the light of the world." (John 8:12)

"I am from above . . . I am not of this world." (John 8:23)

"I am he [the Son of Man]." (John 8:24, 28)

"Before Abraham was, I am." (John 8:58)

"I am the light of the world." (John 9:5)

"I am the gate (for the sheep)." (John 10:7, 9)

"I am the good shepherd." (John 10:11, 14)

"I am God's Son." (John 10:36)

"I am the resurrection and the life." (John 11:25)

"I am in the Father (and the Father is in me)." (John 14:10, 11, 20)

"I am the (true) vine." (John 15:1, 5)

"I am he." (John 18:5, 6, 8)

It is not merely that Jesus makes bold theological claims about himself in these verses in John in ways that are totally uncharacteristic of the Jesus of the synoptic gospel. The issue is even more profound: the author of the Gospel of John appears in these verses to be playing on the words of the divine "I AM," the name of God in the Book of Exodus:

> God said to Moses, "I AM WHO I AM." He said further, "Thus you shall say to the Israelites, I AM has sent me to you.'" (Exod 3:14)

For the author of the Gospel of John, Jesus is the divine I AM, or the incarnation thereof:

> And the [divine] Word (the Logos) became flesh and lived among us, and we have seen his glory, the glory as of a father's only son, full of grace and truth. (John 1:14)

The synoptic gospels present a very different picture of Jesus, one not influenced by the preaching of John's church, probably in Alexandria or Ephesus, sometime toward the end of the first century, where and when the Gospel of John was presumably written. In contrast to the Jesus of the Gospel of John, the Jesus of the synoptic gospels is not the primary focus of his own preaching. The Jesus of the synoptic gospels is, in fact, reluctant to make any claims of the sort that dominate John's theology.

So it is to the synoptic gospels that we turn first in our effort to reconstruct the life, the ministry, and the teachings of the historical Jesus, but these gospels also pose some serious questions. Most prominent, in this regard, is the so-called synoptic problem, the study of the literary relationship among the gospels of Matthew, Mark, and Luke.

Since the late eighteenth century, scholars have recognized that there is a clear literary relationship among these three gospels, because they contain parallel material, often in the same or in very similar words, in a similar narrative framework, and with stories often in the same sequence. Scholars have not, however, always agreed on the nature of that literary relationship.

The most common explanation of the literary relationship among the synoptic gospels is generally referred to as the modified two-source hypothesis or the four source hypothesis.

THE PRIORITY OF MARK

Since the nineteenth century most scholars have argued that the Gospel of Mark is the earliest of the synoptic gospels and that the authors of Matthew and Luke made use of Mark in writing their respective gospels. The arguments advanced in support of the priority of Mark are:[1]

1. The Argument from Shared Content. Matthew reproduces 90% and Luke about 55% of the subject matter of Mark's gospel in language that is largely identical with Mark's language.

2. The Argument from Wording. In those passages found in all three gospels, either Matthew or Luke or both are almost always in close verbal agreement with Mark, including even the grouping of words and the structure of sentences. Matthew and Luke almost never agree together against Mark.

3. The Argument from Order, Arrangement, or Sequence of Incidents. The order or sequence of stories in Mark is clearly the more original and is, in general, supported by both Matthew and Luke. Where either Matthew or Luke departs from the Markan order, the other is usually found supporting Mark's order.

4. The Argument from Editorial Improvement of Mark's More Original or Primitive Character. Matthew and Luke improve upon and refine Mark's more primitive language, style, and grammar.

5. The Argument from the Distribution of Markan and non-Markan Material Throughout Matthew and Luke. The way in which Markan and non-Markan material is distributed throughout Matthew and Luke suggests that the authors of Matthew and Luke were working with Mark independently and were incorporating into the Markan framework additional material from other sources.

---

1. Streeter, *The Four Gospels*, 157–69, 195–97. Reprinted in Bellinzoni, ed., *The Two-Source Hypothesis*, 23–36. Additional arguments both for and against the priority of Mark can be found in Bellinzoni's collection of essays. Suffice it to say that the overwhelming consensus of contemporary New Testament scholarship is that Mark wrote first and was used by Matthew and Luke. An important resource for a review of the synoptic problem can be found at: http://www.ntgateway.com/synoptic/

THE NEW TESTAMENT
THE TRIPLE TRADITION

The chart below reproduces the account of Jesus' healing of Simon Peter's mother-in law, a story that appears in all three of the synoptic gospels, referred to therefore as the so-called triple tradition. Words that are found in both Matthew and Mark are underlined; words that are found in both Mark and Luke are printed in *italics*. Some words in Mark will obviously be both underlined and italicized, meaning that these words are found in all three gospels.

1. Jesus' Healing of Simon's Mother-in-law

Matt 8:14–15	Mark 1:29–31	Luke 4:38–39
	[29]As soon as they left *the synagogue*,	[38]After leaving *the synagogue*
[14]When Jesus <u>entered</u> Peter's <u>house</u>,	they <u>*entered*</u> the <u>house</u> of *Simon* and Andrew, with James and John. [30]*Now*	he *entered* *Simon*'s house. *Now*
he saw his <u>mother-in-law</u> lying <u>in bed</u> <u>with a fever</u>;	*Simon's* <u>mother-in-law</u> *was* <u>in bed</u> <u>with</u> *a* <u>fever</u>, *and they* told *him* about *her* at once.	*Simon's* mother-in-law *was* suffering from *a* high *fever*, *and they* asked *him* about *her*.
[15]<u>he</u> touched <u>her</u> <u>hand</u>,	[31]<u>*He*</u> came and took <u>*her*</u> by the <u>*hand*</u> *and* lifted her up,	[39]Then *he* stood over *her* *and* rebuked *the fever*
and <u>the fever left her</u>, and <u>she</u> got up and <u>began to</u> <u>serve</u> him.	then <u>*the fever left her*</u>, <u>*and she began to*</u> <u>*serve*</u> *them*.	and it *left her*. Immediately *she* got up *and began to* *serve them*.
total words: 33 words underlined: 20 % underlined: 61%	total words: 59 words underlined: 20 % underlined: 34% words in italics: 29 % in italics: 49% words underlined or in italics or both: 33 % words underlined or in italics or both: 56%	total words: 45 words in italics: 29 % in italics: 64%

SOURCE CRITICISM

What exactly does this table illustrate? First of all, there is clearly a literary relationship among the three gospels, requiring that they be looked at together (synoptically), and necessitating an explanation regarding the nature of the literary relationship among them. Specifically, who copied from whom?

The English texts of the New Revised Standard Version of Matthew and Mark share 20 words either exactly or nearly exactly and almost always in the same order.[2] Mark and Luke, on the other hand, share 29 words either exactly or nearly exactly and also almost always in the same order. As we have already noted, most scholars have concluded that Mark is the earliest of the three synoptic gospels and that it served as a source for both Matthew and Luke. Generally, when Matthew departs from Mark, Luke supports the Markan reading; and when Luke departs from Mark, Matthew supports the Markan reading. Matthew and Luke agree against Mark on two details in this story: in omitting the reference to Andrew, James, and John; and in mentioning that following her healing, Peter's mother-in-law got up from bed before she served them.

Some scholars have argued that the so-called minor agreements of Matthew and Luke against Mark prove that Matthew and Luke could not have used Mark as their common source. There are, however, two simple explanations for the agreements of Matthew and Luke against Mark in this story. One explanation is that Matthew and Luke, acting independently, saw no reason for including Andrew, James, and John in this story as their presence serves no function in the story, and both Matthew and Luke independently thought it essential to indicate that Peter's mother-in-law got up from bed, thereby emphasizing her restored health, before she served him/them.

A second explanation might be that Matthew and Luke had access to somewhat different versions of the Gospel of Mark from the version that survives as our presumed best text of Mark. In other words, Mark survives for us in a form different from an earlier form that it had when Matthew and Luke both used it as a source for their respective gospels. This latter explanation addresses the issue of the instability of the text of the Gospel of Mark in the earliest period of its transmission, an issue that we addressed at length in chapter 1.

The argument from order or arrangement shows that Mark and Luke have the same stories both before and after the account of Jesus' Healing of Simon's Mother-in-law, namely The Man with an Unclean Spirit preceding and Other Healings of Jesus following (see the table below). Matthew has the same story as Mark following Jesus' Healing of Simon's Mother-in-Law, but no parallel to Mark's (and Luke's) preceding story (The Man with an Unclean Spirit).

---

2. The comparison of texts is done here on the basis of the New Revised Standard Version, so word counts in this story and in subsequent stories are based on that translation. Scholars ordinarily work with the Greek text, so word counts would obviously be slightly different from what they are here by our undertaking this study from the English translation.

No parallel in Matthew	Mark 1:23–28 The Man with an Unclean Spirit	Luke 4:33–37 The Man with an Unclean Spirit
Matt 8:14–15 Jesus' Healing of Peter's Mother-in-law	Mark 1:29–31 Jesus' Healing of Simon's Mother-in-law	Luke 4:38–39 Jesus' Healing of Simon's Mother-in-law
Matt 8:16–17 Other Healings of Jesus	Mark 1:32–34 Other Healings of Jesus	Luke 4:40–41 Other Healings of Jesus

The evidence points convincingly to the priority of Mark. Assuming that Mark is the earliest of the three gospels, scholars have also noted that Matthew and Luke not only followed Mark's gospel very closely, but both Matthew and Luke also abbreviated Mark substantially in their recasting of this story, presumably to make room for additional material that they wanted to include in their respective gospels. When abbreviating their Markan source, Matthew reproduced 56% of Mark's words and Luke 76% either exactly or almost exactly and almost always in the same order in which those words appear in Mark. Matthew and Luke's dependence on Mark is indisputable.

2. The Rejection of Jesus at Nazareth

Let us examine another story that appears in the triple tradition, a story that we looked at briefly in chapter 1 in connection with the discussion of textual criticism—the story of the rejection of Jesus at Nazareth.

Matt 13:54–58	Mark 6:1–6a	Luke 4:16–24
⁵⁴<u>He</u> <u>came to his hometown</u> and <u>began to</u> teach the people <u>In</u> their <u>synagogue</u>,	¹*He* left that place, and <u>*came to* his hometown</u>, and his disciples followed him. ²*On the Sabbath* *he* <u>began to</u> preach <u>in</u> *the* <u>synagogue</u>,	¹⁶When *he came to* Nazareth, where he had been brought up, he went to *the synagogue* *on the Sabbath* day, as was his custom. He stood up to read, ¹⁷and the scroll of the prophet Isaiah was given to him. He unrolled the scroll and found the place

SOURCE CRITICISM

Matt 13:54–58	Mark 6:1–6a	Luke 4:16–24
		where it was written: [18]"The Spirit of the Lord is upon me, because he has anointed me to bring good news to the poor. He has sent me to proclaim release to the captives and recovery of sight to the blind, to let the oppressed go free, [19]to proclaim the year of the Lord's favor." [20]And he rolled up the scroll, gave it back to the attendant, and sat down. The eyes of all in the synagogue were fixed on him. [21]Then he began to say to them, "Today this scripture has been fulfilled in your hearing."
so that they <u>were astounded</u>	and many who heard *him* <u>were astounded</u>.	[22]All spoke well of *him* and *were* amazed at the gracious words that came from his mouth.
and <u>said</u>, "<u>Where did this man get this wisdom</u> and these <u>deeds of power</u>?	*They* <u>said</u>, "<u>Where did this man get</u> all <u>this</u>? What is this <u>wisdom</u> that has been given to him? What <u>deeds of power</u> are being done by his hands?	*They* said,
[55]<u>Is not this the carpenter's son</u>? Is not his mother called <u>Mary</u>? <u>And</u> are not his <u>brothers James and Joseph and Simon and Judas</u>? [56]<u>And</u>	[3]*<u>Is this not the son</u>* of the <u>carpenter</u> and of <u>Mary and</u> the <u>brother</u> of <u>James and Joses and Judas and Simon, and are not his</u>	"*Is not this* Joseph's *son*?"

73

Matt 13:54–58	Mark 6:1–6a	Luke 4:16–24
are not his sisters with us? Where then did this man get all this? ⁵⁷And they took offense at him.	sisters here with us?³ And they took offense at him.	
		²³He said to them, "Doubtless you will quote to me this proverb, 'Doctor, cure yourself!' and you will say, "Do here also in your hometown the things that we have heard you did in Capernaum.
But Jesus said to them, "Prophets are not without honor except in their own country and	⁴Then Jesus said to them, "Prophets are not without honor, except in their hometown, and among their own kin, and	²⁴And he said, "Truly I tell you no prophet is accepted in the prophet's hometown."
in their own house." ⁵⁸And he did not do many deeds of power there,	in their own house." 5And he could do no deed of power there, except that he laid his hands on a few sick people and cured them.	
because of their unbelief.	⁶And he was amazed at their unbelief.	

It would be useful to compile figures for those verses in the table above for which there are meaningful parallels. Most specifically, I shall not include Luke 4:16c ("He stood up to read"), 16c–21, 23 in the word count, as this material has obviously been added to the Markan framework by the author of the Gospel of Luke, possibly from another source.

---

3. This reading of Mark 6:3 is the proposed reconstruction of the text from Chapter 1.

SOURCE CRITICISM

Matt 13:54–58	Mark 6:1–6a	Luke 4:16ab, 22, 24
total words: 112	total words: 150	total words: 63
words underlined: 78	words underlined: 78	
% underlined: 70%	% underlined: 52%	
	words in italics: 21	words in italics: 21
	% words in italics: 14%	% words in italics: 33%
	words underlined or in italics or both: 86	
	% words underlined or in italics or both: 57%	

Markan priority is particularly evident from the different ways in which both Matthew and Luke deal with the "embarrassment" in Mark 6:5 that Jesus *could do no deed of power there* (in Nazareth). Matthew softened this problematic passage by changing Mark's words to read "And he (Jesus) *did not do many deeds of power there*, a relatively minor but important improvement. Luke, on the other hand, deleted the offending verse entirely when he rewrote the story.

Note that I substituted the reconstructed text of Mark 6:3 in lieu of the reading of the New Revised Standard Version, based on the discussion of textual criticism in chapter 1. It is evident that the version printed above makes much more sense as the reader tries to understand the parallels in Matthew and Luke. Without this emendation of Mark 6:3, it is very difficult to understand why both Matthew and Luke would independently have modified Mark in a way that calls into question Jesus' virgin birth.

The argument for the priority of Mark based on the order or arrangement of stories is less clear in this story than in the one examined previously. It is, nevertheless, still relevant. I pointed out previously that when Luke departs from Mark's order, Matthew usually supports Mark, and vice versa. The stories surrounding the Rejection of Jesus at Nazareth can be summarized as follows:

Matt 13:51–53	Mark 5:21–43	Luke 4:1–15
Treasures Old and New	A Girl Restored to Life and a Woman Healed	The Temptation of Jesus
Matt 13:54–58	Mark 6:1–6a	Luke 4:16–24
The Rejection of Jesus at Nazareth	The Rejection of Jesus at Nazareth	The Rejection of Jesus at Nazareth
	Mark 6:6b–13	Luke 4:25–30
	The Mission of the Twelve	Stories about Elijah And Elisha

Matt 14:1–12	Mark 6:14–29
The Death of John the Baptist	The Death of John the Baptist

Although there is no agreement among Matthew, Mark, and Luke regarding what immediately precedes The Rejection of Jesus at Nazareth, there is near agreement between Matthew and Mark about what follows. The Mission of the Twelve immediately follows in Mark (6:6b–13), and that story in turn is followed in Mark by The Death of John the Baptist (6:14–29), which is the very next story in Matthew's text (14:1–12).

Referring back to the chart on The Rejection of Jesus at Nazareth, apart from Luke's omission of Mark 6:5 and his addition of the material in Luke 4:16c–21, 23, the three versions of the story are very similar. Either Matthew or Luke or both reproduce 57% of Mark's words in almost exactly the same order. Luke 4:16ab, 22, 24 are clearly adapted freely from Mark 6:1–6a. In fact, Luke uses much of Mark's wording. The source of Luke 4:16c–21, 23 is more problematic. This material may come from Luke's special source L (see the discussion of L later in this chapter), or it may be an original Lukan composition. In any case, this portion of the story in Luke is obviously a conflation of two distinct elements. Jesus reads from portions of Isa 61:1–2 and 58:6, which in Luke's gospel are quoted verbatim from the Greek Septuagint. For the author of the Gospel of Luke, the message is clear: Jesus is the fulfillment of scripture and so proclaims himself in the context of his visit to the synagogue in Nazareth. Apparently Luke could not resist inserting this story into this particular context.

The freedom with which both Matthew and Luke edited their Markan source is a clear indication that historical accuracy and faithfulness to written tradition were not primary considerations in their copying or editing the Markan source. We can only imagine that scribes likely took the same kinds of liberties with their written sources as the authors of the gospels of Matthew and Luke took when they rewrote the Gospel of Mark.

LUKE'S GREAT OMISSION OF MARKAN MATERIAL

Of particular concern to scholars in looking at the triple tradition is the question of why, with the exception of a brief saying, Luke has drawn no material from the material in Mark 6:45–8:26, a block of 74+ verses. The exception is the single saying:

Mark 8:15	Luke 12:1
And he cautioned them, saying, "Watch out – *beware of the yeast of the Pharisees* and the yeast of Herod."	He began to speak first to his disciples, *"Beware of the yeast of the Pharisees,"* that is, their hypocrisy."

SOURCE CRITICISM

The only parallel between Mark and Luke in these verses is in the words, "Beware of the yeast of the Pharisees," a phrase that sounds remarkably like a common aphorism that Luke may have drawn from oral tradition or from his special source L. It may even be an authentic saying of Jesus, remembered without regard to its original context. In any case, Luke probably did not draw this isolated saying from Mark.

The large block of Markan material that is missing from Luke contains the following:

Markan Story Missing from Luke	Mark
Jesus Walks on the Water	6:45–52
Jesus' Healings in Gennesaret	6:53–56
Clean and Unclean	7:1–23
The Faith of the Syro-Phoenician Woman	7:24–30
The Healing of the Deaf Man	7:31–37
Jesus Feeds the Four Thousand	8:1–10
The Demand for a Sign	8:11–13
The Yeast of the Pharisees and Herod	8:14–21
Jesus Heals a Blind Man at Bethsaida	8:22–26

How can we best explain the absence of this large block of important Markan material from the Gospel of Luke? There are only two possible explanations, either: (1) Luke consciously chose for whatever reason to omit this material; or (2) this material was not in the copy of Mark to which Luke had access.

It is difficult to explain why Luke would have intentionally omitted such an important body of material if it was in his text of the Gospel of Mark. If the material was not in the text of Mark to which Luke had access, there are two possible explanations, either: (1) Luke had access to a defective manuscript of Mark from which several pages had been lost, or (2) these more than 74 verses were not in the original manuscript of the Gospel of Mark, the one to which Luke had access, and were added to Mark by a later editor, whose enhanced copy of the Gospel of Mark served as the version of Mark to which Matthew (but not Luke) had subsequent access. I would venture to suggest that this block of material, containing these nine stories, was not in the first edition of the Gospel of Mark, the text of Mark to which Luke had access. The material in Mark 6:45–8:26 is generally Gentile-oriented and may very well be a later addition to the Gospel of Mark, the edition known to the author of the Gospel of Matthew. However this block of material was consciously omitted or lost from Mark or added to a second edition of the gospel, this piece of information once against suggests the fluidity of the text of the gospel in its first decades of transmission.

Our review of the two stories from the triple tradition and of the possible reasons for Luke's Great Omission of Markan Material gives little comfort to those who assume that our canonical gospels were preserved largely intact during the first century of their transmission. The distinct and significant rewriting of these Markan stories by the authors of the gospels of Matthew and Luke and the matter of the large missing block of Markan material from Luke's gospel clearly cast doubt on such an assumption.

THE DOUBLE TRADITION

The two stories that we examined above are part of the triple tradition, stories found in all three of the synoptic gospels, Matthew, Mark, and Luke. There are, indeed, dozens of such traditions. We shall now look at two stories from the double tradition, stories that are found in Mark and in either Matthew or Luke, but not in both. The close literary relationship among the synoptic gospels also appears, as we might expect, in these passages in the double tradition.

1. The Healing of the Demoniac in the Synagogue

Mark 1:21–28	Luke 4:31–37
²¹They *went to Capernaum*; *and* when *the Sabbath came*, he entered the synagogue and *taught*. ²²*They were astounded at his teaching*, for *he* taught them as one having *authority*, and not as the scribes. ²³Just then *there was in their synagogue a man* with *an unclean spirit*, ²⁴*and he cried out*, *"What have you to do with us, Jesus of Nazareth? Have you come to destroy us? I know who you are, the Holy One of God."* ²⁵*But Jesus rebuked him, saying, "Be silent, and come out of him!"* ²⁶And the unclean spirit convulsing *him* and crying with a loud voice, *came out of him*.	³¹He *went* down *to Capernaum*, a city in Galilee, *and* was *teaching* them on *the sabbath*. ³²*They were astounded at his teaching*, because *he* spoke with *authority*. ³³In the synagogue there was *a man* who had the *spirit* of *an unclean* demon, *and he cried out* with a loud voice, ³⁴"Let us alone! *What have you to do with us, Jesus of Nazareth? Have you come to destroy us? I know who you are, the Holy One of God."* ³⁵*But Jesus rebuked him, saying, "Be silent, and come out of him!"* When the demon had thrown *him* down before them, he *came out of him* without having done him any harm.

SOURCE CRITICISM

Mark 1:21–28	Luke 4:31–37
²⁷*They were all amazed, and* they *kept on asking one another, "What is this*? A new teaching – *with authority*! *He commands* even *the unclean spirits, and they* obey him." ²⁸At once his fame *began to* spread throughout *the* surrounding *region* of Galilee.	³⁶*They were all amazed and kept saying to one another, "What* kind of utterance *is this*? For *with authority* and power *he commands the unclean spirits, and* out *they* come!" ³⁷And a report about him *began to* reach every place in *the region*.
total words: 147	total words: 154
words in italics: 96	words in italics: 96
% words in italics: 65%	% words in italics: 62%

As for the order or the arrangement of this story in Mark and Luke, the following chart is illustrative:

Mark 1:16–20	Luke 4:16–30
Jesus Calls the First Disciples	Jesus' Preaching at Nazareth
Mark 1:21–28	Luke 4:31–37
The Healing of the Demoniac in the Synagogue	The Healing of the Demoniac in the Synagogue
Mark 1:29–31	Luke 4:38–39
The Healing of Peter's Mother-in-law	The Healing of Peter's Mother-in-law

The stories preceding The Healing of the Demoniac in the Synagogue are different in Mark (1:16–20) and Luke (4:16–30), but the stories immediately following The Healing of the Demoniac in the Synagogue are the same in both gospels (Mark 1:29–31 // Luke 4:38–39).

Moreover, the verbal agreement between Mark and Luke is striking. The word order, the content, and the vocabulary are almost identical, leaving no doubt that the two version of this story reflect the borrowing of one from the other. Although Luke reproduces Mark almost exactly, still 38% of Luke's words do not come from Mark but are part of Luke's editing of his Markan source.

Once again, we must pose the question whether Luke's freedom with his Markan source is characteristic of the way in which the gospels were modified by copyists during the first century of transmission. Even when the texts are as close as these two, still about one-third of Mark's text has been modified by Luke. How characteristic is this of the way in which manuscripts were copied by scribes in the first century after the writing of the Markan autograph? Is this a practice reserved for "new compositions," or does it reflect the way in which early Christian scribes freely edited manuscripts that they were reproducing?

2. The Syrophoenician/Canaanite Woman

Matt 15:21–28	Mark 7:24–30
²¹Jesus left that place <u>and went away to the</u> district <u>of Tyre</u> and Sidon.	²⁴From there he set out <u>and went away to the</u> region <u>of Tyre</u>. He entered a house and did not want anyone to know he was there. Yet he could not escape notice,
²²Just then <u>a</u> Canaanite <u>woman</u> from that region came out and started shouting, "Have mercy on me, Lord, Son of David; my <u>daughter</u> is tormented by a demon." ²³But he did not answer her at all. And his disciples came and urged him, saying, "Send her away, for she keeps shouting after us." ²⁴He answered, "I was sent only to the lost sheep of the house of Israel." ²⁵But <u>she came and</u> knelt before him, saying, "Lord help me."	²⁵but <u>a woman</u> whose little <u>daughter</u> had an unclean spirit immediately heard about him, And <u>she came and</u> bowed down at his feet. ²⁶Now the woman was a Gentile, of Syrophoenician origin. She begged him to cast the demon out of her daughter.
²⁶<u>He</u> answered, "<u>It is not fair to take the children's food and throw it to the dogs</u>." ²⁷<u>She</u> said, "Yes, Lord, yet <u>even the dogs eat the crumbs</u> that fall from their masters' <u>table</u>." ²⁸<u>Then</u> Jesus answered <u>her</u>, "Woman, great is your faith! Let it be done for you as you wish."	²⁷<u>He</u> said to her, "Let the children be fed first, For <u>it is not fair to take the children's food and throw it to the dogs</u>. ²⁸But <u>she</u> answered him, "Sir, <u>Even the dogs</u> under the <u>table eat the</u> children's <u>crumbs</u>." ²⁹<u>Then</u> he said to <u>her</u>, "For saying that, you may go – the demon has left your <u>daughter</u>."

SOURCE CRITICISM

Matt 15:21–28	Mark 7:24–30
And her <u>daughter</u> was healed instantly.	³⁰So she went home, found the child lying on the bed, and the demon gone.
total words: 151	total words: 149
words underlined: 40	words underlined: 40
% words underlined: 26%	% words underlined: 27%

This story supports fully the argument from order or arrangement:

Matt 15:1–20	Mark 7:1–23
The Tradition of the Elders	The Tradition of the Elders
Matt 15:21–28	Mark 7:24–30
The Canaanite Woman's Faith	The Syrophoenician Woman's Faith
Matt 15:29–31	Mark 7:31–37
Jesus Cures Many Others	Jesus Heals a Deaf Man and Many Others

The stories both preceding and following the Canaanite/Syrophoenician's Woman's Faith are identical in both gospels, a strong indication of literary dependence and the priority of Mark.

The verbal agreement is another matter. In fact, were it not for the formal dialogue between Jesus and the (Syrophoenician/Canaanite) woman, it would not be entirely clear that Matthew and Mark are telling the same story in these passages. The verbal agreement between the two gospels is minimal apart from the verbal exchange of what appear to be aphorisms spoken first by Jesus, then by the woman:

> "It is not fair to take the children's food and throw it to the dogs."
> "Even the dogs under the table eat the children's crumbs."

Apart from the strong verbal agreement in these two sayings (which accounts for more than half of the verbal agreement in these two versions of the story), there are just enough words elsewhere, and in the same relative order, in the two texts to indicate that Matthew was apparently editing the Markan gospel. However, Matthew rewrote almost completely the narrative portion of his Markan source in Matt 15:22–25, 28.

Both accounts appear to be dealing with the beginning of the mission to the Gentiles; Mark specifically uses the word "Gentile" in 7:26. Matt 17:24 leaves no ambiguity at all, when Jesus says, "I was sent only to the lost sheep of the house of Israel"—that is, *not* to the Gentiles. But, according to the account in Matt 15:28, it is the faith of the Canaanite woman that led Jesus to perform his first healing outside Israel.

What is particularly evident in these two versions of the story is the substantial liberty that Matthew took in editing, indeed in rewriting, the narrative portion of his Markan source—to such a degree that when Matthew finished, there was little left of Mark's narrative. Only the sayings material remains relatively intact.

THE SAYINGS SOURCE Q

As mentioned earlier in this chapter, the Gospel of Matthew reproduces about 90% and the Gospel of Luke about 55% of the subject matter of Mark's gospel in language that is largely identical with Mark's language. This evidence is generally referred to as the argument from content, and we have reviewed above several instances in support of this argument in both the triple tradition and the double tradition.

Once the Markan material in Matthew and in Luke has been identified and the case has been made that Matthew and Luke copied from (somewhat different?) manuscripts of the Gospel of Mark, it is evident that there are still more than 200 verses, mostly sayings material, that is similar in both Matthew and Luke but that is not found in Mark. There are only three possible explanations for the unambiguous verbal agreement in these more than 200 verses:

1. Matthew copied from Luke; or
2. Luke copied from Matthew; or
3. Matthew and Luke made independent use of a common written or oral source.

The suggestion that Matthew used Luke or that Luke used Matthew fails for two reasons:

1. following the Temptation Story at the beginning of the three synoptic gospels, there is not a single instance in which Matthew and Luke agree in inserting the same saying in the same context in the Markan outline; and
2. it is sometimes Luke and sometimes Matthew who reproduces an individual saying in what appears to be the more original form.

These important observations clearly indicate that Matthew and Luke could not have copied from one another. But these observations make a good deal of sense if Matthew and Luke had individual access to the same source, or to two somewhat different versions of the same source, and were independently incorporating sayings from this source into the framework of the Markan gospel that they were using. Scholars refer to this hypothetical source as Q for *Quelle*, the German word for "source."[4]

---

4. See Streeter, *The Four Gospels*, 182-86, reprinted in Bellinzoni, *The Two Source Hypothesis*, 221-225. Other arguments both for and against the use of the hypothetical source Q are contained in Bellinzoni, 227-433. The case against the Q hypothesis is laid out in a series of essays in Bellinzoni,

SOURCE CRITICISM

That Q was a written source and not simply common oral tradition to which Matthew and Luke had access is supported by the fact that most of the so-called Q material appears in the same order in both Matthew and Luke. To illustrate this point, I list below in their order in the Gospel of Matthew the Q material found in the first seven chapters of that gospel:[5]

Matthew	Luke
3:7–10	3:7–9
3:11–12	3:16b–17
4:2b–11a	4:2b–13
5:2–4, 6	6:20–21
5:11–12	6:22–23
5:13	14:34–35
5:15	11:33
5:18	16:17
5:25–26	12:58–59
5:32	16:18
5:39b–40	6:29
5:42	6:30
5:44	6:27–28
5:47	6:33–34
5:48	6:36
6:9–13	11:2–4
6:19–21	12:33–34
6:22–23a	11:34
6:24	16:13
6:25–33	12:22b–31
7:1–2	6:37–38
7:3–5	6:41–42
7:7–11	11:9–13
7:12	6:31
7:13–14	13:24
7:16, 18	6:43–44
7:21	6:46
7:22–23	13:26–27

319–433. See also Goodacre, *The Case Against Q*.

5. Most scholars assume that Luke followed the sequence of Q more closely and that Matthew rearranged the order of Q in order to create several long discourses. I have followed the order of the Gospel of Matthew in this chart to show that the sequence of Q is evident even in the gospel that followed Q's order less closely.

THE NEW TESTAMENT

Matthew	Luke
7:24–27	6:47–49
7:28a	7:1a
and so forth.	and so forth

In the Lukan column, the parallels that do not appear in more or less the same sequential order are printed father to the right to indicate that they are out of sequence with Matthew. Nevertheless, in spite of these exceptions, the Lukan and Matthean orders persist for the most part, indicating that Q must have been a written source and not merely a body of similar oral tradition.

In the charts below we see two examples of material that is presumed to have come to Matthew and Luke from Q.

DO NOT WORRY

The first block of material appears to be a collection of sayings of Jesus on anxiety. The material appears in very similar form in both Matthew and Luke. Words that are found in both gospels are underlined.

Matt 6:25–34	Luke 12:22–32
	²²He said to his disciples,
²⁵"<u>Therefore I tell you</u>,	"<u>Therefore I tell you</u>,
<u>do not worry about your life</u>,	<u>do not worry about your life</u>,
<u>what you will eat</u>	<u>what you will eat</u>,
or what you will drink,	
<u>or about your body</u>,	<u>or about your body</u>,
<u>what you will wear</u>.	<u>what you will wear</u>.
<u>Is</u> not <u>life more than food</u>,	²³For <u>life</u> is <u>more than food</u>,
<u>and the body more than clothing</u>?	<u>and the body more than clothing</u>.
²⁶Look at the birds of the air: <u>they</u>	²⁴Consider the ravens: <u>they neither</u>
<u>neither sow nor reap</u>	<u>sow nor reap</u>, they have neither
nor gather into <u>barns</u>, <u>and</u>	storehouse nor <u>barn</u>
<u>yet</u> your heavenly Father <u>feeds them</u>.	<u>and yet</u> God <u>feeds them</u>.
<u>Are you</u> not <u>of more value</u>	<u>Of</u> how much <u>more value are you</u>
<u>than</u> they?	<u>than</u> the birds!
²⁷<u>And can any of you by worrying</u>	²⁵<u>And can any of you by worrying</u>
<u>add a single hour to your span of life</u>?	<u>add a single hour to your span of life</u>?
	²⁶If then you are not able to do

Matt 6:25–34	Luke 12:22–32
	so small a thing as that,
²⁸And <u>why do you worry about</u>	<u>why do you worry about</u>
clothing?	the rest?
<u>Consider the lilies</u> of the field,	²⁷<u>Consider the lilies,</u>
<u>how they grow;</u>	<u>how they grow:</u>
<u>they neither toil nor spin;</u>	<u>they neither toil nor spin;</u>
²⁹<u>yet I tell you, even Solomon</u>	<u>yet I tell you, even Solomon</u>
<u>in all his glory</u>	<u>in all his glory</u>
<u>was not clothed like one of these.</u>	<u>was not clothed like one of these.</u>
³⁰<u>But if God so clothes</u>	²⁸<u>But if God so clothes</u>
<u>the grass of the field,</u>	<u>the grass of the field</u>
<u>which is alive today and</u>	<u>which is alive today and</u>
<u>tomorrow is thrown into the oven,</u>	<u>tomorrow is thrown into the oven,</u>
<u>will he</u> not <u>much more clothe you –</u>	how <u>much more will he clothe you –</u>
<u>you of little faith?</u>	<u>you of little faith!</u>
³¹Therefore, <u>do not</u> worry, saying,	²⁹And <u>do not</u> keep striving
'<u>What</u> will we <u>eat</u>?' or	for <u>what</u> you are to <u>eat</u>
'<u>What</u> will we <u>drink</u>?' or	and <u>what</u> you are to <u>drink</u>,
'What will we wear?'	and do not keep worrying.
³²<u>For it is the</u> Gentiles	³⁰<u>For it is the</u> nations of the world
who <u>strive</u> for <u>all these things;</u>	that <u>strive</u> after <u>all these things;</u>
<u>and</u> indeed <u>your</u> heavenly <u>Father</u>	<u>and your Father</u>
<u>knows that you need</u> all these things.	<u>knows that you need</u> them.
³³But <u>strive</u> first <u>for</u> the <u>kingdom of</u>	³¹Instead, <u>strive for</u> his <u>kingdom,</u>
God and his righteousness, <u>and</u> all <u>these</u>	<u>and these</u>
<u>things will be given to you as well.</u>	<u>things will be given to you as well.</u>
³⁴So <u>do not</u> worry about tomorrow,	³²<u>Do not</u> be afraid, little flock,
<u>for</u> tomorrow will bring	<u>for</u> it is your Father's good pleasure
worries of its own.	to give you the kingdom."
Today's trouble is enough for today."	
total words: 240	total words: 242
words underlined: 166	words underlined: 166
% words underlined: 69%	% words underlined: 69%

These passages in Matthew and Luke contain not a single saying but a collection or cluster of sayings that are found in substantially the same form in both gospels, although in very different contexts. In the Gospel of Matthew, this block of material is found in the Sermon on the Mount (Matt 5–7), immediately after sayings On

Treasures in Heaven (Matt 6:19–21), on The Sound Eye (Matt 6:22–23), and on Serving Two Masters (Matt 6:24) and immediately preceding sayings on Judging (Matt 7:1–5) and On Profanity (Matt 7:6).

Matt 6:19–21 Sayings on Treasures in Heaven	
Matt 6:22–23 Sayings on the Sound Eye	Luke 12:13–15 A Warning on Avarice
Matt 6:24 Sayings on Serving Two Masters	Luke 12:16–21 Parable of the Rich Fool
Matt 6:25–34 Sayings on Anxiety	Luke 12:22–32 Sayings on Anxiety
Matt 7:1–5 Sayings on Judging	Luke 12:33–4 Sayings on Treasures in Heaven
Matt 7:6 Saying on Profanity	

In the Gospel of Luke, this cluster is found immediately after two passages that are unique to Luke, a Warning against Avarice (Luke 12:13–15) and the Parable of the Rich Fool (Luke 12:16–21) and immediately before another Q saying On Treasures in Heaven (Luke 12:33–34), which is the Lukan parallel to Matt 6:19–21. The different context in the two gospels supports the hypothesis that Matthew and Luke were working independently with a common block of written material in which these saying had already been combined.

The body of the sayings material is very similar in both gospels, so much so that if one eliminates the introductory words of Luke 12:22 ("He said to his disciples") and the very different final verses in Matt 6:34 and Luke 13:32, the already high incidence of agreement between Matthew and Luke (69%) increases even further to 79% in both gospels. The fact that Matthew and Luke end this cluster with very different sayings may be evidence that they were working from different versions of the Q document.

Whatever else we may conclude about this material, it is evident that Matthew and Luke have not borrowed these sayings from each other but that they have independently inserted this block of sayings material into their separate gospels from a common written source in which these sayings were already grouped together. The agreement indisputably establishes these conclusions; the differences reinforce the view that the evangelists, their sources, and their subsequent copyists all appear to have exercised liberties in copying material. Even in quoting presumed sayings of Jesus, subsequent writers obviously exercised poetic license.

A second example of material that is presumed to come from Q is:

JESUS' EXHORATION TO FEARLESS CONFESSION

Matt 10:26–33	Luke 12:2–9
²⁶"So have no fear of them; for <u>nothing is covered up</u> <u>that will not be uncovered, and nothing secret that will not become known</u>. ²⁷What I say to <u>you</u> <u>in the dark</u>, tell <u>in the light</u>; <u>and what you</u> hear <u>whispered</u>, <u>proclaim</u> <u>from the housetops</u>.	² "<u>Nothing is covered up</u> <u>that will not be uncovered, and nothing secret that will not become known</u>. ³Therefore whatever <u>you</u> have said <u>in the dark</u> will be heard <u>in the light</u>, <u>and what you</u> have <u>whispered</u> behind closed doors will be <u>proclaimed</u> <u>from the housetops</u>. ⁴I tell you, my friends,
²⁸<u>Do not fear those who kill the body</u> but cannot kill the soul; rather <u>fear him who</u> can destroy both soul and body in <u>hell</u>.	<u>do not fear those who kill the body</u>, and after that can do nothing more. ⁵But I will warn you whom to fear: <u>fear him who</u>, after he has killed, has authority to cast into <u>hell</u>. Yes I tell you, fear him!
²⁹<u>Are not</u> two <u>sparrows sold</u> <u>for</u> a <u>penny</u>? <u>Yet not one of them</u> will fall to the the ground apart from your Father. ³⁰And <u>even the hairs of your head</u> <u>are all counted</u>. ³¹So <u>do not be afraid</u>; <u>you are of more value than</u> <u>many sparrows</u>.	⁶<u>Are not</u> five <u>sparrows sold</u> <u>for</u> two <u>pennies</u>? <u>Yet not one of them</u> is forgotten in God's sight. ⁷But <u>even the hairs of your head</u> <u>are all counted</u>. <u>Do not be afraid</u>; <u>you are of more value than</u> <u>many sparrows</u>. ⁸And I tell you,
³²<u>Every<u>one</u> therefore <u>who</u> acknowledges me before others</u>, I <u>also will acknowledge before</u> my Father in heaven; ³³<u>but whoever denies me before others</u>,	<u>everyone who acknowledges me before others</u>, the Son of Man <u>also will acknowledge</u> <u>before</u> the angels of God; ⁹<u>but whoever denies me before others</u>

Matt 10:26–33	Luke 12:2–9
I also <u>will</u> deny <u>before</u> my Father in heaven."	<u>will</u> be <u>denied before</u> the angels of God."
total words: 147	total words: 168
words underlined: 95	Words underlined: 95
% words underlined: 65%	% words underlined: 57%

Once again we have a good example of a cluster of sayings in the gospels of Matthew and Luke that obviously came from the sayings source Q. More than half of the words in Matthew and Luke are identical, and the individual sayings within the cluster appear in the same order.

The sayings cluster in Matt 10:26–33 is preceded by sayings material from Q that speaks to the fate of the disciples (Matt 10:17–25) and is followed by sayings material from Q describing divisions within households (Matt 10:34–36).

Matt 10:17–25	Luke 12:1
The Fate of the Disciples	The Leaven of the Pharisees
Matt 10:26–33	Luke 12:2–9
Exhortation to Fearless Confession	Exhortation to Fearless Confession
Matt 10:34–36	Luke 12:10
Divisions within Households	The Sin Against the Holy Spirit

The sayings cluster in Luke 12:2–9, on the other hand, is preceded by the saying about the leaven of the Pharisees from the triple tradition (Matt 16:5–6 // Mark 8:14–15 // Luke 12:1) and is followed by a story from the triple tradition about the sin against the Holy Spirit (Matthew 12:31–32 // Mark 3:28–30 // Luke 12:10), showing once again that Matthew and Luke did not copy from one another but rather had independent access to the hypothetical sayings source Q.

SPECIAL M AND SPECIAL L

If one removes from the gospels of Matthew and Luke the material that they derived from both Mark and the sayings source Q, there is still a good deal of material that is unique to Matthew and unique to Luke. Scholars generally refer to this material as (Special) M and (Special) L, implying thereby that the authors of the gospels of Matthew and Luke used their own special sources in addition to their common use of Mark and Q. The following tables identify most but not all of the material that is unique to Matthew and to Luke respectively:

Special M (material found only in the Gospel of Matthew)

1:1–17	The Genealogy of Jesus the Messiah
2:13–21	The Flight into Egypt and Return
5:21–24	On Murder and Anger
5:33–37	On Oaths
6:1–4	On Giving Alms
6:5–6	On Prayer
6:16–18	On Fasting
7:6	On Profaning the Holy
11:1	Continuation of the Journey
11:28–30	"Come to Me"
13:24–30	The Parable of the Weeds
13:36–43	Jesus Explains the Parable of the Weeds
13:44–46	The Parables of the Hidden Treasure and the Pearl
13:47–50	The Parable of the Net
13:51–52	Treasures New and Old
17:24–27	Payment of the Temple Tax
18:19–20	"Where Two or Three are Gathered Together"
18:23–35	The Parable of the Unforgiving Servant
21:28–32	The Parable of the Two Sons
27:3–10	The Death of Judas
27:62–66	The Guard at the Tomb
28:11–15	The Report of the Guard
28:16–20	The Great Commission

Special L (material found only in the Gospel of Luke)

1:5–25	John the Baptist's Birth Promised
1:26–38	The Annunciation
1:39–56	Mary's Visit to Elizabeth
1:57–80	The Birth of John the Baptist
2:21–38	Jesus Presented in the Temple
2:41–52	The Child Jesus in the Temple
3:10–14	John the Baptist's Preaching
3:23–38	Jesus' Genealogy

5:1–11	The Miraculous Catch of Fish
6:24–26	The Woes
7:11–17	The Widow's Son at Nain
8:1–3	Galilean Women Minister to Jesus
9:52–56	Rejection by Samaritans
10:29–37	The Parable of the Good Samaritan
10:38–42	Martha and Mary
11:5–8	Parable of the Persistent Friend
11:27–28	Only Those Truly Blessed
12:13–15	Warning against Greed
12:16–21	Parable of the Rich Fool
12:35–38	On Vigilance
13:1–9	Repent or Perish
13:10–17	The Healing of the Crippled Woman
13:31–33	The Third Day
14:1–6	The Healing of a Man with Dropsy
14:7–14	On Humility
14:28–32	Conditions of discipleship
15:8–10	The Parable of the Lost Coin
15:11–32	The Parable of the Prodigal Son
16:1–13	The Parable of the Dishonest Manager
16:19–31	The Parable of the Rich Man and Lazarus
17:7–10	Worthless Slaves
17:11–19	Cleansing of Ten Lepers
17:20–21	On the Coming of God's Kingdom
18:1–8	The Parable of the Unjust Judge
18:9–14	The Parable of the Pharisee and the Tax Collector
19:1–10	Zaccheus
19:41–44	Jesus Weeps Over Jerusalem
21:34–36	On Vigilance
21:37–38	Ministry of Jesus in Jerusalem
23:6–12	Jesus before Herod
23:13–16	Pilate Acquits Jesus of Wrongdoing
24:13–35	Jesus' Appearance on the Road to Emmaus
24:36–43	Jesus' Appearance to Disciples in Jerusalem
24:44–49	Jesus' Final Commission and Ascension

The opening words of the Gospel of Luke imply that the author of that gospel had access to *many* sources:

SOURCE CRITICISM

> ¹:¹Since *many* have undertaken to set down an orderly account of the events that have been fulfilled among us, ²just as they were handed on to us by those who from the beginning were eyewitnesses and servants of the word, ³I too decided after investigating everything carefully from the very first, to write an orderly account for you, most excellent Theophilus, ⁴so that you may know the truth concerning the things about which you have been instructed. (Luke 1:1–4)

The author of the Gospel of Luke makes it clear that his was not the first attempt to write a narrative account about Jesus and that he made use of earlier written sources. In addition to the material that the authors of the gospels of Matthew and Luke drew from the Gospel of Mark and from the sayings source Q, there is material that appears only in Matthew (generally identified as coming from a source called M) and material that appears only in Luke (generally identified as coming from a source called L). Although the existence and nature of M and L is more problematic than is the case for the sayings source Q, a diagram of the literary relationship among the gospels of Matthew, Mark, and Luke looks like this:

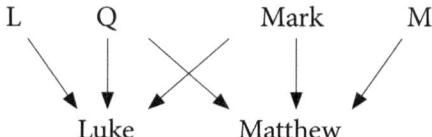

It would be a mistake to ascribe all of the material in M and L to oral traditions or to single written sources available respectively to Matthew and Luke. The nature of the material in M and L is very complex and contains in both cases both narrative and sayings material including genealogies, birth narratives, isolated sayings, parables, accounts of resurrection appearances, and in the case of L miracles stories. Interestingly, the materials in M and L are very different from one another, and the genealogies, the birth and infancy narratives, and the accounts of Jesus' resurrection appearances differ considerably, suggesting independent origins.

It is probably best to think of M and L as symbols for multiple written and possibly oral sources that were available to Matthew and Luke independently. M and L may also serve as symbols for material that the authors of the gospels of Matthew and Luke may have composed independently as they were involved in incorporating material from Q and from their individual sources into the Markan framework.

The distinctive birth narratives and genealogies were likely independent written sources. Moreover, the authors of Matthew and Luke clearly had access to independent accounts of Jesus' resurrection appearances: Matthew reports appearances in Galilee, and Luke reports appearances in and around Jerusalem. Additionally, Matthew and Luke each had access to several different parables of Jesus in addition to the parables that each drew from Mark and Q. Furthermore, L apparently contained some miracle stories; M did not. The varied nature of material drawn from the "sources" M and

L suggests that they were not single written documents but rather multiple written sources and/or oral traditions available to the two evangelists.

CONCLUSIONS

Let it be clear at the outset that this chapter deals with texts, with literary compositions, with documents written by Christians, for Christians, in Christian communities toward the end of the first century. This chapter does not deal with events in the life and ministry of Jesus or with Jesus' message and teaching. We shall have occasion to deal with those issues in due course in a subsequent chapter.

In chapter 1, I argued that establishing the presumed oldest text is a necessary prelude to all study of the New Testament and early Christianity. Without a clear understanding of the nature of the texts that we are reading, we cannot proceed convincingly with other issues of substance. We concluded in that chapter that there are serious challenges to that task and that unfortunately we cannot be completely confident that we are reading the autograph texts of the synoptic gospels when we open our Bibles.

In this chapter, we looked more closely at the synoptic gospels—Matthew, Mark, and Luke—and more specifically at the nature of the literary relationship among these three gospels, the so-called synoptic problem. We observed that there can be no question that there is a clear interdependence among those gospels, and we illustrated elements of the nature of that relationship in the several charts in this chapter.

Simply stated, the synoptic problem is the question of the literary relationship among the gospels of Matthew, Mark, and Luke. It is evident that these gospels share much of the same material, that their organization or ordering of the material is similar, and that parallels among the gospels often extend to exact or nearly exact verbal conformity in the presentation of material. That said, there are also striking dissimilarities and disagreements among the synoptic gospels. Simply stated, the synoptic problem seeks an explanation of the similarities and the dissimilarities, the agreements and the disagreements, the consistencies and the inconsistencies, the congruities and the incongruities, the conformities and the disparities among the gospels of Matthew, Mark, and Luke. The methodology of this chapter is clear; it is to collect, analyze, and explain the data by looking carefully at representative passages.

The regnant hypothesis designed to explain the facts is that Mark is the earliest of the gospels and that the authors of the gospels of Matthew and Luke copied from and modified their Markan source.[6] Although no single argument for Mark's priority is entirely convincing, the cumulative weight of the several individual arguments is overwhelming. The criteria for establishing Markan priority have been tested for more

---

6. In *The Two Source Hypothesis*, 3–14, I looked briefly at several other proposed solutions to the synoptic problem, including the models of Saint Augustine, Johann J. Griesbach, Austin M. Farrer, Robert L. Lindsey, B. C. Butler, and Pierson Parker. Those positions have won few adherents.

than a century and appear to be methodologically sound. To illustrate the case for Markan priority, we analyzed in this chapter several charts showing passages in the triple and double tradition in order to appreciate more fully the nature of that literary relationship, and we observed that the cumulative evidence for Markan priority is persuasive.

Obviously the case for Markan priority is not built on the examination of a handful of passages printed in parallel columns, but on careful examination of the complete texts of the synoptic gospels viewed in parallel columns. Such an effort lies beyond the scope of this volume, but the foundational work has been done and can be reviewed and analyzed in printed synopses of the gospels.[7] The examples afforded in this chapter are representative and illustrative of the larger body of evidence. These examples should leave little doubt regarding Matthew's and Luke's dependence on the Gospel of Mark.

Some scholars have argued that the minor agreements of Matthew and Luke against Mark in the triple tradition render Markan priority impossible, but we have shown how such minor agreements against Mark can be easily explained, especially once the reader recognizes the instability of the gospel texts during the first decades of their transmission and the tendency of Christian copyists to harmonize the gospels.

The case for the sayings source Q is built upon the priority of Mark. Moreover, the existence of a Greek written source of more than 200 verses, primarily of sayings material common to both Matthew and Luke but not found in Mark, is reinforced by the fact that much of the material appears in Matthew and Luke in the same order, although always in different contexts. This latter observation is a clear indication that Matthew did not draw these sayings from Luke or vice versa. It is virtually impossible to imagine a scenario in which, if he were copying from the Gospel of Luke, Matthew would consciously lift these 200+ verses from Luke and then consistently set each saying within his gospel in a context different from the context of his Lukan source.

It is, of course, clear that Q is a hypothetical source, not a document that we have found or are likely to find; however, the discovery of the *Gospel of Thomas* in 1945 confirmed that such a collection of Jesus' sayings without a narrative framework existed in early Christian communities, perhaps as instruction manuals for prospective converts to Christianity. With regard to Q, we again presented detailed tables of parallel verses to illustrate the case for the written source Q.

The case for M and L is more complicated, and it is probably best to look at M and L as symbols for several perhaps written and/or oral sources that were available to Matthew and Luke respectively. The letters M and L may also represent stories or sayings or redactionary materials that were original compositions of Matthew and Luke. Just as the case for Q is based on the priority of Mark, the case for M and L is based on the priority of Mark, the existence of Q as a written source available to Matthew and

---

7. Of the many synopses available, I find most helpful *Synopsis of the Four Gospels*, edited by Kurt Aland.

Luke, and on the fact that there is a good deal of additional material that is unique to Matthew and Luke individually.

To the extent that not all scholars agree with the four-source hypothesis (Mark, Q, M, and L) as illustrated in the table above, the reason lies not in faulty reasoning but in the absence of data that would be sufficient to make a decisive and irrefutable determination about the literary relationship among the gospels.

There is unfortunately no evidence from external sources about the way in which the evangelists composed their gospels. Instead, we are reduced to drawing our conclusions based solely on the data found within the gospels. There is, to be sure, a great deal of data to draw upon, but not quite enough to leave no doubt whatsoever about how to analyze and interpret the data inherent within the documents themselves.

CHAPTER 4

THE APOSTOLIC PREACHING AND ITS DEVELOPMENTS

IN PREVIOUS CHAPTERS, WE looked closely at texts of the New Testament. Our initial challenge was to establish the autograph or the earliest versions of the books of the New Testament by means of the methodology known as textual criticism. We then looked at literary criticism and philology as ways of understanding the books of the New Testament more clearly within their own contexts. In the last chapter, our focus turned to source criticism and most especially to the question of the literary relationship among the synoptic gospels.

In this chapter and the next, we shall attempt to penetrate behind some of the church's written documents into the oral tradition that circulated among Christians before they began to commit their thoughts to writing. This is obviously a particularly difficult challenge. How can we possibly hope to gain access to oral tradition from the first century? There is obviously no way to obtain direct access to such information. There is no one to interview, and the relatively early hypothetical sources that we identified in the last chapter (Q, M, and L) are just that: hypothetical. Moreover, it is not entirely clear whether these hypothetical sources were written or oral or a combination of both.

In the 1930s, there appeared almost simultaneously two very different and seemingly contradictory approaches to the study of early Christianity, one in England and one in Germany. Each is monumental, but in very different ways.

C. H. Dodd published *The Apostolic Preaching and Its Developments* in 1936, based on three lectures that he had delivered the previous year at the University of London, Kings College.[1] A small but meaty book, Dodd isolated a core of primitive preaching common to Paul, Acts, and the canonical gospels and identified that material as the foundational message of apostolic Christianity, the *kerygma*, from the Greek word for "announcement," or "proclamation," or "preaching." In the New Testament, the *kerygma* is, therefore, the proclamation of the gospel (Greek εὐαγγέλιον, *euangĕliŏn*), the "good news" about Jesus the Messiah's victory (over death).

Just a year before Dodd's London lectures, Walter Bauer published in Germany a very different kind of book, *Orthodoxy and Heresy in Earliest Christianity*, which

---

1. C. H. Dodd, *The Apostolic Preaching and Its Developments*.

maintained that from earliest times Christianity existed in different forms in different parts of the Christian world, that in the first Christian centuries heresy was not a perversion of an original orthodoxy, and that the distinction between orthodoxy and heresy was actually a construct based on later standards established by fathers, synods, and councils of the church principally in the third and fourth centuries.[2]

Each of these studies is valuable in its own right. Dodd deals exclusively with the books of the canonical New Testament and is, therefore, looking only at literature that authorities within the church began to consider authoritative beginning in about 200. Bauer, on the other hand, looks at the variety of early Christian movements to demonstrate the striking theological diversity that existed during the early centuries of the faith.

Since our focus in this volume is primarily on the New Testament, Dodd serves our purposes especially well in this chapter, whose objective is to understand the earliest stages in the development of a religious movement that resulted ultimately in the canonization of the twenty-seven books of the New Testament. Bauer's contribution will serve our purposes in a subsequent chapter in which we examine the various trajectories of post-apostolic Christianity.

THE APOSTOLIC PREACHING

The earliest writings in the canonical New Testament are letters of Paul, written between about 52 and 56, or about seventeen to twenty-one years after his conversion to Christianity in about 35. We have no earlier Christian literature, except perhaps for imperfect reconstructions of hypothetical sources underlying the synoptic gospels (namely Q, M, and L) and perhaps the earliest stage of the *Gospel of Thomas*, if, indeed that gospel is as old as some scholars think it is.[3] For now at least, we turn to Paul's letters and to early stages in the development of the Acts of the Apostles to examine what Dodd refers to as "the apostolic preaching."

Clearly the single most important passage in Paul's letters for reconstructing the core of the apostolic preaching, the *kerygma*, is 1 Cor 15:1–8:

> [15:1]Now I would remind you, brothers and sisters, of the good news that I proclaimed to you, which you in turn received, and in which also you stand, [2]through which also you are being saved, if you hold firmly to the message that I proclaimed to you—unless you have come to believe in vain.
>
> [3]For I handed to you as of first importance what I in turn had received: that Christ died for our sins in accordance with the scriptures, [4]and that he was buried, and that he was raised on the third day in accordance with the scriptures, [5]and that he appeared to Cephas, then to the twelve. [6]Then he appeared to more

---

2. Bauer, *Rechtgläubigkeit und Ketzerei*, translated into English as *Orthodoxy and Heresy in Earliest Christianity*.

3. Koester, *Ancient Christian Gospels*, 75–128.

than five hundred brothers and sisters at one time, most of whom are still alive, though some have died. ⁷Then he appeared to James, then to all the apostles. ⁸Last of all, as to one untimely born, he appeared also to me.

In 1 Cor 15:1–3a, Paul states clearly and unequivocally that he is quoting words that he had previously received:

> Now I would remind you [Corinthians], brothers and sisters, of the good news that I proclaimed to you, which you in turn received, ... For I handed to you as of first importance what I in turn had received . . . .

In these introductory words, Paul reminds the Corinthians of the process by which the *kerygma* was transmitted in the early church through a chain of tradition. Paul states that he *received* the *kerygma* from Christians before him and that he in turn *proclaimed* or *handed* it to the Corinthians [and to others]. But it is not clear from whom Paul received the tradition. Paul seems to downplay the importance of that connection in Gal 1:15–20:

> ¹⁵But when God, who had set me apart before I was born and called me through his grace, was pleased ¹⁶to reveal his Son to me (Greek *within me*), so that I might proclaim him among the Gentiles, I did not confer with any human being, ¹⁷nor did I go up to Jerusalem to those who were already apostles before me, but I went away at once to Arabia, and afterwards I returned to Damascus.
> ¹⁸Then after three years I did go up to Jerusalem to visit Cephas [Peter] and stayed with him fifteen days; ¹⁹but I did not see any other apostle except James the Lord's brother. ²⁰In what I am writing to you, before God, I do not lie.

Paul's trip to Jerusalem to see Peter and James was in about 38 (three years after his conversion). Was it on this visit that Paul received the tradition from Peter and James, or did he hear it first from unnamed Christians (e.g., Ananias, see Acts 9:22–19)? Or is Paul claiming that it came to him in his call and commission by the risen Lord? The answer is not self-evident from Paul's testimony. What is evident is that the message was "traditional."

There follows then, beginning in 1 Cor 15:3, the substance of that earliest preaching:

> *that* Christ died for our sins in accordance with the scriptures (15:3b);
>
> *that* he was buried (15:4a);
>
> *that* he was raised on the third day in accordance with the scriptures (15:4b);
>
> *that* he appeared to Cephas, then to the twelve (15:5);
>
> *then* he appeared to more than five hundred at one time (15:6);
>
> *then* he appeared to James (15:7a);
>
> *then* he appeared to all the apostles (15:7b);
>
> *last of all* he appeared to Paul (15:8).

Paul wrote 1 Corinthians from Ephesus in Asia Minor in about 54 to a Christian house church that he had established several years earlier during his visit to Corinth in about 50–52. If Paul's conversion occurred in about 33, roughly three years after Jesus' death in about 30, then his visit to Corinth began about seventeen years after his conversion. This timeframe is important in order to understand more clearly the historical and religious context of the Pauline *kerygma*.[4]

What is especially important in Paul's summary of the *kerygma* in 1 Cor 15 is that there was from the outset a combination of history and theology. That Jesus died and was buried is incontrovertible as basic historical facts. What the earliest church added to that history as an essential part of its *kerygma* is that Jesus' death was "for our sins" and "in accordance with the scriptures" (1 Corinthians 15:3b) and that "he was raised on the third day in accordance with the scriptures" (1 Corinthians 15:4b).

There follows then in verses 5–7 a formulaic list of "witnesses" to the resurrected Christ: (1) Cephas, (2) the twelve, (3) more than five hundred, (4) James, the brother of Jesus, and (5) all the apostles. Then, almost as a requisite afterthought in support of his own apostleship, Paul adds the testimony that the risen Christ appeared also to him, although Paul's vision was certainly not part of the "official" list in the original apostolic preaching.

It is, I believe, best to take up in sequence the issues raised in 1 Cor 1:3b–4b:

1. There can be no doubt that Jesus' death and burial are grounded firmly in history and that they served as the historical basis for the *kerygma*:

    that Christ died (1 Corinthians 15:3b);

    that he was buried (1 Corinthians 15:4a).

2. The *meaning* of Jesus' death and burial was an entirely different matter, once Jesus' earliest followers began to understand these raw events as part of God's purpose in history. The theological purpose of Jesus' death is specified in the words of the *kerygma*:

    for our sins in accordance with the scriptures (1 Corinthians 15:3b; 4b).[5]

3. The words of the *kerygma*, accordingly, provide the key to how the church arrived at an understanding of its most primitive theology. The meaning of Jesus' death was

---

4. The matter of chronology will be discussed in detail later in this book in connection with the discussion of Paul.

5. An interesting question is whether the words "for our sins" in 1 Cor 15:3b was part of the pre-Pauline *kerygma*, or a Pauline addition or redaction. Without that phrase, the pre-Pauline *kerygma* would have read: "For I handed to you as of first importance what I in turn had received: that Christ died in accordance with the scriptures, and that he was buried, and that he was raised on the third day in accordance with the scriptures, and that he appeared to Cephas, then to the twelve." The unanswerable question in this regard is what scriptures the earliest church had in mind when it used the phrase "in accordance with the scriptures." If Pss 22 and 110 were all they had in mind, then the phrase "for our sins" may be a later redaction. If the earliest church also had Isa 53 in mind, then the phrase "for our sins" may have been part of the pre-Pauline *kerygma*. See the discussion immediately following.

revealed to the apostles only as the result of searching for its meaning in the Jewish scriptures (1 Corinthians 15:3b). Moreover, the raising of Jesus from the dead served as God's response to Jesus' seemingly meaningless death, and that response of God, as well, was discovered by Christians who looked for an understanding of Jesus' death in the Hebrew scriptures (1 Corinthians 15:4b).

If I have understood the sequence of events correctly, Jesus' death in Jerusalem came as a surprise to Jesus' disciples, and perhaps even to Jesus himself. The crucifixion seemed to render Jesus' ministry and teaching meaningless, because the Jews and the Romans had won the day. Whatever threat Jesus posed to them and to their leadership had been eliminated. Apparently, the interpretation of Jesus' seemingly meaningless death as having the benefit of atoning for people's sins surfaced in the aftermath of Jesus' death only after some of his followers found the solution in passages in the Hebrew scriptures. Interestingly, the earliest *kerygma*, as expressed in 1 Cor 15, probably did not specify the relevant scriptural passages to which the church was referring, but merely the general "in accordance with the scriptures."

Ps 22 and Isa 53 come immediately to mind:

a. The opening words of Psalm 22 (My God, my God, why have you forsaken me?) prefigure the alleged cry of Jesus from the cross in Matt 27:46 and Mark 15:34, whether or not Jesus actually spoke these words at his crucifixion. The rest of Ps 22 obviously spoke meaningfully to Jesus' followers following his unexpected death and served as an inspiration for details in the passion narratives, as laid out subsequently in the canonical gospels.[6]

b. Isa 52:13—53:12 spoke of the redemptive suffering of the servant of the Lord and apparently informed the church's earliest preaching. Likewise, these verses too subsequently provided details for the account of Jesus' passion, as reported in the synoptic gospels.

Following the death and burial, the next claim of the *kerygma* was that Christ was raised from the dead "on the third day in accordance with the scriptures." In this regard, the specific scriptural passage(s) to which the church was referring are elusive. None speak clearly to Jesus' resurrection. The closest we can come to a specific prooftext that Paul and the primitive *kerygma* may have had in mind is Hos 6:2:

> After two days he will revive us; on the third day he will raise us up, that we may live before him.

---

6. See, for example, the alleged saying of Jesus in Mark 10:45 (= Matt 20:28, but interestingly not reported in Luke): "For the Son of Man came not to be served but to serve, and to give his life as a ransom for many." In this form, the saying clearly echoes the *kerygma* of the early church, although I can imagine behind this Markan saying an authentic saying of Jesus to this effect: "I came not to be served but to serve." It is easy to understand how Mark or the pre-Markan oral tradition might have transformed such a saying into the form in which it appears in Mark's gospel.

Other passages appear to have influenced the church's subsequent understanding of Jesus' life and death, although none of these passages seem to have been a part of the early *kerygma* (for example Deut 18:15, 18;[7] Ps 69:21;[8] Ps 109:25;[9] Prov 31:6;[10] Lam 1:12, 18;[11] Lam 2:15;[12] Wis 2:17–18;[13] etc.). It is unlikely that Paul had any of these passages in mind when he wrote the phrase "according to the scriptures" in 1 Co 15:3–4.

It is eminently clear, however, that relatively soon after Jesus' death, followers of Jesus searched the Hebrew scriptures for an explanation of the events surrounding Jesus' crucifixion and death and found in such passages as these that the final events in Jesus' life had unfolded in detail in accordance with God's purpose. It is important to acknowledge in this regard that early Christians were interpreting these passages not in light of their original contexts but rather in the context of their own time, as they sought meaning in Jesus' crucifixion and death.

For example, the author of Acts 2:27 specifically cites Ps 16:10 when he says, "For you will not abandon my soul to Hades, or let your Holy One experience corruption." Far-fetched as these references may seem, they were convincing to the early Christians, to Paul, and to those to whom Paul subsequently preached. It is important for the modern reader to understand that such interpretations of the Hebrew scriptures were not unusual in first century Judaism and are familiar to us from Essene and rabbinic writings of the period. The early Christian community was engaged in the seemingly common practice in reinterpreting ancient texts in light of their own contemporaneous history. It is likely that the phrase "according to the scriptures" in the earliest *kerygm*a was a general reference to the Hebrew scriptures and may not have originally been an allusion to specific biblical passages.

More detailed citation of the Hebrew scriptures followed in later Christian writings, especially in the written gospels as we shall see in a subsequent chapter. Interestingly, there is in the earliest tradition no allusion to an empty tomb, probably because the tradition of the empty tomb was a later development in the unfolding of the story of what happened following Jesus' death.

---

7. The LORD your God will raise up for you a prophet like me [Moses] from among your own people; you shall heed such a prophet.... I will raise up for them a prophet, like you from among their own people; I will put my words in the mouth of the prophet, who shall speak to them everything that I commanded.

8. They gave me poison for food, and for my thirst they gave me vinegar to drink.

9. I am an object of scorn to my accusers; when they see me they shake their heads.

10. Give strong drink to one who is perishing, and wine to those in bitter distress.

11. Is it nothing to you, all you who pass by? Look and see if there is any sorrow, which was brought upon me, which the LORD inflicted on the day of his fierce anger.... The LORD is in the right, for I have rebelled against his word; but hear, all you peoples, and behold my suffering; my young women and young men have gone into captivity.

12. All who pass along the way clap their hands at you; they hiss and wag their heads at daughter Jerusalem; "Is this the city that was called the perfection of beauty, the joy of all the earth?"

13. Let us see if his words are true, and let us test what will happen at the end of his life; for if the righteous man is God's child, he will help him, and will deliver him from the hand of his adversaries.

THE APOSTOLIC PREACHING AND ITS DEVELOPMENTS

The element in the Pauline *kerygma* in 1 Cor 15 immediately following Jesus' resurrection is a list of his appearances to specific individuals. That list begins with Cephas (Peter), a claim that may explain Peter's position of authority in the early Jerusalem church. Such an appearance is not reported in the gospels, but Luke 24:34 may allude to it.[14] The reference to the Twelve in Paul's list refers to the original followers of Jesus, although the names of the twelve vary from gospel to gospel. In any case, Judas Iscariot would certainly not have been counted as a witness to the resurrection, so the reference to the Twelve may be more traditional than historical. In fact, the use of the expression "The Twelve" is probably a post-resurrection tradition.

Where in 1 Cor 15 does the primitive *kerygma* actually end and Paul begin? Paul himself may provide the clue, as the grammatical construction changes following the appearances to Peter and the Twelve. The earlier statements (1 Cor 15:3b, 4a, 4b, and 5) are all introduced by the word "that" (see above), perhaps indicating that they were all part of the traditional list. With verse 7, Paul shifts from "that" to "then" to introduce the final elements, suggesting that the tradition has ended and that Paul has added at this point additional witnesses (the five hundred, James, and all the apostles,—and ultimately Paul himself):[15]

1. The appearance to "more than five hundred brothers and sisters at one time" appears nowhere else in the New Testament, although there is a reference in Acts 2:1 to an unspecified number of followers who were present in one place at Pentecost. Could this be what Paul is alluding to?

2. The appearance to James (referred to in Gal 1:19 as the brother of Jesus) is unique to this passage. Nowhere else is there a report of such an appearance to James. The canonical gospels imply that members of Jesus' family were not among Jesus' followers during his lifetime. Mark 3:21 says "When his family heard it, they went out to restrain him, for people were saying, 'He has gone out of his mind'"; and John 7:5 reports "For not even his brothers believed in him." Paul and Acts agree in representing Jesus' brother James as a leader of the Jerusalem church (Gal 1:19; 2:9, 12; Acts 1:13; 12:17; 21:18). By listing James here, Paul may be providing the justification for James's ascendancy to a position of leadership in the Jerusalem church: James had his own post-resurrection appearance.

3. Paul's next reference is to an appearance to "all the apostles," a group that was probably more than the Twelve mentioned earlier, but his intention is not clear.

---

14. They were saying, "The Lord has risen indeed, and he has appeared to Simon." Simon Bar-Jona (Simon the son of Jona) was the original Hebrew name of the apostle known later as Cephas or Peter (Aramaic and Greek respectively for "rock").

15. The transition may actually occur in the middle of 1 Cor 15:5: "*that* he appeared to Cephas, *then* to the twelve," in which case only the appearance to Peter would have come from the earliest *kerygma*. Alternatively the *then* in 1 Cor 15:5b may have served as the model for Paul's subsequent additions to the list.

4. Finally Paul mentions Christ's "untimely" appearance to him 1 Cor 15:8), whereby Paul believed that he was called to be an apostle. It sounds here almost as if Paul thought that Christ's appearance to him was the last appearance of the risen Lord.

In addition to 1 Cor 15:1–8, Dodd cites additional passages as presenting the *kerygma* according to Paul, with the passages in italics designating elements of the Pauline *kerygma*:

Rom 1:1–4

> ¹Paul, a servant of Jesus Christ, called to be an apostle, set apart for *the gospel of God,* ²*which he promised beforehand through his prophets in the holy scriptures,* ³*the gospel concerning his Son, who was descended from David according to the flesh,* ⁴*and was declared to be Son of God with power according to the spirit of holiness by resurrection from the dead, Jesus Christ our Lord* . . . .

Rom 2:16

> . . . on the day when, *according to* my *gospel, God, through Jesus Christ, will judge the secret thoughts of all.*

Rom 8:34

> Who is to condemn? It is *Christ Jesus, who died, yes, who was raised, who is at the right hand of God, who indeed intercedes for us.*

Rom 10:8–9

> ⁸But what does it say?
> "The word is near you,
> on your lips and in your heart"
> (that is the word of faith that we proclaim); ⁹because *if you confess with your lips that Jesus is Lord and believe in your heart that God raised him from the dead, you will be saved.*

Gal 1:3–4

> ³ . . . from God our Father and from *the Lord Jesus Christ,* ⁴*who gave himself for our sins to set us free from the present evil age, according to the will of our God and Father,* . . . .

Gal 3:1

> . . . It was before your eyes that *Jesus Christ was publicly exhibited as crucified*!

Gal 4:6

> . . . *God sent the Spirit of his Son into our hearts crying, "Abba! Father!"*

THE APOSTOLIC PREACHING AND ITS DEVELOPMENTS

1 Thess 1:10

> ... and to wait for *his Son from heaven, whom he raised from the dead—Jesus, who rescues us from the wrath that is coming.*

I might add, as well, Phil 2:6–11, where Paul is evidently quoting a Christ Hymn that he drew from earlier Christian tradition, hence a pre-Pauline statement of faith:

> [5]Let the same mind be in you that was in Christ Jesus,
> [6]who, though he was in the form of God,
> did not regard equality with God
> as something to be exploited,
> [7]but emptied himself,
> taking the form of a slave,
> being born in human likeness.
> And being found in human form,
> [8]he humbled himself
> and became obedient to the point of death—
> even death on a cross.
> [9]Therefore God also highly exalted him
> and gave him the name
> that is above every name,
> [10]so that at the name of Jesus
> every knee should bend,
> in heaven and on earth and under the earth,
> [11]and every tongue should confess
> that Jesus Chrst is Lord,
> to the glory of God the Father.

What is particularly interesting in this Christ Hymn is the exaltation theology in Phil 2:9, which appears to have been a very primitive theological statement of what became of Jesus following his death.

In summary, with regard to the *kerygma* according to Acts, Dodd states:

> It is true that the *kerygma* as we have recovered it from Paul's epistles is fragmentary. No complete statement of it is, in the nature of the case, available. But we may restore it in outline somewhat after this fashion:
>
> The prophecies are fulfilled, and the new Age is inaugurated by the coming of Christ.
> He was born of the seed of David.
> He died according to the Scriptures, to deliver us out of the present evil age.
> He was buried.
> He rose on the third day according to the Scriptures.
> He is exalted at the right hand of God, as Son of God and Lord of quick and dead.
> He will come again as Judge and Saviour of men.[16]

---

16. Dodd, Ibid., 107.

Dodd's assessment of what constituted the *kerygma* according to Paul is essentially accurate, although I am less confident than Dodd that the earliest *kerygma* identified Jesus as a descendant of King David. That article, I suspect, came later, and I would eliminate it from Dodd's statement. Although Paul refers to Jesus as Son of David in Rom 1:3, the phrase does not appear in the *kerygma* of 1 Cor 15:3–5 or in any of the passages cited above. The term "Son of David" was used in contemporary Judaism primarily in connection with the popular hope for a political messiah, a role that Jesus certainly did not fulfill.

In addition to his discussion of the apostolic preaching in the letters of Paul, Dodd cites several passages in Acts as constituting the *kerygma* according to the Acts of the Apostles. Although Dodd's case for the *kerygma* according to Paul is geneorally convincing, the situation with Acts is very different. The particular difficulty in Dodd's collection of passages from Acts is that they appear in a series of purported speeches of Peter and Paul that are likely the composition of the anonymous author of the Gospel of Luke and the Acts of the Apostles, both of which were probably written sometime between 85–100.[17]

Scholars have generally assumed that the speeches of Peter and Paul in Acts are literary compositions of the author of Luke-Acts. Speeches in Greek historical writings generally represented the outlook of the author of the writings rather than the outlook of the alleged speakers. It is, therefore, evident that the author of Acts gave the speeches their present form. It is, however, less clear what kind of source or sources he consulted in composing these speeches.

Knowing the way in which the author of Luke-Acts used multiple sources in composing his gospel, it is safe to assume that he used whatever sources were available to him in writing Acts—once again probably multiple sources. But unlike the case with the synoptic gospels, we have no additional written documents with which to compare the final version of Acts. If we had only one gospel, the Gospel of Luke, there would be no way to establish the likelihood that the author of Luke used a gospel like Mark as his source, not to speak of the hypothetical sources Q and L.

It is probably safe to assume that the author of the speeches in Acts had access to primitive oral and/or written material, that he was familiar with the contents of the gospels of Mark and Luke, and that he was writing several decades after the age of the apostolic *kerygma* and after Paul. Unfortunately, the passages in the speeches in Acts that Dodd has collected as "the *kerygma* according to Acts" reflect the preaching of a much later period than the passages that Dodd identified as "the *kerygma* according to Paul." For example, the author of the speeches in Acts was obviously familiar with

---

17. The dating of Luke-Acts is especially problematic. The earliest date would be sometime after the last events described in Acts, namely Paul's two-year imprisonment in Rome at the beginning of the 60s. Moreover Luke makes use of the Gospel of Mark, and Luke 19:43–44; 21:20, 24 afford a rather detailed description of the siege of Titus and the fall of Jerusalem in 70, suggesting a date well after 70. The latest possible date is more difficult, and some scholars consign the gospel to the early second century. A date between 80 and 100 probably best addresses all of the evidence.

THE APOSTOLIC PREACHING AND ITS DEVELOPMENTS

details of the life and ministry of Jesus and believed that John the Baptist had been the precursor of Jesus, elements that are with good reason lacking in the Pauline version of the *kerygma*: more specifically, they were likely not known to Paul.

Accordingly, although there are phrases in the speeches in Acts that may be helpful in reconstructing the apostolic preaching, much if not most of what Dodd has assembled as "the kerygma according to Acts" has little to do with the apostolic preaching. I have printed below the passages in Acts cited by Dodd. Using "the *kerygma* of Paul" as my standard, I have indicated in italics those few phrases in the speeches in Acts that I consider credible material from the early *kerygma*:

Acts 2:14–39 (Peter's Pentecost Speech)

[2:16]This is what was spoken through the prophet Joel (followed by a citation of the Septuagint version of Joel 2:28–32).... [30](David) knew that God had sworn with an oath to him that he would put one of his descendants on his throne.... [22b]*Jesus of Nazareth*, a man attested to you by God with deeds of power, wonders, and signs, that God did through him among you—[23]this man, handed over to you by the definite plan and foreknowledge of God, *you crucified and killed* by the hands of those outside the law. [24]But *God raised him up, having freed him from death* (according to Ps 16:8–11).... [32]*This Jesus God raised up, and of that all of us are witnesses*.... [36b]*God has made him both Lord and Messiah, this Jesus whom you crucified*.... [33]*Being therefore exalted at the right hand of God*, and having received from the Father the promise of the Holy Spirit, he has poured out that which you both see and hear (according to Ps 110:1).... [38]*Repent, and be baptized every one of you in the name of Jesus Christ so that your sins may be forgiven.*

Acts 3:13–26 (Peter's Speech at the Temple)

[18]*In this way God fulfilled what he had foretold through all the prophets, that his Messiah would suffer*.... [24]And all the prophets, as many as have spoken, from Samuel and those after him, also predicted these days.... [13b]The God of our fathers has glorified his servant Jesus, whom you handed over and rejected in the presence of Pilate, though he had decided to release him. [14]But you rejected the Holy and Righteous One and asked to have a murderer given to you, [15]and *you killed* the Author of Life, *whom God raised from the dead.*

Acts 4:10–12 (Peter's Speech before the Council)

[4:10b]*Jesus Christ* of Nazareth, *whom you crucified, whom God raised from the dead.* ... [11]is "the stone that was rejected by you, the builders; it has become the cornerstone" (Ps 118:22). [12]There is salvation in no one else, for there is no other name under heaven given among mortals *by which we must be saved.*

Acts 5:30–32 (Peter's Speech before the Council)

[30]*The God of our ancestors raised up Jesus, whom you had killed* by hanging him on a tree. [31]*God exalted him at his right hand* as leader and Savior.... [32]And *we are witnesses to these things*, and so is the Holy Spirit whom God has given to those who obey him.... [31b]*that he might give repentance to Israel and forgiveness of sins.*

Acts 10:36–43 (Peter's Speech to the Gentiles)

[36]The message he sent to the people of Israel, preaching peace by Jesus Christ . . . . [37]beginning in Galilee after the baptism that John announced: [38]how God anointed Jesus of Nazareth with the Holy Spirit and with power; how he went about doing good and healing all who were oppressed by the devil, for God was with him. [39]We are witnesses to all that he did both in Judea and in Jerusalem. [40]*They put him to death* by hanging him on a tree; [40]but *God raised him on the third day and allowed him to appear,* [41]not to all the people, but to us who were chosen by God as witnesses, and who ate and drank with him after he rose from the dead. [42]He commanded us to preach to the people and to testify that he is the one ordained by God as judge of the living and the dead. [43]*All the prophets testify about him that everyone who believes in him receives forgiveness of sins through his name.*

Acts 13:17–41 (Paul's Speech in the Synagogue in Antioch)

[32]We bring you the good news that what God promised to our ancestors [33]he has fulfilled for us, their children. . . . [[17-22]Election and divine governance of Israel, to the reign of David.] [23]Of this man's posterity God has brought to Israel a Savior, Jesus, as he promised; [24]before his coming John had already proclaimed a baptism of repentance to all the people of Israel. [25]And as John was finishing his work, he said . . . "But one is coming after me; I am not worthy to untie the thong of the sandals on his feet." . . . [27]Because the residents of Jerusalem and their leaders did not recognize him or understand the words of the prophets that are read every Sabbath, they fulfilled those words by condemning him. [28]Even though they found no cause for a sentence of death, they asked Pilate to have him killed. [29]When they had carried out everything that was written about him, they took him down from the tree and *laid him in a tomb.* [30]But *God raised him from the dead;* and for many days *he appeared* to those who came up with him from Galilee to Jerusalem, and they are now his witnesses to the people (according to Ps 2:7; Isa 55:3; Ps 16:10). [38]*Let it be known to you therefore, my brothers, that through this man forgiveness of sins is proclaimed to you;* [39]*by this Jesus everyone who believes is set free from all those sins* from which you could not be freed by the law of Moses (citation of Hab 1:5).

What is particularly noticeable in what I have quoted above is the large amount of material that I do not regard as being part of the church's earliest preaching, but rather as part of the later framework provided by the author of these speeches. In my opinion, Dodd mistakenly includes in the *kerygma* details about John the Baptist, details about the life and ministry of Jesus, details surrounding Jesus' death and resurrection, and specific quotations from the Hebrew scriptures, all of which, I am convinced, reflect a much later stage in the development of the tradition, and probably even familiarity with written gospels.

THE APOSTOLIC PREACHING AND ITS DEVELOPMENTS

As I indicated in the previous section, I find considerable merit in C. H. Dodd's effort to identify the apostolic preaching in select passages in Paul's letters. The earliest formulation of that preaching is probably the words of 1 Cor 1:3b–5:

> 1:3b . . . that Christ died for our sins in accordance with the scriptures, 4and that he was buried, and that he was raised on the third day in accordance with the scriptures, and that he appeared to Cephas, then to the twelve.

This is not the only statement of the apostolic preaching in Paul, but it is one of the earliest. It also has the distinctive and crucial merit of Paul's surrounding language in which he identifies these words as the foundational message that he "had received" and, in turn, "handed on" and "proclaimed" to the Corinthian Christians (1 Cor 15:1, 3).

In this section I intend to show that the development of the *kerygma* in the apostolic age and especially in the post-apostolic age likely received motivation and momentum from a particularly important phrase in the apostolic preaching, repeated not once but twice in the formula in 1 Cor 15: *according to the scriptures* (1 Cor 15:3b, 4).

It is my contention that a systematic search through the Hebrew scriptures served as the basis not only for the development of the *kerygma*, but also for the development of subsequent oral and written tradition about Jesus of Nazareth, leading to the composition of the written gospels.

In this section, I will focus on the passages in the speeches in Acts that Dodd identified as *kerygma* but that reflect, in my opinion, a stage of development beyond the apostolic preaching, informed by the church's systematic search through the Hebrew scriptures:

1. Peter's Pentecostal Speech in Acts 2:14–39 contains three specific references to the Hebrew scriptures:

   a) Acts 2:16–21

   > 2:16No, this is what was spoken through the prophet Joel, (followed in Acts 2:17–21 by a citation of Joel 2:28–32)
   > Acts 2:17In the last days it will be, God declares,
   > that I will pour out my Spirit upon all flesh,
   > and your sons and your daughters shall prophesy,
   > and your young men shall see visions,
   > and your old men shall dream dreams.
   > 18Even upon my slaves, both men and women,
   > in those days I will pour out my Spirit;
   > and they shall prophesy.
   > 19And I will show portents in the heavens above
   > and signs on the earth below,

blood, and fire, and smoky mist.
²⁰The sun shall be turned to darkness
and the moon to blood,
before the coming of the Lord's great and glorious day.
²¹Then everyone who calls on the name of the Lord shall be saved.

This passage in Acts 2:17–21 is almost an exact quotation from the Septuagint version of Joel 2:28–32 with minor but significant changes. Particularly significant is the change of the opening word "afterward" in Joel to "in the last days" in Acts, emphasizing thereby the eschatological claim of the church that it was living in the end-time. Acts 2:18 adds the words "and they shall prophesy," not found, although perhaps implied, in Joel 2:29.

The author of the speech in Acts includes this quotation from Joel to indicate that the coming of the Holy Spirit to the apostles who had assembled in Jerusalem at Pentecost (Acts 2:1) and their subsequent preaching "in other languages, as the spirit gave them ability" (Acts 2:4), fulfilled what was written in the Hebrew scriptures. Acts 2:17, 18 equates the speaking in tongues at Pentecost with prophecy within the church. Moreover, the Lord in Acts 2:21 is, of course, Jesus and not the God of Israel, as in Joel.

As with virtually all such citations of the Hebrew scriptures, this passage takes no account of the original context in the Hebrew scriptures, although this is one of those rare occasions when a passage in the New Testament actually cites its source by name. It is important to ask whether the author of this speech in Acts had the Greek text of Joel in front of him or rather a collection of proof-texts from the Hebrew scriptures already collected in Greek by Christians in a written document. I am inclined to think that the latter, a collection of proof-texts in Greek, served as one of many sources available to the author of the Acts of the Apostles.[18]

b) Acts 2:25–28

²⁵ᵃFor David says concerning him, (followed in Acts 2:25b–28 by a citation of Ps 16:8–11)
^(Acts 2:25b)I saw the Lord always before me,
for he is at my right hand so that I will not be shaken;
²⁶therefore my heart was glad, and my tongue rejoiced;
moreover my flesh will live in hope.
²⁷For you will not abandon my soul to Hades,
or let your Holy One experience corruption.
²⁸You have made known to me the ways of life;
you will make me full of gladness with your presence.

---

18. A document known as *4QTestimonia* was found in cave 4 among the so-called Dead Sea Scrolls. Its name *testimonia* comes from what scholars previously assumed was an early type of Christian writing, specifically a collection of proof-texts or verses from the Hebrew scriptures designed to prove that Jesus was messiah. The *Testimonia* from Qumran proves the existence of such a genre at the time of the early church. *4QTestimonia* is usually dated to the middle of the first century BCE.

Peter makes it clear in his speech in Acts that the words of Ps 16 confirm the fact that God "attested to Jesus of Nazareth with deeds of powers, wonders, and signs that God did through him among you" (Acts 2:22), that Jesus was "handed over to you according to the definite plan and foreknowledge of God" (Acts 2:23a), that he was "crucified and killed by the hands of those outside the law" (Acts 2:23b), but that "God raised him up, having freed him from death" (Acts 2:24a).

The words of Acts 2:25b-28 are an exact quotation from the Septuagint of Ps 16. The phrase "in hope" at the end of Acts 2:26 presumably reflects, for the author of the speech, hope in the resurrection of the dead. The claim that "you will not abandon my soul to Hades" (Acts 2:27) implies that God will not allow Jesus' soul to remain "in death." It does not refer to a journey to Hades, a later notion that some argue first appears in 1 Pet 3:18-20; 4:6, although that interpretation of 1 Peter is itself doubtful.

c) Acts 2:34-35

> [34a]For David did not ascend into the heavens, but he himself says (followed in Acts 2:34b-35 by a citation of Psalm 110:1)
> [Acts 2:34b]The Lord said to my Lord,
> "Sit at my right hand
> [35]until I make your enemies your footstool."

This exact citation within Peter's speech of the Septuagint of Ps 110:1 makes clear that "the Lord" (God) said to "my Lord" (Jesus), "Sit at my right hand." The meaning of that command is eminently clear in Acts 2:32, 36: [32]"This Jesus God raised up, and of that we are all witnesses. . . . [36]Therefore let the entire house of Israel know with certainty that God *has made* him both Lord and Messiah, this Jesus whom you crucified." The exaltation or the raising of Jesus to God's right hand is regarded in this speech as God's reversal or undoing of the event of Jesus' crucifixion and death. The author of Peter's speech is saying that the Jews and Romans were not victorious in their execution of Jesus. Rather, God had the final word when he raised Jesus from the dead and exalted him to the place of honor, the right hand of God.

2. Peter's Speech at the Temple in Acts 3:13-26 contains two specific references to the Hebrew scriptures and two unspecified references:

a) Acts 3:22-23

> [3:22a]Moses said, (followed in Acts 3:22b-23 by a citation of Deut 18:15, 18-19; and possibly Lev 23:29)
>
> [Acts 3:22b]"The Lord your God will raise up for you from your own people a prophet like me. You must listen to whatever he tells you. [23]And it will be that everyone who does not listen to that prophet will be utterly rooted out of the people."

This paraphrase of the Septuagint of Deuteronomy (and possibly Leviticus) within Peter's speech at the temple reflects the belief that Jesus was this "prophet like

Moses," promised by Moses. This passage also contains the somewhat later notion of Paul and others that the Jews who rejected Jesus will, in turn, be rejected by God and will be replaced by Christians as the true Israel. Interestingly, the very same passage from Deut 18 is cited in *4QTestiminia*, the document found among the Dead Sea Scrolls (see footnote 18).

> b) Acts 3:25
>
> 25aYou are the descendants of the prophets and of the covenant that God gave to your ancestors, saying to Abraham (followed in Acts 3:26b by a citation of Gen 22:18; 26:4)
>
> Acts 2:25bAnd in your descendants all the families of the earth shall be blessed.

In this speech in Acts, Peter regards the Christians as the descendants of the prophets of Israel and of the covenant given to the Israelites. Acts 3:25b or the author's source changed the word "nations" in the Septuagint of Genesis to "families" in consideration of his Christian audience.

c) In addition to these two specific citations from the Hebrew scriptures, Acts 3:13 (In this way God fulfilled what he had foretold through all the prophets that his Messiah would suffer) and Acts 3:24 (And all the prophets, as many as have spoken, from Samuel and those after him, also predicted these days) allude to unspecified passages in the Hebrew scriptures, perhaps more in keeping with the earlier stage in the development of the tradition which reported events of the apostolic preaching "in accordance with the scriptures" (1 Cor 15:3, 4) without citing specific passages.

3. Peter's Speech before the Council in Acts 4:8–22 contains one specific reference to the Hebrew scriptures:

> 4:10b . . . Jesus Christ of Nazareth, whom you crucified, whom God raised from the dead. 11aThis Jesus is (followed in Acts 4:11b by a paraphrase of the Septuagint of Ps 118:22)
>
> Acts 4:11bthe stone that was rejected by you, the builders;
> it has become the cornerstone.

Acts 4:12 makes clear that

> "there is salvation in no one else [than Jesus], for there is no other name under heaven among mortals by which we must be saved." Jesus is the cornerstone of the *kerygma*, the cornerstone of the gospel (Acts 4:11b).

4. Peter's Speech before the Council in Acts 5:29–32 contains no specific reference to the Hebrew Scriptures.

5. Peter's Speech to the Gentiles in Acts 10:34–43 contains no specific reference to the Hebrew Scriptures, although this speech concludes with these words in Acts 10:43:

THE APOSTOLIC PREACHING AND ITS DEVELOPMENTS

"All the prophets testify about him [Jesus] that everyone who believes in him receives forgiveness of sins through his name." Once again there is this unspecified reference in the words "all the prophets testify. . . ."

6. Paul's Speech in the Synagogue in Antioch in Acts 13:16–41 contains four specific references to the Hebrew Scriptures and two unspecified references:

a) Acts 13:32–33

> ³²And we bring you the good news that what God promised to our ancestors ³³ᵃhe has fulfilled for us, their children by raising Jesus; as also it is written in the second psalm (followed in Acts 13:33b by a citation of Ps 2:7)

> Acts 13:33b You are my Son;
> today I have begotten you.

The exact citation from the Septuagint of Psalm 2:7 in the context of "raising Jesus" from the dead implies that Jesus became God's Son by virtue of the resurrection. This adoptionist theology, specifically that God "adopted" Jesus as his son, may be one of the earliest theological statements regarding the resurrection and Jesus' divine sonship. We find similar adoptionist statements in Acts 2:36 (Therefore let the entire house of Israel know with certainty that God *has made* him both Lord and Messiah, this Jesus whom you crucified) and Rom 1:4 ([Jesus Christ] *was declared to be* Son of God with power according to the spirit of holiness *by resurrection from the dead* . . .). A similar reference to Ps 2:7 (combined with Isa 42:1) appears in the context of Jesus' baptism (Matt 3:17; Mark 1:11; Luke 3:22), raising the question of whether the church initially traced Jesus' "adoption" as God's Son to the resurrection and then subsequently to the time of Jesus' "call" on the occasion of his baptism by John.[19]

b) Acts 13:34

> ³⁴ᵃAs to his [God's] raising him [Jesus] from the dead, no more to return to corruption, he has spoken in this way, (followed in Acts 13:34b by a citation of Isa 55:3)

> Acts 13:34b"I will give you the holy promises made to David."

The quotation from Isa 55:3 follows the Septuagint, but it is so fragmentary that the meaning of this passage is not really clear, unless the author of the speech in Acts

---

19. Matthew and Luke appear to have borrowed their accounts of Jesus' baptism from the Gospel of Mark, the oldest of the synoptic gospels. Mark has no birth narratives, so he may well have entertained an "adoptionist" theology of Jesus' divine sonship traceable to his baptism (i.e., his call and commission). Matthew and Luke, on the other hand, both have accounts, although very different accounts, of Jesus' birth by a virgin, implying that Jesus' divine "sonship" was traceable to the time of his conception. The inconsistency of having Jesus' "sonship" traceable at the same time to both his conception and his "call and commission" (i.e. his baptism) would not be the only inconsistency in the New Testament and may reflect the complicated way in which the authors of the gospels made use of what may have been inconsistent sources.

is referring to the promise made to David concerning Jesus' resurrection, a promise found elsewhere in the Psalms (Ps 110:1).

c) Acts 13:35

^{35a}"Therefore he has also said in another psalm, (followed in Acts 13:35b by a citation of Ps 16:10)

^{Acts 13:35b}"You will not let your Holy One experience corruption."

This citation from the Septuagint of Psalm 16:10 is also cited in Acts 2:27, 31 in the context of Peter's Pentecostal Speech and was apparently a favored Christian proof-text in support of Jesus' resurrection from the dead.

d) Acts 13:40–41

⁴⁰Beware, therefore, that what the prophets said does not happen to you (followed in Acts 13:41 by a citation of Hab 1:5)

^{Acts 13:41}"Look, you scoffers!
Be amazed and perish,
for in your days I am doing a work,
a work that you will never believe, even if someone tells you.

The warning in anticipation of the Jews' rejection of Jesus (see Acts 13:44–47 and 28:23–28) is drawn from a similar prophetic rejection in the Septuagint version of Hab 1:5. There is clear mention of this rejection of the Jews in Acts 13:39—"by this Jesus everyone who believes is set free from all those sins *from which you could not be freed by the law of Moses.*"

e) In addition to these four specific citations of Hebrew scriptures in Paul's Speech in the Synagogue in Antioch, there are two general references to the Hebrew scriptures in 13:27, 29

> (Because the residents of Jerusalem and their leaders did not recognize him or understand *the words of the prophets that are read every sabbath*, they fulfilled those words by condemning him. . . . When they had carried out *everything that was written about him*, they took him down from the tree and laid him in a tomb).

We have seen in our review of the primitive *kerygma* that, following its earliest practices, the church continued to build on the earliest formulation of its preached message by persisting in searching through the Hebrew scriptures for more and more passages that could inform the church about who this Jesus was and what he had accomplished.

The earliest formulation may have been little more than that Jesus had died, that he was buried, and that he was raised from the dead. The risen Lord's appearances to

Peter and the twelve were likely also very early claims, but the nature of those appearance (perhaps in dreams?) is never very clear.

The notion that Jesus died "for our sins" may represent a next stage in the development of the tradition, whether through Paul's own words in 1 Cor 15:3 or, more likely, in the period before Paul received the *kerygma*. Although the speeches of Peter and Paul in Acts contain some primitive theological formulations, including the claims that Jesus was crucified and died and that God raised him up and made him Lord and messiah (what I have called exaltation theology), those speeches begin to focus increasingly on Jesus' death as atonement for sin, and they increasingly cite more and more passages from the Hebrew scriptures, fleshing out increasingly more "historical" and "theological" details.

Clearly, the search for additional scriptural proof was an important apologetic strategy for early Christian communities. Christians in many communities engaged in searching more and more deeply into the Hebrew scriptures for passages that they believed referred to Jesus and his role as God's anointed one. With that increased practice came more and more specific allusions to the scriptures and often even specific references to these passages.

CONCLUSIONS

In the Introduction, I identified specific criteria that assist historians in their efforts to reconstruct the past. Among the most important of these criteria is the "time and place" criterion, which affirms that the closer in time and place a source or the author of a source is to an event, the more reliable that source is likely to be.

As we proceed in this book to reconstruct the history of the earliest church, our focus in this chapter has not been on recovering events in the life and ministry of Jesus or even in reconstructing events in the history of the earliest church. Our focus has been on reconstructing the preached message of the earliest church, what C. H. Dodd has called the apostolic preaching or the primtive *kerygma*. That piece of the puzzle is particularly important, because it informs our understanding of the way in which tradition evolved in the first decades of the church's history, and it helps us to address "the bias rule," the principle that every source and every piece of evidence must be examined critically to ascertain the nature and degree of its bias.

As we observed previously, no evidence and no testimony can be taken entirely at its face value, especially evidence or testimony whose primary purpose is to advance the agenda of a witness (or an author) or to advance the agenda of the in-group to which a source is addressed. This is a particularly important principle to recall and to observe in the case of the New Testament, because this particular anthology of books is a collection of writings from within the church for readers within the church and does not purport to be objective.

The time and place criterion lends credibility to the reliability of Paul's report of what constituted the earliest *kerygma*, especially the passage in 1 Cor 15:1–5, in which Paul describes the faithfulness with which tradition has been passed along in the early church.

We need, nonetheless, to be mindful of the fact that there is an important difference between *history* and *theology* and that the apostolic preaching was a combination of both. The historical portion of the *kerygma* is incontrovertible, namely that Jesus was crucified, died, and was buried. By themselves and free from theological overlay, these words pass both the time and place criterion and the bias rule, and they describe actual events in real history. There was no reason for the church to have created these data, as Jesus' crucifixion, death and burial clearly posed a serious challenge for Jesus' followers, who were apparently surprised and even disillusioned by what had happened to their leader.

The theological overlay to this basic historical reality is an entirely different matter, namely "that Christ died for our sins in accordance with the scriptures" and "that he was raised on the third day in accordance with the scriptures." With these words, we have moved beyond history, and the words *in accordance with the scriptures* have provided us with the key to unlock the mystery of how it was that Jesus' followers came to understand the *meaning* of Jesus' death as an atoning sacrifice for our sins. This latter component of the *kerygma* belongs not to the realm of history, but to the realm of theology: namely that Jesus "died for our sins in accordance with the scriptures" and "was raised on the third day in accordance with the scriptures."

The general appeal to scriptural passages in this regard (perhaps Isa 52:13–53:12; Hos 6:2; Ps 16:8–11; 110:1) makes it clear that we should look at Jesus' atoning death and resurrection not as events in history, but as a theological formulation of the earliest *kerygma* based on a reading of the Hebrew scriptures, because it was clearly as a result of such a search through these scriptures that Jesus' followers came to believe that Jesus had died for our sins and that God had raised him from the dead.

The atoning death and resurrection are the church's answer to Jesus' death. God has reversed the apparent victory of those who killed Jesus by raising him from the dead. By this claim—and it is a claim—the church was saying that God had ultimately triumphed over the Jews and the Romans. God had the final word: Good triumphed over Evil. Rudolf Bultmann formulated a famous, or perhaps infamous saying to the effect that Jesus died and rose into the *kerygma*. There is some truth to these words as the distinction between history and theology was blurred when theology came to be understood as if it were history.

These observations lead us to a very important question: how much of the early church's message is history, and how much is theological overlay? Or to put it somewhat differently: did the church understand actual events in the life and ministry of Jesus in light of the Hebrew scriptures, or did a reading of the Hebrew scriptures inform and lead to the actual creation of theology and of confessional stories that are theology that simply appears to be history?

It is not only the resurrection that falls into this category of theology rather than history. An examination of the speeches in Acts that Dodd, in my opinion, incorrectly identified as part of the earliest *kerygma* betrays the fact that much of what we read in those speeches and also in the canonical gospels is probably also theology and not history. I am thinking, in particular, of statements in the speeches in Acts that God sent John the Baptist as a precursor of Jesus (Acts 10:37; 13:24), that God anointed Jesus at his baptism with the Holy Spirit (Acts 10:38), that God endowed Jesus with deeds of power, wonders, and signs (Acts 2:22b; 10:38b), that the risen Christ ate and drank with some of his followers after he rose from the dead (Acts 10:41), and that the risen Lord commanded his followers to preach to the people and to testify that Jesus is the one ordained by God as judge of the living and the dead (Acts 10:42). None of these claims belong to the realm of history. They are part of the theology that was gathered over time into the *kerygma* as a result of a careful reading of the Hebrew scriptures with an eye to identifying messianic proof-texts.

There may be some element of truth underlying some of these stories. For example, John probably did baptize Jesus in the Jordan River as a part of his baptism for the remission of their sins, and Jesus may have performed exorcisms as a component of his ministry. But these raw historical events have been substantially reinterpreted and expanded in the accounts found in the speeches in Acts and most especially in the canonical gospels, all of which were written in a much later period than the formative years with which we are concerned in this chapter.

We have also observed that the Hebrew scriptures from which the author of the speeches in Acts frequently quoted was actually the Septuagint Greek translation of those scriptures. This observation raises the question of whether consultation of the Hebrew scriptures for the meaning of Jesus' untimely death was undertaken in the earliest period by a search through the scriptures in their original Hebrew. We cannot answer this question with any degree of certainty. I suspect that Hebrew texts were the basis for the church's initial claims, but that as Christianity, especially Pauline Christianity, moved into the Gentile world, the Septuagint increasingly became the authoritative scriptures of Gentile Christianity, as Greek was at that time the primary *lingua franca* of the Mediterranean world.

We have in this chapter also indicated the complicated process by which the speeches of Peter and Paul in the Acts of the Apostles were assembled. As was mentioned earlier in this chapter, scholars have generally assumed that these speeches are literary compositions of the author of Luke-Acts, inasmuch as speeches in Greek historical writings tended to represent the outlook of the author of the writings rather than the outlook of the alleged speakers. It is, therefore, evident that the author of Acts gave the speeches their present form.

In saying that, we have also suggested some of the sources or building blocks of these speeches. The author of Acts obviously had access to early tradition, such as the exaltation theology evident in Acts 2:32–36; 5:31 (cf. Rom 1:4), as well as to the statements that Jesus died, was buried, and rose on the third day "in accordance with the scriptures." As the author of the Gospel of Luke, the author of these speeches in Acts added to them information about Jesus' baptism by John, his miraculous signs and wonders, and his suffering leading up to his crucifixion, death, resurrection, ascension, and the outpouring of the Holy Spirit.

I have suggested that there likely existed in an early period in the history of the church a *testimona* document, similar to *4QTestimonia* from the Dead Sea Scrolls. Relatively early in the church's history, someone (or many someones) appears to have collected into one place the Greek translation (Septuagint) of passages from the Hebrew scriptures that the church believed predicted the coming of God's messiah. We noted that such passages rarely spoke to the issue of messiah in their original contexts but that Christians so understood them from a very early period. The author of the Acts of the Apostles appears to have had access to such a Christian *testimonia* document and to have incorporated elements of it into the speeches of Peter and Paul.

The fact that these scriptural passages had a very different meaning in their original contexts from what they subsequently meant to Christians was, we have shown, not unusual in first century Judaism; Christians were following practices known to us from Essene and rabbinic circles. Such use of the Hebrew scriptures adds, however, to our doubt regarding the reliability of some of the "history" connected with Jesus' life and ministry, an issue to which we now turn in the context of the canonical gospels.

CHAPTER 5

THE CRUCIFIXION OF JESUS AND THE PASSION NARRATIVE

I INTEND IN THIS chapter to continue to examine how tradition and stories about Jesus developed in the first decades following his death, a particularly critical time in the history of the nascent Christian community. To judge from 1 Thess 4:15–17,[1] Paul and the first generation of Christians lived in expectation of the imminent return of Jesus, an event that would mark the end of history as we know it, and the inauguration of a New Age, the period of God's Rule. This expectation certainly influenced the development of early Christian tradition.

THE EMERGENCE OF A PASSION NARRATIVE

The first decades in the history of the emergent church were primarily a period of oral tradition, especially with regard to events in the life and ministry of Jesus. There was no reason to write for posterity if Christians were living in the end-time. Paul's letters were, of course, an exception, because he wrote not for posterity but to address immediate issues in specific, widely spread churches, many of which Paul had himself established.[2]

As we observed in the previous chapter, the church's earliest preaching focused on Jesus' death, burial, exaltation, and post-resurrection appearances as salvific events—the fundamental elements in the Pauline *kerygma*. There was little initial interest in details of the life and ministry of Jesus. Even Q, which was an early collection of sayings of Jesus, did not attempt to set those sayings into a narrative concerned with elements of Jesus' ministry. Moreover, we learn very little about the life and ministry

---

1. 4:15For this we declare to you by the word of the Lord, that we who are alive, who are left until the coming of the Lord, will by no means precede those who have died. 16For the Lord himself, with a cry of command, with the archangel's call and with the sound of God's trumpet, will descend from heaven, and the dead in Christ will rise first. 17Then we who are alive, who are left, will be caught up in the clouds together with them to meet the Lord in the air: and so we will be with the Lord forever.

2. Some argue that the Q community, which was co-terminus with Paul and which had begun very early to collect sayings of Jesus, represents a non-apocalyptic group, at least in its earliest stage of development. We shall look more closely at that issue in a subsequent chapter on the historical Jesus.

of Jesus from Paul.[3] The focus of his letters was, of course, on issues that arose within specific churches, especially as Paul understood that certain matters required his immediate personal attention. Paul could never have imagined that he was writing epistles for inclusion in a Christian Bible.

All the same, tradition about Jesus began to take shape in the early decades following Jesus' death. Written gospels did not appear out of nothing between about 67 and 100. They emerged from and built upon earlier oral and written traditions. This chapter and the next focus on two subjects that contribute to an understanding of how some of the building blocks of the written gospels emerged in earliest Christianity: namely, the development of the story of Jesus' crucifixion in this chapter, and in the next chapter the scholarly discipline known as form criticism.

We have seen previously that the *meaning* (i.e. the interpretation) of Jesus' life, death, and resurrection was revealed to the church gradually in the period following his death. A dramatic change came to Jesus' followers through the power and inspiration of their belief that God had reversed the tragic and theologically problematic event of the crucifixion by raising Jesus from the dead on the third day *in accordance with the scriptures.*

In a story that appears only in Luke 24:13–35, the resurrected Jesus appeared to two of his disciples on the road from Jerusalem to Emmaus. According to the story, it was the risen Lord who instructed the disciples in the interpretation of the Hebrew scriptures. The significance of what Moses and the prophets had earlier proclaimed about Jesus of Nazareth is evident in Luke's words: "Was it not necessary that the Messiah should suffer these things and then enter his glory?" (Luke 24:26). Luke provides no specific scriptural references to Moses and the prophets in this story, although he does so elsewhere in the gospel: for example, Luke 3:4–6 cites Isaiah 4:3–5, and Luke 7:27 cites Mal 3:1.

The story in Luke 24 culminates with verse 27 ("Then *beginning with Moses and all the prophets, he* [the risen Christ] *interpreted to them the things about himself in all the scriptures*"); and again in verse 32 ("Were not our hearts burning within us . . . while *he* [the risen Christ] *was opening the scriptures to us?*) [italics mine]. It is eminently clear from these passages that Jesus' disciples believed that the risen Christ himself had disclosed to them the meaning of his life, death, and resurrection by interpreting for them the Hebrew scriptures. Or, alternatively, the author of the Gospel of Luke paraphrased the situation in this way, so that the disciples would not have to acknowledge that they themselves had been involved in the intellectual labor of proving from the scriptures that Jesus was the messiah.

Stated differently, the meaning of Jesus' death and resurrection occurred to Jesus' followers only after Jesus had died and, so they believed, had himself revealed it to them. The discovery came to them only as they engaged in searoching through the

---

3. See Paul's words in 2 Cor 5:16: "From now on, therefore, we regard no one from a human point of view; even though we once knew Christ from a human point of view, we know him no longer in that way."

THE CRUCIFIXION OF JESUS AND THE PASSION NARRATIVE

Hebrew scriptures for clues that enabled them to understand more clearly the meaning of what had transpired. This story in Luke 24 reminds us of what we discussed in the last chapter: the Hebrew scriptures informed early Christian history and may have been responsible for encouraging Christians to create stories as if they were history.

There is evidence in the written gospels that suggests that some of the disciples doubted Jesus and deserted him in the hours leading up to his arrest and crucifixion. The apostles' desertion of Jesus is strengthened by the stories of Judas's betrayal (Mark 14:10–11; Matt 26:14–16; Luke 22:3–6; and John 13:2) and of Peter's denial (Mark 14:66–72; Matt 26:69–75; Luke 22:56–62; John 18:25–27). Jesus' disciples appear to have fled before his crucifixion. Only the Gospel of Luke (24:36–49) has the disciples witness the resurrection, perhaps a rehabilitation of the apostles, and an essential element for Luke's subsequent story of the ascension of Jesus in Acts 1:1–11.

There is no mention that any of Jesus' disciples were in attendance at the crucifixion, although the gospels mention the presence of some of his women followers:

1. Mark 15:40 mentions "women looking on from a distance," including Mary Magdalene, Mary the mother of James the younger and of Joses, and Salome;

2. Matt 27:56 names among the women "looking on from a distance" Mary Magdalene, Mary the mother of James and Joseph, and the mother of the sons of Zebedee;

3. Luke 23:49 mentions "the women who had followed Jesus from Galilee," but gives no names;[4] and

4. John 19:25–26 refers to Jesus' mother (although not by name), to his mother's sister (also not by name), to Mary the wife of Clopas, to Mary Magdalene, and to the mysterious and otherwise nameless beloved disciple (probably a symbolic figure in the Gospel of John);

5. Mark 15:42–47; Matt 27:57–61; Luke 23:50–56; and John 19:38–42 mention Joseph of Arimathea as the man who buried Jesus, although only Matthew (27:57) and John (19:38) identify Joseph as a disciple of Jesus.

None of Jesus' disciples were at his tomb on the third day after the crucifixion to witness the resurrection, although Jesus is reported in three of the gospels to have predicted three times and in some detail the events leading to his deliverance to the Gentiles and to his suffering, death, and resurrection:

first in Mark 8:31–33; Matt 16:21–23; Luke 9:21–22;

second in Mark 9:30–32; Matt 17:22–23; Luke 9:43b–45; and

third in Mark 10:32–34; Matt 20:17–19; Luke 18:31–34.

---

4. Luke may have in mind those women mentioned in Luke 8:2–3 (Mary Magdelene, Joanna the wife of Herod's steward Chuza, Susanna, and "many others, who provided for them out of their resources") and in Luke 24:10 (Mary Magdelene, Joanna, Mary the mother of James, and "the other women with them"). Luke 23:49 begins by referring to "all his acquaintances, including the women, etc.," but it is not clear to whom he is referring, whether relatives, friends, or disciples.

It is difficult to imagine why the apostles were not at Jesus' tomb on Easter morning if Jesus had three times predicted in detail the events leading up to his arrest, crucifixion, death, and resurrection. There is obviously something wrong with these accounts in their present form. The likelihood of the matter is that these detailed "predictions" never occurred and that these stories are subsequent creations of the tradition.

A likely reconstruction of the scenario is that the disciples deserted Jesus before his death, probably out of fear, disillusionment, disbelief, and despair. The early Christian community subsequently explained the events surrounding Jesus' final days in light of their subsequent reading of the Hebrew scriptures, sometime after Jesus' death. The accounts of Jesus' predictions of his passion, death, and resurrection developed presumably at an even later date in order to support the view that Jesus, as the divine son of God, must have known in advance what lay ahead of him. It is evident in this regard that Jesus' followers unlocked retrospectively and through a search of the Hebrew scriptures the *meaning* of what had earlier appeared to them as the victory of the Jewish and Roman leadership over their prophetic hero. The Jews and the Romans had succeeded in ridding themselves of this fanatical prophetic nuisance.

This retrospective reinterpretation of history is reinforced in Luke 24:36–49, when following his appearance on the road to Emmaus, Jesus appeared to his disciples in Jerusalem and said (in Luke 24:44–47):

> [44] "These are my words that I spoke to you while I was still with you—that everything written about me in the law of Moses, the prophets, and the psalms must be fulfilled." [45]Then he opened their minds to understanding the scriptures, [46]and he said to them, "Thus it is written, that the Messiah is to suffer and to rise from the dead on the third day, [47]and that repentance and forgiveness of sins is to be proclaimed in his name to all nations, beginning from Jerusalem.

Although these two stories, the walk to Emmaus and Jesus' appearance to his disciples, are found only in the Gospel of Luke, which was probably written more than fifty years after Jesus' death, they clearly betray what had become a common practice among Christians: namely, interpreting continuously since the earliest period of the Christian church the events of Jesus' life and ministry, and especially his death and resurrection, in accordance with the Hebrew scriptures.

There can be no question that the answer to the *meaning* of Jesus' life was revealed to Jesus' followers only after his death through their meticulous reading and retrospective reinterpretation of the scriptures. As a result, the church began to tell the story of Jesus' life, death, and resurrection with the advantage of hindsight and *in accordance with the scriptures.*

The death of Jesus *for our sins* had occurred in fulfillment of Isa 53:4–6, 9–12:

> [53:4]Surely he has borne our infirmities
> and carried our diseases;
> yet we accounted him stricken,

struck down by God, and afflicted.
⁵But he was wounded for our transgressions,
crushed for our iniquities;
upon him was the punishment that made us whole,
and by his bruises we are healed.
⁶All we like sheep have gone astray;
we have all turned to our own way,
and the LORD has laid on him
the iniquity of us all.

. . . .

⁹They made his grave with the wicked
and his tomb with the rich,
although he had done no violence
and there was no deceit in his mouth.
¹⁰Yet it was the will of the LORD to crush him with pain.
When you make his life an offering for sin,
he shall see his offspring, and shall prolong his days;
through him the will of the LORD shall prosper.
¹¹Out of anguish he shall see light;
he shall find satisfaction through his knowledge.
The righteous one, my servant, shall make many righteous,
and he shall bear their iniquities.
¹²Therefore I will allot him a portion with the great,
and he shall divide the spoil with the strong;
because he poured out himself to death,
and was numbered with the transgressors;
yet he bore the sin of many,
and made intercessions for the transgressors.

And Jesus' resurrection *on the third day* had obviously occurred in fulfillment of Hos 6:2:

> After two days he will revive us;
> on the third day he will raise us up,
> that we may live before him.

However improbable we may consider the connection between these verses in Isa 53 and Hos 6 and the events surrounding Jesus' death and resurrection, it is important to observe that early Christians clearly made that connection.

THE CRUCIFIXION OF JESUS IN MARK

The extent of the passion narrative in the Gospel of Mark is disputed by scholars. Some maintain that Mark 14–16 comprises the story of the passion, some that it begins as early as Mark 8:31. Some suggest that Jesus' passion is Mark's focus throughout the gospel and that everything that is reported in the early chapters of Mark points to and anticipates Jesus' passion, death, and resurrection. In fact, toward the end of the nineteenth century, Martin Kähler described the Gospel of Mark as "a passion narrative with an extended introduction."[5]

There is some truth to all of these observations. However, rather than trying to discuss where Mark's passion narrative begins and ends, I will focus instead on just one element within the passion narrative—Mark's account of Jesus' crucifixion—with an eye to understanding the relationship between Mark's account and individual passages in the Hebrew scriptures.

It is evident that the author of the Gospel of Mark (or a source available to him) reported the final moments of Jesus' life with the Hebrew scriptures in mind. Compare the text of Mark's gospel in the column on the left with material in the Hebrew scriptures on the right. I maintain that the material in the Hebrew scriptures was clearly available to Mark or to the author of a written source known to Mark, perhaps from a *testimonia* document, a collection of proof-texts composed early in the church's history to demonstrate that Jesus was God's messiah:

Mark 15:21–37	Hebrew Scriptures
[21]They compelled a passer-by, who was coming in from the country, to carry his cross; it was Simon of Cyrene, the father of Alexander and Rufus.	
[22]Then they brought Jesus to the place called Golgatha (which means the place of a skull),	
[23]And they offered him wine mixed with myrrh; but he did not take it.	Prov 31:6 Give strong drink to one who is perishing, and wine to those in bitter distress.
[24]And they crucified him, and divided his clothes among them, casting lots to decide what each should take.	Ps 22:18 They divide my clothes among themselves, and For my clothing they cast lots.
[25]And it was nine o'clock in the morning when they crucified him.	

---

5. Martin Kähler, *The So-Called Historical Jesus*, 80.

THE CRUCIFIXION OF JESUS AND THE PASSION NARRATIVE

Mark 15:21–37	Hebrew Scriptures
²⁶The inscription of the charge against him read, "The King of the Jews."	
²⁷And with him they crucified two bandits, one on his right and one on his left.	Isa 53:12b . . . he poured out himself to death, and was numbered with the transgressors . . . .ᵃ
[²⁸And the scripture was fulfilled that says, "And he was counted among the lawless."]ᵇ	[see Isa 53:12 and Ps of Sol 16:5]
²⁹Those who passed by derided him, shaking their heads and saying, "Aha! You who would destroy the temple and build it in three days,	Ps 22:7 All who see me mock at me; they make mouths at me, they shake their heads.ᶜ
³⁰save yourself, and come down from the cross!"	Ps 109:25 I am the object of scorn to my accusers; when they see me, they shake their heads. Lam 2:15 All who pass along the way clap their hands at you; they hiss and wag their heads at daughter Jerusalem.
³¹In the same way the chief priests, along with the scribes, were also mocking him among themselves and saying, "He saved others; he cannot save himself.	Wis Sol 2:17–18 Let us see if his words are true, and let us test what will happen at the end of his life; for if the righteous man is God's child, he will help him and will deliver him from the hand of his adversaries.ᵈ
³²Let the Messiah, the King of Israel, come down from the cross now, so that we may see and believe." Those who were crucified with him also taunted him.	Ps 22:8 "Commit your cause to the LORD; let him deliver— let him rescue the one in whom he delights!"

THE NEW TESTAMENT

Mark 15:21–37	Hebrew Scriptures
³³When it was noon, darkness came over the whole land until three in the afternoon.	Amos 8:9 On that day, says the Lord GOD, I will make the sun go down at noon, and darken the earth in broad daylight.
³⁴At three o'clock Jesus cried out with a loud voice, "Eloi, Eloi, lema sabachthani? which means, "My God, my God, why have you forsaken me?"	Ps 22:1 My God, my God, why have you forsaken me?ᵉ
³⁵When some of the bystanders heard it, they said, "Listen, he is calling for Elijah."	
³⁶And someone ran, filled a sponge with sour wine, put it on a stick, and gave it to him to drink saying, "Wait, let us see whether Elijah will come to take him down."	Ps 69:21 They gave me poison for food, and for my thirst they gave me vinegar [sour wine] to drink.
³⁷Then Jesus gave a loud cry and breathed his last.	Ps 18:6 In my distress I called upon the LORD; to my God I cried for help. From his temple he heard my voice, and my cry to him reached his ears.

a. See also Ps 22:16 ("For dogs are all around me; a company of evildoers encircles me.").

b. Mark 15:28 is lacking in our best manuscripts of the Gospel of Mark and was subsequently added to Mark from the parallel passage in Luke 22:37, which includes as a proof-text a quotation from Isa 53:12.

c. See also Pss 22:6 ("But I am a worm, and not human; scorned by others, and despised by the people."); 35:21 ("They open wide their mouths against me; they say, 'Aha, Aha, our eyes have seen it.'"); and 109:25 ("I am an object of scorn to my accusers; when they see me they shake their heads.").

d. See also Ps 22:8 ("Commit your cause to the LORD; let him deliver – let him rescue the one in whom he delights!").

e. See also Ps 22:2 ("O my God, I cry by day, but you do not answer; and by night, but find no rest.").

In this account of Jesus' crucifixion in Mark 15:21–37, an excerpt from Mark's passion narrative, only verses 21–22, 25–26, and 35 have no apparent parallel or source of inspiration in the Hebrew scriptures. There can be little doubt that most of the details in this narrative arose from creative reflection on the Hebrew scriptures.

THE CRUCIFIXION OF JESUS AND THE PASSION NARRATIVE

The only material that is not motivated or colored in some way by biblical "proof-texts" is that Simon of Cyrene helped to carry Jesus' cross to the site of execution at Golgatha (15:21–22), that the crucifixion took place at nine o'clock in the morning (15:25), that there was an inscription on the cross that read "The King of the Jews" (15:26), and that Jesus died (15:37b). The words of the bystanders in Mark 15:35, 36 ("Listen, he is calling for Elijah" and "Wait, let us see whether Elijah will come to take him down") are probably Markan commentary on Jesus' Aramaic/Hebrew words in Mark 15:34a in light of the popular Jewish expectation that Elijah would precede the coming of the messiah (Mal 4:5: "Lo, I will send you the prophet Elijah before the great and terrible day of the LORD comes.").

We cannot, of course, be certain that even these few details in the story are historically reliable simply because there are no apparent sources of inspiration for them in the Hebrew scriptures. Moreover, we should be extremely careful about claiming as historical any of Mark's details that appear to have been inspired or colored by a non-contextual, if not wholly inappropriate reading of the Hebrew scriptures. The recovery of history must always be one of our highest priorities.

There was presumably a brief foundational story about Jesus' crucifixion behind Mark or behind the written source on which Mark probably depended and to which a significant amount of legendary tradition attached itself, most of it based on scriptural proof-texts. From earliest times, Christians understood Jesus' passion as part of the divine plan, as an event foreshadowed in accounts of innocent and unjust suffering in the Hebrew scriptures. Although it is impossible to determine exactly what is historical and what is legendary in the account in Mark 15:21–37, there can be little doubt that in its present form the story has been woven together with the help of passages from the Hebrew scriptures, texts that the early Christian church identified and likely assembled into a *testimonia* document in order to impart theological meaning to Jesus' otherwise meaningless death.

Some scholars have argued that the reference in Mark 15:21 to Simon of Cyrene and his sons Alexander and Rufus suggests that the sons were well known to Mark's readers, presumably in the church at Antioch of Syria, where Mark was probably written. If so, it is possible that Alexander and Rufus personally contributed this detail about their father to the evangelist and that this verse was not part of an earlier passion narrative that served Mark as a source.

It is possible that the author of the Gospel of Mark drew his version of the passion narrative from a written source that had its origin in the worship of the church. It is very likely that Christians who initially focused on the resurrection of Jesus began to develop a liturgy for the celebration of that festive event and that a liturgy of the passion served as an appropriate prelude to the joyous Easter celebration. It was a common practice in ancient Christianity for converts to be baptized on Easter. What better preparation for Christians to celebrate their death to their old lives and their rebirth into Christ than to prepare by a liturgy of dying to their previous lives through a liturgical rehearsal of the events leading up to Jesus' own death.

The times of the day mentioned in Mark 15:25, 33, 34 may provide information about such a liturgy rather than about actual times in the course of Jesus' crucifixion. More specifically, the timing of events in Mark 15:25 (nine o'clock in the morning) and in Mark 15:34 (three o'clock in the afternoon) may be built around the reference to noon (Mark 15:33), which may have been based solely on the passage in Amos 8:9 (see the chart above).

In looking at the text of the passion narrative, an important question comes immediately to mind: Did actual incidents surrounding Jesus' crucifixion evoke the recollection of specific passages in the Hebrew scriptures? Or have passages from the Hebrew scriptures colored or contributed to the creation of details in Mark's account of Jesus' final hours as products of early Christian piety or myth-making?

There can be little doubt that the Hebrew scriptures colored the way in which Mark and his successors presented details in the account of Jesus' crucifixion. It is more difficult to determine whether there is historical memory at the center of these details or whether Mark (or his written *testimonia* source) provided details primarily from a quest for understanding Jesus' crucifixion through the lens of the Hebrew scriptures. I think the latter. The entire account in Mark 15: 21–37 appears to be little more than a rhetorical exercise.

Critical in the table above is the fact that of the twelve allusions to the Hebrew scriptures, seven are allusions to passages in Psalms, and four of the seven are allusions to verses in Psalm 22,[6] a favorite psalm of the early Christian church. We need in this regard only to recall the words of the risen Lord in Luke 24:44: "These are my words that I spoke to you while I was still with you—that everything written about me in the law of Moses, the prophets, *and the psalms* must be fulfilled" [italics mine]. The frequent use of Psalms and, in particular of Psalm 22, raises questions suggesting that the church played a major role in the creation of the passion narrative.

I am convinced that Paul had in mind the early stages of such a process of searching for "proof-texts," when he repeated the early tradition that "Christ died for our sins *in accordance with the scriptures*" (1 Cor 15:3). Indeed, as I mentioned above, the material in these verses in 1 Cor 15:3–5 is obviously pre-Pauline, inasmuch as Paul states unmistakably that he was passing to the Corinthian Christians what he had earlier received.

Conservative Christians like to point to these same passages in the Hebrew scriptures and then to the New Testament to demonstrate that these Old Testament "prophecies" were *fulfilled* in the life and ministry of Jesus. Such examples of prophecy and fulfillment are often regarded as "positive proof" of Jesus' divine origin and

---

6. If we include the references listed in the footnotes to the table above, this sentence would then read: "Critical in the table above is the fact that of the eighteen allusions to the Hebrew scriptures, thirteen are allusions to passages in Psalms, and eleven of the thirteen are allusions to Ps 22."

THE CRUCIFIXION OF JESUS AND THE PASSION NARRATIVE

messiahship. I am now turning that argument on its head and claiming that "events" in the passion narrative have been colored, if not invented, by consciously consulting and appropriating passages from the Hebrew scriptures.

The story of Jesus' crucifixion in Mark 15 was built upon the solid foundation of so many different passages from the Hebrew scriptures that it is no longer possible to say much more about the crucifixion than that Jesus was crucified by the Romans at a place called Golgatha, that a certain Simon of Cyrene (the father of Alexander and Rufus) may have been engaged to carry Jesus' cross, and that Jesus died. The timetable of certain events in the story may be more liturgical than historical, and the inscription on the cross may be nothing more than an irony to illustrate that the Romans were right in identifying Jesus as "King of the Jews," a title that Jesus certainly never claimed for himself, the story of the triumphal entry in Jerusalem in Mark 11:1–11 and the whole of the Gospel of John notwithstanding.

Before bringing this discussion of the crucifixion to a close, I would like to make one more observation. At the time of the composition of the passion narrative by either Mark or by the author of the written source that Mark presumably used, Jewish writers were involved in a similar method of interpretating their scriptures.

Examples of a similar interpretation of the Hebrew scriptures appear among the Dead Sea Scrolls in writings known as *pesherim* (singular *pesher*), meaning "interpretations." Among the Essenes, a *pesher* afforded an "interpretation" of the Hebrew scriptures in a way that implies that all previous interpretations of the passage afforded only partial understanding, and that the true meaning of the passage was now more fully understood. Such an understanding of the Hebrew scriptures appears in the *pesher* on Habakkuk (1QpHab), in which the author maintained that God was only now disclosing to the Teacher of Righteousness, a prominent figure within and perhaps the founder of the Essene community, "all the deeper implications of the words of His servants the prophets."[7] By contrast, the prophets of earlier generations had only a partial and imperfect understanding of what Habakkuk had revealed to them.

Like the Qumanic Essenes, early Christians sought self-understanding and justification for what had recently happened to them in the only foundation that they could understand, the Hebrew scriptures. The discovery of *4QTestimonia* at Qumran established the existence of a string of composite citations of biblical passages, which Christians may have imitated. In this thematic *pesher* from Qumran, the author (or the *pesherist*) brought together passages from different biblical texts for the purpose of developing a theme.

If the role of the interpreter of a *pesher* was to discover the fullness of what God was revealing in a particular passage of the Hebrew scriptures, then the author of these verses in Mark 15 was involved in such a process when he interpreted the scriptural passages cited above as appropriate to an understanding of Jesus' crucifixion. What is especially important in understanding the *pesharim* that were discovered among the

---

7. Gaster, *The Dead Sea Scrolls*, 252.

Dead Sea Scrolls is that the Essenes believed that biblical prophecies were now being fulfilled in the history of their community.

Is this technique of biblical interpretation that is known to us from the Dead Sea Scrolls evident in the verses from the passion narrative cited above? Has the author of these verses in Mark consciously employed the *pesher* technique? If so, and I am convinced that this is the case, the core of the passion narrative must have been composed by someone familiar with this method of interpreting the Hebrew scriptures. The original author of these verses in Mark 15:21–37 must have been a Palestinian Jewish Christian writing in a Jewish Christian community relatively early in the history of the church, perhaps within a decade or two of Jesus' death.

With regard to the *pesharim* from Qumran, Devorah Dimant maintained:[8]

> The distinctiveness of the Qumranic pesharim lies in their peculiar structure and terminology, and in their systematic application of the biblical text to the historical circumstances of the community itself. The immediate purpose of the pesharim is to vindicate the Teacher of Righteousness and his followers in their struggle against their opponents, to strengthen the adherents' faith and their powers of endurance, and to inspire them with hope for the future. The Qumranic pesher should, therefore, be considered as a commentary of a special kind.

The similarities to the passion narrative in Mark 15 are striking. It is very likely that such a written "interpretation" of Jesus' death served to vindicate Jesus and his followers in their struggle against their Jewish and Roman opponents, to strengthen Christians' faith and their powers of endurance in the face of persecution, and to inspire them with hope for the future. It is evident that the passion narrative established for the earliest church that Jesus' death was part of God's purpose in history. It may also have served to justify an annual reenactment of those events, perhaps in the context of the observance of the Eucharist as part of a liturgical celebration and commemoration leading up to Easter.

CONCLUSIONS

The methodological challenges in this chapter are considerable, but fascinating.

There can be no doubt that early Christians scrutinized the Hebrew scriptures for an understanding of the events that had unfolded around the life and ministry, and especially around the death and resurrection of Jesus of Nazareth. The evidence is overwhelming, but it is not always clear exactly what passages from the Hebrew scriptures they had in mind, especially in those instances in which there is no specific citation of the biblical passage.

Some of the references to the Hebrew scriptures are precise and unmistakable; some are highly likely; some are quite possible; and some are feasible if frankly uncertain. The range of the allusions is broad, but their intention is unquestionable and

---

8. Dimant, "Pesharim, Qumran," 250.

unmistakable. Christians were convinced that events had unfolded and were still unfolding as part of God's plan, even to the minutest detail. The table of Mark 15:21–37 and its scriptural parallels is representative of what occurs throughout the gospels to a greater or lesser degree. Paul informs us that the process began very early in the history of the church, probably immediately after Jesus' unanticipated death and almost certainly for the specific purpose of finding meaning in a death that must have seemed meaningless.

Scholars have long speculated that Christians consulted *testimonia* books, collections of relevant proof-texts drawn from the Hebrew scriptures. With the discovery of the Dead Sea Scrolls, that was no longer mere speculation, because the Essenes had such books, such as *4QTestimonia* and *4QFlorilegium*. The Essenes also wrote *pesharim* that resemble the exercise that we illustrated above in the table of Mark 15:21–37.

Christians obviously took their quest for meaning in a different direction, but the Essenes and Christians were both involved in applying the Hebrew scriptures systematically to historical circumstances within their own communities. Essenes were involved in vindicating their leader, the Teacher of Righteousness, just as Christians were involved in vindicating Jesus. To be theologically accurate, both groups were involved in establishing the fact that God had vindicated their respective leaders. What is not entirely clear is whether Christians learned this practice directly from the Essenes. Or was such interpretation of the Hebrew scriptures more widespread than we know from the relatively limited evidence available to us?

What is important in this regard is that Christians were engaged in a practice that was not unique to them. However implausible this interpretation of scriptures may seem to the modern mind, it was current among Jews in the period both before and after the beginnings of Christianity, and it served to convince Jews and even Gentiles to become followers of the prophet from Nazareth.

Perhaps the most challenging task for the student of the Bible is to determine how this practice of searching the Hebrew scriptures for proof-texts influences the question of the historical value of our gospels. Were details of the life and ministry remembered, and those memories then matched to specific passages in the Hebrew scriptures? Or did the search for scriptural passages significantly color the history and lead to the creation of a large body of stories that are more legend than history? This question may be more important to conservative Christians, who often embrace the inerrancy of scripture, than to more liberal Christians, who are not bound by such strictures.

One thing should be clear from this chapter: early Christianity did not entertain concerns about history in the same way in which modern readers generally do. Ancient mythologies regularly reflected the playful imagination of talented poets and authors. Our ancient forbears understood that and accepted it. Jesus was different in that he was an historical figure, but we have already seen that ancient biographies did not conform to modern standards. Historical accuracy was not a criterion in antiquity, although it may be an overriding expectation today. It is unreasonable to expect writings from thousands of years ago to conform to or to meet our rigorous standards of historical verifiability.

From our study of Mark 15:21–37, I would venture to say that we know very little about events surrounding Jesus' crucifixion except that he was crucified by the Romans on a hill called Golgatha and that, for some reason, Simon of Cyrene was apparently enlisted to carry Jesus' cross. We can assume that, according to the custom of the time, Jesus was buried shortly after his death. We know that Christians believed that God raised Jesus from the dead on the third *in accordance with the scriptures*, presumably in accordance with Hos 6:2. This conclusion is drawn in large measure because we know of no other biblical passage to which Christians may have been referring, although Ps 110:1 may have been enlisted as a proof-text for the resurrection (exaltation) even before the passage in Hos 6:2.

In a subsequent chapter, we shall discuss some of the criteria that enable us at least to attempt to recover the historical Jesus. One of these criteria is the criterion of dissimilarity or embarrassment. The criterion of dissimilarity or embarrassment maintains that a tradition about Jesus that does not reflect or conform to the teachings of early Christianity has a greater claim to historicity and authenticity than a tradition that mirrors the church's preaching. By that criterion, we should probably be highly suspicious of details in the story of Jesus' crucifixion and in the larger body of tradition known as the passion narrative.

The evidence suggests overwhelmingly that the account of the crucifixion is more theological than historical. In fact, theology was the primary concern of the early church. It is we who seem more preoccupied with matters of historical accuracy. Inasmuch as there is no unadulterated account of Jesus' crucifixion, the burden is upon us to provide such an account. If we do, the narrative is certain to be scant: Romans crucified Jesus at a hill called Golgotha just outside the walls of Jerusalem.

Although I have argued that the author of the Gospel of Mark composed the story of Jesus' crucifixion primarily by appropriating passages from the Hebrew scriptures as building blocks for his narrative, it seems suitable at this time to mention the important contribution of Dennis R. MacDonald, who has argued convincingly that the author of the Gospel of Mark modeled his gospel after the *Iliad* and the *Odyssey* and composed a Christian anti-epic in which he represented Jesus as a suffering hero fashioned like, although obviously superior to the traditional Greek heroes.[9]

MacDonald observed that everyone who learned to write Greek in the ancient world learned from Homer and that ancient authors commonly borrowed from and recast Homer in their own writings. MacDonald argues convincingly that, in telling the story of Jesus of Nazareth, the author of the Gospel of Mark recast Homer in contemporary Greco-Jewish form: "the earliest evangelist was not writing a historical

---

9. Dennis R. MacDonald, *The Homeric Epics*.

biography, as many interpreters suppose, but a novel, a prose anti-epic of sorts."[10] Even in the story of the crucifixion, MacDonald finds more than eleven parallels between Mark's account of the death of Jesus and Homer's account of the death of Hector, although he acknowledges that Mark is more dependent on the Hebrew scriptures and other Jewish texts in the passion narrative than anywhere else in his gospel. What is amazing is how quickly Christians forgot this allegorical understanding of the gospel and began instead to read the gospel as if it were history, rather than an ancient novel. Identifying this Homeric theme in the Gospel of Mark makes it almost impossible to separate what is fact from what is fiction, a conclusion we already reached in looking at the author's appropriation of Old Testament texts. Can we be certain that Mark fashioned his gospel after the *Iliad* and the *Odyssey*? Obviously not, but MacDonald has collected an abundance of evidence to support his bold thesis, which has gained considerable scholarly approval.

As an historical footnote to this chapter, after a thirty page detailed discussion of the complex issues involved in establishing the date of Jesus' crucifixion, Raymond Brown concludes that the date, translated into the Julian calendar, was most likely April 7, 30,[11] or (as I calculated with help from Tarek Maani and his website[12]) Friday, April 5, 30 CE in the Gregorian calendar.

---

10. Ibid., 7.

11. Brown, *The Death of the Messiah*, 1350–78. Brown's second choice for a date is April 3, 33 (in the Julian calendar), or Friday, April 1, 33 in the Gregorian calendar.

12. http://bennyhills.fortunecity.com/elfman/454/calindex.html

CHAPTER 6

FORM CRITICISM

IN THIS CHAPTER, I intend to continue the discussion of how tradition about Jesus developed in the first decades of the history of Christianity by focusing on the scholarly discipline known as form criticism.[1]

WHAT IS FORM CRITICISM?

Form criticism attempts to reach behind the sources of our written gospels in an effort to reconstruct the underlying oral tradition, which it then identifies, classifies, and relates to its presumed sociological setting in the life of the Greco-Roman world and the life of early Christian communities.

Form criticism of the New Testament originated in 1919 with the publication of Martin Dibelius's *Die Formgeschichte des Evangeliums* (*From Tradition to Gospel*),[2] followed in 1921 by Rudolf Bultmann's *Die Geschichte der synoptischen Tradition* (*The History of the Synoptic Tradition*),[3] and in 1933 by Vincent Taylor's *The Formation of the Gospel Tradition*.[4]

Form critics have made the following observations, based on criteria derived from a scholarly study of the New Testament:

1. Before there were written gospels or even written sources of the gospels, there was a period of oral tradition in the early church.

2. With the exception of the block of material known as the passion narrative,[5] sayings

---

1. The name of the discipline in the original German of both Martin Dibelius and Rudolf Bultmann is *Formgeschichte*, which literally means "the history (German *Geschichte*) of form (German *Form*)," reflecting the original intention of the method—namely, to study the history of the literary "forms" through which the synoptic tradition was transmitted in the early church. The translation of the word *Formgeschichte* into English as "form criticism" is, in my opinion, unfortunate because of the negative connotations of the word "criticism." As a result of this perceived negativity, conservative Christians have often been reluctant to embrace the invaluable methodology advanced by form critics.

2. Dibelius, *Die Formgeschichte des Evangeliums*. English translation *From Tradition to Gospel*.

3. Bultmann, *Die Geschichte der synoptischen Tradition*; English translation *The History of the Synoptic Tradition*.

4. Taylor, *The Formation of the Gospel Tradition*.

5. As indicated in the previous chapter, the passion narrative refers to the accounts in the latter

and narrative material circulated independently as isolated sayings and individual stories, probably in detached or separate units of oral tradition.

3. The material preceding the passion narrative in the synoptic gospels can be classified according to certain identifiable literary forms.
4. The vital factors that gave rise to these literary forms can be found in the practical needs and interests of early Christian communities.
5. The rudimentary material of the synoptic tradition has no biographical, chronological, or geographical value.
6. The original forms of the tradition can be recovered and its history traced by discovering the laws of oral tradition.

Scholars observed many generations ago that, especially in the Gospel of Mark, individual stories frequently begin with the word "and" (Greek καί, *kai*), little more than an awkward connective intended to link a story to the immediately preceding story. This observation led scholars to conclude that each story in the synoptic gospels, or each pericope as scholars came to call them, was originally a free-standing unit of oral tradition during an early period in the history of its transmission.

This insight led to the conclusion that the author of the Gospel of Mark was not an author in the usual sense of that word, but rather a collector of individual units of oral tradition, individual stories that were current in the church at Antioch when and where he probably wrote his gospel. In other words, Mark pulled together existing stories and used them as the building blocks of his gospel. The original units of oral (and later written) tradition survive in Mark (as well as in Matthew and Luke) primarily in the form of the individual pericopes (or units of written tradition) that were the principal components of the synoptic gospels

THE FORMS

Scholars noticed that the material in the synoptic gospels of Matthew, Mark, and Luke tends to fall into five different categories or literary forms:

pronouncement stories

miracle stories

parables

---

chapters of the gospels recording stories of Jesus' triumphal entry into Jerusalem, his betrayal, arrest, trial, crucifixion, death, and resurrection. Although not all scholars agree, the passion narrative probably assumed oral and even written form early in the Church's history, perhaps decades before its appearance in the Gospel of Mark. As Christians remembered and possibly rehearsed annually events leading up to Jesus' crucifixion, death, and resurrection, particularly during the week preceding the celebration of Easter, they may have developed a liturgy for the commemoration of the days before Jesus' crucifixion and their celebration of his resurrection. In this manner, a passion narrative, whether initially oral or written, may have emerged in the years immediately following Jesus' death.

sayings material, and

legends (or stories about Jesus).

PROUNCEMENT STORIES

Pronouncement Stories are short stories generally involving a controversy or discussion in which an opponent of Jesus asks Jesus a question or poses a problem. Following an exchange, a saying or pronouncement of Jesus resolves the issue. There are two main parts to pronouncements stories: the narrative framework and the saying of Jesus. As we shall see in our examples below, the frameworks merely serve to set the scene for the sayings or pronouncements of Jesus. In fact, most if not all of these stories were probably constructed around traditional sayings of Jesus. If that is so, then the frameworks for the sayings are probably inventions of the Christian community and may not be integral to the specific sayings.

In recent years, New Testament scholars have compared the literary form of the pronouncement stories in the synoptic gospels to *chreiai* (singular *chreia*) or concise statements attributed to individuals in classical rhetoric. As we observed earlier in the discussion of literary criticism in chapter 2, it should be no surprise that Christians appropriated existing literary forms in creating what ultimately became the building blocks of the synoptic gospels.

1. Render to the Emperor

An excellent example of a pronouncement story is the passage in Mark 12:13–17, a story copied and reworked in Matt 22:15–22 and in Luke 20:20–26. Based on the conviction that the Gospel of Mark is the oldest of the synoptic gospels, we will now look at this story in its presumed oldest (Markan) form:

> [13]Then they sent to him some Pharisees and some Herodians to trap him in what he said. [14]And they came and said to him, "Teacher, we know that you are sincere, and show deference to no one; for you do not regard people with partiality, but teach the way of God in accordance with truth. Is it lawful to pay taxes to the emperor or not? [15]Should we pay them, or should we not?" But knowing their hypocrisy, he said to them, "Why are you putting me to the test? Bring me a denarius and let me see it." [16]And they brought one. Then he said to them, "Whose head is this, and whose title?" They answered, "The emperor's." [17]Jesus said to them, "Give to the emperor the things that are the emperor's, and to God the things that are God's." And they were utterly amazed at him.

There are some interesting features to this story (or pericope). The opening word "then"[6] is simply the connective that Mark used to link this story, to be sure very

---

6. The word here is actually καί, *kai*, the Greek word "and." Mark uses the conjunction "and" tirelessly to connect individual pericopes in his gospel (see e.g. Mark 1:7; 1:9; 1:12; 1:16; 1:21; 1:23; 1:29;

loosely, to the preceding story (or pericope). It does not mean that this was the "event" in Jesus' life that followed immediately upon the "event" reported in the previous pericope in Mark, namely, the parable of the wicked tenants (Mark 12:1–12). In fact, in Matthew's gospel the preceding pericope is the parable of the wedding banquet. Luke, on the other hand, follows Mark's sequence.

The "they" in verse 13 is no one, in particular. It has no real antecedent, even if the reader looks into the preceding pericopes. It is, rather, little more than Mark's way of setting the stage for a new story. There follows then a dialogue or controversy in which Jesus' enemies, some Pharisees and Herodians, try to entrap him. The point of the story is contained in Jesus' pronouncement at the end of the pericope:

> Give to the emperor the things that are the emperor's, and to God the things that are God's (Mark 12:17).

This pronouncement may have circulated originally as an isolated saying, and the tradition of the early church subsequently provided the narrative framework. In other words, even if we were certain that we were reading an authentic saying of Jesus, the saying was probably not spoken under the circumstances provided in Mark's story. Someone in the church created the framework as an introduction to and contextual setting for Jesus' saying during the period of oral tradition.

Mark concludes the pericope with the closing editorial words: "And they were utterly amazed at him," a characteristic Markan ending to many of his stories (e.g., Mark 1:22, 27; 2:12; 5:20, 42; 6:2; 7:37; 11:18). It would be naïve to think that with these words Mark is describing what actually happened following Jesus' delivery of the pronouncement. Rather, what we see in this pericope is how Mark took a unit of oral tradition and incorporated it stylistically into his gospel between two other pericopes or units of tradition. The expression of the amazement of the crowd is a typical Markan editorial addition, a feature of his redaction of prior tradition.

2. *The Sabbath Was Made for Humankind*

A second example of a pronouncement story is the passage in Mark 2:23–28, a story copied and reworked in Matt 12:1–8 and in Luke 6:1–5. In its presumed oldest form in Mark, the story reads:

> ²³One sabbath he was going through the grainfields; and as they made their way his disciples began to pluck heads of grain. ²⁴The Pharisees said to him, "Look, why are they doing what is not lawful on the sabbath?" ²⁵And he said to them, "Have you never read what David did when he and his companions were hungry and in need of food? ²⁶He entered the house of God, when Abiathar was high

---

1:35; 1:39; 2:1; 2:13; and so on throughout the body of his gospel. Although the King James Version (KJV) consistently translated these "ands," most modern translations (regrettably) do not, or for stylistic reasons change them to some other word, such as "then" in this pericope, thereby masking the awkward way in which Mark connects these distinctive pericopes, or units of oral tradition.

priest, and ate the bread of the Presence, which it is not lawful for any but the priests to eat, and he gave some to his companions." [27]Then he said to them, "The sabbath was made for humankind, and not humankind for the sabbath; [28]so the Son of Man is lord even of the sabbath."

The opening words of this pericope in the original Greek are *kai egeneto*: "and it came to pass that," as in the previous example a simple connective that Mark used to link this story to the preceding story. Once again, this does not mean that this "event" in Jesus' life followed immediately upon the "event" reported in the previous pericope, the question about fasting.

The phrase "one sabbath" provides a loose contextual setting for the incident: the disciples' (and presumably Jesus') violation of the command not to work on the sabbath. It is the Pharisees who challenge Jesus with the rebuke, "Look, why are they doing what is not lawful on the sabbath?" Jesus cites the story in 1 Sam 21:1–6, although erroneously, because it was Ahimelech who was high priest and not his son Abiathar (1 Sam 22:20), suggesting that the author of the Gospel of Mark did not have personal access to the Hebrew scriptures, but that he or his source was merely citing the story from memory. This dialogue or controversy between Jesus and the Pharisees, even with its error in detail, is Mark's way of setting the stage for Jesus' pronouncement at the end of the pericope:

> The sabbath was made for humankind, and not humankind for the Sabbath (Mark 2:27).

In spite of the text of verses 27–28 as cited above, it appears that only the words in verse 27 constitute Jesus' pronouncement. Mark rounds out the pericope with the closing editorial words: "So the Son of Man is lord even of the sabbath." These are probably not Jesus' words, but serve rather as Mark's commentary on the pronouncement story, inasmuch as verses 27 and 28 are obviously not a coherent whole, in spite of the way in which the sentences are punctuated in the English text. In my opinion these verses should be rendered as two sentences, not one:

> [27]"Then he [Jesus] said to them, 'The sabbath was made for humankind, and not humankind for the sabbath.'[28] So the Son of Man is lord even of the sabbath."

What does Mark's final comment imply, even as it blurs the meaning of Jesus' pronouncement?

As in the case of our first example, the pronouncement "The sabbath was made for humankind, and not humankind for the Sabbath" likely circulated as an isolated saying, and it was the early church that provided the narrative framework for the saying. In other words, even if we could be certain that we are reading an authentic saying of Jesus, it is evident that the saying was not spoken by Jesus under the circumstances provided in Mark's narrative account.

Underlying Mark's Greek phrase (*ho anthropos*) rendered in both Greek and English as "humankind" twice in verse 27 but as "Son of Man" (*ho huios tou anthropou*) in both Greek and English in verse 28 is the same phrase *bar-nasha* in Aramaic, the language that Jesus and his disciples presumably spoke. The phrase, which literally means "a son of man" in Aramaic was often used to refer to "humankind," as it is correctly translated twice in verse 27. The phrase was also used to refer to "the Son of Man" or "The Man," the eschatological superhuman figure, who, Jesus and others of his generation believed, would come in the final days to usher in the Age to Come, the period of God's Rule (cf. Dan 7:13).

There is an important implication involved in translating the phrase as "humankind" twice in verse 27 and as "the Son of Man" in verse 28. The modification implies that the author of the Gospel of Mark misunderstood the original saying of Jesus to imply that it was Jesus who, as the (future) eschatological Son of Man, was lord of the sabbath. Instead, what Jesus was apparently implying was that the Jewish law, the Torah, was given by God for humankind; humankind was not created to serve the Torah. The translation above is correct, but in the English translation of the NRSV, verse 28 is a *non sequitur* to verse 27. The mistake was Mark's, not ours, and not the translators of the New Revised Standard Version of the Bible.

What we see in this pericope is the way in which Mark took a unit of oral tradition, this pronouncement story, and incorporated it stylistically into his gospel and added at the end his own special meaning or commentary. Here is an example where philology helps us to make sense of a passage that otherwise makes no sense. In his pronouncement Jesus is talking about humankind, whereas Mark in his commentary is talking about Jesus as the awaited eschatological Son of Man. An Aramaic origin to these two distinct but here conflated verses is evident.

3. Other Examples

Other examples of pronouncement stories in the Gospel of Mark include:

Eating with Tax Collectors and Sinners (Mark 2:15–17 = Matt 9:10–13 = Luke 5:29–32)

The Question about Fasting (Mark 2:18–22 = Matt 9:14–17 = Luke 5:33–39)

Jesus' True Relatives (Mark 3:31–35 = Matt 12:46–50 = Luke 8:19–21)

A Prophet without Honor (Mark 6:1–6a = Matt 13:53–58 = Luke 4:16–30)

Jesus Blesses Little Children (Mark 10:13–16 = Matt 19:13–15 = Luke 18:15–17)

The Rich Young Man (Mark 10:17–22 = Matt 19:16–22 = Luke 18:18–23)

The Sons of Zebedee (Mark 10:35–40 = Matt 20:20–23 [Luke has no parallel to this pericope])

On the Resurrection (Mark 12:18–27 = Matt 22:23–33 = Luke 20:27–40)

The Anointing at Bethany (Mark 14:3–9 = Matt 26:6–13 = Luke 7:36–50)

The fact that there is a grouping of three pronouncement stories in Mark 2

> Eating with Tax Collectors and Sinners (Mark 2:15–17)
>
> The Question about Fasting (Mark 2:18–22)
>
> Plucking Grain on the Sabbath (Mark 2:23–28)

and another grouping of two or perhaps three pronouncement stories in Mark 10

> Jesus Blesses Little Children (Mark 10:13–16)
>
> The Rich Young Man (Mark 10:17–22)
>
> and perhaps The Sons of Zebedee (10:35–40)

may suggest that the author of the Gospel of Mark had access to a written collection of such pronouncement stories as one of several sources that he consulted and made use of in compiling his gospel.

MIRACLE STORIES

The word "miracle" generally means something very different to us than it did to those who lived in the ancient world. We usually understand "miracle" to mean a violation or suspension of the natural order or of the so-called "laws of nature," but our understanding of the natural order was not a feature of the ancient world.

We sometimes use the word "miracle" somewhat loosely:

"My son was in a very serious automobile accident. It's a miracle he survived."

"The tornado destroyed the house next door, but our house was miraculously spared."

"My grandfather's heart stopped beating, but the doctor applied the paddles, and it started to beat again. It's a miracle he's still alive."

This usage of the word does not refer, of course, to suspensions of the natural order, but simply to extraordinary but understandable circumstances.[7]

In the ancient world, a miracle was a wondrous event that was regarded as an act of God. Such wondrous events are attributed not only to Jesus, his apostles, and others in the New Testament and to Moses, Elijah, Elisha, and others in the Old Testament, but to Asklepios, Isis, and others in Hellenistic literature and to the "sons of the Pharisees" in the New Testament. In other words, although cures, exorcisms, and even raisings of the dead are unusual, they are not extraordinary in the literature of the ancient world and are not reserved to figures in the Bible.

---

7. There is also a conscious attempt by some to pass off as "miracles" healings or cures performed on television on Sunday mornings as a component of what I call "the electronic church." These "miracles" are more theater and chicanery than anything else and should be dismissed as such; sadly they are malicious deception disguised as religion.

FORM CRITICISM

In the New Testament, as in the case of any literature, "events" are reported by those who witnessed and interpreted what may have happened. Strictly speaking, miracles pose serious problems for the historian because they fall outside the realm of what can be known empirically. The stories known to us in the gospels as miracle stories about Jesus have been created, mediated, and written by interpreting minds in Christian communities or perhaps by evangelists at a time when there was no understanding of or commitment to the empirical, a relatively recent perspective.

The early Christian community obviously believed that Jesus was able to perform and did perform miracles. That conviction was probably based on a number of factors:

1. Jesus, like many of his generation, may have practiced exorcisms during the course of his ministry.
2. Jesus' freedom with respect to the Jewish law, his disregard for the division between ritual cleanness and uncleanness, and his apparent iconoclasm on many occasions obviously affected people's perceptions of him.
3. The church's appeal to the Hebrew scriptures in understanding the life and ministry of Jesus certainly pointed them at some time to the words of Isa 35:5–6a:

> 35:5Then the eyes of the blind shall be opened,
> and the ears of the deaf unstopped;
> 6then the lame shall leap like a deer,
> and the tongue of the speechless sing for joy.

Surely this passage from Isaiah was in the mind of the author of Q when he wrote the story that survives in similar form in Matthew and Luke:

Matt 11:2–5	Luke 7:18–22
11:2When John heard in prison what the Messiah was doing, he sent word by his disciples 3and said to him, "Are you the one who is to come, or are we to wait for another?"	7:18The disciples of John reported all these things to him. So John summoned two of his disciples 19and sent them to the Lord to ask, "Are you the one who is to come, or are we to wait for another?" 20When the men had come to him, they said , "John the Baptist has sent us to you to ask, "Are you the one who is to come, or are we to wait for another?" 21Jesus had just then cured many people of diseases, plagues, and evil spirits, and had given sight to many

Matt 11:2–5	Luke 7:18–22
	who were blind.
⁴Jesus answered them,	²²And he answered them,
"Go and tell John what you hear	"Go and tell John what you have
and see; ⁵the blind receive	seen and heard: the blind receive
their sight, the lame walk, the lepers	their sight, the lame walk, the lepers
are cleansed, the deaf hear, the	are cleansed, the deaf hear, the
dead are raised, and the poor have	dead are raised, the poor have
good news brought to them.	good news brought to them.

See also Isa 26:19a

> Your dead shall live, their corpses shall rise.

Isa 29:18

> On that day the deaf shall hear
> the words of a scroll,
> and out of their gloom and darkness,
> the eyes of the blind shall see.

Isa 42:6b–7a, 18

> I have given you as a covenant to the people,
> a light to the nations,
> to open the eyes that are blind . . . .

Isa 61:1

> The spirit of the Lord GOD (Yahweh) is upon me,
> because the LORD (Yahweh) has anointed me;
> he has sent me to bring good news to the oppressed,
> to bind up the brokenhearted,
> to proclaim liberty to the captives; . . . .
> and release to the prisoners.

Like the pronouncement stories, the miracle stories of the gospels follow a traditional literary form. There is generally a description of a disorder, followed by an actual healing, followed by the amazement of the crowd.

1. *The Healing of the Leper*

There is an excellent example of a miracle story in Mark 1:40–45, a story copied and reworked in Matt 8:1–4 and in Luke 5:12–16. In its presumed oldest form in Mark, the story reads:

> ⁴⁰A leper came to him begging him, and kneeling said to him, "If you choose, you can make me clean." ⁴¹Moved by pity, Jesus stretched out his hand and touched him, and said to him, "I do choose. Be made clean!" ⁴²Immediately the leprosy left him, and he was made clean. ⁴³After sternly warning him he sent him away at once, ⁴⁴saying to him, "See that you say nothing to anyone; but go, show yourself to the priest, and offer for your cleansing what Moses commanded, as a testimony to them." ⁴⁵But he went out and began to proclaim it freely, and to spread the word, so that Jesus could no longer go into a town openly, but stayed out in the country; and people came from every quarter.

Although it is not clear from the English translation above, this pericope in the original Greek (and in the KJV) begins characteristically with the Greek word καί, *kai* (meaning "and"), the typical Markan way of connecting his pericopes. The previous story in Mark is a description of Jesus' preaching tour through Galilee. In Matthew, the preceding section contains a series of warnings by Jesus. Luke has Jesus' call of his first disciples. Notice how Matthew and Luke both digress from Mark's order or outline, but they do so differently, just as we would expect if they were working independently of each other.

When we read a miracle story in the gospels, it is essential to realize that we are not necessarily reading an account of a *miracle* that Jesus actually performed. What we are reading is rather a *miracle story* that had its origin in the early church, a story whose purpose served the missionary message of the church by reinforcing and intensifying belief in Jesus as the messiah. The distinction between a "miracle" and a "miracle story" is fundamental.

Form critics look at what they call the *Sitz im Leben* of each and every pericope in the synoptic gospels. That is to say they look at the life situation of each story. Did a particular story have its origin in the life and ministry of the historical Jesus or in the preaching (the *kerygma*) of the church. It is probably best to read the miracle stories of the gospels as stories that had their origin and development within the context of the early church, not within the context of the life and ministry of the historical Jesus of Nazareth.[8]

It is, however, not impossible or even improbable that this particular miracle story had its origin within the context of something that Jesus said and did. In this case, we may be dealing with a situation in which Jesus, as was characteristic of him, refused to discriminate between people who, under the Jewish law, were considered to be ritually clean and people who were considered to be ritually unclean, such as women, sinners, lepers, etc. There were very likely occasions in the course of Jesus' ministry when he may have declared lepers to be ritually "clean." It is a small step from such a situation to see how the church's oral tradition would transform such a story

---

8. Form critics do not concern themselves with the question of whether or not Jesus actually performed "miracles." They rather attempt to find a place for individual "miracle stories" in the life and preaching of early Christian communities.

into a story in which a leper whom Jesus had "ritually cleansed" was also physically cleansed or healed of his leprosy.

2. The Healing of the Man with a Withered Hand

Another example of a miracle story is the story of Jesus healing a man with a withered hand in Mark 3:1–6, a story copied and reworked in Matt 12:9–14 and Luke 6:6–11. In its presumed oldest form in Mark, the story reads:

> $^{3:1}$Again he entered the synagogue, and a man was there who had a withered hand. ^{2}They watched him to see whether he would cure him on the Sabbath, so that they might accuse him. ^{3}And he said to the man who had the withered hand, "Come forward." ^{4}Then he said to them, "Is it lawful to do good or to do harm on the sabbath, to save life or to kill?" But they were silent. ^{5}He looked around at them with anger; he was grieved at their harshness of heart and said to the man, "Stretch out your hand." He stretched it out, and his hand was restored. ^{6}The Pharisees went out and immediately conspired with the Herodians against him, how to destroy him.

Once again, it is not clear from the English translation of the word "again" at the beginning of this passage, but this pericope in the original Greek (and in the KJV) begins characteristically with the word "and," the typical Markan manner of connecting pericopes. In Mark (as well as in Matthew and Luke), the preceding pericope is the story of Jesus' pronouncement about the sabbath (Mark 2:23–28; Matt 12:1–8; Luke 6:1–5), a pronouncement story which we examined previously and in which, in the case of the Gospel of Mark, Jesus delivered the saying "The sabbath was made for humankind, and not humankind for the sabbath (see above, pp. 135–137).

This pericope is technically a miracle story inasmuch as there is a description of the man with the withered hand; Jesus commands him to stretch out his hand; and in doing so the man's hand is restored. Yet, it is clear that the healing is not the principal purpose of this pericope. Like the preceding story in all three of synoptic gospels, the focus is on the conflict between Jesus and the his accusers the Pharisees not over the healing *per se*, but over the healing on the sabbath in violation of the commandment not to work on the sabbath.

The implication of some of the details of the story suggest that it is set not at the beginning but toward the end of Jesus' ministry. Mark has apparently misplaced it in setting it at this point in his gospel. The implication of the story is that the Pharisees are determined to collaborate with the Herodians (supporters of the rule of Herod's family in Jerusalem) to present formal charges against Jesus before the Sanhedrin in Jerusalem. This story is understood as part of the conspiracy "how to destroy him" (Mark 3:6). This portion of the story makes no sense in the context of Jesus' Galilean ministry. The primary purpose of this story is whether it is lawful to perform a good deed on the sabbath. The miraculous element in the story is secondary, in fact almost incidental.

3. Other Examples

Miracle stories play an important role in the Gospel of Mark, especially in Mark 1–9. Additional examples of miracle stories in Mark include:

The Exorcism of a Man with an Unclean Spirit (Mark 1:23–28 = Luke 4:31–37; no parallel in Matt)

Jesus Heals Peter's Mother-in-Law (Mark 1:29–31 = Matt 8:14–15 = Luke 4:38–39)

Jesus Heals a Paralytic (Mark 2:1–12 = Matt 9:1–8 = Luke 5:17–26)

Jesus Restores Jairus's daughter to Life and Heals a Woman (Mark 5.21–43 = Matt 9:18–26 = Luke 8:40–56)

Jesus Feeds the Five Thousand (Mark 6:30–44 = Matt 14:13–21 = Luke 9:10–17)

Jesus Walks on Water (Mark 6:45–52 = Matt 14:22–33; no parallel in Luke)

Jesus Heals the Sick in Gennesaret (Mark 6.53–56 = Matt 14:34–36; no parallel in Luke)

Jesus Cures a Deaf Man (Mark 7.31–37 = Matthew 15:29–31; no parallel in Luke)

Jesus Feeds the Four Thousand (Mark 8:1–10 = Matt 15:32–39; no parallel in Luke)

Jesus Cures a Blind Man at Bethsaida (Mark 8.22–26; no parallel in Matt or Luke)

Jesus Heals the Blind Bartimaeus (Mark 10:46–52 = Matthew 20:29–34 = Luke 18:35–43)

We observed previously that passages in the Hebrew scriptures frequently inspired elements in the New Testament, specifically in the apostolic preaching, in the kerygma in Acts, and in the story of the crucifixion. The miracles stories of the gospels reflect the same tendency to appropriate elements in the Hebrew scriptures and adapt them to a new setting in the life of Jesus or the early church.

Specifically, the story of Jesus raising Jairus's daughter from the dead (Mark 5:21–24a, 35–43) appears to have been inspired by the stories of Elijah reviving the widow's dead son in 1 Kgs 17:17–24 and Elisha reviving the widow's dead son in 2 Kgs 4:18–37. The story of Jesus raising the widow's dead son at Nain in Luke 7:11–17 also reflects elements of 1 Kgs 17:17–24.

Moreover, the stories of Elijah multiplying food and oil for the widow of Zarephath in 1 Kgs 17:8–16 and of Elisha multiplying oil for the widow in 2 Kgs 4:1–7 and food for one hundred men in 2 Kgs 4:42–44 probably inspired the stories of Jesus feeding the five thousand in Mark 6:30–44 (= Matt 14:13–21 and Luke 9:10–17) and the four thousand in Mark 8:1–10 (= Matt 15:32–39). In fact, Mark's two miracle chains include stories that echo deeds of Moses (food and water) and Elijah/Elisha (food and healings). Mark's point in these stories is to get his audience to think about Jesus in the context of these ancient Israelite heroes.

PARABLES

Parables were a common form of teaching through illustration in Jesus' time in both Greco-Roman and Jewish circles. The gospel parables are stories that Jesus presumably told to illustrate some detail or truth, generally about the imminent coming of God's Rule (or what is generally referred to as the Kingdom of God). In the parables in the synoptic gospels, Jesus usually compares God's Rule to something that his audience will easily understand, often using images from agriculture or nature. Many of the parables begin with the phrase, "The Kingdom of God (or God's Rule) is like . . . ."

1. The Parable of the Growing Seed

There is an excellent example of a parable in Mark 4:26–29, the parable of the growing seed, the only parable in Mark's gospel without a parallel in either Matthew or Luke. The text of Mark reads:

> 4:26He also said, "The kingdom of God is as if someone would scatter seed on the ground, 27and would sleep and rise night and day, and the seed would sprout and grow, he does not know how. 28The earth produces of itself, first the stalk, then the head, then the full grain in the head. 29But when the grain is ripe, at once he goes in with his sickle, because the harvest has come.

The parables of Jesus are often difficult to understand because the reader is not hearing them in their original physical setting and historical context, where the meaning would have been evident to those who were present. It appears, however, that this parable is one of many so-called parables of growth that Jesus delivered to illustrate that God's Rule was already growing on earth whenever anyone did God's will. Verse 29 appears to refer to the imminent end (the harvest) of history as we know it and the arrival of the end time that would mark the beginning of God's judgment and God's Rule.

2. The Parable of the Mustard Seed

Another very similar parable follows immediately upon the parable of the growing seed, namely the parable of the mustard seed in Mark 4:30–32 with parallels in Matt 13:31–32 and Luke 13:18–19:

> ⁴:³⁰He also said, "With what can we compare the kingdom of God, or what parable will we use for it? ³¹It is like a mustard seed, which, when sown upon the ground, is the smallest of all the seeds on earth; ³²yet when it is sown it grows up and becomes the greatest of all shrubs, and puts forth large branches, so that the birds of the air can make nests in its shade."

Like the previous parable, this too is a parable of growth, presumably emphasizing an element of Jesus' teaching about the Kingdom of God. It is likely that Mark's introduction to the parable in verse 30 is part of his own editorial redaction and that, in the form in which the parable came to Mark, it simply read "The kingdom of God is like a mustard seed, etc."

3. Other Examples

Other examples of synoptic parables that have their roots in the Gospel of Mark include:

The parable of the sower (Mark 4:1–9 = Matt 13:1–9 = Luke 8:4–8)

The parable of salt (Mark 9:49–50 = Matt 5:13 = Luke 14:34–35)

The parable of the laborers in the vineyard (Mark 10:31 = Matt 20:1–16 = Luke 13:30

The parable of the wicked tenants (Mark 12:1–12 = Matt 21:33–46 = Luke 20:9–19)

The parable of the flood (Mark 13:35 = Matt 24:37–44 = Luke 17:26–36)

The parable of the ten virgins (Mark 13:33–37 = Matt 25:1–13 = Luke 12:35–38)

The parable of the talents (Mark 13:34 = Matt 25:14–30 = Luke 19:11–27)

The fact that there is a cluster of parables in Mark 4 (Mark 4:1–9, 26–29, 30–32) suggests that the author of the Gospel of Mark had access to a written source containing some parables attributed to Jesus, not that Jesus delivered these parables seriatim on one occasion.

SAYINGS

Sayings material generally refers to individual sayings or to clusters of sayings attributed to Jesus.

1. A Cluster of Sayings in Mark

There is a good example of such a cluster of sayings in Mark 4:21–25. This material is found largely intact in Luke 8:16–18 with some additional parallels in Luke 6:38;

11:33; 12:2; and 19:26; but Mark's sayings have been scattered throughout the Gospel of Matthew, where they appear in Matt 5:15; 7:2; 10:26; 13:12; and 25:29.

The text of Mark reads:

> $^{4:21}$He said to them, "Is a lamp brought in to be put under a bushel basket, or under the bed, and not on the lampstand? ^{22}For there is nothing hidden, except to be disclosed; nor is anything secret, except to come to light. ^{23}Let anyone with ears to hear listen!" ^{24}And he said to them, "Pay attention to what you hear; the measure you give will be the measure you get, and still more will be given you. ^{25}For to those who have, more will be given; and from those who have nothing, even what they have will be taken away."

As the author of the Gospel of Matthew apparently observed, these sayings in Mark 4:21–25 are distinct and unrelated and could hardly have been delivered by Jesus in this sequence on a single occasion. Rather in their present form, they are connected by key words: *lamp* in verse 21 and *light* in verse 22, *hear* in verses 23 and 24, and *more* and *given* in verses 24 and 25. These sayings were probably remembered in this order in the oral tradition by means of these key words and were apparently known to the author of the Gospel of Mark in this arrangement or were known through a written source available to the author of Mark.

2. Another Cluster of Sayings in Mark

Another interesting cluster of sayings appears in Mark 8:34–9:1 with parallels in Matt 16:24–28 and Luke 9:23–27:

> $^{8:34}$He called the crowd with his disciples, and said to them, "If any want to become my followers, let them deny themselves and take up their cross and follow me. ^{35}For those who want to save their life will lose it, and those who lose their life for my sake and for the sake of the gospel, will save it. ^{36}For what will it profit them to gain the whole world and forfeit their life? ^{37}Indeed, what can they give in return for their life? ^{38}Those who are ashamed of me and my words in this adulterous and sinful generation, of them the Son of Man will also be ashamed when he comes in the glory of his Father with the holy angels." $^{9:1}$And he said to them, "Truly I tell you, there are some standing here who will not taste death until they see that the kingdom of God has come with power."

Like the previous cluster of sayings, this material also appears to be a grouping of sayings with a similar theme, rather than a single coherent statement.

Mark does not have nearly as many individual sayings or clusters of sayings of Jesus as do Matthew and Luke. Remember that more than 200 verses of material common to Matthew and Luke, but not found in Mark, are believed to have been available to them from the sayings source Q.

FORM CRITICISM

3. Other Examples

There are, however, some additional sayings or sayings clusters in the Gospel of Mark:

False Christs and false prophets (Mark 13:21–23 = Matt 24:23–24 = Luke 17:23)

Take heed, watch (Mark 13:33–37 = Matt 25:13; 24:42 = Luke 21:36; 19:12–13; 12:40; 12:38)

As in the case of the parables, we should not conclude from these clusters of sayings in Mark that Jesus delivered these sayings seriatim on a single occasion. Rather these clusters of sayings suggest that one or more of Mark's sources collected into a single place several sayings that were attributed to Jesus and that focused on a common subject or theme.

LEGENDS

Legends or stories about Jesus are stories that purport to relate events in the life of Jesus by surrounding those events with amazing, wondrous, or even supernatural details. Many of these legends appear to be "biographical," but the miraculous elements in these stories reveal their legendary character. The birth and infancy narratives in Matt 1:18–2:3 and Luke 2:1–40, the story of Jesus in the Jerusalem temple at age twelve (Luke 2:41–51), the story of Jesus' baptism in Matt 3:1–17, Mark 1:2–11, and Luke (3:1–22), the temptation of Jesus in Matt 4:1–11, Mark 1:12–13, and Luke 4:1–13, the transfiguration of Jesus in Matt 17:1–9, Mark 9:2–10, and Luke 9:28–36, and the resurrection appearances, especially in Matt 28:9–20 and Luke 24:10–43, are all legends, whose purpose is clearly to enhance or augment the representation of Jesus. There are no formal literary characteristics to these legends about Jesus. They are exactly what the name implies, legends or stories about Jesus. These stories likely have little if any historical value. In fact, we are seeing increasingly that historical accuracy was obviously not an important or overriding criterion in the collection and preservation of Christian tradition.

1. The Birth Narrative in the Gospel of Matthew

I will now discuss several interesting features of Matthew's birth narrative to demonstrate one way in which some of these legendary stories likely originated in fulfillment of the Hebrew scriptures.

a. The Birth of Jesus the Messiah (Matt 1:18–25)

> $^{1:18}$Now the birth of Jesus the Messiah took place in this way. When his mother Mary had been engaged to Joseph, but before they lived together, she was found to be with child from the Holy Spirit. ^{19}Her husband Joseph, being a righteous man and unwilling to expose her to public disgrace, planned to dismiss her quietly.

²⁰But just when he had resolved to do this, an angel of the Lord appeared to him in a dream and said, "Joseph, son of David, do not be afraid to take Mary as your wife, for the child conceived in her is from the Holy Spirit. ²¹She will bear a son, and you are to name him Jesus, for he will save his people from their sins." ²²All this took place to fulfill what had been spoken by the Lord through the prophet:

> ²³"Look, the virgin shall conceive and bear a son,
> and they shall name him Emmanuel,"

which means "God is with us." ²⁴When Joseph awoke from sleep, he did as the angel of the Lord commanded him; he took her as his wife, ²⁵but had no marital relations with her until she had borne a son; and he named him Jesus.

It appears that this entire story has as its only purpose to report that Jesus was born of a virgin, because, according to Matthew, Jesus' birth from a virgin (Matt 1:18–25) took place to fulfill a prophecy in Isa 7:14 (see Matt 1:22–23):

Matt 1:22–23ab	Isa 7:14
²²All this took place to fulfill what had been spoken by the Lord through the prophet: ²³"Look, the virgin shall conceive and bear a son, and they shall name him Emmanuel."	Therefore the Lord himself will give you a sign. Look, the young woman[9] is with child and shall bear a son, and shall name him Immanuel.

This citation from Isaiah follows Matthew's legendary report that Mary was found to be pregnant by the Holy Spirit, not from her husband Joseph, and that Joseph was commanded by an angel to name the child Jesus, because "he will save his people from their sins." The apparent *non sequitur* in the last part of Matthew 1:21 unfortunately makes no sense in English, but it does make sense in Hebrew, where the name Jesus (Hebrew *yasha'*) means "he saves."[10] Matthew introduces in 1:21 and 1:23c word plays on the names Jesus (Hebrew for "he saves") and Emmanuel (Hebrew for "God is with us"), anticipating thereby Jesus' saving act and God's reconciliation with humankind by means of the crucifixion, which is reported later in the gospel.

Matthew's story of Jesus' birth has absolutely no historical merit and should be characterized as a legend, whose purpose it is to enhance or augment the representation of Jesus as God's divine son.

---

9. The Greek text of Isaiah that the author of the Gospel of Matthew would have had access to would have read "virgin" in 7:14 rather than "young woman." The original Hebrew reads "young woman," but it was mistranslated into the Greek Septuagint as "virgin." Hence, Matthew is here dependent on a mistranslation in his use or misuse of this passage as a "proof-text." This argument was made in more detail in chapter 2.

10. See the interesting wordplay on Jesus' name in Matt 8:25, when the disciples cry out when their boat is caught in a severe windstorm on the Sea of Galilee, "Lord, save us."

FORM CRITICISM

b. The Visit of the Wise Men (Matt 2:1–12)

> $^{2:1}$In the time of King Herod, after Jesus was born in Bethlehem of Judea, wise men from the East came to Jerusalem, ^{2}asking, "Where is the child who has been born king of the Jews? For we observed his star at its rising, and have come to pay him homage. ^{3}When King Herod heard this, he was frightened, and all Jerusalem with him; ^{4}and calling together all the chief priests and scribes of the people, he inquired of them where the Messiah was to be born. ^{5}They told him, "In Bethlehem of Judea; for so it has been written by the prophet:
>
>> ^{6}'And you, Bethlehem, in the land of Judah,
>> are by no means least among the rulers of Judah;
>> for from you shall come a ruler
>> who is to shepherd my people Israel.'"
>
> ^{7}Then Herod secretly called for the wise men and learned from them the exact time when the star had appeared. ^{8}Then he sent them to Bethlehem, saying, "Go and search diligently for the child; and when you have found him, bring me word so that I may also go and pay him homage." ^{9}When they had heard the king, they set out; and there, ahead of them, went the star that they had seen at its rising, until it stopped over the place where the child was. ^{10}When they saw that the star had stopped, they were overwhelmed with joy. ^{11}On entering the house, they saw the child with Mary his mother; and they knelt down and paid him homage. Then, opening their treasure chests, they offered him gifts of gold, frankincense, and myrrh. ^{12}And having been warned in a dream not to return to Herod, they left for their own country by another road.

It appears that this long story of the visit of the wise men has as its purpose to report that Jesus was born in Bethlehem of Judea (Matt 2:5–6) in fulfillment of a prophecy in Mic 5:2:

Matt 2:5–6	Mic 5:2
$^{2:5}$They told him, "In Bethlehem of Judea; for so it has been written by the prophet: ^{6}'And you, Bethlehem, in the land of Judah, are by no means least among the rulers of Judah; for from you shall come a ruler who is to shepherd my people Israel.'"	But you, O Bethlehem of Ephrathah who are one of the little clans of Judah, from you shall come forth for me one who is to rule in Israel, whose origin is from old, from ancient days.

2 Sam 5:2b may also be in the mind of the author of Matt 2:5–6:

"The LORD (Yahweh) said to you: 'It is you who shall be shepherd of my people Israel, you who shall be ruler over Israel.'"

The proof text follows Matthew's account of the visit of the wise men, who inquired in Jerusalem "Where is the child who has been born king of the Jews?" (Matt 2:2). According to Matthew's story, Herod was frightened and summoned all the chief priests and scribes to inquire where the Messiah was to be born. The passage in Mic 5:2 combined with 2 Sam 5:2b provided the answer to the wise men's question. In the aftermath of the scriptural citation, Matthew provides for the clandestine departure of the mysterious men back to their unnamed home in the East in order to spare Jesus from Herod's massacre.

c. The Escape to Egypt (Matt 2:13–15)

> 2:13Now after they had left, an angel of the Lord appeared to Joseph in a dream and said, "Get up, take the child and his mother, and flee to Egypt, and remain there until I tell you; for Herod is about to search for the child, to destroy him." 14Then Joseph got up, took the child and his mother by night, and went to Egypt, 15and remained there until the death of Herod. This was to fulfill what had been spoken by the Lord through the prophet,
> "Out of Egypt I have called my son."

The flight of Joseph, Mary, and the infant Jesus to Egypt (Matt 2:13–15) fulfills the prophecy in Hos 11:1:

Matt 2:15b	Hos 11:1
This was to fulfill what had been spoken by the Lord through the prophet,	
	When Israel was a child, I loved him,
"Out of Egypt have I called my son."	and out of Egypt I called him my son.

This proof text follows Matthew's account of an angel's warning to Joseph that the family should flee to Egypt and remain there because Herod intended to search for the child and destroy him. Matthew reports that the family remained in Egypt until the death of Herod, in order that God could call Jesus out of Egypt in fulfillment of Hosea's prophecy.

d. The Massacre of the Infants (Matt 2:16–18)

> 2:16When Herod saw that he had been tricked by the wise men, he was infuriated, and he sent and he killed all the children in and around Bethlehem who were two years old or under, according to the time that he had learned from the wise men. 17Then was fulfilled what had been spoken through the prophet Jeremiah:

¹⁸"A voice was heard in Ramah,
wailing and loud lamentation,
Rachel weeping for her children;
she refused to be consoled,
because they are no more."

The massacre of the children (Matt 2:16–18) fulfills the prophecy in Jer 31:15:

Matt 2:17	Jer 31:15
Then was fulfilled what had been spoken through the prophet Jeremiah:	
	Thus says the LORD:
"A voice was heard in Ramah,	"A voice is heard in Ramah,
wailing and loud lamentation,	lamentation and bitter weeping.
Rachel weeping for her children;	Rachel is weeping for her children;
she refused to be consoled,	she refuses to be comforted
	for her children,
because they are no more."	because they are no more.

According to Matthew, Herod had commanded the wise men to return to him and report where they had found the child messiah. When they did not, he had all the children in and around Bethlehem who were two years and under killed. The author of the Gospel of Matthew regarded that massacre of the children as the fulfillment of Jeremiah's prophecy.

e. The Return to Nazareth (Matt 2:19–23)

> ²:¹⁹When Herod died, an angel of the Lord suddenly appeared in a dream to Joseph in Egypt and said, ²⁰"Get up, take the child and his mother, and go to the land of Israel, for those who were seeking the child's life are dead." ²¹Then Joseph got up, took the child and his mother, and went to the land of Israel. ²²But when he heard that Archelaus was ruling over Judea in place of his father Herod, he was afraid to go there. And after being warned in a dream, he went away to the district of Galilee. ²³There he made his home in a town called Nazareth, so that what had been spoken through the prophets might be fulfilled,
> "He will be called a Nazorean."

The fifth and last of the proof texts in Matthew's birth narrative is problematic. Following their flight to Egypt and the massacre of the children, Joseph, Mary, and the infant Jesus returned not to Bethlehem, the place of Jesus' birth and the family's presumed hometown according to Matthew, but they went instead to Nazareth in Galilee to avoid Herod's son King Archelaus of Judea (4 BCE–6 CE) in fulfillment of the prophecy:

> "There [in Galilee] he [Joseph] made his home in a town called Nazareth, so that what was spoken through the prophets might be fulfilled,
> 'He will be called a Nazorean'" (Matt 2:23).

The problem with this passage in Matthew is that there is no text in the Hebrew scriptures that corresponds to this apparent citation. It is not clear what text the author of the Gospel of Matthew had in mind or, more likely, what text from Hebrew scriptures the author of the Gospel of Matthew was reproducing from his presumed written *testimonia* source.

What is clear, however, from this discussion of Matthew's birth narrative is that most of the themes in Matthew's story were built around passages from the Hebrew scriptures:

Jesus' birth from a virgin (1:18–25) in fulfillment of Isaiah

the site of Jesus' birth in Bethlehem (2:1–12) in fulfillment of Micah and 2 Samuel

the flight to Egypt (2:13–15) in fulfillment of Hosea

the massacre of the children (2:16–18) in fulfillment of Jeremiah

the relocation of the family to Nazareth (2:19–23) in fulfillment of an unknown citation by nameless prophets.

Interestingly, Matthew 1:22 ("spoken by the Lord through the prophet"); 2:5 ("written by the prophet"); 2:15 ("spoken by the Lord through the prophet"); 2:17 (spoken through the prophet Jeremiah"); and 2:23 ("spoken through the prophets") differ only slightly in form:

1. only Matt 2:5 has "written"; the rest all have "spoken";
2. only Matt 2:17 identifies the prophet (Jeremiah) by name;
3. Matt 1:22 and 2:15 add the phrase "by the Lord"; and
4. only our mystery passage Matt 2:23 has the plural "prophets" instead of the singular "prophet," perhaps because the author of the Gospel of Matthew was unable to identify the source of the quotation and so left the citation deliberately vague. The truth of the matter is that we simply do not know what Matthew had in mind in this passage.

As we have seen previously in the Pauline *kerygma*, in the speeches of Peter and Paul in Acts, and in the story of Jesus' crucifixion in Mark's passion narrative, so too there is no question whatsoever that the Hebrew scriptures contributed to and informed the development of legendary tradition surrounding Matthew's account of Jesus' birth, whether it was the author of the gospel or of an earlier source who was initially responsible for shaping this story.

If the information based on Matthew's (or his source's) reading of the scriptures is bracketed or eliminated from the text, the story reveals only the barest outline of Jesus' origin:

1. Jesus' parents were Joseph and Mary.[11]

2. Jesus was probably born in Nazareth (he is always referred to as Jesus of Nazareth, never as Jesus of Bethlehem). The birth in Bethlehem seems to be nothing more than a contrivance in fulfillment of the scriptures.

Apparently there was no flight to Egypt as reported in Matthew; rather Matthew's account of the flight fulfills a scriptural prophecy and models Jesus after Moses, who led the people of Israel out of Egypt during the time of the Exodus. Neither, apparently, was there a massacre of the children, as reported in Matthew; rather the story once again fulfills a prophecy and models Jesus after Moses in Exod 1:22; 11:4–6, when, according to the tradition, the pharaoh ordered the massacre of every boy born to the Hebrews. The Moses typology in the Gospel of Matthew is obviously a major theme of the gospel: Jesus is the new Moses, or the prophet greater than Moses. Matthew even takes Jesus to a mountain to deliver his famous Sermon on the Mount (Matt 5–7), the new law, which fulfills or completes the law of Moses, also delivered from a mountain, Mount Sinai.

Despite its dubious historicity, the story of Jesus' birth does, however, fulfill an important theological purpose in the Gospel of Matthew. It provides a story in fulfillment of several passages from the Hebrew scriptures, and it also traces Jesus' divine sonship not to the resurrection/exaltation (as in Acts and Paul), nor to the baptism (as in Mark), but rather to Mary's conception by the Holy Spirit (when "she was found to be with child from the Holy Spirit" [Matt 1:18]). In these passages, we witnessed in the church's writings a gradual move to an ever "higher" Christology, a more developed theological interpretation of the person of Jesus. We find in Matthew that Jesus was designated Son of God not by virtue of his resurrection from the dead, neither was he designated Son of God at his baptism. Rather he was conceived miraculously as Son of God by the power of the spirit of God.

Like the Gospel of Matthew, the Gospel of Luke also has a legendary birth narrative, but it is completely different from the birth narrative in the Gospel of Matthew. The two gospels agree on the fact that Jesus was born of a virgin (Matt 1:18–21; Luke 1:26–38), that Joseph was Mary's husband (Matt 1:18-19; Luke 2:5; 2:33), and that

---

11. In spite of the birth narratives in both Matthew and Luke, there is a contradictory tradition, even within the New Testament, that identifies Joseph as Jesus' father. In our discussion of Mark 6:3 within the context of textual criticism (see chapter 1, pp. 33–35), we argued that the original text probably read: "Is this not the son of the carpenter and of Mary?" The parallel passage in Matt 13:55a reads: "Is not this the carpenter's son?" The genealogies in both Matthew and Luke trace Jesus' genealogy through Joseph (Matt 1:16 and Luke 3:23); in fact Luke 3:23 obviously recognized the problem: "Jesus was about thirty years old when he began his work. He was the son (*as was thought*) of Joseph . . . ." With the parenthesis, Luke tries to gloss over the problem that he probably found in one of his sources. The Gospel of John, which knows nothing of the tradition about the virgin birth) refers to Jesus twice as the "son of Joseph": see John 1:45 ("Philip found Nathaniel and said to him, 'We have found him about whom Moses in the law and also the prophets wrote, Jesus son of Joseph from Nazareth.'"); and John 6:42 ("They were saying, 'Is not this Jesus, the son of Joseph, whose father and mother we know?'").

the birth took place in Bethlehem (Matt 2:5-6; Luke 2:4). Yet, even in those details on which Matthew and Luke agree, there are major differences.

Most obvious is the fact that in the Gospel of Matthew the family lived in Bethlehem where Jesus was born. From Bethlehem they traveled to Egypt to escape Herod's order to kill the children and subsequently went to Nazareth rather than back to the family home in Bethlehem, following a warning to Joseph in a dream. Luke, on the other hand, locates the family home in Nazareth and then devised the Roman census as the reason for their traveling to Bethlehem, because according to the prophecy in Mic 5:2 and 2 Sam 5:2b the Messiah had to be born in Bethlehem, the city of Israel's great King David. As in Matthew, the author of the Gospel of Luke traces Jesus' title Son of God back to Mary's conception: "The angel said to her, 'The Holy Spirit will come upon you, and the power of the Most High will overshadow you; therefore the child to be born will be holy; he will be called Son of God'" (Luke 2:35).

Luke lacks Matthew's story of the visit of the wise men, and Matthew lacks Luke's story of the angels' proclamation to the shepherds in the field. The two versions of Jesus' birth seem totally independent.

To complete the picture of Jesus' origin, the author of the Gospel of John traces Jesus' divine sonship to a time before creation, the "highest" Christology that we find in the New Testament. He refers to Jesus as the incarnation of the divine *logos*, the *word* of God or the *divine reason*:

> And the Word (*logos*) became flesh and lived among us, and we have seen his glory, the glory as of a father's only son, full of grace and truth (John 1:14).

In the short space of about 70 years, Jesus' divine sonship was pushed backward in time from his exaltation (in Paul and Acts), to his baptism (in Mark), to his conception (in Matthew and Luke), and finally to a time before creation (in John).

2. The Story of Jesus' Baptism in Mark

The baptism of Jesus is reported in Mark 1:9–11 as follows:

> 1:9In those days Jesus came from Nazareth of Galilee and was baptized by John in the Jordan. 10And just as he was coming up out of the water, he saw the heavens torn apart and the Spirit descending like a dove on him. 11And a voice came from heaven, "You are my Son, the Beloved; with you I am well pleased."

One of the most certain historical events in Jesus' life is that John baptized him in the Jordan River. It passes with flying colors the criterion of dissimilarity or embarrassment; it stands in marked contrast to the church's preaching. Mark makes it clear in 1:4–5 that

> "John the baptizer appeared in the wilderness, proclaiming a baptism of repentance for the forgiveness of sins" (1:4) and that "people . . . were baptized by him in the river Jordan, confessing their sins" (1:5).

FORM CRITICISM

It is reasonable to assume that Jesus was one of the many people who submitted to John's "baptism of repentance for the forgiveness of sins." No other explanation is reasonable, although the author of the Gospel of Matthew recognizes the theological dilemma involved in Jesus' baptism and, therefore, amends his Markan source by creating a dialogue between John and Jesus in which he says that "John would have prevented" Jesus from being baptized, "saying, 'I need to be baptized by you'" (Matt 3:14).

It is very likely that Jesus' baptism was the transforming event in his life. In fact, Mark reports that Jesus' own ministry began only after John was arrested (Mark 1:14), implying thereby that Jesus was initially a follower or disciple of John. To the extent that we can know, it appears that the messages of John and Jesus were very similar. Both men seem to have anticipated the imminent end of history and the inauguration of the New Age of God's Rule, perhaps with the imminent arrival of the Son of Man. Identifying the authentic teachings of both John and Jesus is a very serious challenge for students of the New Testament and will be examined in more detail in a subsequent chapter.

The point I wish to make here is that the author of the Gospel of Mark has transformed what was probably an historical event in the life of Jesus into a "legend," by reporting that the Spirit of God descended on Jesus at his baptism and spoke to him, "You are my Son" (Mark 1:11). The words of Jesus' call and commission echo the words of Psalm 2:

Mark 1:11	Ps 2:7
And a voice came from heaven,	I will tell of the decree of the LORD:
	He said to me,
"You are my Son, the Beloved;	"You are my son;
with you I am well pleased."	today I have begotten you."

The author of the Gospel of Mark may also have had in mind Isa 42:1:

> Here is my servant, whom I uphold,
> my chosen, in whom my soul delights;
> I have put my spirit upon him;
> he will bring forth justice to the nations.

In fact, Mark 1:9–11 seems to combine elements of Ps 2:7 and Isa 42:1, with possible allusions to Gen 22:2, 12, 16–17a;[12] and to Exod 4:22–23.[13] The one story is set

---

12. Genesis 22:2He [God] said, "Take your son, your only son Isaac, whom you love, and go to the land of Moriah, and offer him there as a burnt offering on one of the mountains that I shall show you." . . . 12He [God] said, "Do not lay your hand on the boy or do anything to him; for now I know that you fear God, since you have not withheld your son, your only son, from me." . . . 16and [the angel of the LORD] said, "By myself I have sworn, says the LORD: Because you have done this, and have not withheld your son, your only son, 17I will indeed bless you . . . ."

13. Exodus 4:22Then you [Moses] shall say to Pharaoh, "Thus says the LORD: 'Israel is my

in the context of Abraham's sacrifice of his son Isaac, the other in the context of Moses' encounter with the Egyptian pharaoh. However unrelated to Jesus' baptism these stories may be, this kind of typology was frequently in the forefront of contemporary Jewish and Christian writers (e.g., Rom 5:14; 1 Cor 10:1–6, 11; Justin Martyr, *Dialogue with Trypho* 40.1; 41.1; 42.1; 43–44), especially when we realize that the author of the Gospel of Mark was probably intentionally anticipating Jesus' ensuing sacrificial death as God's firstborn son.

3. Other Examples

In addition to the legendary material associated with Jesus' birth and baptism, the Transfiguration story in Matt 17:1-8; Mark 9:2-8 and Luke 9:28-36 and the resurrection appearances in Matt 28 and Luke 24 are also examples of legends.

CONCLUSIONS

Form criticism is the scholarly study of the literary forms that Christians used in developing the building blocks of the synoptic gospels. Not surprisingly Christians used literary forms already current in Greco-Roman and Jewish literature at the time. Pronouncements stories, miracle stories, sayings material, parables, and legends all have antecedents in the Jewish and/or Hellenistic world.

Not surprisingly, sayings material, whether in the form of isolated sayings, clusters of sayings, or parables, show the least influence of the church. By their very nature, pronouncement stories, miracle stories, and legends have substantial narrative material, which necessary reflects the *Sitz im Leben* of the church. Even in those instances in which a pronouncement story enshrines an authentic saying of Jesus, the narrative framework probably originated as an element in the church's preaching.

In the previous chapter, we saw ways in which Christian writers were influenced by Hebrew scriptures in the creation of the story of Jesus' crucifixion. The practice of building stories of contemporary events around passages of the Hebrew scriptures was a Christian method of interpretation similar to the manner in which contemporary Jewish Essenes living at Qumran interpreted the scriptures in relation to events that were unfolding around the sect and its founder in their own time.

We have observed in this chapter a similar method of appropriating the Hebrew scriptures in the creation of the birth narratives in Matthew, the story of Jesus' baptism, miracles stories involving Jesus, etc.[14] In fact, the birth narrative in the Gospel of Matthew appears in its literary form to be a Christian *midrash*,[15] building as it does on

---

firstborn son.'" I said to you, "Let my son go that he may worship me."

14. Although we did not look at the story of the transfiguration of Jesus (Mark 9:2–8) in this chapter, this legend or story about Jesus also makes use of material found in the Hebrew scriptures.

15. Midrash is a process of interpretation by which rabbis created stories, frequently with legendary

texts in the Hebrew scriptures. Some may think that this understanding of Matthew's birth narrative as a legend dismisses the value of the text. In fact, the birth narratives of Matthew and Luke are creative pieces of interpretation, whether or not they have any historical value.

An important consequence of form criticism is that it illustrates not only the kinds of literary forms that Christian tradition assumed in both the oral and the written tradition, but it illustrates once again the creative role of the community in molding that tradition. We have seen that the church played a major role not only in preserving and shaping traditions about Jesus, but that it played a major role in creating tradition about Jesus. For example, the framework of the pronouncements stories reflects the creative role of the church; the tendency of tradition to heighten the role of a popular hero often results in the generation of miracle stories; and that same tendency lead to the development of popular legends surrounding Jesus' birth, baptism, transfiguration, and resurrection.

The role of the Hebrew scriptures in the development of oral and written tradition in Christian communities raises serious questions about the historical value of many, perhaps most of the stories about Jesus of Nazareth. We saw in the previous chapter how the role of the Hebrew scriptures molded not only the form but also the content of the story of the crucifixion of Jesus in the passion narrative. That same creative element was especially operative in the creation of miracle stories and legends and even in the narrative framework of pronouncement stories. Accordingly, many of the stories in the synoptic gospels have little to no historical value, although they obviously had important theological value to the early Christian communities which generated them.

In the course of this chapter we have seen once again how Christian tradition regarding the birth, ministry, death, and exaltation of Jesus of Nazareth reflect not only historic memory, but perhaps more importantly the church's searching diligently through the Hebrew scriptures to find passages or "proof-texts" that might impart meaning to a life that ended abruptly and apparently unexpectedly in a way that left Jesus' followers puzzled and disillusioned about the meaning of what had transpired.

We are so accustomed to thinking of the cross as a symbol of Christianity that we generally fail to recognize the shame and disgrace associated with Jesus' ignominious execution.[16] Imagine that instead of being crucified Jesus had been executed in an electric chair and that Christians today wore gold electric chairs rather than crosses around their necks, and you will then understand better the disappointment, disgrace,

---

parts although based on material from the Hebrew scriptures, in order to fill in missing pieces in the Torah. Midrash is literature that seeks to answer questions.

16. See in this regard Deut 21:22–23: "When someone is convicted of a crime punishable by death and is executed, and you hang him on a tree, his corpse must not remain all night upon the tree; you shall bury him that same day, for *anyone hung on a tree is under God's curse*. You must not defile the land that the LORD your God is giving you for possession" [italics mine].

and ignominy associated with Jesus' death in the minds of his earliest disciples.[17] It is no wonder that Jesus' followers searched through the Hebrew scriptures to find meaning in what otherwise seemed to be a meaningless event—no, rather a disgraceful event (cf. 1 Cor 1:23).

I have obviously not examined exhaustively all of the passages in the synoptic gospels that were formulated or informed "according to the scriptures." I have looked at a few decisive passages, and in so doing I have touched only the surface of the subject. The Hebrew scriptures informed the church's teaching and writings regarding virtually every stage in Jesus' birth and baptism, life and ministry, death and resurrection in synoptic tradition, and presumably also in the oral tradition and in the church's earliest written documents, which likely served as sources for the synoptic evangelists.

Many of those early documents were lost, probably for all time: early Christian sayings collections, collections of parables and pronouncement stories and miracle stories, early Christian catechisms, one or more versions of a passion narrative that may have been composed originally for the celebration of a church liturgy during the week leading up to the celebration of Jesus' crucifixion and resurrection.

There can be no question that the primary purpose of the gospels was *not* to record what we would consider objective history. There is nothing objective or detached about the gospels. They do not pretend to be history, as we understand that word; they are rather confessional compositions; they are proclamations of God's salvific work in the person of Jesus of Nazareth. The Gospel of Mark begins with the words: "The beginning of the good news of Jesus Christ." The word translated as "good news" is the Greek word *euangelion* or "gospel." For the earliest Christian communities the *gospel* was the *good news* that was preached first orally and then later written in books to proclaim that Jesus was the Messiah, the Son of God, the Lord. As the Gospel of John so appropriately states, the gospels were written that "you might believe that Jesus is the Messiah, the Son of God, and that through believing you might have life in his name" (John 20:31).

If Christian stories about the life and ministry of Jesus have been so colored by the beliefs of the early church and so colored by a Christian reading of the Hebrew scriptures, how then can we know anything about Jesus of Nazareth? It is to that difficult task that we will direct our attention in a subsequent chapter. But first we must look once again at the way in which the gospels were put together by examining the method of redaction criticism.

---

17. Many will be surprised to learn that the cross was not a prevalent symbol of Christianity during the church's first two centuries. Rather fish, anchor, and shepherd imagery was dominant in earliest Christianity. See Graydon F. Snyder, *Ante Pacem: Archaeological Evidence of Church Life Before Constantine* (Macon, GA: Mercer University Press, 1985).

CHAPTER 7

REDACTION CRITICISM

WHAT IS REDACTION CRITICISM?

REDACTION CRITICISM IS THE discipline that studies the contribution of the author, editor, or redactor who, using both oral and written sources, composed literary works available to us in the various books of the New Testament, primarily in the synoptic gospels and, to some extent, in the Acts of the Apostles. The discipline attempts to discover the theological motivation of an author or editor in collecting, organizing, and editing traditional material, and in creating new writings for early Christian communities.

As we saw in the previous chapter, form criticism emerged in Germany in the period after the First World War with the work of Martin Dibelius and Rudolf Bultmann and spread to the English-speaking world through the work of Vincent Taylor and the translation of Dibelius's and Bultmann's seminal works into English. Redaction criticism emerged from the circle of form criticism in Germany in the period after the Second World War with the gospel commentaries of Willi Marxsen,[1] Hans Conzelmann,[2] and Günther Bornkamm.[3]

Whereas form criticism concentrates on pre-existing oral tradition that served as the building blocks of the gospels of Matthew, Mark, and Luke, redaction criticism focuses on the ways in which the individual authors made use of oral and written traditions which they inherited and then reshaped into their own literary compositions. Redaction criticism focuses on the fact that the evangelists were not so much authors as they were editors or redactors of earlier oral and written material.[4]

One way to look at the authors of the gospels of Matthew and Luke as redactors is to study the ways in which they changed their Markan source when they incorporated material from Mark into their own gospels. It is relatively easy to assess a gospel's

---

1. Marxsen, *Der Evangelist Markus*.
2. Conzelmann, *Die Mitte der Zeit*.
3. Bornkamm, Gerhard Barth, and Heinz Joachim Held, *Überlieferung und Auslegung im Matthäus-evangelium*.
4. Haenchen (*Der Weg Jesu*, 24) proposed the term *Kompositionsgeschichte* (composition criticism, or composition history) for the discipline in lieu of *Redakionsgeschichte* (redaction criticism, or redaction history). I frankly prefer "composition criticism" as being a more accurate term to describe the discipline, but "redaction criticism" has now won universal favor among New Testament scholars.

editorial and theological emphasis or bias when you can analyze the way in which that author or redactor has edited an existing written source.

In the charts below we can see how redaction criticism produces important information about Matthew and Luke as editors or redactors of the Gospel of Mark. Words that are found in both Matthew and Mark are underlined, and words that are found in both Mark and Luke are printed in italics.

Assuming that the author of the Gospel of Matthew used Mark as his source, material in Matthew that is *not* underlined reflects ways in which Matthew edited his Markan source. It is equally important to observe that Matthew has omitted material found in his Markan source. In similar manner, Luke edited his Markan source and chose not to include certain details found in Mark, even as he added other material of his own.

The changes in Matthew and Luke are what initially interest redaction critics, because such modification can be easily measured. Some of the omissions may be for no reason other than tightening up what some scholars have described as Mark's diffuse style; some changes may be for the purpose of clarification; and some changes may reflect a conscious effort to address particular theological concerns of the evangelist. Obviously, little can be learned by looking at the editorial changes in just a few pericopes of a few of verses, but a great deal can and has been learned about the redaction process by applying this exercise to the synoptic gospels in their entirety.

EXAMPLES OF REDACTION CRITICISM

Let us look at examples of the ways in which Matthew and Luke used their Markan source. The first example is the story of Peter's confession that Jesus is the Christ.

PETER'S CONFESSION

The story of Peter's confession appears in all three of the synoptic gospels, but we will look separately at Luke's and Matthew's redaction of their Markan source. First Luke's redaction of Mark:

Mark 8:27–30	Luke 9:18–21
[27]*Jesus* went on with his *disciples* to the villages of Caesarea Philippi; and on the way *he asked* his disciples, "*Who do* people *say that I am?*" [28]And *they answered* him, "*John and Baptist;*	[18]Once when *Jesus* was praying alone, with only the *disciples* near him, *he asked* them, "*Who do* the crowds *say that I am?*" [19] *They answered*, "*John the Baptist;*

REDACTION CRITICISM

Mark 8:27–30	Luke 9:18–21
and *others, Elijah*; *and still others*, *one of the prophets.*"	but *others, Elijah*; *and still others*, that *one of the* ancient *prophets* has arisen."
²⁹*He asked them*, *"But who do you say that I am?"* *Peter answered* him, *"You are the Messiah."*	²⁰*He said to them*, *"But who do you say that I am?"* *Peter answered*, *"The Messiah* of God."
³⁰And *he sternly ordered them not to tell anyone* about him.	²¹*He sternly ordered* and commanded *them not to tell anyone*, ...

Form critics generally identify this pericope as a legend or a story about Jesus, although in this particular story there is focus on Peter as well as on Jesus. The core of this pericope is nearly identical in both Mark and Luke; the differences appear almost exclusively in the introductions to the dialogue between Jesus and his disciples. The italicized words in Luke indicate what he has drawn from Mark; the words that are not italicized are Luke's redactional element, his editorial modification of his Markan source. Luke reproduces 66% of Mark's words in the entire pericope, and 76% in the dialogue alone, if we exclude from consideration the introductory settings in both gospels.

Luke omits Mark's place reference to "the villages of Caesarea Philippi" and adds in its place a remark that "Jesus was praying alone," something Luke did earlier in the context of Jesus' Baptism (Luke 3:21: "and when Jesus had been baptized *and was praying*") and at the call of the disciples (Luke 6:12: "he [Jesus] went out to the mountain *to pray*"), perhaps implying that on important occasions Luke wanted to show that Jesus prepared himself by praying. This subtle addition is evidently an important element of Luke's redaction of his Markan source, both in this passage and elsewhere. Such observations enable scholars to identify editorial or redactional characteristics of the gospels.

Matthew's redaction of the Markan source is much more significant:

Mark 8:27–30	Matt 16:13–20
²⁷<u>Jesus</u> went on with his disciples to <u>the</u> villages <u>of Caesarea Philippi</u>; and on the way <u>he asked his disciples,</u> "<u>Who do people say that</u> I am?" ²⁸<u>And they</u> answered him,	¹³Now when <u>Jesus</u> came into <u>the</u> district <u>of Caesarea Philippi,</u> <u>he asked his disciples,</u> "<u>Who do people say that</u> the Son of Man is?" ¹⁴<u>And they</u> said,

Mark 8:27–30	Matt 16:13–20
"<u>John and Baptist</u>; and <u>others, Elijah</u>; <u>and still others,</u> <u>one of the prophets</u>." ²⁹<u>He</u> asked <u>them</u>, "<u>But who do you say that I am?</u>" <u>Peter answered</u> him, "<u>You are the Messiah</u>."	"Some say <u>John the Baptist</u>; but <u>others, Elijah</u>; <u>and still others,</u> Jeremiah or <u>one of the prophets</u>." ¹⁵<u>He</u> said to <u>them</u>, "<u>But who do you say that I am?</u>" ¹⁶Simon <u>Peter answered</u>, "<u>You are the Messiah</u> the Son of the living God." ¹⁷And Jesus answered him, "Blessed are you, Simon son of Jonah! For flesh and blood have not revealed this to you, but my Father in heaven. ¹⁸And I tell you, you are Peter, and on this rock I will build my church, and the gates of Hades will not prevail against it. ¹⁹I will give you the keys of the kingdom of heaven, and whatever you bind on earth will be bound in heaven, and whatever you lose on earth will be loosed in heaven
³⁰And <u>he sternly ordered</u> them <u>not to tell anyone</u> about him.	²⁰Then <u>he sternly ordered</u> the disciples <u>not to tell anyone</u> that he was the Messiah.

In the verses in which Matthew is dependent on Mark, there is very little deviation from the Markan source. Matt 19:13 has "the Son of Man is" instead of "I am" in Mark 8:27, a slight Christological upgrade on Matthew's part. Moreover, Matt 16:16 adds the heightened Christological title "the Son of the living God" to "You are the Messiah" in Mark 8:29, a major Christological upgrade by Matthew. In reply to Peter's acknowledgment that Jesus is the Messiah, Jesus says in return in the Gospel of Matthew "You are Peter (Greek Πέτρος, *petros*; Aramaic *kepha*), and on this rock (Greek πέτρα, *petra*; Aramaic *kepha*) I will build my church" (Matt 16:18). In fact, the major difference between the two gospels in this pericope is that Matthew opens up Mark 8:29 from 8:30 to insert Jesus' reply to Peter once Peter has acknowledged Jesus as the Messiah (Matt 16:17–19).

In addition to the heightened Christology of the Matthean version of the story, the pericope in Matthew is as much or even more a legend about Peter than it is about Jesus, focusing, as it does, on Peter's special role in the founding of the early church. The phrases "my Father in heaven" (Matt 16:17) and "the kingdom of heaven" (Matt 16:19) and the use of the word "church" (Matt 16:18) are especially characteristic of the Gospel of Matthew, suggesting Matthean authorship of these verses:

"Father in heaven" appears elsewhere in Matt 5:16, 45, 48; 6:1, 9; 7:11, 21; 10:32, 33; 12:50; 18:10, 14, 19; 23:9;

"the kingdom of heaven"[5] appears in Matt 3:2; 4:17; 5:3, 10, 19 (2x), 20; 7:21; 8:11; 10:7; 11:11, 12; 13:11, 24, 31, 33, 44, 45, 47, 52; 16:19; 18:1, 3, 4, 23; 19:12, 14, 23; 20:1; 22:2; 23:13; 25:1; and

the word "church" appears in the four gospels only in the Gospel of Matthew, in this passage and again twice in Matt 18:17, which, like this passage, also refers to the binding and loosing of sin (18:18).

There is some question about the meaning of the "rock" on which the church was established (Matt 16:18). Was the rock Peter himself, or was it Peter's confession that Jesus was the Messiah? Probably the latter. It is clear from both Acts and from Paul's letters that Peter had no such unchallenged status in the early church:

Acts 11:2–18 holds Peter accountable for preaching to the Gentiles in Caesarea upon his return to Jerusalem.

In Gal 2:9, Paul refers to Peter, James, and John as "acknowledged pillars" of the Jerusalem church, but it is clear that there is sarcasm in Paul's words and that there was a question, if not an outright conflict, over the issue of authority between Paul and the leaders of the Jerusalem church.

In Gal 2:11, Paul says that he opposed Peter to his face in Antioch.

It is rather Peter's confession of Jesus as Messiah that serves as the foundation on which the church was built. Peter was apparently the first to make that claim—not during Jesus' ministry, but after Jesus' death (Acts 2:36–38; cf. Rom 1:1–4). That is probably the meaning of 1 Cor 15:3: that Jesus appeared first to Cephas, then to the twelve. That initial appearance to Peter may be the basis of the belief that Jesus was

---

5. Matthew's phrase "kingdom of heaven" is rendered in other books of the New Testament as "kingdom of God." Although Matthew uses the phrase "kingdom of God" five times in Matthew 6:33; 12:28; 19:24; 21:31, 43, he alone of all the books of the New Testament uses (thirty-two times) the phrase "kingdom of heaven," a phrase which clearly reflects Matthew's redactionary tendency. The change to "kingdom of heaven" is generally understood as a Judaizing tendency on Matthew's part, a reflection of his reverence for and avoidance of the name of God. See Luke 15:18: Father, I have sinned against heaven and before you.

Messiah, although in contradiction to 1 Cor 15, Matt 28:9 reports that, following his death and burial, Jesus appeared first to Mary Magdalene and the other Mary.

Although a study of this pericope in Matthew, Mark, and Luke disclosed several significant redactionary characteristics of the Gospel of Matthew, we found fewer redactionary characteristics of the Gospel of Luke. We can, however, probably discern a very important redactionary characteristic of the Gospel of Mark in this passage: namely, in the final verse, Mark 8:30: "And he sternly ordered them not to tell anyone about him," presumably meaning that following Peter's confession the disciples were ordered not to reveal to anyone that Jesus was the Messiah.

There are similar admonitions elsewhere in the Gospel of Mark, and always at the end of pericopes:

Mark 1:34:

And he cured many who were sick with various diseases, and cast out many demons; and he would not permit the demons to speak, because they knew him.

Mark 1:43–44:

After sternly warning him [the cleansed leper] he [Jesus] sent him away at once, saying to him, "See that you say nothing to anyone . . . ."

Mark 3:11–12:

Whenever the unclean spirits saw him, they fell down before him and shouted, "You are the Son of God!" But he sternly ordered them not to make him known.

Mark 5:43:

He strictly ordered them [the witnesses to the raising of Jairus's dead daughter] that no one should know this, and told them to give her something to eat.

Mark 7:36:

Then Jesus ordered them to tell no one [about the healing of the deaf man]; but the more he ordered them, the more zealously they proclaimed it.

Mark 9:9:

As they were coming down from the mountain [where Jesus had been transfigured], he ordered them [Peter, James, and John] to tell no one about what they had seen, until after the Son of Man had risen from the dead.

Mark 9:30–31:

They went on from there and passed through Galilee. He did not want anyone to know it; for he was teaching his disciples, saying to them, "The Son of Man is to be betrayed into human hands, and they will kill him, and three days after being killed, he will rise again."

REDACTION CRITICISM

These passages all reflect a theme common to the Gospel of Mark: what Wilhelm Wrede called "The Messianic Secret."[6] Wrede regards the messianic secret as a redactionary element in the Gospel of Mark, attached as it is, almost as an afterthought to several pericopes to explain a perplexing dilemma familiar to Mark and to the early church—namely that Jesus never proclaimed his own messiahship during his lifetime but was regarded as Messiah after his death, but only after the disciples had come to believe that Jesus had been raised from the dead.

In the case of the Gospel of Mark, we have seen that the author of the gospel assumes that Jesus' messiahship was traceable to his baptism, but that Jesus kept his messiahship a secret for most of his ministry until Peter first recognized and announced it to Jesus and the other disciples. Following the discovery, Jesus introduced the disciples to the idea of a suffering and dying messiah, although he had already "sternly ordered them not to tell anyone about him" (Mark 8:30).

Wrede identifies the theological source of the messianic secret in the problematic contradiction between what the church remembered Jesus to have proclaimed during his ministry and what the church came to believe about him following his death (and resurrection). According to Wrede, the author of the Gospel of Mark explained Jesus' lack of any explicit declaration about his messiahship during the course of his lifetime by suggesting that Jesus kept his messiahship a secret, even from his disciples for most of his ministry. Jesus admitted his messiahship to them shortly before his death but then urged them to keep it a secret until after his resurrection. In other words, the messianic secret was based not in the ministry of the historical Jesus but was rather an invention of the church, or more likely a redactional device of the author of the Gospel of Mark, designed to account for the dilemma of the memory of Jesus' non-messianic ministry.

The theme of the messianic secret explains why Jesus' messiahship was proclaimed by the church only after Jesus' death, because that is when Jesus' disciples first made the messianic claim about him. What is particularly important about regarding the messianic secret as a redactionary creation of the author of the Gospel of Mark is that this theory presents important evidence in support of the view that Jesus never represented himself as Messiah during his lifetime but that these redactional verses were tacked onto existing pericopes that Mark borrowed from his sources in order to accommodate the dilemma of how to explain Jesus' apparently non-messianic ministry.

Wrede's thesis gives new meaning to the following passages:

Mark 8:31:

> Then he [Jesus] began to teach them [the disciples] that the Son of Man must undergo great suffering, and be rejected by the elders, the chief priests, and the scribes, and be killed, and after three days rise again.

---

6. Wrede, *Das Messiasgeheimnis in den Evangelien*; English edition, *The Messianic Secret*.

Mark 9:30–32:

> They went on from there and passed through Galilee. He did not want anyone to know it; for he was teaching his disciples saying to them, "The Son of Man is to be betrayed into human hands, and they will kill him, and three days after being killed, he will rise again. But they did not understand what he was saying and were afraid to ask him.

Mark 10:32–34:

> They were on the road, going up to Jerusalem, and Jesus was walking ahead of them; they were amazed, and those who followed were afraid. He took the twelve aside and began to tell them what was to happen to him, saying, "See we are going up to Jerusalem, and the Son of Man will be handed over to the chief priests and scribes, and they will condemn him to death; then they will hand him over to the Gentiles; and they will mock him, and spit upon him, and flog him, and kill him; and after three days he will rise again.

Mark 9:9:

> As they were coming down the mountain [following Jesus' transfiguration], he [Jesus] ordered them [Peter, James, and John] to tell no one about what they had seen until after the Son of Man had risen from the dead.

The important function of these passages as redactionary elements in the Gospel of Mark is evident. These verses were added by the author of the Gospel of Mark and are similar to the amazement of the crowd following Jesus' healing, another redactionary feature that we identified in the previous chapter in our discussion of the miracle stories in the Gospel of Mark (see Mark 1:22, 27; 2:12; 5:20, 42; 6:2; 7:37; 11:18; 12:17).

So what significance does Wrede's theory have for understanding Matthew's redactional tendencies? Rudolf Bultmann regarded this story in Matt 16 as a misplaced Easter story, carried back by Mark into the period just before the triumphal entry into Jerusalem.[7] I find Bultmann's position unconvincing, although Bultmann's thesis supports the belief that the disciples claimed that Jesus was messiah only after his death.

However, Bultmann is right to the extent that Mark knew and retrojected the story of Peter's confession from the period after the resurrection to an earlier point in the plot, probably for both literary and theological reasons. The story of Peter's confession is best understood as a Markan story, the turning point in the gospel's drama, the beginning of the end of Jesus' messianic ministry. Moreover, Jesus' question to the disciples in Mark 8:29 ("But who do you say that I am?") is obviously a contrivance, a Markan literary device designed to elicit Peter's confession. Jesus' question makes little sense, except that it is a literary contrivance on the part of Mark to set the stage for Peter's confession that Jesus is the Messiah.[8]

---

7. Rudolf Bultmann, *The History of the Synoptic Tradition*, 258–59, 288–89.
8. Ibid., 257–58.

REDACTION CRITICISM

The story in Matthew may serve another purpose as well: namely, to rehabilitate the character and the intelligence of the disciples, who had denied or had not understood Jesus (cf. Matt 13:51; Matt 13:16 // Mark 4:13; Matt 13:23 // Mark 4:20; Matt 14:33 // Mark 6:52; Matt 16:12 // Mark 8:21).

THE REJECTION OF JESUS AT NAZARETH[9]

Mark 6:1–6a	Matt 13:54-58
¹He left that place and came to his hometown, and his disciples followed him.	⁵⁴He came to his hometown, and
²On the sabbath he began to teach in the synagogue, and many who heard him were astounded. They said,	began to teach the people in their synagogue, so that they were astounded and said,
"Where did this man get all this? What is this wisdom that has been given to him? What deeds of power are being done by his hands?	"Where did this man get this wisdom and these deeds of power?
³Is not this the carpenter, the son of Mary,⁹ and brother of James and Joses and Judas and Simon, and are not his sisters here with us?"	⁵⁵Is not this the carpenter's son? Is not his mother called Mary? And are not his brothers James and Joseph and Simon and Judas? ⁵⁶And are not his sisters with us? Where then did this man get all this?
And they took offense at him. ⁴Then Jesus said to them, "Prophets are not without honor, except in their hometown, and among their own kin, and in their own house."	⁵⁷And they took offense at him. But Jesus said to them, "Prophets are not without honor except in their own country and in their own house.
⁵And he could do no deed of power there, except that he laid his hands on a few sick people and cured them. ⁶And he was amazed at their unbelief.	⁵⁸And he did not do many deeds of power there, because of their unbelief.

---

9. As we saw in the chapter on textual criticism, the original text of Mark 6:3a probably read "Is not this the son of the carpenter and of Mary?"

Matthew reproduces the substance of Mark, although he abbreviates Mark's diffuse style. Mark's 147 words are reduced by Matthew to 112. Otherwise, the only significant editorial change comes in the final two verses of Mark, which Matthew obviously found problematic: "he [Jesus] *could do no* deed of power there....," which Matthew softened to read: "And he [Jesus] *did not d*o many deeds of power there...." The thought that Jesus was unable to perform miracles apparently posed theological problems to the author of the Gospel of Matthew, hence his redactional modification of Mark's text.

The situation is quite different with regard to the way in which the author of the Gospel of Luke edited his Markan source:

Mark 6:1–6a	Luke 4:16–30
¹*He* left that place and *came to* his hometown, and his disciples followed him. ²On the sabbath he began to teach in *the synagogue,*	¹⁶When *he came to* Nazareth where he had been brought up, he went to *the synagogue on the sabbath* day, as was his custom. He stood up to read, ¹⁷and the scroll of the prophet Isaiah was given to him. He unrolled the scroll and found the place where it was written: ¹⁸"The Spirit of the Lord is upon me, because he has anointed me to bring good news to the poor. He has sent me to proclaim release to the captives and recovery of sight to the blind, to let the oppressed go free, ¹⁹to proclaim the year of the Lord's favor." ²⁰And he rolled up the scroll, gave it back to the attendant, and sat down. The eyes of all in the synagogue were fixed on him. ²¹Then he began to say to them, "Today this scripture has been fulfilled in your hearing."
and many who heard him *were* astounded.	²²All spoke well of him *and were* amazed at the gracious words

Mark 6:1–6a	Luke 4:16–30
	that came from his mouth.
They said,	*They said,*
"Where did this man get all this?	
What is this wisdom	
that has been given to him?	
What deeds of power are being	
done by his hands!	
³*Is not this* the carpenter,	"*Is not this* Joseph's son?"
the son of Mary,ᵃ	
and brother of James and Joses	
and Judas and Simon,	
and are not his sisters here with us?"	
And they took offense at him.	
	²³He said to them,
	"Doubtless you will quote to me
	this proverb, 'Doctor, cure yourself!'
	And you will say, 'Do here also in
	your hometown the things that we
	have heard you did at Capernaum.'"
⁴Then Jesus *said* to them,	²⁴And he *said,*
	"Truly I tell you,
"*Prophet*s are *no*t without honor,	*no prophet* is accepted
except *in* their *hometown,*	*in* the prophet's *hometown.*
and among their own kin,	
and in their own house."	
⁵And he could do no deed of power	
there, except that he laid his hands	
on a few sick people and cured them.	
⁶And he was amazed at their unbelief.	
	²⁵But the truth is there were
	many widows in Israel
	in the time of Elijah,
	when the heaven was shut up
	three years and six months,
	and there was a severe famine
	over all the land;
	²⁶yet Elijah was sent to none of them
	except to the widow at Zarephath

Mark 6:1–6a	Luke 4:16–30
	in Sidon. ²⁷There were also many lepers in Israel in the time of the prophet Elisha, and none of them was cleansed except Naaman the Syrian." ²⁸When they heard this, all in the synagogue were filled with rage. ²⁹They got up, drove him out of the town, and led him to the brow of the hill on which their town was built, so that they might hurl him off the cliff. ³⁰But he passed through the midst of them and went on his way.

a. See footnote 9.

Although the passage in Luke 4:16–30 is very different from the material in Mark 6:1–6a, there can be no doubt that Luke was reworking Mark's pericope. The story appears in Mark after Jesus has already begun his Galilean ministry in and around Capernaum (Mark 1:14–5:43) and after he has called his twelve disciples (Mark 1:16–20; 2:13–14; 3:13–19). Luke, on the other hand, relocates the story at the beginning of Jesus' Galilean ministry, immediately following the story of Jesus' baptism by John (Luke 3:1–22) and his temptation by the devil (Luke 4:1–13).

Luke reports in very general terms an early Galilean ministry (Luke 4:14–15)[10] and alludes to a prior ministry in Capernaum (Luke 4:23), although details of the ministry in Capernaum begin in Luke only after the incident in the synagogue in Nazareth (Luke 4:31–42), and Luke's account of Jesus' call of his first apostles does not appear until much later (Luke 5:1–11). Despite these very important differences, the body of the material in Mark and Luke is identical: the visit to the synagogue in Nazareth (Mark 6:1–2a // Luke 4:16); the reaction to Jesus' ministry, initially positive (Mark 6:2b // Luke 4:22a) and subsequently negative (Mark 6:3d // Luke 4:28–30); mention of Jesus' family (Mark 6:3 // Luke 4:22b); the proverb about a prophet who is without honor and unwelcome in his hometown (Mark 6:4 // Luke 4:24); and Jesus' inability to perform deeds of power in Nazareth (Mark 6:5 // by implication in Luke 4:25–30).

---

10. Luke 4:14–15: Then Jesus, filled with the power of the Spirit, returned to Galilee, and a report about him spread through all the surrounding country. He began to teach in their synagogues and was praised by everyone.

Luke produces the substance of his Markan source, although with considerable editing. For example, Luke omits entirely the problematic verse Mark 6:5, which Matthew amended to eliminate Mark's offending words that Jesus "could do no deed of power" in Nazareth. Luke also edited his Markan source by adding in 4:16 the phrase "as was his custom," when mentioning Jesus' appearance in the synagogue on the sabbath day. This phrase is very similar to what Luke repeatedly says about the apostles' and other Christians' custom of visiting the Jerusalem temple during the earliest period of the church (Acts 2:46; 3:1; 4:1; 5:12, 42; 21:26). The addition of this phrase in Luke and the verses cited in Acts obviously reflect similar redactional characteristics of their common author.

Most notably, however, although Luke follows Mark's text as his primary source (Luke 4:16, 22, 24), he introduces three additional elements into the story (Luke 4:17–21, 23, 25–30), and it is these additional verses that most especially reflect Luke's redactional interests.

1. Luke 4:17–21 appears to come from a *testimonia* source. In Luke, Jesus' reading from the Hebrew scriptures comes from a conflation of the Septuagint translation of Isa 61:1abc; 58:6d; and 61:2a with minor variances. The fact that Luke's citation is composed of several verses of Isaiah that are both out of order and that have minor omissions and variances suggests that Luke drew this material not directly from the Septuagint but rather from a source, a *testimonia* document, that had already collected these verses together as a proof-text concerning the coming of Jesus of Nazareth.

What is remarkable about these verses is that it is Jesus himself who quotes this collection of proof-texts, a detail that Luke obviously wants the reader to understand Christologically. In Luke 4:21, it is Jesus himself who indicates that these verses in Isaiah refer to him. Setting these verses within the context of Jesus' earliest preaching at the synagogue in Nazareth indicates that Luke wants his readers to understand Jesus' entire subsequent ministry in light of this initial self-proclamation.

The following chart illustrates how Luke rearranged the earliest chapters of his Markan source:

Luke	Mark	
1:1–4	1:1	Superscription
1:5–2:52	—	Infancy Stories of John the Baptist and Jesus
3:1–6	1:2–6	Introduction of John the Baptist
3:7–14	—	Preaching of John to the Crowds
3:15–18	1:7–8	Proclamation of John the Baptist
3:19–20	6:17–18	Herod's arrest of John the Baptist
3:21–22	1:9–11	The baptism of Jesus

Luke	Mark	
3:23–38	—	The ancestry of Jesus
4:1–13	1:12–13	The temptation of Jesus
4:14–15	1:14–15	Beginning of the Galilean Ministry
4:16–30	6:1–6	The Rejection of Jesus at Nazareth

Moreover, the use of "Spirit" in verse 18 is also characteristically Lukan. From the beginning of his gospel, Luke shows that the Spirit of prophecy had reappeared in Israel after being inactive for many centuries. Even before his birth, John the Baptist was "filled with the Holy Spirit" (Luke 1:15); an angel announced to Mary that the Holy Spirit would come upon her at Jesus' conception (Luke 1:35); John's parents, Elizabeth and Zechariah, were both "filled with the Holy Spirit" (Luke 1:41, 67); "the Holy Spirit rested on" Simeon, a holy man, who was, therefore, able to recognize Jesus as Messiah at his circumcision (Luke 2:25–35); "the word of God came to John . . . in the wilderness" (Luke 3:2); John's baptism of repentance was a preparation for Jesus' baptism "with the Holy Spirit and fire" (Luke 3:16). And in Acts, Luke reports that Jesus gave "instructions through the Holy Spirit to the apostles whom he had chosen" (Acts 1:2), and that it was at Pentecost that Jesus' apostles were "baptized with the Holy Spirit" (Acts 1:5). Consistent with these passages in Luke-Acts, in Luke 4:18, quoting the book of Isaiah, Jesus says, "The Spirit of the Lord is upon me, because he has anointed me to bring the good news to the poor." Luke's redactional predisposition is evident in these verses.

Further word study has sometime led scholars to conclude that the author of the Gospel of Luke shows special concern for the poor. The beatitude in Luke 6:20 is especially significant in this regard: "Blessed are you who are poor, for yours is the kingdom of God," rendered in the parallel passage in Matt 5:3 as "Blessed are the *poor in spirit*, for theirs is the kingdom of Heaven." Luke focuses on the poor as a component of Jesus' mission in Luke 4:18 (the passage under consideration in this paragraph) and again in 7:22; see also Luke 14:13, 21; 16:20, 22; 18:22; 19:8; 21:2–3. A simple word count shows that Matthew uses the word "poor" (Greek πτωχός, *ptōxŏs*) 5 times; Mark, 5 times; John, 4 times; and Luke, 10 times (Luke 4:18; 6:20; 7:22; 14:13, 21; 16:20, 22; 18:22; 19:8; 21:3). Of the 10 occurrences in Luke, only two are derived from Mark (Luke 18:22 // Mark 10:21; Luke 21:3 // Mark 12:43); two come from the sayings source Q (Luke 6:20 // Mattt 5:3; Luke 7:22 // Matthew 11:5); and six are unique to Luke (Luke 4:18; 14:13; 14:21; 16:20, 22; 19:8). The evidence suggests that concern with the poor was evident in both Mark and Q, as well as in Luke's special material. This multiple attestation from three independent sources (Mark, Q, and L) suggests that this concern for the poor was probably an important component of Jesus' own teaching. Luke's apparent special concern with the poor is somewhat compromised by the fact that the word *ptōxŏs* appears nowhere in the Acts of the Apostles, although there is concern in the early chapters of Acts with those having need (Acts 2:45; 4:35).

2. Luke 4:23 contains the proverb "Doctor, cure yourself," a proverb quoted in various forms in both Greek and Jewish literature. Although placed by Luke on Jesus' lips, Jesus implies that these words reflect the cynical thinking of the people of Nazareth, who were apparently not among his earliest followers in contrast to his early success in Galilee, alluded to in the summary statement in Luke 4:14–15, but detailed subsequent to this pericope in Luke 4:31–5:39.[11]

3. Luke 4:25–30 provides Jesus the occasion to remind the people of Nazareth of Elijah and Elisha, prophets who previously turned their backs on disbelieving Israelites and performed miracles outside Israel in Sidon and Syria respectively. Verses 26 and 27 reflect God's earlier rejection of the Jews and the healing of Gentiles, foreshadowing Luke's interest in the theme of God's rejection of the Jews and subsequent blessing of the mission to the Gentiles. This theme of the Jews first and then the Gentiles is a common Lukan motif both in Luke (2:32; 21:24; 22:25) and in Acts (9:15; 10:45; 11:1, 18; 13:46–48; 15:14; 18:6; 28:28).

Whether these three additions to the Lukan pericope were available to the evangelist from one or more sources or were additions of Luke's own creation, we can never know with certainty. But we do know that these three insertions into the Markan framework represent modifications characteristic of redactionary interests of the author of Luke-Acts.

CONCLUSIONS

Redaction criticism goes a step beyond form criticism by examining the ways in which the various units of oral and written tradition that emerged in early Christianity assumed different configurations and forms in the various gospels, especially in the synoptic gospels, Matthew, Mark, and Luke.

In this chapter, we have identified specific redactional tendencies in the gospels of Matthew and Luke by comparing their versions of two pericopes with the parallel passages in their Markan source. Even with the limited number of passages examined in this chapter, we have been able to see how the methodology of redaction criticism works and how it yields important results for understanding the various steps involved in the composition of the gospels.

In the two passages we examined, we were able to detect some specific redactional characteristics of the gospels of Matthew and Luke:

---

11. The metaphors of the physician and the prophet, which appear in Luke 4:23 and 4:24, also appear side by side in the *Gos Thos* 31 (Jesus said, "No prophet is welcome on his home turf; doctors don't cure those who know them."). Either this similarity between Luke and *Thomas* is a coincidence, and these passages reflect parallel traditions, or they show that the author of the *Gospel of Thomas* was dependent on the synoptic gospels, especially in this instance on the Gospel of Luke.

Matthew

In the parallel passages concerning The Rejection of Jesus at Nazareth, we observed that Matthew abbreviated Mark's diffuse style and softened Mark's theologically problematic words "he [Jesus] could do no deed of power there." Matthew's editing of Mark's offensive words is not only evidence that Matthew copied from Mark and not vice versa, but it illustrates important tendencies in Matthew: the tendency to abbreviate Mark, the tendency to improve Mark's literary style, and the tendency to edit theologically problematic passages.

In the story of Peter's Confession, we noted that Matthew elevated Mark's Christology by adding the phrase that Jesus was "the Son of the living God." Matthew also added verses 16:17–19 concerning Jesus' naming Peter as the "rock" and establishing the church during his lifetime, presumably on the foundation of Peter's confession that Jesus was the Messiah. We also observed in these added verses some specifically Matthean vocabulary: "my father in heaven," "the kingdom of heaven," and "church." These Semitisms suggest that these additional verses in Matthew originated in an Aramaic-speaking community.

Key words and phrases in Matthew's redactionary material reveal a propensity for language that is more Jewish than Hellenistic, presumably disclosing something about the author of the gospel and/or something about his audience. As a result of such perceived redactional interests, most scholars believe that the Gospel of Matthew was written by a Jewish Christian for a Jewish Christian community. (See also, p. 164, n. 5)

We know from Paul and, to some extent, from Acts that Peter was a leader of the Jerusalem church (Gal 1:18: 2:1–10; Acts 8:14–25; 11:1–18), hence, the theme of the primacy of Peter in this passage likely had its roots within the Jerusalem Christian community. Following the destruction of Jerusalem by the Romans in 70 CE, the Christian community fled to Pella. We know also that there was an important Jewish Christian community in Antioch of Syria, where the author of the Gospel of Matthew may have been living at the time he composed his gospel.

Luke

In the examination of the parallel passages concerning Peter's Confession, we noted that on important occasions Luke apparently wanted to show that Jesus prepared himself by praying.

Luke consciously moved the story of The Rejection of Jesus at Nazareth to the very beginning of Jesus' ministry at the synagogue at Nazareth, presumably to set the stage for everything that follows in his gospel. At the outset of his ministry, immediately following his baptism by John, by citing passages from the prophet Isaiah, Jesus' proclaims his identity as the one anointed by the Spirit of God. We also observed Luke's characteristic use of "Spirit" in Luke-Acts and his special concern for the "poor," as well as his statement that it was Jesus' custom to pray in the synagogue on the sabbath. Like Matthew, Luke found offensive the words in Mark 6:5 that Jesus "could do no deed of power" in Nazareth and completely eliminated this verse, which Matthew retained but softened.

Perhaps most important, Luke emphasized in this passage God's rejection of the Jews and his blessing of the mission to the Gentiles, presumably disclosing to us something about the author of the gospel and/or something about his audience. Based on his special interests and redactional tendencies, most scholars identify the author of the Gospel of Luke as a Gentile Christian writing for a Gentile Christian community.

Even from our limited study of two pericopes, it is evident that the authors of the synoptic gospels were not so much authors as they were collectors and editors of earlier existing traditions, which they assembled and reworked to suit their own theological perspectives and the needs of the communities for which each wrote. Their redactional processes were obviously very sophisticated. The authors not only improved the style of their written sources, but they made changes that suited their individual efforts to propagate Christianity, weaving together in a very intricate and skillful manner multiple sources.

Although we have examined only a few passages, the value of redaction criticism is eminently clear. To draw more far-reaching conclusions, it would be necessary to look at every passage in every gospel in order to understand fully the method and full benefits of redaction criticism.

Going beyond comparing Matthew and Luke with their Markan source in order to understand their redactional tendencies, there is the concurrent challenge to use the results of that comparison to study Q, the material common to Matthew and Luke but not found in Mark. Such a study can presumably assist in reconstructing that presumed hypothetical source. More specifically, if the results of redaction criticism are consistent, there should be some correlation between the way in which Matthew and Luke edited Mark and the way in which they edited their common source Q and employed their individual sources, M and L, a point illustrated in my examination of "the poor" in Luke.

Source criticism and redaction criticism have demonstrated that the evangelists used multiple sources: Matthew used Mark, Q, and M; and Luke used Mark, Q, and L. Although it may be possible to reconstruct a version of the hypothetical source Q (and this task has, indeed, been attempted more than once), it is obviously much more complicated to make sense of M and L, which are probably little more than symbols for material that is unique to Matthew and Luke respectively. M and L may each be multiple sources and may also include some original literary creations of the final redactors of the gospels of Matthew and Luke respectively.

THE NEW TESTAMENT
Mark

We have also observed that the tools of redaction criticism can be and have been applied successfully to the Gospel of Mark, even though it is more difficult to reconstruct the sources of Mark than it is to identify and construct the sources of Matthew and Luke. In the case of Mark, we have already established the likelihood that the Passion Narrative was at one time a separate free-standing written document that may have originated within the liturgy of the church. Mark may also have had access to a written collection of *testimonia*, similar to what we have found at Qumran, passages from the Hebrew scriptures that Christian scribes collected into one place to serve as proof texts for events in the life and ministry of Jesus.

Scholars have identified some redactional characteristics of the Gospel of Mark. As I mentioned in an earlier chapter, Mark apparently used a number of written sources: a passion narrative, a *testimonia* source, a collection of pronouncement stories, miracle stories, parables, sayings clusters, and legends. We have, however, observed in this chapter some specific redactional characteristics of Mark.

Putting the pieces of his gospel together, the author of the Gospel of Mark appears to have introduced the theme of the Messianic Secret to explain why Jesus' ministry was non-messianic and why his messiahship was disclosed first to Peter, but only *after* Jesus' death. We also observed that just as he added a sentence to existing pericopes in order to introduce the theme of the Messianic Secret, Mark also added a sentence to many of the miracle stories to express the amazement of the crowd at Jesus' works. These two themes, the amazement of the crowd and the Messianic Secret, are very nearly inconsistent and reflect the kinds of theological challenges that the early church generally and the author of the author of the Gospel of Mark specifically faced in affording coherence to existing tradition that he shaped into his gospel.

The process of working methodically through specific passages in the gospels gives substantial credence and support to the method of redaction criticism. The application of the principles yields detailed results that can be tested elsewhere in the gospels until an increasingly clearer picture of each of the synoptic gospels begins to emerge.

CHAPTER 8

JESUS OF NAZARETH: THE ESCHATOLOGICAL PROPHET

JESUS CHRIST STANDS AT the center of Christianity. I say "Jesus Christ" and not simply "Jesus," because it is not the man Jesus who occupies the central place in Christianity, but Jesus the Christ (Greek Χριστός, *Christos*, which translates the Hebrew word *messiah*, "the anointed" of God). Jesus Christ was not his name; it was and still is the Christian church's confessional statement that Jesus is the anointed one, the divine Son of God.

It is not within the scope of the historical method to consider whether Jesus was or is the Messiah of God. That is a confessional statement of Christians and lies beyond the purview of biblical scholarship. Scholars can however, attempt to uncover and understand the man Jesus of Nazareth, the Jesus of history. Scholars can even ask questions such as "What did Jesus teach?" and "Who did Jesus think he was?" Scholars may disagree on the answers to those questions, but they are legitimate questions for scholarly historical investigation.

It was councils of the church at Nicaea (in 325), at Constantinople (in 381), at Ephesus (in 431), and at Chalcedon (in 451) that definitively established the place of Jesus in orthodox Christian theology and that produced some of the most important statements of faith or creeds of Roman Catholic, Protestant, and Orthodox Christianity.

The decree of the Council of Chalcedon in 451 defines the person of Jesus as follows:

> We teach . . . one and the same Christ, Son, Lord, Only-begotten, known in two natures, without confusion, without change, without division, without separation.

For mainstream believing Christians, Jesus is the Messiah of Israel, the divine Son of God, he who is of the same substance as the Father. Jesus is wholly God and wholly man. He is the Deliverer, the Savior, and a host of other titles that establish his role as the ultimate mediator between God the Father (who is regarded in Christian orthodoxy as Jesus' Father) and humankind. Jesus is the incarnation of the divine Logos, the divine Word of God. He is Hagia Sophia (Holy Widsom).

Such confessional statements set the definitions of Christian *orthodoxy*, a word of Greek origin that means "the correct teaching" of the catholic or universal church, as opposed to *heresy*, a word of Greek origin that means "party, or schism, or faction," implying a false or wrong teaching, or another teaching (*heterodoxy*).

The quest for the Jesus of history, for the man Jesus, devoid of the myth and legendary overlay of two thousand years of Christian piety and theology, is riddled with serious challenges, as scholars have tried to develop a methodology that might assist in recovering the man Jesus of Nazareth, devoid of the theological language imposed by the earliest Christians and the multiple additional overlays of ecclesiastical councils and Christian theologians throughout two thousand years of history.

THE QUEST FOR THE HISTORICAL JESUS: THE SOURCES

As we noted in the introductory chapter, the rationalist Enlightenment began to shine on the study of the Bible with the ground-breaking work of Richard Simon in France in the seventeenth century and Johann David Michaelis in Germany in the eighteenth century. Serious historical inquiry into the life of Jesus began in the late eighteenth century with the work of Hermann Samuel Reimarus, who basked in the light of English deism.

It is, of course, essential to understand the methodological presuppositions of historical inquiry, whatever the subject matter. The issue of historical inquiry has been particularly challenging when the object of study has been Jesus of Nazareth. Nevertheless, nineteenth century Liberal Protestant scholarship, especially in Germany, began to suppress, often inconsistently, the supernatural element in the gospels and focused attention increasingly on the ethical component of Jesus' teaching.

David Friedrich Strauss's two-volume *Life of Jesus* (1835–1836) recognized that the gospels contain religious ideas expressed in the literary form of story (or myth), which appear to be history but are not. At about the same time, biblical scholars began to recognize significant differences between the Gospel of John and the synoptic gospels and undertook the challenge of finding a solution to the synoptic problem. The result of this effort established the priority of the Gospel of Mark and the existence of the hypothetical source Q, both of which served as literary sources for the gospels of Matthew and Luke.

The history of the early efforts to recover the Jesus of history is documented in Albert Schweitzer's monumental study *The Quest of the Historical Jesus*. It is worth quoting from Schweitzer's conclusion:

> The Jesus of Nazareth who came forward publicly as the Messiah, who preached the ethic of the Kingdom of God, who founded the Kingdom of Heaven on earth,

JESUS OF NAZARETH: THE ESCHATOLOGICAL PROPHET

and died to give His work its final consecration, never had any existence. He is a figure designed by rationalism, endowed with life by liberalism, and clothed by modern theology in an historical garb.[1]

Schweitzer observed that the failure of the nineteenth century quest for the historical Jesus resulted from the tendencies of historians of the period to attribute to a Jesus of their own making their own opinions and biases.

Schweitzer maintained that the one clear element in Jesus' teaching that had gone unnoticed by scholars who had tried to "modernize" Jesus was the eschatological character of Jesus' preaching. Following the initial insight of Johannes Weiss,[2] Schweitzer claimed that Jesus was a product of popular first century Jewish expectations about the end of history and the inauguration of a new age of God's rule. Schweitzer affirmed that, not surprisingly, Jesus was, first and foremost, a first century Jew and should be understood as such.

Schweitzer's exhaustive study effectively brought an end to the original quest for the historical Jesus, but not until the skepticism of nineteenth century scholarship led some scholars to question whether Jesus had actually ever lived. Biblical scholarship continued to improve in the twentieth century, and there is less of a tendency now, at least in unbiased scholarly circles, to project the thoughts and ideas of this generation onto the Jesus of the canonical gospels.

It has been clear for a long time that we know about Jesus only from the canonical gospels, but scholars have not always understood how to read these ancient sources. We have seen in the past few chapters that the church played a major role in preserving traditions about Jesus and that it significantly colored and altered stories about Jesus to serve the theological needs and biases of the church at every step along the way. Historical accuracy, as we understand that concept, was apparently never an important criterion in the writing of the canonical gospels.

We have already noted that in order to reconstruct the life of any person who lived long ago, historians have had to devise, develop, and refine criteria to sort out what we can and cannot know about that person in his or her historical context. In recent decades we have learned to ask more of the right questions, and we have also learned how better to answer these questions. Our challenges as biblical historians include:

1. the identification and examination of sources that come from a time as close as possible to events themselves—earlier sources are generally less likely to have been influenced by myth and legend;

2. the recovery and identification of multiple sources that were produced independently of one another in order to be able to compare the testimony of different and

---

1. Schweitzer, *Von Reimarus zu Wrede*, translated into English as *The Quest of the Historical Jesus*, 398.
2. Weiss, *Die Predigt Jesu*, translated into English as *The Proclamation of the Kingdom of God*.

independent witnesses;

3. a desire to discover an internal consistency within the multiple and diverse sources; and

4. the admission that our sources are not unbiased and that their authors had a vested interest in the subject matter at hand.[3]

JESUS OUTSIDE THE CANONICAL GOSPELS

When we turn to Jewish, Roman, and even Christian literature outside the four canonical gospels for assistance in recovering the historical Jesus, the results are disappointing. It generally surprises Christians to learn that we know almost nothing about Jesus from ancient non-Christian sources. Jesus apparently had little impact on his own generation or on the generations immediately following his death. His initial impact on Jewish and Roman societies was negligible.

In 112, Pliny the Younger, the Roman Governor of Bithynia-Pontus, provided the earliest surviving pagan reference to Jesus. Writing about eighty years after Jesus' death, Pliny mentioned that Jesus was worshiped by his followers as a God. In fact, Pliny takes little note of Jesus himself because he was actually not particularly interested in Jesus the man. He was, however, very concerned about what the Roman Emperor Trajan would have him do with Christians who were living in the province where Pliny governed.

A few years later (about 119), the Roman historian Suetonius wrote about riots that had occurred in Rome many decades earlier, during the reign of Emperor Claudius (41–54). Suetonius reported that these riots had been instigated by a certain "Chrestos." Did he mean "Christ"? That is not clear. And, if Suetonius meant Christ, then he was mistaken, because Jesus died about twenty years before the riots. Perhaps Suetonius was referring to Jesus' followers, the Christians, but that too is not clear.

At about the same time (115) the Roman historian Tacitus identified Christianity as a "superstition," meaning a religion that was not sanctioned by the Roman Empire. Tacitus reports that when Nero burned Rome, he blamed the Christians for having started the fire and used them as scapegoats. In spite of this morsel of misinformation, Tacitus provides us with the first piece of historical information about Jesus from the pen of a non-Christian writer: "Christus, from whom the Christians derive their name, was executed during the reign of Tiberius at the hands of one of our procurators, Pontius Pilate."

These three men, Pliny the Younger, Suetonius, and Tacitus, provide the only references to Jesus in pagan writings from the century immediately following Jesus' death. Their testimony is late, meager, unreliable, and basically useless, except for the

---

3. Of course, it is unrealistic to expect our ancient gospels to be objective and to have no vested interest in the subject matter, but that is the most serious challenge we face in using the canonical gospels as our only sources for a reconstruction of the life and ministry of Jesus.

fact that it confirms that there was a man named Jesus of Nazareth, who still had a following some eighty years after his death. We learn from them absolutely nothing about what Jesus did or taught, except that he was executed under Pontius Pilate. We do not even learn from them the reason for Jesus' execution.

The situation is not much different when we turn to contemporary Jewish literature. During the century following Jesus' death, there is only one Jewish writer who made any mention of Jesus. In book 18 of *The Antiquities of the Jews*, the Jewish historian Flavius Josephus wrote toward the end of the first century:

> At this time there appeared Jesus, a wise man, *if indeed one should call him a man.* For he was a doer of startling deeds, a teacher of people who receive the truth with pleasure. And he gained a following both among many Jews and among many of Greek origin. *He was the Messiah.* And when Pilate, because of an accusation made by the leading men among us, condemned him to the cross, those who loved him previously did not cease to do so. *For he appeared to them on the third day, living again, just as the divine prophets had spoken of these and countless other wonders about him.* And up until this very day the tribe of Christians, named after him, has not died out (Josephus, *Antiquities* 18.3.3).

Josephus remained a devout Jew throughout his life; he never converted to Christianity. We should, therefore, be suspicious about the authenticity of this testimony, especially with respect to the words printed above in italics. These words sound like the testimony of a Christian, not of a Jew. Once we recognize that it was Christians, and not Jews, who preserved Josephus's writings, it is evident that a Christian scribe probably added these confessional (italicized) words to Josephus's original text. Since these words could not have come from Josephus, they have little value as an independent source for a reconstruction of the life and ministry of Jesus, except perhaps for the words printed without italics, which may possibly be original.[4]

When we turn to Christian sources outside the canonical New Testament, the situation is no different. The non-canonical gospels are of uncertain value. The sayings *Gospel of Thomas* may afford some independent insight into Jesus' teaching, but that is by no means clear. Scholars disagree whether *Thomas* is early and independent of the canonical gospels or written by someone who knew and used the canonical gospels as sources. Some scholars have also argued for an early date for the *Gospel of Peter*, but that too is unclear. It is by no means obvious that any of the extra-canonical gospels are independent witnesses.

Much to the surprise of students of the New Testament, Paul, the earliest Christian writer, is also of little value in reconstructing the life and ministry of Jesus. We glean the following information from Paul: Jesus was "born of a woman" (Gal 4:4); he was "born under the law," meaning he was born a Jew (Gal 4:4). Jesus had "brothers" (1 Cor 9:5), one of whom was named "James" (Gal 1:19). He had "twelve" disciples (1 Cor 15:5). He instituted the Lord's Supper (1 Cor 11:23–25). Jesus "was betrayed"

---

4. That, indeed, is the thesis of Meier, *A Marginal Jew*, vol. 1, 61.

(1 Cor 11:23), although the Greek word in this verse may actually mean "was handed over." And Jesus was "crucified" (1 Cor 2:2). As for Jesus' teaching, Paul provides little detail: Christians should not get divorced (1 Cor 7:10–11) and should pay preachers of the gospel (1 Cor 9:14). Apart from these few passages, Paul tells us virtually nothing about the life, ministry, and teachings of Jesus of Nazareth. If Paul's letters were the only available source for writing a life of Jesus, we might be able to come up with one short paragraph, and even that single paragraph would be devoid of meaningful detail.[5]

Apart from the authors of the four canonical gospels (Matthew, Mark, Luke, and John), other New Testament authors tell us even less than Paul. In other words, we have no choice but to turn to the canonical gospels to begin the task of learning about the life, ministry, and teaching of Jesus. Yet, these gospels meet none of the criteria that we identified above as essential for a reconstruction of the life of any figure from antiquity:

1. The gospels do not come from a time close to the life and ministry of Jesus. Jesus died in about 30; the gospels were likely written between about 67 and 100, forty to seventy years, or two to three generations after Jesus' death.

2. The gospels were not produced independently. At least three of the gospels, Matthew, Mark, and Luke, show a clear literary relationship, with Matthew and Luke likely to have made direct use of Mark. In addition, the Gospel of John presents serious problems of its own and cannot serve as a credible source for historical reconstruction.

3. The four gospels show remarkable inconsistency in their portrayal of Jesus. There are serious differences between the Gospel of John and the synoptic gospels; there are serious differences among the synoptic gospels; and there are internal inconsistencies within individual gospels.

4. The gospels are *not* unbiased and make no claim to be so. The Gospel of John was clearest when the author wrote in 20:31: "These [things] are written that you may come to believe that Jesus is the Messiah, the Son of God, and that through believing you may have life in his name." The gospels are admittedly and unabashedly Christian propaganda. They were written by Christians for Christians to propagate and advance Christianity.

How can the canonical gospels, whose purpose was religious rather than historical, which were written to support and spread the faith, serve scholars as sources for a reconstruction of the life and ministry of Jesus? This is a very serious challenge, for without the canonical gospels we have nothing.

---

5. Cf. 2 Cor 5:16 (From now on, therefore, we regard no one from a human point of view; even though we once knew Christ from a human point of view, we know him no longer in that way).

JESUS OF NAZARETH: THE ESCHATOLOGICAL PROPHET

Scholars have tended in recent decades to embrace two very different pictures of Jesus: an interpretation of Jesus as an eschatological prophet and an interpretation of Jesus as a teacher of wisdom. We shall look in this chapter and the next at each of these views and examine, in particular, the methodologies that lead to such very different interpretations or portraits of Jesus of Nazareth

JESUS, THE ESCHATOLOGICAL PROPHET OF GOD'S IMMINENT RULE

THE QUEST FOR THE HISTORICAL JESUS: THE CRITERIA

We have already examined several scholarly methodologies used in New Testament studies: textual criticism, literary criticism, philological criticism, source criticism, form criticism, and redaction criticism. These tools provide the foundation for all historical investigation of the gospels. In addition, scholars have devised several criteria to assist in the effort to determine what in the gospels is historical and, therefore, what likely happened during the course of the life and ministry of Jesus. More specifically, what exactly did Jesus teach his followers? The following criteria have emerged as being especially useful in such an investigation.[6]

1. *The Criterion of Dissimilarity or Embarrassment*

A saying of Jesus or a tradition about Jesus in the gospels that does not reflect the claims of the early Christian church *about* Jesus has a greater likelihood of being historically accurate than a saying or tradition that mirrors the church's *kerygma* or reflects the theological bias of the church.[7] Such a dissimilar saying or tradition is less likely to have been fabricated by the church. Why, after all, would the church preserve a saying of Jesus or a story about Jesus that contradicts the church's preaching unless that saying or teaching was otherwise genuine? Although this criterion has its limits, it is probably the single most important criterion for assisting scholars in distinguishing between the teaching *of* Jesus and the early church's teaching *about* Jesus. Scholars call this the criterion of dissimilarity or the criterion of embarrassment.

---

6. These criteria are associated especially with the work of Norman Perrin, *Rediscovering the Teaching of Jesus*.

7. Previous chapters make it eminently clear why scholars are suspicious of material in the gospels that suits the theological interests of the early church. The criterion of dissimilarity or embarrassment is the most reasonable response to this dilemma.

THE NEW TESTAMENT

2. The Criterion of Multiple Attestation

For any testimony to be credible, it should be attested by two or more independent witnesses. In a court of law, the testimony of a single witness, without additional independent corroboration, is much less compelling than the testimony of multiple independent witnesses. In the case of the gospel tradition, we do, in fact, have multiple independent witnesses. I do not, of course, mean the gospels of Matthew, Mark, Luke, and John, because two of these gospels are not independent witnesses: the gospels of Matthew and Luke copied freely from the Gospel of Mark. I refer rather to the independent witnesses L, Q, Mark, and M, as illustrated in the chart below:

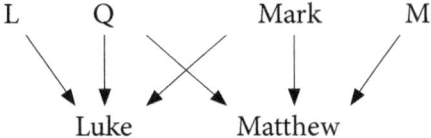

As we have already seen on many occasions in earlier chapters, this diagram illustrates that Luke and Matthew are not independent witnesses. They used Mark as a primary source. However, if a saying of Jesus is found in two or more of the four truly independent witnesses (the Gospel of Mark, and the three hypothetical sources used by Matthew and Luke, namely Q [the sayings source common to both Matthew and Luke], M [the special Matthean material], and L [the special Lukan material]), then there is a greater likelihood that the saying reaches back to the historical Jesus, or at least to the earliest stage in the development of oral tradition about Jesus. Scholars call this the criterion of multiple attestation or independent attestation.[8]

3. The Criterion of Contextual Credibility

Documents must be consistent with the historical, political, social, and religious contexts to which they belong. This means that any reconstruction of the life and ministry of Jesus must be consistent with and conform to the situation in first century Roman Palestine. Whatever else he may have been, Jesus was first and foremost a Galilean Jew. He conducted his ministry in Roman Palestine for a brief period around 30. Scholars must, therefore, make every possible effort to set Jesus within the context of his own time and place. Gospel tradition that places Jesus in a different context has considerably less claim to authenticity. Much of the subject matter of the Gospel of John fails to meet this important criterion, as it places Jesus in a much more Hellenistic than Jewish context. Scholars call this the criterion of contextual credibility.

---

8. In addition to Mark, Q, M, and L, the apocryphal *Gospel of Thomas* may also be an independent witness to tradition about Jesus. We will discuss this issue in more detail in the next chapter.

4. The Criterion of Semitism or Aramaism

Inasmuch as Jesus and his disciples presumably spoke Aramaic as their mother tongue, sayings tradition that reflects, exhibits, or displays Aramaic or Semitic qualities or tendencies has a greater claim to authenticity than material that makes sense only in Greek, the language of the Hellenistic church and of the written gospels. Although this criterion does not necessarily lead us directly to Jesus, it may take us back minimally to Jesus' earliest followers, most of whom also spoke Aramaic. Scholars call this the criterion of Semitism or Aramaism.

5. The Criterion of Coherence

A saying or a teaching of Jesus that is similar to material whose reliability has already been established by one or more of the other criteria listed above may be considered reliable because it is consistent with other presumably authentic material. Scholars call this the criterion of coherence.

In using these criteria, it is essential to admit that the historian of the New Testament can do no more than establish probabilities in reconstructing what Jesus may have said and what may actually have happened during the course of Jesus' life and ministry. Historical criticism is not an exact science with mathematical proofs and absolute certainty. It is impossible to confirm or validate the past with total confidence. Nevertheless, by employing these criteria, scholars have been able to capture a much clearer glimpse into the life, ministry, and teaching of Jesus of Nazareth.

THE QUEST FOR THE HISTORICAL JESUS: A NEW LOOK AT OLD TEXTS

I propose in this section to look at several passages in the synoptic gospels to show how the above-mentioned criteria for authenticity can be applied to gospel tradition in ways that afford meaningful insight into the teachings of the historical Jesus.

1. An Example from Mark

The first of the passages I propose to examine is the cluster of sayings of Jesus in Mark 8:34–9:1:[9]

---

9. This material in Mk. 8:34–9:1 is part of the triple tradition and was incorporated into Matt 16:24–28 and Luke 9:23–27. The saying in Mark 8:35 (= Matt 10:25 and Luke 9:24) is found also in the hypothetical source Q (= Matt 10:39 and Luke 17:33), which will be examined later in this chapter. The saying is also found in a slightly modified, but typically Johannine form in John 12:25, which will also be examined later in this chapter. In addition, the saying in Mark 8:38 (= Matt 10:27 and Luke 9:26) is also found in Q (= Matt 10:32–33 and Luke 12:8–9), which will also be examined later in this chapter.

> ⁸:³⁴He called the crowd with his disciples, and said to them, "If any want to become my followers, let them deny themselves and take up their cross and follow me. ³⁵For those who want to save their life will lose it, and those who lose their life for my sake, and for the sake of the gospel, will save it. ³⁶For what will it profit them to gain the whole world and forfeit their life? ³⁷Indeed, what can they give in return for their life? ³⁸Those who are ashamed of me and of my words in this adulterous and sinful generation, of them the Son of Man will also be ashamed when he comes in the glory of his Father with the holy angels." ⁹:¹And he said to them, "Truly I tell you, there are some standing here who will not taste death until they see the kingdom of God has come with power."

This passage contains five or possibly six independent sayings that relate to the theme of personal sacrifice and loyalty to Jesus. The sayings have been collected into one place by the author of the Gospel of Mark, or more probably by an earlier author whose collection of these sayings was known to and used by the author of the Gospel of Mark. Let us examine the sayings individually by applying to them the five criteria for authenticity.

Mark 8:34. The saying in verse 34 poses some interesting challenges:

> He called the crowd with his disciples, and said to them, "If any want to become my followers, let them deny themselves and take up their cross and follow me."

In this saying, the words "take up their cross" fail the criterion of dissimilarity. The saying clearly reveals, with these suspicious words, the church's reflection on Jesus' crucifixion from its vantage point and reflects an understanding of the crucifixion as the saving event of the Christian *kerygma*.

There is, however, no need to discard the entire saying as unauthentic on account of these few words. Eliminating only the words that fail the test of dissimilarity may be sufficient. The resultant saying would then be, "If any want to become my followers, let them deny themselves and follow me." In this form the saying may, indeed, reflect a genuine call by Jesus to his disciples to follow a life of denial of the material values of this world in preparation for the future time of God's rule. This simpler form of the saying has more balance than the version with the added words "take up their cross":

> If any want to become my followers,
> let them deny themselves and follow me.

"Any" in the first line is balanced by "them" in the second line. "Want to become" is balanced by "deny themselves," and "my followers" is balanced by "follow me." This kind of parallelism is a common feature of Hebrew poetry and is evident in many of the poetic passages in the Old Testament. In this case, we have what scholars call synthetic parallelism; the second line repeats and reinforces the substance of the first line. The saying in this amended form meets the criterion of Aramaism or Semitism and the criterion of contextual credibility, meaning that Jesus could definitely have spoken these words to his followers in Aramaic. The fact that a saying that fails the criterion of dissimilarity, can, with only minor revisions, satisfy the criteria of Aramaism and contextual credibility both validates the amended form of the saying and corroborates the methodology scholars have devised to address the question of authenticity. The words "take up their cross" are obviously redactional additions of either Mark or of one of Mark's written sources.

Mark 8:35. The saying in verse 35 poses a number of interesting problems:

> For those who want to save their life will lose it,
> and those who lose their life for my sake,
> and for the sake of the gospel, will save it."

In this saying, two phrases fail the criterion of dissimilarity: "for my sake," and "and for the sake of the gospel." "For my sake" clearly implies the church's belief in Jesus' special role as God's designated messenger, the savior.[10] Whoever dies for Jesus' sake will save his own life. That phrase echoes early Christian preaching. The same is also true of the phrase "and for the sake of the gospel." The "gospel" was the "good news," the *kerygma*, the preached message of the Christian community. When these two offending phrases are removed, we have the following couplet:

> For those who want to save their life will lose it,
> and those who lose their life will save it.

Once again the two lines balance each other.

> Those who save will lose,
> those who lose will save.

As in the saying in Mark 8:34, this parallelism is a feature of Hebrew poetry evident throughout the Old Testament. In this case, we have what scholars call antithetical parallelism; the second line states the opposite, the antithesis, of what is stated in the first line. In the revised form, the saying meets the criterion of Aramaism and the criterion of contextual credibility. Once again, the fact that a saying that initially failed the criterion of dissimilarity has, with minor modifications, met the criteria of Aramaism and contextual credibility supports both the amended form of the saying and the methodology that scholars have devised to address the issue of authenticity. The words "for my sake and for the sake of the gospel" are obviously redactional additions of either Mark or of one of Mark's written sources.

Mark 8:36–37. The saying or sayings in verses 36 and 37 are somewhat more enigmatic:

---

10. It is also worth noting that the phrase "for my sake" does not appear in several ancient manuscripts, raising the question of whether it actually appeared in the autograph of Mark or was added by a later scribe.

> For what will it profit them to gain the whole world and forfeit their life? What can they give in return for their life?

Verse 36 is an example of what in the Old Testament is incomplete antithetical parallelism, meaning that (1) not every item in the first line is balanced by an item in the second line (hence, incomplete), and (2) the second line states the opposite, the antithesis, of what is stated in the first line:

> For what will it profit them to gain the whole world
> and forfeit their life?

"Gain the whole world" stands in contrast, in antithesis, to "forfeit their life." Once again, as in the sayings in verses 34 and 35, this parallelism is a feature of Hebrew poetry and is found throughout the Old Testament. The saying in its form in Mark 8:36, therefore, meets the criterion of Aramaism and may, indeed, be authentic.

The saying in verse 37 is more problematic:

> What can they give in return for their life?

This saying may be a Markan gloss or an elaboration on verse 36. It adds little to the text and seems to just dangle with no meaningful connection to the other sayings.

Mark 8:38. The saying in verse 38 is particularly interesting:

> Those who are ashamed of me and of my words in this adulterous and sinful generation, of them the Son of Man will also be ashamed when he comes in the glory of his Father with the holy angels."

This saying appears to meet three of the criteria: the criterion of Aramaism, the criterion of contextual credibility, and the criterion of dissimilarity or embarrassment. Once again we have two lines in parallel, a feature of Hebrew poetry:

Those who are ashamed of me and of my words in this adulterous and sinful generation,

the Son of Man will also be ashamed of them when he comes (in the glory of his Father with the holy angels).

I have shifted the order of the words "of them" in the English translation to illustrate more clearly the parallelism between the two lines and to show what might have been the form of the saying in the Aramaic original. The criterion of dissimilarity in this verse is evident in the fact that Jesus is speaking not of himself in the second line when he uses the words "Son of Man," but rather of someone else, presumably the eschatological Son of Man known to us from contemporary Jewish literature. Jesus is clearly announcing, as did others of his generation, probably including John the Baptist, the imminent arrival of the end of history and the inauguration of God's rule, which God's messenger, the Son of Man, would usher in. This saying also meets the criterion of contextual credibility. It is very likely an authentic saying of Jesus on the basis that it fulfills at least three criteria: dissimilarity, contextual credibility, and Aramaism.

JESUS OF NAZARETH: THE ESCHATOLOGICAL PROPHET

The final words of this saying, "in the glory of his Father with the holy angels," may be a Markan interpolation into the text, which is why I have included it in parentheses. In fact, the saying may have survived largely intact in Mark because, following Jesus' death, early Christians interpreted the saying in light of their belief that Jesus would, within their lifetimes, return in glory as the anticipated eschatological Son of Man. Efforts to deny that Jesus is referring in this saying to someone other than himself are theologically motivated and are based not on the evidence but on prior belief. The meaning of the passage is eminently clear: Jesus expected the imminent arrival of the anticipated eschatological Son of Man. This was the cornerstone of Jesus' teaching, and his ethical demands should be understood within the context of this message.

Mark 9:1. The saying in Mark 9:1 is also very interesting:

> Truly I tell you, there are some standing here who will not taste death until they see the kingdom of God has come with power.

This saying clearly meets the criterion of contextual credibility, and it coheres with the previous saying in Mark 8:38. The imminent arrival of God's rule will take place during the lifetime of some who are listening to Jesus' teaching. The fact that the end did not come, as Jesus predicted, is testimony to the saying's dissimilarity with popular early Christian preaching. Accordingly, its authenticity is beyond reasonable doubt.

As we have already seen, shortly after Jesus' death his followers began to proclaim that Jesus had been raised from the dead and exalted to God's right hand and that it was, in fact, Jesus who would soon return as the supernatural Son of Man to usher in the age of God's rule.

Summary of Mark 8:34–9:1. During the period of early oral tradition, followers of Jesus apparently remembered separately these five independent sayings until someone likely grouped them into this cluster because of their similar content. The original form of this written cluster of sayings may have looked something like this:

> If any want to become my followers,
>
> let them deny themselves and follow me.
>
> Those who want to save their life will lose it,
>
> and those who lose their life will save it.
>
> What will it profit them to gain the whole world
>
> and forfeit their life?
>
> Those who are ashamed of me and of my words in this adulterous and sinful generation,
>
> the Son of Man will also be ashamed of them when he comes.
>
> Truly I tell you, there are some standing here who will not taste death
>
> until they see the kingdom of God has come with power.

This may have been the form of five authentic sayings of Jesus collected into a written source that was available to the author of the Gospel of Mark. The sayings in this form are different from the preached message, the *kerygma*, of the early church, which is to say they meet the criterion of dissimilarity or embarrassment. They reflect a clear familiarity with the parallelism of Hebrew poetry and must have assumed their form either in the teaching of Jesus or in the very earliest period of the Aramaic speaking church, long before Jesus' teaching was stripped of its original Semitic form and transformed for a Greek-speaking, Greek-thinking audience.

The sayings fit nicely into the context of first century Judaism; and they cohere, that is they afford a single consistent picture of what Jesus likely preached. These sayings also meet the criterion of multiple attestation because they are similar in form and in content to apparently authentic sayings of Jesus from other independent sources, as we shall see below.

From this analysis of this cluster of five sayings, there emerges a picture of Jesus as an eschatological prophet who preached the imminent end of history and the coming of the Son of Man, who would soon usher in God's rule. Jesus and his followers apparently believed that these events would transpire within the lifetime of many of those who were listening to Jesus' message. To prepare for these impending events, Jesus called upon his followers to renounce the values of this world and to live their lives as if God's rule had already arrived. Jesus may have believed that he was already setting the process in motion through his message and his mission, his teaching, and his action.

2. Examples from Q

Let us turn now to two sayings from the Q source and examine them using the same criteria. The reader is reminded that Q was apparently a written sayings source known to Matthew and Luke, but not to the author of the Gospel of Mark. The first of these Q passages is found in Matt 10:32–33 and Luke 12:8–9, the other in Matt 10:39 and Luke 17:33.

Q (Matt 10:32–33 = Luke 12:8–9)

Matt 10:32–33	Luke 12:8–9
	And I tell you,
Everyone who acknowledges me	everyone who acknowledges me
before others,	before others,
I will also	the Son of Man will also
acknowledge	acknowledge
before my Father in heaven;	before the angels of God;
but whoever denies me	but whoever denies me

JESUS OF NAZARETH: THE ESCHATOLOGICAL PROPHET

Matt 10:32–33	Luke 12:8–9
<u>before others</u>	<u>before others</u>
I <u>will</u> also <u>deny</u>	<u>will</u> be <u>denied</u>
<u>before</u> my Father in heaven.	<u>before</u> the angels of God.
total # words in Matthew: 30	total # words in Luke: 32 (excluding introduction)
# words in Matthew underlined: 19	# words in Luke underlined: 19
% words in Matthew underlined: 63%	% words in Luke underlined: 59%

The agreement between Matthew and Luke in this Q passage is very high, 63% in Matthew and 59% in Luke.[11] The only significant difference between the two texts is the first person "I" in Matthew where Luke has the third person "the Son of Man," and "my Father in heaven," which appears twice in Matthew, where Luke has in both instances "the angels of God." These differences are, however, significant. Was Jesus at the center of his own teaching, as Matthew's text clearly indicates, or was Jesus rather pointing to the coming of someone other than himself, "the Son of Man," as Luke's text implies? With regard to this saying, does Matthew or Luke follow more closely the wording of Q, their hypothetical common written source?

Applying the criterion of dissimilarity or embarrassment, it is evident that Luke preserves the more original version of this saying and that the author of the Gospel of Matthew has changed the words of Q in order to have Jesus point not to someone other than himself, the eschatological Son of Man, as the intermediary between God and man, but rather to have Jesus point indisputably to himself as God's designated intermediary. It is easy to explain why Matthew would have changed the Q source, if Luke's version is more original; it is far more difficult, in fact virtually impossible, to explain why Luke would have modified Q, if Matthew's text preserves the original wording. Likewise, we have seen previously that the phrase "my father in heaven" is a common redactional characteristic of the Gospel of Matthew. Hence, we have here a Q saying for which Luke preserves the more original wording. In fact, Luke may have preserved Q virtually unchanged, given the fact that Matthew supports 63% of Luke's words.

The poetic parallelism of this Q passage is evident in the literary form of the saying, as printed below. The criterion of Aramaism is, therefore, also satisfied.

Everyone who	acknowledges me	before others,
	the Son of Man	will also acknowledge	before the angels of God;
but	whoever denies me	before others
		will be denied	before the angels of God.

---

11. We have done our calculations based on the text of the New Revised Standard Version of the Bible in English, hence our calculations are only approximate, although not unreasonable. Ideally, comparisons should be made by using the Greek texts of the gospels, not English translations.

Not only are the criteria of dissimilarity and Semitisim satisfied by this examination and interpretation of the data, but we now have a saying that likely satisfies all five criteria for authenticity:

1. multiple attestation (Mark and Q);
2. dissimilarity (Jesus points to someone other than himself as the eschatological Son of Man);
3. contextual credibility (the Son of Man was a well-known figure in first century Jewish eschatological circles);
4. Semitism or Aramaism (the passage reflects the form of ancient Hebrew poetry);
5. coherence (the message of this saying is very much like the message in the collection of sayings in Mark 8:34–9:1 that we examined above).

Q (Matt 10:39 = Luke 17:33)

Matt 10:39	Luke 17:33
Those who find their life will lose it, and those who lose their life for my sake will find it.	Those who try to make their life secure will lose it, but those who lose their life will keep it.
total # words in Matthew: 20	total # words in Luke: 20
words in Matthew underlined: 14	words in Luke underlined: 14
% words in Matthew underlined: 70%	% words in Luke underlined: 70%

The agreement between Matthew and Luke in this Q passage is very high, 70% in both gospels. The differences between the two gospels is largely editorial: "find" in Matthew for "try to make secure" in Luke; "and" in Matthew for "but" in Luke; and "find" again in Matthew for "keep" in Luke. The words "for my sake" in Matthew once again compromise the poetic parallelism and are likely a Matthaean addition, just as they were in Mark 8:35. These words fail to satisfy the criterion of dissimilarity. The fact that the phrase "for my sake" occurs in both Mark 8:35 and Matt 10:39 may indicate that the phrase was in Q and that Luke eliminated it, but it is certainly not original to the earliest form of the saying as originally spoken by Jesus. The words "find," "lose," "lose," "find" in Matthew reflect much better the probable poetic structure of the original saying. Luke's changes in the verbs in lines 1 and 4 destroy the poetic balance. I am inclined to propose the following as the version of this saying that was most likely in Q, and therefore most likely reflective of Jesus' teaching:

Those who find their life will lose it,
but those who lose their life will find it.

3. Examples Found in both Mark and Q

When we compare the versions of the sayings discussed above that appear in both Mark and Q, it is not entirely clear what lies behind these two versions:

Q (of Matt 10:32–33 and Luke 12:8–9) and Mark 8:38

Q (Matt 10:32–33 and Luke 12:8–9)	Mark 8:38
Everyone <u>who</u>	Those <u>who</u>
acknowledges me before others,	
<u>the Son of Man</u>	
will also acknowledge	
before the angels of God;	
but whoever denies me before others	are ashamed of me and of my words
	in this adulterous
	and sinful generation
	of them <u>the Son of Man</u>
<u>will</u> be denied	<u>will</u> also be ashamed when he
	comes in the glory of his Father
before <u>the angels</u> of God.	with <u>the</u> holy <u>angels</u>.
total # words in Q: 32	total # words in Mark: 39
words underlined in Q: 8	words underlined in Mark: 8
% words underlined in Q: 25%	% words underlined in Mark: 21%

The incidence of verbal agreement is not sufficient to establish that these passages are two versions of the same saying, although one could probably make that case. The saying in Q has two parts in parallel balance; the saying in Mark parallels only the second part of the Q saying. The appearance of "Everyone who" in the first portion of Q and of "Those who" in Mark, and of "the Son of Man" in the first portion of Q and in Mark, would enable us to reconstruct a single version that combines portions of both, such as:

> Those who acknowledge me before others,
> the Son of Man will also acknowledge before the angels of God;
> but those who deny me before others
> will be denied before the angels of God.

Although possible, this reconstruction is highly speculative and proves very little. What is clear is that we have two very similar accounts of a saying, both versions of which have strong independent claims to authenticity. There are three possible explanations of this data:

1. either the two versions (Mark and Q) stem from a single saying in oral or written form;

2. they are two distinct and independent sayings, both of which were remembered in the oral tradition, or

3. Jesus' sayings were not always remembered verbatim, hence the variation in the two forms.

There is something to be said for all three explanations:

> First, even if the essence of Jesus' teaching was remembered by his followers, no one was taking stenographic notes when Jesus spoke. Repeating the tradition during the period of oral transmission obviously resulted in both accidental and deliberate changes to what Jesus actually said.
>
> Second, Jesus probably had a consistent message, but he would not necessarily use exactly the same words every time he delivered that message. Differences between the saying in Mark and the saying in Q may reflect two distinct versions of the teaching delivered by Jesus on different occasions.
>
> Third, maybe few or none of the so-called "sayings" of Jesus in the synoptic gospels report verbatim what Jesus actually said.

I suspect that there is some truth to all three explanations, but we cannot be sure which addresses best this particular saying tradition in Mark and Q.

We will never know definitively whether this is one or two sayings. We will never know exactly how much the saying has suffered in transmission. We will never know exactly what reflects accurately the words that Jesus actually spoke, and what was changed by the early church during the period of oral and written transmission. Nevertheless, I do believe that we can be confident that the substance of the saying(s) is an authentic teaching of Jesus, because it meets all of the criteria for authenticity identified above.

Q (Matt 10:39 and Luke 17:33) and Mark 8:35

Q (Matt 10:39 and Luke 17:33)	Mark 8:35
<u>Those who</u> find <u>their life</u> <u>will lose it,</u> but <u>those who lose their life</u> <u>will</u> find <u>it</u>.	For <u>those who</u> want to save <u>their life</u> <u>will lose it,</u> and <u>those who lose their life</u> <u>will</u> save <u>it.</u>
total # words in Q: 17	total # words in Mark: 20
total # words underlined in Q: 14	total # words underlined in Mark: 14
% words underline in Q: 82%	% words underlined in Mark: 70%

The verbal agreement between the version of this saying in Q and the version in Mark is very strong: between 70% and 82% respectively. The parallelism in Mark, *save, lose, lose, save* is very similar to what we see in Q, *find, lose, lose, find*. The Q version of the saying seems more original, as the Markan form appears to be talking about *salvation*, a more theological term than Q's *find*.

4. An Example from John

Very similar to this saying in Mark and Q is a saying in the Gospel of John 12:25:

> Those who love their life
> lose it,
> and those who hate their life in this world
> will keep it for eternal life.

The form of this saying in John is quite similar to the synoptic versions, the major difference being the addition of the words "in this world" in the third line and the typically Johannine phrase "for eternal life" in the fourth line.[12] Apart from this characteristically Johannine expression, we have in John the same saying that we have examined already in Mark and in Q. We, therefore, have multiple attestation for this saying in three independent sources: Mark, Q, and John.

A pre-Johannine version of this saying may have read:

> Those who love their life
> (will) lose it,
> and those who hate their life
> (will) keep (or find) it.

Notice once again the formal structure of what may be the original parallelism of the Aramaic poetry that likely underlies the pre-Johannine version of this popular saying.

5. Miscellaneous Apocalyptic Sayings

There are other sayings of Jesus in the synoptic gospels that also reflect this representation of Jesus as an apocalyptic prophet. Among them are:

Mark 1:15:

> The time has been fulfilled, the kingdom of God is near; repent and believe in this good news.

Mark 13:26–27:

---

12. John uses the phrase "eternal life" nine times in his gospel: John 3:15; 4:36; 5:39; 6:54; 6:68; 10:28; 12:25; 17:2; 17:3. Matthew, Mark, and Luke together use the phrase only six times (Matt 19:16; 25:46; Mark 10:17; 10:30; Luke 10:25; 18:18), and even then in passages that reflect Matthew and Luke's literary dependence on Mark, meaning only two independent incidents of the phrase "eternal life" in the synoptic gospels.

Then they will see the Son of Man coming in clouds with great power and glory. Then he will send out the angels, and gather his elect from the four winds, from the ends of the earth to the ends of heaven.

Mark 13:30:

Truly I tell you, this generation will not pass away until all these things have taken place.

Mark 13:32–37:

But about that day or hour no one knows, neither the angels in heaven, nor the Son, but only the Father. Beware, keep alert; for you do not know when the time will come. It is like a man going on a journey, when he leaves his home and puts slaves in charge, each with his work, and commands the doorkeeper to be on watch. Therefore, keep awake—for you do not know when the master of the house will come, in the evening, or at midnight, or at cockcrow, or at dawn, or else he may find you asleep when he comes suddenly. And what I say to you I say to all: Keep awake.

Mark 14:62:

Jesus said, "... you will see the Son of Man seated at the right hand of the Power, and coming with the clouds of heaven."

Matt 19:28 (from Q, cf. Luke 18:28–30):

Jesus said to them, "Truly I tell you, at the renewal of all things, when the Son of Man is seated on the throne of his glory, you who have followed me will also sit on twelve thrones, judging the twelve tribes of Israel."

This collection of passages is by no means exhaustive, but it affords a clear and consistent representation that Jesus, devoid of the overlay of early Christian theology, was an apocalyptic prophet. In fact, Jesus' teaching strongly resembles the teaching of John the Baptist, who was Jesus' predecessor and perhaps his mentor. Many of the parables in the gospels of Matthew, Mark, and Luke reflect Jesus' teaching that God's rule was coming very soon, or that it was already growing and breaking into history whenever and wherever anyone does God's will.

Jesus' radical ethical teaching may have been grounded in his eschatological worldview. He apparently believed that the end of history, as we know it, was coming very soon and that his followers should prepare for this cataclysmic event by loving and serving God unconditionally with their entire beings and by loving their neighbors (meaning "everyone") as themselves. This appears to have been Jesus' single commandment, because for Jesus it was evidently not possible to love God without loving one's neighbor.[13]

---

13. In a famous pericope in Mark 12:28–34 (= Matt 22:34–40 and Luke 10:25–28), a scribe asked Jesus which is the greatest commandment. Jesus answered: the first is to love God, and the second is to love your neighbor. Jesus obviously understood that the two commandments could not be separated; they were, in fact, one commandment. Jesus' teaching consistently supports this conclusion.

CONCLUSIONS

It is helpful at this point, by gathering information from both this chapter and previous chapters, to review the reasons why the quest for the historical Jesus is so riddled with obstacles:

1. Our written sources are limited. There are no relevant contemporary Jewish or Roman sources about Jesus, and there is no meaningful information in the canonical New Testament beyond the four gospels. Extra-canonical Christian sources are generally late and of little to no historical value with the possible exception of the *Gospel of Thomas* and the *Gospel of Peter*, yet there is still no scholarly consensus on the dating of these texts.

2. The canonical gospels pose serious challenges:

    a. There are marked differences between the Jesus of the Gospel of John, who openly proclaims himself as the divine Son of God, and the Jesus of the synoptic gospels, who urges his disciples not to disclose his identity to anyone.

    b. There are significant differences between the birth narratives in the gospels of Matthew and Luke; moreover, the gospels of Mark and John have no birth narratives.

    c. The reports of resurrection appearances in the gospels of Matthew, Luke, and John are very different and essentially irreconcilable; moreover, the Gospel of Mark has no report of resurrection appearances.

    d. In the synoptic gospels Jesus refers to both himself and to someone other than himself as the Son of Man, differences that are fundamentally contradictory.

These important challenges, together with what we have learned from textual criticism, literary criticism, philological criticism, form criticism, and redaction criticism have convinced scholars of the need to identify formal criteria that can assist in determining the authenticity of material attributed to Jesus in the gospels. Scholarly conclusions are obviously only as sound as the foundations on which they are built—in this instance the criteria of authenticity and the detailed arguments based on these criteria.

As we have seen in our analysis of the passages examined in detail in this chapter, the criteria of dissimilarity or embarrassment, multiple attestation, contextual credibility, Semitism, and coherence have yielded significant and valuable results, especially when applied to sayings material. These criteria are less well suited to an examination of narrative material in the gospels, although when coupled with the results of other scholarly methods, especially form criticism and redaction criticism, these criteria can sometimes yield important results for narrative material as well.

In the course of this chapter, we have identified two specific messages in Jesus' teaching:

1. Jesus believed that he was called and commissioned by God to proclaim the imminent arrival of God's rule; and
2. Jesus called upon his followers to deny the material values of this world in anticipation of and in preparation for the time of God's rule.

(1) Among the passages portraying Jesus as an eschatological prophet or a herald of God's imminent imperial rule are:

a. the reconstructed form of the two sayings of Jesus found in Mark 8:38–9:1:

> Those who are ashamed of me and of my words in this adulterous and sinful generation,
> the Son of Man will also be ashamed of them when he comes.
> Truly I tell you, there are some standing here who will not taste death
> until they see the kingdom of God has come with power.

b. the reconstructed form of the Q saying of Jesus underlying Matt 10:32–3 = Luke 12:8–9:

> Everyone who acknowledges me before others,
> the Son of Man will also acknowledge before the angels of God;
> but whoever denies me before others
> will be denied before the angels of God.

c. other examples of apocalyptic sayings of Jesus in the synoptic gospels include:

Mark 1:15:

> The time has been fulfilled, the kingdom of God is near; repent and believe in this good news.

Mark 13:26–27:

> Then they will see the Son of Man coming in clouds with great power and glory. Then he will send out the angels, and gather his elect from the four winds, from the ends of the earth to the ends of heaven.

Mark 13:30:

> Truly I tell you, this generation will not pass away until all these things have taken place.

Mark 13:32–37:

> But about that day or hour no one knows, neither the angels in heaven, nor the Son, but only the Father. Beware, keep alert; for you do not know when the time will come. It is like a man going on a journey, when he leaves his home and puts slaves in charge, each with his work, and commands the doorkeeper to be on watch. Therefore, keep awake—for you do not know when the master of the house will come, in the evening, or at midnight, or at cockcrow, or at dawn, or

else he may find you asleep when he comes suddenly. And what I say to you I say to all: Keep awake.

Mark 14:62:

Jesus said, "... you will see the Son of Man seated at the right hand of the Power, and coming with the clouds of heaven."

Matt 19:28 (from Q, cf. Luke 18:28–30):

Jesus said to them, "Truly I tell you, at the renewal of all things, when the Son of Man is seated on the throne of his glory, you who have followed me will also sit on twelve thrones, judging the twelve tribes of Israel."

(2) Among the passages in which Jesus calls upon his followers to deny the material values of this world in anticipation of and in preparation for the time of God's imperial rule are:

a. the reconstructed form of the three sayings of Jesus in Mark 8:34–36:

If any want to become my followers,
let them deny themselves and follow me.
Those who want to save their life will lose it,
and those who lose their life will save it.
What will it profit them to gain the whole world
and forfeit their life?

b. the reconstructed form of the Q saying of Jesus underlying Matt 10:39 = Luke 17:33:

Those who find their life will lose it,
but those who lose their life will find it.

c. the two sayings of Jesus in Mark 4:24–25:

the measure you give will be the measure you get,
(For) to those who have,
more will be given;
and from those who have nothing,
even what they have will be taken away.

d. the reconstructed version of a pre-Johannine saying in John 12:25:

Those who love their life (will) lose it,
and those who hate their life (will) keep (or find) it.

In trying to reconstruct the life, ministry, and teaching of the historical Jesus, we must obviously look beyond the narrow picture that we have uncovered in this chapter and remember some of what we uncovered in previous chapters as well. We must also muster additional information that we have not yet had an opportunity to discuss in this volume in order to complete the picture. Herewith is a summary of what we can likely know about Jesus of Nazareth, the eschatological prophet.

We should probably begin by acknowledging that we know nothing about Jesus' birth and childhood. The stories in the opening chapters of Matthew and Luke are just that, stories. They are legends, put together by the church. They were sometimes created in fulfillment of the Hebrew scriptures, and they were sometimes merely the creation of story tellers. But, whatever else may be, they are stories with no historical value whatsoever. In fact, contrary to what we read in Matthew and Luke, Jesus was probably born not in Bethlehem of Judea but in Nazareth in the northern Galilee, the son of Miriam (Mary) and Joseph, the oldest of at least seven children, among them four brothers—James, Joses, Judas, and Simon (Mark 6:3)—and at least two unnamed sisters.

What we do know about Jesus begins with his relationship with John the Baptist, who apparently called people to the Jordan River for a baptism of repentance for the forgiveness of sins (Mark 1:4). That Jesus submitted to John's baptism is certain, as the remembrance of Jesus' baptism by John posed embarrassment to the later church to such an extent that Matthew constructed a conversation between John and Jesus to justify Jesus' willingness to be baptized by John (Matt 3:13-15).

Jesus apparently understood his submission to John's message and his baptism by John as the inaugural event of a major personal religious experience in his own life, but we will never fully understand what this event meant to Jesus, because the story comes to us in the canonical gospels in the form of legends. We know that the author of the Gospel of Mark understood this event as God's adoption of Jesus as his anointed (messianic) son (Mark 1: 11: And a voice came [to Jesus] from heaven, "You are my Son, the Beloved, with you I am well pleased."). Although we cannot recover what this baptism by John may have meant to Jesus, it appears likely that Jesus became a follower of John and that Jesus' own ministry began following the arrest of John (Mark 1:14-15: Now after John was arrested, Jesus came to Galilee, proclaiming the good news of God, and saying, "The time is fulfilled, and the kingdom of God has come near; repent, and believe in the good news."). Presumably, Jesus understood that God had called him to continue John prophetic ministry following John's arrest. Jesus apparently continued to proclaim John's message of the imminent arrival of God's rule, although Jesus does not appear to have continued John's practice of baptizing sinners to repentance in the Jordan. That appears to have been John's particular hallmark.

In proclaiming the inauguration the new age of God's rule, Jesus taught his followers that there should be no division, no discord, no hatred, and no discrimination among people. Those who were rich should sell everything to support the poor (Mark 10:17-21). Unconditional love of others was more important than the command of the Mosaic law to observe the Sabbath (Mark 2:23-28; 3:1-6). Dietary laws were meaningless in the new order. God was not concerned about what food went into the body of a person but with what actions came out from that person (Mark 7:18–19).

Not only should Jesus' followers prepare themselves for the imminent judgment; they should also proclaim to others this message of the imminent end of history and the ethic of God's command of unconditional love toward other people (Mark 3:13–19). The occasion for this radical ethic was Jesus' belief in the imminent arrival of God's rule, which would be ushered in by God's mediator, the eschatological Son of Man, who in Jesus' teaching was clearly someone other than himself (Mark 8:38–9:1).

As we have seen, there is nothing in the authentic sayings tradition to support the idea that Jesus was ever the subject of his own teaching. That position is an invention of early Christianity and most consistently of the Gospel of John. It is difficult to know what Jesus understood his own role was in the unfolding eschatological drama. But it appears that he understood himself to be the final precursor of the Son of Man, a herald who would prepare the people for the arrival of God's final messenger, whose coming would signify the end of history, as we know it, and the arrival of the new age of God's rule.

Not only his words, but his actions as well reveal that Jesus thought of himself as an eschatological prophet: his baptism by John the Baptist; his call of twelve disciples probably representing the twelve tribes of Israel; his association with tax collectors, women, sinners, lepers, and the outcasts of society; his ceremonial cleansing of the Temple (Mark 11:15–19) shortly before his arrest and crucifixion; and perhaps even his apparently willing execution at the hands of the Jews and the Romans, thereby pronouncing his (and God's) judgment on the current social, religious, and political order. Even the circumstances of Jesus' crucifixion are uncertain. What was the reason for his arrest and execution? The Jewish authorities and the Roman governor may have considered Jesus as a threat to their authority. Jesus' overturning the tables of the money-changers in the temple precincts may have been the single most horrendous event that sealed his fate (Mark 11:15–19).

Jesus lived his life as if God's rule was already arriving, even though he seems to have awaited its consummation with the arrival of the eschatological Son of Man. Perhaps Jesus believed that he and his followers, by their words and deeds, could help to usher in the Age to Come, the new order of God's rule. In doing God's will in the here and now, Jesus seemingly believed that God's rule was, in fact, already breaking into history.

The Jesus painted here is a far cry from the Jesus of the Gospel of John, who said: "I am the bread of life" (6:35); "I am the light of the world" (8:12; 9:5); "I am from above" (8:23); "I am the gate" (10:9); "I am the good shepherd" (10:11, 14); "I am the resurrection and the life" (11:25); "I am the way, and the truth, and the life" (14:6). The Jesus of the Gospel of John is not Jesus of Nazareth. He is not the historical Jesus. He is a construct of the Christian church, a construct of the author of the Gospel of John, bearing little or no resemblance to the Jesus of history. Yet, it is this Jesus of the Gospel of John who has dominated Christian theology down through the ages.

What I have attempted to accomplish in this chapter is to reach behind the early church's various portraits or representations of Jesus in the gospels, using the criteria of authenticity in an effort to gain a clearer picture of what kind of person Jesus of Nazareth actually was. We cannot be sure of every detail in the portrait of Jesus of Nazareth that we have painted, but we can be confident that our construct reflects a far more accurate portrait of the historical Jesus than do any of the portraits painted in our canonical gospels.

What can we conclude about the gospels and about the historical Jesus from this review?

1. The gospels seldom provide us with the exact words of Jesus or even a faithful version of his life, ministry, and teaching. They provide us with the testimonies of the second and third generations of Christians who received from earlier generations oral and written traditions that were already influenced and conditioned by the beliefs, needs, and biases of nascent Christian communities. To this earlier tradition, the evangelists added their own biases of what they thought Jesus might or should have taught.

2. Only though a rigorous critical examination of Jesus' alleged words, using the sharpest tools of scholarly research, can we hope to understand what Jesus actually said and did in the course of his ministry. It is challenging, but it is not impossible, to move from the gospels to Jesus by using the finest tools of historical criticism. Although difficult and sometimes painful, the task is worthwhile and essential. The results of this effort are promising, as a consistent and coherent picture of Jesus begins to emerge.

3. Critical study of the evidence suggests that Jesus of Nazareth expected the imminent arrival of a figure, whom he and others of his time referred to as the Son of Man (or the Man), a supernatural angelic person who would come riding on the clouds of heaven to usher in the new order of God's rule, which more traditional translations sometimes refer to as the Kingdom of God. Jesus was apparently an eschatological prophet who understood that he was the final precursor of that angelic Son of Man, and that, as such, he was the messenger of a radical ethic that demanded unconditional love of God and unconditional love of one's fellow human beings in preparation for the arrival of the Son of Man and the age of God's rule.

4. This historical reconstruction is supported by the five criteria established at the outset of this chapter: the criteria of dissimilarity or embarrassment, multiple independent attestation, contextual credibility, Semitism, and coherence.

Anyone who ignores this method and approaches the gospels uncritically and who then expects to know what Jesus said on any specific issue by citing out of context individual passages in the gospels is involved in a futile exercise that disregards the established critical tools of biblical scholarship.

In the following chapter, we shall turn our attention to a very different scholarly portrait of Jesus, a representation of the historical Jesus as a teacher of wisdom.

CHAPTER 9

JESUS OF NAZARETH: THE TEACHER OF WISDOM

BIBLICAL SCHOLARSHIP, INDEED ALL scholarship, is an ongoing process. New times often usher in alternative or even unorthodox ways of understanding and interpreting the same old data. Occasionally, new data are available to scholars and result, therefore, in modifications in scholarly opinion.

An important example of such a shift in biblical scholarship has been the relatively recent interpretation of Jesus, not as an eschatological prophet, but as a teacher of wisdom. New insights and new arguments have resulted in new interpretations of well-known material and in the pioneering interpretation of other relatively recent discoveries, such as the *Gospel of Thomas*, both in Greek fragments and in a complete Coptic translation. I hope in this chapter to explore some of these more recent developments in New Testament studies in order to illustrate, at least in part, the tentative nature of biblical scholarship.

THE "SAYINGS GOSPEL" Q

Characteristic of this portrait of Jesus as a teacher of wisdom is the work of Helmut Koester, James M. Robinson, and John S. Kloppenborg. In an essay on the history of Q research in *The Critical Edition of Q*, Robinson traces the evolution of Q scholarship from Schleiermacher's comments about Papias's reference to *logia* (oracles) of Jesus in 1832 to the present.[1]

Since the emergence of redaction criticism in Germany in the decades after World War II, scholars have observed that a study of the ways in which the authors of the gospels of Matthew and Luke edited their Markan source reveals that they reproduced Mark with considerable fidelity. According to Robinson,

> The approach of redaction criticism made it methodologically more possible to reconstruct the critical text of Q, by identifying distinctive Matthean and Lukan traits of syntax, vocabulary, and theology (broadly understood), identified by studying their redaction of Mark, and then using these traits as objective criteria for identifying the redactional alterations in Q. These Matthean and Lukan

---

1. Robinson, "History of Q Research," xix–lxxi.

"fingerprints" on the Q sayings facilitate the reconstruction of the Q text, in that one is often able to identify and peel off the Matthean and Lukan redaction. The reconstruction of a critical text thereby becomes a more feasible undertaking.[2]

This observation led scholars to presume that the authors of the gospels of Matthew and Luke preserved the text of Q with the same measure of fidelity with which they preserved Mark. This presumption allowed that scholars can, therefore, reconstruct Q from the texts of Matthew and Luke with reasonable accuracy.

This is, of course, a presumption, perhaps even a reasonable presumption, but it does raise certain questions. How do we know that Matthew and Luke treated all sources alike? Working backward from Matthew and Luke may enable us to reconstruct a Greek text of Q, but was Q written originally in Aramaic or in Greek? Did the authors of the gospels of Matthew and Luke have access to identical or nearly identical texts of Q? Can we be certain that the differences between Matthew's and Luke's wording of Q material is merely the result of the evangelists' redaction. Depending on how scholars answer these questions, they may or may not be able to reconstruct the archetype of Q.

The reconstructed text of Q begins with John the Baptist's announcement of eschatological judgment and his baptism of Jesus; the beatitudes for the poor, the hungry, the mourning, and the persecuted follow with their eschatological warnings; and Q ends with sayings proclaiming the coming of the Son of Man like lightning. Does this material reflect the teaching of the historical John the Baptist and the historical Jesus of Nazareth, or is this the teaching of the Q community, the message of a Hellenistic Christian community that produced Q in its present form?

It was Heinz Eduard Tödt who first recognized that Q is not simply one more proclamation of the primitive church's kerygma but that it may be the message of a community concerned with preserving sayings of Jesus. Tödt maintained that early Christianity preserved two kinds of tradition: one was the church's preaching of Jesus' passion, death, and resurrection; the other was tradition that sought to preserve Jesus' message. According to Tödt, Q belonged to the second sphere; it preserved Jesus' own message.[3]

Ulrich Wilckens emphasized the element of Wisdom in Q:

> The motif that Wisdom abandons the earth is . . . found in a Q saying, Jesus' threat against Jerusalem: Matt 23:37–39 par. Luke 13:34–35. In Matthew this saying follows upon another threat against "this generation," Matt 23:34–36 par. Luke 11:49–51, where Matthew has retained from Q the sequence of both sayings and Luke the introduction to this last threat ["Therefore also the Wisdom of God said"]. Hence the saying Matt 23:37–39 was originally in Q a saying of Wisdom that Matthew put on Jesus' tongue. ... Here an echo of the myth in 1 Enoch 42 becomes clear: In resignation, Wisdom withdraws back into heaven. She wanted to collect to herself the children of Jerusalem as her children, but

2. Ibid., xlviii.

3. Tödt, *Der Menschensohn in der synoptischen Überlieferung*, 244–45.

they did not want it. Now she withdraws from them and will leave them to themselves until the parousia of the Messiah.[4]

The two sayings (Q 11:49–51 and Q 13:34–35), presumably part of a single unit, based on their Matthean sequence, are reproduced here in the form in which Wilckens believes they would have appeared together in Q:

Q 11:49–51 (= Matt 23:34–36)

Therefore also .. Wisdom said: I will send them prophets and sages, and «some» of them they will kill and persecute, so that «a settling of accounts for» the blood of all the prophets poured out from the founding of the world may be required of this generation, from «the» blood of Abel to «the» blood of Zechariah, murdered between the sacrificial altar and the House. Yes, I tell you, «an accounting» will be required of this generation!

Q 13:34–35 (= Matt 23:37–39)

O Jerusalem, Jerusalem, who kills the prophets and stones those sent to her! How often I wanted to gather your children together, as a hen gathers her nestlings under her wings, but you were not willing! Look, your house is forsaken! .. I tell you, you will not see me until [[«the time» comes when]] you say: Blessed is the one who comes in the name of the Lord![5]

Involved with the group of German scholars at Heidelberg University who promoted some of these new ideas about Q, Robinson proposed that the literary genre of Q might actually be sapiential (wisdom).[6] This observation has influenced many Q scholars, both in Germany and in North America.

Odil Hannes Steck considers the subject of this Jerusalem saying to be the Wisdom of Sirach 24 that was residing in Jerusalem.[7] If the identification of personified Wisdom is correct, and if Wisdom is departing Israel and Jerusalem, then this is likely a reference to the impending fall of Jerusalem to the Romans. Such an interpretation

---

4. Wilckens, *Weisheit und Torhei*, 163–64 (English translation "History of Research," li).

5. The text of Q sayings in this chapter and elsewhere is taken from Robinson *et al*, *The Critical Edition of Q*. Customarily, citations in Q are indicated by the location of the passage in the Gospel of Luke, so Q 13:34–35 refers to the Q form of the passage underlying Luke 13:34–35 and its Matthean parallel, and so forth. Matthew generally rearranged the Q material quite differently from Luke; the Matthean parallels are available for easy reference in Robinson's *The Critical Edition of Q*.

The sigla (signs or marks) in the text of Q throughout this chapter are based on the sigla in *The Critical Edition of Q*; see pp. lxxx–lxxxviii for a full explanation of all of the sigla. Those relevant to the texts cited in this chapter are:

[[the]] — Double square brackets enclose probable but uncertain reconstructions of the text of Q;
<the> — Single angle brackets indicate that the text is an emendation found, as such, neither in Matthew nor in Luke;
«the» — Double angle brackets indicate that there is a Greek text derived from Q in only one gospel, and hence that a critical text cannot be established by the usual comparison of Matthew and Luke;
.. — Two dots indicate that there may be some text here that cannot be reconstituted.

6. Robinson, "The History of Q," lii.

7. Steck, *Israel und das gewaltsame Geschick der Propheten*, 230–32.

would mean that this saying comes from a period some forty years after Jesus' death. Identifying this passage as a late redaction of Q pushes the final date of Q closer to 70 than to the date of 50 usually assigned to Q. Or, is the theory of a later redaction in about 70 of an early version of Q from about 50 a feasible theory? Some scholars have suggested that the Son of Man sayings in Q 17 (17:23–24, 26–30, 34–35) fit best with the final stages of the Jewish Roman war of 66–70, but I am not convinced that this late date for these sayings is necessary. In fact, if these sayings are as late as 66–70 CE, is this expectation of the Son of Man something new, or is it a renewal of an earlier expectation that goes back to Jesus himself? It is not evident that it was during this late period that the Son of Man material was integrated into earlier Q material that was presumably unfamiliar with Christian eschatology.

Examining the evidence in Q, Dieter Lührmann, argued that the redaction of Q should probably be adjusted from the generally accepted mid-century date and that the redaction likely took place "in the Hellenistic congregation of about the 50s or 60s."[8] What we have witnessed is the shifting of the date of Q from sometime around 50 to sometime closer to 70, with the accompanying claim that "earlier compositions were imbedded in Q,"[9] setting thereby the stage for more recent discussions about Q.

Helmut Koester has argued that it is likely that primitive sayings or groups of sayings of Jesus were dominated by wisdom sayings, legal statements (critique of old conduct and pronouncements regarding new conduct), prophetic sayings (including some I-words, beatitudes, and woes), and parables, just as in Jesus' own teaching. As is partly evident from Q, sayings predicting Jesus' suffering, death, and resurrection, and the material reflecting the development of a Christological evaluation of the person of Jesus, were still absent; detailed apocalyptic predictions, such as those contained in Mark 13, were not part of such primitive collections; specific regulations for the life of the church (*Gemeinderegeln*) were equally absent.

What was the theological tendency of such collections of *logoi* [sayings of Jesus]? The answer to this depends entirely upon the Christological post-Easter frame to which they were subjected. Q domesticated the *logoi* [of Jesus] through a kind of apocalypticism which identified Jesus with the future Son of man. According to Koester, Q domesticated the sayings of Jesus through an apocalypticism that identified Jesus with the future Son of Man.[10]

Koester maintains that the Son of Man sayings do not go back to Jesus himself but that they come late in the Q trajectory. What is significant is that Q identifies Jesus as the Son of Man who will return in the near future. That teaching does not go back to Jesus. However, admitting that fact does not undermine the view that Jesus himself taught of the imminent coming of the eschatological Son of Man, who would be someone other than himself. The foundational question is whether Jesus expected

---

8. Lührmann, *Die Redaktion der Logienquelle*, 88.
9. Robinson, "History of Q Research," lv.
10. Koester, "GNOMAI DIAPHOROI, 300–01.

JESUS OF NAZARETH: THE TEACHER OF WISDOM

the Son of Man's imminent arrival, not whether Jesus expected to return as the Son of Man. I find it questionable that the Son of Man references are necessarily secondary and that they obscure the original focus of Q as sapiential.

John Kloppenborg built on the earlier work of Lührmann, Robinson, Koester, and others[11] and has been among the most important of those scholars who have identified layers of tradition in Q. Specifically, Kloppenborg identified three distinct layers:

a first layer of tradition (Q^1) possibly written in the Galilee in the 50s, whose sayings cast Jesus as a teacher of wisdom;

a second layer of tradition (Q^2) possibly added as early as the 60s or 70s, whose sayings cast Jesus as an apocalyptic prophet; and

a third layer of tradition (Q^3) that includes some narrative passages, completed not later than 80.[12]

Kloppenborg maintains that the Q community probably originated in Galilee about twenty years after Jesus' death with a group of Jesus' followers who were unaware of Paul's Hellenistic *kerygma* with its message of Jesus' atoning death and resurrection, as is demonstrated by Q's lack of a passion narrative and stories of Jesus' death and resurrection.

In the previous chapter, I maintained, despite the theological outlook of the Hellenistic *kerygma* and the canonical gospels, that Jesus was not the subject of his own teaching. Rather Jesus proclaimed the imminent coming of the Son of Man who would usher in God's rule. Only by penetrating behind the *kerygma* of the gospels can we recover the historical Jesus, whom we identified in the previous chapter as an eschatological prophet.

There are only two explanations for the survival in the gospels of elements of both an un-messianic teaching of Jesus and the teaching of a Jesus who proclaims his messiahship and divine sonship:

1. either there were at a very early time two distinct portraits of Jesus existing side by side in the *same* Christian community(ies), one non-messianic and one messianic; or

2. there were at a very early time at least two portraits of Jesus existing concurrently but in *different* Christian communities, one non-messianic and one messianic.[13]

The former explanation seems improbable given the small size of Christian communities in the first decades following Jesus' death. The latter seems more likely, given the wide range of interpretations of Jesus' message, even in the earliest decades

---

11. Robinson, "History of Q Research," lxi.

12. Kloppenborg, *The Formation of Q*. See also Kloppenborg Verbin, *Excavating Q*; and *The Critical Edition of Q*.

13. Kloppenborg agrees with these alternatives (*The Formation of Q*, 21).

following his death. Clearly, the messianic and the non-messianic portraits of Jesus are contradictory, and clearly, the non-messianic portrait has, by virtue of the criterion of dissimilarity or embarrassment, the greater claim to historicity.

How does Q fit into the picture of early Christianity? If Kloppenborg is right in placing Q^1 in Palestine (the Galilee) in the 50s among Jesus' earliest followers, then this document (Q^1) might place us a step closer to Jesus and contain sayings with a particularly strong claim to authenticity and reliability. From a methodological perspective, there are however two issues to consider:

1. How certain are we of the existence of the hypothetical source Q? Although we have made numerous references to Q in previous chapters and have developed arguments based on Q, it is important to remember that Q is a hypothetical document. It is one thing to make the case for Q; it is an entirely other matter to reconstruct Q and to then make the claim that it is an identifiable *Sayings Gospel Q*. Perhaps most problematic is the claim that there are several discernible and recoverable strata of Q. Some might consider this observation overly cautious on my part; I consider it sound and suited to the nature of the evidence, especially the matter of the three different strata of Q.

2. Kloppenborg observed that Q contains wisdom (sapiential) sayings and apocalyptic sayings, both of which are attributed to Jesus. He then asks whether Q underwent a "redactional intervention" implying that one of these elements was primary and the other secondary.[14] Kloppenborg then separates the wisdom sayings from the apocalyptic sayings and claims that Q originated as a sapiential (wisdom) document (Q^1) to which apocalyptic sayings of Jesus (Q^2) were subsequently added. The Q document was then further revised with the addition of narrative passages, which Kloppenborg identifies as Q^3.

It would be helpful to look more closely at some of Kloppenborg's work on Q before passing judgment on the credibility of his theory of multiple strata of the *Sayings Gospel*. To that end, Kloppenborg has identified six clusters of wisdom sayings or "sapiential speeches" that, he believes, were in an early written stratum of Q.[15] These speeches were presumably completed units of tradition, written sapiential collections, prior to their incorporation into what amounts to the first edition of Q, or what Kloppenborg identifies as Q^1. I will quote only a few verses from each of these six clusters:

---

14. Ibid., 96.

15. Kloppenborg, "The Sayings Gospel Q," 1–66. Several of these six sayings clusters have also been identified by Dieter Lührmann, Siegfried Schulz, Dieter Zeller, Ronald Piper, Hans Dieter Betz, and others.

JESUS OF NAZARETH: THE TEACHER OF WISDOM

Cluster 1. Q 6:20b–23b, 27–35, 36–45, 46–49[16]

^{6:20b}Blessed are [[«you»]] poor, for God's reign is for [[you]].

^{6:21}Blessed are [[«you»]] who hunger, for [[you]] will eat [[your]] fill.

Blessed are [[«you»]] who [[mourn]], for [[<you> will be consoled]].

^{6:22}Blessed are you when they insult and [[persecute]] you,

and [[say every kind of]] evil [[against]] you because of

the son of humanity.[17]

^{6:23}Be glad and [[exult]], for vast is your reward in heaven. For this is how they [[persecuted]] the prophets who «were» before you.

^{6:27}Love your enemies

^{6:28}and [[pray]] for those [[persecuting]] you.

^{6:29}[[The one who slaps]] you on the cheek, offer [[him]] the other as well;

and [[to the person wanting to take you to court and get]] your shirt,

[[turn over to him]] the coat as well.

[[«And the one who conscripts you for one mile, go with him a second.»]] . . . .

^{6:36}Be full of pity just as your Father .. is full of pity.

^{6:37} .. Do not pass judgment, «so» that you are not judged.

[[For with what judgment you pass judgment,

you will be judged.]]

^{6:38}[[And]] with the measurement you use to measure out,

it will be measured out to you. . . . .

^{6:41}And why do you see the speck in your brother's eye,

but the beam in your own eye you overlook?

^{6:42}How can you say to your brother:

Let me throw out the speck [[from]] your eye,

and just look at the beam in your own eye?

Hypocrite, first throw out from your own eye the beam,

and then you will see clearly to throw out the speck

«in» your brother's eye. . . .

Cluster 2. Q 9:57–60, (61–62); 10:2–11, 16

^{9:57}And someone said to him:

I will follow you wherever you go.

^{9:58}And Jesus said to him:

Foxes have holes, and the birds of the sky have nests;

but the son of humanity does not have anywhere he can lay his head.

^{9:59}But another said to him:

---

16. The text of these six clusters of Q sayings is taken from Robinson, *The Critical Edition of Q*. Once again, citations in Q are customarily indicated by the location of the passage in the Gospel of Luke, so Q 6:20b refers to the Q form of the passage underlying Luke 6:20b and its Matthean parallel, and so forth.

17. "the son of humanity" here and elsewhere in this collection is the translation of the phrase traditionally rendered "the Son of Man."

THE NEW TESTAMENT

Master, permit me first to go and bury my father.
⁹ː⁶⁰But he said to him:
Follow me, and leave the dead to bury their own dead. . . .
¹⁰ː⁸And whatever town you enter and they take you in,
[[«eat what is set before you»]].
¹⁰ː⁹And cure the sick there, and say [[to them]]:
The kingdom of God has reached unto you.
¹⁰ː¹⁰But into whatever town you enter and they do not take you in,
on going out [[from that town]],
¹⁰ː¹¹shake off the dust from your feet.
¹⁰ː¹⁶Whoever takes you in takes me in,
[[and]] whoever takes me in takes in the one who sent me.

Cluster 3. Q 11:2b–4, 9–13

¹¹ː²ᵇ[[When]] you pray, [[say]]:
Father—may your name be kept holy!—
let your reign come:
¹¹ː³Our day's bread give us today;
¹¹ː⁴and cancel our debts for us,
as we too have cancelled for those in debt to us;
and do not put us to the test! . . . .

Cluster 4. Q 12:2–7, 11–12

¹²ː²Nothing is covered up that will not be exposed,
and hidden that will not be known.
¹²ː³What I say to you in the dark, speak in the light;
and what you hear «whispered» in the ear, proclaim on the housetops. . . .
¹²ː¹¹When they bring you before synagogues,
do not be anxious about how or what you are to say;
¹²ː¹²for [[the holy Spirit will teach]] you in that .. hour
what you are to say.

Cluster 5. Q 12:22b–31, 33–34

¹²ː²²ᵇTherefore I tell you,
do not be anxious about your life, what you are to eat,
nor about your body, with what you are to clothe yourself.
¹²ː²³Is not life more than food, and the body more than clothing? . . . .
¹²ː²⁷[[Observe]] the lillies, how they grow
They do not work nor do they spin. Yet I tell you:
Not even Solomon in all his glory was arrayed like one of these.
¹²ː²⁸But if in the field the grass,
there today and tomorrow thrown into the oven, God clothes thus,
will he not much more clothe you, persons of petty faith! . . . .
¹²ː³¹But seek his kingdom,

and [[all]] these things shall be granted to you. . . .

According to Kloppenborg, the collection of sapiential sayings or "sapiential speeches" should probably include, as well:

Cluster 6. Q 13:24; 14:26–27; 17:33; 14:34–35

> ^{14:26}[[<The one who>]] does not hate father and mother <can>not be my <disciple>; and
> [[<the one who>]] <does not hate> son and daughter cannot be my disciple.
> ^{14:27} .. The one who does not take his cross and follow after me
> cannot be my disciple.
> ^{17:33}[[The one who]] finds one's life will lose it,
> and [[the one who]] loses one's life [[for my sake]] will find it.

REFERENCES TO THE SON OF MAN IN KLOPPENBERG'S Q[1]

The phrase "son of man" seems to have three very different meanings in the canonical gospels, and part of the confusion likely arises from the ambiguity of the original Aramaic phrase (*bar ĕnāš*) that underlies the Greek of the New Testament (*hŏ huiŏs tou anthrōpou*). It is important to recall that Jesus and his earliest followers spoke Aramaic. When Jesus' words were translated from Aramaic into Greek by early Christians, the Aramaic phrase that meant "a mere mortal being" (*bar ĕnāš*) was apparently translated into Greek literally as "son of man." As a result this Aramaic phrase that meant merely "man" or "human being" (or sometimes simply "I" or "me") was confused with the honorific title ascribed to the eschatological Son of Man. This issue appears to have become especially confused once the Christian *kerygma* proclaimed that Jesus would return very soon as the eschatological Son of Man.

In these six clusters of sayings, there are only two sayings that refer to the Son of Man ("son of humanity" in the reconstructed text of Q): Q 6:22 and Q 9:58:

> ^{Q 6:22}Blessed are you when they insult and [[persecute]] you,
> and [[say every kind of]] evil [[against]] you because of
> the son of humanity.

> ^{Q 9:58}And Jesus said to him:
> Foxes have holes, and the birds of the sky have nests;
> but the son of humanity does not have anywhere he can lay his head.

Although the Greek phrase used in both of these passages is *hŏ huiŏs tou anthrōpou* (the son of man), it is clear that neither of these passages refers to the eschatological Son of Man, nor to the suffering Son of Man in the passion narrative of the synoptic gospels:

Mark 8:31 = Matt 16:21 = Luke 9:22

Mark 9:12 = Matt 17:12b

Mark 9:31 = Matt 17:22b–23a = Luke 9:44b

Mark 10:33 = Matt 20:18 = Luke 18:31–33

Mark 10:45 = Matt 20:28

Mark 14:21 = Matt 26:24 = Luke 22:22)

Rather, in these two verses in Q, the Greek phrase "son of man (humanity)" is a surrogate term for "me" and "I" respectively and refers to Jesus in his active ministry, emphasizing his humility or lowliness. See also Luke 7:33–34:

> For John the Baptist has come eating no bread and drinking no wine, and you say, "He is a demon"; the Son of Man has come eating and drinking and you say, "Look, a glutton and a drunkard, a friend of tax collectors and sinners."

And also Luke 5:24 and 6:5:

> 5:24"But so that you may know that the Son of Man has authority on earth to forgive sins,"—he said to the one who was paralyzed—"I say to you, stand up and take your bed and go to your home."

> 6:5Then he said to them, "The Son of Man is lord of the sabbath."

With these words, Jesus is not claiming for himself authority on earth to forgive sins or to break the law of the sabbath. He is claiming that the authority to forgive sins and to break the sabbath rests with simple mortal human beings *like* him.

This interpretation is especially clear in the version of this story in Mark 2:27–28, which we examined earlier in this book. After being challenged by the Pharisees for sending his disciples into the fields to gather grain on the sabbath, Jesus said to them:

> The sabbath was made for humankind, and not humankind for the sabbath. So the Son of Man [humankind] is lord even of the sabbath. (my rendering, see above pp. 138–40).

In these passages, the understanding of the phrase "son of man" as any simple mortal being is obviously Markan and probably even pre-Markan, as is evident in these two passages in Q. Underlying these verses in both Mark and Q is a remarkable claim that likely reaches back to Jesus himself: namely, that a simple human being has authority on earth to forgive sins and to break the sabbath law if there is a valid reason.

Further support for this extraordinary claim of Jesus is found in Matt 9:8:

> When the crowds saw it [i.e., Jesus forgiving the sins of the paralytic], they were filled with awe, and they glorified God, who had given such authority [to forgive sins] to human beings (tois anthrōpois).

In summary, the two verses, Q 6:22 and Q 9:58, are not eschatological, in spite of the confusion in the Greek text and in modern English translations. The confusion could be avoided in English if translators would simply render the original intent

JESUS OF NAZARETH: THE TEACHER OF WISDOM

of the Aramaic into English rather than translate literally the confused Greek into confusing English. I would propose something like this in English:

> Q 6:22 Blessed are you when they insult and persecute you,
> and say every kind of evil against you because of me.

> Q 9:58 And Jesus said to him:
> Foxes have holes, and the birds of the sky have nests;
> but I do not have anywhere [I] can lay [my] head.

REFERENCES TO GOD'S KINGDOM IN KLOPPENBERG'S Q¹

The issue with the phrase "God's Kingdom" in Kloppenborg's Q¹ is different. In Kloppenborg's six clusters of presumed wisdom sayings, there are four references to the kingdom (Greek *basileia*) of God, or God's reign, or God's rule. Let us look at each of these passages individually.

> Q 6:20b. Blessed are [[«you»]] poor, for God's reign is for [[you]].

In Q 6:20b, we find the first of the beatitudes, all of which emphasize a reversal of values, probably characteristic of Jesus' teaching: the material values of this world ("wealth" in Q 6:20b) as opposed to the vision of God's reign as preached by Jesus. There is, as well, a paradox in the beatitudes, and especially in this beatitude: the first element (poverty) expresses the current lot of Jesus' followers; the second element expresses their eschatological status in God's (future) reign or rule.

> Q 10:9. And cure the sick there, and say [[to them]]:
> The kingdom of God has reached unto you.

In Q 10:9, Jesus' proclamation of the kingdom of God is a blessing for those who welcome Jesus' disciples and a curse for those who disregard them, because God's kingdom or rule reaches the people in the disciples' preaching about it and in their work on its behalf. The implication of this saying is that the kingdom of God has approached or has drawn near to the people, but that its full manifestation still lies in the future.

In this saying, Q preserves some of the futuristic eschatology of the teaching of Jesus and the earliest Christian community. C. H. Dodd maintained that the verb *ēngiken* in both Mark 1:15 and in this verse in Q 10:9 means "has [already] come,"[18] but Werner Georg Kümmel, James M. Robinson, and others have shown that the verb should be understood as "has approached" or "has drawn near."[19]

---

18. Dodd, *The Parables of the Kingdom*, 28–30.
19. Kümmel, *Promise and Fulfillment*, 24; Robinson, *The Problem of History in Mark*, 72 n. 1; Schlosser, *Le Règne de Dieu*, vol. 1, 106–08; Fitzmyer, *The Gospel According to Luke*, 848–49. Cf. Black, "The Kingdom of God Has Come," 289–90; Hutton, "The Kingdom of God Has Come," 89–91.

In chapter 2, we examined the importance of philological study in biblical scholarship. This verse in Q is an important case in point. Stated simply, in support of his translation of the verb ἐινγίζειν (*eingizein*) as "has [already] come," Dodd cited passages in the Greek Septuagint in which *eingizein* was used to translate the Hebrew word *ngʿ*,[20] or the Aramaic word *mṭ ʾ*.[21] On the other hand, Joel Marcus has shown that "in the Septuagint, however, *engizein* almost always translates two other verbs, *ngš*,[22] and *qrb*,[23] which mean 'to come near,' and this is the most obvious meaning of the Greek verb in the other NT passages as well as in its rare occurrences in nonbiblical Greek."[24] This verse in Q, therefore, means that with the teaching of Jesus and his disciples God's reign or rule has drawn near to or has begun to approach the people. Implied, moreover, is that God's reign or rule will ultimately be consummated with the future coming of the eschatological Son of Man, a conclusion for which we presented substantial evidence in the previous chapter.

> Q 11:2b. [[When]] you pray, [[say]]:
> Father—may your name be kept holy!—
> let your reign come:

In Q 11:2b, we encounter the second petition in what is commonly referred to as the Lord's Prayer. The form in Q (and in Luke) is generally thought to be more original than the more familiar Matthean version and is, therefore, presumably closer to what Jesus may have taught. The meaning is eminently clear: Jesus' followers are urged to pray for the arrival of God's reign, which he and they apparently believed was already manifest through Jesus' teaching and ministry. The Greek verb *elthetō* is a second aorist, third person singular imperative and means "may it [your reign or rule] come," in the words of Joseph Fitzmyer "expressing punctiliar action suited to the eschatological nuance of the wish."[25]

> Q 12:31. But seek his kingdom,
> and [[all]] these things shall be granted to you.

In Q 12:31, Jesus urges his listeners to allow God's kingdom to dominate their lives. In doing so they will receive from God all that they really need in their lives—food, drink, and clothing.

These four verses appear in the material that Kloppenborg identified as the first layer of Q, material that reflects the wisdom teaching of the earliest church and/or possibly of the historical Jesus. It is important to note that even in this selected material there are clear tones of eschatology in these four references to God's kingdom or rule.

20. Meaning "touch, reach, strike." See *A Hebrew and English Lexicon*, 619.
21. Meaning "come." Ibid., 1101, 1083.
22. Meaning "draw near, approach." 620.
23. Meaning "come near, approach." Ibid., 897.
24. Marcus, *Mark 1–8*, 172–73.
25. Fitzmyer, *Luke*, 904.

To remedy this problem, some scholars maintain that material in Q¹ was sometimes subsequently edited by a later redactor and that passages such as these may be redactional layers superimposed on earlier wisdom sayings. Such an interpretation of the data is problematic. From a methodological point of view, it is important to be sure that data is not being manipulated simply to fit presumed conclusions. Interpreting apparently eschatological references as secondary editing is questionable and is an example of circular reasoning.

LOOKING AT Q AS AN INTEGRAL WHOLE

To look at Q as an integral whole does not imply that there were no earlier oral and/or written sources that the author(s) of Q collected and incorporated into the version(s) of the document available to the authors of the gospels of Matthew and Luke. Indeed, the six clusters that Kloppenborg identified as Q¹ may have existed in oral or written form and may have been brought together into Q along with other oral and/or written materials from both wisdom and eschatological teachings of Jesus.

Accordingly, it is appropriate to look more closely at some of the passages in which Q speaks directly about or alludes to the reign or rule of God or to the coming of the Son of Man or otherwise points to the impending end:

Q 3:7–9

> He said to the [[crowds coming to be]] bapti[[zed]]: Snakes' litter! Who warned you to run from the impending rage? So bear fruit worthy of repentance, and do not presume to tell yourselves: We have as «fore»father Abraham! For I tell you: God can produce children for Abraham right out of these rocks! And the ax already lies at the root of the trees. So every tree that is not bearing healthy fruit is to be chopped down and thrown on the fire.

Matt (3:1–17) and Luke (3:1–22) both represent John the Baptist as the precursor of Jesus, who received his call and commission from God on the occasion of his baptism by John. In these verses in Q, however, John the Baptist may be understood as a precursor, not of Jesus, but of the eschatological Son of Man. The text of Q implies that John came to baptize the Jews and to warn them of the imminent danger of God's anger against those who are unprepared for the impending judgment.

Q 6:20–23 (from Kloppenborg's first cluster)

> <..> And [[rais]]ing his [[eyes to]] his disciples he (Jesus) said:
>
> Blessed are [[«you»]] poor for God's reign is for [[you]].
>
> Blessed are [[«you»]] who hunger for [[you]] will eat [[your]] fill.
>
> Blessed are [[«you»]] who [[mourn]], for [[you will be consoled]].

> Blessed are you when they insult and [[persecute]] you, and [[say every kind of]] evil [[against]] you because of the son of humanity.
>
> Be glad and [[exult]], for vast is your reward in heaven. For this is how they [[persecuted]] the prophets who «were» before you.

These verses in Q present beatitudes or declarations of blessedness that are eschatologically-oriented. Jesus addresses those who have abandoned everything in anticipation of God's coming reign. These beatitudes introduce the great sermon, Matthew's Sermon on the Mount (Matt 5–7) and Luke's Sermon on the Plain (Luke 6:17–49).

Q 6:46–49 (from Kloppenborg's first cluster)

> Why do you call me: Master, Master, and do not do what I say? Everyone hearing my words and acting on them, is like a person who built [[one's]] house on bedrock; and the rain poured down and the flash-floods came, [[and the winds blew]] and pounded that house, and it did not collapse, for it was founded on bedrock. And [[everyone]] who hears [[my words]] and does not act on [[them]] is like a person who built [[one's]] house on the sand, and the rain poured down and the flash-floods came, [[and the winds blew]] and battered that house, and promptly it collapsed and its [[fall]] was devastating.

In these verses, Jesus issues an eschatological warning to those who address him as Master but who do not heed his warning by demonstrating the kind of commitment that is necessary to respond to Jesus' call to discipleship.

Q 7:28

> I tell you: There has not arisen among women's offspring anyone who «surpasses» John. Yet the least in God's kingdom is more than he.

With these words, Jesus praises John the Baptist as the greatest of men until the coming of God's rule, at which time those who have submitted to God's rule will surpass in greatness even John.

Q 7:34

> The son of humanity came, eating and drinking, and you say: Look! A person «who» is a glutton and drunkard, a chum of tax collectors and sinners!

Jesus speaks of himself in this saying as the son of man [son of humanity] with the Aramaic meaning "I." The meaning here is not eschatological.

Q 9:58 (from Kloppenborg's second cluster)

> And Jesus said to him: Foxes have holes, and birds of the sky have nests; but the son of humanity does not have anywhere he can lay his head.

Jesus again speaks of himself as the son of man [son of humanity] with the Aramaic meaning "I."

JESUS OF NAZARETH: THE TEACHER OF WISDOM

Q 10:9 (from Kloppenborg's second cluster)

> And cure the sick there, and say [[to them]]: The kingdom of God has reached unto you.

Jesus tells his disciples that God's rule has drawn near to the people as a result of their healing of the sick and that it serves as a blessing to those who accept the disciples and as a judgment against those who reject them.

Q 11:17–18, 20

> But, knowing their thoughts, he said to them: Every kingdom divided against itself is left barren, and every household divided against itself will not stand. And if Satan is divided against himself, how will his kingdom stand? . . . But if it is by the finger of God that I cast out demons, then there has come upon you God's reign.

In these verses, Jesus discusses with the crowd the question of the source of his power and authority. The story addresses the question whether Jesus received his power from Satan (or Beelzebul) and concludes that Jesus' power not only comes from God but that, in exercising that power, Jesus was already introducing God's reign whenever people met Jesus both in his words and in his deeds.

Q 11:30

> For as Jonah became to the Ninevites a sign, so [[also]] will the son of humanity be to this generation.

Jesus speaks to this generation of the coming of the son of man as a sign of the inauguration of God's reign. What is unclear is whether Jesus is referring to himself in the Aramaic sense of the phrase (simply I), or whether he is referring here to the coming of the eschatological Son of Man. It is perhaps this very ambiguity that led to later confusion in the use of the phrase son of man as a title of Jesus as the Son of Man designate, who will return again following his death and resurrection.

Q 11:52

> Woe to you, [[exegetes of the Law,]] for you shut the [[kingdom of <God> from people]]; you did not go in, [[nor]] let in those «trying to» get in.

In this verse, Jesus condemns the scribes and the Pharisees for controlling the Hebrew scriptures through their narrow interpretation of the law, thereby effectively locking people out of or otherwise excluding them from God's kingdom.

Q 12:10

> Jesus says: Whoever blasphemes against the Father, it will be forgiven him. And whoever blasphemes against the Son, it will be forgiven him. But whoever blasphemes against the Holy Spirit, it will not be forgiven him, neither on earth nor in heaven.

Jesus speaks of the unforgivable sin against the Holy Spirit. The later church came to understand this verse as a reference to the Trinity: the Father, the Son, and the Holy Spirit. "Son" here probably means son of man, either in the Aramaic sense of "me" or as a reference to the coming eschatological Son of Man. In Luke-Acts, sins against the Holy Spirit risked harsh judgment (see Acts 5:1–11; 7:51; 8:14–24). The parallel passage in Matt 12:32 makes no mention of the Father and, therefore, appears to be more original than what is cited above as Q 12:10.[26]

Q 12:39–40

But know this: If the householder had known in which watch the robber was coming, he would not have let his house be dug into. You also must be ready, for the Son of Humanity is coming at an hour you do not expect.

Jesus clearly warns that the eschatological Son of Man will come when he is least expected. There is nothing to suggest that Jesus is referring here to his own second coming.

Q 12:42–46

Who then is the faithful [[and]] wise slave who the master put over his household to give [[them]] food on time? Blessed is that slave whose master, on coming, will find him so doing. [[Amen,]] I tell you, he will appoint him over all his possessions. But if that slave says in his heart: My master is delayed, and begins to beat [[his fellow slaves]], and eats and drinks [[with the]] drunk[[ards]], the master of that slave will come on a day he does not expect and at an hour he does not know, and will cut him to pieces and give him an inheritance with the faithless.

Although the phrase "son of man" appears nowhere in this story, the parable of the faithful and unfaithful slave is unmistakably an allegory warning of the unexpected day and hour of the arrival of the Son of Man. The authentic parables of Jesus were generally not full-blown allegories, so there is some question whether this is Jesus speaking of the imminent arrival of the Son of Man or the Christian community speaking of Jesus' imminent return as the eschatological Son of Man. Because of the proximity of this parable to Q 12:39–40, it is evident that both stories focus on the uncertainty of the time of the Son of Man's coming.

Q 12:54-56

[[«But he said to them:» When evening has come, you say: Good weather! For the sky is flame red.]] [[And at dawn: Today «it's» wintry! For the lowering sky

---

26. Matt 12:32: "Whoever speaks a word against the Son of Man (perhaps meaning "against me") will be forgiven, but whoever speaks against the Holy Spirit will not be forgiven, either in this age or in the age to come." The Matthean version "either in this age or in the age to come" is more eschatological and seems to be more original. See also *Did* 11:7: "And every prophet who speaks in the Spirit you shall neither try nor judge; for every sin shall be forgiven, but this sin shall not be forgiven."

is flame red.]] [[The face of the sky you know to interpret, but the time you are not able to?]]

Once again, in this story Jesus speaks about the people's ability to read the signs of the sky and thereby predict the weather, but they are unable to read the signs of the times that will usher in the Age to Come.

Q 13:18

What is the kingdom of God like, and with what am I to compare it?

Q 13:20

[[And again]]: with what am I to compare to kingdom of God?

These words of Jesus in the form of a rhetorical question introduce the parable of the mustard seed (13:18–19) and the parable of the yeast (13:20–21) respectively. The phrase also served as a familiar formula in rabbinical parables.[27]

Q 13:29, 28

[[And many]] shall come from Sunrise and Sunset and recline with Abraham and Isaac and Jacob in the kingdom of God, but [[you will be]] thrown out [[into the]] out[[er darkness]], where there will be wailing and grinding of teeth.

Jesus speaks of the joy that will accompany those who will dine with the Hebrew patriarchs in the future kingdom of God in contrast to the wailing and grinding of teeth on the part of those who are excluded from God's kingdom. To eat in the kingdom of God is a common metaphor for salvation (see Luke 14:15; 22:16; 22:29–30; see also Isa 25:6; Rev 3:20; 19:9).

Q 16:16

.. The law and the prophets «were» until John. From then on the kingdom of God is violated and the violent plunder it.

Jesus says that the Hebrew scriptures were in effect until the coming of John the Baptist, but that the situation has now changed with the coming of John. The meaning of this verse is "one of the greatest riddles of the exegesis of the Synoptics"[28] but, whatever it may mean, the sense is certainly negative, suggesting that the rule of God suffers violence. Ulrich Luz has suggested that it means "Since John the Baptist, violence has been done to the kingdom of God," possibly by the Zealots or more likely by "overzealous followers of the Baptist and of Jesus."[29] Admittedly most suggestions are mere conjectures.

---

27. Fitzmyer, *The Gospel according to Luke*, 679; Jeremias, *The Parables of Jesus*, 101; Strack and Billerbeck *Kommentar zum Neuen Testament*, vol. 2, 8.

28. Luz, *Matthew 8–20*, 140.

29. Ibid., 141.

Q 17:23–24, 26–27, 30

> If they say to you: Look, he is in the wilderness, do not go out; look, he is indoors, do not follow. For as the lightning streaks from Sunrise and flashes as far as Sunset, so will be the Son of Humanity [[on his day]]. . . . . . As [[it took place in]] the days of Noah, so will it be [[in the day<>]] of the Son of Humanity. [[For as in those days they were]] eating and drinking, marrying and giving in marriage, until the day Noah entered the ark and the flood came and took them all, . . . so will it also be on the day the Son of Humanity is revealed.

Jesus warns his listeners that the eschatological Son of Man and the end of history as we know it can come at any time. Jesus is not speaking of his own second coming (parousia).

Q 17:34–35

> I tell you there will be two «men» [[in the field]]; one is taken and one is left. Two «women» will be grinding at the mill; one is taken and one is left.

Jesus warns once again that the end can come at any time and that only some people will share in God's reign.

Q 19:12–13, 15–24, 26

> .. A certain person, on taking a trip, called ten of his slaves and gave them two minas [[and said to them: Do business until I come]]. . . . . [[After a long time]] the master of those slaves comes and settles accounts with them. And the first [[came]] saying: Master, your mina has produced ten more minas. And he said to him: Well done. Good slave, you have been faithful over a pittance. I will set you over much. And the [[second]] came saying: Master, your mina has earned five minas. He said to [[him: Well done, good slave, you have been faithful over a pittance.]] I will set you over much. And the other came saying: Master, [[I knew]] you, that you are a hard person, reaping where you did not sow and gathering up where you did not winnow; and, scared, I [[went «and»]] hid [[your <mina>]] in [[the ground]]. Here, you have what belongs to you. He said to him: Wicked slave! You knew that I reap where I have not sewn, and gather up from where I have not winnowed? [[Then you had to invest]] my money [[with the]] money [[changers]]! And at my coming I would have received what belongs to me plus interest. So take from him the mina and give «it» to the one who has ten minas. . . . [[For]] to everyone who has will be given; but from the one who does not have, even what he has will be taken from him.

Jesus tells a parable of the reckoning that will occur at the time when God's reign arrives.

Although these sayings of Jesus survive in Q without context, it is still incumbent upon biblical scholars to make sense of individual isolated sayings as part of a coherent picture of Jesus' life, ministry, and teaching. Indeed, four of these sayings are embedded in Kloppenborg's six clusters of sapiential teachings.

Kloppenborg himself acknowledges the methodological limitations of his study:

JESUS OF NAZARETH: THE TEACHER OF WISDOM

> To characterize Q as "sapiential" is not, therefore, to imply a depiction of Jesus as a teacher of this-worldly, prudential wisdom, still less to imply an intellectual world that was hermetically sealed against eschatology, prophetic traditions, and the epic traditions of Israel.[30]

Kloppenborg is clear is stating that his analysis of Q is literary and does not lend itself to inferences about the historical Jesus:

> To say that the wisdom components were formative for Q and that the prophetic judgment oracles and apophthegms [pronouncements] describing Jesus' conflict with "this generation" are secondary is not to imply anything about the ultimate tradition-historical provenance of any of the sayings. It is indeed possible, indeed probable, that some of the materials from the secondary compositional phase are dominical or at least very old, and that some of the formative elements are, from the standpoint of authenticity or tradition-history, relatively young.[31]

Helmut Koester has examined Q, or what he calls "The Synoptic Sayings Source,"[32] and has observed that Jesus' Inaugural Sermon to the Disciples in Q 6:20–46 is not simply a "sapiential speech," as Kloppenborg maintains,[33] but it is

> "a prophetic, and thus eschatological, announcement of the presence of the rule of God. However, there is no trace of an apocalyptic perspective which predicts judgment and condemnation."[34]

Likewise, Koester maintains that many of the sayings in Q 12:39–13:21, which describe the coming judgment, speak about the uncertainty of the coming of the Son of Man. Some of these sayings speak to "the presence of the eschatological moment in Jesus and his word," a position that Koester claims "was the original meaning of such sayings in the original version of Q."[35]

Koester argues that the original version of Q included not only wisdom sayings, but eschatological sayings as well.[36] He does not believe, as do Koppenborg and others, that the earliest version of Q "presented Jesus simply as a teacher of wisdom without an eschatological message."[37]

Like Kloppenborg, Koester identifies several stages in the writing of Q. For Koester, these stages include: (1) the first collection of the sayings of Jesus and their assembly into sapiential discourses, (2) an apocalyptic redaction, and (3) a pre-Matthean redaction that produced the Sermon on the Mount.[38] Koester maintains that these stages in

---

30. Kloppenborg, *Excavting Q*, 388.
31. Ibid., 245.
32. Koester, *Ancient Christian Gospels*, 128–71.
33. Kloppenborg, *Formation of Q*, passim.
34. Koester, *Ancient Christian Gospels*, 138.
35. Ibid., 147.
36. Ibid., 150.
37. Ibid.
38. Ibid., 128–71, see especially 170.

the development of Q likely occurred in "Greek-speaking Christian communities in the diaspora of Syria, like that of Antioch."[39]

In the previous chapter, we observed that eschatology appears to frame Jesus' message, yet it is clear that he also taught a great deal that falls more obviously into the category of wisdom. As Koester has shown, these are not necessarily separate and isolated spheres of teaching; they are parts of a coherent whole. Jesus expected the imminent coming of the Son of Man to consummate the present in-breaking of God's reign, which Jesus apparently believed was already evident in his teaching and ministry and in the behavior of his disciples.

Reconstructing Q is a critical component of solving the puzzle. The detailed scholarly reconstruction of Q by a team of almost fifty scholars, however imperfect their work may be, has been enormously helpful to New Testament scholarship, particularly as dedicated Q scholars have worked to discover and reconstitute the text of Q and to determine its date, its place of origin, and its characteristics.

To identify Q as the source of many of the sayings found in Matthew and Luke is an important and enduring contribution to biblical scholarship. Reconstituting Q from parallel verses in Matthew and Luke has been a major endeavor. However, to proceed from this reconstruction of Q and to dissect Q into two or three distinct layers and to then describe in detail the process by which Q came into its present form is especially challenging and may lie beyond the limits of historical reason.

Bart Ehrman has characterized the dilemma well:

> Let me repeat: Q is a source that we don't have. To reconstruct what we think was in it is hypothetical enough. But at least in doing so we have some hard evidence, since we do have traditions that are verbatim the same in Matthew and Luke (but not found in Mark), and we have to account for them in some way. But to go further and insist that we know what was not in the source, for example, a Passion narrative, what its multiple editions were like, and which of these multiple editions was the earliest, and so on, really goes far beyond what we can know.[40]

Some would argue that Ehrman is overly cautious, that we do have the text of Q, even if we do not have a manuscript of Q. I agree with Ehrman's reservations, because I find that it is difficult to pile hypothesis upon hypothesis upon hypothesis; yet, this is exactly what some scholars are doing.

THE *GOSPEL OF THOMAS*

Until the twentieth century, the *Gospel of Thomas* was known only from references in several church fathers, beginning in the early third century. The earliest reference to the *Gospel of Thomas* appears in a writing of Hippolytus of Rome (ca. 170–ca. 236).

---

39. Ibid., 170.
40. Ehrman, *Jesus, Apocalyptic Prophet*, 133.

Writing about 222–235 about a sect known as the Naasenes,[41] Hippolytus wrote, in what some scholars think may be an allusion to saying 5 in the *Gospel of Thomas*:

> [The Naassenes] speak . . . .of a nature which is both hidden and revealed at the same time and which they call the thought-for kingdom of heaven which is in a human being. They transmit a tradition concerning this in the Gospel entitled "According to Thomas," which states expressly, "The one who seeks me will find me in children of seven years and older, for there, hidden in the fourteenth aeon, I am revealed" (Hippolytus, *Refutation of All Heresies* 5.7.20).

Writing about 233 in Alexandria, Origen (ca. 185–ca. 254) referred to the *Gospel according to Thomas* as a heterodox gospel.[42] Perhaps dependent on Origen, other church fathers referred to the *Gospel of Thomas* and the *Gospel according to Matthias* as heretical: Eusebius of Caesarea (ca. 260–ca. 339)[43] and Jerome (ca. 347–420).[44] In his *Catechetical Lectures* (347–348), Cyril of Jerusalem (ca. 315–386) mentioned the *Gospel of Thomas* twice.[45] Moreover, the 5th century *Decretum Gelasianum* also mentions among its list of heretical books "a Gospel attributed to Thomas, which the Manichaean use."[46] And the *Stichometry* of Nicephorus (758–828) provides a list of

---

41. The Naasenes (or Nasoraeans) were one of many baptizing sects located in Galilee, Transjordan, Syria and the area of northern Iraq beginning in about 200 BCE and extending into the first centuries CE. Similar baptizing groups included the Essenes, the Samaritans, the Ebionites, the Sabaeans, and the Elchasaites.

42. "There is I know a Gospel which is called 'according to Thomas,' and one 'according to Matthias,' and there are many others which we read, lest we should seem to be unacquainted with any point for the sake of those who think they possess some valuable knowledge if they are acquainted with them. But in all these we approve nothing else but that which the Church approves, that is, four Gospels only as proper to be received" (Origen, *Homily on Luke* 1).

43. "But we have nevertheless felt compelled to give a catalogue of these also, distinguishing those works which according to ecclesiastical tradition are true and genuine and commonly accepted, from those others which, although not canonical but disputed, are yet at the same time known to most ecclesiastical writers—we have felt compelled to give this catalogue in order that we might be able to know both these works and those that are cited by the heretics under the name of the apostles, including, for instance, such books as the Gospels of Peter, of Thomas, of Matthias, or of any others besides them, and the Acts of Andrew and John and the other apostles, which no one belonging to the succession of ecclesiastical writers has deemed worthy of mention in his writings" (Eusebius, *Church History* 3.25.6).

44. "The evangelist Luke declares that there were many who wrote the gospels, when he says, 'forasmuch as many, etc.' (Luke 1:1), which being published by various authors, gave rise to several heresies. They were such as that according to the Egyptians, and Thomas, and Matthias, and Bartholomew, that of the Twelve Apostles, and Basilides, and Apelles, and others which it would be tedious to enumerate" (Jerome, *Commentary on Matthew*, Prologue). See also Ambrose of Milan (ca. 338–397), *Expositio Evangelii Lucae* 1.2.

45. "The Manichaeans also wrote a Gospel according to Thomas, which being tinctured with the fragrance of the evangelic title corrupts the souls of the simple sort" (Cyril of Alexandria, *Catechesis* 4.36).

"Let none read the Gospel according to Thomas: for it is the work not of one of the twelve Apostles, but of one of the three wicked disciples of Manes" (Cyril of Alexandria, *Catechesis* 6.31).

46. Koester, *Ancient Christian Gospels*, 78. Mani (216–276), the founder of the dualistic religion known as Manichaeism, was a prophet who was raised in the late first century Jewish Christian sect

canonical and apocryphal books of the Old Testament and New Testament and lists the *Gospel of Thomas* as having 1300 lines, implying that *Thomas* was still known in the early ninth century.

Although obviously well-known in antiquity, the *Gospel of Thomas* survived only as a memory in writings of fathers of the church until the discovery in 1897, 1903, and 1904 of three Greek papyrus fragments at the site of an ancient library at Oxyrhynchus, Egypt:

Papyrus	Papyrus Date[47]	Sayings in *Gos Thos*
Oxyr pap 1	about 200	26–30, 77:2–3, 31–33 in that order
Oxyr pap 654	about 250	prologue, 1–7
Oxyr pap 655	before 250	24, 36–39

These three fragments appear to represent portions of three different copies of the *Gospel of Thomas* in what was probably its original Greek.[48] When the papyri were first discovered, some speculated that they might be fragments of the unknown *Gospel of Thomas*, but that was confirmed only with the discovery in 1945 at Nag Hammadi, Egypt of a complete and well-preserved fourth or fifth century Coptic manuscript of the *Gospel of Thomas* with 114 sayings attributed to Jesus, but with little narrative, no stories about Jesus, no miracles, and no account of Jesus' death and resurrection. Although the three earlier fragments are apparently examples of the Greek text underlying the Coptic *Gospel of Thomas*, they differ from the Greek text of the *Gospel of Thomas* that was evidently available to the translator of the Coptic, as the Greek and the Coptic texts are often quite different.

Since its discovery, the *Gospel of Thomas* has been an issue of considerable controversy among New Testament scholars. Dating the *Gospel of Thomas* has been particularly problematic, because it is difficult to know exactly what it is that scholars are dating. Scholarly opinion falls into two very different camps, one camp that dates an early version of the gospel between about 50 and 100, and a second camp that dates the gospel underlying the Coptic translation to sometime in the second century, following the composition and dissemination of the gospels of Matthew, Mark, Luke, and John.

---

known as the Elchasaites.

47. The dates of papyrus 1, 654, and 655 are based on an analysis of scribal handwriting. See Kraft. ed., *The Complete Gospels*, 324.

48. An English translation of the Greek fragments of the *Gospel of Thomas* can be found in Miller, *The Complete Gospels*, 325–29.

JESUS OF NAZARETH: THE TEACHER OF WISDOM
AN EARLY DATE FOR THE *GOSPEL OF THOMAS*

Scholars who favor an early date for the *Gospel of Thomas* point especially to similarities between sayings in the *Gospel of Thomas* and seemingly related sayings in the hypothetical source Q and argue that "sayings gospels" apparently belonged to the earliest stratum of Christian tradition during the period before the writing of our canonical gospels. Some have argued that the form of some of the sayings in the *Gospel of Thomas* is more primitive than the form of their parallel sayings in the canonical gospels, that a shorter, simpler, less developed version of a saying without the redactional characteristics of our canonical gospels is generally more original than a longer, more complex, more developed version with those redactional characteristics, for example:

Gos Thos	Canonical Gospel Parallel
Saying 8	Matt 13:47–50
Saying 9	Mark 4:2–9
Saying 20	Mark 4:30–32
Saying 21	Q/Luke 12:39–40
Saying 31	Mark 6:4–6a
Saying 34	Matt 15:14 = Luke 6:39 (= Q)
Saying 47ab	Q/Luke 16:13 = Matt 6:24
Saying 57	Matt 13:24–30
Saying 63	Luke 12:16–21
Saying 64	Matt 22:1–10=Luke 14:16–24 (=Q)
Saying 65	Mark 12:1–9
Saying 68	Q/Luke 6:22
Saying 95	Q/Luke 6:34
Saying 109	Matt 13:44

A closer look at a just few of these texts might better illustrate the point:

Saying 8	Matt 13:47–50[49]
And he said, "The human one is like a wise fisherman who cast his net into the sea and drew it up from the sea full of little fish. Among them the wise fisherman discovered a fine large fish. He threw all the little fish back into the sea, and easily chose the large fish. Anyone here with two good ears had better listen."	"Again, *the kingdom of heaven* is like *a net* that was thrown into the sea and caught fish *of every kind; when it was full, they threw it ashore, sat down, and put the good into baskets but threw out the bad. So it will be at the end of the age. The angels will come out and separate the evil from the righteous and throw them into the furnace of fire, where there will be weeping and gnashing of teeth.*

Saying 20	Mark 4:30–32
The disciples said to Jesus, "tell us what Heaven's imperial rule is like." He said to them, "It is like a mustard seed. (It's) the smallest of all seeds, but when it falls on prepared soil, it produces a large branch and becomes a shelter for birds of the sky.	He also said, "With what can we compare the kingdom of God, *or what parable will we use for it?* It is like a mustard seed, which, when sown upon the ground, is the smallest of all the seeds *on earth, yet when it is sown it grows up and becomes the greatest of all shrubs,* and puts forth large branches, so that the birds of the air can make nests in its shade.

Saying 34	Q 6:39 = Matt 15:14
Jesus said, "If a blind person leads a blind person, both of them will fall into a hole."	*Can* a blind person show the way to a blind person? *Will not* both fall into a *pit*?

It is difficult to know whether this criterion of brevity and greater simplicity puts us in touch with a more primitive version of a saying, a version earlier in time and perhaps closer to the teaching of the historical Jesus, especially when the results of such analysis sometimes fly in the face of the criteria for historicity outlined in the previous chapter: namely, the criteria of dissimilarity or embarrassment, multiple attestation, contextual credibility, Semitisms, and coherence.

Nevertheless, it is important to penetrate the question of the relationship between the sayings in the *Gospel of Thomas* and parallel traditions in the synoptic gospels. More

---

49. Words printed in italics in these three examples reflect what may be secondary characteristics beyond what may be the more primitive form of these sayings in the *Gospel of Thomas*.

specifically, of the 114 sayings in the *Gos Thos*, 79 have parallels in the synoptic gospels, 46 have parallels to sayings in Q, 27 have parallels to sayings or parables in the Gospel of Mark, 12 have parallels to sayings found only in the Gospel of Matthew (special M?), and 1 has a parallel to a saying found only in the Gospel of Luke (special L?).[50]

Koester argues convincingly that "the materials which the *Gospel of Thomas* and Q share must belong to a very early stage of the transmission of Jesus' sayings. . . . Thus, the *Gospel of Thomas* is either dependent upon the earliest version of Q or, more likely, shares with the author of Q one or several very early collections of Jesus' sayings."[51] Koester makes a strong case in support of the theory that Thomas "had direct access to the traditions which formed the basis of Q's earliest composition" and adds that Thomas "preserved forms of such materials which are more original than the forms in which they are extant in the common sayings source of Matthew and Luke."[52] "The close relationship of the *Gospel of Thomas* to Q cannot be accidental. . . . The *Gospel of Thomas* is either dependent upon Q's earlier version or upon clusters of sayings employed in its composition."[53] Koester also argues that the sources of Mark and the *Gospel of Thomas* were apparently closely related.[54]

It is important to note that the focus of the sayings of Jesus in the *Gospel of Thomas* have no clear Christological message and, therefore, stand in the face of the claim that the early church was of one mind in its proclamation that Jesus' death and resurrection stood at the center of the whole of early Christian faith.

It is also interesting to observe that in *Gos Thos* 12 the leadership of the early church, doubtless of the Jerusalem church, was apparently focused on Jesus' brother James (cf. Mark 6:3; Matt 13:55; Gal 1:19; 2:1–14; and Eusebius, *Church History*, 2.23, 4–7) rather than on Peter, possibly reflecting an early stage in the history of the nascent church that predates the emergence of traditions supporting Petrine supremacy (Matt 16:16–18):

> The disciples said to Jesus, "We know that you are going to leave us. Who will be our leader?"
> Jesus said to them, "No matter where you are, you are to go to James the Just, for whose sake heaven and earth came into being." (*Thomas* 12)

A LATE DATE FOR THE *GOSPEL OF THOMAS*

Looking at other material in the *Gospel of Thomas*, some scholars favor a date sometime in the second century. These scholars usually point to the fact that the *Gospel of*

---

50. Koester, *Ancient Christian Gospels*, 107.
51. Ibid., 95.
52. Ibid., 97. See also 99.
53. Ibid., 150.
54. Ibid., 100–103.

Thomas lacks the eschatological element of earliest Christianity, as manifest in the genuine Pauline letters, in Q, and in the Gospel of Mark. Instead, God's rule in the *Gospel of Thomas* has already taken place and is here and now for those who are prepared to receive Jesus' teaching.

The Jesus of many of the sayings in the *Gospel of Thomas* does not appear to be particularly Jewish and may reflect elements of proto-gnostic thinking. Moreover, in the *Gospel of Thomas*, salvation comes not through Jesus' passion, death, and resurrection, as in the *kerygma* and in the canonical gospels, but through listening to the living Jesus, whose words bring eternal life to those who hear him and understand.

As we observed above, of the 114 sayings in the *Gospel of Thomas*, 79 have parallels in the canonical gospels, a fact that obviously has important consequences. Evidence that the author of the Coptic *Gospel of Thomas* was familiar with the canonical gospels would obviously support a date in the second century. Yet, New Testament scholars disagree sharply about the issue of the relationship of the *Gospel of Thomas* and the canonical gospels. It appears, however, that there are four clusters of sayings in the *Gospel of Thomas* that approximate the order of sayings in the synoptic gospels, an interesting piece of datum:

Gos Thos	Matt	Mark	Luke
32	5:14b		
33:2–3	5:15	4:21	8:16; 11:33
43:3	7:16a, 17–18; 12:33		6:43–44a
44	12:31–32	3:28–30	12:10
45:1	7:16b		6:44b
45:2	12:35		6:45ab
45:3	12:34b		6:45
65	21:33–39	12:1–8	20:9–15
66	21:42	12:10	20:17
92:1	7:7b		11:9b
93	7:6		
94	7:8bc		11:10bc

Before examining these four clusters in the Coptic *Gospel of Thomas*, it is worth noting that only one of the four appears in the Greek fragments from Oxyrhynchus, and even that material is incomplete. *Gos Thos* 32 and 33 appear in Oxyrhynchus

JESUS OF NAZARETH: THE TEACHER OF WISDOM

papyrus 1; however, saying 33 is fragmentary in the Greek and unfortunately does not include the critical verses 33:2–3.

With regard to the parallels to the Coptic *Gospel of Thomas*, although three of the four clusters of sayings are quite small, they reveal a very interesting pattern:

1. The two sayings in the *Gospel of Thomas* (32 and 33:2–3), the first cluster, appear in the same order as in Matthew (5:14b; 5:15). The saying in Matt 5:14b is not found in either Mark or in Luke, suggesting that the author of the *Gospel of Thomas* knew the two unrelated sayings either from the oral tradition, from Matthew's special source M, or more likely from the Gospel of Matthew.

2. The five sayings in the *Gospel of Thomas* (43:3; 44; 45:1; 45:2; and 45:3), the second cluster, are connected in an intricate pattern that cannot be coincidental. *Gos Thos* 43:3 replicates Matt 7:16a and 12:33. Apparently drawing from Matt 12:33, *Gos Thos* 44 then replicates the immediately preceding material in Matt 12:31–32. Then, returning to the order of Matt 7:16a (= *Gos Thos* 43:3), *Gos Thos* 45:1 then replicates Matt 7:16b. Returning once again to the order of Matt 12:31–32, *Gos Thos* 45:2–3 then replicates Matt 12:35 and 12:34b. The pattern is clear and very intricate, and it necessarily presupposes knowledge of our written Gospel of Matthew.

3. *Gos Thos* 65 and 66, the third cluster, replicate the same order as Matthew, Mark, and/or Luke. Since Matthew seems to be the common denominator in these clusters, we should probably assume the use of Matthew here as well.

4. *Gos Thos* 92.1; 93; and 94 replicate the order of Matt 7:7b; 7:6; and 7:8bc in that order. The saying in Matt 7:6 (= *Gos Thos* 93) is not found in either Mark or Luke, suggesting that it came from Matthew's special source M, or more likely from the Gospel of Matthew in light of the evidence in the other clusters.

It is difficult to account for this ordering of the sayings in these four clusters in the *Gospel of Thomas* if the author of *Thomas* did not have access to the texts of the synoptic gospels, or at least the Gospel of Matthew. Familiarity with Q-like material or sources of Q is not sufficient to explain these clusters, unless we assume (without justification) that Matt 5:14b and 7:6 were both derived from Q but that Luke chose not to include these sayings in his gospel.

Another detail, found in the previous chapter (see pp. 168–74) speaks to *Thomas's* use of the Gospel of Luke: saying 31 in the *Gospel of Thomas* links the words "prophet" and "physician," a connection found only in Luke 4:23–24, but not in the parallel passages in Mark 6:1–6a and Matt 13:54–58.

There can be no doubt that there is some relationship between the Coptic version of the *Gospel of Thomas* and the synoptic gospels, although that relationship is not entirely clear. There are two possibilities:

1. The author of the *Gospel of Thomas* had access to one or more of the canonical gospels.
2. The author of the *Gospel of Thomas* had access to oral or written tradition that, in some form, was familiar to the authors of the canonical gospels or to their sources.

At least with respect to the Coptic version of the *Gospel of Thomas*, the first option best explains the evidence.

THE *GOSPEL OF THOMAS*, ESCHATOLOGY, AND GNOSTIC THOUGHT

An especially important question is whether the author of the *Gospel of Thomas* de-eschatologized synoptic or pre-synoptic tradition to which he had access, or whether both the earliest stratum of Q (Q^1) and the Thomasine church, presumably in eastern Syria (Edessa),[55] had access to pre-eschatological tradition, teaching that was actually closer to the teaching of the historical Jesus. Although eschatology is less pronounced in the *Gospel of Thomas* than in other Christian tradition, it is still evident.

In saying 8 above (see p. 228), the reference to "the human one" may actually be a reference to the eschatological Son of Man, although we cannot be certain given the limited context. Moreover, the reference to "Heaven's imperial rule" in the parable of the mustard seed in saying 20 (see p. 228) underscores the theme of the growth of God's rule, a common theme in the synoptic gospels. The reference to the day of the harvest and to "God's imperial rule" in the parable of the seed in saying 57 both point to the time of God's final judgment, as does the warning to be prepared in saying 63.

> *Gos Thos* 57: Jesus said, "The Father's imperial rule is like a person who had [good] seed. His enemy came during the night and sowed weeds among the good seed. The person did not let the workers pull the weeds, but said to them, "No, otherwise you might go to pull up the weeds and pull up the wheat along with them.' For on the day of the harvest the weeds will be conspicuous, and will be pulled up and burned.
>
> *Gos Thos* 63: Jesus said, "There was a rich man who had a great deal of money. He said, "I shall invest my money so that I may sow, reap, plant and fill my storehouses with produce, that I may lack nothing. These were the things he was thinking in his heart, but that very night he died." Anyone here with two ears had better listen!

---

55. As I indicated above, there is evidence in *Gos Thos* 12 that an early stage in the development of the *Gospel of Thomas* or of some of its sayings may point to Jerusalem (or Galilee) as its place of origin, or as the place of origin for some of the sayings. By contrast, the attribution of the gospel to Didymus Judas Thomas points to Edessa in Eastern Syria because the name appears in the same form in the *Acts of Thomas*, which is generally associated with Edessa.

And sayings 65 and 99 both have eschatological themes.

> *Gos Thos* 65: He said, "A [. . .] person owned a vineyard and rented it to some farmers, so they could work it and could collect its crop from them. He sent his slave so the farmers would give him the vineyard's crop. They grabbed him, beat him, and almost killed him, and the slave returned and told his master. His master said, 'Perhaps he didn't know them.' He sent another slave, and the farmers beat that one as well. Then the master sent his son and said, 'Perhaps they'll show my son some respect.' Because the farmers knew that he was the heir to the vineyard, they grabbed him and killed him.' Anyone here with two ears had better listen!
>
> *Gos Thos* 99: The disciples said to him, "Your brothers and your mother are standing outside."
>
> He said to them, "Those here who do what my Father wants are my brothers and my mother. They are the ones who will enter my Father's domain."

Although none of the sayings mentioned above has a Gnosticizing element, we do find Gnosticizing themes, like secret knowledge, the rejection of the physical world and of the female element, hidden truths about human existence, and liberation of the soul from the body in several of the sayings in *Thomas*, for example in sayings 2, 3:4, 21:6–7, 28, 49, 50, 56, 80, 92, 94, and 114, suggesting a later rather than an earlier date for the *Gospel of Thomas* at least in its final form in the Coptic translation.

> *Gos Thos* 2: Jesus said, "Those who seek should not stop seeking until they find. When they find, they will be disturbed. When they are disturbed, they will marvel, and will rule over all."
>
> *Gos Thos* 3:4: Jesus said, ". . . When you know yourselves, then you will be known, and you will understand that you are children of the living Father.
>
> *Gos Thos* 21:6–7: He said, ". . . As for you, then, be on guard against the world. Prepare yourselves with great strength, so the robbers can't find a way to get to you, for the trouble you expect will come."
>
> *Gos Thos* 28: Jesus said, "I took my stand in the midst of the world, and in flesh I appeared to them. I found them all drunk, and I did not find any of them thirsty. My soul ached for the children of humanity, because they are blind in their hearts and do not see, for they came into the world empty, and they also seek to depart from the world empty. But meanwhile, they are drunk. When they shake off their wine, then they will change their ways."
>
> *Gos Thos* 49: Jesus said, Congratulations to those who are alone and chosen, for you will find the (Father's) domain. For you have come from it, and you will return there again."
>
> *Gos Thos* 50: Jesus said, "If they say to you, 'Where have you come from?' say to them, 'We have come from the light, from the place where the light came into being by itself, established [itself], and appeared in their image.' If they say to you, 'Is it you?' say, 'We are its children, and we are the chosen of the living

Father.' If they ask you, 'What is the evidence of your Father in you?' say to them, 'It is motion and rest.'"

Gos Thos 56: Jesus said, "Whoever has come to know the world has discovered a carcass, and whoever has discovered a carcass, of that person the world is not worthy."

Gos Thos 80: Jesus said, "Whoever has come to know the world has discovered the body, and whoever has discovered the body, of that one the world is not worthy."

Gos Thos 92: Jesus said, "Seek and you will find. In the past, however, I did not tell you the things about which you asked me then. Now I am willing to tell you them, but you are not seeking them."

Gos Thos 94: Jesus said, "One who seeks will find, and for [one who knocks] it will be opened."

Gos Thos 114: Simon Peter said to them, "Make Mary leave us, for females don't deserve life." Jesus said, "Look, I will guide her to make her male, so that she too may become a living spirit resembling you males. For every female who makes herself male will enter the domain of heaven."

Gnostizing of the tradition may have emerged intentionally at the price of earlier eschatological elements in some of *Thomas*'s oral or written sources.

Eschatology appears to have belonged to at least some of the sayings in the *Gospel of Thomas*, to some of the earliest material in Q, and to the Gospel of Mark, and, therefore, presumably to the teaching of the historical Jesus. Although there was clearly a wisdom element to Jesus' teaching, the portrait of Jesus as a sapiential teacher of wisdom should probably be framed within the picture of Jesus as an eschatological prophet, who preached the imminent arrival of the Son of Man, God's supernatural messenger who would usher in the period of God's rule. It is virtually impossible to understand Jesus apart from eschatology.

It is, of course, also possible to imagine that Jesus was a wisdom teacher whose message was framed by an eschatological worldview, but whose followers later "apocalypticized" him and his message after he had faced abuse and rejection.

Whatever the origin and history of the *Gospel of Thomas*, we appear to have access to a document that reached its current form sometime in the second century, that at least in its final form knew and used one or more of the canonical gospels, and that had a proto-Gnostic or mystical leaning. It is relatively easy to understand how Jesus' teaching of the denial of the values of the material world could evolve in some Christian circles into a teaching about the denial of the body, and, therefore, account for the mysticism, the asceticism, and the proto-Gnostic element in the *Gospel of Thomas*.

CONCLUSIONS

As we have seen countless times, the canonical gospels are so replete with Christian theology that previous quests for the historical Jesus often reached the conclusion that it is essentially impossible to penetrate the theological overlay in the gospels and recover the historical Jesus. Some theologians have argued that the historical Jesus is actually irrelevant to Christianity and that the quest itself is, therefore, essentially irrelevant. These claims may or may not be valid, but scholars continue to work with the available sources to determine as precisely as possible what Jesus did and did not say and what he did and did not do.

Both Judaism and Christianity are deeply rooted in the claim that God manifested himself in history and that the Bible contains the record of God's acts in history. Stated differently—in terms that are perhaps more relevant to the twenty-first century—history matters, especially as both Judaism and Christianity regard history as an essential vehicle of human understanding. And so, some practitioners of biblical scholarship persist in doing their best, within the limits of historical reason, to take still another turn at penetrating the available sources in the on-going quest for the historical Jesus.

Especially important in this chapter has been study of the *Sayings Gospel Q* and the non-canonical *Gospel of Thomas*, one a hypothetical source, the other a relatively recent archaeological discovery. The effort of a team of scholars to reconstruct Q with the skill and precision of historical reason and the accompanying effort to penetrate the 114 sayings of Jesus in the *Gospel of Thomas* have attempted to open new avenues in our collective effort to reconstruct the earliest decades in the history of Christianity. It is still too early to know how this story will play out over time, but scholars are deeply immersed in the effort and are working to determine whether and where a scholarly consensus will eventually emerge.

Basic to modern study of the New Testament has been the judgment that Mark is the earliest of the canonical gospels, that Mark served as a source for the gospels of Matthew and Luke, that the authors of Matthew and Luke had access to a collection of sayings material called Q and to additional oral and/or written materials that were apparently available to only Matthew or Luke (special M and special L respectively).

The challenge in this chapter and in the previous chapter has been to separate from the accounts of what the gospels purport that Jesus said and did what Jesus may actually have said and done. We have tried to move from the gospels to Jesus by developing methods and tools that will yield results consistent with the canons of historical reason.

We now have the added advantage of broadening our quest by examining a reconstructed Q and the extra-canonical *Gospel of Thomas*. The conclusions of the previous chapter, coupled with the relatively recent work on Q and the *Gospel of Thomas*, remind us of the need to penetrate beyond those sayings in which Jesus speaks of himself in disbelievingly Christian language, when Jesus proclaims for himself the core of the Christian *kerygma*. The criterion of dissimilarity or embarrassment is probably still the single most important tool for penetrating through or beyond theology to discover and embrace history.

What emerged in previous chapters was a Jesus who was baptized by John in the Jordan River, who proclaimed in the Galilee the message of the imminent inbreaking of God's rule, who performed exorcisms and healed the sick, who associated with the outcasts of society and brought hope to the hopeless, who went to Jerusalem with the apparent intention of challenging the Jewish authorities, and who was executed by the Roman authorities under the leadership of the Roman governor Pontius Pilate for reasons that are surprisingly difficult to determine. What is still uncertain from this chapter is a critical question: namely, whether biblical scholarship will abandon the picture of Jesus as an eschatological prophet and embrace instead a portrait of Jesus as the herald of a present sapiential kingdom.

In the previous chapter, I advocated the representation of Jesus as the eschatological prophet of God's future reign. I maintained that the evidence leans heavily in that direction. I find it difficult to understand how the portrait of Jesus as a teacher of wisdom could have threatened the Jewish and Roman establishments in Jerusalem to a degree that required Jesus' crucifixion. Of course, the Romans crucified many people in those days and do not seem to have been particularly discriminating about whom they crucified. Yet, there must have been something that Jesus did that appeared threatening to them. Was Jesus' threat to the Jewish authorities when he cleansed the temple sufficient reason for the Romans to consent to Jesus' execution? We will, of course, never know definitively the answer to this haunting question.

One thing we have learned in this chapter is that early Christianity was remarkably diverse in its multiple interpretations of Jesus. We have only scratched the surface in this regard; we have only alluded to the *Gospel of the Ebionites*, the *Gospel of the Hebrews*, and the *Gospel of the Nazoreans*, in part at least because their portraits of Jesus are mere sketches. We have only fragments of these gospels from church fathers who referred to them in polemical terms. Perhaps future archaeological discoveries will add additional pieces to our giant puzzle.

This chapter discussed the *Sayings Gospel Q* (Kloppenborg's Q^1, Q^2, and Q^3) and the *Gospel of Thomas*. The assumptions and observations involved in a study of these writings, one hypothetical and the other a relatively recent discovery, are problematic and controversial.

It is important to remember that Q is a hypothetical document. Although I applaud the efforts of scholars to use the critical tools available to them to reconstruct Q, the reconstruction is still that—a reconstruction of a hypothetical source. Identifying discernible and recoverable strata of a hypothesis is methodologically challenging, if not dubious. Identifying wisdom sayings and eschatological sayings in Q is one thing; identifying them as reflecting separate strata of Q is quite a different matter.

Moreover, we did find evidence that the Son of Man in Q is, at least sometimes, eschatological, although the phrase also seems at times to mean merely "a human being" or even "I" or "me," when spoken by Jesus. Indeed, the confusion of the meaning of that phrase in Aramaic may have contributed to the belief of early followers of Jesus that it was Jesus himself who would soon return as the eschatological Son of Man.

I identified several verses (Q 6:20b; 10:9; 11:2b; and 12:31) in Kloppenborg's earliest clusters of Q^1 in which the phrase "kingdom of God" (or "God's imperial reign") has an eschatological tone and decried as a contrived theory the effort to label such passages as the subsequent redaction of Q^2. Kloppenborg may be right, but the methodology is essentially flawed, or at least tenuous. The hypothesis of multiple layers of Q may not be built on a foundation of sand, but it is certainly not built on a foundation of rock.

Scholars must determine how far they can go in reconstructing a hypothetical document like Q, whether it is appropriate to try to determine its date, its place of composition, its theology, and especially whether it is appropriate to dissect that hypothetical document into several distinct strata. At what point are hypotheses about a hypothesis still operating within the limits of historical reason? My own observations about Q and the *Gospel of Thomas* are, admittedly, informed in significant measure by the conclusions drawn about Jesus in the previous chapter.

The same questions must be addressed in looking at the "sources" or "strata" of the *Gospel of Thomas*. I identified a number of sayings in *Thomas* that might be older in form than parallels to these saying in the canonical gospels (sayings 8, 9, 20, 31, 34, 57, 63, 64, and 65 to name just a few). But is the criterion that the shorter or simpler form of a saying is always, or even usually, the earlier form valid? And can the results of this study then override conclusions reached in the previous chapter, which used five distinct but complementary criteria—dissimilarity or embarrassment, multiple attestation, contextual credibility, Semitism, and coherence?

A critical study of the *Gospel of Thomas* appears to yield contradictory results. Some evidence points to an early date for the *Gospel of Thomas*; some evidence points to a date subsequent to the writing of the canonical gospels. Can both be right? Are some of the sayings from the period ca. 50–70 and some from the early second century subsequent to the composition of the canonical gospels and at a time when proto-Gnosticism was emerging in the eastern regions of the Christian church? Perhaps!

April DeConick provides interesting insight into the apparent contradictions we observed in the *Gospel of Thomas*.[56] Some scholars have interpreted the *Gospel of Thomas* as an old Jewish-Christian gospel;[57] others have understood it as a late Naas-

---

56. DeConick, "The Gospel of Thomas," 469–79.

57. Puech, "Une Collection de Paroles de Jésus," 146–66; Quispel, "The Gospel of Thomas and the New Testament, 189–207; "Some Remarks on the Gospel of Thomas," 276–90; "L'Évangile selon Thomas et les Clémentines," 181–96; "L'Évangile selon Thomas et le Diatessaron," 87–117; "The 'Gospel of Thomas' and the 'Gospel of the Hebrews,'" 371–82; "The *Gospel of Thomas* Revisited," 218–66; Guillaumont, "Sémitismes dans les logia de Jésus," 113–23; "Les 'Logia' d'Oxyrhynchus sont-ils traduits du copte?" 325–33; "Les sémitismes dans l'Évangile selon Thomas, 190–204.

sene Gnostic gospel,[58] a Valentinian Gnostic gospel,[59] or as a relatively early proto-Gnostic gospel.[60] By contrast, DeConick sees the *Gospel of Thomas* as a rolling corpus of sayings that reflect different moments in the history of the Thomasine community, a trajectory in orthodox Christianity that valued esoteric or mystical teaching.[61] DeConick believes that

> The original *Gospel of Thomas* was urgently and imminently eschatological in its orientation, and may provide us with some valuable information about the theology of the Jerusalem church during the 'dark age' of early Christianity, the years 30-50 CE. It appears that this old speech gospel was taken by the missionaries east into Syria where it was left with the Christian community there. Over the years in this new environment, it was adapted to the changing needs, demands and theology of the Christians in Syria. Accretions gradually developed within the collection, working to reconfigure and reinterpret the older sayings and hermeneutics once they became a liability or irrelevant to the present experience of the Syrian Christians.... [The *Gospel of Thomas*] should be recognized as an early 'Orthodox' Syrian Gospel.[62]

DeConick takes account of an early kernel of material in the *Gospel of Thomas* and of some later material as well in developing a theory that is particularly interesting. It is, however, difficult, with so little information, to be sure of the origin and detailed development of the gospel.

How much credence should we afford to the tradition of Cyril of Jerusalem that the *Gospel of Thomas* was written by one of the three disciples of Mani (who lived between 216 and 276)? Is this charge anything more than standard heresiological polemic against a book of which Cyril disapproved? Probably not. The outright dismissal of books that were perceived as heretical was standard practice of the time. How important is the fact that the ascription of the gospel to Didymus Judas Thomas points to Edessa in eastern Syria as its place of composition? This is probably quite important, at least for some stage in the development of the gospel. How should we weigh the issue of the presumed authority of James in saying 12 and the possible denigration of Peter in saying 13? Can these threads of evidence support the theory of a version of the *Gospel of Thomas* written in Jerusalem under the aegis of James about 50 with a second edition written in Edessa about 60? Was the text of *Thomas* so very fluid as to explain why the three Greek Oxyrhynchus fragments from the first half of the third

---

58. Grant, "Notes on the Gospel of Thomas," 170-80; Grant and Freedman, *The Secret Sayings of Jesus*; Schoedel, "Naasene Themes in the Coptic Gospel of Thomas," 225-34; Smyth, "Gnosticism in 'The Gospel according to Thomas,'" 189-98; Cornélis, "Quelques elements pour une comparison," 83-104.

59. Cerfaux and Garitte, "Les paraboles du Royaume," 307-27; Gärtner, *The Theology of the Gospel of Thomas*.

60. Robinson and Koester, *Trajectories Through Early Christianity*, 158-204.

61. DeConick, "The Gospel of Thomas," 474-79.

62. Ibid., 477, 479.

century differ significantly from the Greek text that was apparently available a century or more later to the translator of the Coptic version?

The conclusions we can reasonably draw from this chapter are, at best, tenuous, if not unconvincing. They are not on a methodological par with the conclusions reached in previous chapters. Scholars who argue for strata of Q and for an early date for a version of the *Gospel of Thomas* have made an important contribution to biblical scholarship, but I am not convinced they have demonstrated conclusively that eschatology was a late-comer to the Jesus tradition. They may, however, have demonstrated that we should be mindful that Jesus was a teacher of wisdom who delivered sapiential teachings within the context of his role as an eschatological prophet.

I find it particularly difficult to accept the thesis that the eschatological layer of tradition is late and that it was added subsequently to a more authentic tradition of Jesus as a teacher of wisdom. I find the effort to promote such a portrait of Jesus and the early church methodologically flawed.

In my opinion, this chapter underscores the uncertainty of many of our conclusions. The flaw lies not in the methodology of biblical scholarship, nor in the lack of rigor and expertise of individual biblical scholars, but rather in the paucity of evidence with which we must often work.

CHAPTER 10

THE EARLY CHRISTIAN CHURCH

It is difficult, if not impossible, to reconstruct the events of the first days, weeks, and even years following Jesus' death. As historians, we cannot simply begin the story by reporting that Jesus rose from the dead on the third day after his crucifixion, as resurrections from the dead fall outside the realm of historical verifiability or falsifiability.

David Friedrich Strauss has shown that resurrection stories belong rather to the literary genre of myth, not to the sphere of modern historical investigation. Historians can, however, say that at some point in time Jesus' earliest followers obviously *came to believe* that Jesus had been raised from the dead on the third day, although belief in Jesus' resurrection clearly came much later than "on the third day" and probably only after a careful search through the Hebrew scriptures, perhaps many months or even years later.

As we have already seen, the words of Hos 6:2 almost certainly served as the basis for the apostles' belief in Jesus' resurrection on the third day:

> $^{6:2}$After two days he will revive us;
> on the third day he will raise us up,
> that we may live before him.

Even Paul's words in 1 Cor 15:3–8 afford scant clues regarding the origin of the church's belief in Jesus' resurrection:

> $^{15:3}$For I handed on to you as of first importance what I in turn received; that Christ died for our sins in accordance with the scriptures, ^{4}and that he was buried, and that he was raised on the third day in accordance with the scriptures, ^{5}and that he appeared to Cephas [Peter], then to the twelve. ^{6}Then he appeared to more than five hundred brothers and sisters at one time, most of whom are still alive, though some have died. ^{7}Then he appeared to James, then to all the apostles. ^{8}Last of all, as to one untimely born, he appeared also to me.

Paul wrote these words in Ephesus in a letter addressed to the church at Corinth about 54, more than twenty years after Jesus' death. These words reflect a tradition that echoes the church's preaching or *kerygma* at a time significantly later than the "events" allegedly reported. But when, where, and from whom Paul heard the report of Jesus' alleged resurrection on the third day and his subsequent appearances is not at all clear. Paul may provide us with some clue when he reports in Gal 1:18 that he visited Peter in Jerusalem for fifteen days (in about 36/37) some three years after his conversion (in about 34), which would be some six or seven years after Jesus' death (in about 30).

THE EARLIEST JESUS MOVEMENT: OUR SOURCES

An important question is what actually happened in the period between Jesus' death and the earliest oral proclamation of the confessional formula that Paul identifies in 1 Cor 15:3 as "traditional." Stated differently, do we have any evidence to assist us in reconstructing what happened in the earliest days within the community of Jesus' followers? The sources that contain the most information about the early church are twofold:

1. the genuine letters of the apostle Paul (Romans, 1 and 2 Corinthians, Galatians, Philippians, 1 Thessalonians, and Philemon[1]), and
2. the Acts of the Apostles.

Paul's letters may be our earliest extant New Testament writings, but it is Luke's second volume, the Acts of the Apostles, that alone in the entire New Testament contains a narrative report of alleged "events" in the history of the early church. Acts was probably written about 85–90 or perhaps even later[2]—some sixty or more years after the beginnings of Christianity—and its value as history is not without serious question. In fact, many scholars remain skeptical about the historical value of Luke's narrative in Acts.

The Acts of the Apostles is, unfortunately, our only source for these earliest years of the church's history, except for what we can glean from Paul's letters, which were written over a period of about six or seven years (about 51 to 58) beginning more than two decades after Jesus' death in about 30. Furthermore, Paul's letters are just that—letters, and do not contain as much historical information as we would like. Acts reports in some detail events from the earliest period in the history of the Christian community, but Acts is the work of someone writing five or more decades after the purported events unfolded and is probably not history, as we today understand the word "history."

Tradition identifies the author of the Gospel of Luke and the Acts of the Apostles as Luke, a physician and an associate of Paul (Col 4:14; 2 Tim 4:11; Phlm 24); however, neither the gospel nor Acts actually claims Lukan authorship. They are both anonymous writings. I will, however, for reasons of convenience refer to the unknown

---

1. We shall discuss in the next chapter which of Paul's letters are authentic and which were more likely written by someone else in Paul's name.

2. Pervo, *Acts*, 5; Pervo, *Dating Acts*; Pervo, "Acts in the Suburbs of the Apologists." Helmut Koester dates Acts not later than 135, a full century after Jesus' death: *Introduction to the New Testament*, volume 2, 310.

author of both books as Luke, a man who was from all appearances a well-educated gentile Christian and who was familiar with the Jewish scriptures. We not only do not know who wrote Acts, but there is nothing in Acts that betrays its place of composition, although scholars have suggested Antioch, Ephesus, Caesarea, Achaia, Macedonia, and Rome.

Although Luke clearly used numerous sources in composing his gospel— most specifically the Gospel of Mark, the sayings source Q, and the special L source—it is difficult, if not impossible, to identify what sources Luke may have used in composing Acts. The material in the Gospel of Luke has parallels in the gospels of Matthew and Mark, hard evidence that has lead scholars to a viable hypothesis to explain the so-called synoptic problem. But the use of written sources for the gospel does not mean that Luke necessarily had access to written sources for Acts; and whatever sources, whether oral or written, that Luke may have used in composing Acts are frankly beyond retrieval or reconstruction.

That said, we are, nevertheless, dependent almost entirely on Acts for a reconstruction of the earliest decades of Christianity. We know that Acts has its challenges as a source for that early history, as it is replete with miracle stories and has multiple accounts of some events, like the conversion of Paul (Acts 9:1–19a; 22:3–21; 26:9–18). Yet, we have no choice but to turn to Acts, for what it is worth, in trying to reconstruct much of that early history. We may, indeed, find that Acts has little historical value and have to admit that we know little to nothing about the beginnings of Christianity.

If, as Paul and the apostolic *kerygma* allege, Peter was the first person to "see" Jesus following his death, and independent tradition appears to support that view (1 Cor 15:5; Luke 24:34), we should probably begin our historical reconstruction by trying to understand what Peter experienced and what significance that experience had for him and for Jesus' other apostles. Perhaps we can draw some inferences regarding Peter's "vision" of the risen Christ from Paul's account of his own "vision" in Gal 1:15–16, where he reports that "God . . . was pleased to reveal his Son to me." The Greek literally says not "to me," but "in me" (*en emoi*) or "within me," emphasizing the inward or subjective nature of Paul's experience. Paul's conversion was, by his own account, a private or inner transformation, a subjective personal experience.

It was not uncommon in the ancient world to interpret dreams in such a way that might suggest that Peter dreamed about Jesus following the crucifixion and came thereby to believe that Jesus was still alive or was once again alive. Such an interpretation of a dream vision would make a good deal of sense if Jesus was an eschatological prophet who preached the imminent coming of God's rule rather than if Jesus was primarily a teacher of wisdom. Peter may have interpreted Jesus' appearance to him in a dream within the larger context of what Jesus had already proclaimed during his active ministry about the imminence of the end-time. It may have been many months or even years after Peter's "vision" of the risen Lord, and likely after many others had shared or otherwise believed in Peter's "vision," that a Christian scribe came upon the passage in Hos 6:2 that lead to the kerygmatic formula that "God had raised Jesus from the dead *on the third day in accordance with the scriptures*" (1 Cor 15:4).

Following an opening preface (Acts 1:1–5), Luke's Acts of the Apostles recounts the mythical story of Jesus' ascension into heaven (Acts 1:6–11), which contains three promises of the risen Lord to his apostles: namely,

1. the coming of the Holy Spirit (Acts 1:8a);

2. the spread of the apostles' witness from Jerusalem to Judea and Samaria, and to the ends of the earth (Acts 1:8b); and

3. Jesus' return to earth at an unspecified time (Acts 1:11).

There follows in Acts 1:12–14 a description of the primitive congregation of Jesus' followers in Jerusalem, the nucleus of which consisted of his apostles Peter, John, James, Andrew, Philip, Thomas, Bartholomew, Matthew, James the son of Alphaeus, Simon the Zealot, Judas the son of James,[3] certain women including Mary the mother of Jesus,[4] and Jesus' brothers.[5] The group is described as devoted to prayer and harmony or unanimity (*homothymadon*) (Acts 1:14).

There then follows in Acts the story of the choice of Matthias to replace Judas as Jesus' twelfth disciple (Acts 1:15–26), a story apparently inspired by Old Testament proof texts (Acts 1:16, 20), therefore indicating that this tradition too may have originated at a time well after the purported event.

PENTECOST

Luke next tells the story of the coming of the Holy Spirit to the apostles at Pentecost (Acts 2:1–13), a Jewish pilgrimage festival that occurred fifty days after Passover, hence about seven weeks after Jesus' death and burial.

It is difficult to know what transpired during the seven weeks between Jesus' death and the festival of Pentecost, assuming that there is at least a modicum of historical merit in Luke's story of the descent of the Holy Spirit at Pentecost. The traditional answer is that the record of at least some of those days immediately following Jesus' death is contained in the accounts of Jesus' resurrection appearances in Matt 28; Mark 16; Luke 24; and John 20–21. But these stories are legendary material with little or no historical value and with obvious contradictions among them. For example, Mark (16:7) and Matt (28:7, 10, 16–20) assume that the apostles returned to Galilee following

---

3. The same apostles are listed in Luke 6:14–16, although in a different order.

4. Luke 8:2–3 includes among Jesus' female followers Mary called Magdalene, Joanna the wife of Herod's steward Chuza, and Suzanna, and "many others." Luke may also have in mind wives of the apostles.

5. Although Mark 6:3 and the parallel in Matth 13:55 identify Jesus' brothers as James, Joses (Joseph), Judas, and Simon, curiously Luke does not name Jesus' brothers in the parallel passage in Luke 4:22, or in this passage in Acts.

Jesus' crucifixion, whereas Luke (24:1–53; Acts 1:1–4) and John (20:1–29)[6] assume that the apostles remained in and around Jerusalem following Jesus' crucifixion. It is not surprising that scholars rarely speak of the intervening period between the crucifixion and Pentecost, because there is no evidence on which to build a credible story.

Like Luke, the author of the Gospel of John apparently received the tradition that God had poured his Spirit upon Jesus' followers.[7] What is not clear is whether the earliest tradition included a story about the apostles' receiving the Spirit at the festival of Pentecost or whether it was Luke who telescoped into the Pentecost story in Acts 2 the apostles' receiving the Holy Spirit. In any event, Luke molded the story in its present form and added Peter's subsequent speech (Acts 2:14–36), which serves in Acts as the occasion for the conversion of some three thousand Jews (Acts 2:41–42), who were presumably in Jerusalem for the pilgrimage festival. Among the writers of the New Testament, Luke and John alone report in dramatized form the outpouring of the Holy Spirit as a discrete event, even though they set it on very different occasions many weeks apart. The new age had begun, initially with the report of Peter's vision of the risen Lord. Now, according to Luke, with the outpouring of the Holy Spirit onto the apostles, the new age apparently began in Jerusalem at Pentecost (Acts 2:1–13).

> 2:1When the day of Pentecost had come, they were all together in one place. 2And suddenly from heaven there came a sound like the rush of a violent wind, and it filled the entire house where they were sitting. 3Divided tongues, as of fire, appeared among them, and a tongue rested on each of them. 4All of them were filled with the Holy Spirit and began to speak in other languages, as the Spirit gave them ability.
>
> 5Now there were devout Jews from every nation under heaven living in Jerusalem. 6And at this sound the crowd gathered and was bewildered, because each one heard them speaking in the native language of each. 7Amazed and astonished, they asked, "Are not all these who are speaking Galileans? 8And how is it that we hear, each of us, in our own native language? 9Parthians, Medes, Elamites, and residents of Mesopotamia, Judea and Cappadocia, Pontus and Asia, 10Phrygia and Pamphylia, Egypt and the parts of Lybia belonging to Cyrene, and visitors from Rome, both Jews and proselytes, 11Cretans and Arabs—in our own languages we hear them speaking about God's deeds of power." 12All were amazed and perplexed, saying to one another, "What does this mean?" 13But others sneered and said, "They are filled with new wine."

In Acts 2, Pentecost serves as the occasion when the apostles collectively began to believe that Jesus was still with them or was once again with them through the power of the Spirit of God, the Holy Spirit. The story in Acts 2:1–13 implies that Pentecost marked in a meaningful way the beginning of the Christian church, the community

---

6. John 21:1–25, which most scholars consider a later addition to the gospel, reports, like Matthew and Mark, Jesus' appearances in Galilee.

7. John 20:22 ("When he [Jesus] had said this, he breathed on them [the apostles] and said to them, 'Receive the Holy Spirit'") and John 20:19 ("When it was evening on that day, the first day of the week . . .") set the outpouring of the Spirit on the apostles on the day of Jesus' resurrection, not seven weeks later at Pentecost, as we read in Luke's account in Acts.

of believers as the new people of God. But is this history, or is it merely story, a story created by Luke?

Penetrating the legendary account in Acts 2 in order to identify even a modicum of history is challenging, if not impossible. Luke may regard the story of the Jews from every nation who were able to understand the apostles as if they were speaking their own native languages as a reversal of the situation at the Tower of Babel in Gen 11:1–9, when God confused the languages of the peoples of the earth. From a theological point of view, just as God had confused the languages of the earth and thereby divided and scattered humankind (Genesis 11:9), God was now reuniting divided and scattered humankind through the outpouring of the Holy Spirit and the establishment of the church. For Luke, the theological point of the story of Pentecost is the universality of the salvation that Jesus had brought to the world. The *kerygma* will be spoken in all languages. The gift of God's spirit is universal; it surpasses all limits.[8]

Behind this legendary account of Pentecost, Luke would have us believe that there is the memory of a transformative moment in the lives of the apostles when they gathered together in Jerusalem for the observance of the Jewish festival of Pentecost, some seven weeks after Jesus' crucifixion. Whatever it is that happened, soon after Jesus' death the apostles' confusion, doubt, and disbelief were, Luke maintains, transformed into belief that Jesus was once again with them, but now apparently through the power of God's Spirit, which settled upon them when they were once again gathered together in the city where, seven weeks earlier, Jesus had been executed. The language of Acts 2:2–3 (see above) is, of course, the language of theophany (see e.g., Exod 3:2; 14:20, 24; 1 Kgs 18:38; 19:11–12; Ps 104:4; Isa 5:24; 6:4; 1 Enoch 14:8–25; 71:5). What Luke is saying in this story is that sometime after Jesus' death, at Pentecost, God made himself manifest to Jesus' apostles.

It is, of course, tempting to ask whether there are some vestiges of history in the legendary accounts of Jesus' resurrection appearances in the gospels (Matt 28:9–20; Mark 16:9–20;[9] Luke 24:12–53; and John 20:11–21:23), as well as in 1 Cor 15:3–8. Perhaps! But it would be difficult to recover vestiges of history from the stories in the legendary form in which they come down to us in the gospels and in Paul's words in 1 Cor 15. The reconstruction I have provided is obviously speculative, but it makes some sense, especially in light of what ensues with Peter's speech in Acts 2:14–36, for it is Peter, who first "saw" the risen Lord and who, according to Luke's account of Acts, was the first to address the crowd of Jews at Pentecost.

---

8. There are, of course, interesting gaps in this story. The apostles do not speak in "one language and the same words" (Gen 11:1). Following the Pentecost experience, Peter addresses the crowd, presumably in Greek, citing the Septuagint and not the Hebrew scriptures (Acts 2:14–36), and everyone in attendance seems to understand what he is saying.

9. These twelve verses in Mark do not appear in the earliest manuscripts of the gospel and are almost universally regarded as a later addition to the gospel, the original text of which apparently ended at Mark 16:8.

The Pentecost story in Acts 2 may contain some kernel of history, although that is not self-evident. Neither can we place credence in the contents of Peter's speech in Acts 2:14–36, which we identified in a previous chapter as a Lukan composition. Luke goes on to report that on Pentecost three thousand Jews accepted Peter's message, were baptized, and "devoted themselves to the apostles' teaching and fellowship, to the breaking of bread and the prayers" (Acts 2:41–42). Although the number of converts to Jesus is probably an exaggeration, there may be some truth to the claim that the enthusiasm of the apostles spilled over to some of the Jews who had assembled in Jerusalem for the pilgrimage festival.

According to Luke, Peter promised the people the forgiveness of their sins and the gift of the Holy Spirit (Acts 2:38) and the salvation promised previously to Israel (Acts 2:39). The text reports that those who accepted Peter's message were then baptized (Acts 2:41). The story in Acts 2 is schematic and formulaic and highly theological; many of the same themes and motifs appear elsewhere in Acts. There may, however, be a vestige of truth in the account that Pentecost marked the occasion of the first Jewish converts to the Jesus movement, which it is still premature to refer to by its later name, Christianity.

EARLY PRACTICES

Acts maintains that at least some members of the early Jesus movement in Jerusalem sold all of their possessions and distributed the proceeds among them all, as each had need. In accordance with what they understood from Jesus' teaching, some of Jesus' followers apparently thought that it was appropriate to hold their possessions in common (Acts 2:44; 4:32–37; 5:1–10; cf. Acts 20:35).[10] What else can we know about this early movement? We know from Acts that Jesus' followers assembled in an area of the Jerusalem temple known as Solomon's portico (Acts 3:11)[11] and that "they broke bread at home" (Acts 2:46).

The earliest members of the Jesus movement were all Jews, who continued to observe Jewish practices, including going up to the temple at the hour of prayer at three o'clock in the afternoon (Acts 3:1). Jesus' followers apparently observed two additional rituals, baptism (Acts 2:38) and the Lord's Supper (Acts 2:46). Rooted in John's baptism of Jesus in the Jordan River and in Jewish rituals of purification and

---

10. The early church's communalism parallels Greco-Roman utopian traditions (Plato, *Republic*, 5.449C; Aristotle, *Nicomachean Ethics*, 8.9.1; 9.8.2). What is not clear is whether communal practice is a Lukan literary creation in an effort to idealize the first generation of Jesus' followers in imitation of Greco-Roman utopian practices, or an actual early Jewish-Christian practice by some of Jesus' followers in Jerusalem, perhaps in imitation this Greco-Roman utopian tradition. The Essenes at Qumran were also communal, so communalism was not unknown among Jews of the period.

11. According to Josephus (*Antiquities* 15.11.3; 20.9.7; *Wars* 5.5) and John 10:23, Solomon's portico was part of Herod's temple complex, a double-columned colonnade with a cedar ceiling on the eastern side of the temple mount overlooking the Kidron Valley.

conversion, baptism by immersion in water apparently served from a very early time as a rite of initiation into the Jesus movement, perhaps in imitation of the baptism of John the Baptist.

The Lord's Supper consisting of bread and wine was evidently celebrated by Jesus' followers as a rite of union with the risen Jesus and with one another. As the accounts of the Last Supper in the canonical gospels make clear, the celebration of the Lord's Supper was apparently rooted in the commemorative Jewish Passover meal, in which Jews celebrated and relived vicariously their ancestors' deliverance from slavery in Egypt (Matt 26:26–30; Mark 14:22–26; Luke 22:14–23. By association and imitation, the Lord's Supper served as a memorial to and vicarious reliving of Jesus' death (1 Cor 11:23–26). From earliest times, the Lord's Supper was celebrated in the homes of more affluent Christians, with the owner of the house and his wife likely presiding. It appears that the leader of the house church was sometimes a woman (Phil 4:2–3; Col 4:15; cf. also the important role women played in the church in Rom 16:1–15; 1 Cor 1:11; 16:19; Phlm 2).

In reflecting on the situation in those first weeks and months following Jesus' death, we should think of this community of believers as a small and almost insignificant phenomenon, based primarily if not exclusively in Jerusalem. Alternatively, the Jesus movement may have begun when and if Peter and the disciples returned to Galilee after Jesus' death, but something may have happened in Jerusalem at Pentecost that gave impetus to the movement and led the apostles to proclaim their earliest message: that God had raised Jesus from the dead and that he still lived with them.

To the extent that members of the Jesus movement differed from Jews in those earliest days and weeks, the difference would probably have been most evident in their practice of Jesus' commandment to love one another as they loved God. At some point even their communal meal was called the *agape* (or love) feast. In virtually every other respect, members of the Jesus movement were otherwise observant Jews and would not have behaved much differently from other observant Jews.

It would be premature, especially in these earliest days and weeks, to think that there was a significant Christological element to the community of believers. Surely it was much too early to suggest that Jesus' followers believed "that Christ died for [their] sins in accordance with the scriptures . . . and that he was raised on the third day in accordance with the scriptures," as formulated subsequently in the oral *kerygma* and as reproduced by Paul more than twenty years later in 1 Cor 15:3–4. Perhaps the early followers of Jesus already believed that Jesus had "appeared to Cephas [Peter], then to the twelve" (1 Cor 15:5). Nevertheless, we should probably see the early Jesus movement as a minimalist sect within Judaism with a minimalist Christology.

THE NEW TESTAMENT
THE HELLENISTS

Acts 6:1 reports that, even as the followers of Jesus were increasing in number, a group known as "the Hellenists complained against the Hebrews because their widows were being neglected in the daily distribution of food." At this point in time, "Hellenists" is likely the term for Jewish Christians from Diaspora regions outside Palestine, Jews who spoke Greek as their native language rather than the Aramaic spoken by Jesus, his earliest disciples, and the first converts to the Jesus movement who may have responded at Pentecost by becoming disciples of Jesus. According to Acts, there were apparently conflicts between Aramaic-speaking Hebrews and Greek-speaking Hellenists, probably based on their cultural and social differences and perhaps on inequities apparent in the "daily distribution of food."[12]

To remedy the situation, Luke reports that Jesus' apostles invited the Hellenists to select from their own number seven men, who were appointed to distribute food to needy Hellenists (Acts 6:3). They chose Stephen, Philip, Prochorus, Nicanor, Timon, Parmenas, and Nicolaus—all Greek names, consistent with their identification as Hellenists. Just as some of the first Hebrew converts had met early opposition from the Jewish authorities (Acts 4:1–22; 5: 17–42), so too the early Hellenists probably met similar opposition, resulting in the stoning of Stephen, the first martyr of the Jesus movement (Acts 7:54–8:1).

Whether this account of the Hellenists and of Stephen's martyrdom reflects actual events in the history of the early church or is simply Lukan "theologized" history with little or no factual content is debated by equally competent scholars. The stories in Acts are permeated by literary, and not necessarily historical concerns, leaving us with little confidence about details of the early history of the Jesus movement.

THE JESUS MOVEMENT IN JUDEA
AND SAMARIA AND BEYOND

Luke reports that, following Stephen's death, "a severe persecution began against the church in Jerusalem, and all except the apostles were scattered throughout the countryside of Judea and Samaria" (Acts 8:1b). More specifically, Luke reports that Philip went to the city of Samaria (probably either Sebaste or Shechem) and converted some of the people (Acts 8:4–6) by proclaiming the good news (Greek *euangelizomenō*) about the kingdom of God and the name of Jesus Christ and by then baptizing the people, both men and women (Acts 8:12). Thereafter, Peter and John went to Samaria and bestowed the Holy Spirit upon the newly converted people (Acts 8:14–17) and then returned to Jerusalem to report to the other apostles on their success, proclaiming the good news (Greek *euēngelizonto*) in many Samaritan villages along the way

---

12. See Acts 4:35, which reports that Jesus' earliest followers brought money and laid it at the apostles' feet for distribution to each of the believers according to his or her need.

(Acts 8:25). After converting and baptizing an Ethiopian eunuch on the road from Jerusalem to Gaza (Acts 8:26–39), Philip proceeded to Azotus (the Greek and Roman name for the Philistine city of Ashdod), a town about twenty-two miles north of Gaza, and continued to proclaim the good news (Greek *euēngelizeto*) to all the cities along the west coast of Palestine until he came to Caesarea (formerly known as Strato's Tower), almost sixty miles to the north (Acts 8:40).

The account in Acts 9 of the conversion of the Pharisee Saul of Tarsus, the church's arch enemy (see Acts 8:1; 9:1), implies that there were already followers of Jesus in Damascus in Syria at a time when Saul had set out to deliver "letters to the synagogues at Damascus, so that if he found any who belonged to the Way [apparently an early term used to refer to the Christian faith],[13] he might bring them bound to Jerusalem" (Acts 9:2). How the Jesus movement spread to Damascus is not clear. Perhaps some Diaspora Jews who had been converted at Pentecost and in the days immediately thereafter and who had fled the persecution in Jerusalem may have returned to their homes in Damascus. Acts reports that the newly converted Saul entered Damascus and began to proclaim Jesus in the synagogues, much to the alarm of the Jews, who plotted to kill him, but that Saul's disciples helped him escape from Damascus by lowering him through an opening in the city wall in a basket (Acts 9:19b–25). According to Luke, Saul then went to Jerusalem to meet with Jesus' disciples, who were understandably suspicious of Paul's intentions until Barnabas intervened on his behalf.[14] Saul encountered difficulty when he argued with Hellenistic Jews, who attempted to kill him, but followers of Jesus apparently helped Saul escape to Caesarea and then to his hometown of Tarsus in Cilicia (Acts 9:26–30).

Once again, we must be cautious in assigning historical value to Luke's narrative. Not only does Luke disagree with Paul about his going to Jerusalem immediately after his conversion, but Luke reports in Acts three very different accounts of Paul's conversion, an issue that we will examine in greater detail in the following chapter.

THE EARLIEST PREACHED MESSAGE: THE PRIMITIVE *KERYGMA*

In Chapter 4, I discussed the apostolic preaching and its development, specifically the work of C. H. Dodd. In subsequent chapters, I reviewed the disciplines of source and form criticism and tried to identify some criteria for historicity to enable us to embark upon a quest for the historical Jesus, a quest that has yielded two very different

---

13. See also Acts 18:25; 19:9, 23; 22:4; 24:14, 22.

14. Paul writes in Gal 1:17 that he did *not* go to Jerusalem immediately after his conversion, but that he went into Arabia and then returned to Damascus, going to Jerusalem only after two years to visit Cephas [Peter] and James, the brother of Jesus (Gal 1:18). Most scholars assume that Paul's account of his own travels is probably more reliable than Luke's account in Acts 9:26–30.

contemporary portraits of Jesus: one of Jesus as an eschatological prophet, the other of Jesus as a teacher of wisdom.

As I said at the time, a study of the apostolic preaching, the *kerygma*, is important, because it informs our understanding of the way in which the church's preaching evolved in the first decades of the church's history and enables us to understand better "the bias rule," the principle that every source and every piece of evidence must be examined critically to ascertain the nature and degree of its bias.

I observed previously that the time and place criterion lends credibility to the reliability of Paul's report regarding what constituted the earliest *kerygma*, most especially the passage in his first letter to the Corinthians, in which Paul described the faithfulness with which he was passing along tradition that he had received from those who came before him: "For I handed on to you as of first importance what I in turn received . . . ." (1 Cor 15:3). We must be mindful, however, that Paul wrote his first letter to the Corinthians in about 54, more than twenty years after Jesus' death. Moreover, there were probably at least a few years between Jesus' death and the emergence of the *kerygma* in the form eventually known to Paul. What form did the *kerygma* assume in the apostles' earliest preaching during the period *before* Paul's conversion? Is it even possible to retrieve or reconstruct the form of the *apostolic preaching* in the days and weeks immediately following the events surrounding Pentecost? Perhaps not.

The historical portion of the early *kerygma* is incontrovertible, namely that Jesus was crucified, died, and was buried.[15] By themselves and free from subsequent theological overlay, these words pass both the time and place criterion and the bias rule: they describe actual events in real history. There was no reason for the church to create these embarrassing data, as Jesus' crucifixion and death posed a serious challenge for Jesus' earliest followers, who were apparently surprised and even disillusioned by what had happened to their leader during his final days in Jerusalem.

As we saw earlier, the theological overlay to these basic historical facts (Jesus' crucifixion, death, and burial) is an entirely different matter, namely "that Christ died *for our sins in accordance with the scriptures*" and "*that he was raised on the third day in accordance with the scriptures.*" With these words, we have moved beyond history. The words *in accordance with the scriptures* provided Jesus' apostles with the requisite clues that enabled early Christians to understand the *meaning* of Jesus' death as an atoning sacrifice for the sins of the people.

The Pauline *kerygma* clearly appealed to specific scriptural passages for meaningful answers to some of the difficult questions posed by Jesus' unexpected and unwelcome death in Jerusalem (such as Isa 52:13–53:12; Hos 6:2; Pss 16:8–11; 110:1). The *kerygma* made it clear that Jesus' followers should look at Jesus' death and resurrection

---

15. Even the "burial" component could be an early Christian addition. Standard Roman procedure was to throw the bodies of crucified criminals in the garbage dump, which would be historically plausible in the case of Jesus, perhaps even more plausible than a kernel from the "theologized" *kerygma*. The truth of the matter is that, shocking as it may seem, either is possible in the case of Jesus.

not simply as events in history, but as salvific events. In fact, referring to Jesus' "atoning" death and "resurrection" obviously move the reader beyond history to theological interpretation.

The atoning death and resurrection were the church's theological answer to Jesus' unanticipated death. These claims are part of the theology that was assembled and inserted over time into the *kerygma* as a result of a careful reading of the Hebrew scriptures with an eye to identifying messianic proof-texts that would enable Jesus' followers to understand the meaning of his unexpected and unwelcome death. In Chapter 4, we observed that the Hebrew scriptures from which the author of the speeches in Acts frequently quoted was the Septuagint Greek translation of those scriptures, not the original Hebrew scriptures.

This observation raises the question of whether the search through the scriptures for the meaning of Jesus' untimely death was undertaken in the earliest period by examining the scriptures in their original Hebrew, or somewhat later by examining the texts of the Greek translation of those Hebrew scriptures. Was the work first undertaken by Aramaic-speaking Hebrews or Greek-speaking Hellenists? We cannot answer this question with certainty. I suspect that Hebrew texts may have been the basis for some of the church's initial claims but that as Christianity, especially Hellenistic and Pauline Christianity, spread into the Gentile world, the Septuagint increasingly became the authoritative scriptures of Gentile Christianity. It was, after all, Greek that served as the *lingua franca* of the Mediterranean world at that time.

An important question to consider at this time is: What was the nature of the apostolic preaching in the two- or three-year period between Jesus' death and the conversion of Paul? More precisely, what was the content of the apostolic preaching in those earliest days and weeks after Jesus' death as we read about them through Luke's lens in the early chapters of Acts? What were Peter and John and Philip telling the people about Jesus in Jerusalem and in Judea and Samaria if there is any truth whatsoever to these Lukan narratives? What had members of the Jesus' movement heard about Jesus in those earliest days and weeks?

It is improbable that the search of the Hebrew scriptures began in the days and weeks immediately after Jesus' death. The apostles were not scribes or Pharisees, learned in the ancient Hebrew texts. That simple fact suggests that the apostolic preaching, as reported by Paul in 1 Corinthians 15 and as discussed previously in Chapter 4 was probably not the most primitive version of what Jesus' earliest disciples proclaimed. The Christological overlay probably implies a later stage in the development of the tradition, a more conscious theological reworking of Jesus' message to make sense retrospectively of Jesus' death as part of God's plan for the Jews and for all humankind.

In spite of Luke's consistent use of the Greek verb *euangelizomai* to characterize that earliest preaching, the "good news" was probably non-Christological in its earliest form. The message may have contained the claim that Jesus was still present in some form within and among the believing community, but the resurrection on the third day was probably not yet a part of the initial message. Those earliest members of the Jesus movement were all Jews, whether Hebrews or Hellenists, and they certainly did not think of themselves as members of a new religion. They probably understood Jesus as a messenger from God, as a prophet who proclaimed the coming of a new order in which God's rule would be manifest. They may even have believed that Jesus would return soon to consummate that new order. They apparently practiced baptism and celebrated a common meal, when they gathered in one another's homes to celebrate not only their love feast but to practice the meaning of the love commandment, as Jesus had taught it.

Just as it was never Jesus' intention to start a new religion, neither did Jesus' earliest disciples nor early converts to the Jesus movement understand that this was the direction in which the movement was headed. What was clear was that following Jesus' teaching often put followers of Jesus into conflict with Jewish authorities, just as it had put Jesus into such conflict throughout his ministry in Galilee and especially in the final days of his life in Jerusalem.

As we have already seen, it is not clear whether the search through the Hebrew scriptures began among Hebrews or Hellenists. What is clear is that citations of the Hebrew scriptures come down to us in the writings of the New Testament only in the form that those citations assumed in the Septuagint. It is also clear that many of the most likely authentic sayings of Jesus, as they come down to us through Q and in the Gospel of Mark are non-Christological, even as we have in the previous chapters reconstructed two portraits of the historical Jesus, both of which are non-Christological. The theological overlay that emerges in the New Testament was the result not of a single event—the resurrection—but was the result of a conscious process that took place over many years, perhaps over many decades, and in different Christian communities.

What is not clear is when that process began, but I doubt that it began immediately after Jesus death and burial or that it was a component of the earliest *kerygma*. I suspect that Acts 2:38–46 contains as untheological a representation of the *kerygma* as we can find in the New Testament: repent; be baptized into the name of Jesus Christ so that your sins may be forgiven; and receive the gift of the Holy Spirit, so that you and your children may receive the benefits of God's promises to Israel. We need to revisit this question of the earliest preaching once again when we try to make sense of the relationship and the subsequent disagreement between Paul and the Jerusalem apostles.

We suggested in Chapter 4 that there existed in an early period in the history of the church a *testimona* document, similar to *4QTestimonia* from the Dead Sea Scrolls. Relatively early in the church's history, someone appears to have collected into one place the Greek translation (Septuagint) of passages from the Hebrew scriptures that the church believed predicted the coming of God's messiah. We noted previously that such scriptural passages rarely, if ever, spoke about the coming of messiah in their original contexts but that Christians so understood these passages from an early period. The author of the Acts of the Apostles probably had access to such a Christian *testimonia* document, elements of which he incorporated into the speeches of Peter and Paul that he, the author of Acts composed, just as other Hellenistic historians were expected to compose such speeches. The important questions that may never be answered are how soon after Jesus' death that process of searching through the Hebrew scriptures began and whether it developed simultaneously in churches in different cities.

THE SPREAD OF CHRISTIANITY

We mentioned previously some of the earliest developments within the Jesus movement, most notably its origin in Jerusalem, the growth of the movement among both Aramaic-speaking and Greek-speaking Jews in Jerusalem, respectively referred to in Acts as Hebrews and Hellenists, and the spread of the movement to Judea and Samaria. I noted that apart from Paul's letters, the Acts of the Apostles is our primary source for this earliest period, so it is helpful to outline details of the spread of Christianity, as reported by Luke in the Acts of the Apostles, even though we cannot assume that we are reading reliable history and not "theologized" history.

Luke reports that some in the Jesus movement who experienced persecution at the hands of Jews in the aftermath of the stoning of Stephen fled to Phoenicia, Cyprus, and Antioch of Syria (Acts 11:19). According to Acts, it was Philip who first proclaimed Jesus as Messiah in Samaria (Acts 8:4–13), although Peter and John subsequently joined Philip in Samaria to bestow the Holy Spirit on the nascent believers (Acts 8:14–24). Thereafter, Peter, John, and Philip returned to Jerusalem, "proclaiming the good news to many villages of the Samaritans" along the way (Acts 8:25). Philip subsequently traveled from Jerusalem to Gaza in southwest Palestine (Acts 8:26), then north along the Mediterranean coast to Azotus (Acts 8:40), and then on to Caesarea, proclaiming along the way "the good news to all the towns" (Acts 8:40).

Acts reports that Saul then went to Damascus to deliver letters to the synagogues in that city for the arrest of members of the Jesus' movement and their delivery to Jerusalem (Acts 9:1–2). It was on this trip, according to Luke, that Saul encountered the risen Jesus, resulting in his conversion, his receipt of the Holy Spirit, and his baptism at the hands of Ananias (Acts 9:3–25). After some time in Damascus, Saul returned to Jerusalem with Barnabas (Acts 9:26–27), although he himself denies such a visit to Jerusalem (Gal 1:17).[16] From Jerusalem, Saul went to Caesarea and then back to his hometown of Tarsus (Acts 9:30). Saul was subsequently joined in Tarsus by Barnabas, who had traveled from Jerusalem to Antioch (Acts 11:22) and then on to Tarsus to look for Saul (Acts 11:25), presumably at the request of the church in Antioch. According to Luke, Barnabas then brought Saul from Tarsus to Antioch (Acts 11:26).

---

16. As stated earlier, scholars generally assume that Paul is the more reliable authority in such matters, indicting once again the problematic nature of relying on the Acts of the Apostles for a reconstruction of the early history.

At this time, Antioch was the third largest city in the Roman Empire, after Rome and Alexandria, and the first major city to house a Christian community. For all intents and purposes, Antioch was the cradle of pre-Pauline Gentile Christianity. Seemingly impressed with the growth of the Christian community in Antioch, leaders of the Jerusalem church designated Barnabas, a Cypriot Jew who had migrated to Jerusalem, to go to Antioch to assess the situation in its flourishing church and report back to them. In the meantime, Peter had traveled to western Palestine to Lydda (Acts 9:32), then to Joppa (Acts 9:38–43), and then to Caesarea (Acts 10:1–33).

These early missionary travels were nothing compared to what was to come. Specifically, the church at Antioch apparently took the usual step of commissioning Barnabas and Saul "for the work to which I [the Holy Spirit] have called them" (Acts 13:2),[17] namely a more systematic effort to win converts among the Gentiles—from among Hellenized Jews, Greek converts or near-converts (proselytes) to Judaism, and pagans in the Greco-Roman world.

Paul's First Missionary Journey (ca. 46 to 48)

According to Luke, the first of these missionary journeys (Acts 13:4–14:28) took Barnabas and Saul, with assistance from John (John Mark), from the commissioning church at Antioch to

> Seleucia (Acts 13:4), also known as Seleucia Pieria, the seaport for Antioch, from which Barnabas, Saul, and John Mark sailed west to Barnabas's homeland of Cyprus,[18] stopping first at
>
> Salamis, where they proclaimed the word of God in the synagogues of the Jews (Acts 13:5), then overland across Cyprus to Paphos (Acts 13:6), where the Roman proconsul Sergius Paulus was converted (Acts 13:7–12). Barnabas, Saul (whose name was changed to Paul), and John Mark then sailed north to
>
> Perga in Pamphylia (Acts 13:13), where John Mark left Barnabas and Paul and returned to Jerusalem for reasons that Luke does not explain. From Perga, Barnabas and Paul traveled inland to
>
> Antioch of Pisidia (Acts 13:14), where Barnabas and Paul went into the synagogue on successive sabbaths and where they converted many Gentiles (Acts 13:14, 42, 44, 48–49). Barnabas and Paul were expelled from Antioch (Acts 13:50–52) and moved onto
>
> Iconium (Acts 14:1), where they went into the Jewish synagogue and made converts among Jews and Greeks and where they were again persecuted by unbelieving Jews and Gentiles (Acts 14:2–5); then to
>
> Lystra (Acts 14:6), where they again made disciples (Acts 14:8–18) but where Jews from Antioch and Iconium stoned Paul and dragged him out of the city (Acts 14:19); then to
>
> Derbe, where they made many disciples (Acts 14:20–21). Paul, who through his preaching skills appears to have become the leader of the mission (Acts

---

17. Once again, we are reading Luke's "theologized" interpretation of Paul's missionary journeys.

18. Col 4:10 implies that John Mark was Barnabas's cousin and presumably, therefore, also a Cypriot. There is no way to assess the reliability of this tradition, which obviously comes to us from a period many decades after the fact.

14:12), and Barnabas then returned to Lystra, Iconium, and Antioch of Pisidia (Acts 14:21), appointing "elders for them in each church" (Acts 14:23); then through the

Province of Pisidia (Acts 14:24), to
Pamphylia (Acts 14:24),
Perga (Acts 14:25), and
Attalia (Acts 14:25), from which they sailed back to
Antioch of Syria (Acts (14:26), presumably by way of Salamis. At Antioch, Paul and Barnabas "called the church together and related all that God had done with them, and how he had opened a door of faith for the Gentiles" (Acts 14:27).[19]

This first missionary journey was presumably the brainchild of the leadership of the church at Antioch of Syria, one of the most important churches in early Christianity and the church where, according to Luke, disciples were first called "Christians" (Acts 11:26). During this first missionary journey, primarily to Cyprus and south-central Anatolia, Barnabas and Paul apparently went first to the Jewish synagogues in each city (Acts 13:5, 14–16, 42–43; 14:1; see also Acts 17:1, 10, 17; 18:4, 7, 8, 19, 26; 19:8), where they won converts from both Jews and proselytes, pagans who were attracted to Judaism and who worshiped in the synagogue but who did not take the final step of conversion to Judaism by submitting to the painful rite of male circumcision. It appears that Barnabas was initially the senior member of the missionary team but that along the way Saul, who assumed the Roman name Paul, perhaps at Paphos on the island Cyprus, apparently moved to center stage because of his eloquence and became the leading figure in spreading the gospel to the Gentiles.

Paul's Second Missionary Journey (ca. 50 to 54)

According to Luke, the second missionary journey (Acts 15:36–18:22) began with the expectation that Barnabas and Paul would again travel together to revisit churches they had established on their first journey. Between the two journeys, Barnabas and Paul had met with the apostles in Jerusalem, who agreed that Gentiles who accepted Jesus and were baptized need not be circumcised, but that they should refrain from eating food that had been sacrificed to idols, from blood and from anything that had been strangled, and from fornication (Acts 15:1–35). However, Paul and Barnabas disagreed over whether to take John Mark with them, inasmuch as he had deserted them in Pamphylia on their previous journey and had not accompanied them in their missionary work (Acts 15:36–41). The disagreement became so heated

---

19. Acts 14:27 may imply that Paul and Barnabas had kept a written report or itinerary, which may have survived in the church at Antioch and which may have served subsequently as a source for Luke in his composition of Acts. That "diary" may also have served as the basis for the report delivered subsequently to the apostles and elders of the Jerusalem church (Acts 15:4—"When they came to Jerusalem, they were welcomed by the church and the apostles and the elders, and they reported all that God had done with them."). It is, of course, impossible to know definitively whether Luke has created this story or has actually relied on a written "diary" that survived as served him as a source for the missionary journeys as reported in Acts.

THE NEW TESTAMENT

that Paul and Barnabas parted company. Barnabas took his cousin John Mark with him from Antioch and sailed for Cyprus, and Paul set out from Antioch with Silas and traveled overland through Syria and Cilicia, strengthening their churches, probably in the regions of Antioch and Tarsus (Acts 15:37–41), and then proceeded to

> Derbe (Acts 16:1) and
>
> Lystra, where Paul met Timothy, the son of a Jewish-Christian mother and a Greek father, had him circumcised to quell the Jews of the region, and then asked him to join them on the rest of their journey, going from town to town to inform the people of the results of the council of Jerusalem (Acts 16:1–5). They then went through the region of
>
> Phrygia and Galatia, having been forbidden by the Holy Spirit to preach the word in the Roman province of Asia (Acts 16:6).[20] They had planned to head from Mysia to visit Bithynia on the Black Sea, but the Spirit of Jesus did not allow them (Acts 16:7),[21] and they headed instead for
>
> Troas (Acts 16:8), where Paul had a vision (a dream?) that he should sail across the Dardanelles to the Roman province of Macedonia. He sailed, therefore, from Troas toward
>
> Samothrace (Acts 16:11) and landed the following day in the port city of
>
> Neapolis (Acts 16:11), from which he traveled overland to
>
> Philippi, a leading city of Macedonia and a Roman colony, where Paul and Silas won some followers and were subsequently stripped, beaten, and thrown into prison; but they were miraculously freed as the result of an earthquake (Acts 16:12-40). Paul and Silas then passed through
>
> Amphipolis and Apollonia (Acts 17:1) and on to
>
> Thessalonica, where they argued with the Jews for three weeks about the meaning of the scriptures and where both Jews and Greeks were persuaded that Jesus was Messiah (Acts 17:1–9). Paul and Silas then traveled to
>
> Beroea, where the Jews of the synagogue and some Greek women and men of high standing were receptive to the message of Paul, Silas, and Timothy. Some Jews from Thessalonica arrived in Beroea to stir up the crowds, and Silas and Timothy remained in the city while Paul was whisked off to the coast (Acts 17:10–15) and taken to
>
> Athens. There Paul was distressed with the pagan religious scene and argued daily in the synagogue and in the market place, proclaiming the good news about Jesus and the resurrection (Acts 17:16–21). Paul left Athens and traveled to
>
> Corinth, where he argued every sabbath in the synagogue trying to convince Jews and Greeks (Acts 18:1–4). It was in Corinth that Paul met the Jewish-Christian couple Aquila and Priscilla who had come from Rome. Silas and Timothy arrived in Corinth from Macedonia to rejoin Paul. Unsuccessful with the Jews in Corinth, Paul turned from them and said that henceforth he would direct his message to the Gentiles. Paul remained in Corinth for a total of eighteen months (Acts 18:5–11). It was from Corinth that Paul probably wrote his first letter to the church at Thessalonica in about 52.
>
> [According to Acts 18:12–17, some Jews of Corinth took Paul before Gallio, the Roman Proconsul of Achaia, sometime during Paul's eighteen month stay in

---

20. Once again, Luke's "theologizing" of history is evident in this verse.
21. And again, the work of the "spirit of Jesus" is an element of Luke's "theologizing" of history.

Corinth, accusing him of encouraging practices contrary to Jewish law. An inscription discovered at Delphi in 1905 dates Gallio's proconsulship to the years 51–52 CE., giving us one of the few firm dates in New Testament chronology. It is from this date that scholars set both backward and forward the approximate dates of Paul's missionary journeys.[22]]

Accompanied by Priscilla and Aquila, Paul set out from Corinth and sailed to

Cenchreae in the Peloponnese in southern Greece, where he had his hair cut (Acts 18:18–19) and then to

Ephesus (Acts 18:18–22), where Paul went to the synagogue to have a discussion with the Jews. Paul may not have established a church in Ephesus on this visit. Perhaps Priscilla and Aquila (Paul's friends from Corinth), and Apollo established the church in Ephesus. Paul left them in Ephesus when he set sail for

Caesarea (Acts 18:22), from which he traveled overland to

Jerusalem (Acts 18:22) and then to

Antioch (Acts 18:22).

Paul's Third Missionary Journey (ca. 54 to 58)

According to Luke, the third missionary journey (Acts 18:23–21:17) began after Paul had spent some time in Antioch and traveled overland from place to place once again through Galatia and Phrygia, probably including Tarsus and Iconium, strengthening the disciples in those regions (Acts 18:23), until he reached

Ephesus, where he remained for three years (Acts 19:1–41; 20:31). Paul taught for three months in the synagogue in Ephesus, but he was not well received. He then continued to preach in the lecture hall of Tyrannus for two years to both Jews and Greeks. Paul sent his helpers Timothy and Erastus to Macedonia, which Paul intended to visit after spending some more time in Ephesus. Gaius and Aristarchus of Macedonia are reported as accompanying Paul in Ephesus (Acts 19:29). It was during this visit in Ephesus that in about 54–55 Paul probably wrote letters to the church at Corinth. After a dispute in the theater over the role of the goddess Artemis in Ephesus (Acts 19:28–41), Paul left and headed to

Macedonia (Acts 20:1), and then on to

Greece, where he remained for three months (Acts 20:2–3), from whence he departed after the Jews plotted against him. Rather than sailing to Syria, as was his intention, he returned to

Macedonia (Acts 20:3), accompanied by Sopater son of Pyrrhus from Beroea, Aristarchus and Secundus from Thessalonica, Gaius from Derbe, Timothy, and Tychicus and Trophimus from Asia (Acts 20:4). Paul's friends preceded him in leaving Macedonia, but he subsequently sailed from Philippi and joined them in

Troas, where they stayed for seven days (Acts 20:6). From Troas Paul's friends then sailed to

Assos (Acts 20:13), where Paul joined them after traveling overland from Troas. Paul and his friends sailed together from Assos to

Mitylene (Acts 20:14), then to

Chios (Acts 20:15), then to

Samos (Acts 20:15) and

---

22. Haacker, "Gallio," 901–03.

Miletus (Acts 20:15), intentionally bypassing Ephesus, so that Paul could be in Jerusalem by Pentecost. However, elders of the church in Ephesus came to Miletus to meet Paul, who bade them farewell, knowing that he would probably never see them again. Paul then made the final stage of his sea voyage to

Cos (Acts 21:1), then to

Rhodes (Acts 21:1) and from there to

Patara (Acts 21:2), and then past

Cyprus (Acts 21:3) and on to

Tyre (Acts 21:3), from which Paul's friends and their families sailed back home. From Tyre, Paul made his way overland through

Ptolemais (Acts 21:7), to

Caesarea (Acts 21:8), and finally to

Jerusalem (Acts 21:17), where Paul apparently expected to die (Acts 21:13).

Paul's Journey to Rome (ca. 58–60)

According to Luke, upon his return to Jerusalem, Paul faced new opposition from Jews from Asia, resulting in charges that he was "a pestilent fellow, an agitator among all the Jews, and a ringleader of the sect of the Nazarenes"[23] (Acts 24:5). The ensuing hostility resulted in an effort on the part of the Jews to kill him (Acts 23:12–15). Successive trials before Jewish and Roman authorities led Paul to exercise his right as a Roman citizen and appeal his case to the emperor's tribunal (Acts 25:10–12). The Roman governor Festus, accordingly, ordered that Paul be sent from Caesarea to Rome (Acts 25:12), and thus began Paul's final journey (Acts 27:1–28:16).

Accompanied by Artistarchus, a Macedonian from Thessalonica, and some other prisoners, Paul embarked on a ship of Adramyttium and set sail from Caesarea to ports along the coast of Asia (Acts 27:2). The following day they arrived in

Sidon (Acts 27:3), where Paul was able to visit friends. From Sidon they sailed around the northern coast of Cyprus, because the winds were against them. Their next port of call was

Myra in Lycia (Acts 27:5–6), where they boarded an Alexandrian ship bound for Italy. Sailing west, their ship arrived with difficulty off the coast of

Cnidus (Acts 27:7) and continued by sailing along the southern coast of Cyrus, passing Salmone with difficulty, until they were able to pull into

Fair Havens near the city of Lasea (Acts 27:8). Sailing west, they encountered a severe storm that threatened their ship and the lives of its two hundred seventy-six passengers (Acts 27:13–38). The ship struck a reef and ran aground (Acts 27:39–44), but everyone on board was able to swim ashore and reach land on the island of

Malta (Acts 28:1). After spending three months on Malta, they set sail on an Alexandrian ship until they reached

Syracuse on the island of Sicily, where they stayed for three days (Acts 28:11–12) and then sailed to

Rhegium (Acts 28:13), a port in the westernmost part of the toe of Italy, and from there sailed north to

---

23. This is the only verse in the New Testament where Jesus' followers are referred to as Nazarenes (or Nazoreans), thereby associating them with Jesus' hometown of Nazareth.

Puteoli (Acts 28:13–14), where they found Christians who invited them to stay for seven days. From Puteoli they traveled to

Rome (Acts 28:14–16), where Acts ends the story by reporting that Paul preached in Rome, where he lived for two years (Acts 28:17–31).

DISAGREEMENTS BETWEEN PAUL AND ACTS

It is tempting to try to determine where Paul's letters fit into the Lukan chronology as outlined in the Acts of the Apostles. Such an exercise assumes that Acts is a relatively reliable historical document and can, therefore, serve as a dependable framework for writing a history of the early church.

Evidence challenges this assumption and shows that in many of the instances in which Paul's letters can be compared with Acts, there are serious discrepancies. Let us look at just a few examples:[24]

1. As seen above in the context of the second missionary journey, Acts states that Silas and Timothy remained in the city of Beroea in Macedonia while Paul was whisked off to the coast (Acts 17:10–15) and taken to Athens and did not meet up with his friends again until he reached Corinth and they arrived from Macedonia (Acts 18:5). By contrast, Paul states in 1 Thessalonians that he was not alone in Athens, but that Timothy (and perhaps also Silas?) was with him. In fact, it was from Athens that Paul sent Timothy back to Thessalonica "to strengthen and encourage you [Thessalonians] for the sake of your faith so that no one would be shaken by these persecutions" (1 Thess 1:1–3).

2. Acts states that following his conversion, Paul left Damascus and went to Jerusalem, where "he attempted to join the disciples," (who were afraid of him) but, through the intervention of Barnabas, Paul wound up going "in and out among them in Jerusalem" (Acts 9:26–30). By contrast, Paul states emphatically that after God "was pleased to reveal his Son to me . . . , I did not confer with any human being, nor did I go up to Jerusalem to those who were already apostles before me" (Gal 1:15–18). For whatever reason Paul was resolute to maintain to the Galatians his distance and independence from the Jerusalem apostles, even as Luke was determined to show that Paul stood in union and continuity with them.

3. Luke attempts in Acts 21–22 and 28:17 to represent Paul as a Jew who observed the Jewish Law in every detail. Yet, in his letters, Paul consistently downplayed the role of the Law for Gentile Christians and criticized Peter for trying to require Gentiles to live like Jews (Gal 2:14). Paul the observant Jew appears to be a Lukan creation.

4. There are in Acts three very different and sometimes even contradictory accounts of Paul's conversion (Acts 9:1–19a; 22:3–21; 26:9–18), and these apparently legendary Lukan accounts differ significantly from Paul's simple statement in Gal 1:15–17.[25]

---

24. See Ehrman, *The New Testament*, 244–45.

25. I will discuss the several accounts of Paul's conversion in greater detail in the following chapter.

THE NEW TESTAMENT
MESSENGERS OF THE GOSPEL

Luke mentions other messengers of the gospel in the Acts of the Apostles, although it is not always clear what role each played. Acts focuses primarily on Paul's mission to the Gentiles, so it is difficult to assess the contribution of these seemingly lesser figures. Nor do we know of other early Christian missionaries, although there were obviously many, including presumably missionaries to Jews in areas surrounding Palestine, where Jewish Christianity apparently flourished.

Barnabas was, apart from Paul, probably the most important early missionary to the Gentiles. In fact, Barnabas may have been the initial leader of the first missionary journey. Like Paul, Barnabas was a Diaspora Jew. According to Luke, Barnabas was a Levite from Cyprus, whose original name was Joseph but who was called Barnabas by the Jerusalem apostles (Acts 4:36). It is not clear where and by whom Barnabas was converted, but he sold a field that belonged to him and donated the proceeds to the Jerusalem church (Acts 4:37), an act that reflects the communal sharing that was typical of some in the earliest Jerusalem community (compare Barnabas's unselfish act to the deception of Ananias and Sapphira in Acts 5:1–11).

According to Acts, the Jerusalem apostles sent Barnabas to Antioch of Syria to inspect the new Christian community in that city and to investigate the report that believers from Cyprus and Cyrene were converting people who spoke Greek, presumably both Hellenistic Jews and Greek-speaking Gentiles (Acts 11:20–22). From Antioch, Barnabas traveled to Paul's hometown of Tarsus to look for Paul and brought him to Antioch, where they taught together for an entire year (Acts 11:25–26). Together, Barnabas and Paul delivered a collection for famine relief from the church at Antioch to believers living in Judea (Acts 11:27–30). Barnabas and Saul then brought Barnabas's cousin John Mark (according to Colossians 4:10) back with them from Jerusalem to Antioch.

Following their trip to Jerusalem, Barnabas and Paul were commissioned by the church at Antioch to undertake a missionary journey to Cyprus and beyond (Acts 13:1–4). On this first missionary journey, Barnabas and Paul generally went first to the synagogues of the Jews where they proclaimed the good news. They founded churches in Antioch of Pisidia, Iconium, Lystra, and Derbe, meeting with success among Jews, devout converts to Judaism (Acts 13:43), Gentiles (Acts 13:48), and Greeks (Acts 14:1).

When they returned to the church at Antioch after their first missionary journey, Paul and Barnabas reported their success, particularly among Gentiles (Acts 14:27). The church at Antioch then sent them to Jerusalem to discuss the issue of the validity of the Jewish law for Gentile converts (Acts 15:1–10). According to Paul's own testimony, he and Barnabas disagreed on the role of Jewish law for Gentile converts. They disagreed specifically when "certain people came from James" in Jerusalem to Antioch to try to impose circumcision and the Jewish dietary laws on Gentile converts (Gal 2:12–13). Barnabas and Peter, who was visiting Antioch at the time, equivocated, but

Paul stood firm in his claim that Gentile Christians were not bound by Jewish law on the basis of an agreement reached previously at the Jerusalem meeting (Acts 15:22–35).

Barnabas and Paul also disagreed whether to take John Mark with them on their second missionary journey and wound up going separate ways, Barnabas and his cousin John Mark to Cyprus, and Paul and Silas to Asia. Whatever the nature of their disagreement, Paul and Barnabas were apparently later reconciled (1 Cor 9:6).

John Mark was a Jew, the son of Mary, a leading figure in the early church. Together with his mother, he was among the first followers of Jesus in Jerusalem (Acts 12:12). Mark was chosen by the Jerusalem church to serve as a companion for Barnabas and Saul when they left Jerusalem for Antioch (Acts 12:25) in order that he could serve them as an attendant on their forthcoming missionary journey (Acts 13:5). Mark remained with Paul and Barnabas through Cyprus on that journey but left them at Perga in Pamphilia and returned to Jerusalem (Acts 13:13), although Luke does not explain the reason for his departure. Barnabas wanted Mark to accompany them on their second journey to revisit cities where they had previously established churches, but Paul refused, creating a misunderstanding with Barnabas. Barnabas and Mark separated from Paul and left for Cyprus (Acts 15:36–41).

Silas[26] was a Jewish Christian prophet and leader of the Jerusalem church, which sent Silas and Judas as delegates to Antioch to deliver and explain the letter clarifying requirements for Gentile Christians with respect to the Jewish law (Acts 15:22–29, 32). Following their visit to Antioch, Silas and Judas returned to Jerusalem (Acts 15:33). After Barnabas and Paul disagreed about whether John Mark should accompany them on their second journey, Barnabas and John Mark departed for Cyprus, and Paul enlisted Silas to join him on the second journey through Syria and Cilicia to strengthen their churches (Acts 15:40–18:22).

The presence of Silas on this journey presumably lent legitimacy to Paul's preaching and to his mission to the Gentiles. In Philippi, Paul and Silas were dragged into the marketplace before authorities, stripped, beaten, and imprisoned (Acts 16:19–24). Acts mentions that Silas, Paul, and Timothy were expelled from Thessalonica after an uprising instigated by Jews and ruffians (Acts 17:1–5) and that Silas and Timothy remained in Thessalonica while Paul moved on (Acts 17:14). They subsequently rejoined Paul in Corinth (Acts 18:5), where Silas actively evangelized with Paul and Timothy (2 Cor 1:19). Silas is listed along with Paul and Timothy as a sender of the Thessalonian correspondence (1 Thess 1:1; 2 Thess 1:1).

Timothy, a native of Lystra in Asia Minor, was chosen by Paul on the occasion of his visit to Lystra during the second journey, apparently on the advice of the church at Lystra, to serve as Paul's assistant and companion during the remainder of the journey (Acts 16:1–3). On the basis of what is probably reliable information, 2 Tim 1:5 identifies Timothy's Jewish mother as Eunice and his grandmother as Lois and identifies

---

26. Silas is called Silvanus in Paul's letters (2 Cor 1:19; 1 Thess 1:1; 2 Thess 1:1), a Latinized form of Silas, which may be the Aramaic form of the Hebrew name Saul.

both as converts to Christianity. Timothy's father was Greek. Although it is not so stated, Paul and Barnabas may have converted Timothy during the first visit to Lystra (Acts 14:6–20; 16:1–2), as Paul apparently claims Timothy as his personal convert ("my beloved and faithful child in the Lord" 1 Cor 4:17).

Paul arranged for Timothy to be circumcised (Acts 16:3), probably because, as the son of a Jewish mother, Timothy was a Jew by birth and was, therefore, not exempt from circumcision according to the agreement reached at the Jerusalem conference (Acts 15: 23–29).[27] According to Acts, Timothy traveled with Paul and Silas through Asia to Troas and then into Macedonia. Paul left Timothy at Beroea, traveled to Athens, and then subsequently sent for Timothy to join him there (Acts 17:14–15).[28] Paul sent Timothy from Athens back to Thessalonica to strengthen that community and to gather news about the Thessalonian church (1 Thess 3:2). Timothy rejoined Paul in Corinth and delivered a favorable report about the church at Thessalonica (1 Thessalonians 3:1–8; Acts 18:5).

When Paul wrote 1 Thessalonians from Athens, he included Timothy in his opening greeting (1 Thess 1:1; see also 2 Thess 1:1[29]). Timothy next appears in Ephesus during the third missionary journey, when Paul sent him from Ephesus back to Macedonia with Erastus (Acts 19:22). Timothy was presumably with Paul still later in Corinth, as his name appears in the greetings that Paul sent from Corinth to the church at Rome (Rom 16:21), or perhaps Ephesus.[30] Timothy appears once again in Troas on the occasion of Paul's journey back to Jerusalem (Acts 20:4–5) and may also have been with Paul when Paul wrote to the church at Philippi from some undesignated city (Phil 1:1).

Aquila and Prisca (or the diminutive Priscilla) were a married couple (Acts 18:2–3; 2 Tim 4:19), who were missionaries and traveling companions of Paul. Aquila was a Jew from Pontus, the northernmost region of modern Turkey, and by trade a tentmaker, who had lived in Rome with Prisca until they were expelled in 49 along with all Jews by order of the Edict of the emperor Claudius (Acts 18:12). It is not clear from the text, but Aquila and Prisca were apparently Christians before they moved to Corinth from Rome, where they had previously belonged to the synagogue. After spending 18 months living in Aquila and Priscilla's house in Corinth and working as a tentmaker in Aquila's workshop, Paul left with them for Ephesus (Acts 18:21), where they established a church in their home (1 Cor 16:19). Aquila and Prisca remained in Ephesus when Paul went to Jerusalem. Following Claudius's death in 54, the couple

---

27. Some scholars, wondering whether Paul would expect a gentile to be circumcised, suggest that this may be a Lukan gloss; but under Jewish law, Timothy was considered a Jew because of his Jewish mother.

28. As mentioned earlier in this chapter in the section on disagreements between Acts and Paul, Paul disagrees with this detail (1 Thess 1:1–3).

29. Many scholars consider 2 Thessalonians as a pseudonymous letter written not by Paul himself but by a later disciple of Paul in Paul's name.

30. Some scholars regard Rom 16 as a separate letter, probably addressed to the church at Ephesus.

returned to Rome, where they headed the church in their home (Rom 16:3–5a). Aquila and Prisca are mentioned in Rom 16:3, which some scholars argue may actually be an original part of the letter to the Romans and not part of a letter to Ephesus.

Apollos (an abbreviation of Apollonius) was an Alexandrian Jew and an itinerant Christian missionary, who was apparently an independent evangelist and not a disciple or associate of Paul. Apollos's preaching at the synagogue in Ephesus attracted the attention of Aquila and Prisca, who seem to have found his preaching deficient, perhaps because it did not contain some of the elements emphasized by Paul. Luke reports that Aquila and Prisca taught Apollos a more accurate message, presumably with a more Pauline emphasis, inasmuch as they were closely associated with Paul's missionary work (Acts 18:26). From Ephesus, Apollos traveled to Corinth, where he preached with so much success that he became the focus of partisan loyalty in that city (1 Cor 1:12; 6:12), but it does not appear that Apollos competed with Paul or tried to subvert his message or his authority (1 Cor 3:10–23).

Erastus was an associate of Paul on his third missionary journey and is referred to as the treasurer of Corinth, assuming that Paul wrote the letter to the Romans from Corinth (Rom 16:23[31]). Paul sent Erastus and Timothy from Ephesus to Macedonia, while he remained in Ephesus somewhat longer before going to Macedonia to join them (Acts 19:22). Erastus is later reported as living again in Corinth (2 Tim 4:20).

Gaius of Derbe accompanied Paul from Greece to Asia on the third missionary journey (Acts 20:4). He had previously served as Paul's host in Corinth, where Paul converted and baptized him (Rom 16:2; 1 Cor 1:14). In fact, Gaius was among the first people Paul baptized in Corinth on the second missionary journey. Although a native of Derbe, Gaius lived in Corinth and was apparently a man of means. Paul reports that Gaius's house could host "the whole church" in Corinth (Rom 16:23), a phrase that may imply that Christians generally met in several smaller house churches in Corinth. While traveling with Paul, Gaius was among those who were seized in the riot in Ephesus (Acts 19:29).

Aristarchus was a Greek Macedonian from Thessalonica who traveled with Paul from Thessalonica to Macedonia on his third missionary journey (Acts 19:29; 27:2) and who, according to Col 4:10–11, was a Jewish Christian. Along with Gaius, Aristarchus was seized by the mob during the riot in Ephesus and was taken to the theater (Acts 19:29). He accompanied Paul on his final journey from Greece (probably Corinth) to Jerusalem (Acts 20:4) and also embarked on Paul's final journey from Caesarea to Rome, although it is not clear whether Aristarchus sailed on the final leg from Myra in Lycia to Rome (Acts 27:2).

---

31. This point is not affected by the theory that Rom 16 was actually addressed to Ephesus from Corinth.

THE NEW TESTAMENT
THE MESSAGE OF THE EARLIEST APOSTLES

In a previous chapter, I summarized the work of C.H. Dodd in identifying the content of the *kerygma*, the apostolic preaching. I have, however, shown in this chapter that it is not exactly clear what the earliest version of that preaching was and that 1 Cor 15:1–7 does not indicate at what point the various components of the *kerygma* emerged, or how the message may have grown and evolved.

Perhaps the earliest component of the message preached by the Jerusalem apostles was that God raised Jesus from the dead and exalted him to a position of honor at his right hand. As we saw, that message is probably grounded in an early interpretation of Ps 110:1. In fact, Ps 110 may have been the earliest proof text in what later became a portfolio of *testimonia* that the church identified and collected to serve as the basis for its evolving message that Jesus had been raised from the dead and had been made Lord and Messiah.

The claim that Jesus was raised *on the third day in accordance with the scriptures* probably came somewhat later, after a more thorough search through the scriptures and the discovery of Hos 6:2. Moreover, the identification of the suffering servant passages in Isa 53 probably served subsequently as a justification for showing how Jesus could have been messiah, even though during his lifetime he did virtually nothing that first century Jews expected of their messiah. The early church obviously redefined the role of messiah on the basis of details in Jesus life and on the basis of passages in Isaiah that fit and explained what was already known about Jesus, namely that he had suffered and been crucified. The redemptive quality of human suffering, a central message of Isa 53, came to serve as a major theme for the foundling Jesus movement, but it was probably not a component of the earliest preaching.

And what served as the basis for the belief that Jesus would soon return? What was the source of that belief? Jesus' own teaching, or something that the church found in the Hebrew scriptures? As I argued in chapter 8, it is unlikely that Jesus claimed to be messiah. If that observation is correct, then how could Jesus' followers have come to believe not only that Jesus was messiah but that he would return again? If Jesus had been made Lord and messiah, as the church believed based on Ps 110:1, then it was equally clear to them that the messiah was supposed to suffer, die, and be raised from the dead; and so the church searched and found the necessary proof texts in Isa 53 to support that claim.

But there was nothing about Jesus' life and death that required that he return again, simply because God had made him Lord and messiah following his death and exaltation. The key to belief in Jesus second coming may also lie in the words of Ps 110:1:

> The LORD says to my Lord,
> "Sit at my right hand
> *until I make your enemies your footstool*" (italics mine).

Perhaps this verse also recalled for the church the words of Dan 7:13:

> I saw one like a human being [Aramaic: one like a son of man]
> coming with the clouds of heaven.
> And he came to the Ancient One [Aramaic: the Ancient of Days]
> and was presented before him.

Perhaps Jesus' exaltation to God's right hand, as interpreted in light of Ps 110:1, was then also interpreted in light of Dan 7:13 as the "coming" of the Son of Man to the Ancient of Days (God). It was there at God's right hand that the exalted Jesus would sit *until* God made Jesus' enemies into a footstool for him, which would happen only when Jesus returned to earth as Son of Man.

We learn from Acts that Paul (and presumably others) engaged Jews in the synagogues in discussions about the meaning of the Hebrew scriptures.[32] It was presumably through such exchanges that Jews and those involved in the Jesus movement argued about the meaning of specific scriptural passages. Such discussions were not a single event but were presumably part of a drawn-out process through which the church built its primitive Christology based on the interpretation of critical scriptural passages that were discovered in the course of deliberations and argumentations with Jews. As a Pharisee (Acts 23:6; 26:5; Phil 3:4b–6), Paul must have been a major figure in discovering some of those passages and in developing the scriptural case in city after city, building and improving his message along the way, even though the original message was presumably based on the preaching of the earliest Jerusalem apostles.

It is easy to understand how members of the Jesus movement would have made the transition from believing that Jesus had been elevated to God's right hand to believing that he would return as the Son of Man if, during his lifetime, Jesus had preached the imminent coming of the Son of Man. It is also easy to understand the next step in the process through which some of Jesus' teaching about the imminent coming of the Son of Man would be transformed into Jesus' teaching that he would return soon as the Son of Man. The fact that the gospels contain sayings in which Jesus speaks of someone other than himself as the coming Son of Man and sayings in which Jesus speaks of his own future coming as the Son of Man is most easily explained by this hypothesis. It is far more difficult to understand this transition if Jesus never spoke during his lifetime of the coming of the Son of Man. It is also difficult to explain how Paul could have spoken of Jesus' second coming in 1 Thessalonians in about 51/52, long before the composition of Q^2, which was presumably written later.[33] Yet Paul writes to the Thessalonians about how Christians should live in the face of the imminent return of Jesus the Lord (1 Thess 4:1–5:11)

---

32. Interestingly, the word "synagogue" appears in none of the Pauline letters, leading some scholars to conclude that Paul's visits to synagogues during his missionary journeys are an invention of Luke.

33. Proponents of Q2 might argue that Paul and the author of Q2 would have had no contact and no linear connection with one another, thereby invalidating my argument. That may be true, but did Q2 and Paul then independently introduce the element of the Son of Man into early Christianity.

THE NEW TESTAMENT
HOUSE CHURCHES

It is tempting to think when we read the word "church" in the New Testament that we are reading about a designated edifice in which Christians met to worship. Nothing could be further from the truth. There were no churches per se in the first century.

As we have seen, according to Luke, Jesus' earliest followers met in the temple in Jerusalem, gathering in an area called Solomon's Portico, a colonnade on the eastern side of the temple complex (Acts 3:11; 5:12). It is important to remember that Jesus' earliest followers were observant Jews, whether Aramaic-speaking Jews from Palestine or Greek-speaking Jews from the diaspora.

Early followers of Jesus also presumably met in synagogues, Jewish places of worship and instruction. Acts reports that Paul went to synagogues in Jerusalem and elsewhere to persecute followers of Jesus, who obviously gathered there (Acts 26:11). Before his conversion, Paul was on his way to synagogues in Damascus to continue his persecution of Jesus' followers (Acts 9:1–2); and shortly after his conversion, it was to those same synagogues in Damascus that Paul went to proclaim Jesus (Acts 9:19b–20).

On his missionary journeys to convert both Jews and Gentiles, Paul and his companions appear to have gone initially to synagogues in the diaspora to proclaim Jesus. According to Acts, Paul, Barnabas, and John Mark visited the synagogues at Salamis in Cyprus, the first stop on their first journey (Acts 13:5). Paul and Barnabas subsequently went to the synagogue in Antioch in Pisidia (Acts 13:14–43) and to the synagogue in Iconium (Acts 14:1–7). On the second missionary journey, Paul and Silas went to the synagogue in Thessalonica (Acts 17:1–9), to the synagogue in Beroea (Acts 17:10–12), to the synagogue in Athens (Acts 17:16–17), to the synagogue in Corinth (Acts 18:1–8), and to the synagogue at Ephesus (Acts 18:19–20; 19:8–10). Apollos too went to the synagogue in Ephesus when he first preached in that city; in fact, it was in the synagogue at Ephesus that Apollos met Aquila and Prisca (Acts 18:24–26). Although not mentioned specifically, and certainly not by Paul himself, it is reasonable to assume that Paul first visited the synagogue in virtually every city where he preached, at least wherever there was one.

In addition to gathering in Solomon's Portico in the Jerusalem temple or synagogues in Jerusalem and in the diaspora, members of the Jesus movement or the Way typically met in the larger homes of wealthier members of the church in the first century. Several passages are informative:

Acts 2:46

> Day by day, as they spent much time together in the temple, *they broke bread at home and ate their food with glad and generous hearts, praising God* and having the goodwill of all the people (italics mine).

Acts 20:7–8

On the first day of the week, when we met [in Troas] *to break bread,* Paul was holding a discussion with them; since he intended to leave the next day, he continued speaking until midnight. *There were many lamps in the room upstairs where we were meeting* (italics mine).

Rom 16:3–5a

Greet Prisca and Aquila, who work with me in Christ Jesus, and who risked their necks for my life, to whom not only I give thanks but also the churches of the Gentiles. *Greet also the church in their house* (italics mine).

1 Cor 16:19

The churches of Asia send greeting. Aquila and Prisca, *together with the church in their house*, greet you warmly in the Lord (italics mine).

Col 4:15

Give my greetings to the brothers and sisters in Laodicea, and to Nympha *and the church in her house* (italics mine).

Phlm 1–2

Paul, a prisoner of Christ Jesus, and Timothy our brother,
To Philemon our dear friend and co-worker, to Apphia our sister, to Archippus our fellow soldier, *and to the church in your house* (italics mine).

From these passages we learn that believers in Jesus gathered in the homes of members of the church, perhaps regularly on the first day of the week [Sunday, presumably in celebration of the day of Jesus' resurrection], to break bread [i.e. to celebrate the Eucharist, probably in the context of a full meal], to praise God through prayer and perhaps song, and to hold discussions [about Jesus and the work of the church]. Within these meeting in house churches, we witness the beginnings of a liturgy, probably modeled after the liturgy in Jewish synagogues.

AUTHORSHIP, AUDIENCE, AND THE PLACE AND DATE OF COMPOSITION OF THE ACTS OF THE APOSTLES

Before drawing our conclusions about the book of Acts and what we do and do not, can and cannot know about the earliest church, it seems appropriate to say something about the authorship, the audience, and the place and date of composition of Acts.

Authorship. Tradition identifies the author of the Gospel of Luke and the Acts of the Apostles as the same person, and most scholars agree with this tradition, based on a study of the vocabulary, the literary style, the theology, and the themes of the two books. In addition, the introductions to both books (Luke 1:1–4; Acts 1:1–2) tie them together, most specifically their common dedication to an otherwise unknown

Theophilus (Luke 1:3; Acts 1:1) and the reference in Acts 1:1 to "the first book" (obviously the Gospel of Luke).

Tradition identifies the author as Luke, a physician and traveling companion of Paul, but nowhere in either Luke or Acts does the author identify himself.[34] The author's familiarity with the Septuagint may suggest that he was a Hellenistic Jew or a gentile who converted to Christianity after a long association with the diaspora synagogue as a proselyte, but his familiarity with Greek rhetorical conventions and his command of the Greek language suggest that the author was well educated in Greek language and culture.

It is the so-called "we passages" in Acts 16:10–17; 20:5–16; 21:1–18; 27:1–28:16 in which the narrative shifts abruptly and without explanation from the third person to the first person plural that led initially to the tradition that a traveling companion of Paul (specifically Luke) wrote Luke and Acts.[35] Although these "we passages" do not establish Lukan authorship, they may indicate that the author of Acts had access to a written "travel diary" of an eye-witness who had traveled with Paul. One argument against Luke's use of such a source is that the vocabulary and literary style of the "we passages" are similar to the vocabulary and style of the rest of Acts, but Luke's admitted use of sources in writing the gospel (Luke 1:1–3) suggests the likelihood of his use of sources in composing Acts. It should not surprise us if Luke adapted his written sources to conform to his own literary style and vocabulary. I frankly find the theory that Luke may have used a written "travel diary" in compiling the stories of Paul's four journeys interesting, if not compelling.

Audience. The dedication of both Luke and Acts to Theophilus raises the question of who this Theophilus was. The name means in Greek "lover of God" or "beloved of God," suggesting to some that the name is symbolic, that the two books are dedicated to anyone who believes in Jesus as messiah, but there is little evidence for symbolic dedications in the ancient world. If Theophilus was an individual, he may have been Luke's patron for the writing of the two books, but he is otherwise unknown to us.

The audience of Acts is evidently Greek-speaking believers, whether gentile or Jewish, indeed probably both, who would likely have heard the book read in their local churches, as literacy was low, and the labor and cost of copying manuscripts were great. It is difficult to say much more than this about the book's audience.

Place of Composition. Scholars have suggested Antioch, Ephesus, Caesarea, Achaia, Macedonia, and Rome is the place of composition for the Acts of the Apostles.

---

34. The fact that the author is a man is established by the masculine form of the adjective "after investigating" (Greek παρηκολουθηκότι, parēkolouthēkoti) in Luke 1:3 — "I too decided, *after investigating* everything carefully from the very first, to write an orderly account for you, most excellent Theophilus... (italics mine).

35. The first of these passage Acts 16:10 is illustrative of the situation: "When he [Paul] had seen the vision, *we* immediately tried to cross over to Macedonia, being convinced that God had called *us* to proclaim the good news to them" (italics mine).

The most honest answer is that there is little internal evidence to suggest its precise place of composition.

Date of Composition. It is likewise difficult to establish a date of composition for Acts. Luke's mention of Paul's missionary activity in Rome but with no mention of Paul's trial and death has led some scholars to suggest a date as early as 62–64, sometime before Paul's trial and death, but this date is certainly too early. Presumably the author wrote the Gospel of Luke before he wrote the Acts of the Apostles. In fact, Acts 1:1 alludes to the gospel, and the gospel was presumably written after the destruction of the Jerusalem temple in 70 (see Luke 19:41–44; 21:20–24), so the earliest possible date for the composition of Acts might be sometime around 80 or 85.

The latest date of composition can be set by the earliest references to Acts in Irenaeus's *Against Heresies*, written about 180. An earlier date might be supported by a passage in Polycarp of Smyrna's *Letter to the Philippians*, of which chapters 1–12 were probably written about 135–138.[36] Some scholars have argued that *Philippians* 1:2 ("whom God raised up, having released the pangs of Hades") may be citing Acts 2:24 ("But God raised him up, having freed him from death"[37]) but that is by no means certain.[38] It is difficult to establish a date of composition based on such tenuous evidence.

The aforementioned evidence suggests a *terminus a quo* ("end from which," or an earliest possible date) of about 80–85 and a *terminus ad quem* ("end to which," or a latest possible date) of about 135 and certainly no later than about 150. It is difficult to narrow that wide range, but if Pervo is right, a date of composition closer to 130 may be more justified. We must, however, be mindful of the fact that the dates of composition of Luke and Acts cannot be too far apart if they were both written by the same person.

CONCLUSIONS

Reconstructing the very early history of Christianity is especially challenging, because the historical record for the first twenty years following Jesus' death is scant. The earliest extant Christian writing is presumably Paul's first letter to the church at Thessalonica, written in about 51/52, some twenty years after Jesus' death. Luke's second volume, the Acts of the Apostles, the only document that reports events from

---

36. It is the view of Harrison (*Polycarp's Two Epistles to the Philippians*, 286) that Polycarp's letter, in the form in which we know it, is actually two letters that were addressed to the church at Philippi at different times. The earlier letter, consisting of *Philippians* 13 and perhaps 14, can be dated to 110–17. *Philippians* 1–12, on the other hand, and hence *Philippians* 1:2, reflects a later historical situation toward the end of Emperor Hadrian's reign, or about 132–35.

37. Some ancient manuscripts of Acts 2:24 read "the pangs of Hades," a reading much closer to the text of Polycarp.

38. Richard I. Pervo thinks that it is "quite possible" that Polycarp, *Philippians* 1:2 is based on Acts 2:24 and that "if Acts is dated to the second decade of the second century, the probability that Polycarp attests the original text [of Acts 2:24] is rather high" (*Acts: A Commentary*, 81).

the earliest period was written much later, some scholars say in the late 80s, others sometime before 135. The dating of Acts is clearly not resolved.

Historians of early Christianity cannot examine their written sources and decide whether they are reliable or unreliable because we do not have access to actual events *except* through those sources. Historians can, however, explain how their ancient sources arose within their cultural and religious environments and then, perhaps, infer some of the events that may have generated our written texts.

Historians have also compared Acts to other "histories" from the Greco-Roman world. But, as Bart Ehrman reminds us,

> On the whole, histories from Greco-Roman antiquity were creative literary exercises . . . ; historians were necessarily inventive in the ways they collected and conveyed the information that they set forth. . . . This aspect of limited objectivity is particularly obvious in the case of historians living in antiquity. Theirs was a world of few written records but abundant oral tradition. . . . Historians quite consciously made the speeches up themselves, composing discourses that seemed to fit both the character of the speaker and the occasion. . . . They strove not for absolute objectivity but for verisimilitude.[39]

The same limitations and challenges that are evident in Greco-Roman histories are also evident in Acts. The author of the Acts of the Apostles, whom we have referred to as Luke, probably used written sources in the composition of Acts, just as he did in the making of the Gospel of Luke, which he presumably wrote sometime before Acts. Luke writes in Acts 1:1–2:

> In the first book [the Gospel of Luke], Theophilus, I wrote about all that Jesus did and taught from the beginning until the day when he was taken up to heaven, after giving instruction through the Holy Spirit to the apostles whom he had chosen.

We previously identified the sources of the Gospel of Luke as the Gospel of Mark, the Sayings Source Q, and Special L. It is reasonable to assume that some of the redactionary characteristics that scholars have identified in examining the ways in which Luke edited his Markan and Q sources were repeated in the composition of the Acts of the Apostle. More specifically, the vocabulary, the literary style, and the theological predisposition of both books are the same, affording scholars an important tool to distinguish Luke's redactional elements in Acts from what might have appeared in any written sources that he may have used.

The detailed nature of Paul's three missionary journeys and of his final trip to Rome have led some scholars to conclude that Luke may have had access to "travel diaries" composed by one or more of Paul's traveling companions. The detail with which Luke reports visits to different cities on those journeys and specific incidents at many of those destinations may suggest access to written reports from an eyewitness, although it is certainly not clear who may have written those "travel diaries." Paul

---

39. Ehrman, *The New Testament*, 116.

himself, Barnabas, Silas, an unknown assistant, or the scribe who wrote the letters to churches that Paul presumably dictated?[40] Moreover, scholars do have some check on Luke's accounts of Paul's journeys in Paul's own letters, so we can see how well material in the genuine Pauline letters fit into the Lukan chronology and scheme. There are some serious challenges, but Paul's letters and the Acts of the Apostles are reasonably compatible, even if they do disagree in important details.

Even if Luke had access to written diaries of the four journeys, it is quite clear that he did not have access to written documents concerning the events surrounding Pentecost and the days immediately following Jesus' crucifixion, namely the period of the first twenty years of the history of the church. Whatever written or oral sources Luke may have had access to for any portions of Acts are lost to us and are beyond recovery or reconstruction from an analysis of the text of Acts. Luke may have been aware that Paul wrote letters to some of the churches he had established or visited, but it is not clear that Luke had access to any of those letters, although Luke twice refers to other sorts of written letters (Acts 15:23–29 and 18:27).

Depending on the date one assigns to the composition of Luke-Acts, whether sometime in the late 80s or sometime before 135, the status of Paul's letters was certainly quite different in Christian communities over that fifty year interval. An earlier date for Acts would obviously put Luke in closer proximity to actual events or to early sources that he might have used. Whatever else might be said, there are serious limitations involved in using Acts to reconstruct pre-Pauline and even Pauline Christian history.

Scholars have long recognized that the letter in Acts 15 and the speeches of Peter and Paul do not derive from ancient sources but that they are in their present form Lukan compositions, although Luke probably used traditional Christian material in composing these speeches.

The existence of three different and to some extent contradictory accounts of Paul's conversion (Acts 9:1–19; 22:6–16 and 26:12–18) may point to the use of distinct sources for these three passages, but it is not clear that any of these accounts brings us closer to the "event" of Paul's conversion, which Paul describes quite differently in Gal 1:15–16. We will discuss the issue of these passages and of Paul's conversion in greater detail in the next chapter.

Acts and the Gospel of John both have accounts of the outpouring of the Holy Spirit on the apostles, Acts at Pentecost, seven weeks following the resurrection (Acts 2:1–4); and John on the evening immediately following Jesus' resurrection (John 20:19–22), leaving us to wonder whether Pentecost is in any sense of the word "history," or a story created by Luke to telescope the beginnings of Christianity into a

---

40. See, for example, 1 Cor 16:21: "I, Paul, write this greeting with my own hand"; Gal 6:11: "See what large letters I make when I am writing with my own hand"; Col 4:18: "I, Paul, write this greeting with my own hand"; 2 Thess 3:17 "I, Paul, write this greeting with my own hand. This is the mark in every letter I write; it is the way I write"; Phlm 19: "I, Paul, am writing this with my own hand"). These remarks at the end of several letters indicate that Paul had dictated the earlier portion of the letter to a secretary.

single moment. Both accounts of the outpouring of the Holy Spirit are legendary, and neither has a greater claim to historicity.

We have seen in this chapter the difficulty involved in reconstructing a pre-Pauline *kerygma*. There is a temptation to identify something like Acts 2:38 as an early formulation of the earliest preaching:

> Peter said to them, "Repent and be baptized every one of you in the name of Jesus Christ so that your sins may be forgiven; and you will receive the gift of the Holy Spirit."

It is, however, less clear whether we can actually reconstruct a pre-christological *kerygma* devoid of scriptural proof texts. What was the earliest preached message of Jesus' first apostles? The most honest answer is that we do not know.

Like the Gospel of Luke, Acts has its share or miracle stories, and the supernatural element is particularly evident throughout Acts, especially in what is perceived as the work of the Holy Spirit. The challenge is how to assign value to Acts as history, and how to penetrate behind the text to recover the events that gave rise to the earliest Christian communities and to their preached message, whatever it might have been.

The broad brushstrokes of Acts may be somewhat reliable. The challenge is what value to assign to the detail. Probably not a great deal!

CHAPTER 11

PAUL: THE MAN, THE MISSION, AND THE MESSAGE

PAUL OF TARSUS IS the central figure in the Acts of the Apostle. He is also the purported author of fourteen of the twenty-seven books of the New Testament, although most scholars are inclined to assign the authorship of about half that number to Paul. By any reckoning, Paul is, apart from Jesus, probably the single most important figure in the history of early Christianity, perhaps in the two thousand-year history of Christianity. Although Paul was relatively inconsequential until the mid-second century, it is not an exaggeration to suggest that there might be no Christianity today were it not for Paul of Tarsus.

Our knowledge of Paul comes primarily from his seven undisputed letters: Romans, 1 and 2 Corinthians, Galatians, Philippians, 1 Thessalonians, and Philemon. Three letters, 2 Thessalonians, Colossians, and Ephesians, are disputed and are probably pseudonymous letters that provide useful information about the subsequent generation of Pauline interpretation.[1] 1 and 2 Timothy and Titus are almost universally considered Deutero-Pauline letters, written pseudonymously in Paul's name in the early second century by a later disciple of Paul. Few scholars would assign the Letter to the Hebrews to Paul, although early church tradition increasingly considered it part of the Pauline corpus.

As we shall see later in this chapter, even the seven undisputed letters are not without their own literary challenges, and many scholars have questioned the unity of several of them. The literary unity of 1 Corinthians and 1 Thessalonians has been questioned, although the evidence is less than convincing. It is, however, quite likely that Romans, 2 Corinthians, and Philippians in their present form contain elements of several originally separate letters, albeit all of them probably genuine letters of Paul.

Information from Paul's letters alone is unfortunately not sufficient to provide a detailed and accurate portrait of Paul's life, his mission, and his message. Paul's letters are, after all, not autobiographies or even theological treatises. They are personal correspondence from Paul to nascent Christian communities and, in one case, to an individual fellow Christian, Paul's friend Philemon. The Acts of the Apostles is, on the other hand, a secondary source, written decades later by the author of the Gospel of

---

1. For some more detailed information on the dubious nature of Colossians and Ephesians, see the detailed discussion in chapter 2.

Luke, and scholars disagree with respect to the reliability of Acts as a credible source for Paul's life. As we have already seen, Luke was more of an author than he was a careful historian.

However limited our sources and however challenging the task, we have no choice but to proceed to try to reconstruct what we can know about Paul: the man, the mission, and the message.

PAUL THE MAN

THE EARLY YEARS

We know virtually nothing about Paul's life before his call and commission, so we must extrapolate information about that earliest period indirectly from Paul's letters and occasionally from Acts, although, as we have seen, Acts is certainly less reliable than the Pauline letters regarding details of Paul's life.

Paul tells us nothing in his letters about the date and place of his birth, his childhood, or his education. It seems reasonable to assume that Paul was born fairly close to the time of Jesus' birth, a few years BCE.[2] According to Acts, Paul was a diaspora Jew who was born in Tarsus (Acts 9:11; 21:39; 22:3), an important cosmopolitan city with Greco-Roman education. Tarsus was in the Roman province of Cilicia on the main road between Syria and Anatolia at the crossroad between east and west. Luke may be reliable in reporting that Paul came originally from Tarsus, but we should understand that Paul neither confirms nor refutes this information.

In his letters, Paul provides some details about his life before his conversion. He tells us that he was "circumcised on the eighth day [following his birth], a member of the people of Israel, of the tribe of Benjamin, a Hebrew born of Hebrews; as to the law, a Pharisee; as to zeal, a persecutor of the church; as to righteousness under the law, blameless" (Phil 3:5–6). In Rom 11:1, Paul reminds us again that he was "an Israelite, a descendant of Abraham, a member of the tribe of Benjamin." In Gal 1:14, he says: "I advanced in Judaism beyond many among my people of the same age, for I was far more zealous for the traditions of my ancestors." Luke's claim that Paul was a Roman citizen (Acts 22:25–26) is questionable, as is his claim that Paul was raised in Jerusalem "at the feet of [the famous rabbi] Gamaliel" (Acts 22:3). Also questionable is Luke's claim that Paul was present in Jerusalem at the martyrdom of Stephen (Acts 7:58b), inasmuch as Paul wrote that before his conversion and for several years thereafter he was "still unknown by sight to the churches of Judea that are in Christ" (Gal 1:22).

Although Paul always refers to himself by his Roman name Paulus (Greek Paulos), Acts tells us that his Jewish name was Saul,[3] a distinct possibility as diaspora

---

2. It is worth noting that when Paul refers to himself as "an old man" in Phlm 9, he was probably in his mid- to late-fifties.

3. See Acts 7:58; 8:1, 3; 9:1, 4, 8, 11, 17, 22, 24; 11:25, 30; 12:25; 13:1, 2, 7, 9; 22:7, 13; 26:14.

Jews often had both Hebrew and Greek or Roman names that were similar to their Hebrew names. The change from a Hebrew to a Greek name was, however, probably not associated with Paul's conversion, or with his missionary travels, as Luke implies in Acts 13:9.[4]

As a Hellenistic Jew growing up in Tarsus, a vibrant center of Cynic and Stoic philosophies, Paul's first language would have been Greek, and he would have known the Jewish scriptures in the Septuagint Greek, not in the original Hebrew. In fact, we can be certain of that because Paul used the Septuagint whenever he quoted in his letters from the Hebrew scriptures. Paul's mastery of written Greek attests to the likelihood that he was educated in Greek schools, where he also acquired familiarity with popular Greek philosophy. Paul's identity and his thinking clearly bridged two worlds, the one Jewish, the other Hellenistic. Nevertheless, whatever transpired as a result of Paul's conversion experience, Paul was born a Jew; he lived his life as a Jew; and he died as a Jew.

Paul's conversion should be understood first and foremost within the context of his Jewish origins. Although an early persecutor of Christians, Paul came to believe that Jesus was God's messiah (Greek Χριστός, *Christos*). Paul amended his Judaism to accommodate his conversion experience and what he believed was Jesus' commission for him to preach the good news (the gospel) to the Gentiles. Paul's conversion was not a transition from one religion to another, from Judaism to Christianity, but a modification of his Judaism to accept the role of Jesus as messiah and to include the Gentiles as an important component of God's chosen people.

That Paul persecuted Christians is clear from his own testimony (1 Cor 15:9; Gal 1:13, 23; Phil 3:6), but it is unlikely that Paul was involved in persecuting Christians in Jerusalem or that he asked the Jerusalem high priest for letters to take to Damascus so that he could arrest any who belonged to the Way and bring them back to Jerusalem for punishment (Acts 9:1–2). Luke has probably fabricated these stories. The high priest in Jerusalem never had authority over diaspora Jews. It is more likely that Paul persecuted Christians wherever it was that he was living, whether in Tarsus or Damascus or elsewhere. Local synagogues probably persecuted and expelled Christian deviants, and Paul was apparently involved in such persecutions and marginalizations wherever he was living before his conversion, a matter that is not entirely clear.

THE CONVERSION OF PAUL AND THE ACTS OF THE APOSTLES

Luke's three accounts of Paul's conversion in Acts 9, 22, and 26 probably tell us more about Luke than they could possibly tell us about Paul:

---

4. Moreover, if the Jewish name Saul is rendered in Greek, it sounds like Saulos. The Greek word *saulos* means "the loose, wanton gait of courtesans [female prostitutes] or Bacchantes [boisterous revelers]" or "of a prancing horse," a good reason for him to call himself Paul (*A Greek-English Lexicon*, compiled Liddell and Scott, 1586).

Acts 9:1–19a	Acts 22:2b–18a, 21	Acts 26:1b, 9–18
¹Meanwhile Saul, still breathing threats and murder against the disciples of the Lord, went to the high priest ²and asked him for letters to the synagogues at Damascus, so that if he found any who belonged to the Way, men or women, he might bring them bound to Jerusalem. ³Now as he was going along and approaching Damascus, suddenly a light from heaven flashed around him. ⁴He fell to the ground and heard a voice saying to him, "Saul, Saul, why do you persecute me?" ⁵He asked, "Who are you. Lord?" The reply came, "I am Jesus, whom you are persecuting. ⁶But get up and enter the city, and you will be told what you are to do." ⁷The men who were traveling with him stood speechless because they heard the voice but saw no one. ⁸Saul got up from the ground, and	²²:²ᵇThen he [Paul] said: ³"I am a Jew, born in Tarsus in Cilicia, but brought up in this city at the feet of Gamaliel, educated strictly according to our ancestral law, being zealous for God, just as all of you are today. ⁴I persecuted this Way up to the point of death by binding both men and women and putting them in prison, ⁵as the high priest and the whole council of elders can testify about me. From them I also received letters to the brothers in Damascus, and I went there in order to bind those who were there and to bring them back to Jerusalem for punishment. ⁶"While I was on my way and approaching Damascus, about noon a great light from heaven suddenly shone about me. ⁷I fell to the ground and heard a voice saying to me, 'Saul, Saul, why are	²⁶:¹ᵇThen Paul stretched out his hand and began to defend himself: . . . ⁹"Indeed, I myself was convinced that I ought to do many things against the name of Jesus of Nazareth. ¹⁰And that is what I did in Jerusalem; with authority received from the chief priests, I not only locked up many of the saints in prison, but I also cast my vote against them when they were being condemned to death. ¹¹By punishing them often in all the synagogues, I tried to force them to blaspheme; and since I was so furiously enraged at them, I pursued them even to foreign cities. ¹²"With this in mind, I was traveling to Damascus with the authority and commission of the chief priests, ¹³when at midday along the road, your Excellency, I saw a light from heaven, brighter than the sun, shining around me and

PAUL: THE MAN, THE MISSION, AND THE MESSAGE

Acts 9:1–19a	Acts 22:2b–18a, 21	Acts 26:1b, 9–18
though his eyes were wide open, he could see nothing; so they led him by the hand and brought him into Damascus. ⁹For three days he was without sight, and neither ate nor drank. ¹⁰Now there was a disciple in Damascus named Ananias. The Lord said to him in a vision, "Ananias." He answered, "Here I am Lord." ¹¹The Lord said to him, "Get up and go to the street called Straight, and at the house of Judas look for a man of Tarsus named Saul. At this moment he is praying, ¹²and he has seen in a vision a man named Ananias come in and lay his hands on him so that he might regain his sight." ¹³But Ananias answered, "Lord, I have heard from many about this man, how much evil he has done to your saints in Jerusalem; ¹⁴and here he has authority from the chief priests to bind all who invoke your name." ¹⁵But the Lord said to him, "Go, for he is an instrument whom I have chosen to bring my name before Gentiles	you persecuting me?' ⁸I answered, 'Who are you Lord?' Then he said to me, 'I am Jesus of Nazareth whom you are persecuting.' ⁹Now those who were with me saw the light but did not hear the voice of the one who was speaking to me. ¹⁰I asked, 'What am I to do, Lord?' The Lord said to me, 'Get up and go to Damascus; there you will be told everything that has been assigned for you to do. ¹¹Since I could not see because of the brightness of that light, those who were with me took my hand and led me to Damascus. ¹²A certain Ananias, who was a devout man according to the law and well spoken of by all the Jews living there, ¹³came to me and standing beside me, he said, 'Brother Saul, regain your sight!' In that very hour I regained my sight and saw him. ¹⁴Then he said, 'The God of our ancestors has chosen you to know his will, to see the Righteous One and to hear his own voice; ¹⁵for you will be his witness to	my companions. ¹⁴When we had all fallen to the ground, I heard a voice saying to me in the Hebrew language, 'Saul, Saul, why are you persecuting me? It hurts you to kick against the goads.' ¹⁵I asked, 'Who are you, Lord?' The Lord answered, "I am Jesus whom you are persecuting. ¹⁶But get up and stand on your feet; for I have appeared to you for this purpose, to appoint you to serve and testify to the things in which you have seen me and to those in which I will appear to you. ¹⁷I will rescue you from your people and from the Gentiles—to whom I am sending you ¹⁸to open their eyes so that they may turn from darkness to light and from the power of Satan to God, so that they may receive forgiveness of sins and a place among those who are sanctified by faith in me.'"

Acts 9:1–19a	Acts 22:2b–18a, 21	Acts 26:1b, 9–18
and kings and before the people of Israel; ¹⁶I myself will show him how much he must suffer for the sake of my name." ¹⁷So Ananias went and entered the house. He laid his hands on Saul and said, "Brother Saul, the Lord Jesus, who appeared to you on your way here, has sent me so that you might regain your sight and be filled with the Holy Spirit." ¹⁸And immediately something like scales fell from his eyes, and his sight was restored, Then he got up and was baptized, ¹⁹and after taking some food, he regained his strength.	all the world of what you have seen and heard. ¹⁶And now, why do you delay? Get up, be baptized, and have your sins washed away, calling on his name.' ¹⁷After I had returned to Jerusalem and while I was praying in the temple, I fell into a trance ¹⁸ᵃand saw Jesus saying to me, . . . ²¹Then he said to me, 'Go, for I will send you far away to the Gentiles.'"	

Although similar in many ways, Luke's accounts of Paul's conversion in Acts 9, 22, and 26 are also quite different.

Acts 9 reports the transformation of Saul from someone who was an arch-persecutor of Christians to someone who was a steadfast witness of the risen Christ. The story in Acts 9 is an audition (9:4–7), an auditory experience and not a vision; however, both Acts 9:17 ("the Lord Jesus, who *appeared to you* on your way here") and Acts 9:27 ("But Barnabas took him [Paul], brought him to the apostles, and described for them how on the road *he had seen the Lord*, who had spoken to him") clearly imply that Paul had a vision of the risen Lord. Moreover, Acts reports that Paul's traveling companions "heard the voice but saw no one" (9:7). Acts 9 identifies Ananias as the person who gave legitimacy to Saul following his conversion and as the person to whom the risen Jesus said that he had selected Saul as "an instrument whom I have chosen to bring my name before Gentiles and kings and before the people of Israel" (Acts 9:15). Yet, Paul nowhere in his letters mentions Ananias as someone who was instrumental in his conversion and commission.

Acts 22 also reports a private audition, not a vision (Acts 22:7–8), and not a public revelation as in Acts 9:7. Acts 22:9 states "Now those who were with me [Paul] saw the light but did not hear the voice of the one who was speaking to me," a statement that stands in sharp contradiction to Acts 9:7 with respect to who saw and who heard what. As in Acts 9, Ananias plays an important role in Acts 22. It is, in fact, Ananias who says to Paul, "The God of our ancestors has chosen you to know his will, to see the Righteous One, and to hear his own voice; for you will be his witness to all the world of what you have seen and heard" (Acts 22:14–15). In addition to hearing about the commission to the Gentiles from Ananias (Acts 22:15), Paul hears of his missionary commission to the Gentiles a second time, directly from Jesus in the Jerusalem temple ("Then he [Jesus] said to me, "Go, for I will send you far away to the Gentiles" [Acts 22:21]). This story is obviously a Lukan composition (Acts 22:17–21). In Acts 22:21, Luke is consciously pointing away from the temple and Jerusalem to the Gentiles; for Luke, the gospel belongs to the Gentiles, not to the Jews.

Acts 26 is also a Lukan composition, purportedly a speech of Paul delivered to King Agrippa II, to Agrippa's sister Bernice with whom he allegedly had an incestuous relationship,[5] to Porcius Festus, the procurator of Judea, to the Roman military tribunes, and to the prominent men of Caesarea (Acts 25:23). There is no mention of Ananias in Act 26, and it is the risen Lord who delivers to Paul the missionary commission to the Gentiles while Paul is praying in the Jerusalem temple (Acts 26:16–18a, 21).

We see in these three conversion stories that Luke has exercised considerable liberty in reporting the story to such an extent that he is not concerned with historical accuracy or with the inconsistencies he has incorporated into the three accounts. History, as we understand that word, was not Luke's objective. He is rather a story-teller in the mold of other ancient historians, and our observations in the case of the three reports of Paul's conversion must give us pause about how we should understand and evaluate the rest of Acts. Luke has, undoubtedly, used the same imaginative creativity in composing the whole of the Acts of the Apostles. These three stories reveal the degree to which Luke is the creator of the Acts of the Apostles and how freely he adapted whatever oral and/or written sources to which he may have had access.

Quite obviously, all three Lukan accounts of Paul's conversion are far more legendary than Paul's own very simple account of his call and commission in Gal 1:15–16, a passage that is reminiscent of the call of some of the Hebrew prophets:

> But when God, who had set me apart before I was born and called me through his grace, was pleased to reveal his Son to me [or *in me*, or *within me*, (Greek ἐν ἐμοί)], so that I might proclaim him among the Gentiles, . . .

Perhaps, the single most important vestige of truth in the accounts in Acts may be the role of Ananias, which Paul may have intentionally omitted in order to elevate his own importance as an apostle. It is difficult to know why Luke would otherwise

---

5. Juvenal, *Satires*, 6.156–58; Josephus, *Antiquities of the Jews*, 20.7.3.

diminish his favored hero, Paul, by inventing the role of Ananias in Paul's call and commission unless there is some modicum of truth to Ananias's role in Paul's conversion. Although sometimes a bit ambivalent to Paul, Luke does devote more than half of the chapters in Acts to him.

THE PSYCHOLOGY OF PAUL

Although it may be beyond the role of the historian to understand exactly what motivated Paul in his mission and his message, there is some evidence in Paul's letters that affords us with a glimpse into the mind of Paul.

Paul's account of someone's vision in 2 Cor 12:1–10 is generally assumed to be an account of Paul's own experience. Paul's words, especially in 2 Cor 12:6b–7a, make that eminently clear:

> ¹It is necessary to boast; nothing is to be gained by it, but I will go on to visions and revelations of the Lord. ²I know a person in Christ who fourteen years ago was caught up to the third heaven—whether in the body or out of the body I do not know; God knows. ³And I know that such a person—whether in the body or out of the body I do not know; God knows—⁴was caught up into Paradise and heard things that are not to be told, that no mortal is able to repeat. ⁵On behalf of such a one I will boast, but on my own behalf I will not boast, except of my weaknesses. ⁶But if I wish to boast, I will not be a fool, for I will be speaking the truth. But I refrain from it, so that no one may think better of me than what is seen in me or heard from me, ⁷even considering the exceptional character of the revelations. Therefore, to keep me from being too elated, a thorn was given me in the flesh, a messenger of Satan to torment me, to keep me from being too elated. ⁸Three times I appealed to the Lord about this, that it would leave me, ⁹but he said to me, "My grace is sufficient for you, for power is made perfect in weakness." So, I will boast all the more gladly of my weaknesses, so that the power of Christ may dwell in me. ¹⁰Therefore I am content with weaknesses, insults, hardships, persecutions, and calamities for the sake of Christ; for whenever I am weak, then I am strong.

The "person in Christ" to whom Paul refers in 2 Cor 12:2 is Paul himself, who had experienced a revelation from the risen Lord "fourteen years ago." If Paul was writing these words in 2 Cor in 54 or 55, then his ecstatic "vision and revelation" must have been in 40 or 41, presumably during the period of his mission travel in Syria and Cilicia. Paul's ascent into Paradise or entry into heaven (2 Cor 12:4) apparently occurred about five years after his earlier ecstatic call and commission and about a decade before his first visit to Corinth.

It is important to note that the account of this experience contains no description of what Paul *saw* in Paradise, but it does contain auditory elements: Paul "*heard* things that are not to be told, that no mortal is able to repeat" (2 Cor 12:4). One wonders what it was that Paul *heard* and why he was forbidden to repeat what he *heard* to any mortal being. Paul was obviously not a stranger to extraordinary religious experiences. Paul's conversion in the form of a call and commission from the risen Lord, presumably also an ecstatic religious experience, or perhaps in a dream, had occurred just five years earlier.

In the course of this same story, Paul mentions that he had a "thorn in the flesh" that served to keep him from being too elated. Apparently this affliction affected him continuously, and Paul prayed to the Lord three times that it would leave him (2 Cor 12:7). The nature of this affliction has been a topic of discussion since ancient times. Speculation has focused on three possible explanations:[6]

1. Paul's "thorn in the flesh" was some type of personal anxiety or spiritual torment, a weakness on Paul's part, or temptation to sin, perhaps as the result of harassment by a demon or a malevolent angel.

2. Paul's thorn in the flesh was a physical or mental illness—malarial fever, some form of epilepsy, solar retinitis, a speech impediment, hysteria, or a state of depression.

3. Paul's thorn in the flesh should be associated with the persecution and torture that Paul experienced throughout the course of his mission travels.

Furnish maintains that the evidence favors the second explanation, a physical or mental illness, and I agree.[7]

Moreover, Paul reports in Gal 1:11–12 that he had earlier received his gospel "through a *revelation* of Jesus Christ"; and in Gal 1:15–16 that God "was pleased to *reveal* his Son to [or *within*] me": and in Gal 2:2 that he went up to Jerusalem "in response to a *revelation*." By his own admission, "revelations" were nothing unusual to Paul.

There is often no physical examination or laboratory test that can definitively diagnose mental illnesses. Psychiatrists often rely on clinical symptoms. Moreover, it is difficult to diagnose most mental illnesses, even when the patient is at hand. Notwithstanding, Paul's propensity to hallucinations, delusions, revelations, and auditory experiences suggests the possibility that Paul may have suffered from schizophrenia.

PAUL'S MISSION

PAUL'S EARLY TRAVELS

There is little information about Paul's missionary activity immediately following his conversion. We do, however, know firsthand of some of Paul's earliest travels from the account in Gal 1:15–2:1:

> [1:15]But when God, who had set me apart before I was born and called me through his grace, was pleased [16]to reveal his Son to me [or *within* me], so that I might proclaim him among the Gentiles, I did not confer with any human being, [17]nor

---

6. Furnish, *II Corinthians*, 547–52.
7. Furnish, Ibid, 549–50.

did I go up to Jerusalem to those who were already apostles before me, but I went away at once into Arabia, and afterwards I returned to Damascus.

[18]Then after three years I did go up to Jerusalem to visit Cephas and stayed with him fifteen days; [19]but I did not see any other apostle except James the Lord's brother. [20]In what I am writing to you, before God, I do not lie! [21]Then I went into the regions of Syria and Cilicia, [22]and I was still unknown by sight to the churches of Judea that are in Christ; [23]they only heard it said, "The one who formerly was persecuting us is now proclaiming the faith he once tried to destroy." [24]And they glorified God because of me.

[2:1]Then after fourteen years I went up again to Jerusalem with Barnabas, taking Titus along with me.

Paul's account implies that his commission to preach to the Gentiles was a component of his conversion experience (Gal 1:16). Paul also makes it clear that he conferred with no human being and that he did *not* go to Jerusalem immediately following his call and commission to meet with the Jerusalem apostles but that he went "at once into Arabia" (Gal 1:17). Could this disclaimer be an allusion to the role of Ananias, about whom we know only from Luke? Or is this rather Paul's vehement response to the accusations from Christian-Jews or Judaizing missionaries that he had received his message from the apostles but deviated from it, or that Paul's gospel was inconsistent with the gospel of those apostles who had actually known Jesus? Whatever the reason, Paul makes it clear to the Galatians at this point that the Jerusalem apostles were not the source of his commission or of his message. The call, the commission, and the message came to Paul from God through his Son.

Unlike Acts 9, 22, and 26, Paul does not specify where his conversion took place, or even whether it took place somewhere near Damascus. Neither does he specify where exactly he went after his conversion, but Arabia may be a reference to the Nabataean Kingdom, the region south of Damascus and east of the Jordan River, an area known at the time as the Roman province of Arabia.[8] It would be interesting to know whether Paul went to Nabataea to begin his missionary work among the Gentiles or to withdraw into the desert in order to try to understand more clearly the meaning of his call and commission, but Paul does not tell us this important detail. Neither is it clear whether there were already Christian churches in any Nabataean cities prior to Paul's arrival.

In any case, after an unspecified but relatively brief period of time in Arabia, Paul returned to Damascus, or perhaps this is when he went to Antioch. Then after three years, Paul went to Jerusalem to visit Peter and stayed with him for two weeks (Gal 1:18). During that visit, Paul did not see any other apostles, except Jesus' brother James (Galatians 1:19). Paul is intent on making it clear to the Galatians that he is not

---

8. Archaeological excavations reveal that there was in the territory of Roman Arabia, and most especially in the cities of Petra and Bostra, a prosperous civilization with strong Hellenistic influence at the presumed time of Paul's visit. See Betz, *Galatians*, 73–74.

now—at the time he wrote the letter to the Galatians—nor has he ever been subject to the authority of Peter, or James, or any of the Jerusalem apostles. Paul makes that point again in Gal 2:6, when he says that "those who were supposed to be acknowledged leaders" of the Jerusalem church, presumably the Jerusalem apostles, "contributed nothing" to his understanding of his call and commission. What transpired between Paul and Peter and between Paul and James during this initial visit to Jerusalem is not clear, but it is clear that Paul did not consider whatever was exchanged between them to be authoritative instruction from Jesus' apostles. From Paul's perspective, although in general terms, he and the Jerusalem church had reached a consensus, and the pillars had approved his gospel (Gal 2:9–10). This visit to Peter may be the same visit referred to in Acts 9:26–30, although that is by no means certain, because the passage in Acts implies that Paul visited with virtually all of the Jerusalem disciples. Luke is either lying or is, more probably, ignorant of the issue.

Paul mentions that following this visit to Peter (and James) in Jerusalem he next "went into the regions of Syria and Cilicia," although he "was still unknown by sight to the churches of Judea" (Gal 1:21). Paul was apparently already based in Antioch of Syria at this point in time, a detail assumed by Acts.

Gal 2:1 mentions that, together with Barnabas, Paul went to Jerusalem once again after fourteen years, presumably to the Apostolic Council (see Acts 15:1–21), which resulted in the acknowledgment that Peter was "an apostle to the circumcised" Jews and that Paul was entrusted with the gospel for the uncircumcised Gentiles (Gal 2:7–9).

The chronology of events is somewhat uncertain because of two factors: (1) the custom of the period was to count any portions of both the first and the last years as full years in measuring time; and (2) it is unclear whether the dates in these verses in Galatians are measured sequentially or are measured from the time of Paul's conversion. Accordingly, the "three years" of Gal 1:18 could be as little as slightly more than one year, and the "fourteen years" of Gal 2:1 could be as little as slightly more than twelve years. In other words, the period in question in these verses in Galatians might be as little as twelve years after Paul's conversion, or as much as seventeen years. There is a general consensus among scholars that the time in question in Galatians should probably be measured from the date of Paul's conversion.

A PROPOSED CHRONOLOGY

And so, with some uncertainty about the chronology and with grave reservations about the reliability of Acts as history, herewith is a proposed chronology of Paul's ministry, based on Paul's letters and select information gleaned from the Acts of the Apostles:

THE NEW TESTAMENT

Proposed Chronology of Paul's Ministry

Event	Date[a]	Paul's Letters	Relevant Biblical Citations
Jesus' Death	30		
Paul's conversion	35		Gal 1:15–16
Paul's visit to Arabia/Nabataea	35–37		Gal 1:17
Paul's return to Damascus (and/or perhaps Antioch)	37-38		2 Cor 11:32-33
Paul's first trip to Jerusalem to visit Peter and see James	38		Gal 1:18-19; Acts 9:26-30 (?)
Paul's missionary travel to Syria and Cilicia	38-48		Gal 1:21
Paul's trip to Jerusalem with Barnabas and Titus for the Apostolic Council	48		Gal 2:1-10; Acts 15:1-21
Peter's visit to Paul in Antioch, and the arrival of certain people from James	48–49		Gal 2:11–14
Paul's mission journey in Phrygia and Galatia	49		Acts 16:6
Claudius expels Jews from Rome	49		Acts 18:2
Paul's mission journey to Philippi, Thessalonica, and Boroea; and his travel to Corinth via Athens	50–52		Acts 16:11–17:15; 18:1
Paul's arraingment before proconsul Gallio in Corinth	51-52		Acts 18:12-17
Paul wrote from Corinth	52	1 Thessalonians	
Paul's travel to Antioch; then through Asia Minor to Ephesus, with a second visit to Galatia along the way	52		Acts 18:18–23; Gal 4:13
Paul's mission in Ephesus	52–55		Acts 19:1, 8–10, 22
Paul wrote from Ephesus	54	Galatians	
Paul wrote from Ephesus	54	Lost letter to Corinth	1 Cor 5:9
Paul wrote from Ephesus	54	1 Corinthians	

Proposed Chronology of Paul's Ministry

Event	Date[a]	Paul's Letters	Relevant Biblical Citations
Paul wrote from Ephesus	54–55	Material in fragments of 2 Corinthians	2 Cor 2:14–6:13; 7:2–4
Imprisonment in Ephesus	54–55		Phlm 1, 9
Paul wrote from Ephesus	54–55	Three Philippian letters	
Paul wrote from Ephesus	54–55	Philemon	
Paul wrote from Ephesus	54–55	Painful letter to Corinth	2 Cor 2:4; 10:1–13:13
Paul wrote from Macedonia	55	Reconciling letter to Corinth	2 Cor 1:1–2:13; 7:5–16
Paul wrote from Macedonia	55	Two collection letters	2 Cor 8 and 9
Paul wrote from Corinth	55–56	Romans	
Paul departed for Jerusalem with the collection for the poor	56		Acts 20:1–38; 21:15–26
Paul imprisoned in Caesarea	56–58		Acts 25:13–27
Replacement of Felix by Porcius Festus as Roman governor of Judea	58		Acts 24:27; 25:13–14
Paul's voyage to Rome	58		Acts 27:1–28:16
Paul imprisoned in Rome	58–60		Acts 28:30
Paul's martyrdom in Rome	60		*Acts of Paul and Thecla* 11:1–7[b]

a. All dates are approximate. The evidence for some of the events cited in this chart is at best tentative.
b. Hennecke, *New Testament Apocrypha*, vol 2, 383–87.

THE ETHNIC COMPOSITION OF THE EARLY CHARISTIAN COMMUNITY

Luke traces the origin of Hellenistic Christianity to the earliest period in the church's history, specifically to Hellenistic Christians in Jerusalem who complained against Hebrew Christians because the widows of Hellenistic Christians "were being neglected in the daily distribution of food" (Acts 6:1). The solution to this problem was for the Jerusalem apostles to allow the Hellenists to select from among their numbers "seven men of good standing, full of the Spirit and of wisdom, whom [they] may appoint to this task" (Acts 6:3). Although this detail in Acts may not be historically reliable, it is likely that Hellenistic Christianity had its origin among Greek-speaking Jews living in Jerusalem or otherwise visiting the city.

At about the same time, according to Acts, Jews in Jerusalem strongly opposed Stephen, one of the Hellenists, dragged him out of the city, and stoned him to death (Acts 7:54–60), leading to the outbreak of a severe persecution against the church in Jerusalem and the scattering of everyone except the apostles throughout the countryside of Judea and Samaria (Acts 8:1b). According to Luke,

> Now those who were scattered because of the persecution that took place over Stephen traveled as far as Phoenicia, Cyprus, and Antioch, and they spoke the word to no one except Jews. But among them were some men of Cyprus and Cyrene who, on coming to Antioch, spoke to the Hellenists also, proclaiming the Lord Jesus. The hand of the Lord was with them, and a great number became believers and turned to the Lord (Acts 11:19–21).

Whether this information in Acts is entirely accurate, it is clear that there was a Christian community, comprised of both Jews and Gentiles, in Antioch at a relatively early date, probably well before 35, the likely date of Paul's conversion (cf. Gal 2:11–14). The Antioch church was doubtless the principal seat of Hellenistic Christianity at this time.

The older Jerusalem church was comprised primarily, if not exclusively, of Aramaic-speaking Jewish Christians, who met in the Jerusalem temple and in people's homes and who observed the Jewish law, including the practice of male circumcision and the observance of Jewish dietary laws. The Jerusalem church was engaged in missionary activity primarily among Jews in Judea, Samaria, and perhaps elsewhere.

By contrast, the church in Antioch was comprised of Greek-speaking circumcised Jewish Christians and uncircumcised Gentile Christians who apparently did not observe the Jewish law. The Antioch church was apparently involved in missionary activity among both Hellenistic Jews and Gentiles. However, even in the Antioch church there were probably more Jewish Christians than Gentile Christians in these earliest years of its history.

Believers in Jerusalem and Antioch clearly represented very different positions on the role of the Jewish law in the Jesus movement. By 48, about eighteen years after Jesus' death and about thirteen years after Paul's conversion, the question of the role of the Jewish law among Gentile Christians was still unresolved, and Jewish Christianity and Hellenistic Christianity appeared to be heading in different directions.

THE JERUSALEM COUNCIL

Gal 2:1–10

> ¹Then after fourteen years I went up again to Jerusalem with Barnabas, taking Titus along with me. ²I went up in response to a revelation. Then I laid before them

(though only in a private meeting with the acknowledged leaders) the gospel that I proclaim among the Gentiles, in order to make sure that I was not running, or had not run, in vain. ³But even Titus, who was with me, was not compelled to be circumcised, though he was a Greek. ⁴But because of false believers secretly brought in, who slipped in to spy on the freedom we have in Christ Jesus, so that they might enslave us—⁵we did not submit to them even for a moment, so that the truth of the gospel might always remain with you. ⁶And from those who were supposed to be acknowledged leaders (what they actually were makes no difference to me; God shows no partiality)—those leaders contributed nothing to me. ⁷On the contrary, when they saw that I had been entrusted with the gospel for the uncircumcised, just as Peter had been entrusted with the gospel for the circumcised ⁸(for he who worked through Peter making him an apostle to the circumcised also worked through me in sending me to the Gentiles), ⁹and when James and Cephas and John, who were acknowledged pillars, recognized the grace that had been given to me, they gave to Barnabas and me the right hand of fellowship, agreeing that we should go to the Gentiles and they to the circumcised. ¹⁰They asked only one thing, that we remember the poor, which was actually what I was eager to do.

There is nothing to suggest that the church in Jerusalem had any authority over the church in Antioch. Each was autonomous and independent of the other. Nevertheless, Christians in Antioch apparently decided to seek clarification regarding the role of the Jewish law for Gentile converts, and so in about 48 the church at Antioch sent to Jerusalem as its official representatives Paul, the Cypriot Jewish-Christian Barnabas, and the uncircumcised Gentile-Christian Titus to engage "in a private meeting with the acknowledged leaders" of the Jerusalem church, namely Jesus' brother James, Cephas (Peter), and John. Perhaps begging the question, Paul says that he "went up in response to a revelation" (Gal 2:2).⁹ The two groups met so that Paul, Barnabas, and Titus could, on behalf of the church at Antioch, lay before the leadership of the Jerusalem church the gospel that Paul and others had been proclaiming among the Gentiles. The objective was for Paul and the church at Antioch to be sure that everyone was in agreement about the acceptability of the message that Paul and other missionaries from the church at Antioch had been delivering to the Gentiles (Gal 2:2).

Paul was not looking to the Jerusalem leaders to *approve* his message, as he believed that his gospel had come to him in a revelation from God (Gal 1:12). But Paul was determined that the representatives from Antioch and the Jerusalem leaders be in agreement that the Jewish law was not binding on Gentile Christians. Paul makes the important point in Gal 2:3 that the leadership in Jerusalem did not require the Gentile-Christian Titus to be circumcised, thereby affirming the Antioch church's

---

9. Although Paul does not say specifically that it was a revelation to him personally, that is presumably what he intended for the Galatians to understand. This is the third such revelation to which Paul refers in this brief memoir (cf. Gal 1:12, where Paul claims that he received the gospel through a revelation of Jesus Christ; and Gal 1:16, where Paul claims that God revealed his Son to [or *within*] him. It is important to note that Paul understood that he was susceptible to revelations from God, presumably in the form of visions or auditions (or, perhaps, dreams).

position regarding Gentile converts. It is also clear from Paul's account that there was a strong faction of Christian Jews in the Jerusalem church who did not agree with the gospel of freedom from the Jewish law and the decision regarding the acceptance of the uncircumcised Titus. Paul describes them as "false believers" who had "slipped in to spy" on the freedom of Gentile Christians, presumably in an effort to impose the Jewish law, and specifically the law of circumcision, on Gentile Christians living in Antioch and elsewhere (Gal 2:4).

Jesus' brother James, Cephas (Peter), and John, "who were the acknowledged pillars" of the Jerusalem church (Gal 2:9) confirmed the distinction between and the legitimacy of the separate missions of Jewish Christianity (or should we say Christian Judaism?) and Gentile Christianity, specifically that Jesus had called Peter as an apostle to the Jews and Paul as a missionary to the Gentiles (Gal 2:7–9).[10] It was presumably now clear that Gentile Christianity, as represented by the church in Antioch, was free from the Jewish law and had its own independent legitimacy and integrity. This meeting is often referred to as the Apostolic Council or the Jerusalem Council. There is a less reliable but nonetheless important secondary account of this council in Acts 15:1–29.

However clear the meaning of the Apostolic Council may have been to Paul, the matter was not clear to everyone in the Jerusalem church, which was obviously not unanimous in its understanding of or support for what the parties had formally agreed to. The Jerusalem church was, according to Paul, divided between the "leaders" who agreed concerning the legitimacy of Paul's gospel, and "false believers" who did not. The leaders agreed to acknowledge the separate spheres of influence of both parties:

1. the church in Jerusalem and Jewish Christianity (or Christian Judaism), which would remain under the Jewish law; and
2. the church in Antioch and Gentile Christianity, which would be free from the Jewish law.

The division within Jewish Christianity was very real and substantive. The issue is particularly important because at the time of the Jerusalem Council, Jewish Christianity was probably significantly larger in number than Gentile Christianity. Even the church at Antioch likely had more Jewish Christians than Gentile Christians. At the

---

10. It is important to note Paul's language at this point, as it may reflect the language of a formal agreement approved at the Jerusalem Council. God "who worked through Peter making him an *apostle* to the circumcised . . . worked through [Paul] in *sending [him]* to the Gentiles" (Gal 2:8). By his own admission, Paul acknowledges Peter as an *apostle* but was apparently not acknowledged in return as an apostle by the Jerusalem leadership, or Paul would certainly have made that point most emphatically. Paul calls himself an apostle on numerous occasions (Rom 1:1; 11:13; 1 Cor 1:1; 9:1, 2; 15:9; 2 Cor 1:1; 12:12; Gal 1:1; Eph 1:1; Col 1:1; 1 Thess 2:7; 1 Tim 1:1; 2 Tim 1:1; Tit 1:1) in both the authentic and in the deutero-Pauline letters. No other book of the New Testament specifically calls Paul an "apostle." The reference to *apostles* in Acts 14:4, 14 probably appeared in one of the sources used by Luke in composing the Acts of the Apostles with the meaning of "envoys" or "delegates" (See Pervo, ibid., 350).

meeting in Jerusalem, Paul may have succeeded, at least temporarily, in convincing James, Peter, and John of the legitimacy of his Gentile mission of freedom from the Jewish law, but others were not persuaded. Paul may have convinced the Jerusalem leadership in two ways:

1. Paul was intellectually their superior, being far better educated and more sophisticated than the apostles, who served as the pillars of the Jerusalem church; and
2. Paul claimed, and they probably believed him when he said it, that he had received his call and commission, his gospel, and the command to go to Jerusalem to meet with the apostles directly from God through the risen Lord.

As a final note regarding the Jerusalem Council, one has to wonder about the meaning of Gal 2:10: "They [James, Peter, and John] asked only one thing, that we remember the poor, which was actually what I was eager to do." Was the leadership of the Jerusalem church prepared to accept money in exchange for recognizing the legitimacy of Paul's mission to the Gentiles apart from the Jewish law? And was Paul prepared to commit the church at Antioch to such a financial arrangement, an acknowledgment of the legitimacy of the Gentile mission in exchange for money? There is probably significance to the fact that late in his ministry Paul was still delivering such funds to the Jerusalem church from churches far beyond Antioch.

THE INCIDENT AT ANTIOCH

According to the very next story in Gal 2:11–14:

> [11]But when Cephas came to Antioch, I opposed him to his face, because he stood self-condemned; [12]for until certain people came from [Jesus' brother] James, [Peter] used to eat with Gentiles. But after they came, [Peter] drew back and kept himself separate for fear of the circumcision faction. [13]And the other Jews joined him in this hypocrisy, so that even Barnabas was led astray by their hypocrisy. [14]But when I saw that they were not acting consistently with the truth of the gospel, I said to Cephas [Peter] before them all, "If you, though a Jew, live like a Gentile, and not like a Jew, how can you compel the Gentiles to live like Jews?"[11]

Interestingly, Paul's account of this incident in Antioch tells of "certain people [who] came from [Jesus' brother] James," implying that James himself may have been less than convinced of what Paul maintains they had agreed to at the Jerusalem Council. Or perhaps James simply changed his mind and withdrew his support for Paul's

---

11. Some have suggested that Paul's quote to Peter may extend through Gal 2:16: "[15]We ourselves are Jews by birth and not Gentile sinners; [16]yet I know that a person is justified not by the works of the law, but through faith in Jesus Christ. And we have come to believe in Christ Jesus, so that we might be justified by faith in Christ, and not by doing the works of the law, because no one will be justified by the works of the law." The lack of clarity with regard to where Paul's comments to Peter end and Paul's own words begin may be intentional, as Paul tried to make his case as forcefully as possible to the Galatians.

mission of uncircumcision to the Gentiles. The division between Jewish Christianity and Gentile Christianity was on-going and had obviously not been fully resolved at the Jerusalem Council in spite of Paul's allegations in Gal 2. The "circumcision faction" represented a rift within the Jerusalem church, a group that disagreed with and openly opposed James, Peter, and John, the "acknowledged leaders" of the Jerusalem church regarding the agreement presumably reached at the Jerusalem Council. And now Jesus' brother James appears to have joined the opposition.[12]

The stakes were very high. If Paul's claim (and the claim of the Antioch church) of freedom from the Jewish law was not valid, there were two possible directions in which Christianity could move:

1. Paul and the church at Antioch would have to abandon their claim of freedom from the Jewish law for Gentile Christians and live within the Jewish law, effectively becoming Christian Jews, a course that would have been unthinkable, at least for Paul; or

2. Christianity could proceed along two separating or dividing paths, Jewish Christianity (or Christian Judaism) under the Jewish law and Gentile Christianity free from the Jewish law, the one not acknowledging the legitimacy of the other. Such a path was probably also unthinkable from Paul's perspective. Paul had already been granted legitimacy for his gospel by the leadership of the Jerusalem church, or so he thought, and he was clearly not prepared to revisit this critical issue.

Although the circumcision of Titus was the issue of "the circumcision faction" during the visit of Paul, Barnabas, and Titus to Jerusalem, the issue when Peter visited Antioch was the observance of Jewish dietary laws, and more specifically whether Jewish Christians in Antioch should participate in the Eucharistic meal together with uncircumcised Gentile Christians. Apparently Peter had participated in the common meal with Gentile Christians during his visit to Antioch until representatives from James unexpectedly arrived from Jerusalem. Peter then equivocated and withdrew from the Eucharistic meal, and Jewish Christians in Antioch, including even Barnabas, followed Peter in withdrawing. Paul publicly opposed Peter before the Antioch church, but the Jewish Christians of the "circumcision faction" prevailed, causing a serious rift between Paul and the Antioch church, resulting perhaps in a decision for Paul to leave that church and embark on his own missionary activity to the Gentiles. The details of what followed are not clear, but Paul was adamant and uncompromising in advocating the freedom of Gentile Christians from the Jewish law.

At about the same time, James appears to have replaced Peter as the head of the Jerusalem church, perhaps representing a challenge to Peter's authority during Peter's absence from Jerusalem. The conservative position of James and the "circumcision faction" suggests that they are better characterized as Christian Jews than as Jewish

---

12. These developments make it clear that the account of the Jerusalem Council in Acts 15:1–35 is unreliable.

Christians. Their position on the Jewish law meant that members of the circumcision faction were in every respect Jews, but they were Jews who acknowledged Jesus as Lord and as God's appointed messiah. Yet, the role of the Jewish law remained central to their everyday lives.

The unpleasant and divisive incident in Antioch was not the final word on this subject. In spite of the agreement at the Jerusalem Council, the battle continued. Jewish Christianity persisted, and the "false believers" (Gal 2:4) or members of the "circumcision faction" (Gal 2:12) continued to haunt Paul in his missionary work throughout the Gentile world, most specifically now in the churches in Galatia to which he addressed his Letter to the Galatians.

THE COLLECTION

Although only the church at Antioch seems to have been obligated to the collection for the poor of the church in Jerusalem, Paul extended this obligation to other Gentile churches that he established. Specifically, the churches in Macedonia and Achaia (Rom 15:25–29), including the church at Corinth (1 Cor 16:1–4), participated in this collection. In fact, 2 Cor 8 and 9 may be distinct fund-raising letters addressed to the churches in Macedonia and Achaia respectively (see below, p. 295).

Paul intended to deliver this collection personally to the church in Jerusalem on the occasion of his final visit in about 56 (cf. Acts 11:29). Paul's arrival in Jerusalem was apparently unwelcome, and the Jerusalem church may have refused to accept Paul's collection. In the course of events, Paul was arrested and taken to Rome (cf. Acts 11:29; 24:17–28:31). Is it possible that the Jerusalem church refused Paul's offering because the leadership in Jerusalem no longer accepted the legitimacy of Paul's mission to the Gentiles? Unfortunately, we cannot answer that question with certainty, but it is an interesting thought and certainly a possible scenario.

Although Paul's brand of Gentile Christianity ultimately prevailed, Jewish Christianity in one form or another persisted independently for another century or two. In spite of Paul's claim, the agreement that he believed had been sealed with the Jerusalem leadership at the Jerusalem Council in 48 did not go unchallenged. Although Jesus' brother James and some of his associates apparently equivocated, and even Peter, Barnabas, and others in Antioch seem to have vacillated during the unpleasant encounter in Antioch, and although the "circumcision faction" challenged Paul in many of the Gentile churches he had established, Paul remained unrelenting and uncompromising about the legitimacy of his gospel of freedom. Freedom from the Jewish law was at the heart of Paul's mission to the Gentiles and remained so to the end. Paul never equivocated and never compromised on this central issue.

THE NEW TESTAMENT
PAUL'S MESSAGE

It is important to remember that Paul was not a systematic theologian, that he did not write theological treatises. Paul wrote letters to churches he had founded or, in the case of Rome, to a church that he intended to visit sometime soon. It is, therefore, from his letters that we must garner an understanding of the message that Paul preached to the churches that he founded. What exactly was at the core of Paul's gospel?

We will approach the question of Paul's message by looking first at what most scholars consider to be Paul's genuine letters in the probable order in which he wrote them: 1 Thessalonians, Galatians, 1 Corinthians, 2 Corinthians, Philippians, Philemon, and Romans.[13]

1 THESSALONIANS

Paul (together with Timothy and Silvanus) wrote this letter, the oldest book of the New Testament, from Corinth to the nascent church in Thessalonica, a Greek city in the Roman province of Macedonia on the north shore of the Aegean Sea. In about 51, Paul, Timothy, and Silvanus (Silas) arrived in Thessalonica from Philippi, where they had recently "suffered and been shamefully treated" (1 Thess 2:2). In Thessalonica they founded a church composed primarily, if not entirely, of Gentiles (1 Thess 1:9; cf. Acts 16:11–40[14]).

We do not know from Paul's letter under what circumstances he met and engaged his Gentile converts in Thessalonica, or where the church met, or how long Paul remained in Thessalonica, but we can speculate. Paul and his associates apparently set up shop in Thessalonica as leather workers and probably began to proselytize people they met in or near their shop.

Their message to Gentiles in Thessalonica urged their listeners to give up their pagan gods and to worship the one true God, the creator of the world, who would soon send his Son, Jesus of Nazareth, who had died, been raised from the dead and exalted to heaven. Those who accepted this message and believed that Jesus was Lord and messiah and were baptized formed the church (Greek *ekklesia*), the body of believers, who probably met in the home of one of their members to celebrate a common meal, to pray and sing hymns, and to practice Jesus' command to love one another. Gentile Christians presumably did not meet in synagogues. In fact, Paul never uses the work "synagogue" in any of his letters.

---

13. Recognizing, of course, that 2 Corinthians, Philippians, and perhaps even Romans probably contain multiple letters.

14. Luke's format in Acts is generally to report that Paul went first to synagogues to preach to Jews. When that failed, Paul turned to preaching to Gentiles. Luke's scheme does not appear to conform to the agreement reached at the Apostolic Council in Jerusalem: namely, that Peter was the *apostle* to the Jews, and Paul the *missionary* to the Gentiles.

Phil 4:16 implies that Paul and his friends stayed in Thessalonica for several months. We do know that harsh opposition brought persecution to the church in Thessalonica (1 Thess 2:14–15) and forced Paul, Timothy, and Silvanus to leave for Beroea. Luke states that the opposition in Thessalonica came initially from Jews (Acts 17:1–6); Paul, on the other hand, implies that it came from anti-Christian Gentile Thessalonians (1 Thess 2:14: "you suffered the same thing *from your own compatriots*"). We should probably believe Paul and not Acts.

Timothy and Silas apparently remained in Beroea, while Paul traveled to Athens (Acts 17:10–15). When Timothy rejoined Paul in Athens, Paul immediately sent him back to Thessalonica to find out what was happening to the young church in that city (1 Thess 3:1–2). Timothy's report was favorable (1 Thess 3:6–7); however, the Thessalonians expressed concern that Paul had not returned to visit them. Timothy's encouraging report prompted Paul to write 1 Thessalonians from Corinth in about 52.

After reminiscing about his visit to Thessalonica, Paul rehearsed some of his original teaching by reminding the Thessalonians how they should live their lives (1 Thess 4:1–12) in anticipation of Jesus' imminent return (1 Thess 1:10; 2:19; 3:13; 4:15; 5:1–2, 23), and how they should strengthen one another in their communal lives (1 Thess 5:12–22). Paul reminded the Thessalonians that he had taught them to imitate Timothy, Silvanus, himself, and of course Jesus (1 Thess 1:6). He also praised them for having served as examples to fellow-believers in Macedonia and in Achaia (1 Thess 1:7).

1 Thessalonians is a window on the day-to-day life of one of the first churches that Paul established in Europe and certainly the earliest of Paul's churches about which we know anything. Regrettably, we know nothing about churches that Paul may have established much earlier in Arabia, Syria, and Cilicia during what was presumably his earliest missionary activity following his call and commission.

1 CORINTHIANS

When Paul and his friends left Thessalonica in about 51, they headed south to Corinth, the capital of the Roman province of Achaia and a cosmopolitan Greek city with a diverse population, a diversity that was reflected in those who responded to Paul's message. In Corinth, Paul met Aquila and Priscilla, a Jewish couple who had apparently converted to Christianity before they left Rome when Emperor Claudius expelled the Jews in 49. Together Paul, Timothy, Silvanus, Aquila, and Priscilla preached in Corinth a message similar to what Paul had preached to the Thessalonians, and they succeeded in converting a sizable number of Gentiles, perhaps a few dozen. However, in spite of initial success, the church at Corinth proved to be a major challenge for Paul.

The letter known as 1 Corinthians is actually at least the second letter that Paul wrote to the church at Corinth (1 Cor 5:9 states: "I wrote to you in my [previous] letter not to associate with sexually immoral persons . . ."). That letter is lost, or fragments of it may survive in 2 Cor 6:14–7:1.[15]

In about 54, Paul wrote 1 Corinthians from Ephesus to the church at Corinth, which he, Timothy, and Silvanus had established a few years earlier in about 51–52 (1 Cor 2:1–5; 2 Cor 1:19). Paul apparently planned to travel from Ephesus through Macedonia to Corinth, where he thought he would spend the winter before moving on to his next destination, wherever that may be (1 Cor 11:34; 16:5–9). In the meantime Paul had sent Timothy to Corinth (1 Cor 4:17; 16:10–11).

Paul (together with Sosthenes[16]) wrote 1 Corinthians in answer to a lost letter that the Corinthians had written to him (1 Cor 7:1). In addition, Paul addressed other matters that had come to his personal attention from Chloe's people,[17] including divisive quarrels (1 Cor 1:10–17), sexual immorality (1 Cor 5:1–13), and divisions within the Corinth church (1 Cor 11:18–19). Some members of the Corinth church had come to believe that they were already experiencing the state of resurrection and exaltation and were boasting of their superior position within the church (1 Cor 4:8).

In the church at Corinth, there seem to have been different factions that were loyal to Paul, to Cephas, to Apollos, and even to Christ (1 Cor 1:12).[18] Some in the church had even begun to question Paul's authority (1 Cor 3:1–4:5; 9:1–27). The issues in Corinth were complicated by the diversity of the church's members. To address these challenges, Paul called for unity, the general theme of the letter (1 Cor 1:10–17), that could best be accomplished though the love that Paul had already commanded to his congregations (1 Cor 8:1–3; 13:1–13; 16:4).

2 CORINTHIANS

The letter known as 2 Corinthians is one of the most difficult of Paul's letters to understand. It is disjointed and disorganized; its tone is sometimes conciliatory and sometimes argumentative. Many scholars have, therefore, argued that 2 Corinthians is actually a composite of several different letters or of parts of different letters written to Corinth from Ephesus and Macedonia in about 54 or 55. There are many theories about the Corinthian correspondence, but none has gained universal approval. The

---

15. Koester maintains that these verses were not written by Paul but that they are a piece written by a Jewish Christian, which somehow found their way into the Pauline corpus (Koester, *Introduction to the New Testament*, vol 2, 120).

16. A Sosthenes is mentioned in Acts 18:17 as an official of the synagogue in Corinth, but it is not clear that they are the same person.

17. Given Paul's assumption that the Corinthians know who Chloe is, we can safely assume that she was a prominent woman in the church in Corinth.

18. The exact nature of these divisions is uncertain, but Paul's words in 1 Cor 1:12 call attention to the problem: "What I mean is that each of you says, 'I belong to Paul,' or 'I belong to Apollos,' or 'I belong to Cephas,' or 'I belong to Christ.'" What the Corinthians meant by these slogans is unclear, but they seem to reflect factions or divisions within the Corinth church.

model that I adopt here is that the separate letters or fragments of letters to the Corinthians collected into what is called 2 Corinthians include:

2 Cor 2:14–6:13 and 7:2–4: a portion of a letter written from Ephesus to Corinth in response to a report that foreign apostles had visited the Corinth church, but they were apparently not the Jewish Christians of 1 Corinthians.

2 Cor 10–13: a portion of a letter written from Ephesus to Corinth after the previous letter, implying that Paul had visited Corinth in response to the above-mentioned crisis, but that it was Titus's personal intervention that brought reconciliation to the situation in Corinth.

2 Cor 1:1–2:13 and 7:5–16: written perhaps from Macedonia to Corinth, this letter reflects the fact that Paul had received news from Titus about the reconciliation.

2 Cor 8: probably written from Macedonia to accompany the third letter; this letter speaks about the collection received from the Corinth church for the church in Jerusalem.

2 Cor 9: probably also written from Macedonia to accompany the third letter, this letter speaks about the collection received from the churches in Achaea for the church in Jerusalem.

GALATIANS

Paul wrote this letter from Ephesus to the churches in Galatia in about 54. Paul had obviously founded several churches in Galatia (Gal 1:2; 4:13–14) about five years earlier during a visit in 49, shortly after the Apostolic Council in 48. It is, however, not clear how many churches Paul founded in Galatia or in what cities he founded them.[19] Paul's letter to the Galatians offers no clues for answering either question, and we probably should not rely on Acts for help in answering these questions.

At the time Paul wrote this letter, his gospel to the Galatians was being undermined by unspecified Judaizing (Jewish Christian) missionaries, whom Paul considered to be troublemakers and agitators (Gal 5:12). These troublesome missionaries had appealed to Paul's Gentile converts (Gal 4:8–9) to be circumcised (Gal 5:2–12; 6:12–13) and to observe other requirements of the Jewish law (Gal 4:10, 17; cf. 2:12). These Judaizing missionaries resemble the "circumcision faction" in Jerusalem who had previously challenged Paul both in Jerusalem (Gal 2:1–10) and subsequently in Antioch (Gal 2:11–14). Although they are not necessarily the same people, they were clearly promoting the same agenda (Gal 2:1–14). These rivals to Paul's gospel were urging Paul's Gentile converts in Galatia to complete the process of conversion to

---

19. Scholars do not agree whether Paul's Galatian churches were in North Galatia, where Celtic people designated as Galatians originally settled in the region around Ancyra (modern Ankara, Turkey), or in South Galatia toward the Mediterranean Sea, into which area the Roman province of Galatia extended. Modern scholarship tends to favor the North Galatia theory.

Christ by undergoing circumcision and becoming, like them, Christian Jews (see Gen 17:9–14).

The letter to the Galatians is angry and argumentative as Paul tried to dissuade his Galatian converts from compromising "the truth of the gospel" (Gal 2:5, 14). Paul sees himself as the true apostle of Jesus Christ (Gal 1:1) and the true and faithful interpreter of the law and the gospel (Gal 4:21; 5:14). He is outraged at recent developments in Galatia and betrays his anger and disappointment with his Gentile converts in the churches in Galatia:

Gal 1:6–7

> [6]I am astonished that you are so quickly deserting the one who called you in the grace of Christ and are turning to a different gospel—[7]not that there is another gospel, but there are some who are confusing you and want to pervert the gospel of Christ.

Gal 3:1–3

> [1]You foolish Galatians![20] Who has bewitched you? [2]The only thing I want to learn from you is this: Did you receive the Spirit by doing the works of the law or by believing what you heard? Are you so foolish? Having started with the Spirit, are you now ending with the flesh?

Paul's Letter to the Galatians makes it clear that the Jerusalem Council and the incident in Antioch involving Peter and the emissaries from James failed to resolve the issue of the role of the Jewish law in Gentile Christianity. The "circumcision faction" (or their allies) and Paul were still struggling five or six years after Paul thought that this matter had been resolved at the Jerusalem Council. Paul would not yield on this critical issue "even for a moment" (Gal 2:5). His chastisement of his Gentile converts in Galatia represents only the latest round in what was a long struggle to resolve the role of the Jewish law in Gentile Christianity (Gal 3:1). As we have already seen, Paul was determined not to compromise on this fundamental question.

PHILIPPIANS

We learn very little from Paul's Letter to the Philippians about the church in Philippi, a colony in the Roman province of Macedonia that he, Silvanus, and Timothy had visited in about 50. In 1 Thess 2:2, Paul reports that he and his friends "had already suffered and been shamefully treated in Philippi" prior to going to Thessalonica. Accordingly, it seems that the visit to Philippi was probably brief, barely long enough to make a few converts.

Paul (together with Timothy) later wrote to the church at Philippi. It is clear that Paul was in prison at the time (Phil 1:7, 13–14, 17). A date of 54–55 during an

---

20. I would be inclined to translate this phrase even more strongly as "You stupid Galatians!"

otherwise unknown imprisonment in Ephesus is likely but by no means certain. Philippians and Philemon have sometimes been assigned to a later Roman imprisonment in about 58–60, but that place and date of composition pose other challenges.

A sharp change in the tone of the letter beginning in Phil 3:2, the fact that different sections of the letter reflect different circumstances and that it takes Paul a long time to thank the Philippians for a gift they sent him (beginning in Phil 4:10) have led some scholars to question the unity of Paul's Letter to the Philippians and to propose that we have before us the whole or parts of three different letters:

> Phil 4:10–20 is a thank-you note from an imprisoned Paul to the church at Philippi written from Ephesus in 54–55 after Paul received from the Philippians a gift of money delivered by Epaphroditus, who shortly thereafter fell very seriously ill.
>
> Phil 1:1–3:1a; 4:4–7, 21–33 was written by Paul from prison in Ephesus to the church at Philippi somewhat later in 54–55 and was delivered to the Philippians by Epaphroditus shortly after he recovered from his serious illness.
>
> Phil 3:1b–4:3; 4:8–9 is a fragment of a longer letter, also written in about 54–55, dealing with controversies between Paul and competing Jewish or Jewish-Christian missionaries with gnostic tendencies, who had invaded the church at Philippi and who were similar in many ways to the opponents in Corinth (see 2 Cor 2:14–6:13 and 7:2–4).

PHILEMON

The letter to Philemon is the only correspondence to a single individual in the entire corpus of Paul's letters. As in the case of Philippians, Paul (together with Timothy) wrote to Philemon from prison (Phlm 1, 9, 10, 13, 23), probably during the same imprisonment reflected in the letter to the Philippians. Accordingly, Philemon was probably written about 54–55 from Ephesus to a Christian living in Colossae.[21]

Philemon's slave Onesimus had apparently escaped from his master and was subsequently converted by Paul. Onesimus wanted to remain with Paul and continue to serve him, but Paul decided to return Onesimus to Philemon to obtain the master's approval and perhaps Onesimus's freedom (Phlm 14–15).

ROMANS

Paul wrote this letter in about 55–56 from Corinth to the church in Rome. Paul was about to leave Corinth for Jerusalem to deliver the collection to the Jerusalem church in fulfillment of the pledge he had made at the Jerusalem Council seven or eight years

---

21. Paul's Letter to Philemon is clearly related to the Deutero-Pauline Letter to the Colossians. Both contain greetings by some of the same people, and both refer to Onesimus by name (Col 4:9–14, 17; Phlm 2, 23).

earlier (Gal 2:1–10). From Jerusalem, Paul apparently planned to visit the church at Rome on his way to Spain (Rom 15:22–26).

The beginnings of Roman Christianity are unclear, although Christian missionaries probably reached Rome by 48–49 CE. Writing in 119, the Roman historian Suetonius reported that the Emperor Claudius had expelled the Jews from Rome in 49 because of disturbances surrounding a certain Chrestus—probably a misunderstanding for Christus or Christ.[22] Inasmuch as Jesus never traveled to Rome, Suetonius may be referring to a disturbance caused by Jews in Rome upon the arrival of Christian missionaries. Paul's friends Aquila and Priscilla, who had already converted to Christianity, were among the Jews expelled by Claudius in 49. Many Roman Jews, including Aquila and Priscilla, subsequently returned to Rome after the assassination of Claudius in 54.

In writing Romans, probably the last of the genuine Pauline letters, Paul defends his gospel to Christians whom he has never met but intends to visit in the near future. The theme of this letter is summarized in Rom 1:16–17:

> For I am not ashamed of the gospel; it is the power of God for salvation to everyone who has faith, to the Jew first and also to the Greek. For in it the righteousness of God is revealed through faith for faith; as it is written, "The one who is righteous will live by faith."

Rom 16 may be a separate letter to the church at Ephesus that was later appended to Paul's Letter to the Romans, which seems to conclude in Rom 15:33 ("The God of peace be with all of you. Amen"). Because Paul did not found the church at Rome, neither had he ever visited it, the Letter to the Romans presents to his audience the most developed theological statement found in any of his letters. More specifically, Paul is trying in his Letter to the Romans to defend himself against Jewish missionaries who disparaged Paul's law-free gospel.

SUMMARY OF PAUL'S GOSPEL

A good way to begun our summary of Paul's preaching—Paul's gospel—is to examine the three titles of Jesus that he most frequently uses in his letters: Jesus is Lord, Jesus is Messiah, and Jesus is Son of God. He uses the title Lord in 154 different verses in his genuine letters, sometimes more than once in a single verse, Messiah in 250 different verses, and Son of God in 17 different verses.

1. Jesus is Lord

It was apparently the Jerusalem church that first used the title Lord for the risen Christ. In 1 Cor 16:22, Paul cites an old prayer in the original Aramaic, *marana tha*

---

22. Suetonius, *Life of Claudius*, 25. 4.

(Our Lord, come),[23] to a Gentile audience that otherwise would have had no understanding of Aramaic. We can only assume that the Aramaic words were commonplace in both Aramaic- and Greek-speaking Christian churches, perhaps spoken by Jewish and Gentile Christians in an effort to hasten Jesus' second coming.

The Greek word for Lord (*kyrios*) can connote simply "master," as a slave might refer to his master, or "sir," as a respectful form of address. Paul refers to himself as a servant or slave (Greek *doulos*) of Christ (Rom 1:1; Gal 1:10), invoking thereby the slave-master imagery. Paul may also be using the title as a way of identifying Jesus in his eschatological role (Phil 3:20; 4:5; 1 Thess 3:13), inasmuch as the term seems always to refer to the risen, exalted, and glorified Jesus of the post-resurrection period (cf. Acts 2:36).

The title κύριος, *kyrios* (Lord or master) was frequently applied to gods and deified rulers in the Hellenistic world, beginning in the first century BCE.[24] Accordingly, a title that originally had relatively limited meaning to Jewish Christians (master or sir) may have had a very different and more exalted meaning for Gentile Christians when applied to the risen Christ. In fact, the latter part of Paul's words in 1 Cor 8:5–6 may have served as an early Christian creed or confession:

> [5]Indeed, even though there may be so-called gods in heaven or on earth—as in fact there are many gods and many lords—[6]yet for us there is one God, the Father, from whom are all things and for whom we exist, and one Lord, Jesus Christ, through whom are all things and through whom we exist.

2. Jesus is Messiah = Greek Χριστός or Christ

The title Christ also reaches back to the Jerusalem church: the term "messiah" is thoroughly Jewish. By using this term, early Jewish Christians were claiming for Jesus the hopes and expectations associated with an eschatological savior. Messiah is certainly one of the earliest titles ascribed to Jesus following his death and alleged exaltation, through which Jesus' followers claimed that God had *made* Jesus Lord and Messiah. Christ is Paul's favorite Christological term. The 270 times Paul's uses the term Christ in his genuine letters represent 51% of the uses of this title in the New Testament. In fact, in Paul's letters, the phrase Jesus Christ virtually reaches the level of being a name rather than a title, Jesus Christ rather than Jesus is the Christ, the anointed of God, the messiah.

---

23. The Aramaic can also be read as *maran atha* (meaning "Our Lord has come"). The reading *marana tha* (Our Lord, come) is supported in Rev 22:20, where the prayer is found in Greek, not Aramaic: "Come, Lord Jesus."

24. *Theological Dictionary of the New* Testament, edited by Kittel and Friedrich, 487–88.

3. Jesus is Son of God

This title also appears to have originated in Jewish circles in Jerusalem. In the Old Testament, the term is applied to Israel's kings, to high priests, to prophets, and to others as a sign that God has bestowed his favor on a beloved figure. Israel, too, is referred to as God's son.

The term Son of God, which appears only 17 times in Paul's genuine letters, reflects Jesus' special relationship to God as God's adopted son (see Ps 2:7). In 1 Thess 1:9–10, the title reflects Jesus' status as the resurrected messiah, the agent of rescue or salvation from God's wrath. In Paul's letters, Jesus' sonship serves as the precursor for everyone who accepts Jesus as Lord and messiah and who will, therefore, also be adopted as a child of God:

Rom 8:15–17

> [15]For you did not receive a spirit of slavery to fall back into fear, but you have received a spirit of adoption. When we cry "Abba! Father!" [16]it is that very Spirit bearing witness with our spirit that we are children of God, [17]and if children, then heirs, heirs of God and joint heirs with Christ—if, in fact, we suffer with him so that we may also be glorified with him.

Rom 8:22–23

> [22]We know that the whole creation has been groaning in labor pains until now; [23]and not only the creation, but we ourselves who have the first fruits of the Spirit, groan inwardly while we wait for adoption, the redemption of our bodies.

Gal 3:26

> For in Christ Jesus you are all children of God through faith.

Gal 4:4–7

> [4]But when the fullness of time had come, God sent his son, born of a woman, born under the law, [5]in order to redeem those who were under the law, so that we might receive adoption as children. [6]And because you are children, God has sent the Spirit of his Son into our hearts, crying "Abba! Father!" [7]So you are no longer a slave but a child, and if a child then also an heir, through God.

Rom 1:4[25] makes it clear that Jesus was *declared to be* Son of God or was *installed* as Son of God by virtue of his resurrection from the dead.[26] Scholars refer to this type of christology as Adoptionism, i.e. Jesus was *made* Son of God or *adopted* as Son of God by God by virtue of his death and resurrection. In turn, by confessing that Jesus

---

25. Rom 1:3–4 ". . . the gospel concerning his Son who was descended from David according to the flesh and was *declared* to be Son of God with power according to the spirit of holiness *by resurrection from the dead*, Jesus Christ our Lord . . . ."

26. Sons of God are not unknown in myths and legends in the Hellenistic world, but human figures were also so designated: Pythagoras and Plato, and deified rulers, most especially the Roman emperors beginning with Augustus (27 BCE–14CE).

is Lord and Messiah, Christians were promised that they too would, like Jesus, be adopted as God's children and heirs.

In a previous chapter, we reviewed C. H. Dodd's contribution in identifying the principal elements in the apostolic preaching. In examining the Pauline *kerygma*, Dodd focused primarily on the passage in 1 Cor 15:3–7:

> ³For I handed on to you as of first importance what I in turn had received: that Christ died for our sins in accordance with the scriptures, ⁴and that he was buried, and that he was raised on the third day in accordance with the scriptures, ⁵and that he appeared to Cephas, then to the twelve. ⁶Then he appeared to more than five hundred brothers and sisters at one time, most of whom are still alive, though some have died. ⁷Then he appeared to James, then to all the apostles.

In addition, Dodd cites other passages that present the *kerygma* according to Paul, among them passages in Rom 1:1–4; 2:16; 8:34; 10:8–9; Gal 1:3–4; 3:1; 4:6; 1 Thess (see above Chapter 4, pp. 96–104).

With regard to the Pauline *kerygma*, Dodd states:

> It is true that the *kerygma* as we have recovered it from Paul's epistles is fragmentary. No complete statement of it is, in the nature of the case, available. But we may restore it in outline somewhat after this fashion:
>
> The prophecies are fulfilled, and the new Age is inaugurated by the coming of Christ.
>
> He was born of the seed of David.
>
> He died according to the Scriptures, to deliver us out of the present evil age.
>
> He was buried.
>
> He rose on the third day according to the Scriptures.
>
> He is exalted at the right hand of God, as Son of God and Lord of quick and dead.
>
> He will come again as Judge and Saviour of men.²⁷

Dodd's assessment of the elements that constituted the gospel or the *kerygma* according to Paul is particularly helpful. Rudolf Bultmann provides a similar but somewhat fuller version of Paul's gospel, a modified version of which might read:²⁸

> In the fullness of time God sent forth his Son, a pre-existent divine Being, who appeared on earth as a man (2 Cor 8:9; Gal 4:4; Phil 2:6–11). He died the death of a sinner (Rom 8:3; 2 Cor 5:21) on the cross and made atonement for the sins of [humankind] (Rom 3:23–26; 4:25; 8:3; 2 Cor 5:14, 19). His resurrection (exaltation) marked the beginning of the cosmic catastrophe. Death, the consequence

---

27. Dodd, *The Apostolic Preaching and Its Development*, 17.
28. Bultmann, "New Testament and Mythology," 2.

of Adam's sin, has been abolished (Rom 5:12–14; 1 Cor 15:21–22), and the demonic forces have been deprived of their power (1 Cor 2:6; cf. Col 2:15). The risen Christ has been exalted to the right hand of God in heaven (Rom 8:34) and made "Lord" and "King" (1 Cor 15:25; Phil 2:9–11). He will come again on the clouds of heaven to complete the work of redemption, and the resurrection and judgment of [humankind] will follow (1 Cor 15:23–24, 50–57). Sin, suffering, and death will then be finally abolished. All this is to happen very soon; indeed, Paul thinks he himself will live to see it (1 Cor 1:7–8; 4:5; 7:29; 11:26; 15:51–52; Phil 1:6,10; 2:16; 3:20; 1 Thess 4:15–17).

In addition to identifying this reconstruction of Paul's *kerygma*—the Pauline gospel—we must also repeat as a major component of Paul's message his proclamation to the Gentiles that they were no longer bound by the Jewish law and that their justification, vindication, and salvation had been secured by their faith in Jesus as Lord and messiah apart from works of the law.

PROBLEMS AND CONCLUSIONS

Although we are fortunate to have seven presumably genuine letters of Paul among the books of the canonical New Testament, and therefore important primary source material from Paul himself, the challenges involved in reconstructing the life, mission, and message of Paul are, nevertheless, still real. This chapter has identified a number of specific challenges facing scholars, a few of which I will address in these concluding remarks.

CHRONOLOGY

The chronology proposed in this chapter is based on a number of assumptions: (1) the date of Jesus' death in 30 CE, as proposed in an earlier chapter (see chapter 5, p. 131); (2) the reliability of Paul's personal testimony in his seven genuine letters, most especially Rom 11:1; 1 Cor 15:8–9; Gal 1:14–2:14; and Phil 3:5–6; (3) the dating of the Gallio inscription of Acts 18:12–17 in the year 51–52 and its coincidence with Paul's first visit to Corinth; and (4) the assumption that Acts has at least some value as an historical source.

In proposing a chronology of Paul's missionary activities, we have assumed that Paul's testimony is most important and have worked with Acts only when it suits the historical framework otherwise established through Paul's letters. Paul offers a reasonable but limited amount of autobiographical detail in four of his seven genuine letters. To the extent that the proposed chronology in this chapter contradicts the chronology proposed in chapter 10, the chronology in this chapter is preferred because it is based on evidence gathered from Paul's letters.

On a related matter, it is apparent that Luke's account of three missionary journeys beginning and ending in Antioch is probably a Lukan construct. There is nothing in Paul's letters to suggest that he used Antioch as a home base beyond the mid- to late-forties. Quite the contrary, evidence in Galatians suggests that Paul may have been permanently estranged from the Antioch church following Peter's visit in 48–49 and the unsatisfactory resolution, from Paul's perspective, of the confrontation with the emissaries from James.

As we have observed, the matter of the chronology is further complicated by:

1. the custom of counting years inclusive of parts of the first and the last years as if they were full years;
2. the question of whether references to time in Gal 2 is sequential or measured in every instance from Paul's conversion; and
3. the challenge of trying to integrate or reconcile Paul's genuine letters with the Acts of the Apostles.

PAUL AND ACTS

As we have seen, the relationship between Paul's letters and Acts is problematic. It is impossible to reconcile Paul and Acts on many details regarding Paul's travels. More importantly, our examination of Paul's conversion betrays the fact that much of the material in Acts is legendary. Contradictions within the three accounts of Paul's conversion in Acts 9, 22, and 26 make it clear that Luke is more of a story-teller than he is a historian, at least as we think of history today. Furthermore, it is doubtful that Paul was in Jerusalem for the stoning of Stephen, and it is evidently a Lukan fabrication that Paul was traveling to Damascus with letters from the high priests when he "saw" the risen Lord.

A related question might be whether Luke had access to some of Paul's letters and used them among his sources in composing the Acts of the Apostles. The multiple versions of Paul's conversion in Acts 9, 22, and 26 with their inconsistencies and contradictions reveal the imaginative creativity of Luke in composing Acts. Perhaps the most reliable detail in Luke's accounts of Paul's conversion is the role of Ananias in interpreting Paul's call and commission. The criterion of embarrassment speaks in support of the historicity of this detail, but quite obviously we cannot know for sure. Why would Luke have invented a human intermediary between the risen Lord and Paul if independent oral tradition did not otherwise support this somewhat compromising detail?

THE PAULINE LETTERS AND THEIR TRANSMISSION

The New Testament attributes thirteen letters to Paul. Of these thirteen letters, seven are similar in style, vocabulary, and theology; and the situations and issues discussed in these seven letters reflect situations and issues of the Jesus movement in the 40s and the 50s, the period of Paul's missionary activity (Romans, 1 and 2 Corinthians, Galatians, Philippians, 1 Thessalonians, and Philemon). The other six books identified as letters of Paul are probably the writings of later authors who consciously wrote in the name of Paul (Ephesians, Colossians, 2 Thessalonians, 1 and 2 Timothy, and Titus). The style, vocabulary, and theology of these six letters are somewhat different from Paul's seven genuine letters, and the situations and issues discussed in them reflect a later time, a period resembling the end of the first and the beginning of the second centuries.

Moreover, a study of the seven genuine letters of Paul has lead many scholars to claim that at least three of them are composite letters, namely Romans, 2 Corinthians, and Philippians. It is not entirely clear how these letters achieved their current form, but it is possible that someone decided to make a collection of Paul's letters, probably sometime toward the end of the first century when Paul's status had grown in some Christian churches, and material in two or more extant letters were then combined by scribes who prepared material for the collection.

By his own admission, Paul was a controversial figure during the period of his missionary activity and confronted challenges from recognized authorities, sometimes from the church in Jerusalem, including Jesus' brother James. It was probably only later and long after his death that many Christians began to value Paul's letters. It is also likely that Paul wrote additional letters, which are lost to us—letters to churches he had founded or visited, and personal correspondence of the sort that we see in Philemon.

THE PERIOD BEFORE 49

Paul offers little information about the period before 52, the presumed date of the writing of 1 Thessalonians, his earliest letter and the oldest book of the New Testament. Paul offers limited information about the Jerusalem church during its formative period, inasmuch as his first trip to Jerusalem occurred about thirteen or fourteen years after his conversion, or in about 48.

At that time, the Jerusalem church was clearly divided over the issue of what role the Jewish law should play for Gentile converts. The Jerusalem church's leadership of Jesus' brother James, Cephas [Peter], and John initially allowed, at least at the Jerusalem Council, that the Jewish law was not binding on Gentile Christians, whereas the so-called circumcision faction in the Jerusalem church maintained an opposing view by adhering to the position that the Jewish law was binding on *all* followers of Jesus, both Jews and Gentiles.

We also know from Paul that following his conversion in about 35, he traveled to Arabia, perhaps to the Natataean Kingdom south of Damascus and east of the Jordan River, for unspecified reasons. From Arabia, Paul returned to Damascus or perhaps Antioch in about 37–38 and then went to Jerusalem in 38 for two weeks to visit Peter, during which visit he briefly saw Jesus' brother James. Following that visit, Paul preached his gospel for several years in the Roman provinces of Syria and Cilicia (38–48), probably working from the sponsoring base of the Antioch church. Exactly where and what Paul preached in Arabia, Syria, and Cilicia during that early period is not clear.

Paul, together with Barnabas and Titus, went from Antioch to Jerusalem in about 48, some thirteen years after his conversion and some ten years after his previous visit, to represent the views of the Antioch church in what is often called the Jerusalem Council or the Apostolic Council. There in Jerusalem, the Jerusalem leadership and Paul agreed that that Peter would serve as the *apostle* to circumcised Jews and Paul as the *missionary* to uncircumcised Gentiles.

It is also clear that there was a serious confrontation between Paul and Peter in Antioch shortly thereafter in about 48–49, when Peter was visiting the Antioch church, probably for the first time. During that visit Peter ate with uncircumcised Gentile Christians who did not follow Jewish dietary laws. A delegation from Jesus' brother James arrived subsequently from Jerusalem and challenged Peter's practice of eating with Gentiles. Under pressure Peter withdrew, as did Barnabas and other Jewish Christians in the Antioch church, causing a rift, the long-term consequences of which are unclear. Following this disagreement, Paul may have departed the Antioch church and have headed out on his own to evangelize Gentiles further west in the regions of Phrygia and Galatia, marking the beginning of what may have been Paul's independent mission travel.

THE ANTIOCH QUESTION

It is unclear whether Paul was permanently estranged from the Antioch church following the confrontation with the delegation from James, but the division between the Antioch and Jerusalem churches and even within the Jerusalem church remained a serious thorn in Paul's flesh and continued to haunt him in his travels to Galatia and Greece. Acts assumes throughout that Paul returned to his home base in the sponsoring Antioch church after each of three missionary journeys, but Paul's letters do not support Luke's scheme of three missionary journeys. Paul's disagreement with the Antioch church may have persisted. The evidence is not entirely clear.

PAUL'S MESSAGE

Paul's earliest message from 35–50 is not documented—exactly where and what did Paul preach during these fifteen formative years? Even for the period after 50, gleaning Paul's preaching from his letters means that what we know of the Pauline *kerygma* is always incomplete. All of Paul's letters were written to specific circumstances in specific churches, which would already have understood quite clearly the content of Paul's gospel. We have no single account of what Paul said when he preached to the Gentiles. Neither do we know that Paul's message was always the same from the time of his conversion in 35 to his death twenty-five years later in 60. It is likely that Paul's message evolved over that quarter century of his mission work. Most notably, the emphasis on Jesus' second coming, highly charged in 1 Thessalonians, appears to have lessened over time, when Jesus' second coming was "delayed." Reconstructions of Paul's *kerygma* by C. H. Dodd, Rudolf Bultmann, and others are helpful, but they are just that—scholarly reconstructions.

PAUL'S DEATH AS A MARTYR

The final item in the proposed chronology detailed earlier in this chapter is the martyrdom of Paul in Rome in about 60 during Nero's persecution of Christians. Information concerning Paul's martyrdom is reported in the *Acts of Paul and Thecla*, a portion of the apocryphal *Acts of Paul*, but the historical value of this material is questionable.

The earliest reference to this apocryphal literature appears in Tertullian's *De Baptismo* 17, written in about 200:

> If those who read the writings that falsely bear the name of Paul adduce the example of Thecla to maintain the right of women to preach and to baptize, let them know that the presbyter in Asia who produced this document, as if he could of himself add anything to the prestige of Paul, was removed from his office after he had been convicted and had confessed that he did it out of love of Paul. (*Corpus Scriptorum Ecclesiasticorum Latinorum*, volume 20, p. 215)

The legendary character of the *Acts of Paul and Thecla* is self-evident. What is not clear is how much was invented by the unnamed presbyter in Asia and how much already circulated in oral tradition that developed around Paul after his death. Scholars have long been puzzled by the lack of information in the Acts of the Apostles regarding Paul's time in Rome, assuming that Acts was written decades after Paul's death.

We should probably be skeptical of every detail in the *Acts of Paul and Thecla*, including the proposed date and manner of Paul's death by beheading in Rome during the Neronian persecutions. It may well be that Paul simply died quietly in a time and place that we shall never know. It is not unlikely that the details of Paul's death in the *Acts of Paul and Thecla* were influenced decisively by Christian martyrological literature of the second century.

CHAPTER 12

EARLY CHRISTIAN GOSPELS, PART 1

IN THIS CHAPTER AND the next, we will look at several early Christian gospels in an effort to understand how scholars identify the authors, the dates and places of composition, and the purposes of the gospels. We will include in our study not only the canonical gospels, which we will examine in this chapter, but we will also consider in the next chapter some non-canonical or apocryphal gospels, including the *Gospel of the Nazoreans*, the *Gospel of the Ebionites*, the *Gospel of the Hebrews*, the Coptic *Gospel of Thomas*, the *Gospel of Peter*, the *Infancy Gospel of Thomas*, the *Infancy Gospel of James*, the *Gospel of Mary*, the *Gospel of Truth*, and Tatian's *Diatessaron*.

Although obviously related in some way, the four canonical gospels represent Jesus of Nazareth in very different ways. Bart H. Ehrman appropriately entitles the chapters covering the canonical gospels in *The New Testament: A Historical Introduction to the Early Christian Writings* as follows:

> Jesus, The Suffering Son of God: The Gospel According to Mark
>
> Jesus, The Jewish Messiah: The Gospel According to Matthew
>
> Jesus, The Savior of the World: The Gospel According to Luke
>
> Jesus, The Man Sent from Heaven: The Gospel According to John.

In so doing, Ehrman makes the important point that what we have in the New Testament are not four independent and faithful testimonies regarding what transpired during the life and ministry of Jesus of Nazareth. Rather, we have in the canonical gospels four distinct theological portraits of Jesus that represent different ways in which early Christian communities understood, imagined, or recreated Jesus, often in their own image and with little regard to history—at least as we understand history today.

A dozen or more additional gospels paint still different theological portraits of Jesus, but the church accepted only the four canonical gospels and excluded many more from the canon of the New Testament. Like the canonical gospels, the non-canonical gospels portray Jesus in ways that were consistent with the views of at least some Christians in the communities that generated these gospels. In every instance, whether we are dealing with canonical or non-canonical gospels, we learn more about the community or the individual author who created each gospel than we can possibly hope to learn about Jesus himself. The theological inclinations of the gospels pose dilemmas and challenges shared by canonical and non-canonical gospels alike.

THE CANONICAL GOSPELS

This chapter will focus exclusively on the canonical gospels: Matthew, Mark, Luke, and John. Although all four of these gospels are anonymous, by the middle of the second century Christians had begun to assign the authorship of each of these gospels either to an apostle and, therefore, a presumed eyewitness to the life and ministry of Jesus—as in the case of Jesus' apostles Matthew and John—or to a disciple of an apostle and, therefore, a secondary witness to Jesus—as in the case of Mark, a disciple of Peter; and Luke, a disciple of Paul. None of the four canonical gospels claims authorship in any manner or form. The familiar titles "the Gospel According to Matthew," "The Gospel According to Mark," etc. were inventions of Christians in the second century, probably for the purpose of combating some theological tendencies that had developed during that period with accompanying proliferation of gospels. By identifying certain teachings as apostolic and, therefore, authentic and authoritative, and by identifying other teachings or tendencies as divisions and deviations from the teaching of the apostolic church, Christians embarked on the road to defining what was the "right" or "correct"—namely the "orthodox"—portrait or representation of Jesus..

EARLY WITNESS TO THE FOUR CANONICAL GOSPELS

It is helpful at the outset to look at some of the earliest witnesses to the canonical gospels, all from the mid- to late-second century.

PAPIAS OF HIEROPOLIS

Papias (ca. 70–ca. 155–160), whom Irenaeus identified as bishop of Hierapolis of Asia, likely wrote sometime between 110 and 150. Our information about Papias is provided by a secondary source, Eusebius of Caesarea (260–339), who wrote his *Church History* in about 325, almost two hundred years after Papias's death. Eusebius purports to quote from writings of Papias to which he presumably had access, but it is not entirely clear whether Eusebius quoted Papias accurately or edited Papias's writings to suit his own (later) purpose. With regard to Papias, Eusebius wrote the following in *Church History* 3.39.15–16:

> Mark became the interpreter of Peter and wrote down accurately all that he remembered of the things said and done by the Lord, not indeed in the (right) order, because he had not heard the Lord nor had he followed him, but later on, as I said, he had followed Peter who used to give his teachings as demanded by necessity, not, however, in order to make a composition of the words of the

Lord. Thus Mark did nothing wrong in writing down individual pieces just as he remembered them. For only to one thing he gave his attention, to leave out nothing of what he had heard and to make no false statements in them.

Matthew composed the sayings (Greek *ta logia*) in the Hebrew language [Aramaic?], and each translated them as best he could.

It may be that Papias is alluding to the canonical Gospel of Mark, although this is not self-evident. However, although Papias uses Matthew's name, it is not at all clear that he is referring to the canonical Gospel of Matthew, or to anything resembling what we call the Gospel of Matthew, which was almost certainly not written originally in "the Hebrew language" (Aramaic?), but rather in Greek. Neither does Eusebius report that Papias mentioned by name the gospels of Luke and John.

MARCION, JUSTIN MARTYR, TATIAN AND OTHERS

Marcion

Writing in Rome in the middle of the second century, Marcion (ca. 85–ca. 160), a Christian from Sinope of Pontus on the Black Sea, sought to separate Christianity entirely from its Jewish roots. Marcion wrote only a single work, *Antitheses* (or *Contradictions*), in which he set forth his views.

Marcion's work survives only in the writings of his opponents, the most important of whom was the North African Tertullian (ca. 155–ca. 230), who wrote a five-volume work against Marcion, *Adversus Marcionem*, in about 208. We learn from Tertullian that among Marcion's most important teachings was his rejection of the Hebrew Scriptures (the Old Testament), and his acceptance of what was probably the earliest Christian canon, consisting of the Gospel of Luke and ten letters of Paul (Galatians, 1 and 2 Corinthians, Romans, 1 and 2 Thessalonians, Ephesians, Colossians, Philemon, and Philippians; but not 1 and 2 Timothy and Titus). Marcion specifically rejected the gospels of Matthew and John from his canon but apparently made no mention of Mark.

Marcion believed that he was following in the tradition of Paul, who had earlier fought against Judaizers, by purging from the Gospel of Luke and Paul's letters what he believed were unoriginal Judaizing interpolations. Hence, Marcion's canon was actually a truncated version of these eleven books.

Justin Martyr

Justin Martyr (ca. 110–ca.165) was born a pagan in Flavia Neapolis (ancient Shechem) in Roman Palestine. Following his conversion to Christianity, Justin established a school in Rome to advance the spread of Christianity. Justin's mid-second-century writings reveal that he knew the gospels of Matthew and Luke (and perhaps Mark).

He did not, however, use these gospels as his authoritative sources or identify them by name. For the many sayings of Jesus that Justin cited in his *Apology* and his *Dialogue with Tyrpho*, he quoted these sayings in a way that indicates that he was not using the gospels of Matthew and Luke (and perhaps Mark) directly but that he was using a carefully constructed harmony of the gospels of Matthew and Luke (and perhaps in a few instances Mark).[1] Justin apparently had no knowledge of nor did he make use of the Gospel of John. If Justin knew the Gospel of John, he may have regarded it as somewhat "gnosticizing" and, therefore, unorthodox.

Tatian

Tatian (ca. 120–ca. 185) was born in Assyria and found his way to Rome, where he studied under Justin Martyr. Like Justin, Tatian opened a catechetical school in Rome. Tatian's most important writing was the *Diatessaron* (his "One-Through-Four" Gospel), a harmony or synthesis of the gospels of Matthew, Mark, Luke, and John that he composed sometime after the mid-second century. It is possible that Tatian first learned about harmonies of the gospels from his teacher Justin Martyr.

Tatian's *Diatessaron* was widely disseminated and was apparently the only text of the gospels used in Syria during the third and fourth centuries. It is important that Tatian knew our canonical gospels, but it is not clear that he knew them by name or that he recognized their authority. He obviously did not value them as apostolic. If he did, he would not have harmonized them into his "one-through-four" gospel, the *Diatessaron*.

Other Harmonies

Like Justin and Tatian, the author of *Second Clement*, also writing in Rome in the mid-second century, knew a harmony comprised of portions of the gospels of Matthew and Luke.[2] So too Clement of Alexandria (ca. 150–ca. 215), Origen (ca. 185–ca. 254), Irenaeus (the first half of the second century to ca. 202), and the author of the *Pseudo-Clementine Homilies* (third century?) were also aware of harmonized materials from the gospels of Matthew and Luke.

IRENAEUS

Irenaeus of Lyons (died ca. 202) was probably a Greek born in Smyrna in Asia Minor sometime during the first half of the second century. He subsequently settled in Lyon in Gaul, where he was elected bishop and where he wrote his magnum opus, *Against*

---

1. See the detailed discussion in Bellinzoni, *The Sayings of Jesus in the Writings of Justin Martyr*, especially 134–38. See also Koester, *Ancient Christian Gospels*, 360–402.

2. Bellinzoni, ibid., 141–42; Koester, ibid., 351–60.

Heresies, in about 180, primarily to combat the tendency in Christianity referred to as Gnosticism. With respect to the canonical gospels, Irenaeus is the first person to mention all four by name in about 180 (*Against Heresies*, 3.1.1):

> Matthew also issued a written Gospel among the Hebrews in their own dialect [Aramaic?], while Peter and Paul were preaching at Rome, and laying the foundations of the Church.
>
> After their departure [probably meaning the deaths of Peter and Paul?], Mark, the disciple and interpreter of Peter, did also hand down to us in writing what had been preached by Peter.
>
> Luke also, the companion of Paul, recorded in a book the Gospel preached by him [i.e. Paul].
>
> Afterwards, John, the disciple of the Lord, who also had leaned upon His breast, did himself publish a Gospel during his residence at Ephesus in Asia Minor.

Irenaeus reflects the traditional view (the view first reflected in Papias?) that Jesus' apostle Matthew wrote his gospel first in the Hebrew dialect (Aramaic?), followed by Mark who wrote a gospel that reflected the teaching of the apostle Peter. Irenaeus adds to Papias's testimony that Luke subsequently "recorded" the gospel according to Paul and that the apostle John "did publish" his gospel last from Ephesus in Asia.

The most that can be said about this testimony is that Irenaeus apparently knew the four canonical gospels by name, but the rest of what he wrote has little merit as history. Irenaeus is unfortunately not an independent reliable witness, because he is merely reporting an earlier tradition that had no evidence to support it and because what he is reporting is so evidently apologetic. Irenaeus argued that the four gospels are the four "Pillars of the Church." "It is not possible that there can be either more or fewer than four" he stated, presenting as his evidence the four corners of the earth and the four winds (*Against Heresies* 3.11.8).

The assignment of apostolicity or discipleship of apostolicity to these four gospels was critical in the fight against what were regarded as errant Christian tendencies or heresies, which may actually be the original basis for the apostolic naming of the four gospels, and for the subsequent naming of several other gospels that were ultimately excluded from the Christian canon.

THE MURATORI CANON

The Muratori Canon is an eighth century manuscript of a seriously flawed Latin translation of a catalogue of New Testament books, probably composed in Palestine or Syria in the fourth century. In its original Greek, this catalogue may have served as an introduction to a collection of the books of the New Testament. The Canon refers to Bishop Pius of Rome (who served ca. 142–ca. 157) as being quite recent, but this may be a device to try to place the canon in Rome sometime around 200.

Unfortunately, nothing remains of what the author said about the Gospel of Matthew, and only one line remains of what he said about the Gospel of Mark. In its present form, the text of the Muratori Canon begins:[3]

> ... at which however he was present and so he has set it down.
> The third Gospel book, that according to Luke.
> This physician Luke after Christ's ascension (resurrection?),
> since Paul had taken him with him as an expert in the way (of the teaching),
> composed it in his own name
> according to (his) thinking. Yet neither did he himself see
> the Lord in the flesh; and therefore, as he was able to ascertain it, so he begins
> to tell the story from the birth of John.
> The fourth of the Gospels, that of John, (one) of the disciples.
> When his fellow-disciples and bishops urged him,
> he said: Fast with me from today for three days, and what
> will be revealed to each one
> let us relate to one another. In the same night it was
> revealed to Andrew, one of the apostles, that,
> whilst all were to go over (it), John in his own name
> should write everything down.[4]

The Muratori Canon goes on to mention the Acts of all apostles, thirteen of Paul's letters (1 Corinthians, Ephesians, Philippians, Colossians, Galatians, 1 Thessalonians, Romans, 2 Corinthians, 2 Thessalonians, Philemon, Titus, 1 and 2 Timothy); Jude; two letters of John (1 and 2 John?); the Wisdom of Solomon; and the Revelation of John.

Inasmuch as the Muratori Canon speaks of Luke as the third gospel, the missing lines at the beginning of the text obviously referred to the first Gospel of Matthew and the second Gospel of Mark. We can safely conclude that the fourth century Muratori Canon knew and approved the four canonical gospels by name, and an additional nineteen other books. The Wisdom of Solomon is a curiosity in this list, because it is a pre-Christian or non-Christian composition, written by a Hellenized Jew in Alexandria, probably between about 30 BCE and 50 CE. Missing from the Muratori Canon are five books that eventually found their way into the canonical New Testament: Hebrews, James, 1 and 2 Peter, and one additional letter of John (3 John?).

Although our focus in this chapter is on the canonical gospels, it is worth noting that as late as 350 the canon of the New Testament was still quite fluid.

THE SYNOPTIC GOSPELS

As we have seen, the canonical gospels tell us nothing about their authors or about the times and places of their composition. Accordingly, we are dependent on internal and

---

3. Hennecke, *New Testament Apocrypha*, vol 1, 42–45.

4. The Muratori Canon works hard to legitimize the Gospel of John, which may suggest that this gospel was still controversial in many Christian circles.

external evidence to identify the author and the time and place of composition, as well as the purpose of each of these gospels.

External evidence, on the one hand, is relatively straightforward. It refers to evidence found outside the gospels, generally in early Christian writings, that affords meaningful clues about each gospel—whether a clear citation of a gospel by an early church father, a reference to a specific gospel by name, and so on. We have already looked above at some external evidence in Papias, Marcion, 2 Clement, Justin, Tatian, Irenaeus, and the Muratori Canon.

Internal evidence, on the other hand, refers to clues within the gospels that afford us insights into the minds of their authors and the times and places of composition of each of the writings. Unlike the study of external evidence, the examination of internal evidence is more like detective work, and it is easy to see why scholars sometimes disagree on the value or the significance of particular clues.

THE GOSPEL OF MARK

As we have already observed, scholars generally regard the Gospel of Mark as the earliest of the written gospels and probably as the first literary interpretation of the life and ministry of Jesus. As early as the second century, Christian tradition attributed this anonymous gospel to John Mark.[5] Yet, nowhere in this gospel is its anonymous author identified; neither does the gospel even pretend to be apostolic. Although the "author" was apparently no one of special consequence, it is safe to conclude that he was a person of authority in his own community and that he was obviously literate.

Just as the authorship of the Gospel of Mark is uncertain, neither is it clear where and when the gospel was written. The author's conscious effort to explain Jewish customs and to translate Aramaic words for his Greek-speaking readers indicates a place of origin for the gospel somewhere other than Palestine, where such clarification would have been unnecessary. For example:

Mark 3:16–17

"So he [Jesus] appointed the twelve: Simon (to whom he gave the name Peter); James son of Zebedee and John the brother of James (to whom he gave the name Boanerges, *that is, Sons of thunder;* . . . .");

Mark 5:41

[Jesus] took [the dead girl] by the hand and said to her, "Talitha cum," *which means, "Little girl, get up!"*

---

5. See 1 Pet 5:13, which refers to Mark as Peter's son, a phrase that indicates Mark was a disciple or follower of Peter. This verse in 1 Peter may be the sole inspiration for the tradition in Papias and other church fathers that Peter's disciple Mark wrote the gospel that bears his name.

Mark 7:2–4

[The Pharisees and the scribes] noticed that some of [Jesus'] disciples were eating with defiled hands, that is without washing them. (*For the Pharisees, and all the Jews do not eat unless they thoroughly wash their hands, thus observing the tradition of the elders, and they do not eat anything from the market unless they wash it; and there are also many other traditions that they observe, the washing of cups, pots and bronze kettles.*)

Mark 7:11

But you [Pharisees and scribes] say that if anyone tells father or mother, "Whatever support you might have had from me is Corban," (*that is, an offering to God*) . . . ."

Mark 7:34

Then looking up to heaven, [Jesus] sighed and said to them, "Ephphatha," *that is, "Be opened."*

Mark 14:36

He said, "Abba, *Father*, for you all things are possible; . . . ."

Mark 15:22

Then they brought Jesus to the place called Golgatha (*which means the place of a skull*).

Mark 15:34

At three o'clock Jesus cried out with a loud voice, "Eloi, Eloi, lema sabbachthani?" which means, "*My God, my God, why have you forsaken me?*"

Mark 15:42

When evening had come, and since it was the Day of Preparation, *that is, the day before the Sabbath,* . . . .

See also Mark 7:31

"Then he returned from the region of Tyre, and went by way of Sidon towards the Sea of Galilee, in the region of the Decapolis."

[*This verse betrays lack of familiarity with the geography of Palestine.*]

The Gospel of Mark also uses Latin loan words, suggesting that it was written either in Rome or in a Roman province, either in Italy, in Syria, or elsewhere within the Roman Empire:

Mark 5:9

Then Jesus asked [the Gerasene demoniac], "What is your name?" He replied, "My name is *Legion*; for we are many."

[n.b.: A Legion was a Roman regiment of 3,000 to 6,000 soldiers and 100 to 200 cavalry troops.]

Mark 10:11–12

[Jesus] said to [the Pharisees], "Whoever divorces his wife and marries another commits adultery against her; and if she divorces her husband and marries another, she commits adultery.

[n.b.: Under Jewish law, a woman could not initiate divorce against her husband; however, a woman could divorce her husband under Roman law.]

Mark 12:42

A poor widow came and put in two small copper coins [Greek *lepta duo*], which are worth a penny.

[n.b.: Mark says literally, "which are worth a *quadrans*," the smallest denomination of Roman coins. Perhaps Mark was providing the equivalent of the smallest Roman coin for the benefit of his readers. The quadrans would have been known in Rome, and also in Syria and Judea. The *lepton*, on the other hand, was the smallest denomination of coins in Syria-Nabataea.][6]

Rome is an obvious candidate for the place of composition of the Gospel of Mark and was the view of some early church fathers. For example, Irenaeus, writing in Lyons in about 180, seems to assume that Mark was written in Rome:

> After their [Peter and Paul's] departure [from Rome] (i.e., their death), Mark, the disciple and interpreter of Peter, did also hand down to us in writing what had been preached by Peter. (Irenaeus, *Against Heresies*, 3.1.1)

It is difficult to assess the value of Irenaeus's testimony. The statement that Mark wrote down what had been preached by his teacher Peter appears to have little to no historical value. In fact, Peter's Christianity (Gal 2:11–14) is certainly different from Mark's on the important issue of the role of the Jewish dietary law (Mark 7:17–19).[7] As we have seen in earlier chapters, the composition of the Gospel of Mark was a complicated process involving the development of oral and written tradition over a

---

6. Collins, *Mark*, 589.

7. Gal 2:11–14 reads: 11But when Cephas [Peter] came to Antioch, I [Paul] opposed him to his face, because he stood condemned; 12for until certain people came from James, he used to eat with the Gentiles. But after they came, he drew back and kept himself separate for fear of the circumcision faction. 13And the other Jews joined him in this hypocrisy, so that even Barnabas was led astray by their hypocrisy. 14But when I saw that they were not acting consistently with the truth of the gospel, I said to Cephas before them all, "If you, though a Jew live like a Gentile and not like a Jew, how can you compel the Gentiles to live like Jews?"

Mark 7:17–19 reads: 17When he [Jesus] had left the crowd and entered the house, his disciples asked him about the parable [of the sower]. 18He said to them, "Then do you also fail to understand? Do you not see that whatever goes into a person from outside cannot defile, 19since it enters, not the heart but the stomach, and goes out into the sewer? (Thus he declared all foods clean.)

period of several decades following Jesus' death. Nothing within the gospel suggests a meaningful connection to Peter.

On the other hand, by the end of the second century the church was apparently involved in assigning apostolic authorship to anonymous books that had come down from a much earlier time, perhaps even a century earlier. Irenaeus identifies the author of the gospel as John Mark, associated in Acts 12:12, 25 and 1 Pet 5:13 with the apostle Peter. It may be that this development is a conscious power play by the church in Rome to gobble up traditions and identify them as their own.

As we have seen, Rome is a possible place of composition of the Gospel of Mark. The case for Syria may actually be stronger, although the internal evidence on which we are basing the case is meager and quite tenuous, most specifically the reference to the coins (lepta and quadrans) in Mark 12:42. It is impossible to know how much weight we can legitimately assign to the external evidence in Irenaeus, and quite frankly the internal evidence is slight. The value in this discussion is to recognize what might be clues or evidence and to indicate how tentative some of our scholarly arguments are because of the paucity of meaningful evidence. That said, I lean toward Syria as the likely place of composition of the Gospel of Mark; and if Syria, then probably Antioch, the most cosmopolitan city in Roman Syria and a city in which many Christians would likely have spoken both Aramaic and Greek, thereby accounting for both the preservation and the translation of the many Aramaisms in the Gospel of Mark.

If the situation described in Mark 13:5–23 was intended to reflect circumstances that would have been familiar to Mark's readers, then the gospel may have been written in the wake of Nero's persecution of Christians in Rome (i.e., sometime after 64) and perhaps leading up to the time of the Jewish revolt against Rome (in 66–70). A specific date and place of composition is not proved by this internal evidence, but these events are certainly consistent with the evidence available in Mark 13. And so, Antioch of Syria in about 67 is my best estimate for the place and date of composition of the Gospel of Mark, based on scant yet real internal evidence.[8]

The sources that Mark used are not entirely clear, but evidence that we identified in previous chapters suggests that the author of the gospel likely used:

> a collection of *testimonia* containing both implicit and explicit references to the Old Testament (i.e. proof texts, Mark 1:2–3, 11; 15:24, 29, 34);

written sources containing collections of

> sayings (e.g. Mark 9:42–50),
>
> parables (e.g. Mark 4:3–32),
>
> miracle stories (e.g. Mark 4:35–5:43),
>
> pronouncement stories (e.g. Mark 3:22–30; 12:13–17); and probably

---

8. Many scholars date Mark to 70 or even slightly later, arguing that evidence in Mark 13 is prediction *after* the fact (*vaticinium ex eventu*, Latin for "foretelling after the event").

a written passion narrative containing an account of Jesus' final days in Jerusalem (Mark 14:1–15:39), a document that may have emerged as a component of a liturgy leading up to the celebration of Easter (Jesus' resurrection) and that was based on Old Testament "proof texts" (see chapter 5, pp. 122–28).

The evidence suggests that the author of the Gospel of Mark was a collector and editor of preexisting written sources rather than an author per se. In fact, we can see how Mark stitched together these sources by examining his editorial style, which is quite transparent. For instance, Mark's frequent use of the simple word "and" (Greek καί, *kai*) to connect or to provide a transition between individual stories in his gospel implies that Mark was probably collecting existing *pericopes* (or units of oral and mostly written tradition), which he used as building blocks for most of his gospel, leading up to the passion narrative, the clear focus of Mark's story.[9]

The Gospel of Mark begins with an account of Jesus' baptism by John and ends with the report of the empty tomb and the amazement of the women who had gone to Jesus' tomb to anoint his body. The material between these bookend events is filled with sayings, parables, miracle stories, pronouncement stories, legends, and a passion narrative that Mark found in his written sources and incorporated into his narrative.

Whoever he was, the person responsible for writing the Gospel of Mark seems to have created the literary genre that we know as Gospel, although his gospel was probably modeled after Hellenistic biographies already familiar to him and his readers. In its present form, the Gospel of Mark is a theological announcement of professed events in the life of Jesus, but its real purpose is to announce "the good news," the "gospel" about Jesus the messiah (Mark 1:1). From beginning to end, the Gospel of Mark is a confessional recital of Jesus' life, ministry, teaching, and death and was never intended to be otherwise.

Bart Ehrman's designation of Mark as the gospel that introduces the reader to "Jesus: The Suffering Son of God" focuses clearly on an underlying theme of the gospel. In this regard, the words of the Roman centurion who stood facing Jesus at the crucifixion as Jesus breathed his last breath are salutary: "Truly this man was God's Son" (Mark 15:39). This is the first time in the Gospel of Mark that these words are uttered by a human being, and a Gentile Roman no less.[10]

One additional word about the Christology of the Gospel of Mark is in order. After John baptized Jesus in the waters of the Jordan River (Mark 1:9–11), the Spirit of God descended on Jesus like a dove, and a voice came from heaven, saying "You are my Son,

---

9. Although most modern translations do not translate the "and" (*kai*) at the beginning of most stories in Mark, the King James Version does. For example, the stories (pericopes) in Mark 1:9; 1:12; 1:16; 1:21; 1:23; 1:29; 1:35; 1:39; 1:40; 2:1; 2:13; 2:15; 2:18; 2:23; 3:1; 3:7; 3:13; 3:20; 3:22; 3:23; 3:31; etc. all begin with "and" in the original Greek.

10. There are three earlier references to Jesus as God's Son: Mark 1:1 in which the words "Son of God" appear only in late manuscript tradition and are probably not original to the gospel; Mark 1:11 in which the voice from heaven at Jesus' baptism calls him "my Son"; and Mark 3:11 in which unclean spirits call Jesus "Son of God" whenever they see him.

the Beloved; with you I am well pleased." Scholars have long observed that the author of the Gospel of Mark probably understood Jesus' baptism as the moment when God *adopted* Jesus as his Son and set him on his course as messiah. If this interpretation is correct, then like the adoptionist theology in Rom 1:4, where Paul says that "Jesus was *declared* to be Son of God with power according to the spirit of holiness *by resurrection from the dead*," the Gospel of Mark employs the same adoptionist brand of Christology, except that Mark moves the moment of God's adoption of Jesus as Son backwards from Jesus' resurrection (Rom 1:4) to the time of Jesus' baptism (Mark 1:11), thereby introducing the notion that Jesus' entire ministry was messianic from the moment of his adoption by God as his Son at the time of his baptism by John.

Mark's decision to move Jesus' adoption as God's Son from the resurrection to the baptism may explain the reason for what scholars refer to as the theme of the Messianic Secret in Mark. Beginning with Wilhelm Wrede,[11] scholars have understood that Jesus' command to his followers not to reveal to others that he is messiah is actually a literary device of the Gospel of Mark and not grounded in the actual teaching of the historical Jesus.

According to Wrede's thesis, Mark devised the theme of the messianic secret to explain why Jesus was not regarded as messiah during his ministry and why his messiahship was revealed only by virtue of his resurrection from the dead. According to Wrede, if Jesus was messiah and if he was recognized as messiah only after his resurrection, then his messiahship must have been a secret during the course of his ministry.

Perhaps the single most obvious example of Mark's theme of the messianic secret appears in the story of Peter's confession in Mark 8:27–30:

> [27]Jesus went on with his disciples to the villages of Caesarea Philippi; and on the way he asked his disciples, "Who do people say that I am?" And they answered him, "John and Baptist; and others, Elijah; and still others, one of the prophets." He asked them, "But who do you say that I am?" Peter answered him, "You are the Messiah." *And he sternly ordered them not to tell anyone about him.*

In still other stories in Mark, Jesus commands his followers to be silent after he performs exorcisms and healings:

Mark 1:34b

> ... and [Jesus] would not permit the demons to speak, because they knew him.

Mark 1:43–44a

> After sternly warning [the leper whom he had just healed], [Jesus] sent him away at once, saying to him, "See that you say nothing to anyone . . . ."

Mark 3:12

> But [Jesus] sternly ordered [the unclean spirits] not to make him known.

---

11. Wrede, *Das Messiasgeheimnis in den Evangelien*. English edition, *The Messianic Secret*.

Mark 5:43a

[Jesus] strictly ordered [the people] that no one should know this . . .

Mark 7:36a

Then Jesus ordered [the people] to tell no one . . .

Mark 8:26

Then [Jesus] sent [the blind man whom he had healed] away to his home, saying, "Do not even go into the village."

Mark 9:9

As [his disciples] were coming down the mountain, [Jesus] ordered them to tell no one about what they had seen, *until after the Son of Man had risen from the dead.*

Coming at the end of miracle stories, these commands of silence appear unmistakably as Mark's editorial additions to written pericopes to which Mark had access in one of his written sources, probably a collection of miracle stories. The addition of commands of silence at the ends of these stories serves to explain the dilemma of why God's Son and messiah was not recognized as such until *after* his resurrection from the dead. Every time someone recognized Jesus as messiah during the course of his ministry, Jesus silenced that person and ordered him or her not to tell anyone. The italics in the last entry above (Mark 9:9) are particularly revealing as Mark seems to allow that Jesus was not recognized as messiah, or Son of God, or Son of Man designate until he *had risen from the dead*.

The assembled evidence makes it clear that the Gospel of Mark is certainly not a reliable record of the life and ministry of Jesus. Apart from the Baptism at the beginning of the story and the crucifixion and resurrection at the end, there is no value either to the sequence of the purported events or to the geography. Mark collected material from many written sources and provided the framework and the order for these stories. Whether these "stories" or collections of material have any historical value is obviously debatable.

THE GOSPEL OF MATTHEW

Like the Gospel of Mark, the Gospel of Matthew is built on earlier written sources:

1. As we observed at several points earlier in this book, the author of the anonymous Gospel of Matthew used a version of the Gospel of Mark as his primary source. Matthew used most of the material in Mark, generally but not always in exactly the same order.

2. In addition, Matthew used a written source, called Q (= German *Quelle* or "source") containing about 240–260 verses of sayings of Jesus, a source that was also known

to the author of the Gospel of Luke. No copies of Q survive, but scholars have reconstructed the hypothetical source Q with a fair measure of confidence.

3. Matthew also had access to other material, collectively known as M or Special Matthew, which he also wove into the Markan framework:

   a. A fair amount of the material in so-called M is sayings material that is not found in either Mark or Q but that is unique to Matthew, much of it woven into the Sermon on the Mount (Matt 5–7). Although some of this material may have been in the redaction of Q available to Matthew, most of these M sayings were probably available to Matthew in one or more written sources.

   b. There are, in addition, a number of parables that may have been available to Matthew in a separate source:

   > The Parable of the Tares (Matt 13:24–30, 36–43)
   >
   > The Parables of the Hidden Treasure (Matt 13:44)
   >
   > The Parable of the Pearl (Matt 13:45–46)
   >
   > The Parable of the Net (Matt 13:47–50)
   >
   > The Parable of the Unforgiving Servant (Matt 18:23–35)
   >
   > The Parable of the Two Sons (Matt 21:28–32)

   c. Matthew also had available to him written narratives about the birth of Jesus (Matt 1–2), material that is unrelated to the birth and infancy narrative found in Luke 1–2.

   d. In addition, Matthew also had access to a resurrection story of Jesus' appearances in Galilee and of his commissioning his disciples (Matt 28), material unlike the resurrection story found in Luke 24.

The material referred to collectively as M or special Matthew was, therefore, probably *at least* four different written sources: sayings material, a collection of parables, a birth narrative, and an account of resurrection appearances in Galilee.

It may be that the Gospel of Matthew should actually be understood as a second edition of the Gospel of Mark, an "updated" version that was written to include material that was unknown when the first edition, the Gospel of Mark, was written in Antioch in about 67 but that was later available for incorporation into an update or rewriting of Mark's gospel.

As we observed earlier, Papias reports that

> Matthew composed the sayings (Greek *ta logia*) in the Hebrew language [Aramaic?], and each translated them as best he could.

Inasmuch as these words follow immediately upon Papias's comments about the Gospel of Mark, it seems safe to assume that Papias was referring to the Gospel of Matthew. However, scholars have been reluctant to identify the canonical Gospel of Matthew with Papias' "*logia* in the Hebrew language." Although Matthew clearly reflects Semitic influence, the Greek text of Matthew is not a translation from an Aramaic original. Rather, Matthew obviously used the Greek text of Mark as his primary source. Some have suggested that ancient tradition may have assigned the sayings material in special M to the apostle Matthew and that the use of this sayings material eventually gave rise to the belief that Matthew wrote the gospel attributed to him by later generations.

Material in the Gospel of Matthew seems to suggest that the author was aware of the Roman destruction of Jerusalem in 70:

Matt 21:41

[The chief priests and the elders of the people] said to [Jesus], "[The landowner of the vineyard] will put those wretches [the tenants of the vineyard] to a miserable death, and lease the vineyard to other tenants who will give him the produce at the harvest time."

[n.b.: some think that the "miserable death" in this passage refers to the Roman destruction of Jerusalem in 70.]

Matt 22:7

The king was enraged. He sent his troops, destroyed those murderers, and burned their city.

[n.b.: this more detailed description of the ensuing punishment refers quite clearly to the Roman destruction of Jerusalem in 70.]

Matt 24:15–16

"So when you see the desolating sacrilege standing in the holy place, as was spoken by the prophet Daniel (let the reader understand), then let those in Judea flee to the mountains.

[n.b.: Matthew may have understood the "desolating sacrilege," which appeared originally in Dan 9:27 as a reference to an altar of Zeus set up in 167 BCE in the Jerusalem temple by the Seleucid King Antiochus IV Epiphanes, to refer in this instance to the presence of the Roman general Titus in the Jerusalem temple in 70. The parenthetical "let the reader understand," found also in the Markan source (Mark 13:14), would presumably have been clear to the reader, even if it is somewhat puzzling to modern readers of the gospel.]

However tenuous these allusions to the fall of Jerusalem may be, they point us clearly toward a date of composition sometime after the fall of Jerusalem, and certainly after the writing of the Gospel of Mark. Moreover, Jesus' principal opponents in the Gospel of Matthew are the Pharisees, a Jewish sect that acquired greater importance only after the fall of Jerusalem in 70. Scholars incline toward a date sometime after 80, perhaps between 80 and 90.

Bishop Ignatius of Antioch, writing about 110–117 (Ignatius's *Letter to the Smyrneans* 1:1), may contain a specific reference to Matt 3:13–15, affording us the latest possible date for the writing of the Gospel of Matthew:

Matt 3:13–15

> ¹³Then Jesus came from Galilee to John at the Jordan, to be baptized by him. ¹⁴John would have prevented him, saying, "I need to be baptized by you, and do you come to me?" ¹⁵But Jesus answered him, "Let it be so now; for *it is proper for us in this way to fulfill all righteousness.*"

Ignatius, *Letter to the Smyrneans* 1:1

> [Jesus] was truly of the seed of David according to the flesh, and the Son of God according to the will and power of God; that He was truly born of a virgin, was baptized by John, *in order that all righteousness might be fulfilled by Him.*

It is not entirely clear from the citations above that Ignatius knew the written text of the Gospel of Matthew. Perhaps both Matthew and Ignatius were independently aware of the same Antioch tradition that tried to explain why a sinless Jesus would have submitted to John's baptism *for the remission of sins* (Matt 3:6). In either case, the evidence probably points once again to Antioch as the place of composition of the Gospel of Matthew.

Circumstances surrounding the writing of the Gospel of Matthew seem to suit the situation in the Antioch church, a church composed of both Gentile Christians and Jewish Christians. The statement in Matt 4:24 that Jesus' "fame spread throughout all Syria" (not found in Mark's parallel) may reflect the gospel's special interest in Syrian Christianity.

Passages in Matthew suggest that the Pharisees were Jesus' principal opponents and that the author of the gospel was writing to a group of Jewish Christians or Christian Jews who had separated themselves from the Pharisaic Judaism of the period following the destruction of Jerusalem, a situation that probably suits the church in Antioch:

Matt 9:10–13

> ¹⁰And as [Jesus] sat at dinner in the house, many tax collectors and sinners came and were sitting with him and his disciples. ¹¹When the Pharisees saw this, they said to his disciples, "Why does your teacher eat with tax collectors and sinners?" ¹²But when he heard this, he said, "Those who are well have no need of a physician, but those who are sick. ¹³Go and learn what this means, 'I desire mercy, not sacrifice.' For I have come to call not the righteous but sinners."

Matt 9:32–34

> ³²After they had gone away, a demoniac who was mute was brought to him. ³³And when the demon had been cast out, the one who had been mute spoke; and the crowds were amazed and said, "Never has anything like this been seen in Israel." ³⁴But the Pharisees said, "By the ruler of demons he casts out the demons."

Matt 12:1–2

¹At that time Jesus went through the grainfields on the sabbath; his disciples were hungry, and they began to pluck heads of grain and to eat. ²When the Pharisees saw it, they said to him, "Look, your disciples are doing what is not lawful to do on the sabbath."

Matt 27:62–63

⁶²The next day, that is, after the day of Preparation, the chief priests and the Pharisees gathered before Pilate ⁶³and said, "Sir, we remember what that impostor [Jesus] said while he was still alive, 'After three days I will rise again.'"

These passages all reflect a strain between the Pharisees and the community to which the Gospel of Matthew is addressed. Likewise, virtually the whole of Matt 23 is a scathing and unrelenting attack against the hypocrisy of the scribes and Pharisees:

³[The scribes and the Pharisees] do not practice what they teach. . . . ⁵They do all their deeds to be seen by others; for they make their phylacteries broad and their fringes long. . . . 13But woe to you, scribes and Pharisees, hypocrites! For you lock people out of the kingdom of heaven. . . . ²³Woe to you scribes and Pharisees, hypocrites! For you tithe mint, dill, and cummin, and have neglected the weightier matters of the law: justice and mercy and faith. . . . 25Woe to you, scribes and Pharisees, hypocrites! For you clean the outside of the cup and of the plate, but inside they are full of greed and self-indulgence. . . . ²⁷Woe to you, scribes and Pharisees, hypocrites! For you are like whitewashed tombs, which on the outside look beautiful, but inside they are full of the bones of the dead and all kinds of filth. . . . ³³You snakes, you brood of vipers! How can you avoid being sentenced to hell? ³⁴Therefore I send you prophets, sages, and scribes, some of whom you will kill and crucify, and some you will flog in your synagogues and pursue from town to town.

Matthew's condemnation of the Pharisees is vitriolic, and his reference in 23:34 to Jesus' crucifixion and to the persecution of Christians is transparent. The gospel reflects certain knowledge of these events and circumstances in both the past and the present.

An especially interesting detail is that the word "church" appears only in the Gospel of Matthew among the four canonical gospels, and even then only twice, in Matt 16:18 and 18:17. The passage in Matt 16 is particularly important because of the authority granted to Jesus' disciple Peter in these verses:

¹⁶:¹³Now when Jesus came into the district of Caesarea Philippi, he asked his disciples, "Who do people say that the Son of Man is?" ¹⁴And they said, "Some say John the Baptist, but others Elijah, and still others Jeremiah or one of the prophets." ¹⁵He said to them, "But who do you say that I am?" ¹⁶Simon Peter answered, "You are the Messiah, the Son of the Living God." ¹⁷And Jesus answered him, "Blessed are you Simon, son of Jonah! For flesh and blood have not revealed this to you, but my Father in heaven. ¹⁸And I tell you, you are Peter (Greek Πέτρος, *petros* = Aramaic *kephas*), and on this rock (Greek πέτρα, *petra* = Aramaic *kepha*) I will build my church, and the gates of Hades will not prevail

against it. ¹⁹I will give you the keys of the kingdom of heaven, and whatever you bind on earth will be bound in heaven, and whatever you loose on earth will be loosed in heaven." ²⁰Then he sternly ordered the disciples not to tell anyone that he was the Messiah.

Matthew drew portions of this story (Matt 16:13–16, 20) from his Markan source (Mark 8:27–30). It is verses 17–19 that Matthew added to his Markan source. In these verses, the play on the name "Peter" and the word "rock" in both Greek and Aramaic is clear, although the pun does not come through in English.[12] Peter, in Matthew's words, is the rock on which the church was founded. Peter's preeminence among Jesus' disciples and especially in the early Christian community in Jerusalem is evident and may be based on the belief that it was Peter who through a direct revelation from God first saw the risen Lord (1 Cor 15:5; cf. Luke 24:12; John 20:2–9)[13] and who was, therefore, the first to call Jesus *messiah* or Lord.

The use of the word "church" on Jesus' lips is surely anachronistic, although Paul frequently used the word in his letters some twenty to thirty years before Matthew wrote his gospel. But Jesus' message to Peter in the Gospel of Matthew is clear: the powers of evil will not be able to destroy or even contain the church. Jesus gives to Peter the keys, the symbol of administrative authority over the disciplinary affairs of the Jesus community.

Perhaps this passage reflects, retrospectively, the fact that Peter had a position of preeminence not only in the Jerusalem church, but also in the church at Antioch. Is it possible that Peter remained in Antioch after the famous incident at Antioch when Paul confronted him over the issue of the role of the Jewish dietary laws among Gentile Christians (Gal 2:11–14)?

The Jewish-Christian or Christian-Jewish character of Matthew is also born out by other material in the gospel:

1. The author clearly represents Jesus as the new Moses:

    a. Jesus and his parents escape from Judea into Egypt in order that, like Moses, Jesus may be called out of Egypt (Matt 2:13–15).

    b. Jesus narrowly escapes murder as an infant when Herod orders the massacre of all children in and around Bethlehem two years old and younger (Matt 2:16–18), just as Moses escaped pharaoh's massacre of Hebrew male children (Exod 1:15–22).

    c. Like Moses at Mount Sinai, Jesus delivers the New Law from a mountain in material commonly known as the Sermon on the Mount (Matt 5–7).

---

12. The name Cephas or Peter actually does not appear as a name before Christian times. In fact, it is more of an appellation than a name. It would be as if in English Jesus had said, "And I tell you, you are Rocky, and on this rock I will build my church."

13. In the gospels, the earliest witnesses to the empty tomb (and in Matt 28:9–10 and John 20:14–18 the earliest witnesses to the risen Lord) were women, who were not necessarily regarded as reliable witnesses.

d. Jesus delivers five great discourses (Matt 5:1–7:27; 10:5–42; 13:1–52; 18:1–35; 24:3–25:46), probably reminiscent of the five books of Moses that constituted the Jewish Torah.

2. Jesus' life and ministry fulfilled the Jewish law and the prophets (see Matt 1:22–23; 2:5–6; 2:15; 2:17–18; 3:3; 4:14–16; etc.).

3. In delivering the New Law, Jesus states unequivocally: "Do not think that I have come to abolish the law or the prophets; I have come not to abolish but to fulfill" (Matt 5:17), meaning that Matthew understood that Jesus came to compete the law and the prophets, or to give them their full meaning.

4. In a series of contrasts in the Sermon on the Mount in Matt 5:21–47, Jesus juxtaposes the law of Moses ("You have heard that it was said") with his own teachings that begin, "But I say to you." Jesus concludes his new interpretations of the Jewish Law by saying "Be perfect, therefore, as your heavenly father is perfect" (Matt 5:48).

Bart Ehrman has appropriately characterized the Gospel of Matthew as presenting "Jesus, the Jewish Messiah." It is, nevertheless, important to note the universal tone at the end of the gospel, when the risen Lord appears to his disciples for the final time (Matt 28:16–20):

> [16]Now the eleven disciples went to Galilee, to the mountain to which Jesus had directed them. [17]When they saw him, they worshiped him; but some doubted. [18]And Jesus came and said to them, "All authority in heaven and on earth has been given to me. [19]Go therefore and make disciples of all nations, baptizing them in the name of the Father and of the Son and of the Holy Spirit, [20]and teaching them to obey everything that I have commanded you. And remember, I am with you always to the end of the age."

If the Gospel of Matthew was written in Antioch sometime between 80 and 90, it affords meaningful insight into the way in which Antioch Christianity evolved in the period following the confrontation between Peter and Paul some thirty or so years earlier.

If Matthew was writing primarily to Jewish Christians or Christian Jews in Antioch about 80–90, he was apparently addressing some of the circumstances that distinguished them from the emergent Pharisaic Judaism of the period after the fall of Jerusalem. This Antioch church, composed of both Jewish Christians and Gentile Christians, was apparently still struggling with the issue of the relationship of the church to the Jewish Torah.

THE GOSPEL OF LUKE

Like the Gospel of Mark and the Gospel of Matthew, the Gospel of Luke is built on earlier written sources:

1. As we observed at several points earlier in this book, the author of the anonymous Gospel of Luke used a version of the Gospel of Mark as one of his primary sources.[14] Luke used a great deal of the material in Mark, generally but not always in the same order.

2. In addition, Luke used a written source, called Q (= German *Quelle* or "source") containing about 240-260 verses of sayings of Jesus, a source that was also known in some form to the author of the Gospel of Matthew. No copies of Q survive, but scholars have reconstructed the hypothetical source Q with a fair measure of confidence.

3. Luke also had access to other material, collectively known as L or Special Luke, which he also wove into the Markan framework.

    a. Some of the material in so-called L or Special Luke is sayings material that is not found in either Mark or Q but that is unique to Luke. Some of this material, especially individual sayings, could have been in the redaction of Q available to Luke. In addition, some sayings identified as L or Special Luke may have been available to Luke in one or more additional written sources. Material in L includes not only individual sayings but also:

        1. Miracle Stories:

            The Raising of the Widow's Son at Nain (Luke 7:11–17)

            The Healing of the Crippled Woman (Luke 13:10–17)

            The Healing of the Man with Dropsy (Luke 14:1–6)

            The Healing of Ten Lepers (Luke 17:11–19)

        2. Parables:

            The Good Samaritan (Luke 10:29–37)

            The Barren Fig Tree (Luke 13:6–9)

            The Lost Coin (Luke 15:8–10)

            The Prodigal Son and His Brothers (Luke 15:11–32)

            The Dishonest Manager (Luke 16:1–9)

            The Rich Man and Lazarus (Luke 16:19–31)

            The Widow and the Unjust Judge (Luke 18:1–8)

            The Pharisee and the Tax Collector (Luke 18:9–14)

        3. Pronouncement Stories:

            Forgiving the Sinful Woman (Luke 7:36–50)

            Jesus and Beelzebul (Luke 11:14–50)

---

14. The version of the Gospel of Mark available to Luke was obviously not identical to the version available to Matthew. No two manuscripts of the gospels, as they have come down to us, are ever identical. Hence, we cannot know precisely what the manuscripts of Mark that were available to Matthew and Luke looked like, word for word.

Calling for Repentance (13:1–5)

    b. Luke also had available to him written narratives about the birth of John the Baptist and Jesus and about Jesus' early childhood (Luke 1–2), material that is unrelated to the birth narrative found in Matt 1–2.

    c. In addition, Luke also had access to stories of the appearance of the risen Jesus in and around Jerusalem (Luke 24), material that is quite different from the resurrection stories found in Matt 28.

The material referred to collectively as L or Special Luke may, therefore, have been from six or more different written sources: four or more sources containing sayings, miracle stories, parables, and pronouncement stories; birth and infancy narratives; and an account of resurrection appearances in and around Jerusalem.

A comparison of the birth and resurrection stories in Matthew and Luke reveals their independent character and, hence, the fact that they used different sources:

The Birth Narratives in Matthew and Luke

Events	Matthew	Luke
Genealogy of Jesus	Matt 1:1–17	Luke 3:23–28
Birth of John the Baptist Foretold		Luke 1:5–25
Birth of Jesus Foretold		Luke 1:26–38
Mary Visits Elizabeth		Luke 1:39–56
Birth of John the Baptist		Luke 1:57–80
Birth of Jesus	Matt 1:18–25	Luke 2:1–7
Visit of the Magi	Matt 2:1–12	
Shepherds and Angels		Luke 2:8–20
Jesus is Presented in the Temple		Luke 2:21–40
Escape to Egypt	Matt 2:13–15	
Massacre of the Children	Matt 2:16–18	
Return to Nazareth	Matt 2:19–23	
Jesus in the Temple at Age 12		Luke 2:41–42

Although most of us are accustomed to hearing a birth story that is a conflation of material in Matthew and Luke, the two birth narratives are actually very different (as the table indicates) and in some respects even contradictory. Both Matthew and Luke agree that Mary and Joseph were Jesus "parents," that Jesus was born of a virgin, and that the birth took place in Bethlehem. That is the limit of their agreement.

Whereas Matthew assumes that the family was originally living in Bethlehem, then fled to Egypt, and thereafter moved to Nazareth, Luke assumes that Joseph and Mary were originally living in Nazareth and, therefore, devised the census of Caesar Augustus as a device to get the family to Bethlehem in time for Jesus' birth. The traditions of the virgin birth and the birth in Bethlehem were apparently developed relatively early in fulfillment of passages in the Hebrew scriptures: respectively Isa 7:14b; and Mic 5:2 combined with 2 Sam 5:2b:

Isa 7:14b

> Look, the young woman is with child and shall bear a son, and shall call him Immanuel.
>
> [n.b.: The Greek Septuagint version of this passage, which would have been available in the early Christian community, probably read something like: "Look, the virgin shall conceive and bear a son, and they shall name him Emmanuel."]

Mic 5:2

> But you, O Bethlehem of Ephrathah,
> who are one of the little clans of Judah,
> from you shall come forth for me
> one who is to rule in Israel,
> whose origin is from of old,
> from ancient days.

2 Sam 5:2b

> The LORD said to you:
> "It is you who shall be shepherd of my people Israel,
> you who shall be ruler over Israel."

The table above indicates that most of the components of the birth and infancy narratives appear in only one gospel. There is essentially no overlap whatsoever between the accounts in Matthew and Luke, suggesting that these stories developed independently by building on the historical recollection that Mary was Jesus' mother and Joseph his father. Both gospels share the legend of the virgin birth (probably from a misreading of Isa 7:14 carried forward in oral tradition) and the legendary belief that Jesus should have been born in Bethlehem in fulfillment of the scripture in Mic 5:2. As we have seen in an earlier chapter, it is more likely that Jesus was actually born in Nazareth, as he was always known as Jesus of Nazareth.

Just as Matthew and Luke contain independent stories about Jesus' birth, so too do they contain independent stories about his resurrection, revealing their independence and, hence, the fact that they used different sources:

The Resurrection Narratives in Matthew and Luke

Events	Matthew	Luke
Resurrection of Jesus	Matt 28:1–10	Luke 24:1–12
Report of the Guard at the Tomb	Matt 28:11–15	

Events	Matthew	Luke
Walk to Emmaus		Luke 24:13–35
Appearance to the Disciples		Luke 24:36–49
Commissioning of the Disciples	Matt 28:16–20	
Ascension of Jesus		Luke 24:50–53

The similarities between the accounts in Matthew and Luke are essentially limited to the material about the arrival of Mary Magdalene and other women at the empty tomb, material that both Matthew and Luke drew from the brief account in Mark 16:1–8. Yet even in their treatment of Mark's material they differ: "the young man" whom the women found in the empty tomb in Mark 16:5 becomes "an angel" in Matt 28:2–5 and "two men" in Luke 24:4 (and "two angels" in John 20:12). Although Matthew assumes appearances to the disciples in Galilee (Matt 28:10), Luke reports appearances only near or in Jerusalem (Luke 24:13-49). Moreover, only Matthew reports the commissioning of the disciples (Matt 28:16–20), and only Luke reports Jesus' ascension into heaven (Luke 24:50–53). Apart from the material both Matthew and Luke knew from Mark 16:1–8, the authors of the gospels of Matthew and Luke clearly had access to very different and presumably relatively late legendary accounts of Jesus' resurrection appearances.

As in the case of the Gospel of Matthew, it may be argued that the Gospel of Luke can be understood as a second edition of the Gospel of Mark, an "updated" version that was written to include material that was unknown when the first edition was written in Antioch in about 67 but that was now available and that, therefore, demanded a revised version of Mark's gospel. This point is made quite clearly in Luke 1:1–4, when the author refers to the many who had written before him.

Luke gives no direct indication of its time and place of composition or of the audience to whom his gospel was addressed. Assuming that Luke made use of the Gospel of Mark, it was obviously written sometime after Mark. Moreover, the following passages probably refer to the destruction of Jerusalem by the Roman Titus in 70, at times echoing scriptural forewarnings of God's earlier judgments:

> Luke 19:41–44
>
> [41]As [Jesus] came near and saw the city, he wept over it, [42]saying "If you, even you, had only recognized on this day the things that make for peace! But now they are hidden from your eyes. [43]Indeed, the days will come upon you, when your enemies will set up ramparts around you and surround you, and hem you in on every side. [44]They will crush you to the ground, you and your children

within you, and they will not leave within you one stone upon another; because you did not recognize the time of your visitation from God."

Luke 21:20–24

> [20]"When you see Jerusalem surrounded by armies, then know that its desolation has come near. [21]Then those in Judea must flee to the mountains, and those inside the city must leave it, and those out in the country must not enter it; [22]for these are days of vengeance, as a fulfillment of all that is written. [23]Woe to those who are pregnant and to those who are nursing infants in those days! For there will be great distress on the earth and wrath against this people; [24]they will fall by the edge of the sword and be taken away as captives among all nations; and Jerusalem will be trampled on by the Gentiles, until the times of the Gentiles are fulfilled.

The dating of Luke is particularly challenging. Certainly, sometime after 80 is most likely, but how much later than 80 is not at all clear—certainly not later than 130, but that leaves about a fifty year margin. The place of composition is also uncertain: certainly not Palestine, and probably not Antioch (like Mark and Matthew). Luke is obviously more focused on the Gentile mission than either Mark or Matthew. Corinth is a reasonable candidate,[15] but so too are Rome and Asia Minor, and perhaps other cities that served as important centers of Gentile Christianity. Luke is, of course, volume one of the larger work Luke-Acts, but acknowledging that does not help us to locate the gospel more specifically in either time or place. The fact that the author of Luke-Acts knows a great deal about Ephesus, especially in Acts, suggests Ephesus as a possible place of composition.

We must be mindful of the fact that the Gospel of Luke is only half of the larger work Luke-Acts that was probably first written on two scrolls simply as a matter of convenience. The separation of the two volumes and the placing of the Gospel of Luke separately among the gospels probably did not conform to the author's original intention. The Gospel of John now separates Luke from Acts in the Christian canon.

Luke is the only gospel that explicitly acknowledges that its author had access to earlier sources:

> [1:1]Since many have undertaken to set down an orderly account of the events that have been fulfilled among us, . . . [3]I too decided, after investigating everything carefully from the very first, to write an orderly account . . .

Following a formal prologue and dedication of the gospel to Theophilus (Luke 1:1–4), Luke begins his gospel with birth narratives about both John the Baptist and Jesus (Luke 1:5–2:52, material he presumably drew from L) and then proceeds in the main body of his gospel to pick up material from Mark, Q, and L:

Luke 3:1–9:50 follows Mark 1:2–9:50 closely;

---

15. The tradition that the Gospel of Luke was written in Achaia survives from the second half of the second century in the so-called *Anti-Marcionite Gospel Prologues* (Koester, *Ancient Christian Gospels*, 335.

Luke 9:51–18:14 uses material drawn primarily from Q and L;

Luke 18:15–24:12 follows closely material in Mark 10:13–16:8; and

Luke 24:13–53 goes beyond the Markan source to include resurrection appearances from L, the final portion of which (the story of the ascension in Luke 24:50–53) ties Luke with Acts through the repetition of the ascension story in Acts 1:6–11.

Not surprisingly, Ehrman identifies his chapter on Luke as "Jesus, the Savior of the World," emphasizing thereby Luke's interest in and special focus on the Christian mission to the Gentiles, in both his gospel and in the Acts of the Apostles.

THE GOSPEL OF JOHN

The Gospel of John is significantly different from the gospels of Matthew, Mark, and Luke, and that difference has been obvious since antiquity. Although John follows the synoptic gospels' practice of telling a purported story of Jesus' life, ministry, teaching, death, and resurrection, the tone and character of the Gospel of John are very different from that of the synoptic gospels. If it is appropriate to refer to the synoptics as "theologized history," then the Gospel of John might properly be characterized as "historicized theology." The Gospel of John has little to no interest in history per se, at least as we understand history today as a narrative account that provides a chronological record of what likely transpired at some time in the past. In fact, John could be characterized as so unhistorical as to be, in fact, anti-historical.

There is little to nothing in John that we can identify as history and little to nothing that reflects the teaching of the historical Jesus. If we apply the criterion of dissimilarity to the sayings attributed to Jesus in the Gospel of John, there is virtually nothing among those sayings that can be considered as likely authentic. The Jesus of John is, instead, a mythic, self-proclaiming God-man, who bears little or no resemblance to the Jesus of Nazareth we attempted to reconstruct in earlier chapters from evidence in the gospels of Matthew, Mark, and Luke. We debated earlier in this book whether Jesus was an apocalyptic prophet or a teacher or wisdom. In the Gospel of John, Jesus is neither.

John's developed Christology is evident from the very beginning of the gospel. The Gospel of John opens with a prologue that introduces the central theme of the gospel: namely, that the divine Son of God entered the world, was rejected by many, but has granted eternal life to all who will receive him. In its original form, the prologue or a pre-Johannine Christian hymn underlying the prologue may have read (John 1:1–4, 10–14, 16):

> [1]In the beginning there was the Logos, and the Logos was close to God, and the Logos was divine. [2]The Logos was in the beginning together with God. [3]All things came into being through the Logos, and without the Logos nothing came

> into being. What has come into being ⁴in the Logos was life, and the life was the light of humankind. The light shines in the darkness, and the darkness did not comprehend it.
> ¹⁰The Logos was in the world, and the world came into being through the Logos; yet the world did not know the Logos. ¹¹The Logos came to what was its own, and its own people did not accept it. ¹²But to all who received the Logos, . . . it gave power to become children of God, ¹³who were born, not of blood nor of the will of the flesh nor of the will of humankind, but of God.
> ¹⁴And the Logos became flesh and pitched its tent among us, and we have seen his glory, the glory as of a father's only son, full of grace and truth. . . .
> ¹⁶From his fullness we have all received, grace upon grace. (my translation)

The reader sees immediately in these opening verses the significant difference between John and the synoptics. Yet the actual meaning of these verses is generally lost to the modern reader. The opening words, of course, recall Gen 1:1 "In the beginning, when God created the heavens and the earth . . . ." But in John it was the Logos, the divine Word, that was in the beginning. The Greek says λόγος (or *logos*), which probably conjured up in the ancient reader (or listener) multiple meanings. Logos would have reminded Hellenistic Jewish readers or listeners of the divine word spoken by God at creation, through which God had created the heavens and the earth. It might also have reminded Hellenistic Jewish readers or listeners of the divine word that God had spoken to Israel's prophets. But it would also have reminded more Hellenized Gentile Christian readers or listeners of the Logos, which in Greek philosophy was the divine principle or divine reason that provided order to the universe. There is, of course, no single word in English that can possibly communicate the richness of the concept of Logos, this Logos that was close to God (John 1:1b), that was itself divine (John 1:1c), that was in the beginning with God (John 1:2), and by means of which God created everything that has ever come into being (John 1:3).

The prologue goes on to say that in the Logos there was divine life (John 1:4a), and the divine life was the light of everyone (John 1:4b). In verse 5, the word translated as "comprehend" can also mean "overcome," implying that the darkness could not "destroy" the light, but neither could the darkness fully "understand" the light. That ambiguity might be preserved if we translate verse 5: "The light shines in the darkness, but the darkness did not master the light," a feeble and awkward effort to capture in inadequate English the rich nuances of the original Greek. The Logos came into the world (John 1:10a), presumably now in the person of Jesus of Nazareth, but the world did not recognize the Logos (John 1:10b). But, John says, that Jesus gave, to all who believe in his name, the power to become children of God (John 1:12).

Verse 14 is the heart of the hymn: "And the Logos became flesh and lived among us," literally "and pitched its tent in our midst," an allusion to the temporary nature of the visit of the divine Logos in the person of Jesus of Nazareth. John introduces here what later became the Christian concept of the Incarnation, the "in-fleshness" of the divine Logos, who (or which?) revealed "his (or its?) glory, the glory of a father's only son" (John 1:14b). This revelation of the incarnate divine Logos in the God-man Jesus of Nazareth has made God known to humankind.

What follows in the Gospel of John is a series of stories, miracle stories, and monologues through which Jesus, the incarnation of the divine Logos, reveals the glory of all that we can possibly know about God.

It could be argued that the Jesus of the Gospel of John, who proclaims himself rather than the message of the synoptic gospels, bears no resemblance to the historical Jesus of Nazareth. Examples in the Gospel of John of a Jesus who focuses on his own identity in ways that are reminiscent of the divine I AM in Exod 3:14 include:

I am the bread of life that came down from heaven	John 6:35, 41, 48, 51
I am the light of the world	John 8:12; 9:5; 12:46
I am the Son of Man	John 8:28
Before Abraham was, I am	John 8:58
I am the gate for the sheep	John 10:7, 9
I am the good shepherd	John 10:14
I am the resurrection and the life	John 11:25
I am the way, and the truth, and the life	John 14:6
I am the true vine	John 15:1, 5

These were, of course, not claims of the historical Jesus, but they are claims of the risen Christ of the Gospel of John, because it is the risen Christ who walks through the pages of the Gospel of John. Although John places these words on the lips of Jesus in his gospel, he is actually claiming on behalf of the church that Jesus is the bread of life; Jesus is the light of the world; Jesus is the resurrection and the life; etc.

The Gospel of John has no parables, a teaching device found in the synoptic gospels and probably employed by the historical Jesus. Instead of the brief sayings that we find in the synoptic gospels, we find in the Gospel of John extended monologues on Jesus' lips, proclaiming his relationship to God and the need for his followers to believe in him. The Jesus of the Gospel of John is not the historical Jesus of Nazareth. He is from the very outset of the gospel the risen Christ of the church's developed *keryma* of the second or third generation of Christians in the community to which John is writing.

Although the Gospel of John may not tell us much about the historical Jesus, it certainly says a great deal about the Johannine community. The Gospel of John may have been written toward the end of the first century in a Christian community that had already undergone or was currently undergoing a painful separation from the Judaism to which many of its members had probably at one time belonged. Several passages in the gospel suggest such a separation from or break with Judaism:

John 7:13

Yet no one would speak openly about [Jesus] for fear of the Jews.

John 9:22

[The parents of the blind man whom Jesus had healed] said [they did not know who had healed their son] because they were afraid of the Jews; for the Jews had already agreed that anyone who confessed Jesus to be the Messiah would be put out of the synagogue.

John 12:42

Nevertheless, many, even of the authorities, believed in [Jesus]. But because of the Pharisees they did not confess it, for fear that they would be put out of the synagogue.

John 16:2

[The Jews] will put you out of the synagogues. Indeed, an hour is coming when those who kill you will think that by doing so they are offering worship to God.

John 19:38a

After these things, Joseph of Arimathea, who was a disciple of Jesus, though a secret one because of his fear of the Jews, asked Pilate to let him take away the body of Jesus.

John 20:19

When it was evening on that day, the first day of the week, and the doors of the house where the disciples had met were locked for fear of the Jews, Jesus came and stood among them and said, "Peace be with you."

The hostility between Jesus and the Jews in the Gospel of John probably mirrors a conflict between Jews (most especially authorities of the synagogue) and the Jewish Christian community in which and to which this gospel was probably addressed. The story of Jesus' encounter with the Pharisee Nicodemus (John 3: 1–21) probably addresses the question of the encounter of members of the Johannine community with Pharisees.

The purpose of the Gospel of John is summarized at the end of what was probably the original version of the gospel in John 20:30–31:

> [30]Now Jesus did many other signs in the presence of his disciples, which are not written in this book. [31]But these are written so that you may come to believe that Jesus is the Messiah, the Son of God, and that through believing you may have life in his name.

This gospel was written to encourage its readers (or, more probably, its listeners) to believe that Jesus was the Jewish messiah, the Son of God, at a time when many in the community were presumably suffering persecution, probably from the leadership of the local synagogue to which they had earlier belonged.

Like the synoptic gospels, the Gospel of John is anonymous; and as in the case of the synoptics, the author of the Gospel of John presumably made use of earlier written sources, but not the same sources as were available to the authors of the gospels of Mark, Matthew, and Luke, with a couple of exceptions. Neither did the author of the Gospel of John likely know the synoptic gospels, although there is some overlap. If anything, he may have known some stories that appear also in the synoptic gospels, such as the Feeding of the Five Thousand (John 6:1–15; cf. Matt 14:13–21; Mark 6:32–44; Luke 9:10–17) and the Walking on the Water (John 6:16–21; cf. Matt 14:22–33; Mark 6:45–52; no parallel in Luke). The "coupling" of these two stories in both Mark (6:32–44, 45–52) and John (6:1–15, 16–21) suggests that these two stories were apparently so coupled in an earlier written source that may have been available to the authors of both gospels.

Moreover, similarities between the passion narratives in Mark 14–16 and John 18–20 suggest that John probably used a written source similar to a source available to the author of the Gospel of Mark, both of which were obviously developed on the basis of a Christian interpretation of the Hebrew scriptures.[16]

Among the most obvious written sources used by the author of the Gospel of John was a collection of miracle stories not unlike what we saw previously in the Gospel of Mark. Such a written source is evident in Mark 4:35–6:52, which includes the following six miracle stories:

Mark 4:35–42	Jesus Stills the Storm
Mark 5:1–20	Jesus Heals the Gerasene Demoniac
Mark 5:22–24, 35–43	Jesus Raises Jairus's Daughter from the Dead
Mark 5:25–34	Jesus Heals the Woman with a Hemmorhage
Mark 6:30–44	Jesus Feeds the Five Thousand
Mark 6:45–54	Jesus Walks on the Water

The written source of John's miracle stories is even more transparent. Following the first of seven signs (σημεία, *semeia*), The Changing of the Water into Wine at the Wedding in Cana in John 2:1–10, John says (in John 2:11): "Jesus did this, the *first* of his signs in Cana of Galilee, and revealed his glory; and his disciples believed in him." Likewise following the second of Jesus' signs, The Healing of the Official's Son in John 4:43–53, John says (in John 4:54): "Now this was the *second* sign that Jesus did after coming from Judea to Galilee." The complete collection of Jesus' *signs* in the Gospel of John includes the following seven stories:

John 2:1–11	Jesus Changes the Water to Wine
John 4:43–53	Jesus Heals the Official's Son

---

16. The apocryphal *Gospel of Peter* may also have had access to such a written source (see chapter 13).

John 5:2–9	Jesus Heals the Lame Man
John 6:5–14	Jesus Feeds the Five Thousand
John 6:16–25	Jesus Walks on the Water
John 9:1–7	Jesus Heals the Blind Man
John 11:1–45	Jesus Raises Lazarus from the Dead

As Helmut Koester says,

> "The miracles of Jesus [in the Gospel of John] are more than miracles, they are epiphanies," manifestations or appearances of the God-Man Jesus of Nazareth "not as magician but as a god."[17]

As mentioned earlier, this *signs* material comes to a conclusion in John 20:30, which probably marked the end of the original gospel—"And Jesus did many other signs in the presence of his disciples, which are not written in this book."

In its present form, the Gospel of John has some serious "fault lines" or material that is evidently out of order. The first such section is John 4–7. John 4:54 states that Jesus performed his second sign, the Healing of the Official's Son (John 4:46–53), "after coming from Judea to Galilee." In John 5:1, "Jesus went up to Jerusalem" for "a festival of the Jews." Yet in John 6:1, "Jesus went to the other side of the Sea of Galilee, also called the Sea of Tiberias"; and John 7:1 reports that "Jesus went about in Galilee. He did not wish to go about in Judea because the Jews were looking for an opportunity to kill him." These difficulties would be resolved if the text were rearranged as John chapters 4, 6, 5, 7, but such a reordering probably does not address satisfactorily the problem of why these "fault lines" exist.

A second such "fault line" may be evident in John 14:30–31 and 18:1, two separate bits of material that may actually belong together:

> [14:30]I will no longer talk much with you, for the ruler of this world is coming. He has no power over me; [31]but I do as the Father has commanded me, so that the world may know that I love the Father. Rise, let us be on our way. . . . [18:1]After Jesus had spoken these words, he went out with his disciples across the Kidron Valley to a place where there was a garden, which he and his disciples entered.

Chapters 15–17, which separate this material, continue Jesus' farewell discourses in spite of the rather abrupt "Rise, let us be on our way" in John 14:31. Clearly, material is out of order, or perhaps chapters 15–17 are a later interpolation into the gospel, added at the time when John 21 was also added to a gospel that almost certainly originally ended with John 20:31.

A few verses of the Gospel of John appear in the oldest surviving papyrus fragment of any Christian writing. Specifically, John 18:31–33, 37–38 survives—perhaps from as early as the first half of the second century—in a papyrus fragment known as

---

17. Koester, *Ancient Christian Gospels*, 205.

p^{52}, which was discovered in Egypt in about 1920.[18] Another Egyptian papyrus know as p^{66} containing almost the entire text of the Gospel of John was probably written in ca. 200, and a portion of John 1–15 survives in p^{75}, a papyrus text from the third century. That the Gospel of John was apparently widely known in Egypt at an early date does not necessarily indicate that the gospel was written in Egypt, although I find the possibility of an Egyptian (Alexandrian) origin of the gospel appealing, inasmuch as the Christology of the Gospel of John appealed to many Gnostic Christians who lived in Egypt.

Second century tradition places the writing of the Gospel of John in Ephesus, and this is possible, although by no means certain. For whatever reason, Ignatius of Antioch, writing in the early second century to the church at Ephesus, is noticeably silent about the Gospel of John in his *Epistle to the Ephesians*. Ignatius may not have known the gospel, or he may have questioned its "orthodoxy."

The church at Ephesus was presumably established and/or nurtured by Paul and some of his missionary traveling companions; yet Johannine Christianity is qualitatively different from Pauline Christianity—to be sure not an impossible evolution over a thirty or forty year period between Paul's visits to Ephesus and the writing of the gospel. Is it possible that Pauline Christianaity lost out to Johanning Christianity in Ephesus?

As for its date of composition, the gospel's highly developed Christology suggests a date late in the first century, probably in the 90s, or maybe even in the first decade of the second century. The dating of the gospel affects the dating of the three Johannine letters (1, 2, and 3 John), which were presumably written sometime after the gospel.

Referring to the Gospel of John, Bart Ehrman entitles his chapter "Jesus, the Man Sent from Heaven." This phrase captures the essence of the gospel and of the Jesus of John's gospel. I would, however, amend Ehrman's title to read: "Jesus, the God-Man Sent from Heaven."

CONCLUSIONS

It is apparent that the process that resulted in the writing of our canonical gospels was long and complex, although we can only surmise the details of that process based on evidence within the gospels themselves. Jesus died in about 30, and oral tradition about Jesus certainly started to circulate almost immediately after his death. After Peter and others "saw" Jesus following his death and claimed that God had raised Jesus from the dead and exalted him to his right hand, stories about Jesus obviously spread even more widely within the circle of Jesus' followers.

It is, of course, not self-evident exactly how tradition about Jesus originated and evolved and what forms it took at what time. We can reconstruct that process only

---

18. Some scholars have recently rejected this early dating of p52 and have, thereby, pushed the possible date of composition of the Gospel of John into the second century. The dating of ancient papyri is based on paleographical evidence, which is not necessarily definitive.

from the written documents, our gospels, that survive from the period between about 67 and about 100, two and three generations removed from the "events" ostensibly reported in the gospels.

The gospels of Matthew, Mark, Luke, and John have traditionally been regarded as the best sources for reconstructing the life and ministry of Jesus, but their value as history is not clear. These gospels are all anonymous writings; they do not reflect the reliable written testimony of eyewitnesses, whether unbiased or not, to actual events in the life and ministry of Jesus. The gospels are rather four very different theological portraits crafted by second and perhaps third generation followers of the Jesus movement, and they were written in different Christian communities for very different audiences.

From the four canonical gospels, we almost certainly learn more about their authors and the audiences to which they were written than we will ever know about Jesus of Nazareth, their purported subject. These four theological images of Jesus pose serious challenges for modern historians, when they try to move from the gospels to reconstruct the Jesus of history, a quest that may actually be a lost cause. The gospels are not "history," as we understand history today. They are *kerygma* or proclamation, and their purpose was not to preserve an accurate record of Jesus' life and ministry. The gospels are what their name suggests: proclamations of the "good news," the Christian *kerygma* of the second and third generation of believers.

The earliest testimony about the four canonical gospels survives from the mid- to late-second century, and it is largely unreliable and presents a romanticized and legendary picture of what Christians of that period wanted to believe about these four gospels. Mid-second century testimony from Marcion, Justin Martyr, and Tatian demonstrates that the four gospels had no canonical "status" either in the mid-second century, either in the Roman church, where they all lived, or anywhere else for that matter. On the contrary, these authors and presumably others as well were still involved in rewriting, editing, and harmonizing two or three or four of these gospels, a process that continued in subsequent generations as well.

Some of the building blocks of the gospel tradition are, however, evident within the written gospels themselves. Those building blocks consisted, perhaps initially, of a written Passion Narrative (a story of events leading up to the suffering, death, and resurrection of Jesus), built not on historical memory, but on a systematic search through the Hebrew scriptures for *testimonia* or "proof texts" on which the story of Jesus' passion was initially built and subsequently developed. Such a written Passion Narrative might have been used as part of a liturgical celebration during the week leading up to the annual commemoration of Jesus' resurrection, later known as Easter.

It was probably within the context of the preaching and the teaching of individual early Christian churches that followers of Jesus also began independently to formulate oral traditions about the Lord, some built at least in part on historical memory, in the forms of sayings, pronouncement stories, parables, miracle stories, legends, and myths about Jesus, imitating oral and literary forms known from Jewish, Greek, and

Roman oral and written traditions and literature. But, from the outset, it appears that historical reliability, as we understand that term, was not a primary consideration of those who told and later collected stories about Jesus.

Some of these units of oral tradition likely found their way into written sources, so that we find in our gospels evidence for the existence of written collections of parables, written collections of pronouncement stories, written collections of miracle stories, written collections of purported sayings of Jesus, written accounts of Jesus' birth and infancy, and written accounts of appearances of Jesus following his death.

Such written sources served as the building blocks of our canonical gospels, but they now survive only in scholarly reconstructions based on evidence within the written gospels themselves. We have no ancient Passion Narrative used in an early Christian liturgy; no manuscript of Q (the hypothetical sayings source known to the authors of Matthew and Luke); we have no manuscript of a collection of parables available to Mark, Matthew, or Luke; no manuscript of a collection of miracle stories or of "signs" of Jesus known to Mark, Matthew, Luke, or John; etc. Yet evidence in our canonical gospels points to the existence of such written sources during the first decades of the early church.

The identification of the building blocks of the written gospels is a scholarly construct formulated within the limits of historical reason over a period several generations, based upon knowledge of the growth of the Jesus movement over several generations. We can paint this process with broad strokes, although we cannot know in detail how it unfolded over the forty to seventy or eighty years before the writing of our four gospels.

The task of identifying the dates and the places of composition of the four gospels is especially challenging. There are internal clues, for what they are worth. But none of these clues points clearly and unequivocally in a single direction. Equally competent scholars often read the same evidence in a very different way and, therefore, reach different conclusions. The challenge and the disagreement lie not in poor scholarship but in the paucity of evidence that is so often available to scholars.

With some reservation, I suggested in this chapter that

1. the Gospel of Mark was written anonymously in Antioch of Syria for a mixed Jewish-Christian and Gentile-Christian community in about 67;

2. the Gospel of Matthew was written anonymously in Antioch of Syria, probably as an "updated" version of the Gospel of Mark, primarily for a Jewish-Christian community in about 80–90;

3. the Gospel of Luke was written anonymously in Corinth for a Gentile-Christian community in about 85–110; and

4. the Gospel of John was written anonymously in Ephesus or Alexandria for a formerly Jewish-Christian community in about 90–110.

It is, of course, easier to attempt to date the gospels, at least approximately, inasmuch as scholars generally offer a range of dates of composition. It is far more difficult to pinpoint the places of composition, especially in the cases of the gospels of Luke and John.

We also understand better than before that the authors of our four gospels were collectors of existing oral and written traditions. In that respect they copied and edited their sources; they were redactors. But we also know that the evangelists were much more than editors of earlier sources. They were truly creative authors and not just copyists, because they cast very different stamps on their own works.

We have already shown that the earliest evangelist, whom we call Mark, probably had access to a written Passion Narrative and to written collections of parables, miracle stories, pronouncement stories, sayings of Jesus, and myths and legends about Jesus. But it was Mark who gave order to the material he used and thereby created a seeming chronology of "events." And it was Mark who framed his gospel with the motif of the Messianic Secret, a device that Mark needed because he was doing something very different and creative from what came before.

We know from Paul (Rom 1:4) that Jesus was "declared to be Son of God with power . . . by resurrection from the dead." This *adoptionist* theology (God *adopted* Jesus as his Son) appears also in Acts 2:32–36, which states that God raised up Jesus and exalted him to his right hand and *made* him Lord and Messiah. Mark took this earlier Christian *adoptionist* theology and moved the time of Jesus' adoption backward from the resurrection/exaltation to Jesus' baptism by John (Mark 1:11). In so doing, Mark illustrates that historical fidelity is not his concern. His objective is rather to illustrate that Jesus' entire ministry was messianic, even if Jesus' followers did not understand it and did not realize it until *after* Jesus' death. Mark's gospel, his "good news," was about Jesus the Messiah, not about Jesus who *became* the Messiah by virtue of his resurrection. To the extent that there is history in Mark, at least as we are inclined to understand history, it is obviously subordinated to Mark's theological scheme.

In the cases of both Matthew and Luke, Jesus' messiahship is traced by both gospels back to Jesus' birth, although the two gospels contain very different birth narratives. It is evident that the birth and infancy narratives in Matthew and Luke have no value whatsoever as history, but they make the important theological point that, even before Jesus' birth, God identified and consecrated Jesus for a special mission. Like the sixth century BCE prophet Jeremiah, who cites the word of God to him at the time of his call and commission (Jer 1:5),

> "Before I (God) formed you (Jeremiah) in the womb I knew you,
> and before you were born I consecrated you,"

so too God already knew and consecrated Jesus in his mother's womb. Not because there was an accurate record of Jesus' birth, but rather in fulfillment of the prophecy in Isa 7:14, the spirit of God impregnated Jesus' mother when she was still a virgin. There is no doubt that the texts of Jeremiah and Isaiah were known to the evangelists or to their precursors, whose sources they may have used. In any case, the authors of the gospels of Matthew and Luke took considerable liberties for the sake of advancing a Christology that was clearly "higher" than what they found in their Markan source. Unlike Mark, who claimed that Jesus was *adopted* as Son of God at the time of his baptism by John, the authors of the gospels of Matthew and Luke claim that Jesus was Son of God from the moment of his conception.

Matthew and Luke freely edited their Markan source. They even modified or changed alleged sayings of Jesus, a practice that continued well into the mid-second century with Marcion using an abbreviated version of Luke, and Justin Martyr, Tatian, 2 Clement, and others using or composing harmonies of two, three, or four gospels. The evangelists were story-tellers not historians. They were creating Christian literature. History, as we understand that word, was never a criterion in the writing of any of the gospels. The gospels are first and foremost *kerygma*, and the evangelists make no pretense that they are writing anything other than gospels, theological proclamations about the "good news" about Jesus the Christ. The gospels are *kerygma*, not history, although elements of history survive within the *kerygma* at least in the earliest of our gospels.

The Gospel of John is a totally different matter. John traces Jesus' messiahship, indeed his divine Sonship to a time even before creation. It is the divine Logos that was with God from the beginning and that served as the very instrument of God's creation that became flesh in the person of the God-man Jesus of Nazareth. The exalted Christology of the Gospel of John essentially purges the gospel of any concern for history that may survive in the synoptic gospels. Apart from the broad strokes of the Passion Narrative, John has little interest in history, a fact that is already evident in the prologue to the gospel. Interestingly, John has no birth narratives but moves from the prologue directly to John's baptism, although Jesus is never actually baptized in the Gospel of John.

We should understand unequivocally from this chapter and the previous chapters on which this chapter is built that the canonical gospels are exactly what the church has called them: "gospels." They are nothing more and nothing less. They are literary creations designed by Christian writers to portray Jesus as Messiah, Lord, and Savior. They are not biographies, as we understand that term, and one must use the gospels carefully and critically in trying to recover the Jesus of history who lies somewhere behind them.

CHAPTER 13

EARLY CHRISTIAN GOSPELS, PART 2

NON-CANONICAL OR APOCRYPHAL GOSPELS

MATTHEW, MARK, LUKE, AND John are not the only early Christian gospels. There were perhaps another two dozen or perhaps even more additional gospels, some of which survive in names only, some in fragmentary form, and some in complete manuscripts, many of which are from relatively recent discoveries.

The second century was a time when competing forms of Christianity engaged in the process of self-definition, a tendency that resulted in the great variety of Christian literature from the period. The numerous gospels articulated faith positions of various sorts, an activity that some Christian leaders found problematic, resulting in efforts on the part of some church fathers to circumscribe the teachings of the faith.

As some Christians began to oppose certain movements or tendencies in the mid- to late-second century and throughout the third century, there were conscious efforts to suppress or destroy gospels that grew out of some of those movements. The attempt of some to define a *correct* or *orthodox* teaching resulted in identifying some movements or tendencies within the church as *incorrect* or *heterodox* (literally the *other teaching*), or as *heresies* (meaning *divisions* or *parties* or *factions*). At the time of the writing of most, if not all, of the gospels discussed in this chapter, the very concept of orthodoxy and heresy was anachronistic. It is only a later generation looking back at this period that used such labels to characterize movements that were vibrant and flourishng in the second century.

A look at some of the most important of the apocryphal gospels illustrates some of the various Christian tendencies or movements in the second century.

THE *GOSPEL OF THOMAS*

Until relatively recently, the earliest reference to the *Gospel of Thomas* was in a citation in Hippolytus (ca. 170–ca. 236) in his *Refutation of All Heresies* (5.7.20). Referring to the Naassenes' doctrine concerning "a happy nature" within a man, Hippolytus wrote:

> Concerning this (happy) nature, [the Naassenes] hand down an explicit passage, occurring in the Gospel inscribed "According to Thomas," expressing themselves

thus: "He who seeks me will find me in children from seven years old; for there concealed, I shall be revealed in the fourteenth aeon."

This alleged saying of Jesus, supposedly quoted by the Naassenes[1] from the *Gospel of Thomas*, appears nowhere in either the Coptic *Gospel of Thomas* or the *Infancy Gospel of Thomas*, at least in the forms in which these gospels have come down to us. The phrase "a little child of seven" appears in saying 4 of the Coptic *Gospel of Thomas*, a possible although by no means certain connection.

We now possess the complete text of the *Gospel of Thomas* in Sahidic Coptic in a papyrus codex discovered in 1945 near Nag Hammadi, Egypt (known in antiquity as Chenoboskion) on the west bank of the Nile, about 50 miles north of Luxor. Scholars generally agree that the Coptic text is a translation of an original Greek text. We now know that Oxyr Pap 1, 654, and 655, which were discovered in Egypt between 1897 and 1904 and which date from about 200, contain portions of the Greek text of the *Gospel of Thomas*. The fact that the sayings are found in three different papyri suggests that the *Gospel of Thomas* was in wide circulation in the second century.

Unlike the canonical gospels, the *Gospel of Thomas* is not a narrative account of the life and ministry of Jesus. It contains no mention of Jesus' birth, life, death, and resurrection. The *Gospel of Thomas* is rather a collection of 114 relatively short sayings with no systematic arrangement, but all attributed to "the Living Jesus."

As we observed previously, some of the sayings in the *Gospel of Thomas* are similar to and probably related to sayings in the canonical gospels. Some scholars are convinced that material shared by the *Gospel of Thomas* and the sayings source Q may come from an early stage in the development of the Jesus tradition. *Thomas* may have had access to some of the same traditions that were available to the collectors of the sayings in Q. In fact, some of the sayings in *Thomas* may be more original than the form in which these sayings appear in Q.[2] It is, however, less clear whether *Thomas* had access to sayings that found their way into written sources that were available to the author of the Gospel of Mark.[3]

The *Gospel of Thomas* may have been composed over a long period of time. In fact, there are indications that the author(s) of *Thomas* may have incorporated into this gospel several earlier collections of sayings. There is evidence of separate collections in the duplicate form of several sayings in *Thomas*:[4]

---

1. The Naassenes (probably from the Hebrew word *na'ash*, meaning snake), also known as Ophites (from the Greek word *ophis*, also meaning snake) were a Gnostic sect dating from about 100 CE (?) to the early third century. The Hebrew form of their name may reflect an early stage of Jewish Gnosticism or Jewish Christian Gnosticism. The Naassenes claimed to have received their teaching from Mariamne, a disciple of Jesus' brother James.

2. See e.g., Koester, *Ancient Christian Gospels*, 95, 98.

3. Koester, pp. 107–13.

4. Unless otherwise noted, citations from the *Gospel of Thomas* and other apocryphal gospels discussed in this chapter are from Miller, *The Complete Gospels*.

Gos Thos 3:1–5

¹Jesus said, "If your leaders say to you, 'Look, the (Father's) imperial rule is in the sky,' then the birds of the sky will precede you. ²If they say to you, 'It is in the sea,' then the fish will precede you. ³Rather, the (Father's) imperial rule is inside you and outside you. ⁴When you know yourselves, then you will be known, and you will understand that you are children of the living Father. ⁵But if you do not know yourselves, then you live in poverty, and you are the poverty."

Gos Thos 113:1–4

¹His disciples said to him, "When will the (Father's) imperial rule come?" ²"It will not come by watching for it. ³It will not be said, 'Look, here!' or 'Look, there!' ⁴Rather, the Father's imperial rule is spread out upon the earth, and people don't see it."

Gos Thos 5:1–2

¹Jesus said, "Know what is in front of your face, and what is hidden from you will be disclosed to you. ²For there is nothing hidden that won't be revealed."

Gos Thos 6:2–6

²Jesus said, "Don't lie, ³and don't do what you hate, ⁴because all things are disclosed before heaven. ⁵After all, there is nothing hidden that won't be revealed, ⁶and there is nothing covered up that will remain undisclosed.

Gos Thos 6:1

¹His disciples asked him and said to him, "Do you want us to fast? How should we pray? Should we give to charity? What diet should we observe?

Gos Thos 14:1–3

¹Jesus said to them, "If you fast, you will bring sin upon yourselves, ²and if you pray, you will be condemned, ³and if you give to charity, you will harm your spirits.

Gos Thos 48

Jesus said, "If two make peace with each other in a single house, they will say to the mountain, 'Move from here!' and it will move."

Gos Thos 106:1–2

¹Jesus said, "When you make the two into one, you will become children of Adam, ²and when you say, 'Mountain, move from here!' it will move."

Gos Thos 55:1–2

¹Jesus said, "Whoever does not hate father and mother cannot be my disciples, ²and whoever does not hate brothers and sisters, and carry the cross as I do, will not be worthy of me."

Gos Thos 101:1–3

¹"Whoever does not hate [father] and mother as I do cannot be my [disciple], ²and whoever does [not] love [father and] mother as I do cannot be my [disciple]. ³For my mother [. . .], but my true [mother] gave me life."

Gos Thos 56:1–2
¹Jesus said, "Whoever has come to know the world has discovered a carcass, ²and whoever has discovered a carcass, of that person the world is not worthy."

Gos Thos 80:1–2
¹Jesus said, "Whoever has come to know the world has discovered the body, ²and whoever has discovered the body, of that one the world is not worthy."

Gos Thos 111:3
³Does not Jesus say, "Those who have found themselves, of them the world is not worthy"?

Gos Thos 87:1–2
¹Jesus said, "How miserable is the body that depends on a body, ²and how miserable is the soul that depends on these two."

Gos Thos 112:1–2
¹Jesus said, "Damn the flesh that depends on the soul. ²Damn the soul that depends on the flesh."

Like the book of Psalms in the Old Testament, the existence of doublets (and in one instance a triplet) probably indicates the incorporation of more than one source into the *Gospel of Thomas*, at least in the form in which it exists in the Coptic text. In bringing together several sources, the collector(s) of earlier sources appear to have included some sayings more than once, probably as an oversight, and certainly without an eye to consistency.

As for its message, the *Gospel of Thomas* is sometimes "world renouncing" (64:12; 95; 110), and it sometimes retreats into an abstruse, austere, and mystical faith. Like the canonical gospels, *Thomas* speaks about the nature of God, the human self, and the world, and about the interrelationship among them. Although there may be Gnostic elements in the gospel, *Gospel of Thomas* is not a full-blown Gnostic gospel. Elements of Gnosticism appear in *Thomas*'s denunciation of the world and the body (*Gos Thos* 21:6; 56; 80; 111) and in a road map for finding the way home (*Gos Thos* 49; 50). Minimally, the *Gospel of Thomas* in its final form may represent an early stage in Christianity's flirtation with Gnosticism, a flirtation that resulted in a full-blown marriage with Gnosticism among many Christians by the late second and into the third century. The esoteric element in the *Gospel of Thomas*, a feature of some Gnostic literature, is evident in the gospel's opening words: "These are the *secret* sayings that the living Jesus spoke."

Scholars disagree regarding the date and place of composition of the *Gospel of Thomas*. Some date it in the first century and see in it a tradition that runs parallel to the hypothetical source Q. Others regard *Thomas* as later than and dependent on the canonical gospels and, therefore, date it between about 140 and 180. Some see it as a work written relatively early and added to over a period of time, accounting thereby for elements in the gospel that seem both early and late.

Unlike the canonical gospels, all of which are anonymous, the *Gospel of Thomas* actually claims in the prologue to have been written by one of Jesus' apostles:

> These are the secret sayings that Jesus spoke and Didymus Judas Thomas recorded.

The name Didymus Judas Thomas appears in this form only here and in the eastern Syrian *Acts of Thomas*, suggesting to most scholars an eastern Syrian origin for the gospel—at least in its final form.[5] By contrast, *Gos Thos* 12:2 appeals to the authority of Jesus' brother James the Just—not Thomas—suggesting perhaps a Jerusalem or Palestinian origin for an early layer of the gospel's tradition:

> Jesus said to them, "No matter where you are, you are to go to James the Just, for whose sake heaven and earth came into being.

Some date an early stratum of the gospel to Jerusalem as early as 60. However, Thomas tradition was especially popular in Edessa in eastern Syria, which may be where some later sayings were added to an early version of the gospel and where the gospel as a whole was first associated with Thomas. Clearly the gospel was also popular in Egypt in the second century, as the Greek Oxyrhynchus papyri and the subsequent Coptic translation attest.

THE *GOSPEL OF PETER*

The earliest reference to the *Gospel of Peter* comes from Serapion, who served as patriarch of Antioch from 191 to 211. In his *Church History* (6.12.2), Eusebius of Caesarea (ca. 260–339) quotes Serapion with regard to what he considered the docetic Gospel of Peter.[6]

The *Gospel of Peter* was known only by name until 1886, when archaeologists discovered a Greek codex of the gospel in the grave of a Christian monk in Akhmim on the east bank of the Nile in Upper Egypt. Moreover, two papyrus fragments discovered at Oxyrhynchus (identified as Oxyrhynchus Papyrus 2949) dated ca. 200 also belong to the *Gospel of Peter*, providing a latest possible date of composition of sometime before 200.

What survives as the *Gospel of Peter* is a passion narrative that begins with Pilate's washing of his hands and that gives an account of Jesus' trial, suffering, crucifixion,

---

5. The only portion of the name Didymus Judas Thomas that is actually a name is Judas. Didymus means "twin" in Greek, and Thomas is based on the Aramaic or Syriac word for "twin." The Judas referred to here is "Judas the brother of James" (Jude 1), and, therefore, the brother of Jesus. It was in eastern Syria (Edessa) that Jesus' brother Judas was regarded as a twin. In the *Acts of Thomas*, Judas is actually regarded as Jesus' twin-brother.

6. The term Docetism derives from the Greek verb δοκέω (*dokeo*), meaning "to seem." The docetic heresy was associated especially with Christian Gnostics, who maintained that Jesus was not fully human, that he only "seemed" to have a human body and only "seemed" to have died on the cross.

death, burial, and three appearances of the risen Lord: first, the guards at the tomb witness the resurrection; then, Mary Magdalene and the women find the empty tomb; and finally, Peter, Andrew, and other unnamed disciples see Jesus by the lake (the Sea of Galilee?). Ornamental crosses at the beginning and the end of the manuscript indicate that the scribe of the Akhmim codex regarded this text as the complete gospel.[7] The text represents Jesus' apostle Simon Peter as the author of the gospel (*Gos Pet* 7:2; 14:3).

The *Gospel of Peter* has numerous parallels to the accounts of the passion, death, and resurrection in all four canonical gospels, but scholars do not agree on the relationship of the *Gospel of Peter* to the four gospels. Some see the *Gospel of Peter* as a subsequent piecing together of accounts the author found in the canonical gospels, whereas others regard it as an early independent account of Jesus' passion, based on relevant passages in Psalms and the prophets and composed as early as the middle of the first century. In the form in which it comes down to us, the *Gospel of Peter* probably reflects use of the canonical gospels. However, it may be that underlying our text is an earlier edition of the gospel that was subsequently reworked in light of the canonical gospels.

Scholars generally place the *Gospel of Peter* within the broader Petrine tradition of the Syrian church, perhaps Antioch. In its present form, the gospel was written or completed not later than about 150, thereby providing time for its circulation to Egypt before the writing of the Oxyrhynchus fragments sometime before 200.

The question of the gospel's alleged docetic or heretical character is less than clear and is generally based on two passages:

Gos Pet 4:1

And they brought two criminals and crucified the Lord between them. But he himself remained silent, as if in no pain.

This verse is probably modeled after Isa 53:7 and is, therefore, not specifically or consciously docetic.[8] Isa 53 was widely-used as a messianic proof text in early Christianity. In fact, it is tempting to wonder whether this passage in Isaiah and in the *Gospel of Peter* might have served as the basis for subsequent Christian Docetism.

Gos Pet 5:5

And the Lord cried out, saying, "My power, (my) power, you have abandoned me?" When he said this, he was taken up.

---

7. The ornamentation of the Akhmim codex suggests that the scribe was copying what was already an incomplete text, as the gospel begins in the middle of a sentence.

8. Isa 53:7 He was oppressed, and he was afflicted,
yet he did not open his mouth;
like a lamb that is led to the slaughter,
and like a sheep that before its shearers is silent,
so he did not open his mouth.

The verb *taken up* was interpreted by Docetists to mean that Jesus' divine nature left Jesus' body before his death, so that the Lord only "seemed" to have died. But *taken up* might suggest the "orthodox" position of the ascension or exaltation of the Lord into heaven.

In other words, although ancient theologians considered the *Gospel of Peter* as docetic, the references are ambiguous, even though they were interpreted as docetic by later church fathers, both orthodox and heterodox (Gnostic).

JEWISH CHRISTIAN GOSPELS: THE TESTIMONY

The matter of Jewish Christian gospels is enormously complex. Jewish Christian gospels were in circulation in some Christian communities by the early second century, but it is not clear how many such gospels there were. Unfortunately, we have no manuscripts nor do we have even fragments of manuscripts from any of the Jewish Christian gospels. We know about them only from polemical references or citations in the writings of some church fathers. Depending on how we understand or interpret the scant evidence, there may have been three Jewish Christian gospels: the *Gospel of the Ebionites*, the *Gospel of the Hebrews*, and the *Gospel of the Nazoreans*.

IRENAEUS (before 137–ca. 202)

The earliest testimony regarding Jewish Christian gospels comes from Irenaeus, who reports (*Against Heresies* 1.22; 3.21.10) that the Ebionites used only one gospel, the Gospel of Matthew. Yet, it is clear that the gospel to which Irenaeus was referring was not the canonical Gospel of Matthew, as the Ebionite gospel contained no reference to the virgin birth. It is also clear that Irenaeus never saw this apparently nameless gospel, now commonly referred to by scholars as the *Gospel of the Ebionites*.

CLEMENT OF ALEXANDRIA (ca. 150–ca. 215)

Clement provides the next evidence about Jewish Christian gospels, when he refers to a *Gospel according to the Hebrews*, from which he quotes an otherwise unknown saying of Jesus (*Miscellanies* 2.9.45; 2.14.96). This saying also appears in Oxyrhynchus Papyrus 654, along with five other sayings, all six of which belong to the *Gospel of Thomas*, revealing the challenges scholars face in trying to identify what does and what does not belong to each of the Jewish Christian gospels.

EARLY CHRISTIAN GOSPELS, PART 2

ORIGEN (ca. 185–254)

Origen also quotes from the *Gospel according to the Hebrews* (*Commentary on John* 2.12 and *Homily on Jeremiah* 15.4). The story cited by Origen is the story of the temptation of Jesus, but with substantial deviations from the parallel accounts in the canonical gospels. Specifically, in Origen's *Gospel according to the Hebrews*, the Holy Spirit is the mother of Jesus, and Joseph is his father. Origen identifies this gospel as coming from the Ebionites, posing additional questions.

EUSEBIUS OF CAESAREA (ca. 260–ca. 339)

Eusebius speaks specifically about a *Gospel according to the Hebrews*, when he writes (*Church History* 3.25.5):

> To these [spurious writings] some reckon the *Gospel according to the Hebrews*, in which especially those Hebrews who have become converted to Christ find delight.

With reference to the Ebionites, Eusebius wrote (*Church History* 3.29.17):

> ... as they use only the so-called *Gospel according to the Hebrews*, they attach little value to the rest.

Concerning Hegesippus (ca. 120–ca. 180) and his "Memoirs," Eusebius wrote (*Church History* 4.22.8):

> He (Hegesippus) quotes both from the *Gospel according to the Hebrews* and from the Syriac (Gospel) and in particular some words in the Hebrew tongue, showing that he was a convert from the Hebrews.

According to Eusebius, Hegesippus quoted from two different gospels: the *Gospel according to the Hebrews* and a second gospel, the "Syriac Gospel," presumably written in Aramaic.

Two other quotations from Eusebius are relevant to our discussion:

> ... as we have found in a place in the Gospel existing among the Jews in the Hebrew language ... (*Theophania* 4.12)

> Since the gospel that has come down to us in the Hebrew script turns the threat not against him who ..., I put myself the question whether according to Matthew ... (A. Mai, *Nova Patr. Bibl.* 4.1.155).[9]

The reference in these passages in Eusebius is presumably not to the *Gospel according to the Hebrews*, but to another gospel, apparently written in Aramaic. Eusebius and Hegesippus seemingly knew or knew about two gospels, the *Gospel according to the Hebrews* and an unnamed gospel written in Aramaic, probably the *Gospel of the Nazoreans*.

---

9. Quoted from Hennecke, *New Testament Apocrypha*, vol 1, 123.

EPIPHANIUS (ca. 315–403)

Epiphanius was aware of two Jewish Christian sects known as the Nazoreans and the Ebionites (*Against Heresies*, 29). Epiphanius says of the gospel used by the Nazoreans that:

> They [the Nazoreans] have the Gospel according to Matthew complete and in Hebrew [Aramaic?]. For this is evidently still preserved among them, as it was originally written, in Hebrew script. But I do not know whether they have removed the genealogy from Abraham to Christ (*Against Heresies* 29.9.4).

According to Epiphanius, the *Gospel of the Nazoreans* was the Gospel of Matthew in Aramaic, although it is clear that Epiphanius had not himself seen the gospel, because he is uncertain whether the gospel contained the genealogy of Jesus. Epiphanius's *Gospel of the Nazoreans* was probably a translation into Aramaic of the Greek Gospel of Matthew and may have been identical to Hegesippus's Syriac Gospel (see above).

Epiphanius (*Against Heresies*, 30.14.3) says even more about the *Gospel of the Ebionites* and actually quotes some portions of it:

> By mutilating Matthew's genealogy, they make the beginning say, as we have already stated:
>
> In the days of Herod, king of Judea, during the high priesthood of Caiaphas,
>
> they say,
>
> this man named John appeared in the Jordan river baptizing with a baptism that changes people's hearts,
>
> and so on.

Not only does this *Gospel of the Ebionites* lack the genealogy of Jesus; it also lacks the birth narratives in Matt 1–2. It appears that Epiphanius saw a copy of this gospel, although it is unlikely that the Ebionites referred to this "mutilated" version of Matthew as the *Gospel of the Ebionites*. That is the modern scholarly name for an otherwise nameless gospel.

JEROME (ca. 347–420)

There are more references to Jewish Christian gospels in Jerome than in any other church father, but the evidence in Jerome is unfortunately confused and perhaps even contradictory. Jerome seems to have in mind just one Jewish Christian Gospel, although he refers to it by different names: the *Gospel according to the Hebrews*, the *Gospel of the Hebrews*, the *Hebrew Gospel*, the *Hebrew Gospel according to Matthew*, and the *Gospel according to the Apostles*. Jerome obviously thought that he was referring to the Aramaic original of the Gospel of Matthew, an idea that circulated since the time of Papias. However, Jerome does not seem to have had direct access to this

Aramaic Jewish Gospel, whatever its name, and he seems to be relying on evidence and citations from earlier church fathers.

JEWISH CHRISTIAN GOSPELS: THE FRAGMENTS

Despite the sometimes inscrutable information among the early fathers, the general consensus among scholars is that from the first half of the second century until the early fifth century there were several gospels that were used in Christian circles that were still deeply rooted in Judaism. None of these gospels has survived. We know of them only from references and citations in the writings of church fathers, most of which are polemical references.

In all likelihood there were three Jewish Christian gospels:

1. the *Gospel of the Hebrews*, a gospel with Gnosticizing tendencies that is very different from the canonical gospels;

2. the *Gospel of the Nazoreans*, an Aramaic gospel related in some way to the Gospel of Matthew; and

3. the *Gospel of the Ebionites*, a gospel based on the synoptic gospels.

In spite of uncertainties, it is helpful to look at some the characteristics of these three Jewish Christian gospels, recognizing that our information is often confused and sometimes even contradictory.

THE *GOSPEL OF THE HEBREWS*

The *Gospel of the Hebrews* is the most widely cited Jewish Christian gospel. Passages assigned to it come from citations in five church fathers: Clement of Alexandria (ca. 150–ca. 215), Origen of Alexandria and later of Caesarea (ca. 185–254), Didymus the Blind of Alexandria (ca. 313–ca. 398), Cyril of Jerusalem (ca. 315–386), and Jerome of Stridon in Dalmatia (ca. 347–420).

This gospel appears to have opened with an account of the pre-existence of both Mary and Jesus, followed by the birth of Jesus (*Gospel of the Hebrews* 1), although in a manner quite different from the prologue in John and the birth narratives in Matthew and Luke. Also included in this gospel were stories of the baptisms of Jesus, his mother, and his brothers (*Gospel of the Hebrews* 2–3); the temptation of Jesus (*Gospel of the Hebrews* 4a); the call of Matthias/Levi (*Gospel of the Hebrews* 5); Jesus' arrest and crucifixion (*Gospel of the Hebrews* 1); Jesus' ascension into heaven (*Gospel of the Hebrews* 1); and an appearance of the risen Lord to his brother James, who is reported to have been present at the Last Supper (*Gospel of the Hebrews* 9). The Jewish Christian character of this gospel is evident in the story about James at the Lord's Supper and in the account of the risen Christ's appearance first to James, a story whose seed may have been sown in Paul's account of an appearance of Jesus to James in 1 Cor 15:7.[10]

The *Gospel of the Hebrews* has Gnostic elements, most evident in the claim that Michael, a mighty power in heaven, came to earth in the form of Jesus' mother Mary and in the account that it was the Holy Spirit (Michael/Mary) and not God who spoke to Jesus at his baptism (*Gos Heb* 1:1–3; 3):[11]

> It is written in the Gospel of the Hebrews that
>
>> 1:1 When Christ wanted to come to earth, the Good Father summoned a mighty power in the heavens who was called Michael, and entrusted Christ to his care. ²The power came down into the world, and it was called Mary, and Christ was in her womb for seven months. ³She gave birth to him and he grew up and he chose the apostles who preached him everywhere.
>
> In the Hebrew gospel that the Nazarenes read it says,
>
>> 3:1 The whole fountain of the holy spirit comes down on him. For the Lord is the spirit and where the spirit is, there is freedom.
>
> Later on, in the same gospel, we find the following:
>
>> ²And it happened that when the Lord came up out of the water, the whole fountain of the holy spirit came down on him and rested on him. ³It said to him, "My Son, I was waiting for you in all the prophets, wanting for you to come so I could rest on you. ⁴For you are my rest; you are my first-begotten Son who rules forever."

The *Gospel of the Hebrews* was apparently written for Greek-speaking Jewish Christians, probably in Alexandria, Egypt, where Clement, Origen, and Didymus were among its earliest witnesses. The fact that this gospel was known to Hegesippus (ca. 110–ca. 180), according to Eusebius of Caesarea, suggests a date of composition in the first half of the second century.

THE *GOSPEL OF THE NAZOREANS*

Passages assigned to the *Gospel of the Nazoreans* come from citations in four church fathers: Hegesippus, probably originally from Palestine or Syria (ca. 120–ca. 180), Eusebius of Caesarea (ca. 260–ca. 339), Epiphanius of Salamis in Cyprus (ca. 315–403), and Jerome of Stridon in Dalmatia (ca. 347–420).

It appears that the *Gospel of the Nazoreans* was related to the Gospel of Matthew. *Nazoreans* probably had Matthew's birth narrative, the temptation of Jesus, the

---

10. The primacy of James as found in the *Gospel of the Hebrews* is echoed in the *Gos Thos* 12, both of which emphasize the special role that James played in Jewish Christianity, and most especially James's leadership in the early Jerusalem church.

11. The text of the *Gospel of the Hebrews* 1 is quoted or paraphrased (it is not clear which) by Cyril of Jerusalem, *Discourse on Mary, the Mother of God*. The text of the *Gos Heb* 3 is quoted by Jerome, *Commentary on Isaiah 4* (in a comment on Isa 11:2).

Sermon on the Mount, and other stories characteristic of Matthew. In other words, the *Gospel of the Nazoreans* was an Aramaic version of the Greek Gospel of Matthew. Although several early fathers assumed that *Nazoreans* was the original Aramaic text of Matthew referred to by Papias, the reverse was apparently true: the *Gospel of the Nazoreans* was an Aramaic translation of the original Greek Matthew. An analysis of the fragments of the *Gospel of the Nazoreans* shows dependence on the Greek text of the Gospel of Matthew.

When quoting the *Gospel of the Nazoreans*, church fathers seem to have focused on passages in which *Nazoreans* was different from Greek Matthew. The differences are, however, insignificant, not much more than what one would expect from any relatively free translation. Most of the differences that we are able to observe are the result of the *Gospel of the Nazoreans* expanding or clarifying details in Greek Matthew.

If the *Gospel of the Nazoreans* is an Aramaic version of the Gospel of Matthew, then it was obviously composed after Matthew had been written and circulated. That information, together with the reference to the *Gospel of the Nazoreans* in Hegesippus, (ca.110–180), suggests that the *Gospel of the Nazoreans* was written in the first half of the second century, probably in Syria among the sect known as the Nazoreans, perhaps in Beroea (Aleppo) in Coelesyria.

THE *GOSPEL OF THE EBIONITES*

All of the quotations from the *Gospel of the Ebionites* come from Epiphanius of Salamis in Cyprus (ca. 315–403). We do not actually have a name for this gospel, except for the fact that Epiphanius quotes from a gospel that was in use among the Jewish Christian sect know as the Ebionites. Epiphanius refers to it as the *Gospel of the Hebrews*, or the *Hebrew Gospel*.

Although we know little about this gospel, as we have only seven fragments of it in quotations from Epiphanius, the available evidence suggests that this gospel was a harmonized version of the gospels of Matthew, Mark, and Luke. Quotations from Epiphanius refer to the work of John the Baptist (*Gos Ebion* 1a-b, 3), Jesus' baptism by John (*Gos Ebion* 4), the call of the twelve disciples (*Gos Ebion* 2), and the last supper. Epiphanius notes specifically that the gospel did not contain an account of Jesus' genealogy and birth, but began like the Gospel of Mark with the appearance of John the Baptist (*Gos Ebion* 1b).

The *Gospel of the Ebionites* was written in Greek, as it follows closely the Greek text of the synoptic gospels. The Ebionites apparently denied the Virgin Birth of Jesus, hence their deletion of the birth narrative. As in Mark, it is at Jesus' baptism that the Holy Spirit descended on Jesus, creating the union of a heavenly being with the man Jesus, resulting thereby in the Christ, the Son of God, and reflecting an adoptionist, Gnostic, or Docetic tendency in the gospel (*Gos Ebion* 5), different from the simpler adoptionism in the Gospel of Mark. The Ebionites believed in a Gnosticizing christology, regarded Paul as a heretic, disliked cultic sacrifices (*Gos Ebion* 6), practiced circumcision, were vegetarians (*Gos Ebion* 7), and prayed facing toward Jerusalem.

The *Gospel of the Ebionites* was apparently written in the first half of the second century, since Irenaeus (before 137–202) knew of its existence, even if only from hearsay (*Against Heresies* 1.22; 3.21.10). This information, along with the fact that the author of the gospel knew all three synoptics, suggests a date in the first half of the second century. Although we do not know its place of origin, scholars lean toward an area east of the Jordan, where Epiphanius probably first saw the gospel.

JEWISH CHRISTIAN COMMUNITIES: THEIR SOCIAL LOCATION

The origin of Jewish Christian sects in the area east of the Jordan is uncertain, but there may be a clue about their origin in Eusebius (*Church History* 3.5.3), who reports that before the fall of Jerusalem in 70 members of the Jerusalem church departed to an area about five miles east of the Jordan River, where they settled in a city of Perea called Pella. Jewish Christians living in Galilee may also have fled from the invading Roman army and have crossed into Transjordan.

It is possible that the Ebionites and the Nazoreans could trace their origin to Jesus' brother James or to other first generation Jewish Christians in Jerusalem or Galilee. The name Ebionites recalls "the poor" (Hebrew *'ebyônîm*), a term that Paul used to refer to some early Jerusalem Christians (Rom 15:26 "the poor among the Jerusalem saints"; and Gal 2:10 "that we remember the poor"). Likewise Nazoreans (or Nazarenes) was a name used to refer to Jews who believed in Jesus but who still observed the law of Moses (Acts 24:5; cf. Matt 2:23). Among early church fathers, Tertullian, writing in about 200, reports that "the Jews call us Nazarenos" (*Against Marcion* 4. 8). The name Christians eventually replaced the name Nazarenes, apparently first in Antioch (Acts 11:26) and subsequently within the Greek and Latin speaking Gentile church.

THE *INFANCY GOSPEL OF JAMES*

The *Infancy Gospel of James* survives in the Bodmer Papyrus V, a Greek manuscript from the third century, found in 1952 at Pabau, Egypt, the site of the ancient headquarters of the cenobite Pachomian monks. There are, as well, about a hundred thirty manuscripts from the tenth century and later— all very different, indicating the fluidity of the text. The gospel also survives in Old Syriac, Armenian, Georgian, Ethiopic, Sahidic Coptic, and Old Slavonic translations, but not in Latin, presumably because the gospel was condemned in the West.

The *Infancy Gospel of James* deals primarily with the miraculous birth of Mary and with Mary's upbringing in the Jerusalem temple as a virgin, a situation that was not compromised either by intercourse with Joseph or by the birth of Jesus. Although Jesus' birth occupies the final third of the gospel, the gospel's real interest lies in Mary. The story of Mary's aged and childless parents, Anna and Joachim, is reminiscent of the story of Abraham and Sarah and the birth of Isaac in the Hebrew Bible.

The author of the gospel purports to be James, the half-brother of Jesus (through Joseph's previous marriage).[12] The gospel was allegedly written shortly after the death of Herod the Great in 4 B.C.E. (*Inf Jas* 25:1), but it is clear that the gospel knows the birth narratives of both Matthew and Luke, which are woven into the gospel. The gospel was known by Origen (185–232) and probably also by Clement of Alexandria (ca. 150–ca. 215), suggesting a date of about 150 for its composition. The author was obviously not Jewish Christian, as he was unfamiliar with the geography of Palestine and with Jewish customs, including the fact that the Jerusalem temple was not home to young Jewish virgins. Beyond this, there is nothing in the gospel to suggest its place of composition.

The gospel has as its purpose the glorification of Mary and is probably responsible for the development of Mariology, even at the relatively early date of its composition. The gospel was especially popular in the East because of its glorification of virginity and has had a significant influence on Christian art that depicts the young Mary and her parents, Joachim and Anna.

THE *INFANCY GOSPEL OF THOMAS*

Evidence for the *Infancy Gospel of Thomas* comes from several late and unreliable Greek manuscripts of the fourteenth to the sixteenth centuries. There are also Armenian, Georgian, Ethiopic, and Slavonic versions, some of which may actually be closer to the original text. A Syriac version from the sixth century is our oldest complete text of the gospel, although there is an incomplete and somewhat uncertain older Latin version from the fifth or the sixth century. Scholars disagree whether the gospel was composed originally in Greek or Syriac, although most lean toward a Greek original. Unfortunately, the evidence in the rather late Greek manuscripts and the numerous versions makes reconstructing the earliest form of the gospel particularly challenging.[13]

The purpose of the *Infancy Gospel of Thomas* was evidently to fill the gap between Jesus' birth and his visit to Jerusalem with Joseph and Mary at age twelve, as reported in Luke 2:41–52 (=*Inf Thos* 19:1–12). The gospel contains stories about Jesus at age five (*Inf Thos* 2:1), age six (*Inf Thos* 11:1), age eight (*Inf Thos* 12:4), and age twelve (*Inf*

---

12. Rather than identifying James as Jesus' full brother, as is assumed elsewhere in early Christian literature, the *Gospel of James* introduces the device of Joseph's earlier marriage, thereby making James and Jesus merely half brothers. According to the *Gospel of James*, Jesus and James had different mothers.

13. Gero, "The Infancy Gospel of Thomas," 46–80.

Thos 19:1). The earliest of these stories in the gospel reflect a playful, prodigious, and sometimes ill-tempered Jesus:

Inf Thos 2:1–7[14]

¹When this boy, Jesus, was five years old, he was playing at the ford of a rushing stream. ²He was collecting the flowing water into ponds and made the water instantly pure. He did this with a single command. ³He then made soft clay and shaped it into twelve sparrows. He did this on the sabbath day, and many other boys were playing with him.

⁴But when a Jew saw what Jesus was doing while playing on the Sabbath day, he immediately went off and told Joseph, Jesus' father: "See here, your boy is at the ford and has taken mud and fashioned twelve birds with it, and so has violated the Sabbath."

⁵So Joseph went there, and as soon as he spotted him he shouted, "Why are you doing what's not permitted on the Sabbath?"

⁶But Jesus simply clapped his hands and shouted to the sparrows: "Be off, fly away, and remember me, you who are now alive!" And the sparrows took off and flew away noisily.

⁷The Jews watched with amazement, then left the scene to report to their leaders what they had seen Jesus doing.

Inf Thos 4:1–4

¹Later he was going through the village again when a boy ran by and bumped him on the shoulder. Jesus got angry and said to him, "You won't continue your journey." ²And all of a sudden he fell down and died.

³Some people saw what had happened and said, "Where has this boy come from? Everything he says happens instantly."

⁴The parents of the dead boy came to Joseph and blamed him, saying, "Because you have such a boy, you can't live with us in the village, or else teach him to bless and not curse. He's killing our children."

Inf Thos 5:1–6

¹So Joseph summoned his child and admonished him in private, saying, "Why are you doing all this? These people are suffering and so they hate and harass us." ²Jesus said, "I know that the words you spoke are not your words.[15] Still, I'll keep quiet for your sake. But those people must take their punishment. There and then his accusers became blind.

³Those who saw this became very fearful and at a loss. All they could say was, "Every word he says, whether good or bad, has become a deed—a miracle, even!" ⁴When Joseph saw that Jesus had done such a thing, he got angry and grabbed his ear and pulled very hard. ⁵The boy became infuriated with him and replied, "It's one thing for you to seek and not find; it's quite another for you to act this unwisely. ⁶Don't you know that I don't really belong to you? Don't make me upset."

14. This story was surprisingly known to Mohammad, as there are two allusions to it in the Qu'ran (Sura 3:49 and Sura 5:113).

15. This sentence appears to make little sense and should probably be amended to read: "I know that the words your spoke are not your words."

Hard pressed to comment on Jesus' earliest years, Christian tradition saw the young boy Jesus as typically mischievous but also supernatural. These stories of Jesus' early childhood reflect elements of both.

A version of the *Infancy Gospel of Thomas* may have existed in the second half of the second century, but this was a popular work, and it was probably modified over a long period of time. The gospel was known in the late second century to the author of the *Epistle of the Apostles* 4, which knows *Thomas's* story of Jesus discussing the alphabet with the teacher at school (*Inf Thos* 6:1–23). Irenaeus (before 137–ca. 202), writing in about 185, lists the gospel among the "spurious and apocryphal writings" that were used by the Marcosians (*Against Heresies* 1.20.1).[16] Hippolytus (ca. 170–ca. 236) in *Refutation of All Heresies* 5.2 and Origen (ca. 185–254) in *Homily in Luke* 1:1 both mention by name a *Gospel of Thomas*, but it is unclear to which *Gospel of Thomas* they are referring, the Coptic *Gospel of Thomas* or the *Infancy Gospel of Thomas*.

We know nothing about the place or circumstance of the gospel's writing. Although some scholars have identified Gnostic or docetic tendencies in the *Infancy Gospel of Thomas*, the gospel probably originated in proto-orthodox circles. Its understanding of Jesus and his work reflects a natural development in the popular traditions of the Christian movement that began in the late first century and continued through the second century and beyond among ordinary Christians. Interest in childhood narratives had already begun by the end of the first century (Luke 2:41–52).

Some of the stories of Jesus' childhood imitate miracle stories in the canonical gospels:

violation of the sabbath law (*Inf Thos* 2:3–4)

healings of the sick:

>healing the young man who accidently cut off the bottom of his foot with an ax (*Inf Thos* 10:1–4)

>healing Jesus' brother James when he was bitten by a viper (*Inf Thos* 16:1–2)

raisings of the dead:

>raising the child who fell from the roof of a house (*Inf Thos* 9:1–6)

>raising a neighbor's dead infant (*Inf Thos* 17:1–4)

>raising the man who died while working on the construction of a building (*Inf Thos* 18:1–3).

Some of the stories go well beyond the miracle stories in the canonical gospels, especially the almost vindictive punishment miracles in the *Infancy Gospel of Thomas*, some of which is evident in the examples cited above.

There is nothing specifically Christian about the stories attributed to Jesus in the *Infancy Gospel of Thomas*. Rather, the stories elaborate on the missing years of Jesus'

---

16. The Marcosians were a sect of Gnostics, founded by Valentinus's disciple Marcus and active in Lyons and southern Europe from the second to the fourth centuries.

childhood and reflect familiarity with Hellenistic legends and the pious imagination of unsophisticated Hellenistic Christians.

THE *GOSPEL OF MARY*

The *Gospel of Mary*, the only gospel attributed to a woman, survives in three incomplete manuscripts from Egypt:

> a Greek manuscript, John Rylands Papyrus 453, from the early third century, published in 1938;

> a Greek manuscript, Oxyr Pap 3525, from the third century, published in 1983;

> a Sahidic Coptic codex, Berlin Papyrus 8502, from the fifth century, published in 1955.

Less than half of the text of the gospel survives. The longest of the three manuscripts, Berlin Papyrus 8502, originally had nineteen pages, but pages 1–6 and 11–14 are missing, leaving us with just nine pages.

Lacking the beginning, the *Gospel of Mary* begins in the middle of a situation in which the risen Christ, referred to throughout the gospel as the Savior, is engaging his disciples in a discussion and answering their questions on the nature of matter, the nature of sin and spirit, the nature of salvation, and the nature of true humanity as it exists within each individual. The Savior then departs leaving the disciples troubled and concerned about what they are to do and how they are to fulfill the Savior's commission to go forth and preach the gospel.

Following Jesus' departure, Mary Magdelene speaks to the disciples with words of support and reassurance (*Gos Mary* 5:4–8). Peter then asks Mary to share with the disciples any exceptional or esoteric teaching that the Savior may have delivered to her:

> [6:1]Peter said to Mary, "Sister, we know that the Savior loved you more than any other woman. [2]Tell us the words of the Savior that you know, but which we haven't heard."

Mary replies to Peter and the other disciples by relating a discussion she had with the Savior about visions:

> [7:1]She said, "I saw the Lord in a vision [2]and I said to him, 'Lord, I saw you today in a vision.'
>
> [3]He said to me, "Congratulations to you for not wavering at seeing me. [4]For where the mind is, there is the treasure."
>
> [5]I said to him, "Lord, how does a person who sees a vision see it—[with] the soul [or] with the spirit?"

> ⁶The Savior answered, "The <visionary> does not see with the soul or with the spirit, but with the mind which exists between these two—that is [what] sees the vision and that is w[hat . . .]" [four pages of the codex are then missing]

When the text resumes, Mary is reporting the revelation given to her in her vision. The vision describes the challenging ascent of the soul through the seven Powers of Wrath on its way to its rest in silence.

Mary's vision meets with disapproval from two of the apostles:

> ¹⁰:¹Andrew sai[d, "B]rothers, what is your opinion of what was just said? ²I for one don't believe that the Savior said these things, be[cause] these opinions seem to be so different from h[is th]ought."
>
> ¹⁰:³After reflecting on these ma[tt]ers, [Peter said], "Has the Sa[vior] spoken secretly to a wo[m]an and [not] openly so that [we] would all hear? ⁴[Surely] he did [not wish to indicate] that [she] is more worthy that we are?"

Mary Magdelene wept in disappointment at Andrew's and Peter's disbelief, but Levi defended her and accused Peter of having an inclination to anger.

The ascent of the soul through the seven cosmic powers and the esoteric insight of Mary Magdelene are evidence that the *Gospel of Mary* is Gnostic in character. Moreover, the gospel deals with an important related problem in the early church: namely whether the apostles, as represented by Andrew and Peter, faithfully preserved Jesus' teachings. It is significant that the gospel calls into question the reliability of the teachings of Peter and Andrew, while confirming the value of the teachings of Mary Magdelene, a woman.

There are important differences between the Greek and the Coptic texts, most obvious of which is the question of the legitimacy of women's leadership in the later Coptic version, a development that reflects the subsequent exclusion of women from positions of leadership that they had shared in early Christian communities.

The *Gospel of Mary* was probably written in Greek either in Egypt or Syria sometime in the early second century.

THE *GOSPEL OF TRUTH*[17]

The earliest information about the *Gospel of Truth* comes from Irenaeus (before 137– ca. 202) in a highly polemical passage in his *Against Heresies* 3.11.9, written about 175–185:

> But those who are from Valentinus, being, on the other hand, altogether reckless, while they put forth their own compositions, boast that they possess more Gospels than there really are. Indeed, they have arrived at such a pitch of audacity, as to entitle their comparatively recent writing "the Gospel of Truth," though it

---

17. The text of the *Gospel of Truth* is from the translation of Attridge and MacRae in *The Nag Hammadi Library*.

agrees in nothing with the Gospels of the Apostles, so that they have really no Gospel which is not full of blasphemy. For if what they have published is the Gospel of Truth, and yet is totally unlike those which have been handed down to us from the apostles, any who please may learn, as is shown from the Scriptures themselves, that that which has been handed down from the apostles can no longer be reckoned the Gospel of Truth.

The *Gospel of Truth*, attributed to the Gnostic Valentinus (ca. 100–ca. 160) or to one of his disciples, was probably written about 140–180, probably in either Rome or Egypt. The gospel is known to us in two Coptic translations discovered in 1945 near Nag Hammadi, Egypt. The entire gospel survives in a Subachmimic Coptic (a dialect of Upper Egypt or southern Egypt) translation and also in a few fragments in Sahidic Coptic. Both texts were probably translated from an original Greek text.

The opening words of the text make it clear that the author regarded his work as an inspired statement of the gospel:

> The gospel of truth is joy for those who have received from the Father of truth the grace of knowing him, through the power of the Word that came forth from the pleroma,[18] the one who is in the thought and mind of the Father, that is, the one who is addressed as the Savior, (that) being the name of the work he is to perform for the redemption of those who were ignorant of the Father, while in the name [of] the gospel is the proclamation of hope, being discovery for those who search for him *(Gos Truth 16:31–17:3)*.

Although not a narrative of the birth, life, teaching, passion, death, and resurrection of Jesus in the manner of the canonical gospels, the *Gospel of Truth* is, nevertheless, an entwining of doctrinal principles and allusions to episodes in the life of Jesus. However, history is clearly not a concern of the author, who moves freely between cosmic, historical, and psychological domains. Like most of the Gnostic literature, elements of the *Gospel of Truth* are obscure to the modern reader, as it weaves together elements of Platonic philosophy and early Christian theology.

The gospel tells the story of how the Savior (the risen Lord, the Son, the Logos) mediates the transformation from ignorance to knowledge (*gnosis*) to rest in the Father. Some quotes from the *Gospel of Truth* will illustrate most effectively the message of the gospel and the somewhat elusive nature of its language and its thought:

> Ignorance of the Father brought about anguish and terror; and the anguish grew solid like a fog, so that no one was able to see. For this reason error became powerful *(Gos Truth 17:10–15a)*.

> Jesus, the Christ, enlightened those who were in darkness through oblivion. He enlightened them; he showed (them) a way; and the way is the truth which he taught them *(Gos Truth 18:16–21a)*.

---

18. Pleroma (πλήρωμα) is a Greek word meaning "fullness." It refers to the totality of all divine powers and to the divine space, which in Gnostic thought is usually divided into metaphysical aeons, spheres. or personified powers.

For this reason error grew angry at him, persecuted him, was distressed at him (and) was brought to naught. He was nailed to a tree (and) he became a fruit of the knowledge (*gnosis*) of the Father (*Gos Truth* 18:21b–26a).

And the Spirit ran after him, hastening from waking him up. Having extended his hand to him who lay upon the ground, he set him up on his feet, for he had not yet risen. He gave them the means of knowing the knowledge (*gnosis*) of the Father and the revelation of his Son. For, when they had seen him and had heard him, he granted them to taste him and to smell him and to touch the beloved Son (*Gos Truth* 30:17–31a).

For that very reason he brought him forth in order to speak about the place and his resting-place from which he had come forth, and to glorify the pleroma, the greatness of his name and the sweetness of the Father (*Gos Truth* 40:30–41:3).

Therefore, all the emanations of the Father are pleromas, and the root of all his emanations is in the one who made them all grow up in himself (*Gos Truth* 41:15–19).

The *Gospel of Truth* maintains that each person has the ability to change and to awaken to the truth, making it clear that there is really no need for the organized church, which actually serves as a barrier to rather than as a mediator of knowledge (*gnosis*).

TATIAN'S *DIATESSARON*

Although the *Diatessaron* is not regarded as one of the apocryphal gospels, it is important to consider this gospel in this chapter because of the major role it played in early Christianity, especially in Syria and other regions of the East. The Christian apologist Tatian composed the *Diatessaron*, the most important gospel harmony ever written, in Syriac, a northern dialect of Aramaic, probably in Rome between 163 and 172. Tatian's teacher Justin had previously composed a harmony of the synoptic gospels, but Tatian went a step further and incorporated the Gospel of John into a harmony that appears to have used the Gospel of Matthew as its principal framework.[19]

There is insufficient evidence to determine the degree to which Justin's harmony influenced Tatian in his creation of the *Diatessaron*, but it is clear that the work of composing gospel harmonies was not limited to Justin and Tatian. Many Christians composed or otherwise used gospel harmonies, perhaps under the assumption that there could be only one authoritative gospel. Rather than assigning authority to any single proto-canonical gospel, some church fathers apparently worked diligently to provide the single, most complete or authoritative rendering of the gospel tradition. In addition to Justin and Tatian, Second Clement, the *Gospel of the Ebionites*, Clement of Alexandria, Ammonius of Alexandria, Origen, the Pseudoclementine *Homilies*,

---

19. The source of most of the information in this section is Peterson, *Tatian's Diatessaron* and Peterson's chapter "Tatian's Diatessaron" in Koester, *Ancient Christian Gospels*, 403–30.

and others composed or used harmonies of the gospels. Furthermore, the practice of writing and using harmonies continued well beyond the time of Irenaeus, who maintained toward the end of the second century, on the basis of a curious cosmological argument, that there should be four gospels, just as there are four winds and four corners of the earth.

The differences among the four gospels posed a challenge to Tatian, who created a new sequence for the stories and eliminated disagreements among the four gospels. For example, in order to resolve discrepancies between the genealogies of Jesus in Matt 1:1–17 and Luke 3:23–38, Tatian omitted the genealogies entirely. Apart from the genealogies, the only material not included in the *Diatessaron* is the story of the Jesus' ascension into heaven (Luke 24:50–53) and the story of Jesus' encounter with the adulteress (John 7:53–8:11), a passage that is lacking in our most ancient manuscripts of the Gospel of John and that may, in fact, not have been in the original text of John (see Theodoret, *Haereticarum Fabularum Compendium* 1.20).

Although a harmony of the four gospels,[20] the *Diatessaron* illustrates the authority accorded to the four gospels in the middle of the second century, at least in Rome. Although the four increasingly became the accepted gospel canon in much of the church by the end of the second century, the *Diatessaron* persisted for many centuries in being the accepted gospel in Syriac-speaking churches.

In fact, the *Diatessaron* was the standard gospel text of most Syrian churches throughout the fourth and even into the fifth century, when Theodoret, the Syrian bishop of Cyrrhus, thinking that Tatian was a heretic, removed from Syrian churches between 423 and 427 two hundred manuscripts of the *Diatessaron* and substituted instead the four gospels. Gradually, with no copies of the *Diatessaron* available in Syria, the four gospels achieved canonical status in the Syrian church, and the *Diatessaron* was increasingly considered as heretical.

Although no text of Tatian's *Diatessaron* survives in either Greek or Syriac, there is abundant evidence for the text. Western witnesses to the *Diatessaron* include the Latin Codex Fuldensis (sixth century),[21] and Middle High German, Middle Dutch, Early Italian, and Middle English versions. Eastern witnesses include the Syrian father, Ephrem (ca. 306–373), who composed a commentary on the *Diatessaron* (called *Commentary on the Gospel of the Mixed*), a copy of which was discovered in 1957 (the late fifth or early sixth century Chester Beatty Syriac manuscript 709).[22] Although

---

20. Some scholars think that Tatian may also have had access to the apocryphal *Gospel of the Hebrews*, but it may be that some of the material not found in our copies of the canonical gospels was available to Tatian in a version of the proto-canonical gospels that varied somewhat from what survives in our best manuscripts of Matthew, Mark, Luke, and John.

21. Codex Fuldensis is not only an important early witness to Jerome's Latin Vulgate, but it is also a valuable witness to Tatian's *Diatessaron*, which appears in this Latin manuscript of the New Testament in lieu of the four gospels.

22. Chester Beatty manuscript 709 was missing 41 pages, which were subsequently recovered in 1987.

he did not comment on every passage in Tatian's *Diatessaron* or quote in full all of the passages on which he commented, Ephrem does, nevertheless, provide a reliable witness to Tatian's original text, at least in the passages that he quotes. Other Eastern witnesses include Arabic, Persian, Old Armenian, and Old Georgian versions.

Syriac Christianity is particularly important to a study of the early church, because it is an old Christian community and because it does not reflect many of the features of Christianity as it evolved in the west—in Rome, in Corinth, in Ephesus, and even in Alexandria, the areas where Christian orthodoxy was beginning to take shape.

Although some scholars have maintained that the *Diatessaron* was written originally in Latin or Greek, it appears that the original language was Syriac, as Syrianisms or Semitisms appear even in some Western witnesses to the text. The place of composition was probably Rome, where there was a Syriac-speaking Christian community in the second century. In fact, there are Diatessaronic readings in Roman witnesses from the second and third centuries. Following Justin's death in 165, Tatian continued to work in Rome until 172, when he was expelled from the Roman church for being an Encratite[23] and a follower of Valentinus (Irenaeus, *Against Heresies* 1.28.1). Shortly thereafter, Tatian left Rome and returned to the East, where the *Diatessaron* flourished for many centuries.

CONCLUSIONS

The ten gospels discussed in this chapter are not the only apocryphal gospels that circulated in the early church. Among other such gospels, some of which are known only by name, are the *Gospel of Marcion* (second century), the *Gospel of Judas* (second century), the *Gospel of the Egyptians* (second century), the *Gospel of Apelles* (second century), the *Gospel of Basilides* (second century), the *Gospel of Cerinthus* (second century), the *Gospel of Matthias* (second century), the *Gospel of the Twelve (Apostles)* (second century), the *Gospel of Mani* (third century), the *Gospel of Bardesanes* (third century), the *Gospel of Bartholomew* (third century?), the *Life of John the Baptist* (fourth century), and the *History of Joseph the Carpenter* (fifth century). In this chapter, we have discussed a representative sample of the most important of the apocryphal gospels that have survived in whole or in part.

The evidence of the apocryphal gospels illustrates that the writing of gospels continued well beyond the four that eventually achieved canonical status. In fact, it may be that the assignment of names to many of the apocryphal gospels gave rise to the tradition of assigning apostolic names to the gospels attributed by the mid-second century to Matthew (an apostle of Jesus), Mark (a disciple of Jesus' apostle Peter),

---

23. The Encratites (or the "self-controlled") were a second century Gnostic-leaning ascetic Christian sect that forbade marriage and advocated abstinence from meat. Eusebius says that Tatian was the person responsible this heresy (Irenaeus, *Against All Heresies* 1.28; Eusebius, *Church History* 4.28.29).

Luke (a disciple of the self-proclaimed apostle Paul), and John (an apostle of Jesus), all of which were actually anonymous writings.

The apocryphal gospels also continued along a trajectory of moving even farther away from what little the church knew about the historical Jesus and incorporating instead more popular legendary material or more theology specific to the author or to the community that produced the various gospels. That tendency was evident already in our prior discussion of the composition of the proto-canonical gospels, whose historical value is by no means clear, but the problem is even more evident in the abundance of gospels from the second and third centuries.

The gospels were exactly what the word *gospel* implies: they were proclamations of the "good news" of various churches or individuals. The gospels, whether canonical or apocryphal, were not faithful guardians of reliable evidence about the life and ministry of Jesus. Some core of historical material may survive, but it is particularly difficult to identify historical material, even in the earlier gospels, if history is our primary criterion. As we have previously observed, we know far more about the authors of the various gospels than we can ever hope to know about Jesus himself. There is probably little to no evidence for the historical Jesus in any of the apocryphal gospels, except for the minor details that Joseph and Mary were Jesus' parents, that Jesus was baptized by John, and that Jesus suffered and was crucified.

As we have observed in this chapter, some of the apocryphal gospels pose particularly serious challenges to scholars. Most especially, the Jewish Christian gospels, the *Gospel of the Hebrews*, the *Gospel of the Nazoreans*, and the *Gospel of the Ebionites*, are known only from polemical allusions and citations in early church fathers. Even then, we cannot be certain that there were three Jewish Christian gospels and that scholars have assigned each saying correctly to each gospel. At best, we have skeletal parts of three such gospels. However good the scholarship of those specialists who have labored over the maze of information that is available to us about Jewish Christian gospels, the evidence is meager, and the results at best tentative. It would be a great archaeological discovery if any of the Jewish Christian gospels were found largely intact.

The situation is much better with the reconstruction of Tatian's *Diatessaron*, because there are more witnesses to the *Diatessaron* in many different languages in both the East and in the West. Yet we posses no complete text of the *Diatessaron* in what was presumably its original Syriac, except as we are able to reconstruct that text from Ephrem's *Commentary* and the multiple versions.

The history of the texts of both the proto-canonical and the apocryphal gospels is complicated, especially the early history. Scholars have worked diligently to identify various layers or strata of the *Gospel of Thomas*, one of which may reach back to the first century to the Jerusalem community of Jesus' brother James or to traditions that may have had their origin in the Galilee as early as the 50s or 60s. Other material may have been added as the *Gospel of Thomas* was carried to Syria, where it may have been reworked. Still other material may have been added, when the gospel was taken to Egypt and translated into Coptic. A similar complicated situation may be evident with respect to the *Gospel of Peter*, where there may be evidence of a first century stratum and evidence of subsequent editing based on the four proto-canonical gospels sometime around the mid-second century.

Frankly, the more complicated the process of composition, the higher the risk involved in building scholarly consensus around a single theory or hypothesis, with the important words being *theory* or *hypothesis*. A *theory* or a *hypothesis* is, after all, a scholarly construct. There are many presuppositions and a good deal of speculation, especially when the data are thin and when the construct model is complex. There is so very much that we simply do not know. It is facile for scholars to move from good theories or hypotheses to unfounded assumptions, as they reconstruct the past based on all too meager evidence.

Even in those cases where we have complete manuscripts, we can never be sure that we are working with a text that is close to the autograph. It is eminently clear that copyists and translators willingly and knowingly modified the text each and every time it was copied, often although not always intentionally.

We spent a good deal of time in this chapter trying to identify the date, place, and original language of composition of each of the ten gospels discussed. We also summarized some of the qualities or characteristics of each gospel. The results of our discussion are summarized below. In the case of the *Gospel of Thomas* and the *Gospel of Peter*, we have broken down the results based on the possibility that there may have been more than one "edition" of those gospels.

Gospel	Date	Place	Language	Character
Thomas[1st ed.]	ca. 60	Palestine	Greek (?)	sayings of Jesus
Thomas[2nd ed.]	140–180	Syria (Edessa)	Greek	proto-Gnostic (?)
Thomas[3rd ed.]	140–180	Egypt	Coptic	Coptic translation
Peter[1st ed.]	60–70	Antioch	Greek	passion narrative
Peter[2nd ed.]	pre-150	Antioch	Greek	may be Docetic?
Hebrews	1st half of 2nd cent.	Alexandria	Greek	contains Gnostic elements
Nazoreans	1st half of 2nd cent.	Syria (Beroea)	Aramaic	Aramaic translation of Greek Matthew
Ebionites	1st half of 2nd cent.	Transjordan	Greek	Docetic harmony of synoptic gospels

THE NEW TESTAMENT

Gospel	Date	Place	Language	Character
Infancy James	ca. 150	unknown, but not Palestine	Greek	Mary's birth and childhood
Infancy Thomas	2nd half of 2nd cent.	unknown	Greek	stories of Jesus, ages 5–12
Mary	early 2nd century	Egypt or Syria	Greek	Gnostic
Truth	140–180	Rome	Syriac	Gnostic homily
Diatessaron	163–172	Rome	Syriac	harmony of the four gospels

The conclusions are clearer in some instances and less clear in other instances, depending upon the evidence that is available. When it comes to the apocryphal gospels, scholars sometimes have to rely on the polemical testimony of early church fathers, but that testimony is usually secondary, and it is often conditioned more by an individual father's theological purpose than by the facts, further complicating the challenges scholars have to face. As we have seen repeatedly, finding something in an early written source does not guarantee the accuracy of the information, so scholars must look critically at the sources.

We have often mentioned in this chapter the dates of some of the manuscipts or the fragments of manuscripts that have survived from antiquity without discussing how scholars determine the dates of those extant manuscripts. The dating of manuscripts is based on the opinion of papyrologists, specialists in the study of papyrus manuscripts or fragments, who evaluate the paleographical evidence and assign a date base on various criteria, most especially on the style of writing.

Paleography (Greek for *ancient writing*) is the science of studying ancient manuscripts written on papyrus or animal skin in order to classify the different methods of writings and to identify the dates of writing of each manuscript. Because different scripts were current at different times, specialists are able to date ancient manuscripts based on the handwriting of the individual scribes. Simply stated, there were different characteristics of writing, different punctuations, different patterns of abbreviation, different methods of binding, and many other characteristics of manuscripts at different times. Trained specialists, known as papyrologists or codicologists, have turned this information in a reasonably exact science.[24]

Stated simply, good scholarship is a combination of hard science and judicious art, and it is important to distinguish between the two and to understand the

---

24. Mathisen, "Paleography and Codicology," 140–65.

limitations of the methodologies that scholars employ in drawing, and sometimes even overdrawing, their conclusions.

The special value of studying the non-canonical or apocryphal gospels is to see the proliferation of perspectives that these gospels reveal: specifally, the vibrant nature of second-century Christian thinking about Jesus. In other words, the findings in this chapter expose an ongoing positive interaction with Jesus rather than a static, fixed notion or a stable Christology.

CHAPTER 14

POST-APOSTOLIC CHRISTIANITIES

ALMOST FROM THE BEGINNING, Christianity assumed different forms. There was, of course, the Jewish Christianity that took shape in Jerusalem and Galilee around such figures as Peter, John, and Jesus' brother James. Those who personally knew Jesus, his mission, and his message and who followed him during his lifetime and became his disciples belong to the category of Jewish Christians or Christian Jews in the period following Jesus' death.

There was no "orthodoxy" among Jesus' earliest followers, no single authority to whom everyone turned for answers to questions concerning what Jesus taught or who Jesus was. That would come much later. Jesus' disciple Peter and Jesus' brother James assumed some authority relatively early, at least in Jerusalem, but the Jesus movement at that time was still little more than a small sect within Judaism. Those who followed the Way were initially Aramaic-speaking Jews.

There soon arose another movement: Hellenistic Christianity, a movement associated with Greek-speaking and Greek-thinking followers of Jesus, associated in the Acts of the Apostles initially with Stephen and subsequently and most importantly with the Hellenistic Jew Paul of Tarsus, a figure from the Jewish Diaspora, those Jews who lived outside Palestine.. As we know from Acts and from some of Paul's letters, Paul and the Jerusalem apostles did not always see eye to eye on critical issues regarding the role of the Jewish law in the lives of Hellenistic converts to the Way.

In the earliest years of the Jesus movement, Jewish Christians and Gentile Christians were sometimes headed in very different directions. In fact, decisions taken at the Jerusalem Council in about 50, about twenty years after the death of Jesus, effectively allowed the two movements to coexist side by side. Peter was the designated *apostle* to the Jews, and Paul the *messenger* to the Gentiles (Gal 2:8). That arrangement was fragile, and Jewish Christians, perhaps delegates from James, appear sometimes to have followed in the footsteps of Paul to "correct" his message by trying to impose on his converts a brand of Christianity that upheld the authority of the Jewish law, including the law of circumcision and Jewish dietary laws, as obligatory even for Gentile Christians. It was an uneasy time. The diversity within the Jesus movement was not always cordial. Jewish Christianity and Gentile Christianity were sometimes in competition and even in stark disagreement regarding important issues.

Christianity's stunning early success in the Gentile world and its relative lack of success among Jews during the generation of the apostles between about 30 and 70 determined the course that Christianity would follow in subsequent generations. This chapter focuses on some of the forms that Christianity assumed in the generations immediately following the apostolic age—the period of Peter, James, John, and Paul—when Christianity became increasingly more diverse. In fact, instead of speaking about sub-apostolic or post-apostolic Christianity during the period after 70, I would call this the period of post-apostolic Christiani*ties*, thereby emphasizing the diversity within the church, a diversity that sometimes betrayed greater differences than similarities among the various movements or sects that considered themselves Christian.[1]

We shall look in this chapter at five of these movements, recognizing that there are important differences even within each group. In fact, identifying them as distinct movements or tendencies sometimes begs the question, because these categories are modern constructs and are somewhat amorphous, and they sometimes overlap. Nevertheless, it is helpful to group some of the Christian tendencies in order better to understand the ways in which Christianity or Christianities evolved in the period after 70 C.E. and through most of the second century.

JEWISH CHRISTIANITIES

Unfortunately we know little about Jewish Christianity beyond what we find in a few books in the canonical New Testament, in some Christian apocryphal writings, and in the testimony of some church fathers. As history would have it, Jewish Christianity did not succeed in challenging the movement or movements that eventually evolved into orthodox Christianity. What we know about many movements within Jewish Christianity survives primarily in the form of polemic, limited information from church fathers who opposed certain Jewish Christian movements or sects that survived into the second and third centuries. Accordingly, information about Jewish Christianity is limited, and it is difficult to know how significant some of these groups were.

Jesus was born a Jew, lived as a Jew, and died a Jew. He never intended to establish a new religion; he sought to bring reforms to Judaism. So too Jesus' family, his disciples, and his earliest followers were Jews. Jewish Christians during the apostolic and the post-apostolic periods were primarily observant Jews, whose only distinguishing characteristic was that they acknowledged that Jesus was the Jewish messiah. For all Jewish Christians of the first generation, the Hebrew scriptures were authoritative, and the Judaism(s) of the period afforded the theological framework for emerging Christian theology and Christology.[2]

---

1. When speaking of sub-apostolic or post-apostolic Christianity (or Christianities), I am referring to the period after 70, the date by which most of the first generation of Jesus' apostles had died, and coincidentally the date of the fall of Jerusalem to the Romans.

2. In referring to the Judaisms of the first century, I want to call attention to the diversity evident

The Acts of the Apostles does not refer to this group as Jewish Christians or Christian Jews. The early Jewish followers of Jesus, who were apparently led by Jesus' apostles Simon Peter and John and Jesus' brother James, the "pillars of the church" in Jerusalem, are known in Acts as "the Way" (Acts 9:2; 18:25; 19:9, 23; 22:4; 24:14, 22). Early Jewish followers of Jesus assumed that non-Jews who followed the Way would become Jews, undergo adult circumcision, and adopt Jewish customs, such as the dietary laws.

Paul challenged that assumption when he confronted Peter in Antioch regarding the role of the Jewish law for Gentile converts (Gal 2:11–14). Scholars disagree about how the confrontation between Peter and Paul in Antioch was ultimately resolved. Some maintain that Peter recognized the legitimacy of Paul's rebuke, backed off, and served subsequently as the mediator between the opposing positions of Paul and Jesus' brother James. Others maintain that Paul's challenge to Peter at Antioch failed miserably and that Paul departed from Antioch shortly thereafter as a *persona non grata*, never again to return to the Antioch church. We do not know how that confrontation was ultimately resolved.

The controversy regarding Paul and Jewish Christians was fought largely between opposing groups, both of which were ethnic Jews. Although both agreed that Jesus was messiah, they disagreed about whether conversion to Judaism was a prerequisite for conversion to Christianity. Paul's position on the issue was clear. He maintained that Jesus was much more than the Jewish messiah and that Christianity was much more than a Jewish sect. The risen Lord, Paul believed, offered salvation to everyone, both Jews and Gentiles, apart from works of the Jewish law. Paul maintained uncompromisingly that obedience to the Jewish law was not an obligation for converted Gentiles.

Christians who continued to maintain the importance of the Jewish law are often referred to not as Jewish Christians, but as Christian Jews. There is evidence in the gospels of Matthew, Luke, and John of controversies between Jesus and the Jews that may actually reflect the ongoing influence of Jews and Christian Jews on the church through the end of the first and even into the beginning of the second century.

THE LETTER OF JAMES

Although it is difficult to assign a specific date to the Letter of James, it appears that sometime toward the end of the first century someone wrote this book, the most Jewish document in the New Testament. The book is written in the name of Jesus' brother James, although few scholars believe that James was its author. Neither is it really a letter. Although the book begins with an appropriate epistolary greeting, it has no comparable epistolary ending.

---

in Palestinian Judaism and Hellenistic Judaism, and to various sects or parties in Palestinian Judaism, most evidently Pharisees, Sadducees, and Essenes.

There are only two references to Christ in the entire book (Jas 1:1 and 2:1), leading some scholars to argue that these verse may be nothing more than Christian editorial additions to an otherwise Jewish writing, whose examples of patience during times of suffering are drawn from the Hebrew prophets and Job rather than from the life of Jesus, as one would expect in a Christian book (Jas 5:10–11).

Perhaps most important, this book appears to challenge a core element in Paul's teaching, one that was sometimes misrepresented in Deutero-Pauline circles, Paul's doctrine of justification by faith (Jas 2:14–26). Key to the author's argument is Jas 2:14: "What good is it, my brothers and sisters, if you say you have faith but do not have works? Can faith save you?" The Letter of James won canonical status slowly. Although James was accepted as scripture by the church in Alexandria in the third century, it won acceptance in the Western church only in the fourth century, and in the Syrian church only in the fifth century. Martin Luther questioned the authority of James because it challenged an important element in his interpretation of Paul: justification by faith *alone* (*fide sola*).

Although it is difficult to assign a date and place of composition to the Letter of James, it appears that it was written sometime after the fall of Jerusalem, perhaps as a reflection of a Jewish-Christian position in opposition to Pauline Christianity.

THE GOSPEL OF MATTHEW

The Gospel of Matthew is the most Jewish of the proto-canonical gospels and may have been written to afford a mediating position between Jewish Christianity and Gentile Christianity. The gospel is heavily dependent on the Greek Septuagint translation of Hebrew scriptures. It sees Jesus as the fulfillment of promises in the Law and the Prophets, and it represents Jesus as the New Moses who delivers the new law in the Sermon on the Mount (Matt 5–7), just as Moses received the original law on Mount Sinai. The gospel is clearly at odds with Pharisaic Judaism, the group that emerged as a major religious influence in Judaism following the fall of Jerusalem in 70. Jesus accuses the Pharisees of being "hypocrites" (Matt 23:13-15, 27, 29) and calls for righteousness that exceeds that of the scribes and Pharisees (Matt 5:17–20). Yet Jesus is said to have come not to abolish the Law and the Prophets, but to fulfill them (Matt 5:17).

Matthew's Christology moved beyond the adoptionist Christology of the Gospel of Mark, which traced Jesus' Messiahship from his baptism by John. Instead, Matthew introduces the theme of the virgin birth, whereby Jesus is the child of Mary and the Holy Spirit and who is, therefore, both human and divine from the moment of his conception. Matthew's account of Jesus birth is built around a number of "proof texts" from the Hebrew scriptures (Matt 1:22–23 cites Isa 7:14; Matt 2:5b–6 cites Mic 5:2 combined with 2 Sam 5:2; Matt 2:15b cites Hos 11:1; Matt 2:17–18 cites Jer 31:15; but

Matt 2:23b cites no known Hebrew scripture).[3] Moreover, Matthew also traces Jesus genealogy (Matt 1:1–17) back to Abraham, the father of the Jews.

THE LETTER TO THE HEBREWS

The Letter to the Hebrews is also thoroughly Jewish in tone. The Septuagint Greek translation of the Hebrew scriptures may be the writer's principal source. Yet, it is not self-evident that the intended audience was Jewish Christians. The Jewish foundation of Christianity was evident to Gentile Christians early in the history of the movement, when followers of Jesus first began the search through the Septuagint for passages that helped them to understand Jesus, most especially his passion, death, and resurrection. Hebrews may be addressing a community familiar with the Hebrew scriptures, but not necessarily Jewish Christian.

Hebrews makes no claim of apostolic authorship. Although some early fathers, especially in the East, attributed it to Paul, others, including Origen, recognized that Hebrews is quite different from Paul's letters. In fact, Hebrews is probably not a letter, although it has an epistolary ending (Heb 13:19–25), similar to what we find in Rom 16:20–27; Phil 4:20–23; and 1 Thess 5:23–28. Hebrews is probably better characterized as a sermon, a "word of exhortation" (Heb 13:22). Neither is the title "A Letter to the Hebrews" original to the work. It was probably added to the text by a second century scribe, a mere conjecture based on the scribe's understanding of uncertain internal evidence.

The references most often cited as evidence of the book's Jewish character include the comparison of Moses and Jesus (Heb 3:1–6); the identification of Jesus as the great high priest of the order of Melchizedek (Heb 4:14–5:10; 7:1–28); the role of Jesus as the mediator of a better covenant (Heb 8:1–13); the comparison of the earthy and the heavenly sanctuaries (Heb 9:1–22); the discussion of Christ's one-time sacrifice (Heb 10:1–18); and the comparison of the faith of Israelite heroes (Abel, Enoch, Noah, Abraham, Moses, and many others with the example of Jesus (Heb 11:4–12:13).

Hebrews is first cited by Clement of Rome (*1 Clement* 36:2–6) in about 96, perhaps suggesting Rome as either the place of composition or the destination of Hebrews, and a date of composition before 95. This anonymous homily contains some of the most sophisticated Greek in the New Testament and has a developed Christology. Its author is clearly a second generation Christian (Heb 2:3–4). It is perhaps most prudent to suggest that the anonymous author was a highly educated Hellenistic

---

3. In addition to these four (or five) citations of scriptural "proof texts" in the birth narrative, Matthew cites scriptural "proof texts" nine additional times elsewhere in his gospel (Matt 3:3 cites Isa 40:3; Matt 4:14–16 cites Isa 9:1–2; Matt 8:17 cites Isa 53:4; Matt 12:17–21 freely cites Isa 42:1–4; Matt 13:14–15 cites Isa 6:9–10; Matt 13:35 cites Ps 78:2; Matt 21:4–5 combines Isa 62:11 and Zech 9:8; Matt 26:56 [see Matt 26:54] does not cite a specific text; and Matt 27:9–10 loosely cites Zech 11:13, mistakenly identified as Jeremiah).

Christian, perhaps a Hellenistic Jewish Christian, thoroughly familiar with the Septuagint and with Christianity's Jewish roots.

It is equally difficult to speculate about the original readers or listeners of Hebrews, except that they must have had some familiarity with the Septuagint Hebrew Bible. Rome and Alexandria probably have the strongest claim to the book's destination. Both cities had Hellenistic Jewish Christian populations late in the first century, Alexandria probably more than Rome. It is, however, impossible to know definitively where the original recipients of Hebrews lived. Hebrews is an example of the finest blending of Hellenism, Judaism, and Christianity in the latter part of the first century.

THE *DIDACHE*

The *Didache*, or the *Teaching of the Twelve Apostles*, is one of the oldest surviving Christian writings that did not become part of the Christian canon or the New Testament. In its current form, the *Didache* is a Jewish Christian book, probably a composite of earlier writings that were combined in the late first or early second century. In its present form, the *Didache* has four parts:

1. *Did* 1–6, the Two Ways, the Way of Life and the Way of Death, may have been drawn from a Jewish manual of the same name that was used in the synagogue for the initiation of proselytes and that was subsequently modified for use as a Christian manual of instruction for those preparing for Christian baptism. *Didache* 1 reflects most clearly Christian additions to what probably had previously been a Jewish manual.

2. *Did* 7–10 contains a description of early Christian rituals including baptism, fasting, and the celebration of the Eucharist. Baptism should be in the name of the Father, the Son, and the Holy Spirit, preferably in living (i.e. flowing) water. Fasts are to be observed not on Mondays and Thursdays with the hypocrites (i.e. non-Christian Jews), but on Wednesdays and Fridays. Prayer is not to be undertaken in the manner that Jews pray, but Christians should recite the Lord's Prayer three times a day. The Eucharist should be celebrated with the cup first, then the bread, and only by those who have been baptized.

    This section of the *Didache* concludes with the prayer *maranatha* (*Did* 10:6), Aramaic for "Lord Come," an ancient Christian prayer for Jesus' quick return recited by Christians to hasten the Second Coming (see also 1 Cor 16:22 for the only reference to this Aramaic prayer in the New Testament; and Rev 22:20, where a version of the same prayer appears in Greek: "Amen. Come, Lord Jesus!").

3. *Did* 11–15 deals with issues regarding Christian ministry, how to deal with traveling apostles, ministers, teachers, and prophets, and how to appoint worthy bishops and deacons.

4. *Did* 16 contains a brief apocalypse, proclaiming the resurrection of the dead at the last day and the coming of the Lord and all his holy ones with him in the clouds of heaven.

Identifying a date and place of composition of the *Didache* is difficult. Most scholars date the *Didache* to the end of the first century or the beginning of the second century. The *Didache* is still tied to its Jewish roots and reflects a simplicity characteristic of an early stage in the development of Jewish Christianity. The lack of any Christology and the repetition of the ancient prayer *maranatha* in Aramaic point to a date probably not later than 100.

I would suggest Syria or Palestine as the most likely place of composition, but Kurt Niederwimmer has stated correctly, "Regarding the provenance [of the *Didache*], we are completely in the dark."[4]

JEWISH CHRISTIANITIES IN THE EAST

Later Jewish Christian groups, perhaps descendants of the Jerusalem church who fled just before the Romans destroyed the city in 70 and settled east of the Jordan River in Transjordan, included Nazoreans, Ebionites, and Elchasaites, probably isolated Jewish Christian or Christian Jewish sects that continued to survive by embracing their Jewish ways.

1. Nazoreans

Although we cannot be sure of the reliability of his information, Epiphanius described the Nazoreans as an early Jewish Christian group that fled Jerusalem and settled in Pella in 70. The Nazoreans observed the Jewish law. The few fragments of the *Gospel of the Nazoreans* that survive indicate that this gospel was an Aramaic translation of the Gospel of Matthew, including the birth narrative, the temptation of Jesus, the Sermon on the Mount, and other stories characteristic of Matthew. In other words, the Aramaic-speaking Nazoreans appear to have entertained a proto-orthodox Christology and, therefore, to have been proto-orthodox Christians. Their strict adherence to the Jewish law may indicate that they could, indeed, have been descendants of the Jerusalem church that was associated most closely with Peter, James, and John.

2. Ebionites

The Ebionites also appear to have remained faithful adherents of the Jewish law. Although only seven fragments of the *Gospel of the Ebionites* survive in quotations from Epiphanius, it is clear that the Ebionites used a harmonized version of the synoptic

---

4. Niederwimmer, *The Didache*, 53.

gospels, that included a reference to the Baptism of Jesus, the call of the twelve apostles, and the last supper. Epiphanius notes specifically that the *Gospel of the Ebionites* did not contain an account of the genealogy and birth of Jesus but that it began, like the Gospel of Mark, with the appearance of John the Baptist (*GosEbion* 1a-b, 3, 4):

> [1a]Now the beginning of their gospel [of the Ebionites] goes like this:
>
> In the days of Herod, king of Judea, John appeared in the Jordan river baptizing with a baptism that changed people's hearts. He was said to be a descendant of Aaron the priest, a son of Zechariah and Elizabeth. And everybody went out to him.
>
> [1b]By mutilating Matthew's genealogy, they [the Ebionites] make the beginning say, as we have already stated:
>
> In the days of Herod, king of Judea, during the high-priesthood of Caiaphas,
>
> they say,
>
> this man named John appeared in the Jordan river baptizing with the baptism that changed people's hearts,
>
> and so on. (Epiphanius, *Heresies* 30)[5]
>
> [3]And
>
> It so happened that John was baptizing, and Pharisees and all Jerusalem went out to him and got baptized. And John wore clothes made of camel hair and had a leather belt around his waist. His food,
>
> it says,
>
> consisted of raw honey and tasted like manna, like a pancake cooked with oil.
>
> Thus they change the word of truth into a lie and instead of "locusts" (Greek *akris*), they put "pancake cooked with honey" (Greek *enkris*).
>
> [4]After saying many things, it adds:
>
> When the people were baptized, Jesus also came and got baptized by John. As he came up out of the water, the skies opened and he saw the holy spirit in the form of a dove coming down and entering him. And there was a voice from the sky that said, "You are my beloved son—I fully approve of you." And again, "Today I have become your father."
>
> And right away a bright light illuminated the place. When John saw this,
>
> it says,
>
> he said to him, "Who are you?" And again a voice from the sky said to him, "This is my favored son—I fully approve of him."
>
> it says,
>
> John knelt down in front of him and said, "Please, Lord, you baptize me."

---

5. Miller, editor, *The Complete Gospels*.

> But he stopped him and said, "It's all right. This is the way everything is supposed to be fulfilled."

This surviving fragment, especially fragment 4, indicates that Jesus became God's son at his baptism, an adoptionist Christology, which probably explains why the gospel omitted the genealogy and the birth narratives. According to the Ebionites, Jesus was not divine by birth but was adopted by God at his baptism, a theology similar to what we find in the Gospel of Mark.

In fragments 5 and 6, Epiphanius comments that the Ebionites "deny that he [Jesus] was human and that (Christ) was not born of God the Father, but created like one of the archangels." These two statements may appear to be contradictory, but they reflect a Christology that distinguishes between the humanity of Jesus before his baptism and the semi-divine Christ following God's "adoption" of Jesus at his baptism. This particular Christology is referred to as Docetism (from the Greek verb δοκέω, *dokeo*, meaning "to seem"), because the semi-divine Christ "seemed" to be human between his baptism and his death, at which time the divine nature left Jesus when he said in Aramaic, "*Eloi, Eloi, lema sabachthani* . . . My God, my God, why have you forsaken me?" (Mark 15:34 // Matt 27:46).

By affirming that Joseph and Mary were Jesus' parents, the *Gospel of the Ebionites* may reflect a reliable tradition that goes back to the Jerusalem church and specifically to Jesus' brother James.

3. Elchasaites

The Elchasaites were members of a second and third century Jewish Christian sect from Syria, who claimed that their teaching originated in Parthia with a man named Elchasai. Elchasai had reportedly received a revelation from an enormous angel, named the Son of God, who was accompanied by his sister, the Holy Spirit, also of enormous dimensions.

The Elchaisites taught the necessity of circumcision and of a second baptism, condemned continence and virginity and required marriage of all members, prayed facing Jerusalem, and condemned sacrifice. They also condemned the prophets and the apostles, and especially Paul and his letters, based perhaps on the position of Jesus' brother James. The Elchasaites seem to have interwoven elements of Judaism (circumcision and praying facing Jerusalem) with Gnosticism (the pairing of the angel named the Son of God and his sister the Holy Spirit).

Continuing differences persisted in the second and third centuries between Gentile Christianity and some more radical elements of Jewish Christianity or, perhaps more accurately, some forms of Christian Judaism often associated with Jesus' brother James. Differences focused on but were certainly not limited to ongoing disagreement over the authority of the Jewish law and the question of the authority of Paul, the nemesis of many Christian Jews. These differences may reflect and perpetuate early disagreements between Paul and Jesus' brother James.

DEUTERO-PAULINE OR POST-PAULINE CHRISTIANITY

There is an understandable tendency to assume that the evolution of Christianity from Jesus to Paul to Christian orthodoxy is a single straight line, and that alternative Christianities were heterodox or deviant heresies, consciously developed to oppose the apostolic faith. The truth is, of course, far more complicated.

As we have already seen, the transition from the historical Jesus to earliest Christianity is more complicated than most Christians are prepared to admit. Although Jesus' disciples may already have deviated significantly from the teaching of Jesus by focusing on the claim that Jesus had been raised from the dead and made Lord and Messiah, the differences between the teachings of the historical Jesus and the message of the Paul was probably even greater.

A brief review of the relationship between some of the teachings of Jesus and Paul is appropriate before we consider the relationship of post-Pauline Christianity to the teachings of Paul. There are several areas in which the teachings of the historical Jesus and Paul are markedly different, although we should remember that it is not an easy matter to reconstruct what we can know about the teachings of the historical Jesus:

1. Whereas Jesus probably understood that he was a prophetic messenger whom God had designated to proclaim the imminent coming of the eschatological Son of Man and the new age of God's rule, Paul taught that Jesus had already ushered in God's rule through his death and resurrection and that he would soon return as the eschatological judge.

2. Whereas Jesus apparently taught that Jews should live according to the basic principles of the Jewish Law as he represented and interpreted the Law in his command to love God and one another, Paul taught that belief in the death and resurrection of Jesus the messiah was the single path to salvation and that Jesus had brought an end to the role of the Jewish Law.

3. Whereas God was always at the center of Jesus' teaching, Jesus the Christ was always at the center of Paul's teaching.

4. Whereas Jesus taught that unqualified obedience to God's will would help to inaugurate the new age of God's rule, Paul believed that trust in Jesus' death and resurrection would precipitate the period of God's rule.

5. Whereas Jesus taught that the period of God's rule was already present in the lives of his followers whenever they listened to and lived according to his teaching, Paul believed that the period of God's rule began when Jesus defeated the power of sin through his death and resurrection.

THE NEW TESTAMENT

The differences between the teachings of Jesus and Paul are sufficiently evident that many scholars have stated the situation succinctly by maintaining that Paul changed the religion *of* Jesus into a religion *about* Jesus. Paul was, of course, not the only follower of Jesus to do so, but it was clearly Paul who laid the most solid theological foundation for Christianity to evolve into a new religion that would ultimately break with and be different from and distinct from its mother religion, Judaism. That may not have been Paul's intention, but it may have been the inevitable outcome of Paul's teaching since his fellow Jews did not universally embrace his message.

Scholars have generally understood Paul through a study of the seven letters that are almost universally recognized as genuine: Romans, 1 and 2 Corinthians, Galatians, Philippians, 1 Thessalonians, and Philemon. The term post-Pauline or deutero-Pauline is reserved for letters attributed to Paul whose authenticity is either disputed or rejected: three disputed letters, Ephesians, Colossians, and 2 Thessalonians; and three letters attributed to Paul that are almost universally rejected as non-Pauline: 1 and 2 Timothy and Titus. We will not consider in this section the anonymous Letter to the Hebrews, which was erroneously considered a letter of Paul by some early Christian fathers.

PSEUDEPIGRAPHY IN THE ANCIENT WORLD

Pseudepigraphy (from Greek ψευδεπίγραφος, *pseudepigraphos*, meaning "falsely ascribed"; comprised of ψευδής, *pseudes*, meaning "false"; ἐπί, *epi*, meaning "upon"; and γράφω, *grapho*, meaning "to write") is the false attribution of a writing to someone in order to afford greater authority and, perhaps, greater antiquity to that writing. The (false) attribution of a writing to a famous or respected ancient figure presumably afforded the writing and its contents a prestige it would not otherwise merit.

An example of pseudonymity (false naming) in the Hebrew Bible is the Book of Daniel, written in the second century BCE but purporting to come from the period of the Babylonian Exile four centuries earlier. Pseudepigraphy is especially evident in the books of the Old Testament Apocrypha and Pseudepigrapha.

Imitation was widespread in classical antiquity. In fact, it was taught as part of rhetorical training in schools in ancient Greece and Rome. It is, therefore, not surprising that some of the books of the New Testament are also pseudepigraphical, falsely ascribed to Paul or to some other person with apostolic authority. It is, however, important to distinguish between anonymous writings, such as Matthew, Mark, Luke, John, and Acts, which were attributed to important figures by a later generation, and writings that falsely claim authoritative authorship, such as those discussed below, as well as many of the apocryphal gospels discussed in the previous chapter.

EPHESIANS

The earliest and best manuscripts of the so-called Letter to the Ephesians lack the words "in Ephesus" in the salutation in Eph 1:1,[6] suggesting perhaps that this letter may have been intended originally as a circular letter for several churches. The addressees are identified as Gentiles by birth (Eph 2:11; 3:1), although they are exhorted not to continue to live in the ways that Gentiles live, "in the futility of their minds" (Eph 4:17), but rather to live in unity—both Jewish and Gentile Christians:

> [4:4]There is one body and one Spirit, just as you were called to the one hope of your calling, [5]one Lord, one faith, one baptism, [6]one God and Father of all, who is above all and through all and in all.

> [4:22]You were taught to put away your former way of life, your old self, corrupt and deluded by its lusts, [23]and to be renewed in the spirit of your minds, [25]and to clothe yourselves with the new self, created according to the likeness of God in true righteousness and holiness.

> [4:31]Put away from you all bitterness and wrath and anger and wrangling and slander, together with all malice, [32]and be kind to one another, tenderhearted, forgiving one another, as God in Christ has forgiven you. [5:1]Therefore be imitators of God, as beloved children, [2]and live in love, as Christ loved us and gave himself up for us, a fragrant offering and sacrifice to God.

Scholars have long recognized that there are significant differences of vocabulary, literary style, sentence structure, and theological perspective between Ephesians and the seven genuine letters of Paul and often maintain that a disciple of Paul wrote this circular letter in Paul's name, presumably sometime after Paul's death. The situation in Ephesians implies a later stage in the development of the church (Eph 3:1–5:20), more reminiscent of post-apostolic Christianity than of the nascent churches that Paul founded, visited, and addressed in his genuine letters.

A date in the last decades of the first century seems probable, but the author, the place of composition, and the intended destination(s) of the letter remain uncertain.

COLOSSIANS

The Letter to the Colossians purports to be a letter from Paul, written to address a situation in the Gentile church in Colossae in Asia Minor, a church that was apparently established by Epaphras and not Paul (Col 1:7–8).

Colossians maintains that Christians already share in Christ's resurrection (Col 2:12–13; 3:1), a view quite different from what we find in Paul's genuine letters.

---

6. Paul, an apostle of Christ Jesus by the will of God, to the saints who are (*in Ephesus and are*) faithful in Christ Jesus. [The words between parenteses and in italics were probably not in the original text of the letter.]

Moreover, Colossians shares many of the literary features of Ephesians, most especially long complex sentences and a good deal of common vocabulary (see chapter 2, pp. 60–65).

The controversy in the church at Colossae that this letter addresses is a "philosophy" and "empty deceit" (Col 2:8) that encouraged asceticism (Col 2:21, 23); circumcision (Col 2:9–11); observance of special holy times, such as festivals, new moons, or sabbaths (Col 2:13–17); self-abasement and worship of angels or elemental spirits of the universe (Col 2:8; 2:18–19); and a very different kind of Christianity that was being promoted by "false teachers" (Col 2:4).

The heart of the letter is the Christ hymn (Col 1:15–20), whose Christology goes beyond what we find in the genuine Pauline letters. Christ is the "image (Greek *eikon*) of the invisible God, the firstborn of all creation; for in him all things in heaven and on earth were created, things visible and invisible, whether thrones or dominions or rulers or powers—all things have been created through him and for him" (Col 1:15–16). Furthermore, the reference to Christ as "the head of the body, the church" (Col 1:18) occurs in none of the indisputably authentic letters of Paul.

As with Ephesians, it is impossible to assign a precise date, place of composition, and author to Colossians. And, as with Ephesians, it is likely that a disciple of Paul wrote Colossians in Paul's name, probably sometime after Paul's death in the final third of the first century.

2 THESSALONIANS

Although 2 Thessalonians purports to be the second letter addressed by Paul to the church at Thessalonica, many scholars have questioned whether it is actually a letter from Paul. Two verses in 2 Thessalonians are often cited to indicate that the letter is a forgery:

> . . . $^{2:2}$not to be quickly shaken in mind or alarmed, either by spirit or by word or *by letter, as though from us*, to the effect that the day of the Lord is already here.

Many scholars regard the words "by letter, as though from us" as evidence that 2 Thessalonians is a forged letter. This phrase presumably refers to 1 Thessalonians, which the author of 2 Thessalonians is apparently discrediting as a forgery probably because it has an apocalyptic eschatology different from that of 2 Thessalonians.

> $^{3:17}$I, Paul, write this greeting with my own hand. This is the mark in every letter of mine; it is the way I write.

Although Paul wrote closings with *his own hand* in 1 Cor 16:21; Gal 6:11; and Phlm 19, the particularly strong language in 2 Thess 3:17 is unusual (cf. also Col 4:18, also assumed to be pseudonymous).

Moreover, 2 Thessalonians has two thanksgivings (1:3 and 2:13), just like 1 Thessalonians (1:2 and 2:13), a feature that we find in no other Pauline letters, suggesting that 2 Thessalonians was consciously written in imitation of 1 Thessalonians.

Furthermore, the similarities between the opening words of 1 and 2 Thessalonians are so striking that many have seen in 2 Thessalonians a mimicking of 1 Thessalonians by a later pseudonymous author:

1 Thess 1:1–3	2 Thess 1:1–4
[1:1]Paul, Sylvanus, and Timothy, to the church of the Thessalonians in God the Father and the Lord Jesus Christ: Grace to you and peace.	[1:1]Paul, Sylvanus, and Timothy, to the church of the Thessalonians in God our Father, and the Lord Jesus Christ: [2]Grace to you and peace from God our Father and the Lord Jesus Christ.
[2]We always give thanks to God for all of you and mention you in our prayers,	[3]We must always give thanks to God for you, brothers and sisters, as is right, because your faith is growing abundantly, and the love of everyone of you for one another is increasing.
constantly [3]remembering before our God and Father your work of faith and labor of love and steadfastness of hope in our Lord Jesus Christ.	[4]Therefore we ourselves boast of you among the churches of God for your steadfastness and faith during all your persecutions and the afflictions that you are enduring.

Striking is the difference between 1 and 2 Thessalonians regarding Jesus' second coming (Greek παρουσία, *parousia*). Whereas 1 Thess 4:13–5:11 assumes that Jesus' second coming is imminent, 2 Thess 2:2 sets aside the imminence of Jesus' second coming by saying that "the day of the Lord is already here," even as it lists everything that must happen before Jesus' second coming (2 Thess 2:3–12), implying that it is still far in the future and no longer imminent. Perhaps the words in 2 Thess 2:2 (*by letter, as though from us*) was a device of the author, intended to discredit Paul's warning of Jesus' imminent second coming in 1 Thessalonians. The author of 2 Thessalonians was perhaps trying to "interpret" or "correct" 1 Thessalonians by stating that the day of the Lord was already here. After all, 1 Thess 5:4–5 states that the Thessalonians are already "children of light and children of the day" and are not "children of the night or of darkness."

If both 1 and 2 Thessalonians are genuine letters of Paul, the second letter must have been written shortly after the first to the same church at Thessalonica, but the differences between the two letters regarding Jesus' second coming make a close dating improbable. If, on the other hand, 2 Thessalonians is a pseudonymous letter, it was probably written much later than 1 Thessalonians, perhaps sometime in the last decades of the first century to "reinterpret" or "correct" the earlier Pauline eschatology.

1 AND 2 TIMOTHY AND TITUS

These three letters should be looked at together, as they appear to be from the same time and place, and probably the same author. Although they purport to be from Paul, 1 and 2 Timothy and Titus are very different from the indisputably genuine letters of Paul, and scholars are almost unanimous in regarding them as Deutero-Pauline. These three letters are different in language and literary style as well as in their understanding of basic Pauline concepts, such as law, faith, and righteousness. The three so-called Pastoral Letters also focus on church order and governance and on the matter of good works in a way that is quite different from Paul and that obviously reflects a later stage in the development of the church during the post-apostolic age.

The author of the Pastoral Letters was likely familiar with some of the genuine letters of Paul, but he also made use of other sources: rules regarding church order (1 Tim 2:1–2; 2:8–12; 3:1–13; Titus 1:5–9), rules regarding appropriate behavior (1 Tim 5:1–6:2; Titus 2:1–15; 3:1–11), and lists of virtues and vices of the sort familiar from Hellenistic philosophy of the period (1 Tim 1:9–10; 6:4–5; 2 Tim 3:2–5; Titus 3:3).

The three letters address two common problems: the emergence of false teachers who are creating problems in their respective churches, and the matter of authority in the churches, most specifically the matter of church leadership and internal organization.

The Pastoral Letters are generally dated to the first quarter of the second century, possibly in Ephesus, if there is any significance to the frequent mention of Ephesus in the letters (1 Tim 1:3; 2 Tim 1:18; 4:12). The letters are addressed to Timothy, whom Paul left in Ephesus to minister to the church in that city, and to Titus, whom Paul left in Crete for the same purpose. Timothy and Titus were two of Paul's most respected co-workers. Like the authorship, the addressees are also fictitious.

1 Timothy

It appears that 1 Timothy was written primarily to suppress a form of Christian Gnosticism:

1 Tim 1:3–4

> I urge you . . . [to] instruct certain people . . . not to occupy themselves with myths and endless genealogies that promote speculations rather than the divine training that is known by faith.

1 Tim 4:3

> They forbid marriage and demand abstinence from foods, which God created to be received with thanksgiving by those who believe and know the truth.

1 Tim 6:20–21

> Timothy, guard what has been entrusted to you. Avoid the profane chatter and contradictions of what is falsely called knowledge (Greek *gnosis*); by professing it some have missed the mark as regards the faith.

The letter also speaks to the issue of women leaders in the church and directs that there be only male leaders who are morally upright (1 Tim 2:11–15; 5:11–13). This opposition to women leaders is quite different from circumstances in the churches that Paul established with women in positions of leadership (Rom 16:1–2, 3, 6, 7, 12; 1 Cor 1:11; 16:19; Gal 3:28; Phil 4:2–3).

2 Timothy

2 Timothy was written to combat opponents (2 Tim 3:2–5) who maintained that the resurrection had already taken place in the church, a situation similar to what we found in other Deutero-Pauline letters. This is an especially interesting point, because it reveals that there was diversity even within the Pauline camp.

Titus

The letter to Titus is similar in tone to 1 Timothy. It too appears to be combating a form of Christian Gnosticism (Titus 1:5–9; 1:10–16) as well as dealing with matters involving the appointment of elders (Titus 1:5–9).

MARCION

According to an account in Hippolytus (ca. 170–ca. 236), Marcion was born in about 85 in Sinope on the Black Sea, the son of Sinope's bishop. It is not clear whether it was in Asia or in Rome that Marcion developed his view that Christianity should be distinct from Judaism, but in ca. 142 Marcion traveled from Ephesus to Rome, where he continued to teach and where he launched a rival church with strong ascetic leanings. Marcion was excommunicated from the Roman church ca. 144.

Marcion was a radical Paulinist and stressed the discontinuity between Judaism and Christianity. As such, he maintained that the Creator God of Judaism was different from the Father of Jesus. He further taught that the teachings of Paul were incompatible with prevailing Christian teaching, which misrepresented and even subverted Paul's gospel. Consistent with what he believed was a correct understanding of Paul, Marcion rejected the authority of the Old Testament and published in its place the earliest canon of Christian writings, consisting of one gospel and one apostle: an edition of the Gospel of Luke expurgated of all references to the Old Testament and ten letters of Paul—Romans, 1 and 2 Corinthians, Galatians, Ephesians, Philippians, Colossians, 1 and 2 Thessalonians, and Philemon, but not including the Pastoral Letters, 1 and 2 Timothy and Titus. To this canon, Marcion attached his own *Antitheses*, a catalogue of contradictions between the Old Testament and the teachings of Jesus.

At a time before Docetism had been formally condemned by church fathers, Marcion promoted a docetic Christology, denying Jesus' full humanity.

Paul's teaching of the universality of Jesus' message and of the Christian gospel had a significant influence on Marcion's theology. Marcion took Paul's position to what he believed was its logical conclusion: a total rejection of Christianity's Jewish roots. Marcion was a radical Paulinist, who took Pauline theology to a new level, a view which won him many followers, on the one hand, and excommunication from the Roman church in about 144, on the other hand. Following comments in Justin Martyr, some scholars maintain that there were probably more Marcionites than non-Marcionities in many areas of the Roman world in the late second century and even into the fourth and fifth centuries.

Marcion's significance is that Marcionism was the earliest Pauline reform in the history of Christianity and that it assured a permanent place for Paul's letters in the canon at a time when Paul was not always in favor in many regions of the Christian world. It is surprising that it was a Christian "heretic," someone excommunicated from the Roman church, who played a major role in legitimizing Paul. Moreover, it is ironic that the influence of Marcion's canon survives in the structure of the canonical New Testament.

JOHANNINE CHRISTIANITY

The literary evidence for Johannine Christianity is characterized first and foremost in the Gospel of John, and secondarily and perhaps subsequently in the letters know as 1, 2, and 3 John. The relationship of the Revelation of John to Johannine Christianity is less clear and will be addressed separately in the next chapter.

The complex nature of the Johannine literature makes it difficult to trace the origins, the history, and the essential character of Johannine Christianity. Nevertheless, the Gospel of John reveals that there was apparently a relatively early community of Jesus' followers who took a stand against the Jewish background in which they arose and against which they subsequently defined and defended themselves. Where this community lived is unclear, although Ephesus, Syria, and Alexandria are possible locations for Johannine Christianity.

The Johannine community believed that Jesus was the definitive revelation of God's will and that they were in intimate contact with both God and Jesus through the guidance and the inspiration of the Comforter (the Paraclete, Greek παράκλητος, *parakletos*), God's Holy Spirit. And through their relationship with God and Jesus, they knew of their intimate relationship with one another and with fellow believers elsewhere with whom they were also in communion.

THE GOSPEL OF JOHN

Although the author of the Gospel of John used traditional written sources in composing his gospel, the essence of this community's faith was expressed in a distinctive and markedly different way in both its ironic and symbolic language and in its insightful Christology that explored new ways of characterizing the community's faith in the risen Christ. In fact, the Christ of Johannine Christianity is significantly and substantively different from the Jesus of the synoptic gospels. The Jesus of the Gospel of John is the self-proclaiming divine Son of God, the incarnation of the divine Logos, who was present with God before creation. He bears little to no resemblance to the Jesus of the Gospel of Mark's Messianic Secret.

Everyday life in the Johannine community probably included the rituals of baptism and the eucharist that were known to other followers of Jesus, yet the Gospel of John makes no specific mention of either Jesus' baptism or the celebration of the eucharist at the Last Supper. The focus seems rather to be on the spiritual value of traditional Christian rituals. Sometimes, the Jesus of John is almost docetic. From start to finish, he is the risen Lord, who although human ("and the divine Logos became flesh" in John 1:14) appears more obviously divine from the very beginning of the gospel. Furthermore, there are in the Gospel of John no genealogy of Jesus and no birth or infancy narratives, and Joseph of Nazareth appears to be Jesus' biological father (John 1:45; 6:42).

The Johannine Christian community apparently experienced serious conflict with synagogue authorities of the Jewish community in which members of the Johannine circle had their origin. In fact, synagogue authorities appear to have expelled from the synagogue members of the Johannine community, probably sometime after 80, in what was clearly a painful experience (John 9:22; 12:42; 16:2). It is likely that the group that was expelled were Jews of the Jewish Christian variety.

The purpose of the Gospel of John is stated clearly in John 20:31

> But these things are written so that you (plural) may come to believe that Jesus is the Messiah, the Son of God, and that through believing you may have life in his name.[7]

---

7. The phrase "may come to believe that Jesus is the Messiah" is puzzling, because it suggests that the audience did not yet believe that Jesus was the Messiah, the Son of God. Was the gospel addressed initially to Jews within the Johannine community who had not yet accepted Jesus? Some ancient manuscripts read "may *continue* to believe" instead of what appears to be the more original "may *come* to believe." Were later scribes clarifying the meaning of the original, or were they altering the earlier reading to conform the gospel's message to a later and more clearly believing community of Johannine Jewish Christians?

Mention of the Johannine community's expulsion from the synagogue together with the gospel's highly developed Christology point to a date for the gospel late in the first or early in the second century. Moreover, passages like John 12:16; 14:25–26; and 16:12–13 may indicate not only a significant passage of time but the conscious development or evolution of the message as the author acknowledged that his gospel, expressed through the risen Lord and the inspiration of the Holy Spirit and informed by prophecies in the Hebrew scriptures, was different from what Jesus and the earliest church had taught previously.[8] In John, the historical Jesus clearly reinterprets the past in light of what was subsequently revealed to the church by the Holy Spirit.

THE JOHANNINE LETTERS

The Johannine letters suggest that divisions caused disputes in the Johannine community in the early second century. Most scholars maintain that the author of the Johannine letters is different from the author of the Gospel of John, because of differences in their ideas and respective styles of writing. Yet similarities and commonality among the Johannine writings suggest that they all originated in the same circle or school.[9]

From 1 John 2:18–27 and 4:1–3, we learn of the situation that occasioned the writing of 1 John.[10] The problem described is the departure from the church of a group or faction, who are identified as "antichrists" or "liars" (1 John 2:18, 22), who denied "that Jesus is the Christ" (1 John 2:22) and believed that Jesus Christ had not come in the flesh (1 John 4:2). This group or faction that left the Johannine circle apparently believed that Jesus was a spirit and not a physical human being, a belief generally referred to as Docetism (from the Greek δοκέω, *dokeo*, meaning "to appear" or "to seem").[11]

---

8. John 12:16 His disciples did not understand these things at first; but when Jesus was glorified, they remembered that these things had been written of him and had been done to him.
John 14:25–26 [Jesus said,] "I have said these things to you while I am still with you. But the Advocate, the Holy Spirit, whom the Father will send in my name, will teach you everything, and remind you of all that I have said to you."
John 16:12–13 [Jesus said,] "I still have many things to say to you, but you cannot bear them now. When the Spirit of truth comes, he will guide you into all truth, for he will not speak on his own, but will speak whatever he hears, and he will declare to you the things that are to come."

9. We know of the existence of schools with teacher-student relationships among the Pythagoreans, the Stoics, and the Essenes. Philo of Alexandria and Rabbi Hillel also established schools. Among Christians, there was apparently a school of Paul as suggested by the Deutero-Pauline literature; and Krister Stendahl has written about a Matthean school (in *The School of Saint Matthew*). So too, Justin and Irenaeus established schools in Rome and Lyons respectively; and it is common to refer to Antiochene and Alexandrian schools of Christianity.

10. 1 John is actually a sermon or an essay or a polemic treatise, not a letter. It contains none of the customary epistolary greetings or conclusions.

11. Docetists believed that Jesus only *appeared* or *seemed* to have a physical body. In reality Jesus was for them pure spirit, so his physical body was simply an illusion. So too, Jesus' death by crucifixion was also an illusion, because, as pure spirit, Jesus could not have physically died on the cross.

In 2 John, which is a letter addressed to a community, the author identifies himself as an elder (2 John 1), a recognized leader within the community he is addressing. The anonymous writer appears to be referring to the same situation regarding false teachers as that described in 1 John.[12] Such similarity of situation and literary style suggest that 1 and 2 John were written by the same author.

Like 2 John, 3 John was also written by an elder, presumably the person who wrote both 1 and 2 John; but 3 John is addressed to an individual named Gaius and not to a community. Although 3 John does not describe the historical circumstances that occasioned the letter, both 2 and 3 John use similar vocabulary, and in both letters the elder announces his intention to visit sometime soon (2 John 12; 3 John 13–14). In an effort to link the three Johannine letters, some have argued that Diotrephes, mentioned in 3 John 9, may be the person who led the walkout alluded to in 1 and 2 John, but this is mere conjecture. The Demetrius referred to in 3 John 12 may be the person who delivered the letter to Gaius, but that too is unclear.

We know that by the middle of the second century some gnostic communities had a high regard for the Gospel of John. The gospel's symbolic language often enabled Gnostics like Heracleon, a member of the Valentinian school who flourished about 175–180, to extend a gnostic interpretation to the gospel by means of the method of spiritual or symbolic interpretation that he used in his commentary on the Gospel of John.[13]

By the end of the second century, Johannine Christianity had gained acceptance in wider Christian circles. Consequently, Johannine Christianity made a substantial contribution to the subsequent emergence of Christian orthodoxy. It was, in fact, Johannine Christology that eventually set the tone for many of the theological and Christological formulas that by the fourth and fifth centuries resulted in the orthodox formulations of the Trinity and the nature of Jesus Christ as wholly God and wholly man, formulations that led to some of the creeds of the church.

The question of where we should locate the center of the Johannine community remains elusive. Eusebius reports (*Church History* 3.23.1–4) that Irenaeus, writing in about 200, believed that John, the disciple of Jesus, was the author of the Gospel of John, and that he lived in Ephesus into the reign of Emperor Trajan (98–117):

> [1]At that time the apostle and evangelist John, the one whom Jesus loved, was still living in Asia, and governing the churches of that region, having returned after the death of Domitian from his exile on the island. [2]And that he was still alive at that time may be established by the testimony of two witnesses. They should be trustworthy who have maintained the orthodoxy of the Church; and such indeed were Irenæus and Clement of Alexandria. [3]The former in the second book of his work *Against Heresies*, writes as follows [Irenaeus, *Against Heresies* 2.22.50]: "And all the elders that associated with John the disciple of the Lord in Asia bear

---

12. 2 John 7 "Many deceivers have gone out into the world, those who do not confess that Jesus Christ has come in the flesh; any such person is the deceiver and the antichrist!"

13. We know about Heracleon's *Commentary on the Gospel of John* from about fifty references to the work in the writings of Origen.

witness that John delivered it to them. For he remained among them until the time of Trajan." ⁴And in the third book of the same work he attests the same thing in the following words [*Against Heresies* 3.3.4]: "But the church in Ephesus also, which was founded by Paul, and where John remained until the time of Trajan, is a faithful witness of the apostolic tradition."

Although second century tradition identifies Ephesus as the place of composition of the Johannine corpus, there are difficulties with this view. Johannine Christianity is really quite different from the Pauline Christianity that might have characterized Ephesian theology and Christology.

Helmut Koester identifies Syria as the center of Johannine Christianity and argues that the Gospel of John combined traditions of Johannine communities with traditions from Syrian Christianity, some of which may have emerged from circles under the authority of Peter.[14]

I continue to think that Egypt, and specifically Alexandria, may be a possible place of composition for the Johannine writings. The John Rylands papyrus (p^{52}), which contains a few verses of the Gospel of John and which dates from before the middle of the second century, was discovered in Egypt. So too, Papyrus Egerton 2, which bears some resemblance to the Gospel of John and which may "be a text that is older than the Gospel of John"[15] is also from Egypt from the early second century. Moreover, the Nag Hammadi writings include "very rich material of revelation discourses and dialogues with many analogies to the Johannine speeches."[16] In addition, the writings of Philo of Alexandria may have informed the Johannine community, most specifically regarding the concept of the divine Logos, so evident in the prologue to the Gospel of John.

Clearly, we do not know with certainty where Johannine Christianity originated, but we do know that wherever it originated, whether in Ephesus, or in Syria, or in Alexandria, it was an important component in second century Christianity and played a major role in the subsequent emergence of catholic Christianity.

PETRINE CHRISTIANITY

Jesus' apostle Peter is a relatively elusive figure in the early church, especially considering his apparent importance both during Jesus' ministry and in the events subsequent to Jesus' death and burial.

---

14. Koester, *Introduction to the New Testament*, vol 2, 178.
15. Koester, volume 2, 182.
16. Koester, volume 2, 179.

The Primacy of Peter

Peter is listed, along with his brother Andrew, as the first of the apostles whom Jesus called (Matt 4:18-20; Mark 1:16-18; Luke 5:1-11). Along with James and John, Peter was also identified as part of an inner circle of three in the Gospel of Mark (Mark 3:16-17; 5:37; 9:2-13; 13:3-8; 14:33-41). In the synoptic gospels, it was Peter who first confessed that Jesus is messiah (Matt 16:13-16; Mark 8:27-29; Luke 9:20) and who, following that confession in the Gospel of Matthew, is identified as the rock on which the church is founded (Matt 16:17-19). Peter denied Jesus before his arrest and crucifixion (Matt 26:69-75; Mark 14:66-72; Luke 22:55-62), and it is reported that the risen Christ first appeared to Peter (1 Cor 15:5a; Luke 24:34).

Peter was apparently part of the early leadership of the Jerusalem church, together with John and Jesus' brother James (Gal 2:9). He is identified by Paul as the apostle to the Jews, even as Paul was considered the missionary to the Gentiles (Gal 1:8). Peter may have been the first leader of the Jerusalem church (Gal 1:8), but he was also associated subsequently with the church in Antioch (ca. 50–60), where Paul confronted him for his hypocrisy in withdrawing from celebrating the eucharistic meal with Gentile Christians after emissaries from James arrived from Jerusalem and criticized Peter for violating Jewish laws of purity by associating with uncircumcised Gentile Christians (Gal 2:11-14). Whether the disagreement with Paul was ever fully resolved is not clear, but Paul apparently moved from Antioch to the Gentile mission field, whereas Peter seems to have remained in Antioch for an unknown period of time.

Peter eventually found his way to Rome, probably about 60 just a few years before he was martyred during the persecution of Christians during the reign of the Emperor Nero in 64 (John 21:18-19; *1 Clement* 5:4-5). However, Peter was not a founder of the Roman church; neither was he bishop (Greek *episcopos*) of the Roman church, a second century tradition (Irenaeus, *Against Heresies* 3.1.5; Eusebius, *Church History* 2.14.6; 2.25.5-8).[17]

Tradition attributes the Gospel of Mark to Peter's disciple John Mark (Eusebius, *Church History* 2.15.2). Although the Gospel of Mark is anonymous, there may be some validity to the tradition that it comes from followers of Peter in Antioch, a couple of decades after Peter presumably left Antioch for Rome. Moreover, two letters in the New Testament canon are attributed pseudepigraphically to Peter, 1 and 2 Peter.

1 Peter

Allegedly written by Peter from Rome to churches in the Roman provinces of Pontus, Galatia, Cappadocia, Asia, and Bithynia, the pseudonymous author of 1 Peter wrote in very elegant Greek to address issues in Christian communities in Asia Minor several decades after Peter's martyrdom in 64.

17. 1 Pet 5:1 refers to Peter as an elder (Greek πρεσβύτερος, *presbyteros*)

1 Peter obviously addresses developments late in the first or early in the second century, most specifically challenges that Christian were experiencing as a result of their Christian faith. It is evident that at the time of the writing of 1 Peter Christianity was relatively widespread in Asia, followers of Jesus were now commonly referred to as Christians (1 Pet 4:16), and Rome was referred to by Christians as Babylon (1 Pet 5:13). It was clearly many decades after Peter's death.

Christian readers of 1 Peter were living under the threat of sporadic persecution (1 Pet 1:6; 5:9–10), probably primarily verbal abuse (1 Pet 3:9, 15), not systematic persecution or martyrdom. Christianity was not banned during this period, but it was difficult for Christians to participate in activities involving Roman deities at a time when religion and politics were essentially inseparable (1 Pet 3:13–17). The author of 1 Peter understood that Christians in Asia were essentially exiles and aliens and that living in a Greco-Roman culture posed challenging threats to Christians, who could not participate in such pagan activities, hence the occasion for this letter.

2 Peter and Jude

The pseudonymous author of 2 Peter was obviously familiar with both 1 Peter and Jude, His opening salutation reflects a blending of both letters: "Simeon Peter, a servant (Jude 1) and apostle (1 Pet 1:1) of Jesus Christ." Moreover, 2 Pet 3:1 refers specifically to 1 Peter: "This is now, beloved, the second letter I am writing to you." Furthermore, Pet 2:1–22 is obviously dependent on Jude 4–16.

In the first section (1 Pet 1:3–21), Peter maintains that God has made known to believers his expectations in order for them to gain immortality. Specifically, the apostles were "eyewitnesses of his majesty" (1 Pet 1:16) and bearers of "the prophetic message" (1 Pet 1:19), which everyone should follow.

The second section (1 Pet 2:1–22) deals with the emergence, the deception, and the punishment of false prophets and false teachers, even as God punished such persons in the past.

The third section (1 Pet 3:1–10) is concerned with issues surrounding Jesus' second coming (Greek παρουσία, *parousia*), which "will come like a thief" (1 Pet 3:10) in spite of the denial of some false teachers.

The author of 2 Peter was clearly an educated Hellenist, not a Galilean fisherman, who stood solidly in the Petrine tradition, emphasizing true prophecy and its apostolic (= Petrine) origin:

> 3:1This is now, beloved, the second letter I am writing to you; in them I am trying to arouse your sincere intention by reminding you ²that you should remember the words spoken in the past by holy prophets, and the commandments of the Lord and Savior spoken through your apostles.

2 Peter was probably written in the first quarter of the second century, clearly after 1 Peter and Jude had been written and circulated. Although it is impossible to determine its place of origin, Rome is likely, as it seems to have been the center of Petrine Christianity. 2 Peter was first cited by Origen of Alexandria (ca. 185–254) as quoted in Eusebius's *Church History* 6.25.8:

> And Peter, on whom the Church of Christ is built, 'against which the gates of hell shall not prevail' (Matt 16:18), has left one acknowledged Epistle; possibly also a second, but this is disputed.

Other Petrine Writings

There are several Christian writings from the second century and later that also reflect Peter's influence and that were probably written by followers or admirers of Peter:

Gospel of Peter (early- or mid-second century)

Apocalypse of Peter (mid-second century)

Preaching of Peter (second century)

Acts of Peter and the Twelve Apostles (late-second century)

Acts of Peter (ca. 170–190)

Martyrdom of Peter (ca. 170–190)

Acts of Peter and Paul (sixth or seventh century)

Martyrdom of Peter and Paul (sixth or seventh century)

GNOSTIC CHRISTIANITIES

THE ORIGINS OF GNOSTICISM

The origins of Gnosticism and, more specifically, of Christian Gnosticism are unclear, but by the middle of the second century there were a number of features that appeared with some frequency in the full blown Gnosticism of that period. More specifically, Gnostic writings of the second and third centuries engaged in speculative mythologies, sometimes based on early chapters of Genesis, that included many of the following elements:

> a radical ontological dualism of good and evil;
>
> the belief in an "unknown" God or Father, who is different from the God of the Old Testament;
>
> the offspring of this God and his female consort or Mother in the form of many generations of pairs of male and female beings, who served as intermediaries between the "unknown" God and humankind;

the role of these intermediaries in producing the evil, material world;

the spirit or soul as a divine "spark" imprisoned in this evil material world; and

the necessity of supernatural knowledge (Greek γνῶσις, *gnosis*) mediated to Gnostics through special revelation in order to free the divine "spark" from the material world and enable it to return to its source in the light or in the highest good.

No single Gnostic writing contains all of these components, but these elements seem to reflect the underlying myth of developed Gnosticism.

Until relatively recently, we knew about Gnosticism almost exclusively from heresiologists, fathers of the church who wrote to criticize and suppress Gnosticism as a heresy. Among these heresiologists, Irenaeus (ca. 137–ca. 202) and Origen (ca. 185–254) regarded Gnosticism as a deviant form of Christianity. Our understanding of Gnosticism grew considerably with the discovery in 1945 of the Nag Hammadi library, a collection of twelve codices or books, plus eight pages of a thirteenth book tucked inside the front cover of one of the other books. These thirteen books contain fifty-two tractates or individual writings.[18] Accordingly, we now have a clearer picture and a more unbiased understanding of Gnosticism from Gnostic writings and are not dependent only on the testimony of early Christian polemicists.

Although the monks who preserved the Nag Hammadi library were presumably Christians, or more specifically Christian Gnostics or Gnostic Christians, the Nag Hammadi writings are not all Christian and reflect the community's use of books from Jewish, Greek, Zoroastrian, and Hermetic Gnosticism, in addition to some books that are specifically Christian, such as the *Gospel of Thomas*, which appears to be a collection of older sayings of Jesus with a Gnostic overlay. As James M. Robinson states,

> Gnosticism seems not to have been in its essence just an alternative form of Christianity. Rather it was a radical trend of release from the dominion of evil or of inner transcendence that swept through late antiquity and emerged within Christianity, Judaism, Neoplatonism, Hermetism, and the like. As a new religion it was synchretistic, drawing upon various religious heritages. But it was held together by a very decided stance, which is where the unity amid the wide diversity is to be sought.[19]

Although our understanding of full-blown Gnosticism is now richer as a result of the discovery at Nag Hammadi, we still have no clear picture of the origin and early development of Christian Gnosticism.

REFERENCES TO GNOSTICISM IN THE NEW TESTAMENT

There are, however, references in the New Testament to what may perhaps be characterized as Gnostic threats to Christianity. Most specifically, 1 and 2 Timothy and Titus

---

18. Robinson, *The Nag Hammadi Library*, 10.
19. Robinson, p. 10.

address the matter of false teachers, some of whose teaching may reflect elements of a mature Gnosticism, if these letters are dated about 125:

1 Tim 1:3-4

> I [Paul] urge you [Timothy], as I did when I was on my way to Macedonia, to remain in Ephesus so that you may instruct certain people not to teach any different doctrine, and not to occupy themselves with myths and endless genealogies that promote speculations rather than the divine training that is known by faith.

The "myths and endless genealogies that promote speculations" may refer to proto-Gnostic genealogies of the male and female pairs of intermediaries between God and humankind. If so, this verse may mark the first reference in the New Testament to Gnosticism as a threat to a proto-orthodox Christianity.

Other possible references or allusions in the Pastoral Letters to Gnostic genealogies and myths, often drawn from the early chapters of Genesis, include 1 Tim 4:7a; 2 Tim 4:3-4; Titus 1:13-14; 3:9.

1 Tim 6:20-21

> Timothy, guard what has been entrusted to you. Avoid the profane chatter and contradictions of what is falsely called knowledge (Greek, *gnosis*); by professing it some have missed the mark as regards the faith.

1 Timothy's final exhortation to hold fast to the apostolic instructions (see 1 Tim 1:18) and to reject the false teachers characterizes their false teaching as knowledge (Greek *gnosis*). If this is a reference to Gnosticism, then this is the oldest such use of the word *gnosis* in Christian literature.

2 Tim 2:16-18

> Avoid profane chatter, for it will lead people into more and more impiety, and their talk will spread like gangrene. Among them are Hymenaeus and Philetus, who have swerved from the truth by claiming that the resurrection has already taken place. They are upsetting the faith of some.

The author names two false teachers, Hymenaeus and Philetus, whose teaching that the resurrection is a present reality and not a future hope, may reflect a stage of Gnostic teaching.

There are, in addition, two reference in Revelation to an otherwise unknown group or sect called the Nicolaitans. The author of Revelation refers to "the works of the Nicolaitans" in Rev 2:6 and to "the teaching of the Nicolaitans" in Rev 2:15. Were the Nicolaitans a proto-Gnostic sect in Asia Minor at the time that Revelation was written in that region about 95? According to accounts in Irenaeus (before 137–ca.202), *Against Heresies* 1.26.3; 3.11.1; Clement of Alexandria (ca. 150–215), *Stromata* 2.20; Hippolytus (ca. 170–ca. 236), *Refutation of All Heresies* 7.24; and Epiphanius (ca. 315-403), *Against Heresies* 1.2.25, the Nicolaitans were a Gnostic sect that was founded by the proselyte Nicolaus of Antioch (Acts 6:5) and that offered insult to the Holy Spirit, practiced fornication, and allowed the eating of food that had been offered to idols. It is, however, not entirely clear that the church fathers have not created and then subsequently built on this story simply to clarify the references to the mysterious Nicolaitans in Rev 2.

The references in 1 and 2 Timothy, Titus, and Revelation are, to be sure, somewhat ambiguous and obviously open to very different interpretations, but what is certain is that there must have been some form of Christian Gnosticism or proto-Gnosticism by the late first or early second century, several decades before we find records of full-blown Christian Gnosticism toward the middle of the second century.

Some have seen evidence of Christian proto-Gnosticism as early as the mid-first century in Paul's church in Corinth (e.g., 1 Cor 8:1–3),[20] but the evidence is insufficient to make such a case. As Conzelmann says,

> We have to make a methodological distinction between ideas and concepts which *in themselves* are Gnostic and those which may have been taken over by Gnosticism but were of earlier origin and arose in a totally different speculative context. The concepts and motifs in 1 Corinthians belong without exception to the second group.[21]

CHRISTIAN GNOSTICS

Early Christian Gnostics may have included Cerinthus from the Roman province of Asia and Carpocrates of Alexandria, but the accounts about these men are from several centuries later and may be little more than second- and third-hand hearsay and, hence, unreliable. The earliest clear reference to a Christian Gnostic teacher is to Basilides, who was active in Alexandria about 120–140. Basilides was known for his mythological systems and is reputed to have composed a gospel known as the *Gospel of Basilides*, no trace of which survives. Basilides and his son and disciple Isadore claimed that the apostle Matthias had delivered to them teachings that he had previously received in secret from the Savior, the risen Lord.

The most important figure in the history of Christian Gnosticism is Valentinus (ca. 100–ca. 175), who was born in Egypt's Nile Delta and educated in Alexandria, where he apparently came under the influence of the Gnostic Basilides and the Hellenistic Jewish philosopher Philo of Alexandria. Valentinus moved from Alexandria to Rome, where he flourished between ca. 140–160.

---

20. "Now concerning food sacrificed to idols: we know that all of us possess knowledge (γνῶσιν, *gnosin*). Knowledge (γνῶσις, *gnosis*) puffs up, but love builds up. Anyone who claims to know (ἐγνωκέναι, *egnokenai*) something does not yet have the necessary knowledge (οὔπω ἔγνω, *oupo egno*); but anyone who loves God is known (ἔγνωσται, *egnostai*) by him" (1 Cor 8:1–3). Cf. Schmithals, *Gnosticism in Corinth*.

21. Conzelmann, *1 Corinthians*, 15.

Valentinus was the most influential Christian Gnostic and one of the intellectual giants of second century Christianity as he tried to accommodate the Gnostic myth to the emerging Roman proto-orthodoxy. According to Tertullian (ca. 155–230), Valentinus was actually considered for the position of bishop of Rome ca. 143. Valentinus or one of his disciples is usually credited with writing the *Gospel of Truth*, which survives among the tractates of the Nag Hammadi library. Following Valentinus's death in about 175, the Valentinian "school" split into two branches: an Eastern branch based in Alexandria, which produced Axionicus of Antioch, Marcus, Kolorbasos, Marcus, Theodotus, Ambrose, and Candidus; and a Western branch based in Rome, which produced Heracleon, Ptolemy, Hermogenes, Monoimus the Arab, Prodicus, Secundus, Alexander, Flora, Florinus, and Theotimus.

Attacks against Valentinus began about 150 with Justin Martyr and continued into the late seventh century at the Trullan Synod in Constantinople in 692, showing the persistence of diverse Christianities even after the Council of Nicaea in 325. Nicaea had supposedly settled issues of orthodoxy and heresy in Christianity of the period, but apparently not to everyone's satisfaction.

CONCLUSIONS

Writing a history of post-apostolic Christianity poses considerable challenges for historians. The writing of history generally depends on the reliability of our primary sources and on the ability to determine their date and place of composition. As we have seen in this chapter, it is often difficult to assign precise dates and places of composition to many of our primary sources in the sub-apostolic period, and authorship often involved pseudonymity, basically a form of forgery. Moreover, evidence suggests that the writings of the church fathers were not always reliable as sources of the church's early history. They were often more polemicists than historians, so we need to be cautious in using information drawn from fathers of the church. Writing a history of post-apostolic Christianity poses considerable challenges for historians.

That said, what we have seen in second and third century Christianity is evidence of many Christianities that were sometimes headed in very different directions. Even within the different Christian groups or movements identified in this chapter—Jewish Christianity, Deutero-Pauline Christianity, Johannine Christianity, Petrine Christianity, and Gnostic Christianity—there were sometimes different camps or sects or schools even within a single group. In fact, even these five categories are not without their problems. Christianity was fluid during the second century, and we must be cautious not to pigeonhole movements by our scholarly constructs. In the second and third centuries, there was never a single Christianity or a single movement within Christianity that was unequivocally the "right" or the "orthodox" form. Multiple Christianities existed side by side, sometimes within the same individual community or church.

From the perspective of church fathers, many of whom wrote several centuries later, some of these post-apostolic movements represented, but only in retrospect, "heresies" or deviant forms of Christianity. However, scholars now recognize that *orthodoxy* and *heresy* are later terms that were applied retrospectively and inappropriately to earlier movements, based upon decisions taken by formal synods or councils of the church several centuries later. In the second century, there was not yet "one holy, catholic, and apostolic church"; neither was there a universally recognized ecclesiastical authority in place to determine what sect or what movement within the church or churches represented most faithfully the teaching of Jesus of Nazareth, the alleged Lord and founder of this new religion. In fact, fidelity to the teaching of Jesus was not an important consideration in the first and second centuries, because none of the early movements within the church preserved or even reflected closely the teachings of the historical Jesus.

Some early Christianities were regional or were restricted to specific churches. For example, Jewish Christianity was most evident in churches whose members had previously been Jews who believed that Jesus was the Jewish messiah. Many Jewish Christians continued to observe the Jewish ritual of male circumcision and Judaism's dietary regulations, but some did not. Not all Jewish Christians agreed on the critical issue of the role of the Jewish law. When disagreements broke out, some reached out to an apostolic authority to justify a particular position. Others made a different case by appealing to a different apostolic authority or to the authority of the Holy Spirit or to someone to whom the risen Lord had disclosed a new revelation. We have already have seen that Peter and Paul sometimes disagreed regarding the authority of the Jewish law, and Jesus' brother James certainly took an even stronger stand within Judaism than did either Peter or Paul.

Jewish Christianity was a small movement in Jerusalem in the immediate aftermath of Jesus' death, perhaps initially under the leadership of Peter. There may also have been Jewish Christian churches within a few years after Jesus' death in Galilee, the scene of most of Jesus' ministry. Jewish Christianity also spread to the area east of the Jordan River, probably in the aftermath of the fall of Jerusalem to the Romans in 70, when the Jerusalem church was scattered, primarily to the east. Not only did Pharisaic Judaism reorganize following the fall of Jerusalem, but so too did Jewish Christianity and, perhaps more specifically, Christian Judaism.

By contrast Pauline and Deutero-Pauline Christianity advocated a Christianity free from the Jewish law. In spite of his claim to apostleship, Paul was not recognized in all Christian churches as an apostle. Even as late as the fourth century, the *Pseudo-Clementine Homilies* and *Recognitions* polemicized against Paul and his followers. Paul never knew Jesus of Nazareth during the course of his ministry, so he could not claim the authority of Peter or John, who had been with Jesus from the beginning of his ministry, or of James, whose authority was probably based on the fact that he was Jesus' brother.

Paul's claim to apostleship was suspect in non-Pauline circles. But for those who were followers of Paul, his authority was based on an appearance of the risen Lord, an appearance that according to Paul's own testimony in 1 Cor 15 came to him much later than appearances to Jesus' apostles. Paul's enormous influence on Christianity was based, no doubt, on the fact that he traveled through Syria, Asia Minor, Macedonia, and Greece, establishing and nurturing nascent churches over which he exercised authority and to which he wrote hortatory letters of advice that were widely circulated among many of Paul's churches sometime after his death.

Followers of Paul's teaching effectively constituted a Pauline "school," even if there was no geographical center for these disciples of Paul. After Paul's death, some continued to write in Paul's name, thereby exercising Paul's authority, because in their minds they were continuing Paul's work in his absence. It was some of these individuals who were apparently responsible for writing Ephesians, Colossians, 2 Thessalonians, 1 and 2 Timothy, and Titus, six presumably Deutero-Pauline letters, to complement the seven letters that Paul himself had penned—Romans, 1 and 2 Corinthians, Galatians, Philippians, 1 Thessalonians, and Philemon. In fact, 2 Thessalonians may have been written by a follower of Paul to correct Paul's claim in 1 Thessalonians that Jesus would come again very soon. Disappointment over Jesus' failure to return needed to be addressed and corrected, even if that meant discrediting 1 Thessalonians as a forgery.

In connection with Deutero-Pauline Christianity, I discussed in this chapter the work of Marcion. Some see Marcionism as a distinct movement, especially since it survived for several centuries. Others consider Marcion a Gnostic because of the cosmic dualism characterized by his two gods, the Creator god of the Old Testament and the god who was Jesus' father. I consider Marcionism as a logical consequence of Paul's early break with the Jewish law and consider Marcion's use of Paul's letters as the core of his Christian canon as a major step in the creation of the New Testament. For these reasons, I regard Marcionism as an important outgrowth of Deutero-Pauline Christianity. As we have said above, efforts to categorize or pigeonhole Christian teachers or Christian movements have their limitations, and Marcion is an important case in point. He does not easily fall into a single category.

Characterizing Johannine Christianity is relatively easy, because it is limited to the canonical books of the Gospel of John and the letters known as 1, 2, and 3 John. The issue of Johannine Christianity became complicated toward the middle of the second century, when the Gospel of John was suspect in some proto-orthodox circles, even as its popularity grew among Egyptian Gnostics. Justin Martyr appears to have rejected the Gospel of John when he was teaching and writing in Rome in the mid-second century, but his pupil Tatian included John in his *Diatessaron*, his harmony of Matthew, Mark, Luke, and John. Part of the difficulty with the Gospel of John may have been that the gospel sometimes seems almost Docetic in its Christology and engages in a theology and Christology that reaches in the direction of Gnosticism, even as it consciously sought to maintain its base in proto-orthodox Christianity. The decision of proto-orthodoxy eventually to embrace the Gospel of John in the second half of the second century opened Christianity to a very different kind of spirituality from what we find in the synoptic gospels.

Petrine Christianity seems to have remained unusually elusive, especially since it evolved into a dominant movement by the end of the second century. Presumably the Petrine circle had its origins in Antioch after Peter moved to Antioch from Jerusalem in about 50. The Gospel of Mark, perhaps a Petrine gospel may have been written in Antioch about 67, but Peter's move to Rome ca. 60 presumably shifted the circle of Petrine Christianity from Antioch to Rome. There it generated after Peter's death two canonical pseudepigraphical writings, 1 and 2 Peter, and a number of later apocryphal books. The association of Peter with Rome would by the end of the second century give rise to the tradition that Peter was one of the founders of the Roman church and its first bishop.

And finally, there is Gnosticism, a pan-Hellenic movement that opened new avenues for Christianity but that probably went too far in its inwardness and individualism, almost to render the church itself irrelevant. It was primarily against Gnosticism and Gnostic fathers that heresiologists of the second, third, and fourth centuries directed most of their attacks.

As we have seen, the second century brought increasingly more diversity to Christianity. There were many Christianities, some of them significant and widespread, others relatively local and less important. In addition to the five principal movements discussed above, we mention again Adoptionism and Docetism, which were eventually declared heresies, although adoptionist tendencies survive in some of Paul's genuine letters and in the Gospel of Mark.

Second century Christianity was rich in its diversity. With recent discoveries, we now understand better the complexities and the flourishing varieties of second century Christianities.

CHAPTER 15

THE REVELATION OF JOHN

THE APOCALYPSE OR THE Revelation of John (Greek Ἀποκάλυψις Ἰωάννου, *Apokalypsis Iōannou*) is one of the most difficult books of the New Testament to understand, primarily because *apocalypse* is a literary form unfamiliar to modern readers and because it often includes characteristics such as secrecy, esotericism, and symbolism.

Apocalypticism has been defined as "the dualistic, cosmic, and eschatological belief in two opposing cosmic powers, good and evil, God and Satan (or his equivalent); and in two distinct ages—the present, temporal, and irretrievably evil age under Satan, who now oppresses the righteous but whose power God will soon act to overthrow; and the future, perfect and eternal age under God's own rule, when the righteous will be blessed forever."[1]

The dualism that we find in Jewish and Christian apocalypticism juxtaposes good and evil as forces that are engaged in a cosmic struggle for power in the universe. However, the monotheism that characterizes both Judaism and Christianity has resulted in a modified dualism, meaning that the biblical God is necessarily more powerful than the opposing forces of evil and will ultimately triumph in the final celestial struggle. Combined with this cosmic dualism, Jewish and Christian apocalypses also generally focus on eschatology, meaning that they have a distinct concern about end time (the *eschaton*) or the end of history as we know it.[2]

Jewish and Christian eschatology consider the present age to be irretrievably evil, because it is under the dominion of Satan, or Belial, or Beliar, or the devil (or whatever other name he may be called), who tempts and seduces humankind. Yet, there is generally the hope or expectation among Jews and Christians that God will intervene to engage and destroy the forces of evil.[3]

In the Hebrew scriptures, there are several examples of early or proto-apocalyptic texts in Ezekiel, Zech 1–8, Isa 24–27, Zech 9–14, and Joel 2:28–3:21. More developed examples of Jewish apocalypticism appear in Daniel in the Old Testament and in some books of the Old Testament Apocrypha and Pseudepigrapha, specifically in *1 Enoch*,

---

1. Rist, "Apocaylpticism," 157.

2. The Apocalyptic Group of the Society of Biblical Literature actually settled on "apocalypticism" as a subset of "eschatology." See Collins, *Apocalypse*.

3. Bellinzoni, *The Old Testament*, 313–15.

2 *Baruch*, *4 Ezra*, the *Sibylline Oracles*, as well as in some of the Dead Sea Scrolls, all of which writings come from the second century BCE or later.[4]

Earlier in this book, I maintained that Jesus should probably be understood primarily as an eschatological prophet, a prophetic figure who proclaimed the imminent arrival of the end-time. Late Jewish and intertestamental apocalypses contribute significantly to a proper understanding of Jesus and his message. Moreover, Jesus' precursor John the Baptist is represented in the New Testament as an eschatological prophet; and in I Thessalonians, Paul proclaimed to the Thessalonians that Jesus would return very soon, the earliest eschatological proclamation in the canonical New Testament. These two eschatological bookends, John the Baptist and the apostle Paul, corroborate the interpretation of Jesus as an eschatological prophet, a first century Jew influenced by contemporary Jewish apocalypticism. Additionally, many early Christian writings, including most of the books of the New Testament, contain eschatological elements. Nevertheless, although there are other apocalypses in the New Testament, for example Mark 13 and its synoptic parallels, the Revelation of John is the only complete example among the twenty-seven books of the New Testament of the apocalyptic literature that was so popular in both Jewish and Christian circles at the beginning of the Christian era.

The Apocalypse of John is probably the best example of an apocalypse with its presentation of a theology of history that discloses what John has seen of "what is, and what is to take place after this" (Rev 1:19) as elements of God's plan for humankind and for the salvation of humanity. As is often the case in Jewish apocalypses, to secure authority for his book, John attributes everything in it to a "revelation" that he received through Jesus Christ or his angel (Rev 1:1; 4:1; 22:8).

AUTHORSHIP, DATE AND PLACE OF COMPOSITION, AND LITERARY GENRE OF REVELATION

AUTHORSHIP

The Revelation of John purports to have been written by someone named John (Rev 1:1, 4, 9; 22:8), a Christian seer and prophet who received visions and auditions while he was imprisoned on the island of Patmos off the western coast of Asia Minor. There is probably no merit to the tradition in some early Christian fathers that the John of Revelation was also the author of the Gospel of John and of the three Johannine letters, whose eschatology is very different from what we find in Revelation, or that he was John the son of Zebedee, one of Jesus' twelve apostles. The author of Revelation never claims that he was an apostle of Jesus or that he even knew Jesus.[5] John, or Johanan, was a common Hebrew name at the time.

---

4. Bellinzoni, Ibid., 316–47.
5. If, as most scholars believe, the twenty-four elders in Revelation 4:10 are the leaders of the

Although John never calls himself a prophet, he refers to his writing as prophecy (Rev 1:3; 22:7, 9). In fact, the Revelation of John is a thoroughly prophetic writing.[6] This otherwise unknown John was probably an itinerant prophet, which is not to say that he was a prognosticator of the future but that he was someone who, in the tradition of Israel's great prophets, condemned sin and called for repentance and, as a Christian prophet, demanded faithfulness to Jesus and to God. John says, "For the testimony of Jesus is the spirit of prophecy" (Rev 19:10), meaning that the testimony *about* Jesus, or the preaching of the gospel, is the spirit of Christian prophecy.

Prophets and prophecy were not unique to Judaism and Christianity. Prophets were familiar figures throughout the Greco-Roman world, the oracle at Delphi being the most famous prophetic figure. Both Jewish Christians and Gentile Christians would, therefore, have been familiar with prophets.

We know from Paul's letters that there were church prophets in many early Christian communities in the Gentile world (Rom 12:6–8; 1 Cor 12:8–11, 28–30; 13:1–2; 14:29–32; 1 Thess 5:19–20). We learn from the *Did* 11–13 about a different category of prophet: itinerant prophets who moved from place to place, proclaiming revelations they had received.

It seems reasonable to assume that John was known at least to the seven churches in Asia to which he addressed his Revelation. Why John was on Patmos is less clear. He may have gone to Patmos to continue his prophetic ministry, although Patmos was a remote island location where there was likely not yet a Christian community or even sufficiently fertile ground for the creation of one. The possibility remains that John was exiled to Patmos for preaching the Gospel, but that too is uncertain. We actually do not know what John was doing on Patmos, except that it was there that he received the prophetic "visions" about which he wrote in his letter to the seven churches in Asia.[7]

The author of Revelation was obviously familiar with the Hebrew scriptures. Although he never quotes the scriptures exactly, there are more than four hundred allusions to the Old Testament, far more than in any other book of the canonical New Testament.[8] Moreover, Semitic characteristics in the Greek of Revelation suggest

---

twelve tribes of Israel and Jesus' twelve apostles, then this passage too serves as evidence that the John of Revelation is not John the apostle, unless John was able to look at himself.

6. The 1973 Seminar on Early Christian Prophecy of the Society of Biblical Literature states: "The early Christian prophet was an immediately-inspired spokesperson for God, the risen Jesus, or the Spirit who received intelligible oracles that he or she felt impelled to deliver to the Christian community or, representing the community, to the general public" (Eugene Boring, "Prophecy, Early Christian, 496.

7. John's own words in Rev 1:9 are not particularly informative: "I, John, your brother who shares with you in Jesus the persecution and the kingdom and the patient endurance, was on the island called Patmos because of the word of God and the testimony of Jesus." This verse has sometime been understood to imply that John was imprisoned on Patmos by the Romans, but there is no evidence that Patmos was ever a Roman penal colony. It is, however, possible that John was banished from Asia to Patmos because of his prophetic preaching.

8. Ford, *Revelation*, 27.

that John may have been a Jewish native of Palestine and that his mother tongue was probably Aramaic.⁹ John may have been a Palestinian Jew who left Palestine for Asia Minor at the time of the Jewish revolt against Rome (66–73). In fact, he may already have been active as a Jewish prophet in Galilee before his presumed conversion to Christianity.

Stated simply, the author of Revelation cannot be identified with any other known John from the early Christian church. Neither can we assume that the Revelation of John comes from the Johannine community that produced the Gospel of John and the three Johannine letters, often associated in early Christian tradition with John the apostle. The author of the Revelation of John is simply an otherwise unknown John, probably of Palestinian Jewish origin.

DATE

John probably wrote Revelation sometime between 80 and 100. A more precise date is highly speculative. Writing in Rome about 150, Justin Martyr mentions Revelation by name, providing the earliest specific reference to the Apocalypse and, therefore, the latest possible date for the composition of Revelation.[10] An earlier date is probable, as it would have taken some decades for Revelation to have won acceptance in Asia Minor and to have traveled to Rome, where Justin wrote.

Most scholars identify the beast of Rev 13:2, 12, 14, who has died and come back to life, as the Roman Emperor Nero, whose return was expected according to a rumor that circulated throughout the eastern Mediterranean toward the end of the first century.[11] Moreover, the references to Rome by the codename Babylon in Rev 17:5, 9, 18

---

9. Writing in the first half of the third century, Dionysius of Alexandria (ca. 200–265) observed: "Moreover, it can be shown that the diction of the Gospel and Epistle [of John] differs from that of the Apocalypse, for they were written not only without error as regards the Greek language, but also with elegance in their expression, in their reasonings, and in their entire structure. They are far indeed from betraying any barbarism or solecism [a non-standard usage or grammatical construction (*author's note*)], or any vulgarism whatever. For the writer had, as it seems, both the requisites of discourse—that is, the gift of knowledge and the gift of expression—as the Lord had bestowed them both upon him. I do not deny that the other writer saw a revelation and received knowledge and prophecy. I perceive, however, that his dialect and language are not accurate Greek, but that he uses barbarous idioms, and, in some places, solecisms. It is unnecessary to point these out here, for I would not have any one think that I have said these things in a spirit of ridicule, for I have said what I have only with the purpose of showing clearly the difference between the writings" (Eusebius, *Church History*, 7.25.26–27).

10. Justin Martyr, *Dialogue with Trypho*, 81.4.

11. Rev 13:18 states that the beast described in Rev 13:11–17 has "the number of a person. Its number is six hundred sixty-six." This cryptic statement is generally understood to refer to Nero. Nero's name in Hebrew is נרון קסר (*Neron Caesar*). Hebrew numbers are actually the letters of the Hebrew alphabet, as if A=1, B=2, etc. in English. The numerical value of Nero's name is determined by adding the value of the seven letters/numbers in his name: נ = 50, ר = 200, ו = 6, ן = 50, ק = 100, ס = 60, ר = 200. Thus 50 + 200 + 6 + 50 + 100 + 60 + 200 = 666. The words of Revelation 13:18a are an understatement: "This calls for wisdom: let anyone with understanding calculate the number of

was a common theme in Jewish apocalyptic writings following the Roman destruction of Jerusalem in 70, indicating a probable date of composition for Revelation in the late first century.[12] Irenaeus's testimony (*Against Heresies* 5.30.3) that John saw his visions toward the end of the reign of the Roman Emperor Domitian, who died in 96, has led some scholars to date Revelation more precisely about 95–96, but the reliability of Irenaeus's tradition is uncertain.

PLACE OF COMPOSITION

We know from a letter that Pliny the Younger, the Roman governor of Pontus/Bithynia from 111–13, wrote to Emperor Trajan that he was encountering Christians, apparently for the first time (Pliny, *Letter* 10.96). Pontus/Bithynia was northeast of the Roman Province of Asia, so relatively close to the region to which John addressed his seven letters. In his letter, Pliny implies that there had been trials of Christians before he arrived in the area and was required to deal with Christians, but we do not know how widespread and how serious these earlier persecutions were.

According to his own testimony, John received his vision while he was on the island of Patmos in the Aegean Sea about thirty-seven miles southwest of Ephesus. His statement that he was on Patmos "because of the word of God" (Rev 1:9) may imply that John had been exiled by the Romans to an island because of his preaching, the sort of earlier incident to which Pliny may have been referring in his letter.

John wrote Revelation to the seven churches in the Roman province of Asia, specifically to the churches in Ephesus, Smyrna, Pergamum, Thyatira, Sardis, Philadelphia, and Laodicea (Rev 1:4a, 11; 2:1–3:22). The occasion for John's writing his Revelation may have been the persecution of Christians in Asia Minor at the hands of their Jewish and Gentile neighbors, perhaps with the consent of local Roman governors. However, despite claims to the contrary, there is no evidence for a systematic Roman persecution of Christians in Asia in the late first century.

Patmos or Ephesus is usually considered the place of John's composition of Revelation.

---

the beast." Virtually every important and controversial figure in history has at one time or another been identified as the beast of Revelation 13. It is, however, essential to identify the beast within the historical context of the book, namely with someone who was known to the readers or listeners of Revelation at the time the book was written. Presumably, the audience knew exactly to whom the author was referring.

12. Babylon is a name for Rome in the apocalypse of Ezra (*4 Ezra* = *2 Esdras* 3–14), in the Syriac apocalypse of Baruch (*2 Baruch*), and in Book 5 of the *Sibylline Oracles*, probably because of the Roman destruction of Jerusalem in 70 CE and the Babylonian destruction of Jerusalem in 587–86 BCE.

THE NEW TESTAMENT
GENRE: APOCALYPSE, LETTER, AND PROPHECY

Although written in the literary form of an apocalypse (the disclosure of something that has been hidden), John addresses the seven churches in what is clearly a letter. John's call for the blessing of "the one who reads aloud the words of the prophecy" (Rev 1:3) indicates that the author intended Revelation to be read in the seven churches in Asia within the context of Christian worship (see also Col 4:16 and 1 Thess 5:27 for similar instructions). Following its title or superscription (Revelation 1:1–2), the book opens with a traditional epistolary greeting to the community (Rev 1:4–6):

> Grace to you and peace from him who is and who was and who is to come, and from the seven spirits who are before his throne, and from Jesus Christ, the faithful witness, the firstborn of the dead, and the ruler of the kings of the earth. To him who loves us and freed us from our sins by his blood, and made us to be a kingdom, priests serving his God and Father, to him be glory and dominion forever and ever. Amen.

There is also a brief epistolary conclusion in the final benediction (Rev 22:21):

> The grace of the Lord Jesus be with all the saints. Amen.

Revelation is also called a prophecy (Rev 1:3; 19:10; 22:7, 10, 18–19), and portions of John's book describe visionary experiences of the type associated with Israel's prophets (Rev 1:8; 4:1–11; 21:1–22:5). Hence, the Revelation of John presents itself as all three: an apocalypse, a letter, and a prophecy. Knowing and understanding these three genres helps in our understanding the book in its original historical and social context.

STRUCTURE OF THE REVELATION OF JOHN

The Revelation of John has a complex structure, an understanding of which is important to a proper understanding of the book's contents and message. John probably first wrote the dramatic apocalypse (Rev 1:1–2; 1:7–22:20) and then superimposed upon the apocalypse the form of a letter (Rev 1:3–6; 22:21) in order to deliver his message to the audience in the seven churches in Asia Minor. This is evident by the way in which the form of the letter (Rev 1:4–6 and 22:1) simply frame the original apocalypse almost as an afterthought. The original title of the book is, of course, not The Revelation of John, but rather the whole of the superscription found in the opening verses, Rev 1:1–2:

> [1]The revelation of Jesus Christ, which God gave him to show his servants what must soon take place; he made it known by sending his angel to his servant John, [2]who testified to the word of God and to the testimony of Jesus Christ, even to all that he saw.

Verse 1a is probably the actual title, and verses 1b–2 ("he made it known, etc.") a further elaboration to explain to the reader or listener the divine authority of John's revelation.

The author of Revelation is clearly preoccupied with numerology. From very ancient times, the number seven symbolized to the Semitic and the Hellenistic mind wholeness or completeness or perfection, probably based on the four phases of the moon that divided twenty-eight day months into four seven-day period or weeks. Examples of an interest in numerology, and most especially in the number seven, appear in the Revelation of John in the seven churches in Asia (Rev 1:4, 11, 20); the seven seals (Rev 5:1, 5); the seven spirits of God (Rev 1:4; 3:1; 4:5; 5:6); the seven golden lampstands (Rev 1:12, 13, 20; 2:1); the seven horns (Rev 5:6); the seven eyes (Rev 5:6); the seven stars (Rev 1:16, 20; 2:1); the seven flaming torches (Rev 4:5); the seven angels (Rev 8:2, 6; 15:1, 6, 7, 8; 16:1; 17:1; 21:9); the seven trumpets (Rev 8:2); the seven thunders (Rev 10:3, 4); the seven heads (Rev 12:3; 13:1; 17:3, 7, 9); the seven diadems (Rev 12:3); the seven plagues (Rev 15:1, 6, 8; 21:9); the seven golden bowls (Rev 15:7; 17:1; 21:9); the seven mountains (Rev 17:9); the seven kings (Rev 17:9); and the like.

In fact, the number seven may be the formative principle of John's Revelation. Although there are different ways of outlining the book, it can be divided into seven sections, each of which has seven parts. To borrow language from the genre of the theater, the Revelation of John can be seen as a drama in seven acts, each of which contains seven parts, a division that is particularly attractive considering the author's preoccupation with numbers, and most especially with the number seven:

Superscription identifying the book's contents (Rev 1:1–2)

Epistolary Introduction and Greeting (Rev 1:3–5a)

Opening Doxology (Rev 1:5b–8)

Prologue (Rev 1:7–8)

Act 1 — Christ's Message to His Church (Rev 1:9–3:22)

Includes messages to the seven churches in Asia

Act 2 — God Reveals His Final Plan for the World (Rev 4:1–8:1)

Includes the opening of the seven seals by the lamb (Jesus)

Act 3 — The Tribulation of the Church (Rev 8:2–11:19)

Includes the sounding of the seven trumpets introducing God's judgment

Act 4 — The Salvation of Christ's Church (Rev 12:1–15:4)

Includes the showing of the seven great signs or portents: the woman, the red dragon, the beast, the lamb, the angels, the one like a Son of Man, and God's reign

Act 5 — The World in Tribulation (Rev 15:5–16:21)

Includes the pouring out of the seven bowls of God's wrath

Act 6 — God's Judgment of the World (Rev 17:1–20:3)

> Includes the unfolding of the seven plagues (first mentioned in Rev 15:1, and again in Rev 18:4, 8)

Act 7 — The Unfolding of the Millennium (Rev 20:4–22:5)

> Includes the unfolding of God's sevenfold plan (see Act 2 above), including the millennial kingdom, the first resurrection (of Christian martyrs), the defeat of Satan, the final judgment, the new heaven and the new earth, the descent of the New Jerusalem, and the appearance of the river of the water of life and the tree of life, symbolizing the return to the order of creation

Conclusion or Epilogue (Rev 22:6–20)

Closing Epistolary Benediction (Revelation 22:21)

Unlike any other book of the Hebrew Bible or the New Testament, the structure of Revelation seems particularly formal, as the author lays out for the reader his vision of "what is and what is to take place after this" (Rev 1:19).

UNDERSTANDING THE MESSAGE OF REVELATION

As mentioned at the beginning of this chapter, John's Apocalypse is particularly difficult to understand, because the literary genre "apocalypse" is unfamiliar to modern readers. There has been a tendency for many Christians to read the Revelation of John as a prognostication of the future, as if it were speaking to our own time or to the immediate or more distant future. Consequently, every contemporary flood, earthquake, or natural disaster finds a place in the unfolding of John's drama in the thinking of many fundamentalist Christians. People have identified the number of the beast (666) with Roman Catholic popes, with the likes of Adolph Hitler and Joseph Stalin, and even with American Presidents. From the perspective of modern historical criticism, all such efforts to read modern history *into* the Revelation of John are misguided, misinformed, and misdirected. They represent a naïve understanding of Christianity, and most especially of John's Apocalypse. The Apocalypse of John is not a prognostication of contemporary and/or future history. This view of Revelation as history written in advance of its unfolding is simply wrong and reflects a misunderstanding of the intention of the original author.

By contrast, modern historical critics treat Revelation as the ancient text that it is and try to understand that ancient text in its own late first century context, as an example of the Jewish and Christian literary genre of "apocalypse" to which it belongs. Scholars understand Revelation in its present form as an address to the seven historical communities in Asia Minor named in the book: the Christian churches in Ephesus, Smyrna, Pergamum, Thyatira, Sardis, Philadelphia, and Laodicea (Rev 1:4a, 11; 2:1–3:22). With this is mind, the assertion in Rev 1:3 "for the time is near" (ὁ γὰρ καιρὸς ἐγγύς, *ho gar kairos engus*) was meant to be taken literally by those communities. John obviously expected the end of history to come very soon, perhaps within his own lifetime or the lifetime of his readers or listeners. Hence, he intended his vision to serve as a warning for these churches not to conform to the contemporary Greco-Roman society which John "unveils" as beastly, demonic and subject to divine judgment.

Rome, in particular, is the enemy of the readers, the enemy of the church, and the enemy of God, who is about to move quickly to punish Rome and the Roman Empire for their apostasy. Rome is the modern Babylon of old that conquered Israel centuries earlier in 587/86 BCE In fact, John may have written Revelation in somewhat cryptic language to protect Christians in the event that the book should fall into Roman hands. It is, therefore, helpful to review or summarize in greater detail the message of the Revelation of John, most especially the content and meaning of John's seven visions.

In the first of John's visions (Rev 1:9–3:22), Christ appeared to John as an imposing, stately, supernatural figure who delivered to each of the seven churches in Asia words of reprimand for their laxity, assimilation, and complacency, as well as words of support for their love, faith, service, and patient endurance.

John's second vision (Rev 4:1–8:1) occurred in the heavenly throne room, where John saw Christ in the form of a Lamb that had been slaughtered and yet lived. After taking a scroll from God's hand, the Lamb opened each of the seven seals that bound the scroll, and with the opening of each a different menace appeared until, with the opening of the seventh seal, there was silence.

John's third vision (Rev 8:2–11:19) opens with the appearance of seven angels who stood before God in the heavenly throne room with seven trumpets. As the angels blew their trumpets, God's judgments were unleashed upon the earth; the sea; the rivers and springs; the sun, the moon, and the stars; the bottomless pit; and one-third of humankind. With the sounding of the seventh trumpet, the scene shifts once again to the heavenly throne room, where the twenty-four elders (representing the twelve tribes of Israel and Jesus' twelve apostles) worshiped God and where the heavenly temple and the ark of the covenant were revealed.

John's fourth vision (Rev 12:1–15:4) also took place in heaven. John saw first a woman clothed with the sun (i.e., a cosmic queen), a symbol of both Israel and the church. Second he saw a great red dragon (Satan) with seven heads, symbolizing seven successive rulers, who sought to destroy the woman and her child (the Davidic Messiah of Israel) and the rest of her children (persecuted Christians). Third he saw a beast rise out of the sea, symbolizing Rome and the Roman emperors. Fourth John saw a vision of the Lamb and the 144,000 who would be saved. Fifth he saw the vision of three angels delivering three messages of salvation. Sixth John saw one like the Son of Man (a common title for Jesus), gathering together with his angels the righteous for salvation and judging the wicked for damnation. And finally John saw a vision of God's rule.

John's fifth vision (Rev 15:5–16:21) was a vision of the heavenly tabernacle (the temple or the tent) out of which came seven angels with seven bowls from which they poured out seven plagues, reminiscent of the plagues of Egypt in Exodus, indications of God's wrath, ending with the punishment of Babylon (Rome).

John sixth vision (Rev 17:1–20:3) is of seven angels who portray Rome as a great whore, drunk with the blood of Christian martyrs. The angels condemn Rome and her seven kings and proclaim the coming of an eighth king, probably Nero, whom Christians believed would return as the Antichrist (Rev 13:3, 18). This vision ends with heaven rejoicing at the fall of Rome and the casting of Satan into the fiery pit for a thousand years.

John's seventh and final vision (Rev 20:4–22:5) is the unfolding of God's millennial kingdom, including the first resurrection of Christian martyrs, the final defeat of Satan, the last judgment, the vision of a new heaven and a new earth, including the descent from heaven of the New Jerusalem with the Lamb (Christ) as its temple, and finally the river of the water of life flowing from the throne of God and of the Lamb (Christ), together with the tree of life, representing the return to the order of God's creation.

The unfolding of John's drama is reminiscent of both the Jerusalem Temple and the Greco-Roman stage, complete with scenery and stage props. These two familiar locations appear to serve as the settings for John's seven visions. John's theme is, of course, the gospel of Christianity with particular focus on the present (the late first century) and on the immediate future of the end-time of history as John understood it would unfold. John is aware of the present suffering of the church and the persecution of its martyrs, but he focuses more specifically on God's redemptive purpose for his church, especially in its present time of need. For John, the church, even in times of faithlessness and ineffectiveness, continues to serve as the agent of God's redemption in this world and beyond.

The Revelation of John is deeply rooted in the Hebrew scriptures. Its author may have been a Palestinian Jew who had converted to Christianity and who had moved from Palestine to the Roman province of Asia, perhaps after the fall of Jerusalem in 70. John's audience was also probably Jewish Christians, perhaps even a mix of exiled Palestinian Jews and Hellenistic Jews who had worshiped previously in synagogues in communities that, at the time of the writing of Revelation, constituted the seven churches in Asia. John's message to those seven churches was his vision, perhaps his dream, of "what is and what is to take place hereafter" (Rev 1:19).

THE LETTERS TO THE SEVEN CHURCHES

The occasion for John's writing the revelation was twofold. First and foremost, John was convinced that he was living in the last days and that the end was near (Rev 1:3; see also Rev 3:11; 16:15; 22:12, 20). Second, and an obvious consequence of the first,

John was convinced that, in a final judgment, the unjust earthly powers would be judged and punished and that the Christian faithful would be rewarded.

John addresses faithful Christians in a series of seven edicts or decrees, often referred to as John's letters to the seven churches, although the messages are not in the traditional form of ancient letters with epistolary introductions and conclusions. In these seven edicts or proclamations, John identifies some of the evildoers in the individual churches:

> False apostles (Rev 2:2), those who have fallen from the faith (Rev 2:5), and the works of an otherwise unknown sect known as the Nicolaitans (Rev 2:6)[13] in his message to the church in Ephesus;
>
> Jews who betray Christians to Roman officials (Rev 2:9) in his message to the church in Smyrna (cf. Acts 18:12–17);
>
> Christians who follow the teachings of Balaam and of the Nicolaitans and who teach Balak (Rev 2:14–15), implying idolatry and sexual immorality, in his message to the church in Pergamum;
>
> Christians who tolerate a false prophetess, whom John calls Jezebel,[14] who promotes fornication and the eating of food sacrificed to idols (Rev 2:20) in his message to the church in Thyatira;
>
> Christians who are not "alive" but who are "dead" in their faith (Rev 3:1–2) in his message to the church in Sardis;
>
> Jews who betray Christians to Roman officials (Rev 3:9; cf. the situation in the church in Smyrna in Rev 2:9) in his message to the church in Philadelphia; and
>
> Christians whom John describes as neither "cold" not "hot" but as "lukewarm" or indifferent—"wretched, pitiable, poor, blind, and naked" (Rev 3:15–17)—in his message to the church in Laodicea.

To everyone who has an ear to listen to what the Spirit is saying to the seven churches, John offers the opportunity to repent and change their ways so that they may receive a permanent place in the heavenly temple.

JOHN'S REVELATION AND ANCIENT LITERATURE

Many images in Revelation were drawn from Old Testament and Greco-Roman mythologies, evidence that mythic thinking was very much alive in early Christian circles. Although he never quotes the Hebrew scriptures from a recognized Hebrew or

---

13. According to Hippolytus, ca. 170–ca. 236 (*Refutation of All Heresies* 7.24) and Epiphanius, ca. 315–403 (*Against Heresies* 1.2.25), the Nicolaitans were a Gnostic sect that engaged in immoral practices.

14. Jezebel was the Canaanite queen of King Ahab of Northern Israel (1 Kgs 18–19; 2 Kgs 9), who promoted the worship of Canaanite deities in Israel a thousand years earlier in the ninth century BCE.

Greek version, John paraphrases or alludes to passages in the Old Testament hundreds of times, particularly to passages in Ezekiel, Daniel, Isaiah, and Psalms.

John also drew from Greco-Roman mythology in the story in Rev 12:1–17 of the woman who is clothed with the sun (a cosmic queen who may be related to tradition about Isis) and who bears a child while a dragon stands by ready to devour him (which may be related to the story of Leto bearing Apollo). There may also be Greco-Roman allusions in references to Jesus as the morning star (the planet Aphrodite or Venus) in Rev 2:28 and 22:16 and in the reference to Jesus as the one who has the keys of Death and of Hades in Rev 1:18.

The significance of these allusions to the Old Testament and to Greco-Roman mythology is clear. John shows that Christianity is the outgrowth and, indeed, the fulfillment of both Judaism and of Greco-Roman religion. By appealing to familiar images, John makes the connection between the old order and the new order for both his Jewish and his Greco-Roman audiences.

CONCLUSIONS

With the possible exception of Paul and his genuine letters, we know more about the author and the date and place of composition of the Revelation of John than we do about most authors and books of the canonical New Testament. An otherwise unknown Christian prophet named John wrote Revelation from the island of Patmos, or perhaps from Ephesus, to seven churches in the Roman province of Asia about 80–100.

We have seen that prophecy was a common phenomenon in the Jewish, the Greco-Roman, and the Christian worlds of the first century and that it has left an important mark in Christian literature. We find evidence of prophecy not only in Paul's letters and in the Revelation of John, but in many sayings attributed to Jesus in the canonical gospels. Christians made no distinction between the earthly Jesus and the risen or heavenly Lord, so many post-Easter sayings mediated to the church through Christian prophets were considered every bit as authentic as sayings of the historical Jesus,[15] even though the church wrestled with how to distinguish between its own true and false prophets.

The occasion for writing Revelation was that John was convinced that the end was near (Rev 1:3) and that, in an imminent and final judgment, Christ would return to judge and punish the unjust powers of the earth and to reward the Christian faithful. In anticipation of Christ's imminent return and that final judgment, John was issuing a final call for repentance even as he described in a series of visions the consequences of the day of God's and Christ's final judgment. John drew from contemporary Jewish

---

15. Paul admits as much in 2 Cor 5:16—"From now on, therefore, we regard no one from a human point of view; even though we once knew Christ from a human point of view, we know him no longer in that way."

and Greco-Roman mythic imagery in his description of what would "take place after this" (Rev 1:19) by way of rewards and punishments in the end time that he expected to unfold very soon.

Ancient readers or listeners of Revelation would likely have understood the book on several different levels. They would have thought that the book was predicting events that would unfold sometime soon, not in the distant future. They would also have interpreted many of the events described in the text in light of their own historical circumstances. And lastly, they would have thought about events described in Revelation as symbols of the struggle between good and evil and as reflections of timeless truths.

Second and third century Christians were ambivalent about Revelation. Church fathers not only disagreed about the authorship of the book, they also disagreed about the role of apocalyptic currents in the church. Apocalypticism remained popular in some Christian circles, but others thought that apocalypticism was counterproductive as the church increasingly realized that it was going to live in the world for a much longer time than most early Christians expected. The "end time" obviously did not arrive as soon as many Christians, including John the author of Revelation, expected.

CHAPTER 16

THE CANON OF THE NEW TESTAMENT

REACHING BACK TO ANCIENT Mesopotamia, people in the Ancient Near East commonly believed that there was a heavenly book that recorded God's future plans and the destiny of humankind. This heavenly book, it was believed, contained not only divine knowledge and decrees; it also contained divine laws and wisdom, a book of works, and a book of life.[1] It was belief in such heavenly books that probably lead to the conviction that there were earthly books that served as repositories of such heavenly decrees and laws and of divine wisdom. In Judaism this belief manifested itself in trust in authoritative holy books or sacred scriptures.[2]

It is the responsibility of historians of early Christianity to explain how and why Christians came to attribute to twenty-seven Christian writings from a period of about one century after Jesus' death an authority equal to and perhaps even greater than the authority attributed to the scriptures that the church inherited from Judaism. The decision to assign such authority to a limited collection of Christian writings involves an understanding of the expansion of Christian preaching and teaching, especially in reaction to conflicts with perceived schismatic or heretical movements within the church, most especially in the second and third centuries. The study of the emergence of the New Testament canon parallels the movement toward unity in early Christianity.

The importance of the New Testament canon cannot be overemphasized, because this is an area in which Christians reached a universal agreement that survived the ninth-century schism into Eastern and Western Christianity (Orthodox and the Roman Catholic Christianity) and the sixteenth century division of the Western church into Roman Catholic and Protestant Christianity. Contemporary ecumenical dialogue within the universal church is somewhat easier because all Christians recognize the authority of the same twenty-seven books.

The Greek word κανών, *canon*, refers to a tool for measurement and comes from a Semitic word (*qāneh* in Hebrew, *qanû* in Assyrian, *qin* in Akkadian, meaning a *reed*

---

1. For example, Hartman and Di Lella, *The Book of Daniel*, 273) comment that the reference to "the book" in Dan 12:1 is similar in content to the Babylonian "tablets of fate." There are additional references or allusions to such a heavenly book in Exod 32:32–33; Pss 69:28; 139:16; Isa 4:3; Dan 12:1; *1 Enoch* 108:3; and in Phil 4:3 and Rev 20:12, 15 in the New Testament.

2. McDonald, "Canon of the New Testament," 537. Gamble, "Canon, New Testament," 852-61. These two articles are the source of much of the detail outlined in this chapter.

or a *rod*, something firm or straight that could be used as a measuring stick—what we might call a *ruler*. From this word came the term for the specific collection of Christian documents that were considered authoritative for the life and the faith of Christian communities. When the term was first applied to certain Christian writings in the fourth century, it implied a specific "list" or "catalogue" of writings that could or should be read in assemblies of Christian worship.

Christians inherited from Judaism a rich collection of authoritative writings, including:

the Law of Moses (the Torah),

the books of the prophets (*nevi'im*), and

other writings that were considered authoritative (*ketuvim*).

But there was not yet a *canon* of Jewish scriptures, inasmuch as an exact *list* of authoritative books had not yet been determined. The Bible of early Christianity was generally a Greek translation of Hebrew books known as the Septuagint, which included many more books than the Old Testament currently considered authoritative by Protestant Christians. It is generally not known that Christians previously used all of the books of the Greek Septuagint. It was primarily in the nineteenth century that Protestants began to exclude from the Bible those books that were not part of the Hebrew Bible and that are now commonly referred to as the Apocrypha or as Deutero-Canonical books.

THE BEGINNINGS OF CHRISTIAN WRITINGS

During the apostolic age, the period of about forty years from the death of Jesus in about 30 until the fall of Jerusalem and the death of the first generation of Christians in about 70, the scriptures of nascent Christian communities were the Hebrew scriptures that the church had inherited from Judaism, Christianity's mother religion. There were, moreover, two modifying factors in the nascent churches:

the belief that the Holy Spirit was currently present within the church, and

the special authority that Christians assigned to words of Jesus and to words of the risen Lord as spoken by Christian prophets.

The century between 50 and 150 marks the time of the writing and circulation of the books that later became the canon of the New Testament. The earliest Christian writings that survive are Paul's genuine letters: 1 Thessalonians (ca. 52, Galatians (ca. 54), 1 and 2 Corinthians (ca. 54 and 54–55 respectively), Philemon (ca. 54-55), Philippians (ca. 54-55), and Romans (ca. 55-56) were probably all written over about a five-year period between ca. 52–ca. 56. Somewhat later, someone apparently made a collection of Paul's letters, including probably the Deutero-Pauline letters: Ephesians (last third of the first century), Colossians (last third of the first century), and 2 Thessalonians (impossible to date with any precision). This collection of ten letters was likely distributed to several churches, affording to Paul's letters a special status. In fact, there many have been multiple mini-collections that eventually coalesced into the ten, and then thirteen books.

At the same time, other disciples of Jesus were assembling sayings of Jesus into written collections, perhaps for purposes of instructing converts to Christianity. Such sayings collections existed in the form of Q (the hypothetical sayings source used subsequently by the authors of the gospels of Matthew and Luke) and perhaps in sayings that were collected into the earliest version or stratum of the *Gospel of Thomas*. Christians also collected from the Hebrew scriptures "proof-texts" or *testimonia* that they believed foretold or foreshadowed the coming of Jesus and that were then used in developing stories about Jesus, including Passion Narratives of the sort incorporated into the canonical gospels and the *Gospel of Peter*. There were also written collections of parables, miracle stories, and pronouncement stories associated with Jesus; and written birth narratives apparently surfaced in some churches. Copies of these early writings have not survived, probably because they served as the basis for other writings in which they effectively continue to exist.

Although Christians believed that the gospel (*to euangelion*), the *kerygma* or the preached message, was one, there were many written gospels, an issue that posed a challenge for some Christians. The earliest written gospel was probably the Gospel of Mark, likely written in Antioch in the late 60s. The Gospel of Matthew (a revision or second edition of Mark?) and the Gospel of Luke followed between about 80 and 90 (or perhaps somewhat later in the case of Luke), perhaps in Antioch and Corinth respectively; but the dates and places of composition of the canonical gospels are disputed by reputable scholars. Most agree, however, that the Gospel of John was written last, between 90–100, perhaps in Alexandria or Ephesus. These gospels reflected and addressed the needs of the individual churches in which and for which each was written.

In addition to the great four, other gospels appeared in the late first and into the second century and even later, gospels under the name of an apostle or an otherwise important authority. Gospels that did not become part of the canon include (in alphabetical order): the *Gospel of Barnabas*, the *Gospel of Bartholomew*, the *Gospel of Basilides*, the *Diatessaron*, the *Gospel of the Ebionites*, the *Gospel of the Egyptians*, the *Gospel of the Hebrews*, the *Protevangelium of James*, the *Gospel of Joseph the Carpenter*, the *Gospel of Judas*, the *Gospel of Marcion*, the *Gospel of Mary*, the *Gospel of Matthias*, the *Gospel of the Nazoreans*, the *Gospel of Nicodemus*, the *Gospel of Peter*, the *Gospel of Philip*, the *Gospel of Thomas*, the *Infancy Gospel of Thomas*, the *Gospel of Truth*, etc. Some of these gospels survive in their entirety, some in fragments, and some only as names.

These so-called apocryphal or non-canonical gospels had largely local or regional appeal. During the second century, there seems to have been a question whether there should actually be only one gospel, so some church fathers composed harmonies of two, or three, or four, or more gospels in an effort to present the requisite authoritative One Gospel. But by 200, the authority of the great four (Matthew, Mark, Luke, and John) was relatively secure, with the emphasis on "relatively."

OTHER CHRISTIAN WRITINGS OF THE PERIOD

In addition to Paul's letters (including the Deutero-Pauline letters) and the gospels of Matthew, Mark, Luke-Acts, and John, there were other important writings from this period beside the long list of gospels identified above.

Of those additional writings, the following eventually became part of the Christian canon:

Acts (now separated from the Gospel of Luke)[3]

the Pastoral Letters: 1 and 2 Timothy and Titus

the so-called Catholic Letters: James; 1 and 2 Peter; 1, 2, and 3 John; and Jude

Hebrews

The Revelation of John

There were also several relatively early marginal Christian writings that were eventually rejected, although not for reasons of their content or the unorthodoxy of their teaching, but probably because of their lack of connection to an apostolic figure. The following early rejected writings are often referred to collectively as the Apostolic Fathers:[4]

1 Clement (from about 95–96)

2 Clement (from about 150)

Letter of Barnabas (from about 130)

Didache (from about 100)

the *Shepherd of Hermas* (from about 150)

Letters of Ignatius of Antioch (from about 115) (seven letters addressed to the Ephesians, the Magnesians, the Trallians, the Romans, the Philadelphians, the Smyrnaeans, and to Polycarp)

the *Letter to Diognetus* (about 150)

---

3. It is not clear that Luke and Acts were actually ever joined. There is no manuscript evidence that Luke and Acts were included consecutively in early Christian collections.

4. Although two of these writings, 1 Clement and Didache, are probably earlier than some of the books that were eventually included in the Christian canon, their relatively early date was not sufficient reason for their inclusion in the canon. The dates listed for these books are approximate and are widely disputed by reputable scholars. There is usually little significant internal evidence to assist in assigning a specific date of composition of the writings of the Apostolic Fathers.

THE NEW TESTAMENT
THE FORMATION OF THE CANON

The canon of the New Testament was determined primarily by usage, not by formal authority of officials of the church. Although Judaism of the period was a scriptural religion, early Christianity was not. Instead, it focused on Jesus, or more precisely on the risen Lord. It was in the preaching of the Church, not in books, that early Christians encountered Christ. That began to change in the second century, when we find some evidence of interest in early Christian writings in early second century writings (e.g., 1 Tim 5:18, which may be influenced by Matt 10:10 or Luke 10:7;[5] and 2 Pet 3:15–16, which shows familiarity with Paul's letters).

The Hebrew scriptures were important to Christians to the extent that they served the church's exposition of the gospel and the development of oral and written traditions about Jesus and the risen Christ.[6] Apart from Paul's letters and some pre-synoptic written sources including Q, known Christian writings appeared relatively late, beginning with Mark sometime in the late 60s, almost forty years after Jesus' death. It was Christian communities testing the importance and function of these writings in their daily life over a period of several centuries that resulted in the identification of twenty-seven books by common consent.

EARLY COLLECTIONS OF CHRISTIAN BOOKS

PAUL'S LETTERS

Ironically, the earliest writings to be collected by the church were letters of Paul written to individual churches and, in one instance, to an individual person. Paul's letters were the least likely candidates for inclusion in a collection of Christian scriptures, because they were real letters, written to address specific circumstances in individual Christian communities. As such, they were not well suited for every Christian audience.

It is not clear whether someone made a conscious effort to collect Paul's letters or whether churches routinely made copies of Paul's letters and simply decided to circulate them to other Christian communities (see Col 4:16). It is, however, clear that Paul had supporters even after his death and that these followers of Paul were probably

---

5. The phrase in 1 Tim 5:18 ("the laborer deserves to be paid") is reminiscent of Matt 10:10 ("for laborers deserve their food") or Luke 10:7 ("for laborers deserve to be paid"), but there is nothing like this in the Hebrew scriptures. The unusual fact is that 1 Timothy identifies this saying as "scripture" at a time when the gospels were certainly not yet regarded as such. Some scholars have suggested that this is evidence of 1 Timothy's late date. Yet, Luke 10:7 sounds as if it too is quoting scripture or at least a familiar saying. Perhaps the author of 1 Timothy is quoting a familiar authoritative saying from memory and simply assumes mistakenly that he is quoting a Hebrew scripture.

6. In the New Testament, the Greek word γραφή (*graphē*) is used fifty-one times to refer to the Hebrew scriptures, usually with reference to the Law, or to the Law and the Prophets, and on one occasion (Luke 24:44) to Psalms.

involved in copying and collecting Paul's letters, even as they engaged in editing Paul's genuine letters and in writing pseudonymous letters in Paul's name.

Whatever the process, Paul's authentic letters had probably been gathered by about 100 and were known collectively by Clement of Rome (fl. 96),[7] Ignatius of Antioch (d. ca. 117),[8] and Polycarp of Smyrna (ca. 69–ca. 155).[9] Among the books in the New Testament canon, the author of 2 Peter was also familiar with Paul's letters to Rome, Corinth, and Thessalonica. The language of 2 Pet 3:15b-16 (written about 100–150) suggests that the author regarded Paul's letters as scripture, even though he does not identify the letters specifically:

> [3:15b]So also our beloved brother Paul wrote to you according to the wisdom given to him, [16]speaking of this as he does *in all his letters*. There are some things in them hard to understand, which the ignorant and unstable twist to their own destruction, *as they do the other scriptures* [italics mine].[10]

Subsequent editing of Paul's genuine letters and the writing of pseudonymous letters are evidence that Paul had supporters and followers long after his death. It was obviously admirers of Paul who collected, preserved, and disseminated Paul's letters and who added their own pseudonymous letters to the Pauline corpus, writing, as they presumably believed, in the spirit of their teacher.

It is not clear who first arranged the Pauline corpus in the letters' presumed chronological order: Galatians, 1 and 2 Corinthians, Romans, 1 and 2 Thessalonians, Ephesians (= Laodiceans), Colossians (+ Philemon), and Philippians. This is the order attested to by Marcion (ca. 140), by Syrian sources, and also by prologues to Paul's letters in many Latin manuscripts. The presumed chronological order was superseded already in the second century by a collection of thirteen letters of Paul that placed the letters in the order of longest to shortest with the Pastoral Letters (1 and 2 Timothy, and Titus) placed at the end of the original collection, except for Philemon, the shortest letter, placed after the Pastorals at the very end. This sequence survives in modern Bibles.

With the exception of Marcion and some Gnostics, Christian writers of the second century show little knowledge of or interest in Paul's letters, although the reasons

---

7. In a letter that Clement wrote to the church at Corinth in about 95-96, he says (*1 Clement* 47:1): "Take up the epistle of the blessed Paul the Apostle," in what is a clear reference to 1 Cor 1:10-17. *1 Clement* may also contain allusions to passages in Romans, Galatians, and Philippians, and perhaps also to the Deutero-Pauline letter to the Ephesians.

8. Writing in about 117, Ignatius seems to have been familiar with 1 Corinthians, and perhaps also with the Deutero-Pauline letter to the Ephesians. In fact, he may have known the entire collection of Paul's letters.

9. In his *Letter to the Philippians*, Polycarp may be imitating Paul's Philippians, which he occasionally quotes.

10. Although it is not clear which letters of Paul the author of 2 Peter knew, he seems to have minimally known Romans (Rom 2:4 = 2 Pet 3:9, 15) and possibly 1 Thessalonians (1 Thess 5:2 = 2 Pet 3:10). Neyrey (*2 Peter, Jude*, 133-34) identifies at least sixteen specific terms and four themes that 2 Peter may have drawn from at least five of Paul's letters: Romans, 1 and 2 Corinthians, Philippians, and 1 Thessalonians. Moreover, the phrase *in all his letters* in 2 Pet 3:16 obviously implies several letters.

for this are not clear. It is uncertain whether the use of Paul in some communities (e.g. Marcionism) steered some writers away from his letters, but most writers of the second century show no animosity toward Paul. Such animosity was, however, prevalent in Jewish Christian circles. By the end of the second century, Paul's letters gained considerable favor with three important Christian writers, Clement of Alexandria (ca. 150–ca. 215), Tertullian in North Africa (ca. 160–ca. 220), and Irenaeus in Lyons (2nd century–ca. 202). The scriptural status of the thirteen letters of the Pauline corpus was evident by about 200, based on usage alone, not on formal decisions of councils or synods of the church.

The Letter to the Hebrews, which does not claim Pauline authorship, became attached at the end of the thirteen Pauline letters, although its authorship was disputed. Hebrews was accepted as authoritative relatively early by churches in Egypt, but Western churches, most especially Rome, showed little interest in Hebrews until the fourth century.

THE GOSPELS

It was in oral tradition that the teaching of Jesus and teachings about Jesus were initially transmitted. In fact, even after some began to commit Jesus tradition to writing, some fathers of the church, including Papias of Hierapolis, still preferred the oral tradition well into the second century. Nevertheless, beginning about 50, or perhaps even earlier, and extending through the next few decades, there were written collections of sayings, parables, pronouncement stories, and miracle stories, containing tradition about Jesus, as well as passion narratives, birth narratives, and accounts of appearances of the Risen Lord. These oral and written traditions became the building blocks of the gospels, both the canonical and some of the the non-canonical gospels.

The earliest of the gospels, probably written in the late 60s, perhaps in Antioch of Syria, was probably the anonymous gospel attributed in the second century to Mark. Building on Mark and on other written sources, other anonymous gospels attributed in the second century to Jesus' apostle Matthew and to Paul's traveling companion Luke were written. Matthew was probably written between about 80–90 in Antioch (perhaps as a revision or second edition of Mark), and Luke sometime after Matthew perhaps as late as the early second century, perhaps in Corinth. The anonymous gospel attributed in the second century to Jesus' apostle John is generally considered the last of the four canonical gospels, and was written about 100, perhaps in Alexandria or in Ephesus.

Living in Rome about 140, Marcion obviously preferred just one gospel, the most Gentile of all the gospels, the Gospel of Luke, but in a form purged of all Jewish elements. A few decades later, and also in Rome, it was Justin Martyr's pupil Tatian who in about 170 created the *Diatessaron*, a harmony of most of the contents of the four gospels, Matthew, Mark, Luke, and John, and perhaps material from the oral tradition.

The widespread dissemination and popularity of the *Diatessaron* speak volumes for the challenges posed by the numerous gospels. The fact that even the four gospels that eventually achieved canonical status could be edited, added to, rewritten, and even harmonized into one gospel indicates that the four gospels did not have sacrosanct, static, or fixed status during the first several decades of their transmission. In addition to relatively minor editorial changes, copyists or editors added two different endings to the Gospel of Mark, and editors added John 7:53–8:11[11] and chapter 21 to the Gospel of John.

The priority of the Great Four (Matthew, Mark, Luke, and John) surfaced only toward the end of the second century, and even then initially in the Western church. In *Against Heresies* 3.11.8, Irenaeus of Lyons, writing about 180, presented a lengthy cosmological argument for the authority of the quadriform or fourfold gospel:

> It is not possible that the Gospels can be either more or fewer in number than they are. For, since there are four zones of the world in which we live, and four principal winds, while the Church is scattered throughout all the world, and the "pillar and ground" of the Church is the Gospel and the spirit of life; it is fitting that she should have four pillars, breathing out immortality on every side, and vivifying men afresh. From which fact, it is evident that the Word, the Artificer of all, He that sitteth upon the cherubim, and contains all things, He who was manifested to men, has given us the Gospel under four aspects, but bound together by one Spirit. As also David says, when entreating His manifestation, "Thou that sittest between the cherubim, shine forth." For the cherubim, too, were four-faced, and their faces were images of the dispensation of the Son of God. For, [as the Scripture] says, "The first living creature was like a lion," symbolizing His effectual working, His leadership, and royal power; the second [living creature] was like a calf, signifying [His] sacrificial and sacerdotal order; but "the third had, as it were, the face as of a man,"—an evident description of His advent as a human being; "the fourth was like a flying eagle," pointing out the gift of the Spirit hovering with His wings over the Church.... For the living creatures are quadriform, and the Gospel is quadriform, as is also the course followed by the Lord. For this reason were four principal covenants given to the human race: one, prior to the deluge, under Adam; the second, that after the deluge, under Noah; the third, the giving of the law, under Moses; the fourth, that which renovates man, and sums up all things in itself by means of the Gospel, raising and bearing men upon its wings into the heavenly kingdom.

Irenaeus's convoluted argument sounds somewhat defensive, but he basically set in motion the idea of the quadriform gospel: the gospels of Matthew, Mark, Luke, and John rather than any single gospel or any harmony of more than one gospel. Nevertheless, the authority of the *Diatessaron* persisted in the East, most especially in Syria.

---

11. Some ancient manuscripts include these verses after John 7:36 or after John 21:25 or after Luke 21:38 with some variation in the text.

THE NEW TESTAMENT
THE CATHOLIC LETTERS

The seven so-called Catholic Letters are James, 1 and 2 Peter, 1, 2, and 3 John, and Jude. This was the collection of books that received acceptance most slowly. 1 Peter and 1 John were known and referred to already in the second century, whereas James, 2 Peter, 2 and 3 John, and Jude appear to have had only local or regional use until the fourth century in spite of claims regarding their apostolic authorship. James and Jude were attributed to brothers of Jesus, 1 and 2 Peter and 1, 2, and 3 John to apostles of Jesus. The presumed authority of Peter, James and John, the pillars of the Jerusalem church according to Paul's own testimony in Galatians 2:9, may have led to the formation of this collection of seven letters in order to afford both apostolic credibility and balance to the already authoritative Pauline corpus.

ACTS AND REVELATION

The Acts of the Apostles, the second volume of Luke-Acts, and the Revelation of John complete the collection of twenty-seven books. Although Luke and Acts were composed originally as two volumes of a single work, Luke gained acceptance and credibility much earlier. Justin Martyr is the first writer to cite Acts, but it was probably not until the end of the second century that Acts achieved importance in its own right.

The Revelation of John was well received in the second century in the Western church. In the Eastern churches, Revelation was usually read allegorically. In the third century, Egyptian fathers disagreed about whether Revelation should be read literally or allegorically, leading Eastern churches to question the authority of Revelation, which was accepted in the East very slowly.

CANONICAL LISTS

The process of selecting specific Christian books for inclusion in a canon of sacred literature had its roots in Judaism and, in the case of Christianity, in the decision of someone to create a collection of Paul's letters, probably before the end of the first century. By the end of the second century, the fourfold gospel was acknowledged, but not universally. Yet, there was still no canon of Christian scripture, no authoritative catalogue or list of Christian writings that the church as a whole agreed upon. Although some church fathers began to identify lists of authoritative writings as early as the second century, it was not until the third and fourth centuries that there were actual lists of authoritative books. Let us look at some of the critical developments that led to the formation of the New Testament canon. It is important in this connection to note that the canonical lists referred to below are really quite different, a detail that mitigates against a simple linear development of the New Testament canon as it comes down to us today. Historical research trumps uncritical assumptions on this important subject.

THE CANON OF THE NEW TESTAMENT

MARCION

The process of identifying specific Christian books as authoritative probably began in the mid-second century with Marcion of Sinope, who had moved from Asia to Rome and who was by about 140 a member of one of the Christian churches in Rome. Marcion wrote only a single book, *Antitheses*, or *Contradictions*, in which he set forth his teaching that the Hebrew scriptures should be rejected by Christians because they reflected the teaching of the inferior God of Judaism, whereas Jesus was the messenger of the Supreme God of goodness. For his teaching, the clergy of Christian congregations in Rome excommunicated Marcion in 144.

Marcion believed that the Hebrew scriptures were incompatible with the teaching of Jesus and with Christianity and accepted in their stead and in this order the following Christian writings, the first such "list" or "canon" in Christian history: the Gospel of Luke, Galatians, 1 and 2 Corinthians, Romans, 1 and 2 Thessalonians, Ephesians (which Marcion called Laodiceans), Colossians, Philemon, and Philippians.

Marcion further believed that Jesus' apostles had misunderstood Jesus' teaching by claiming that he was the Messiah of the Jewish God. The apostles then falsified Jesus' teaching by adding Judaizing interpolations, which Marcion expurgated from the text of Luke to make the single authentic gospel available to the church. With this expurgation, the Gospel of Luke became the *Euangelion*, and the ten letters of Paul, amended by Marcion of material that he regarded as later additions, became the *Apostolikon*.

Marcion's importance cannot be overestimated. It was he who set in motion the idea of a Christian canon, or a New Testament, and it was in opposition to Marcion that other fathers of the church became aware of the church's inheritance of apostolic writings. Marcionism thrived and survived until the middle of the fifth century, when its books were burned in an effort to stamp out what was then perceived by many as a heresy.

THE CANON OF ORIGEN

An account of the canon of Origen of Alexandria (ca. 185–254) survives in Eusebius's *Church History* 6.25.3–14:

> [3]In the first book of his [Origen's] *Commentary on the Gospel according to Matthew*, defending the canon of the Church, he [Origen] testifies that he knows only four Gospels, writing somewhat as follows:
>
> [4]"Among the four Gospels, which are the only indisputable ones in the Church of God under heaven, I have learned by tradition that first was written that according to Matthew, who was once a tax collector but afterwards an apostle of Jesus Christ, who published it for those who from Judaism came to believe, composed as it was in the Hebrew language. [5]Secondly, that according to Mark, who composed it in accordance with the instructions of Peter, who in

the catholic Epistle acknowledges him as a son, saying, 'She that is in Babylon, elect together with you, salutes you, and so does Mark, my son' (1 Pet 5:13). [6]And thirdly, that according to Luke, the Gospel commended by Paul (cf. 2 Cor 8:18) and composed for those who from the Gentiles [came to believe]. After them all, that according to John."

[7]And in the fifth book of his Expositions on the Gospel according to John, the same person [Origen] says this with reference to the Epistles of the apostles:

"But he who was made sufficient to become a minister of the new covenant, not of the letter but of the Spirit (cf. 1 Cor 3:6), that is, Paul, who 'fully preached the gospel from Jerusalem and round about even unto Illyricum' (Roms 15:19), did not write to all the churches which he had instructed; and even to those to which he wrote he sent but a few lines. [8]And Peter, on whom the Church of Christ is built, 'against which the gates of hell shall not prevail' (Matt 16:18), has left one acknowledged Epistle; possibly also a second, but this is disputed. [9]Why need I speak of him who leaned back on Jesus' breast (John 13:23), John, who has left behind one Gospel, though he confessed that he could write so many that even the world itself could not contain them (John 21:25)? And he wrote also the Apocalypse, being ordered to keep silence and not to write the voices of the seven thunders (Rev 10:4). [10]He has left also an Epistle of a very few lines; and, it may be, a second and a third; for not all say that these are genuine but the two of them are not a hundred lines long."

[11]In addition, he [Origen] makes the following statements concerning the Epistle to the Hebrews, in his Homilies upon it: "That the character of the diction of the Epistle entitled 'To the Hebrews' has not the apostle's rudeness in speech, who acknowledged himself to be rude in speech (1 Cor 11:6), that is, in style, but that the Epistle is better Greek in the framing of its diction, will be admitted by everyone who is able to discern differences of style. [12]But again, on the other hand, that the thoughts of the Epistle are admirable, and not inferior to the acknowledged writings of the apostle, this also everyone who carefully examines the apostolic text will admit."

[13]Further on he [Origen] adds: "If I gave my opinion, I should say that the thoughts are those of the apostle, but the style and composition belong to someone who remembered the apostle's teachings and wrote down at his leisure what had been said by his teacher. Therefore, if any church holds that this Epistle is by Paul, let it be commended for this also. For it is not without reason that the men of old time have handed it down as Paul's. [14]But who wrote the Epistle, in truth, God knows. Yet the account that has reached us [is twofold], some saying that Clement, bishop of the Romans, wrote the Epistle, and others, that it was Luke, the one who wrote the Gospel and the Acts."

By the mid-third century, Origen listed four gospels (Matthew, Mark, Luke, and John), an indeterminate number of letters of Paul, 1 (and possibly 2) Peter, the Apocalypse of John, 1 (and possibly 2 and 3) John, Hebrews (although not written by Paul, but perhaps by Clement of Rome or by Luke). Assuming Origen acknowledged thirteen letters of Paul (which is not clear from the text), his list contained as few as twenty-one and as many as twenty-four books (depending on whether 2 Peter and 2 and 3 John are included}.

Missing from Origen's list are Acts, James, and Jude. The omission of Acts is curious, because he mentions it in his discussion of Hebrews (see verse 14 above), unless Origen knew Luke-Acts as a single book in two parts. But in his discussion of Luke, Origen does not specifically mention part two (The Acts of the Apostles). In any event, he also omits James and Jude.

THE MURATORI CANON

Until relatively recently, scholars believed that the Muratori Canon had been written in Rome, or perhaps elsewhere in Italy, by about 200 or early in the third century. More recently, it has been proposed, with good reason, that the Muratori Canon could not have been assembled as early as 200 and that it is more likely an Eastern canonical list from the fourth century, perhaps from Palestine or Syria.[12]

The Muratori Canon is fragmentary and was badly translated into Latin [the original Greek has not survived]; however, it lists the following books: four gospels (Matthew, Mark, Luke, and John), Acts, thirteen letters of Paul (Romans, 1 and 2 Corinthians, Galatians, Ephesians, Philippians, Colossians, 1 and 2 Thessalonians, 1 and 2 Timothy, Titus, and Philemon), Jude, 1 and 2 John, the Wisdom of Solomon, the Revelation of John, and the *Apocalypse of Peter*.

Notable in the Muratori Canon is the absence of Hebrews, James, 1 and 2 Peter, and 3 John, and the inclusion of the pre-Christian Wisdom of Solomon in a list of Christian books, and of the *Apocalypse of Peter*. The canon specifically rejects by name the *Shepherd of Hermas*, pseudo-Pauline letters to the Laodiceans and to the Alexandrians, and additional unnamed books attributed to heterodox groups.

In other words, the Muratori Canon included twenty-four books, including two that did not become canonical (the Wisdom of Solomon and the *Apocalypse of Peter*), and omitting five that did eventually become canonical (Hebrews, James, 1 and 2 Peter, and 3 John).

EUSEBIUS OF CAESAREA

Writing in Caesarea in the early decades of the fourth century (probably about 325), Eusebius, bishop of Caesarea, provides a list of early Christian writings in three categories (*Church History* 3.25):

Acknowledged Books (Greek *homologoumenoi*), or books accepted without qualification:

four gospels (Matthew, Mark, Luke, and John), Acts, the fourteen letters of Paul (Romans, 1 and 2 Corinthians, Galatians, Ephesians, Philippians

---

12. Sundberg "Canon Muratori," 1–44; Ferguson, "Canon Muratori," 677–83. The similarity of the Muratori Canon to Eusebius of Caesarea's list suggests a similar provenance.

Colossians, 1 and 2 Thessalonians, 1 and 2 Timothy, Titus, Philemon, Hebrews), 1 John, 1 Peter, the Revelation of John ("if it is considered appropriate")

Disputed Books (Greek *antilegomenoi*), or books whose authenticity or authority is uncertain or questioned:

James, Jude, 2 Peter, 2 and 3 John ("the work of the Evangelist or of someone else of the same name")

Spurious Books (Greek νόθοι, *nothoi*), or books that are totally rejected:

the *Acts of Paul*, the *Shepherd of Hermas*, the *Revelation of Peter*, the "alleged" *Epistle of Barnabas*, "the so-called teaching of the Apostles" (*Didache*), and the Revelation of John "if appropriate here"; and "some have included the *Gospel of the Hebrews* in the list," and "writings published by heretics under the names of the apostles, such as the Gospels of Peter, Thomas, Matthias, and others, or the Acts of Andrew, John, and other apostles"

In other words, Eusebius listed twenty-one acknowledged books (or twenty-two if Revelation is included), ten disputed books, and omitted five books that eventually became canonical (James, 2 Peter, 2 and 3 John, and Jude), which he lists as "disputed books." It is interesting that the Revelation of John shows up on the lists of "acknowledged books" and "spurious books," rather than among the "disputed books." Clearly, Revelation was still a problem even at this relatively late date.

Eusebius's list obviously reflects the situation in churches with which he was most familiar at the beginning of the fourth century, presumably churches in and around Caesarea.

CONSTANTINE

In 331, the Roman Emperor Constantine commissioned Eusebius to deliver fifty copies of the Bible for the Church of Constantinople. According to the *Apostolic Constitutions* 4, Athanasius of Alexandria, writing about 340, reports that Alexandrian scribes were preparing Bibles for the Emperor Constans, Constantine's third and youngest son. It is not clear that this project was in fulfillment of Constantine's original commission. Neither is it clear what exactly was included in these Bibles. It seems reasonable to assume that, in fulfillment of Constantine's commission, Eusebius would have provided copies of the New Testament without the Revelation of John in accordance with his own preference stated above.

Constantine's commission may have been the motivation for such manuscripts as Codex Sinaiticus, Codex Vaticanus, and Codex Alexandrinus, our earliest extant biblical manuscripts.

THE CANON OF THE NEW TESTAMENT

THE CATALOGUE OF UNCERTIAN DATE AND PROVENANCE INSERTED IN CODEX CLAROMONTANUS

Codex Claramontanus is a sixth century manuscript of Paul's letters with Greek and Latin texts on opposing pages. This Western codex contains additional early information, possibly from the fourth century, including a catalogue of the Old Testament and the New Testament canons inserted between Philemon and Hebrews.

The catalogue lists the following books: the four gospels (Matthew, Mark, Luke, and John), ten letters of Paul (not including Philippians and 1 and 2 Thessalonians), the seven "Catholic Letters" (James, 1 and 2 Peter, 1, 2, and 3 John, and Jude), *Barnabas*, the Revelation of John, Acts, the *Shepherd of Hermas*, the *Acts of Paul*, and the *Apocalypse of Peter*. The omission of Philippians and 1 and 2 Thessalonians is usually considered an oversight. The matter of Hebrews, which is also not included, is less clear.

If we include the three overlooked letters of Paul (Philippians and 1 and 2 Thessalonians, but not Hebrews), the catalogue lists thirty books. The status of Hebrews is uncertain, but four of the works listed in the catalogue were ultimately not included in the New Testament canon (*Barnabas*, the *Shepherd of Hermas*, the *Acts of Paul*, and the *Apocalypse of Peter*).

Inasmuch as the catalogue is a stichometry or a measurement of ancient texts by στίχοι, *stixoi*, meaning "rows" or "verses," it is not entirely clear that the author of the catalogue thought that these four works were necessarily canonical. Their inclusion may be due to nothing more than the fact that they were in a source whose principal purpose was to measure the length of important books, perhaps for purposes of future copyists, and that the Catalogue included these four books simply because they were in his source. We cannot, of course, be sure. Neither do we know that the omission of Hebrews was accidental. Hebrews was not always popular in Western churches.

THE CHELTENHAM CANON

The Cheltenham Canon is a Latin list that apparently originated in North Africa shortly after the mid-fourth century.

With reference to the New Testament, the Cheltenham Canon, a stichometry like the catalogue inserted in the Codex Claramontanus, lists:

Four Gospels:	Matthew	2700 lines
	Mark	1700 lines
	John	1800 lines
	Luke	3300 lines

All the lines make 10,000 lines

Epistles of Paul, 13 in number

The Acts of the Apostles	3600 lines
The Apocalypse	1800 lines
Three Epistles of John	350 lines
One only	
Two Epistles of Peter	300 lines
One only	

The meaning of "one only" (*una sola*) immediately following the three letters of John and the two letters of Peter is unclear. Perhaps the author was implying that he personally acknowledged as canonical only one letter of John and one letter of Peter, although he was reporting the cumulative length of all three letters of John and of both letters of Peter, because that information was available in his source. Stated simply and honestly, the meaning of "one only" in both instances is uncertain.

Missing from the Cheltenham Canon are James, Jude, and Hebrews.

ATHANASIUS'S LIST

In a Festal Letter issued on Easter in 367, Athanasius (ca. 293–373), bishop of Alexandria, was the first person to list clearly and unequivocally the twenty-seven books that eventually constituted the New Testament canon. In doing so, Athanasius acknowledged the authority of Revelation at a time when it was still suspect in the East.

Yet, in spite of Athanasius, Tatian's *Diatessaron* continued to be popular in the East, especially in Syria, until the sixth century. In fact, the Syrian church generally acknowledged the following books as canon through the fifth century: the *Diatessaron*, Acts, Paul's letters, and then only recently and somewhat reluctantly James, 1 Peter, and 1 John.

THE CANON OF CYRIL OF JERUSALEM

Cyril of Jerusalem (315–386) delivered Catechetical Lectures in preparation for baptism on Easter Saturday. In Catechetical Lecture 4.36, Cyril wrote:

> Then of the New Testament there are four Gospels only, for the rest have false titles and are harmful. The Manicheans also wrote a *Gospel according to Thomas*, which being smeared with the fragrance of the name "Gospel" destroys the souls of those who are rather simple-minded. Receive also the Acts of the Twelve Apostles; and in addition to these the seven Catholic Epistles of James, Peter, John, and Jude; and as a seal upon them all, and the latest work of disciples, the fourteen Epistles of Paul.
>
> But let all the rest be put aside in a secondary rank. And whatever books are not read in the churches, do not read these even by yourself, as you have already heard [me say concerning the Old Testament apocrypha].

Missing from Cyril's list is the Revelation of John.

THE CANON OF THE NEW TESTAMENT
THE CANON OF THE SYNOD OF LAODICEA[13]

A synod held in Laodicea in Phrygia Pacatiana in about 363, "in which many blessed fathers from diverse provinces of Asia were gathered together," took action regarding a canon, but the precise decision taken at that synod is unclear.

Thirty or so clerics in attendance at the synod issued several "canons," as decrees of a synod were commonly called. Canon 59, which is found in all accounts of the synod with only minor variations, states that only canonical books should be read in the church. This statement is followed in later and probably secondary manuscripts by Canon 60, a list of specific canonical books. However, the list is absent from most of the earlier Latin and Syriac versions of the decree, and most scholars consider the list to be a latter addition:

> Canon 59. No psalms composed by private individuals nor any uncanonical books may be read in the church, but only the Canonical Books of the Old and New Testaments.
>
> Canon 60. [After listing the books of the Old Testament] And these are the books of the New Testament: Four Gospels, according to Matthew, Mark, Luke, and John; the Acts of the Apostles, Seven Catholic epistles, namely, one of James, two of Peter, three of John, one of Jude; Fourteen Epistles of Paul, one to the Romans, two to the Corinthians, one to the Galatians, one to the Ephesians, one to the Philippians, one to the Colossians, two to the Thessalonians, one to the Hebrews, two to Timothy, one to Titus, and one to Philemon.

Canon 60 was almost certainly not original to the Synod of Laodicea. Nevertheless, missing from the list of Canon 60, whenever it was written, is the Revelation of John.

THE CANON APPROVED BY THE APOSTOLIC CANONS

In about 383, a series of 85 Canons (or decrees) attributed to the apostles was compiled by a redactor of the *Apostolic Constitutions*. This is the concluding Canon as translated from the Latin version:

> Canon 85. Let the following books be esteemed venerable and holy by all of you, both clergy and laity. [A list of books of the Old Testament . . .]
>
> And our sacred books, that is, of the New Testament, are the four Gospels, of Matthew, Mark, Luke, John; the fourteen Epistles of Paul; two Epistles of Peter; three of John; one of James; one of Jude; two Epistles of Clement; and the *Constitutions* dedicated to you, the bishops, by me, Clement, in eight books, which is not

---

13. A synod (Greek σύνοδος, *synodos*, Latin *consilium*) *is* a local or regional ecclesiastical assembly under hierarchical authority, for the discussion and decision of matters relating to faith and morals, or discipline. Synod and council are synonymous terms.

appropriate to make public before all, because of the mysteries contained in them; and the Acts of us, the Apostles.

Note in this canon, attributed pseudonymously to Clement of Rome, the omission of the Revelation of John and the addition of the two letters of Clement (1 and 2 Clement), and of the *Apostolic Constitutions* (although not to be made public to all).

THE CANON OF GREORY OF NAZIANUS

Toward the end of his life (ca. 329–390), Gregory of Nazianus drew up in iambic verse (perhaps as an aid for the memory of his readers) a catalogue of Biblical books. The lineation but not the rhythm of the original Greek verse is preserved in this translation:

> [List of books of the Old Testament . . .]
>
> But now count also [the books] of the New Mystery;
> Matthew indeed wrote for the Hebrews the wonderful works of Christ,
> And Mark for Italy, Luke for Greece,
> John, the great preacher, for all, walking in heaven.
> Then the Acts of the wise apostles,
> And fourteen Epistles of Paul,
> And seven Catholic [Epistles], of which James is one,
> Two of Peter, three of John again.
> And Jude's is the seventh, you have all.
> If there is any besides these, it is not among the genuine [books].

Gregory omits the Revelation of John from his list, although he obviously knew of Revelation, because, on rare occasions, he quotes from it in some of his other writings.

In 692, the Trullan Council of two hundred fifteen bishops of the Eastern Roman Empire was convened in Constantinople under Byzantine auspices to confirm as orthodox some practices of the church at Constantinople that were not normative in Rome. Among those decisions, the Trullan Council upheld Gregory of Nazianus' canonical list, omitting the Revelation of John.

THE CANON OF AMPHILOCHIUS OF ICONIUM

A list of biblical books from sometime after 394 is included in a poem generally attributed to Amphilochius, a Cappadocian by birth and bishop of Iconium in Lycaonia. The poem, entitled *Iambics for Seleucus*, instructs Seleucus how to follow a life of study and virtue and urges him to apply himself to the Scriptures more than to any other writing. Once again, as in the case of the Canon of Gregory of Nazianus, the form of a poem may have served as an aid to remembering Amphilocius's list.

THE CANON OF THE NEW TESTAMENT

[List of books of the Old Testament . . .]

It is time for me to speak of the books of the New Testament.

Receive only four evangelists:

Matthew, then Mark, to whom, having added Luke

As third, count John as fourth in time,

But first in height of teachings,

For I call this one rightly a son of thunder,

Sounding out most greatly with the word of God.

And receive also the second book of Luke,

That of the catholic Acts of the Apostles.

Add next the chosen vessel,

The herald of the Gentiles, the apostle

Paul, having written wisely to the churches

Twice seven Epistles: to the Romans one,

To which one must add two to the Corinthians,

That to the Galatians, and that to the Ephesians, after which

That in Philippi, then the one written

To the Colossians, two to the Thessalonians,

Two to Timothy, and to Titus and to Philemon,

One each, and one to the Hebrews.

But some say the one to the Hebrews is spurious,

not saying well, for the grace is genuine.

Well, what remains? Of the Catholic Epistles

Some say we must receive seven, but others say

Only three should be received — that of James, one,

And one of Peter, and those of John, one.

And some receive three [of John], and besides these, two

of Peter, and that of Jude a seventh.

And again the Revelation of John,

Some approve, but the most

Say it is spurious, This is

Perhaps the most reliable (literally, most unfalsified)

canon of the divinely inspired Scriptures.

In this poem, Amphilochius reports the earlier difference of opinion regarding Hebrews, the Catholic Epistles, and the Revelation of John. In fact, he not only reports the differences of opinion concerning 2 Peter, 2 and 3 John, Jude, and the Revelation of John, but he himself appears to reject these four Catholic Letters, and he almost certainly rejects the Revelation of John. Having expressed doubt about these five books, the author ends with the unusual phrase "This is perhaps the most reliable canon of the divinely inspired Scriptures." What is especially interesting about the Canon of Amphilochius is that this bishop, writing in Asia Minor sometime after 394, seems to be uncertain about the exact extent of the canon.

THE CANON OF THE THIRD SYNOD OF CARTHAGE

The first council that accepted the New Testament canon of twenty-seven books was the Synod of Hippo Regius in North Africa in 393; however, the formal decisions taken by that council have been lost. A brief summary of the acts of the Synod of Hippo Regius was read at and accepted in Canon 24 of the third Synod of Carthage in North Africa in 397:

> Canon 24. Besides the canonical Scriptures, nothing shall be read in church under the name of divine Scriptures. Moreover, the canonical Scriptures are these: [then follows a list of Old Testament books].
>
> The [books of the] New Testament:
>
> the Gospels, four books; the Acts of the Apostles, one book; the Epistles of Paul, thirteen; of the same to the Hebrews, one Epistle; of Peter, two; of John, apostle, three; of James, one; of Jude, one; the Revelation of John.
>
> Concerning the confirmation of this canon, the transmarine Church shall be consulted. On the anniversaries of martyrs, their acts shall also be read.

In reviewing this list it is interesting to note that Hebrews is listed separately from the thirteen epistles attributed to Paul, perhaps reflecting uncertainty regarding its authorship. The reference to the "transmarine Church" in the final section is presumably a reference to the Church of Rome, which will be consulted about Canon 24 of the synod, perhaps hoping for or expecting Rome's approval.

In 419 in another Synod held at Carthage, the relevant words appear in the following form:

> ... Fourteen Epistles of Paul ... the Revelation of John, one book.
>
> Let this be sent to our brother and fellow-bishop, Boniface [of Rome], and to the other bishops of those parts, that they may confirm this canon, for these are the things that we have received from our fathers to be read in church.

At this synod, the fourteen letters are credited to Paul. Moreover, once again Carthage looks to Rome for confirmation of its decision.

THE CANON OF THE NEW TESTAMENT
THE DECRETUM GELASIANUM

The *Decretum Gelasianum de libris recipiendis et non recipiendis* (*The Gelasian Decree concerning the Books Received and Not-Received*), is traditionally attributed to Gelasius, bishop of Rome 492–496; however, in its present form it is generally considered to be of South Gallic origin from the sixth century. Several parts of the *Decretum* can, however, be traced back to Pope Damasus I (366–383) and, therefore, probably reflect Roman tradition.

The second part of the *Decretum* is a canon catalogue that lists all twenty-seven books of the New Testament:

Part 2 — A Catalogue of the Canon

Likewise it was said: Now indeed the issue of the divine scriptures must be discussed, which the universal Catholic church receives or which it is required to avoid.

1. This is the Order of the Old Testament: [There then follows a list of the books of the Old Testament in three divisions. . . .]

4. Likewise the order of the Scriptures of the New Testament, which the Holy and Catholic Roman church upholds and is venerated:

Four books of the Gospels	
according to Matthew	one book
according to Mark	one book
according to Luke	one book
according to John	one book
Likewise the Acts of the Apostles	one book
The letters of the apostle Paul in number fourteen	
To the Romans	one letter
To the Corinthians	two letters
To the Ephesians	one letter
To the Thessalonians	two letters
To the Galatians	one letter
To the Philippians	one letter
To the Colossians	one letter
To Timothy	two letters
To Titus	one letter
To Philemon	one letter
To the Hebrews	one letter
Likewise the Apocalypse of John	one book
Likewise the canonical letters in number seven	
Of the apostle Peter	two letters

Of the apostle James	one letter
Of the apostle John	one letter
Of the other John the elder	two letters
Of the apostle Judas the Zealot	one letter

Here ends the Canon of the New Testament

Although the *Gelasian Decree* lists the twenty-seven books of the canonical New Testament, there are some curiosities in the list. What is particularly interesting is the order of Paul's letters and of the so-called "canonical letters" (the Catholic Letters), the placement of the Revelation (the Apocalypse) of John before the seven "canonical letters," and the attribution of 1 John to John the apostle, and of 2 and 3 John to John the Elder.

THE CATALOGUE OF SIXTY CANONICAL BOOKS

This list, which probably originated in the seventh century, reflects the view, widely held in the Greek Church at a later time, of a canon of sixty books, thirty-four Old Testament books and twenty-six New Testament books, because the Revelation of John was not included.

THE STICHOMETRY OF NICEPHORUS

Nicephorus, the Patriarch of Constantinople 806–815, wrote a *Chronography* extending from Adam to the year of his death in 829. To this *Chronography*, Nicephorus appended a canon list, whose origin is uncertain, but which may have been Jerusalem. It is uncertain whether the original list is actually older that 800.

What is striking about the Stichometry of Nicephorus is that there was still in the ninth century a list of New Testament books that omitted the Revelation of John. In fact, the catalogue of Old and New Testament books is followed by a list of *antilegomena* (rejected books), which includes the Revelation of John as part of the New Testament apocrypha. Inasmuch as this work is a stichometry, next to each book in the list is the count of its *stichoi* (lines).

JEROME AND AUGUSTINE

Two individuals who were particularly responsible for the final catalogue of the New Testament canon of twenty-seven books were Jerome and Augustine.

About 383, Pope Damasus I (366–384) engaged Jerome, his personal secretary, to translate the Bible into Latin, the translation commonly known as the Vulgate. Jerome's translation of the New Testament, which appeared in 385, included twenty-seven books. This translation was instrumental in fixing the New Testament canon in the West, as the Vulgate became the official Bible of the Roman Catholic Church.

At about the same time, Augustine of Hippo in North Africa settled on the same twenty-seven book canon. In 393, the First Council of Hippo approved the twenty-seven book canon of the New Testament, together with the Greek Septuagint of the Old Testament, a decision that was subsequently confirmed by the third Synod of Carthage in 397 (see above). Augustine was present at both councils and thereafter considered the matter of the canon closed.

From the fourth century, the canon of the New Testament was essential fixed in the West. By the fifth century the Eastern Church, with few exceptions, had accepted the Revelation of John and was, therefore, in agreement with the West regarding the canon of the New Testament. The only holdout was the Syrian Church, which finally accepted the twenty-seven book canon in 508.

Formal confirmation (or reconfirmation) of the twenty-seven book canon of the New Testament came much later with the Council of Trent in 1546 for Roman Catholicism, the Thirty-Nine Articles of 1563 for the Church of England, the Westminster Confession of Faith of 1646 for British Calvinism, and the Synod of Jerusalem of 1672 for Greek Orthodoxy. Although these various denominations within Christianity did not always agree on the canon of the Old Testament, specifically on the status of the deutero-canonical or apocryphal books found in the Greek Septuagint but not in the Hebrew Bible, they did all agree on the twenty-seven books of the New Testament.

FACTORS INFLUENTIAL IN THE FORMATION OF THE NEW TESTAMENT CANON

Inasmuch as the establishment of the New Testament was not an event but a process, it is worthwhile to identify some of the factors that led to the creation of the canon. There is no single overriding cause. There were rather several influences at work over more than four centuries, some of them operating concurrently, that led to the formation of the New Testament.

First, the formation of the Jewish canon, the Old Testament, was unfolding at about the time that Christianity arrived on the scene. The creation of the Old Testament was also a process, not an event. Shortly before the emergence of Christianity, a collection of Hebrew scriptures was translated into Greek between about 250–150 BCE in Alexandria, Egypt. The so-called Septuagint contained about fifteen more books than what rabbis in Palestine and Babylonia eventually included in the Hebrew Scriptures, a process determined by usage over time, not by a formal decision of some religious authority. In many ways, Christianity paralleled the relatively long process in Rabbinic Judaism over some of the same period of time. Christians were certainly aware of the process that led to the establishment of the Hebrew Bible, even as they wrestled with the status of some of their own early Christian writings.

Secondly, the collection and dissemination of Paul's letters toward the end of the first century was obviously an acknowledgment that there were "authoritative" Christian writings worth preserving, copying, collecting, and disseminating to several churches, a process that foreshadowed what would subsequently unfold centuries later with the creation of formal lists or "canons" of authoritative Christian writings.

Thirdly, Marcion's decision in about 140 to create a collection of books that included an expurgated version of the Gospel of Luke and ten letters of Paul probably set wheels in motion, because, shortly thereafter, other church fathers began to take action in reaction to Marcion. Gospels harmonies evident in 2 Clement, the writings of Justin Martyr, and the *Diatessaron* about mid-second century were almost certainly motivated by Marcion's "canon."

A fourth factor, evident in the writings of some church fathers against second- and third-century heresies, such as Gnosticism and Montanism, was that the formation of the New Testament canon served as a reaction against the appearance of a large number of "heretical" books, especially gospels. Irenaeus's case for the fourfold gospel served as one response to the conviction in some circles that there should, on the one hand, be only One Gospel (reflected in the creation of gospel harmonies and most especially Tatian's *Diatessaron*), and, the realization, on the other hand, that there were as many as two dozen gospels floating around in different churches. Irenaeus was obviously addressing this situation with his cosmological argument for the fourfold gospel. Yes, there could be more than One Gospel, but there could be no more nor less than four.

In the end, the formation of the canon was determined primarily by usage, by the common consent of Christian communities that engaged in identifying those writings that best served the teaching and the worship of Christian assemblies. Although there were a few efforts to set the canon of the New Testament by formal authority in synods of the church, those decisions apparently had only local or regional jurisdiction.

The issue of a canon was not considered at the first Ecumenical Council of the church, the Council of Nicaea in 325. In fact, it was the long process of testing the books in the everyday life of the church that was the determining factor. The writings that became most valued were those that proved over time to be most useful in nourishing, supporting, and guiding the church in its preaching, in its teaching, and in its worship. Establishing a formal list of writings to read in worship services was, in significant measure, a matter of formalizing what was already common practice.

CONCLUSIONS

Paul wrote letters to churches he had either founded or visited or intended to visit; or in one case (Philemon) he wrote to an individual. His writings were personal letters, nothing more and nothing less. Paul could not have imagined that he was writing letters that would someday carry for Christians the same authority as the Hebrew scriptures. Although Paul regarded himself as an apostle of the risen Lord and claimed that he spoke with the authority of the Spirit, he could not possibly have envisaged that his letters would one day be considered part of the Bible.

Moreover, the authors of the manifold gospels could never have imagined that they were writing books for the Bible. The authors of the gospels wrote their own versions of the *euangelion*, the "gospel" or the "good news" for Christian communities that they presumably already knew in order to strengthen these churches in their faith, or in their special brand of the faith. Hence, the plethora of gospels—more than two dozen that we know either in whole or in part, or whose names we simply know from writings of early Christian fathers.

Most of the non-canonical gospels were written after the writing of what subsequently emerged as the four canonical gospels. The *Gospel of Thomas* and the *Gospel of Peter* may be exceptions, although I am inclined to believe that these gospels, at least in their present form, are much later. An early version of the *Gospel of Thomas*, or more likely an early written source of the *Gospel of Thomas*, may have been written in the first century. The same may be true of the *Gospel of Peter*. Moreover, some of the tradition that found its way into Jewish Christian gospels is likely quite early and may reach back to Peter or to James, the brother of Jesus. It is difficult to draw conclusions about the Jewish Christian gospels, because only fragments survive in polemical writings of several church fathers.

In spite of the fact that there were about two dozen gospels circulating in various churches by the mid- to late-second century, there was apparently a tendency in some churches to think that there should be only One Gospel. The tradition that the gospel was "one" was apparently strong within some communities, even though many churches probably had their own gospel, or perhaps several gospels. One way of working toward the "oneness" or the "unity" of the gospel was to create harmonies or two or more gospels. We know of such harmonies from 2 Clement and the Pseudo-Clementine literature, and from Justin Martyr, who about 150 was apparently working with a harmony of Matthew and Luke and, possibly, Mark, perhaps a harmony that Justin himself composed.

Justin either did not know or, more probably, did not like the Gospel of John, as he made no use of it. During the second century it was Gnostics who valued the Gospel of John most highly, perhaps rendering it somewhat suspect in Justin's judgment. It was Heracleon, a Gnosic who flourished about 175, probably in the south of Italy, who was the first to write a commentary on a gospel, namely the Gospel of John. And it was Justin's pupil Tatian who in about 160 composed the *Diatessaron* the fullest gospel harmony, containing most of the material found in the gospels of Matthew, Mark, Luke, and John.

The formation of the canon of the New Testament is just one component in the history of the early church, from the time that the earliest Christian writings first appeared in the mid-first century until the universal church agreed on the twenty-seven book canon in 508. There were four criteria that the church applied in establishing the canon:

1. Was a book "apostolic"? In other words, was the book written by one of Jesus' apostles, could it be traced to one of Jesus apostles, or was it written during the time of the apostles or in a manner consistent with the teachings of the apostles? By the mid-second century the four *anonymous* gospels that would eventually be considered as canonical had been attributed to Matthew, Mark, Luke, and John. Matthew and John had been apostles of Jesus; Mark was identified as a disciple of Jesus' apostle Peter; and Luke was considered a traveling companion of Paul, an apostle by virtue of his claim to have seen the risen Lord.

    Yet this criterion was not always decisive, because many of the apocryphal gospels were attributed to apostles or to figures otherwise known to have been associated with Jesus: (in alphabetical order) the *Gospel of Barnabas*, the *Gospel of Bartholomew*, the *Protevangelium of James*, the *Gospel of Joseph the Carpenter*, the *Gospel of Judas*, the *Gospel of Mary*, the *Gospel of Matthias*, the *Gospel of Nicodemus*, the *Gospel of Peter*, the *Gospel of Philip*, the *Gospel of Thomas*, and the *Infancy Gospel of Thomas*. A *claim* to apostolicity was obviously not sufficient for these pseudonymous gospels to gain inclusion in the canon. It was assumed that canonical writings came from the church's earliest period, and many of the apocryphal books were known to be later pseudonymous compositions.

2. Was the book "orthodox"? The terms "orthodox" and "heretical" are, of course, later terms, sometimes used by the church retrospectively to judge theological opinions of earlier generations. "orthodoxy" refers to the "correctness" of the teachings embedded in the texts. However, since the canon was not fixed until a relatively late date, the criterion of "orthodoxy" could be and was applied to earlier writings with the benefit of hindsight.

    For inclusion in the canon, a book had to conform to, or at least not contradict, what the church considered its normative or standard teaching, the so-called rule of faith in Tertullian and Irenaeus. This was a difficult criterion to apply in practice, because there were not yet Christian scriptures against which to "measure" a book's "orthodoxy." However, in 325, the universal Church assembled at the First Ecumenical (or worldwide) Council in Nicaea and endorsed the Nicene Creed to resolve disagreements about the understanding of the One God in Three Persons (most especially the relationship of the Son to the Father). With pressure from the Roman Emperor Constantine who presided over the Council of Nicaea, the church formally identified what had worldwide or universal (catholic) theological appeal in order to bring unity to what was a divided church. The timing of the council is critical, because it came in the midst of the dispute over whether certain books should or should not be included the canon. Although the canon was not formally at issue at the Council of Nicaea, the council's decisions affected subsequent discussion about the canon.

    The rule of faith included beliefs about God, his relationship to Jesus, the nature of Jesus' earthly life, death, resurrection, and ascension. It was the test of orthodoxy or the rule of faith that prevented some texts that were attributed to apostles from becoming canonical (e.g. the gospels of Thomas, Peter, and Philip).

3. Was the book "catholic" or "universal"? To be considered "catholic," a book had to be relevant for the universal church or the church at large. Local or regional appeal was insufficient. The church rejected books that were regarded as esoteric or sectarian. "Universality" implied a book's value to the whole, the universal (i.e. catholic) church.

4. Was the book in "traditional use"? Had the book been known and used from a very early time, most especially in the worship services of many or most churches? Sometimes the importance of the community or the city in which a text was used was influential. Like the criterion of "orthodoxy," this criterion was applied retrospectively from the vantage point of the third and the fourth centuries.

These criteria were more functional than prescriptive or regulatory. That is, these criteria were not formally adopted and then applied rigorously or consistently. Scholars actually infer these criteria from Christian writings of the period. In discussing the criteria for establishing canonicity, it is important to note that "inspiration" was *not* a criterion, because individual Christians and the church as a whole benefited from the presence and the power of the Holy Spirit. Inspiration was not limited to the scriptures.

Like the Old Testament, the New Testament is a collection of books—twenty-seven to be exact, written by sixteen or more different authors over a period of about seventy to one hundred years, in many different cities, primarily in the eastern regions of the Roman Empire. As such, the New Testament reflects both the unity and the diversity of early Christianity. Yet, the establishment of the canon proscribed or limited the diversity by effectively excluding some movements or tendencies that the majority of churches regarded as schismatic or heretical.

Our knowledge of the Christian canon is drawn from two sources: (1) from within the books themselves, where we see the theological positions of different individuals and different churches unfolding; and (2) from early fathers of the church, many of whom left a rich repository of writings in which they discussed and commented on ancient Christian writings and the formation of the canon. In fact, beginning just before the middle of the second century, Christian writers began to refer to or even quote from some of the books that eventually became the canon of the New Testament, thereby reflecting use of some of these books in their churches because people considered them authoritative.

We know a great deal about the process that led to the formation of the canon, as it is well documented over a period of a few hundred of years in the writings of church fathers and in canonical lists. Yet, however important the formation of the canon is, it is just one element in the rich and sometimes controversial development of the early church.

BIBLIOGRAPHY

Aland, Kurt, editor. *Synopsis of the Four Gospels,* Greek-English Edition of the Synopsis Quattuor Evangeliorum, tenth edition. London and New York: United Bible Societies, 1993.

Bauer, Walter. *Rechtgläubigkeit und Ketzerei im ältesten Christentum.* Tübingen: Mohr/Siebeck, 1934. Translated into English as *Orthodoxy and Heresy in Earliest Christianity* by a team from the Philadelphia Seminar on Christian Origins, edited by Robert A. Kraft and Gerhard Krodel. Philadelphia: Fortress, 1971.

Bellinzoni, Arthur. "The Gospel of Luke in the Apostolic Fathers: An Overview," In *The New Testament and the Apostolic Fathers: Trajectories through the New Testament and the Apostolic Fathers*, edited by Andrew F. Gregory and Christopher M. Tuckett. 45–68. Oxford: Oxford University Press, 2005.

―――. *The Old Testament: An Introduction to Biblical Scholarship.* Amherst, NY: Prometheus, 2009.

―――. *The Sayings of Jesus in the Writings of Justin Martyr.* Leiden: E. J. Brill, 1967.

―――, editor. *The Two Source Hypothesis: A Critical Appraisal.* Macon, GA: Mercer University Press, 1985.

Betz, Hans Dieter. *Galatians: A Commentary on Paul's Letter to the Churches in Galatia.* Hermeneia. Philadelphia: Fortress, 1979.

Black, Matthew. The Kingdom of God Has Come," In *Expository Times* 63 (1951–52) 289–90.

Bornkamm, Günther, Gerhard Barth, and Heinz Joachim Held, *Überlieferung und Auslegung im Matthäus-evangelium.* Neukirchen: Neukirchener Verlag, 1960. Translated into English by Percy Scott as *Tradition and Interpretation in Matthew*. Philadelphia: Westminster, 1963.

Bovon, François. *Luke 1: A Commentary on the Gospel of Luke 1:1–9:50.* Hermeneia. Minneapolis: Fortress, 2002.

Brown, Francis, S. R. Driver, and Charles A. Briggs, editors. *A Hebrew and English Lexicon of the Old Testament with an Appendix Containing the Biblical Aramaic*; based on the lexicon of William Gesenius as translated by Edward Robinson. Oxford: Clarendon, 1955.

Brown, Raymond E. *The Death of the Messiah: From Gethsemane to the Grave.* New York: Doubleday, 1994.

Bultmann, Rudolf. *Die Geschichte der synoptischen Tradition*, third edition. Göttingen: Vandenhoeck & Ruprecht, 1958. English translation *The History of the Synoptic Tradition*, translated by John Marsh. Oxford: Basil Blackwell, 1962.

―――. "New Testament and Mythology," In *Kerygma and Myth*, edited by Hans Werner Bartsch, translated by Reginald H. Fuller, 1-44. London: SPCK, 1957.

BIBLIOGRAPHY

Cerfaux, L. and G. Garitte, "Les paraboles de Royaume dans l'Évangile de Thomas," In *Le Muséon* 70 (1957) 307–27.

Collins, Adela Yarbo. *Mark: A Commentary*. Hermeneia. Minneapolis: Fortress Press, 2007.

Collins, John Joseph, editor. *Apocalypse: The Morphology of a Genre*. Semeia 14. Atlanta: Scholars, 1983.

———. *The Apocalyptic Imagination: An Introduction to Jewish Apocalyptic Literature*, second edition. Grand Rapids, MI: Wm. B. Eerdmans Co., 1998.

Conzelmann, Hans. *Die Mitte der Zeit: Studien zur Theologie des Lukas*. Tübingen: J. C. B. Mohr [Paul Siebeck], 1954. Translated into English by G. Buswell as *The Theology of Saint Luke*. New York: Harper and Row, 1960.

———. *1 Corinthians: A Commentary on the First Epistle to the Corinthians*, translated by James W. Leitch. Hermeneia. Philadelphia: Fortress, 1975.

Cornélis, E.M.J.M. "Quelques elements pour une comparison entre l'Évangile de Thomas et la notice d'Hippolyte sur les Naassènes," In *Vigiliae Christianiae* 15 (1961) 83–104.

DeConick, April D. "The Gospel of Thomas," In *The Expository Times* (2007), volume 118, 469–79.

Dibelius, Martin. *Die Formgeschichte des Evangeliums*, third edition, edited by Günther Bornkamm. Tübingen: Vandenhoeck & Ruprecht, 1958. English translation of the second edition, *From Tradition to Gospel*, translated by B. L. Wolff. London: Ivor Nicholson & Watson, 1934.

Dimant, Divorah. "Pesharim, Qumran," In *The Anchor Bible Dictionary*, volume 5 (O–Sh), edited by David Noel Freedman, 244–51. New York: Doubleday, 1992.

Dodd, C. H. *The Apostolic Preaching and Its Developments*. New York and London: Harper and Brothers, 1954.

———. *The Parables of the Kingdom*. New York: Scribner's, 1961.

Ehrman, Bart. *Jesus, Apocalyptic Prophet of the New Millennium*. New York: Oxford University Press, 1999.

———. *The New Testament: A Historical Introduction to the Early Christian Writings*. New York: Oxford University Press, 1997.

———. *The Orthodox Corruption of Scripture: The Effect of Early Christological Controversies on the Text of the New Testament*. New York: Oxford University Press, 1996.

Epp, Eldon J. *Junia: The First Woman Apostle*. Minneapolis: Fortress, 2005.

———. "Textual Criticism (New Testament)," In *The Anchor Bible Dictionary*, volume 6 (Si–Z), David Noel Freedman, editor in Chief. 412–35. New York: Doubleday, 1992.

Ferguson, Everett, "Canon Muratori: Date and Provenance," In *Studia Patristica* 18 (1982) 677–83.

Fitzmyer, Joseph A. *The Gospel According to Luke (X-XXIV): Introduction, Translation, and Notes*. The Anchor Bible. Garden City, NY: Doubleday, 1958.

Ford, J. Massyngberde. *Revelation: A New Translation with Introduction and Commentary*. The Anchor Bible. Garden City, NY: Doubleday & Company, 1975.

Furnish, Victor Paul. *II Corinthians: A New Translation with Introduction and Commentary*. The Anchor Bible. Garden City, NY: Doubleday & Company, Inc., 1984.

Gärtner, Bertil, *The Theology of the Gospel of Thomas*, translated from the Swedish by Eric J. Sharpe. London: Collins, 1961.

Gaster, Theodor. *The Dead Sea Scrolls in English Translation*. Garden City, NY: Doubleday Anchor Books, 1957.

Gero, Stephen. "The Infancy Gospel of Thomas: A Study of the Textual and Literary Problems," In *Novum Testamentum* 13 (1971) 46–80.

Goodacre, Mark. *The Case Against Q: Studies in Markan Priority and the Synoptic Problem.* Harrisburg, PA: Trinity Press International, 2002.

Grant, Robert M. "Notes on the Gospel of Thomas," In *Vigiliae Christianae* 13 (1959) 170–80.

Grant, Robert M. and David Noel Freedman. *The Secret Sayings of Jesus: The Gnostic Movement which Challenged Christianity and its "Gospel of Thomas" Recently Discovered in Egypt.* Garden City, NY: Doubleday, 1960.

Guillaumont, Antoine. "Les 'Logia' d'Oxyrhynchus sont-ils traduits du copte?," In *Le Muséon* 73 (1960) 325–33.

———. "Les sémitismes dans l'Évangile selon Thomas: Essai de classement," In *Studies in Gnosticism and Hellenistic Religions presented to Gilles Quispel on the Occasion of his 65th Birthday*, Études preliminairies aux religions orientales dans l'Empire romain 91, edited by R. van den Broek and M. J. Vermaseren, 190–204. Leiden: E. J. Brill.

———. "Sémitismes dans les logia de Jésus retrouvés à Nag-Hammadi," In *Journal Asiatique* 246 (1958) 113–23.

Haacker, Klaus. "Gallio," In *The Anchor Bible Dictionary*, volume 2 (D–G), 901–03. New York: Doubleday, 1992.

Haenchen, Ernst. *Der Weg Jesus.* Berlin: Alfred Töpelmann, 1966.

The HarperCollins Study Bible. New Revised Standard Version of the Bible: With the Apocryphal/Deuterocanonical Books, Wayne A. Meeks general editor. London and New York: HarperCollins Publishers, 1993.

Harrison, Percy. *Polycarp's Two Epistles to the Philippians.* Cambridge: Cambridge University Press, 1936.

Hartman, Louise F. and Alexander A. DiLella. *The Book of Daniel.* The Anchor Bible. Garden City, NY: Doubleday & Company, 1978.

Hennecke, Edgar, *New Testament Apocrypha: Writings Relating to the Apostles; Apocalypses and Related Subjects*, edited by Wilhelm Schneemelcher, English translation edited by R. McL. Wilson. Philadelphia: The Westminster Press, 1964.

Hutton, W. R. "The Kingdom of God Has Come," In *Expository Times* 64 (1952–53) 89–91.

Jeremias, Joachim. *The Parables of Jesus*, revised edition. New York: Scribner, 1963.

Jewett, Robert. *Romans.* Hermeneia. Minneapolis: Fortress, 2007.

Kähler, Martin. *The So-Called Historical Jesus and the Historic Biblical Christ*, English translation of *Der sogennante historische Jesus und der geschichtliche, biblische Christus.* Translated into English by Karl E. Braaten. Philadelphia: Fortress Texts in Modern Theology, 1988.

Kittel, Gerhard and Gerhard Friedrich, editors. *Theological Dictionary of the New Testament*, translated by Geoffrey W. Bromiley, abridged in one volume by Geoffrey W. Bromiley. Grand Rapids, MI: William B. Eerdmans, 1985.

Kloppenborg Verbin, John S. *Excavating Q: The History and Setting of the Sayings Gospel.* Minneapolis: Fortress, 2000.

Kloppenborg, John S. *The Formation of Q: Trajectories in Ancient Wisdom Collections.* Studies in Antiquity and Christianity. Harrisburg, PA: Trinity University Press, 1987.

———. "The Sayings Gospel Q: Literary and Stratigraphic Problems," In *Symbols and Strata: Essays on the Sayings Gospel Q*, edited by Risto Uro. Helsinki: 1–66. SES and Göttingen: Vandenhoeck und Ruprecht, 1996.

BIBLIOGRAPHY

Koester, Helmut. *Ancient Christian Gospels: Their History and Development*. London: SCM; Harrisburg, PA: Trinity International, 1990.

———. "GNOMAI DIAPHOROI: The Origin and Nature of Diversification in the History of Early Christianity," In *Harvard Theological Review* 58 (1965) 279–318.

———. *Introduction to the New Testament: History and Literature of Early Christianity*. Volume 2. Philadelphia: Fortress, 1982.

———. "The Text of the Synoptic Gospels in the Second Century," In *Gospel Tradition in the Second Century: Origins, Recensions, Text, and Transmission*, edited by William L. Petersen. Christianity and Judasim in Antiquity, 19–37. Notre Dame, IN: University of Notre Dame Press, 1989.

Krentz, Edgar. *The Historical-Critical Method*. Philadelphia: Fortress, 1975.

Kümmel, Werner Georg. *Promise and Fulfillment: The Eschatological Message of Jesus*. Studies in Biblical Theology 23. Naperville, IL: Allenson, 1957.

Liddell, Henry George and Robert Scott. *A Greek-English Lexicon*, A New Edition Revised and Augmented throughout by Henry Stuart Jones, with the Assistance of Roderick McKenzie. Oxford: Clarendon, 1948.

Lohse, Eduard, *Colossians and Philemon*, translated by William R. Poehlmann and Robert J. Karris, edited by Helmut Koester. Hermemeia. Philadelphia: Fortress, 1971.

Lührmann, Dieter, *Die Redaktion der Logienquelle*. WMANT 33. Neukirchen-Vluyn: Neukirchener Verlag, 1969.

Luz, Ulrich. *Matthew 8–20*, translated into English by James E. Crouch, edited by Helmut Koester. Hermeneia. Minneapolis: Fortress, 2001.

MacDonald, Dennis R. *The Homeric Hymns and the Gospel of Mark*. New Haven, CT: Yale University Press, 2000.

MacDonald, Lee Martin. "Canon of the New Testament," In *The New Interpreter's Dictionary of the Bible*, Volume 1 (A–C), 536–47. Nashville: Abingdon, 2006.

Marcus, Joel. *Mark 1–8: A New Translation with Introduction and Commentary*. The Anchor Bible. New York: Doubleday, 2000.

Marxsen, Willi. *Der Evangelist Markus. Studien zur Redaktionsgeschichte des Evangeliums*. Göttingen: Vandenhoeck & Ruprecht, 1959. Translated into English by James Boyce, Donald Juel, William Poehlmann, and Roy A. Harrisville as *Mark the Evangelist, Studies on the Redaction History of the Gospel*. New York and Nashville: Abingdon Press, 1969.

Mathisen, Ralph W. "Paleography and Codicology," In *The Oxford Handbook of Early Christian Studies*, edited by Susan Ashbrook Harvey and David D. Hunter, 140–65. Oxford: Oxford University Press, 2008.

Meier, John. *The Marginal Jew: Rethinking the Historical Jesus*. New York: Doubleday, 1991.

Metzger, Bruce. *A Textual Commentary of the New Testament: A Companion to the United Bible Societies' Greek New Testament*. London and New York: United Bible Societies, 1971.

Miller, Robert J., editor. *The Complete Gospels: Annotated Scholarly Version*, revised and expanded edition. Sonoma, CA: Polebridge, 1994.

Niederwimmer, Kurt. *The Didache*, translated by Linda M. Maloney, edited by Harold Attridge. Hermeneia. Minneapolis: Fortress, 1998.

Page, T.E. et al., *The Apostolic Fathers*, 2 volumes. The Loeb Classical Library. Cambridge, MA: Harvard University Press, 1948, 1952.

———, *Clement of Alexandria*, The Loeb Classical Library. Cambridge, MA: Harvard University Press, 1953.

———, *Eusebius: The Ecclesiastical History*, 2 volumes. The Loeb Classical Library. Cambridge, MA: Harvard University Press, 1953, 1957.

Perrin, Norman. *Rediscovering the Teaching of Jesus*. New York: Harper & Row, 1967.

Pervo, Richard I. *Acts*. Hermeneia. Minneapolis: Fortress, 2009.

———. "Acts in the Suburbs of the Apologists," In *Contemporary Studies in Acts*, edited by Thomas E. Phillips, 29–46. Macon, GA: Mercer University Press, 2009.

———. *Dating Acts Between the Evangelists and the Apologists*. Santa Rosa, CA: Polebridge, 2006

Petersen, William L. "Tatian's Diatessaron," In Helmut Koester's *Ancient Christian Gospels: Their History and Development*, 403–30. London: SCM Press; Harrisburg, Pennsylvania: Trinity Press International, 1990.

———. *Tatian's Diatessaron: Its Creation, Dissemination, Significance, and History in Scholarship*. Supplements to *Vigiliae Chriustianae* 25. Leiden E. J. Brill, 1994.

———. "What the Apostolic Fathers Tell Us about the Text of the New Testament in the Second Century," In *The New Testament and the Apostolic Fathers: The Reception of the New Testament in the Apostolic Fathers*, edited by Andrew F. Gregory and Christopher M. Tuckett, 29–46. Oxford: Oxford University Press, 2005.

Peuch, H.-Ch. "Une Collection de Paroles de Jésus Récemment Retrouvée: L'Évangile selon Thomas," In *Comptes rendus des séances – Academie des inscriptions & belles letters* (1957) 146–66.

Pfeiffer, Robert H. *Introduction to the Old Testament*. New York: Harper & Brothers, 1948.

Quispel, Gilles. "L'Évangile selon Thomas et le Diatessaron," In *Vigiliae Christianae* 13 (1959) 87–117.

———. "L'Évangile selon Thomas et les Clémentines," In *Vigiliae Christianae* 12 (1958) 181–96.

———. "The 'Gospel of Thomas' and the 'Gospel of the Hebrews,'" In *New Testament Studies* 12 (1966) 371–82.

———. "The Gospel of Thomas and the New Testament," In *Vigiliae Christianae* 11 (1957) 189–207.

———. "The Gospel of Thomas Revisited," In *Colloque International sur les Textes de Nag Hammadi. Québec, 22–25 août 1978*. La Bibliothèque Copte de Nag Hammadi, I, edited by B. Barc, 218–66. Quebec: Laval University Press, 1981.

———. "Some Remarks on the Gospel of Thomas," In *New Testament Studies* 5 (1958/1959) 276–90.

Rist, Martin. "Apocalypticism," In *The Interpreter's Dictionary of the Bible*, volume 1 (A–C), 157–61. New York: Abingdon Press, 1962.

Robinson, James M. "History of Q Research," In *The Critical Edition of Q: Synopsis including the Gospels of Matthew and Luke, Mark and Thomas with English, German, and French Translations of Q and Thomas*, edited by James M. Robinson, Paul Hoffmann, and John S. Kloppenborg, xix–lxxxi. Minneapolis: Fortress; and Leuven: Peeters, 2000.

———. *The Problem of History in Mark and Other Markan Studies*. Philadelphia: Fortress, 1982.

Robinson, James M. and Helmut Koester. *Trajectories Through Early Christianity*. Philadelphia: Fortress, 1971.

Schlosser, Jacques. *Le Règne de Dieu dans les Dits de Jesus*, 2 volumes. Études bibliques. Paris: Gabalda, 1980.

Schoedel, William. "Naassene Themes in the Coptic Gospel of Thomas," In *Vigiliae Christianae* 14 (1960) 225–34.

Schweitzer, Albert. *The Quest of the Historical Jesus*, translated by W. Montgomery, with a new introduction by James M. Robinson. New York: Macmillan Company, 1968.

Smyth, Kevin. "Gnosticism in 'The Gospel according to Thomas,'" In Heythrop Journal 1 (1960) 189–98.

Snyder, Graydon F. *Ante Pacem: Archaeological Evidence of Church Life Before Constantine.* Macon, GA: Mercer University Press, 1985.

Spinoza, Baruch. *Tractatus Theologico-Politicus* [*Theological Political Treatise*], translated by Samuel Shirley. Leiden: Brill Academic, 1997.

Steck, Odil Hannes. *Israel und das gewaltsame Geschick der Propheten: Untersuchungen zur Überlieferung des deuteronomistischen Geschichtsbildes im Alten Testament, Spätjudentum und Urchristentum.* WMANT 23. Neukirchen-Vluyn: Neukirchener Verlag, 1967.

Stendahl, Krister. *The School of Saint Matthew, and its Use of the Old Testament,* Uppsala: C. W. K. Gleerup, 1954: 2nd edition 1968.

Strack, H. and P. Billerbeck, *Kommentar zum Neuen Testament aus Talmud und Midrashim*, 6 volumes. Munich: Beck, 1922–61.

Streeter, Burnett Hillman, "The Priority of Mark," *The Four Gospels: A Study of Origins.* London: Macmillan and Co., 1924. Reprinted in Arthur J. Bellinzoni, editor. *The Two-Source Hypothesis: A Critical Appraisal*, 23–36. Macon, GA: Mercer University Press, 1985.

Sundberg, A. C. "Canon Muratori: A Fourth Century List," In *Harvard Theological Review* 66 (1973) 1–44.

Tarnas, Richard. *The Passion of the Western Mind: Understanding the Ideas That Have Shaped Our World View.* New York: Ballantine Books, 1991.

Taylor, Vincent. *The Formation of the Gospel Tradition.* London: Macmillan & Co. Ltd., 1933.

Tödt, Heinz Eduard. *Der Menschensohn in der synoptischen* Überlieferung. Gütersloh: Gütersloher Verlagshaus Mohn, 1959.

Weiss, Johannes. *Die Predigt Jesus vom Reiche Gottes.* Göttingen, 1892; second revised and enlarged edition 1900. English translation, *The Proclamation of the Kingdom of God.* Mifflintown, PA: Sigler, 1999.

Wilkins, Ulrich. *Weisheit und Torheit: Eine exegetisch-religionsgeschichtliche Untersuchung zu 1 Kor. 1 und 2.* Beiträge zur Historischen Theologie 26. Tübingen: Mohr-Siebeck, 1959.

———. "Über die Bedeutung historischer Kritik in der modernen Bibelexegese," In *Was heist Auslegung der Heiligen Schrift?* Regensburg: Friedrich Pustet, 1966; English translation by Edgar Krentz, *The Historical Method*. Philadelphia: Fortress, 1975.

Wrede, Wilhelm. *Das Messiasgeheimnis in den Evangelien: Zugleich ein Betrag zum Verständnis des Markusevangeliums.* Göttingen: Vandenhoeck & Ruprecht, 1901; translated into English by J. C. G. Grieg as *The Messianic Secret*. Cambridge: James Clark & Company, 1971.

SCRIPTURE INDEX

Biblical References are listed according
to their order in the Bible.

OLD TESTAMENT

Genesis

22:2	155, 155n12
22:12	155
22:16–17	155
22:18	110
26:4	110

Exodus

1:15–22	322
3:2	243
3:14	68
4:22	155n13
4:22–23	155
14:20	243
14:24	243
32:32–33	410n1

Leviticus

23:29	109

Deuteronomy

18	110
18:15	100, 100n7, 109
18:18	100, 100n7
18:18–19	109
21:22–23	157n16
34	4

1 Samuel

21:1–6	136
22:20	136

2 Samuel

5:2,	149, 154, 326, 369

1 Kings

17:8–16	143
17:17–24	143
17:17–24	143
18—19	407n14
18:38	243
19:11–12	243

2 Kings

4:1–7	143
4:18–37	143
4:42–44	143
9	407n14

Psalms

2:7	106, 111, 123, 155, 298
16	109
16:8–11	105, 108, 114, 249
16:10	100, 106
18:6	124

Psalms (continued)

22	98n5, 99, 126, 126n6
22:1	124
22:2	124ne
22:6	123nc
22:7	123
22:8	123, 124nd
22:16	124na
22:18	122
35:21	124nc
69:21	100, 100n8, 124
69:28	410n1
78:2	370n3
104:4	243
109:25	100, 100n9, 123, 124nc
110	98n5, 262
110:1	105, 109, 112, 114, 130, 249, 262, 263
118:22	105, 110
139:16	412n1

Proverbs

31:6	100, 100n10

Isaiah

4:3	410n1
4:3–5	118
5:24	243
6:9–10	370n3
7	58
7:14	58, 59 60, 65, 66, 148, 326, 338, 361
9:1–2	370n3
11:2	350n11
24—27	397
26:1	140
29:18	140
35:5–6	139
40:3	370n3
42:1	111, 155
42:1–4	370n3
42:6–7	140
42:18	140
52:13—53:12	99, 114, 249
53	98n5, 99, 121, 262, 345
53:4	370n3
53:4–6	120
53:7	345, 345n8
53:9–12	120
53:12	123, 124nb
55:3	106, 111, 112
58:6	76, 172
61:1	140, 170
61:1–2	76
61:2	170
62:11,	370n3

Jeremiah

1:5	338
31:15	151, 369

Lamentations

1:12	100, 100n11
1:18	100, 100n11
2:15	100, 100n12

Daniel

7:13	137, 263
9:27	319
12:1	410n1

Hosea

6	121
6:2	99, 121, 130, 238, 246
11:1	150, 369

Joel

2:28–32	105, 107
2:29	108

Amos

8:9	124

Micah

5:2	149–50, 154, 326, 369

SCRIPTURE INDEX

Habakkuk

1:5	106, 112

Zechariah

1—8	397
9:8	370n3
9—14	397
11:13	372n3

Malachi

3:1	118
4:5	125

OLD TESTAMENT APOCRYPHA

Wisdom of Solomon

2:17–18	100, 100n13, 123

OLD TESTAMENT PSEUDEPIGRAPHA

1 Enoch

14:8–25	243
71:5	243
108:3	410n1

NEW TESTAMENT

Matthew

1:1–17	89, 325, 360, 370	3:1–17	147, 215
1:16	153n11	3:2	164
1:18	153	3:3	323, 370n3
1:18–19	153	3:6	320
1:18–21	153	3:7–10	83
1:18–25	147–48, 152, 334	3:11–12	83
1:21	148	3:13–15	200, 320
1:22	152	3:14	155
1:22–23	323, 369	3:17	111
1:23	58, 60n7, 65, 48	4:1–11	147
2:1–12	149–50, 152	4:2b–11a	83
2:2	150	4:14–16	323, 370n3
2:5	152	4:16	323
2:5–6	149–50, 154, 323, 369	4:17	163
2:13–15	150, 152, 322, 325	4:18–20	387
2:13–21	89	5—7	85, 153, 216, 318, 322, 369
2:15	150, 152, 323, 369		
2:16–18	151, 322, 325	5:1—7:27	323
2:17	151, 152	5:2–4	83
2:17–18	323, 369	5:3	163, 172
2:19–23	151–54, 325	5:6	83
2:23	152, 352, 370	5:10	163

445

Matthew (continued)

Reference	Pages
5:11–12	83
5:13	83, 145
5:14	229, 231
5:15	83, 228
5:16	163
5:17	323, 365:
5:17–20	369
5:18	83
5:19	163
5:20	163
5:21–24	89
5:21–47	323
5:25–26	83
5:32	83
5:33–37	89
5:39–40	83
5:42	83
5:44	83
5:45	163
5:47	83
5:48	83, 163, 323
6:1	163
6:1–4	89
6:5–6	89
6:9	163
6:9–13	83
6:16–18	89
6:19–21	83, 86
6:22–23	83, 86
6:24	83, 86, 225
6:25–33	83
6:25–34	84–87
6:33	163n4
6:34	86
7:1–2	83
7:1–5	86
7:3–5	83
7:6	86, 89, 228, 229
7:7	228, 229
7:7–11	83
7:8	228
7:11	163
7:12	83
7:13–14	83
7:16	83, 228
7:17–18	228
7:18	83
7:21	84, 163
7:22–23	83
7:24–27	84
7:28	84
8:1–4	140
8:11	163
8:14–15	70–72, 143
8:16–17	72
8:17	370n3
8:25	148n10
9:1–8	143
9:8	212
9:10–13	320
9:14–17	137
9:18–26	143
9:32–34	320
10:5–42	323
10:7	163
10:10	414, 414n5
10:17–25	88
10:25	185n9
10:26–33	88
10:27	185n9
10:32	163
10:32–33	185n9, 190–91, 193, 198
10:33	164
10:34–36	88
10:39	185n9, 192, 194, 199
11:1	89
11:2–5	139–40
11:5	172
11:11	163
11:12	163
11:28–30	89
12:1–2	321
12:1–8	135, 142
12:9–14	142
12:17–21	370n3
12:28	163n5
12:31–32	88, 228
12:32	218, 218n26
12:33	228
12:34	228
12:35	228
12:46–50	137
12:50	164
13:1–9	145
13:1–52	323
13:11	163
13:14–15	370n3
13:16	167
13:23	167
13:24	163
13:24–30	89, 225, 318
13:31	163
13:31–32	144
13:33	163
13:35	370n3
13:36–43	89, 318

SCRIPTURE INDEX

13:44	163, 225, 318	18:18	163
13:44–46	89	18:19	163
13:45	163	18:19–20	89
13:45–46	318	18:23	163
13:47	163	18:23–35	89, 318
13:47–50	89, 225, 318	19:12	163
13:51	167	19:13	162
13:51–52	89	19:13–15	137
13:51–53	75	19:14	163
13:52	163	19:16	195n12
13:53–58	137	19:16–22	137
13:54–58	72–77, 229	19:23	163
13:55	34, 152n11, 227, 241n5	19:24	163n5
14:1–12	76	19:28	196, 199
14:13–21	143, 333	20:1	163
14:22–33	143, 333	20:1–16	145
14:33	167	20:17–19	119
14:34–36	143	20:18	212
15:1–20	81	20:20–23	137
15:14	225, 226	20:28	99n6, 212
15:21–28	80–82	20:29–34	143
15:22–25	81	21:4–5	370n3
15:28	82	21:28–32	89, 318
15:29–31	81, 142	31:31	163n5
15:32–39	142	21:33–39	228
16	166, 321	21:33–46	145
16:5–6	88	21:41	319
16:12	167	21:42	228
16:13–16	322	21:43	163n5
16:13–20	161–62, 321–22	22:1–10	225
16:16	162	22:2	163
16:16–18	227	22:7	319
16:17	163	22:15–22	134
16:17–19	162, 174, 322, 387	22:23–33	137
16:18	162, 163, 321, 420	22:34–40	196n13
16:19	164	23	321
16:20	322	23:3	321
16:21	211	23:5	321
16:21–23	119	23:9	163
16:24–28	185n9	23:13	163
17:1–8	156	23:13–15	369
17:1–9	147	23:23	321
17:12b	213	23:25	321
17:22–23	119	23:27	321
17:22b–23a	212	23:33–34	321
17:24	81	23:34	321
17:24–27	89	23:34–36	204, 205
18:1	163	23:37–39	204, 205
18:1–35	323	24:3—25:46	323
18:3	163	24:15–16	319
18:4	163	24:23–24	147
18:10	163	24:36	36
18:14	163	24:37–44	145
18:17	163, 321	24:42	147

Matthew (continued)

25:1	163
25:1–13	145
25:13	147
25:14–30	145
25:46	195n12
26:6–13	137
26:14–16	119
26:24	212
26:26–30	54, 245
26:54	370n3
26:56	370n3
26:69–75	119, 387
27:3–10	89
27:46	99, 374
26:56	119
27:57	119
27:57–61	119
27:62–63	321
27:62–66	89
28	156, 241, 318
28:1–10	326
28:2–5	327
28:7	242
28:9	164
28:9–10	322n13
28:9–20	147, 243
28:10	242
28:11–15	89, 326
28:16–20	89, 242, 323, 329

Mark

1—9	143
1:1	32, 171, 315n10
1:2–3	314
1:2–6	171
1:2–11	147
1:2—9:50	328–29
1:4	200
1:4–5	154
1:7	134n6
1:7–8	171
1:9	134n6, 315n9
1:9–11	154–56, 171
1:11	35, 111, 155, 200, 315n10, 324
1:12	134n6, 315n9
1:12–13	147, 173
1:14	155
1:14–15	200
1:14—5:43	170
1:15	195, 198, 215
1:16	134n6, 315n9
1:16–20	80, 169
1:21	134n6, 315n9
1:21–28	79–80
1:22	135, 166
1:23	134n6, 315n9
1:23–28	72, 142
1:27	135, 166
1:29	134n6, 315n9
1:29–31	70–72, 79, 143
1:32–34	72
1:34	164
1:34b	316
1:35	135n6, 315n9
1:39	135n6, 315n9
1:40	315n9
1:40–45	140
1:43–44	164, 316
2:1	135n6, 315n9
2:1–12	143
2:12	135, 166
2:13	135n6, 315n9
2:13–14	170
2:15	315n9
2:15–17	138
2:18	315n9
2:18–22	138
2:23	315n9
2:23–28	135–38, 142, 200
2:27	136, 137
2:27–28	136, 212
2:28	137
3:1	315n9
3:1–6	141, 200
3:7	315n9
3:11	35, 315n10
3:11–12	164
3:12	316
3:13	315n9
3:13–19	170, 201
3:16–17	311, 387
3:20	315n9
3:21	101
3:22	315n9
3:22–30	314
3:23	315n9
3:28–30	88
3:31	315n9
3:31–35	137
4	145
4:1–9	145
4:2–9	225
4:3–32	314

SCRIPTURE INDEX

Reference	Pages	Reference	Pages
4:13	167	8:1–10	77, 143, 144
4:20	167	8:11–13	77
4:21–25	145–46	8:14–15	88
4:24–25	199	8:14–21	77
4:26–29	144–45	8:15	76–77
4:30–32	145, 225	8:21	167
4:35–42	333	8:22–26	77, 143
4:35—5:43	314	8:26	317
4:35—6:52	333	8:27	162
5:1–20	333	8:27–30	160–66, 316, 322
5:7	35	8:29	162, 166
5:9	212, 312	8:30	162, 163, 165
5:20	135, 166	8:31	121, 165, 211
5:21–24a	143	8:31–33	119
5:21–43	75, 143	8:34	186–87, 188
5:22–24	333	8:34–36	199
5:25–34	333	8:34—9:1	146, 185–90, 185n9. 192
5:35–43	143, 333	8:35	185n9, 187, 188, 192, 194–95
5:37	387	8:36	188
5:41	311	8:36–37	187–88
5:42	135, 166	8:38	185n9, 188, 193
5:43	164, 317	8:38—9:1	198, 201
6:1–2a	170	9:1	189
6:1–6	137, 172	9:2–8	156, 156n14
6:1–6a	72–76, 137, 167–73	9:2–10	147
6:2	135, 166	9:2–13	387
6:2b	170	9:7	35
6:3	35–37, 74n3, 75, 170, 200, 227, 241n5	9:9	164, 166, 317
6:3d	170	9:12	212
6:4	170	9:30–31	164
6:4–6a	225	9:30–32	119, 166
6:5	75, 170, 171, 175	9:31	212
6:6b–13	75	9:42–50	314
6:14–29	76	9:49–50	145
6:17–18	171	10:11–12	313
6:30–44	143, 333	10:13–16	137, 138
6:32–44	333	10:13—16:8	329
6:45–52	77, 143, 333	10:17	195n12
6:45–54	333	10:17–21	200
6:45—8:26	77	10:17–22	137, 138
6:52	167	10:21	172
6:53–56	77, 143	10:30	195n12
7:1–23	77, 81	10:31	145
7:2–4	311–12	10:32–34	119, 166
7:11	312	10:33	212
7:17–19	313, 313n7	10:35–40	137, 138
7:18–19	201	10:45	99n6, 213
7:24–30	77, 80–82	10:46–52	143
7:31	312	11:1–11	127
7:31–37	77, 81, 143	11:15–19	201
7:34	312	11:18	135, 166
7:36	164, 317	12:1–9	225
7:37	135, 166	12:1–12	135, 145

Mark (continued)

12:6	35
12:13	135
12:13–17	134, 314
12:17	135, 166
12:18–27	137
12:28–34	196n13
12:42	313, 314
12:43	172
13	314
13:3–8	387
13:5–23	314
13:14	319
13:21–23	147
13:26–27	195–96, 198
13:30	196, 198
13:32	36
13:32–37	196, 198–99
13:33–37	145, 147
13:34	145
13:35	145
14—16	121, 333
14:1—15:39	314
14:3–9	137
14:10–11	119
14:21	212
14:22–26	245
14:33–41	387
14:36	312
14:61	35
14:62	196, 199
14:66–72	119, 387
15	127, 128
15:21	125
15:21–22	124
15:21–37	122–126, 128
15:22	312
15:24	324
15:25	125, 126
15:25–26	124
15:26	125
15:28	124nb
15:29	314
15:33	126
15:34	99, 125, 126, 312, 314, 374
15:35	124
15:36	125
15:37b	125
15:39	35
15:40	119
15:42	312
15:42–47	119
16	242
16:1–8	327
16:5	327
16:7	242
16:8	244n9
16:9–20	244

Luke

1—2	318, 325
1:1	323n44
1:1–3	267
1:1–4	28n4. 91, 171, 327, 328
1:3	266n34
1:5–25	89
1:5–26	325
1:26–38	325
1:5—2:52	171, 328
1:15	172
1:26–38	89, 153, 325
1:35	172
1:39–56	89, 325
1:41	172
1:57–80	80, 89, 325
1:67	172
2:1–7	325
2:1–40	147
2:4	154
2:5	153
2:7	34
2:8–20	325
2:21–38	89
2:21–40	325
2:25–35	172
2:32	173
2:33	153
2:35	154
2:41–42	325
2:41–51	147
2:41–52	89
3:1–6	171
3:1–22	147, 170, 215
3:1—9:50	328
3:2	172
3:4–6	118
3:7–9	83
3:7–14	171
3:10–14	89
3:15–18	171
3:16	172
3:16b-17	83
3:19–20	171
3:21	161

SCRIPTURE INDEX

3:21–22	171	6:34	225
3:22	111	6:36	83
3:23	153n11	6:37–38	83
3:23–28	325	6:38	145
3:23–38	89, 172, 360	6:39	225
4:1–13	147, 172	6:41–42	83
4:1–15	75	6:43–44	83
4:2b-13	83	6:43–44a	228
4:14–15	170, 170n10, 172	6:44b	228
4:16	171	6:45	228
4:16ab	76, 77	6:45ab	228
4:16c-21	76, 77	6:46	83
4:16–24	75–76	6:47–49	84
4:16–30	79, 137. 168–72	7:1a	84
4:17–21	171	7:11–17	90,, 143, 324
4:18	172	7:18–22	139–140
4:21	171	7:22	172
4:22	35, 76, 171, 241n5	7:27	118
4:22a	170	7:33–34	212
4:22b	170	7:36–50	137, 324
4:23	76, 171, 173, 173n11	8:1–3	90
4:23–24	229	8:2–3	119n4, 241n4
4:24	76, 171, 173n11	8:4–8	145
4:25–30	75, 171, 173n11	8:16	228
4:28–30	170	8:16–18	145
4:31–37	78–79, 143	8:19–21	137
4:31–42	170	8:40–56	143
4:31—5:39	173	9:10–17	143
4:33–37	72	9:18–21	160–67
4:38–39	70–72, 79, 143	9:21–22	119
4:40–41	72	9:22	211
5:1–11	90, 170	9:23–27	146, 185n9
5:12–16	140	9:24	185n9
5:17–26	143	9:26	185n9
5:24	212	9:28–36	147, 156
5:29–32	137	9:43b-45	119
5:33–39	137	9:44b	212
6:1–5	135, 142	9:51—18:14	329
6:5	212	9:52–56	90
6:6–11	142	10:7	414, 414n5
6:12	161	10:25	195n12
6:14–16	241n3	10:25–28	196n13
6:17–49	216	10:29–37	90, 324
6:20	172	10:38–42	90
6:20b	209n16	11:2–4	83
6:20–21	83	11:5–8	90
6:22	225	11:9b	228
6:22–23	83	11:9–13	83
6:24–26	90	11:10bc	228
6:27–28	83	11:14–50	324
6:29	83	11:27–28	90
6:30	83	11:33	83, 146, 228
6:31	83	11:34	83
6:33–34	83	11:49–51	204

451

Luke (continued)

12:1	76–77	18:1–8	90, 324
1:2	146	18:9–14	90, 324
1:2–9	87–88	18:15–17	137
12:8–9	185n9, 190–92, 193	18:15—24:12	329
12:10	88, 228	18:18	195n12
12:13–15	86, 90	18:18–23	137
12:16–21	86, 90, 225	18:22	172
12:22	86	18:28–30	196, 199
12:22–32	84–87	18:31–33	212
12:22b-31	83	18:31–34	119
12:33–34	83, 86	18:35–43	143
12:35–38	90, 145	19:1–10	90
12:38	147	19:8	172
12:39–40	225	19:11–27	145
12:40	147	19:12–13	147
12:58–59	83	19:26	146
13:1–5	325	19:41–44	90, 267, 327–28
13:1–9	90	20:9–15	228
13:6–9	324	20:9–19	145
13:10–17	90, 324	20:17	228
13:18–19	144	20:20–26	134
13:24	83	20:27–40	137
13:26–27	83	21:3	172
13:30	145	21:20–24	267, 328
13:31–33	90	21:24	173
13:32	86	21:34–36	90
13:34–3	204	21:36	147
14:1–6	90, 324	21:37–38	90
14:7–14	90	21:38	417n11
14:13	172	22:3–6	119
14:15	219	22:14–23	54, 245
14:16–24	225	22:16	219
14:21	172	22:22	212
14:28–32	90	22:25	173
14:34–35	83, 145	22:29–30	219
15:8–10	90, 324	22:37	124nb
15:11–32	90, 324	22:56–62	119
15:18	163n5	23:6–12	90
16:1–3	90	23:13–16	90
16:1–9	324	23:49	119, 119n4
16:13	83, 225	23:50–56	119
16:17	83	24	118, 156, 242, 318, 325
16:18	83	24:1–12	326
16:19–31	90, 324	24:1–53	242
16:20	172	24:4	327
16:22	172	24:10	119n4
17:7–10	90	24:10–43	147
17:11–19	90, 324	24:12	322
17:20–21	90	24:12–53	244
17:23	147	24:13–35	90, 118
17:26–36	145	24:13–49	327
17:33	185n9, 192, 194, 199	24:13–53	339
		24:26	118
		24:27	118

SCRIPTURE INDEX

24:32	118
24:34	101
24:36–43	90
24:36–49	119, 120, 327
24:44	414n6
24:44–47	120
24:44–49	90
24:50–53	327, 329, 360

John

1:1b	330
1:1c	330
1:1–4	329
1—15	335
1:2	330
1:3	330
1:4a	330
1:4b	330
1:5	330
1:10a	330
1:10b	330
1:10–14	329
1:12	330
1:14	154, 330, 383
1:14b	331
1:16	329
1:45	153n11, 383
2:1–10	333
2:1–11	333
2:11	333
3:1–21	332
3:15	195n12
4	334
4—7	334
4:26	67
4:36	195n12
4:43–53	333
4:46–53	333, 334
4:54	333, 334
5	334
5:1	334
5:2–9	334
5:39	195n12
6	334
6:1	334
6:1–15	333
6:5–14	334
6:16–21	333
6:16–25	334
6:35	67, 201, 331
6:41	67, 331
6:42	153n11, 383
6:48	67
6:48–58	54
6:51	67, 331
6:54	195n12
6:68	195n12
7	334
7:1	334
7:5	101
7:13	332
7:28	68
7:29	68
7:36	417n11
7:53—8:11	360, 417
8:12	68, 201, 331
8:23	68, 201
8:24	68
8:28	68, 331
8:58	68, 331
9:1–7	334
9:5	68, 201, 331
9:22	332
10:7	68, 331
10:9	68, 201, 331
10:11	68, 201
10:14	68, 201, 331
10:28	195n12
10:36	68
11:1–45	334
11:25	68, 201, 331
12:16	397, 397n8
12:25	185n9, 195n12, 199, 331
12:42	332, 383
13:1–5	54
13:2	119
13:23	420
14:6	201, 331
14:10	68
14:11	68
14:20	68
14:25–26	384, 384n8
14:3–31	334
14:31	334
15—17	334
15:1	68, 331
15:5	68, 331
16:2	332, 383
16:12–13	384, 384n8
17:2	195n12
17:3	195n12
18—20	333
18:1	334
18:5	68
18:6	68
18:8	68

John (continued)

18:25–27	119
18:31–33	334
18:37–38	334
19:25–26	119
19:38	119
19:38a	332
19:38–42	119
20:1–29	242n7
20:11—21:23	244
20:12	327
20:14–18	322n13
20:19	242n7, 332
20:22	247n7
20:30	334
20:30–31	332
20:31	182, 334, 383
21	334, 417
21:1–25	247n6
21:18–19	387
21:25	417n11, 420

Acts of the Apostles

1:1	266
1:1–2	266
1:1–4	242
1:1–5	241
1:1–11	119
1:2	172
1:5	172
1:6–11	241
1:8a	241
1:8b	241
1:11	241
1:12–14	241
1:13	101
1:14	241
1:15–26	241
1:16	241
1:20	241
2	244, 248
2:1	101, 108
2:1–4	270
2:1–13	241, 242
2:2–3	243
2:4	108
2:14–36	242, 243n8, 244
2:14–39	105, 107–8
2:16–21	107–8
2:17	108
2:17–21	108
2:18	108
2:21	108
2:22	109
2:22b	115
2:23a	109
2:23b	109
2:24	268n37
2:24a	109
2:25–28	108–9
2:25b–28	108, 109
2:26	109
2:27	100, 109, 112
2:32	109
2:32–36	116, 338
2:34–35	109
2:36	109, 111, 297
2:38	244, 245, 270
2:38–46	251
2:39	244
2:41	244
2:41–42	242, 244
2:44	249
2:45	173
2:46	245, 265
3:1	245
3:11	245, 264
3:13	110
3:13–26	105, 109
3:22–23	109
3:22b–23	109
3:24	110
3:25	110
3:25b	110
3:26b	110
4:1–22	246
4:8–22	110
4:10–12	105
4:11b	110
4:32–37	244
4:35	173, 250n12
4:36	258
4:37	258
5:1–10	244
5:1–11	218, 258
5:12	264
5:17–42	246
5:29–32	110
5:30–32	105–6
5:31	116
6:1	246, 283
6:3	246, 284
7:51	218
7:54–60	284
7:54—8:1	246

7:58	272n3	11:18	173
7:58b	272	11:19	251
8:1	247, 272n3	11:19–21	284
8:1b	247, 284	11:20–22	259
8:3	272n3	11:22	252
8:4–6	247	11:25	252, 272n3
8:4–13	251	11:25–26	259
8:12	247	11:26	252, 253, 352
8:14–17	247	11:27–30	259
8:14–24	218, 251	11:29	289
8:14–25	174	11:30	272n3
8:25	247, 251	12:12	259, 314
8:26	251	12:17	101
8:26–39	247	12:25	259, 272n3, 314
8:40	247, 252	13:1	272n3
9	247, 276, 280	13:1–3	54
9:1	247, 272n3	13:1–4	259
9:1–2	252, 264	13:2	252, 272n3
9:1–19	270	13:4	252
9:1–19a	240, 258, 274–76	13:4—14:28	252
9:1–2	252, 264	13:5	253, 259, 265
9:2	247, 368	13:6	253
9:3–25	252	13:7	272n3
9:4	272n	13:7–12	253
9:4–7	276	13:9	272n3, 273
9:7	276	13:13	253, 259
9:8	272n3	13:14	253
9:11	272, 272n3	13:14–16	253
9:15	173, 276	13:14–43	265
9:17	272n3, 276	13:16–41	111
9:19b-20	264	13:17–41	106
9:19b-25	247	13:24	115
9:22	272n3	13:27	112
9:22–29	97	13:29	112
9:24	272n3	13:32–33	111
9:26–27	252	13:33b	111
9:26–30	247, 247n14, 258, 281, 282	13:34	111
		13:35	112
9:27	276	13:35b	112
9:32	252	13:36–41	259
9:38–43	252	13:39	112
10:1–33	252	13:40–41	112
10:34–43	110–11	13:41	112
10:36–43	106	13:42	253
10:37	115	13:42–43	253
10:38	115	13:43	259
10:38a	115	13:44	253
10:41	115	13:44–47	112
10:42	115	13:46–48	173
10:43	110	13:48	259
10:45	173	13:48–49	253
11:1	173	13:50–52	253
11:1–18	174	14:1	253, 259
11:2–18	163	14:1–4	52

Acts of the Apostles (continued)

14:1–7	265
14:2–5	253
14:4	286
14:6	253n10
14:6–20	260
14:8–18	253
14:12	253
14:14	296n14
14:19	253
14:20–21	253
14:21	253
14:23	253
14:24	253
14:25	253
14:26	253
14:27	253, 253n19, 259
15	270
15:1–10	259
15:1–21	282
15:1–29	286
15:1–35	254
15:4	253n19
15:14	173
15:22	260
15:22–29	260
15:22–35	259
15:23–29	260, 269
15:32	260
15:33	260
15:36–41	254
15:36—18:22	254, 259
15:37–41	254
15:40—18:22	260
16:1	254
16:1–2	260
16:1–3	260
16:1–5	254
16:3	260
16:6	254, 282
14:6–20	260
16:7	254
16:8	254
16:10	266n35
16:10–17	266
16:11	254
16:11—17:15	282
16:11–40	290
16:12–40	254
16:19–24	260
17:1	253, 255
17:1–5	260
17:1–6	291
17:1–9	255, 265
17:10	253
17:10–12	265
17:10–15	255, 257, 291
17:14	260
17:14–15	260
17:16–17	265
17:16–21	255
17:17	253
18:1	282
18:1–4	255
18:1–8	265
18:2	282
18:2–3	261
18:4	253
18:5	257, 260
18:5–11	253
18:6	173
18:7	253
18:8	253
18:12	261
18:12–17	255, 282
18:17	292n16
18:18–19	255
18:18–22	255
18:18–23	282
18:19	253
18:19–20	265
18:22	255
18:23	255
18:23—21:17	255
18:24–26	265
18:25	247n13, 368
18:26	253, 261
18:27	269
19:1	255, 282
19:1–41	255
19:8	253
19:8–10	265, 282
19:9	247n13, 368
19:22	261, 262, 282
19:23	247n13, 368
19:28–41	256
19:29	256, 262
20:1	256, 283
20:1–38	283
20:2–3	256
20:3	256
20:4	256, 262
20:4–5	261
20:5–16	266
20:6	256
20:7–8	265
20:13	256

SCRIPTURE INDEX

20:14	256	27:8	257
20:15	256	27:13–38	257
20:31	255	27:39–44	257
20:35	244	28:1	257
21—22	258	28:11–12	257
21:1	256	28:13	257
21:1–18	266	28:13–14	257
21:2	256	28:14–16	257
21:3	256	28:17	258
21:7	256	28:17–31	257
21:8	256	28:23–28	112
21:15–26	283	28:28	173
21:17	256	28:30	283
21:18	101		
21:39	272		
22	277, 280, 301		
22:2b-18a	274–76		

Romans

1:1	286n10, 297
1:1–4	102, 116, 163, 299
1:3–4	298n25
1:4	111, 298, 316, 338
1:16–17	296
2:16	102, 299
3:23–26	299
4:25	299
5:12–14	300
5:14	156
8:3	299
8:15–1	298
8:22–23	298
8:34	102, 299, 300
10:8–9	102, 299
11:1	300
11:13	286n10
12:5	55
12:6–8	399
15:25–29	289
15:26	352
15:33	296
16	261n30, 296
16:1–2	381
16:1–15	245
16:2	262
16:3	261, 381
16:3–5a	261, 265
16:6	381
16:7	51–52, 52n4, 65, 381
16:12	381
16:20–27	370
16:21	261
16:23	261, 262

22:3	272
22:3–21	240, 258
22:4	247n13, 368
22:6–16	270
22:7	272n7
22:7–8	277
22:9	277
22:13	256, 272n7
22:14–15	277
22:15	277
22:21	274–76, 277
22:17–21	277
22:25–26	272
23:12–15	256
24:5	256, 352
24:14	247n13, 368
24:17—28:31	289
24:22	247n13, 368
24:27	283
25:10–12	256
25:12	256
25:13–14	283
25:13–27	283
25:23	277
26	277, 280, 301
26:1b	274–76
26:9–18	240, 258, 274–76
26:11	264
26:12–18	270
26:14	272n7
26:16–18a	277
26:21	277
27:1—28:16	256, 266, 283
27:2	257, 262
27:3	257
27:5–6	257
27:7	257

SCRIPTURE INDEX

1 Corinthians

1:1	286n10	11:23–25	181
1:3b-4b	98	11:23–26	243
1:7–8	300	11:25	55
1:10–17	292, 415n7	11:26	55, 300
1:11	53, 245, 381	11:33	56
1:12	25, 261, 292, 292n18	11:34	292
1:14	262	12:1–31	53
1:17	48	12:8–11	399
1:23	158	12:13	55
2:1–5	292	12:27	55
2:2	182	12:28–30	399
2:6	300	13:1–2	399
3:1—4:5	292	13:1–13	292
3:4–6	25	14:1–40	53
3:6	420	14:29–32	399
3:10–23	261	15	98, 101, 107, 164, 244, 250, 395
3:22	25	15:1	107
4:5	300	15:1–3a	97
4:6	25	15:1–5	114
4:8	292	15:1–7	262
4:17	260, 292	15:1–8	96–97, 102
5:1	53	15:3	97, 107, 110, 113, 126, 163, 239, 245
5:1–13	292	15:3b	97, 98, 98n5, 100, 107
5:9	53, 282, 291	15:3–4	100, 246
6:12	261	15:3b-4b	98, 99
7:1	53, 292	15:3–5	104, 126
7:1–40	53	15:3b–5	107
7:10–11	182	15:3–7	299
7:29	300	15:3–8	238, 244
8:1–3	292, 392n20	15:4	107, 110, 241
8:1–13	53	15:4a	97, 98, 101
8:5–6	297	15:4b	97, 98, 99, 101
8:1–13	53	15:5	97, 101, 101n15, 181, 240, 246, 322
9:1	286n10	15:5b	98n5, 101n15
9:1–27	292	15:5–7	51, 98
9:2	286n10	15:5–9	52
9:5	34, 52, 181	15:6	97
9:6	52, 259	15:7	34, 52, 350
9:14	182	15:7a	97
10:1–6	156	15:7b	97
10:11	156	15:8	97, 102
10:14–32	53	15:8–9	52, 300
10:16–17	55	15:9	273, 286n10
11	54	15:12–57	53
11:6	420	15:21–22	300
11:18	53	15:23–24	300
11:18–19	292	15:25	300
11:18–34	53–54, 56	15:50–57	300
11:20	54	15:51–52	300
11:21	54	16:1–4	89
11:21–22	55	16:4	292
11:23	182		

SCRIPTURE INDEX

16:5–9	292
16:8	53
16:10–11	292
16:19	245, 261, 265, 381
16:21	269n40, 378
16:22	296, 371
16:24	56

2 Corinthians

1:1	286n10
1:1—2:13	283, 293
1:19	259n26, 260, 292
2:4	283
2:14—6:13	283, 293, 295
5:14	299
5:16	118n3, 182n5
5:19	299
5:21	299
6:14—7:1	53, 292
7:2–4	283, 293, 295
7:5–16	283, 293
8	283, 289, 293
8:9	299
8:18	420
8:23	52
9	283, 289, 293
10—13	293
10:1—13:13	283
11:32–33	282
12:1–10	278
12:2	278
12:4	278
12:6b-7a	278
12:7	279
12:12	286n10

Galatians

1:1	286n10, 294
1:2	293
1:3–4	102, 299
1:6–7	294
1:10	297
1:11	48
1:11–12	50, 279
1:12	285, 285n9
1:13	273
1:14	272
1:14—2:14	300
1:15–16	50, 240, 270, 277, 279, 282
1:15–17	258
1:15–18	258
1:15–20	97
1:15—2:1	279–80
1:16	280, 285n9
1:17	247n14, 280, 282
1:18	174, 239, 247n14, 281
1:18–19	282
1:19	34, 52, 101, 181, 280
1:21	281, 282
1:22	272
1:23	273
2	288, 301
2:1	281
2:1–10	174, 184–85, 282, 293, 293, 296
2:1–14	293
2:2	279, 285
2:3	285
2:4	286, 289
2:5	294
2:6	281
2:7–9	281, 286
2:8	286n10, 366
2:9	101, 163, 286, 418
2:9–10	281
2:10	287, 352
2:11	163
2:11–14	282, 284, 287–89, 293, 313, 313n7, 322, 365
2:12	101, 289, 293
2:12–13	259
2:14	258, 294
2:16	287n11
3:1	102, 294, 299
3:1–3	294
3:26	298
3:28	381
4:4	181, 299
4:4–7	298
4:6	102, 299
4:8–9	293
4:10	293
4:13	282
4:13–14	293
4:17	293
4:21	294
5:2–12	293
5:12	293
5:14	294
6:11	269n40, 378
6:12–13	293

Ephesians

1:1	286n10, 377
1:22–23	55
2:11	377
3:1	377
3:1—5:20	377
4:4	55
4:11	52
4:12	55
4:16	55
4:17	377

Philippians

1:1	261
1:1—3:1a	295
1:6	300
1:7	294
1:10	300
1:13–14	294
1:17	294
2:6–11	103, 299
2:9	103
2:9–11	300
2:16	300
3:1b—4:3	295
3:2	295
3:5–6	272, 300
3:6	273
3:20	297, 300
4:2–3	245, 381
4:4–7	295
4:5	297
4:8–9	295
4:10	295
4:10–20	295
4:20–23	370
4:21–33	295

Colossians

1:1	286n10
1:5	61, 62
1:7	62
1:7–8	377
1:9	63
1:10	61
1:11	62, 63
1;12	62
1:14	63
1:15–16	378
1:15–20	378
1:16	61, 62, 63
1:17	62
1:18	55, 61, 378
1:19	63
1:20	61, 64
1:21	63, 64
1:22	63, 64
1:23	61, 63
1:24	61
2:3	62
2:4	61, 62, 378
2:5	61
2:7	64
2:8	61, 63, 378
2:9	61, 63
2:9–11	378
2:11	61
2:12	64
2:12–13	377
2:13	64
2:13–17	377, 378
2:14	61, 62, 63
2:15	61, 62, 300
2:16	61, 62
2:17	62
2:18	61, 62
2:18–19	378
2:19	55, 62, 63, 64
2:20	62
2:21	62, 378
2:22	62
2:23	62, 378
3:1	62, 377
3:3	62
3:8	62, 63
3:9	61
3:11	62
3:13	62
3:14	62, 63
3:15	55, 62
3:16	62, 63, 64
3:19	62
3:21	62
3:22	64
3:24	62
4:6	62
4:7	62
4:9–14	295n21
4:10	62, 259
4:10–11	262
4:11	62
4:13	62
4:14	62, 240

4:15	245, 265
4:16	414
4:17	295n21
4:18	269, 378

1 Thessalonians

1:1	259n26, 260, 261
1:1–3	258, 260n28, 379
1:2	379
1:5	48
1:6	291
1:7	291
1:9	290
1:9–10	298
1:10	103, 291, 298
2:2	290, 294
2:7	286n10
2:13	379
2:14	291
2:14–15	291
2:19	291
3:1–2	291
3:1–8	260
3:2	260
3:6–7	291
3:13	291, 297
4:1–12	291
4:1—5:11	264
4:13—5:11	379
4:15	291
4:15–17	117, 300
5:1–2	291
5:2	415n10
5:4–5	379
5:12–22	291
5:23	291
5:23–28	370

2 Thessalonians

1:1	259n26, 260, 261
1:1–4	379
1:3	379
2:2	379
2:3–12	379
2:13	379
3:17	269n40, 378

1 Timothy

1:1	286n10
1:3	380
1:3–4	380, 391
1:9–10	380
1:18	391
2:1–2	380
2:8–12	380
2:11–15	381
3:1–13	380
4:3	380–81
4:7a	391
5:1—6:2	380
5:11–13	381
5:18	414, 414n5
6:4–5	380
6:20–21	380–81, 391

2 Timothy

1:1	286n10
1:5	260
1:18	380
2:16–18	391
3:2–5	380, 381
4:3–4	391
4:11	240
4:12	380
4:20	262

Titus

1:1	286n10
1:5–9	380, 381
1:10–16	381
1:13–14	391
2:1–15	380
3:1–11	380
3:3	380
3:9	391

Philemon

1	295
2	245, 295n21
9	272n2, 295
10	295
13	295
14–15	295
23	295, 295n21
24	240

Hebrews

2:3–4	370
3:1–6	370
4:14—5:10	370
7:1–28	370
8:1–13	370
9:1–22	370
10:1–18	370
11:4—12:13	370
13:19–25	370
13:22	370

James

1:1	369
2:1	369
2:14	369
2:14–26	369
5:10–11	369

1 Peter

1:1	388
1:3–21	388
1:6	388
1:16	388
1:19	388
2:1–22	388
3:1	388
3:1–10	388
3:9	388
3:10	388
3:13–17	388
3:15	388
3:18–20	109
4:6	109
4:16	388
5:1	387n17
5:9–10	388
5:13	311n5, 314, 388, 420

2 Peter

2:1–21	388
3:1	388
3:9	415n10
3:10	415n10
3:15	415n10
3:15–16	414
3:15b-16	414
3:16	415n10

1 John

2:18	384
2:18–27	384
2:20	38n29
2:22	384
2:24	38n29
2:27	38n29
4:1–3	384
4:2	384
4:7a	38
4:11	37
4:19	40–41

2 John

1	385
7	385n12
12	385

3 John

9	385
12	385
13–14	385

Jude

1	344n5, 388
4–6	388

Revelation

1:1	50, 398
1:1a	403
1:1–2	402, 403
1:1b-2	403
1:3	399, 402, 404, 406, 408
1:3–5a	403
1:3–6	402
1:4	398, 403
1:4a	401, 404
1:4–6	402
1:5b-8	403
1:7–8	403
1:7—22:20	402
1:8	402
1:9	398, 399n7, 401
1:9—3:22	403, 405
1:11	401, 403, 404

SCRIPTURE INDEX

1:12	403	13:2	400
1:13	403	13:3	406
1:16	403	13:11–17	400n11
1:18	421	13:12	400
1:19	399, 402, 404, 406, 409	13:1	400
1:20	403	13:18	400n11, 406
2	392	13:18a	400,n13
2:1	403	15:1	403, 404
2:1—3:22	401, 404	15:5—16:21	403, 406
2:2	407	15:6	403
2:5	407	15:7	403
2:6	391, 407	15:8	403
2:9	407	16:1	403
2:14–15	407	16:15	406
2:15	391	17:1	403
2:20	407	17:1—20:3	404, 406
2:28	408	17:3	403
3:1	403	17:5	400
3:1–2	407	17:7	403
3:9	407	17:9	400, 403
3:11	406	17:18	400
3:15–17	407	18:4	404
3:20	219	18:8	404
4:1	398	19:9	219
4:1–11	402	19:10	399, 402
4:1—8:1	403, 405	20:4—22:5	404, 406
4:5	403	21:1—22:5	402
5:1	403	21:9	403
5:5	403	22:1	402
5:6	403	22:6–20	404
8:2	403	22:7	399, 402
8:2—11:19	403, 405	2:8	398
8:6	403	22:9	399
10:3	403	22:10	402
10:4	403, 420	22:12	406
12:1–17	408	22:16	408
12:1—15:4	403, 405	22:18–19	402
12:3	403	22:20	297n31, 406
13	401n11	22:21	402, 404
13:1	403		

APOCRYPHAL GOSPELS

Coptic Gospel of Thomas

prologue	224, 343, 344	6:2–6	342
1—7	224	8	225, 226, 230, 345
2	231	9	225, 233
3:1–5	342	12	227, 230n55
3:4	231	12:2	344
4	341	14:1–3	342
5:1–2	342	20	225, 226, 230, 235
6:1	342	21	225

SCRIPTURE INDEX

Coptic Gospel of Thomas (continued)

21:6	343
21:6–7	231
24	224
26—30	224
28	231
31	225, 229, 235
31—33	224
32	228, 229
33	228, 229
33:2–3	228, 229
34	225, 226, 235
36–39	224
43:3	228, 229
44	228, 229
45:1	228, 229
45:2	228, 229
45:3	228, 229
47ab	225
48	342
49	231, 343
50	231–32, 343
55:1–2	342
56	231, 232, 343
56:1–2	343
57	225, 230, 235
63	225, 230, 235
64	225, 235
64:12	343
65	225, 228, 229, 231, 235
66	228, 229
68	225
77:2–3	224
80	231, 232, 343
80:1–2	343
87:1–2	343
92	231, 236
92:1	228, 229, 232
93	228, 229
94	228, 229, 231, 232
95	225, 343
99	231
101:1–3	342
106:1–2	342
109	225
110	343
111	343
111:3	343
112:1–2	343
113:1–4	342
114	231, 232

Gospel of the Ebionites

1a-b	351, 373
1b	351
2	351
3	351, 373
4	351, 373
5	351
6	352
7	352

Gospel of the Hebrews

1	349, 350n11
1:1–3	350
2–3	349
3	350n11
3:2–4	350
4a	349
5	349
9	349

Gospel of Mary

5:4–8	356
6:1	356
7:1–6	356–57
10:1–2	357
10:3–4	357

Gospel of Peter

4:1	345
5:5	345
7:2	345
14:3	345

Gospel of Truth

16:31—17:3	358
17:10–15a	358
18:16–21a	358
18:21b–26a	359
30:17–31a	359
40:30–41:3	359
41:15–19	359

Infancy Gospel of James

25:1	353

Infancy Gospel of Thomas

2:1	353
2:1–7	354
2:3–4	355
4:1–4	354
5:1–6	354
6:1–23	355
9:1–6	355
10:1–4	355
11:1	353
12:4	353
16:1–2	355
17:1–4	355
18:1–3	355
19:1	353–54
19:1–12	353

EARLY CHURCH FATHERS

1 Clement

47:1–3	25

Clement of Alexandria, *Miscellanies*

2.9.45	346
2.14.96	346

Cyril of Alexandria, *Catechesis*

4.36	223n45
6.31	223n45

Didache

1—6	371
7—10	371
10:6	371
11—15	371
16	372
11:3–6	52n5

Epiphanius, *Adversus Haereses* (*Against Heresies*)

1.2.25	407n13
1.28	361n23
1.28.1	361
29.9.4	348
30.14.3	348

Epistle of the Apostles

4	355

Eusebius

Church History (Ecclesiastical History)

2.23	227
3.5.3	352
3.23.1–4	385
3.25	421
3.25.5	347
3.25.6	223n43
3.29.17	347
3.39.15–16	306–7
4.22.8	347
4.28.29	361n23
6.25.3–14	419–20
7.25.26–27	400n9

Theophanies

4.12	347

Hermas

Similitudes

9.15.4	52n5
9.16.5	52n5
9.25.2	52n5

SCRIPTURE INDEX

Vision

3.5.1	52n5

Hippolytus, *Refutation of All Heresies*

5.2	355
5.7.20	340
7.24	407n13

Ignatius, *Letter to the Smyrneans*

1:1	320

Irenaeus, *Against Heresies*

1.20.1	355
1.22	346, 352
2.22.50	385
3.1.1	309
3.3.4	389
3.11.8	309, 417
3.11.9	357–58
3.21.10	346, 352

Jerome, *Commentary on Matthew*

Prologue	223n44

Justin Martyr

Apology

66:3	25

Dialogue with Trypho

10:2	25
100:1	25
101:3	25
103:8	25
104:1	25
105:5	25
106:2	25
107:1	25

Origen

Commentary on John

2.12	347

Homily on Jeremiah

15.4	347

Homily on Luke

1	223n42
1.1	355

Polycarp, *Letter to the Philippians*

1—12	267, 267n36
1:2	267n36
13	267n36
14	267n36

Serapion, *Ecclesiastical History*

6.12.2	344

Tertullian

De Baptismo

17	304

Against Marcion

4.8	352

Theodoret, *Haereticarum Fabularum Compendium*

1.20	360

OTHER ANCIENT WRITINGS

Josephus, *Antiquities*

11.6.13   55

Suetonius, *Life of Claudius*

25.4   296n22

Qu'ran

Sura 3:49   354n15
Sura 5:113   354n15

AUTHOR INDEX

Aland, Barbara and Kurt, 41, 52
Astruc, Jean, 9
Attridge, Harold W., 357n17

Bauer, Walter, 57, 95–96, 96n2
Bellinzoni, Arthur J., 1n1, 27n1, 28n4, 69n1, 82n4, 92n6, 317n1, 317n2, 409n3, 410n4
Betz, Hans Dieter, 208n15, 280n8
Billerbeck, P., 219n27
Black, Matthew, 213n19
Blout, Charles, 9
Bodenstein, Andreas Rudolph, 4, 13
Boring, M. Eugene, 399n6
Bornkamm, Günther, 159n3
Bovon, François, 28, 28n5, 39
Brown, Raymond E., 131, 131n11
Bruno, Giordano (Filippo), 8, 9
Bultmann, Rudolf, 114, 132, 132n1, 132n2, 166, 166n7, 299, 299n28, 304
Butler, B. C., 92n6

Cappel, Louis, 4, 7, 13
Carlstadt, Andreas, (see Bodenstein, Andreas Rudolph)
Cerfaux, L., 235n57, 236n59
Collins, Adela Yarbo, 313n6
Collins, Anthony, 9
Collins, John Joseph, 397n2
Conzelmann, Hans, 159n2, 392n21
Copernicus, Nicholas, 8
Cornélis, E., 236n58

Darwin, Charles, 14n19, 21
DeConick, April D., 235, 235n56, 241, 241n62
Descartes, René, 5
Dibelius, Martin, 132, 132n1, 132n2
DiLella, Alexander A., 410n1
Dimant, Divorah, 128, 128n8
Dodd, C. H., 95, 95n1, 96, 103, 103n16, 104, 106, 107, 113, 115. 213, 213n18, 214, 299, 299n27, 304

Ehrman, Bart, 33n16, 38n22, 36, 223, 223n40, 257n24, 268, 268n39, 305, 315, 323
Eichhorn, Johann Gottfried, 9, 14
Epp, Eldon J., 30n7, 30n12, 30–32, 33, 34, 35, 36, 37, 38, 40, 54n4
Erasmus, Desiderius, 29

Farrer, Austin M., 92n6
Ferguson, Everett, 421n12
Fitzmyer, Joseph A., 213n19, 214n25, 219n27
Ford, J. Massyngberde, 399n8
Freedman, David Noel, 238n58
Friedrich, Gerhard, 297n24
Furnish, Victor Paul, 279, 279n6, 279n7

Galilei, Galileo, 8–9
Gamble, Harry Y., 410n2
Garitte, G., 236n59
Gärtner, Bertil, 236n59
Gaster, Theodor, 127n7
Gero, Stephen, 353n13
Goodacre, Mark, 83n4
Grant, Robert M., 236n58
Griesbach, Johann J., 92n6
Guillaumont, Antoine, 235n57

Haacker, Klaus, 255n22
Haenchen, Ernst, 159n4
Harrison, Percy, 267n36
Hartman, Louise F., 401n1
Hennecke, Edgar, 283nb, 310n3, 347n9
Hobbes, Thomas, 6, 13
Hume, David, 14
Hutton, W. R., 213n19

Jeremias, Joachim, 219n27
Jewett, Robert, 51n3

Kähler, Martin, 122, 122n5
Karlstadt (see Bodensein, Andreas Rudolph)
Kepler, Johannes, 8–9

469

AUTHOR INDEX

Kittel, Gerhard, 57, 297n24, 297n24
Kloppenborg, John S., 204, 207, 207n12, 207n13, 208, 208n14, 208n15, 211, 213, 214, 215, 216, 217, 220, 221, 221n30, 221n33, 234
Koester, Helmut, 26n1, 27, 27n3, 39, 96n3, 203, 206, 206n10, 221, 221n32, 221n34, 222, 227n46, 230, 230n50, 239n2, 240n60, 300n15, 308n1, 308n2, 334, 334n17, 341n2, 341n3, 372n19, 386n14–16
Krentz, Edgar, 13n17
Kümmel, Werner Georg, 213, 213n19

Lachmann, Karl, 29, 32, 40
Lessing, Gotthold Ephraim, 10, 14, 20
Liddell, Henry George, 273n4
Lindsey, Robert L., 92n6
Lohse, Eduard, 61, 61n8
Lührmann, Dieter, 206, 206n8, 207, 208n15
Luther, Martin, 4, 51, 369
Luz, Ulrich, 219, 219n28

MacDonald, Dennis R., 130, 130n9, 131, 131n10
MacDonald, Lee Martin, 410n2
MacRae, George W., 357n17
Marcus, Joel, 214, 214n24
Marxsen, Willi, 159, 159n1
Mathisen, Ralph W., 364n24
Meier, John, 181n4
Metzger, Bruce, 30n7
Michaelis, Johann David, 178
Miller, Robert J., 228n48, 341n4, 373n5
Morin, Jean, 5, 7, 13

Nestle, Eberhard and Erwin, 41, 52
Niederwimmer, Kurt, 372, 372n4

Paris, Matthew, xiv
Parker, Pierson, 92n6
Perrin, Norman, 183n6
Pervo, Richard I., 239n2, 274n38, 296n10
Petersen, William L., 28, 28n6, 39, 359n19

Peuch, H.-Ch., 235n57
Peyrère, Isaac La, 5
Pfeiffer, Robert H., 2–3, 3n3
Piper, Ronald, 208n15
Pope, Alexander, 56

Quispel, Gilles, 235n57

Reimarus, Herman Samuel, 10–11, 20, 67, 178
Rist, Martin, 397n1
Robinson, James M., 203, 203n1, 205, 205n5, 205n6, 206n9, 207, 207n11, 209n16, 213, 213n19, 236n60, 401n18

Schleiermacher, Friedrich, 203
Schlosser, Jacques, 213n19
Schmithals, Walter, 392n20
Schoedel, William, 238n58
Schultz, Siegfried, 208n15
Schweitzer, Albert, 10, 10n10, 178–79, 179n1
Scott, Robert, 273n4
Simon, Richard, 7, 178
Smyth, Kevin, 238n58
Snyder, Graydon F., 158n17
Spinoza, Baruch, 6, 6n8, 7
Steck, Odil Hannes, 205, 205n7
Stendahl, Krister, 384n9
Strack, H., 219n27
Strauss, David Friedrich, 11–13, 178, 238
Streeter, Burnett Hillman, 69n1, 83n4
Sundberg, A. C., 421n12

Tarnas, Richard, 13n18
Taylor, Vincent, 132, 132n4
Tödt, Heinz Eduard, 204 204n3
Weiss, Johannes, 179, 179n2

Wilkins, Ulrich, 15, 15n21, 205n4
Wrede, Wilhelm, 165, 165n6, 166, 316

Zeller, Dieter, 208n15

www.ingramcontent.com/pod-product-compliance
Lightning Source LLC
Chambersburg PA
CBHW080531300426
44111CB00017B/2682